Dennis McNally

Desolate Angel

Jack Kerouac, the Beat Generation, and America

DA CAPO PRESS

A Member of the Perseus Books Group

Copyright © 1979, 2003 by Dennis McNally

Cataloging-in-Publication data for this book is available from the Library of Congress.

First Da Capo Press edition 2003
Reprinted by arrangement with the author
ISBN 0–306–81222–3

Published by Da Capo Press
A Member of the Perseus Books Group
http://www.dacapopress.com

Da Capo Press books are available at special discounts for bulk purchases in the U.S. by corporations, institutions, and other organizations. For more informa-tion, please contact the Special Markets Department at the Perseus Books Group, 11 Cambridge Center, Cambridge, MA 02142, or call (800) 255-1514 or (617) 252-5298, or e-mail j.mccrary@perseusbooks.com.

1   2   3   4   5   6   7   8   9   10—06   05   04   03

Grateful acknowledgment is made to the following for permission to reprint previously published material:

City Lights Books: Excerpt from *Kaddish and Other Poems* by Allen Ginsberg. Copyright © 1961 by Allen Ginsberg. Excerpt from *Howl and Other Poems* by Allen Ginsberg. Copyright © 1956, 1959 by Allen Ginsberg. Excerpt from *The Yage Letters* by William S. Burroughs and Allen Ginsberg. Copyright © 1963 by William S. Burroughs and Allen Ginsberg. Excerpt from *Mishaps, Perhaps* by Carl Solomon. Copyright © 1966 by Carl Solomon. Excerpt from *Scattered Poems* by Jack Kerouac. Copyright © 1970, 1971 by The Estate of Jack Kerouac. Reprinted by permission of City Lights Books.

Coward, McCann & Geoghegan, Inc.: Excerpt from *Desolation Angels* by Jack Kerouac. Copyright © 1960, 1965 by Jack Kerouac. Excerpt from *Vanity of Duluoz* by Jack Kerouac. Copyright © 1968 by Jack Kerouac.

E. P. Dutton & Co., Inc.: Excerpt from *Nothing More to Declare* by John C. Holmes. Copyright © 1967 by John C. Holmes. Reprinted by permission of the publishers, E. P. Dutton.

Dwarf Music: Excerpt from "Absolutely Sweet Marie" by Bob Dylan. Copyright © 1966 by Dwarf Music. Used by permission. All rights reserved.

Grove Press, Inc.: Excerpts from *Mexico City Blues* and *The Subterraneans* by Jack Kerouac.

Harcourt Brace Jovanovich, Inc.: Excerpts from *The Town and the City* by Jack

When a society becomes afraid of its poets, it is afraid of itself.

—Lenore Kandel

You road I enter upon and look around, I believe you
                    are not all that is here,
I believe that much unseen is also here . . .

. . .

From this hour I ordain myself loos'd of limits and
                    imaginary lines,
Going where I list, my own master total and absolute . . .

. . .

To know the universe itself as a road, as many roads, as
                    roads for traveling souls.

—Walt Whitman

Preface

> History is hard to know, because of all the hired bullshit, but even without being sure of "history" it seems entirely reasonable to think that every now and then the energy of a whole generation comes to a head in a long fine flash, for reasons that nobody really understands at the time—and which never explain, in retrospect, what actually happened.
>
> —Hunter Thompson

Though Thompson's comments were meant for another era, they seem to apply as well to the activities of Jack Kerouac, Allen Ginsberg, Neal Cassady, John C. Holmes, and William S. Burroughs—the members of the so-called "Beat Generation." This small group of writers and poets created a body of profoundly significant art that deserves study if only for aesthetic reasons. But even more to the point of this work, their art and their lives are dramatic reflections of the historical changes of the United States in the period following World War II, and it is to that end that I undertook this labor, working more as an historian than as a literary critic.

The truth of a book entails far more than the accurate rendition of facts; I do not think it is a breach of my respect for scholastic accuracy to acknowledge that I regard these alienated American prophets as my spiritual and intellectual ancestors. In a world that faces a potential ecological and spiritual apocalypse, I respectfully submit that the legend of these psychic pioneers is necessary in order that we might understand our present reality. Within my personal limits, I have attempted to act as a channel for something very like wisdom.

• • •

This work has spanned madness and death and love, and ineradicably altered my life. Quite often, I gained most not from what I read, however illuminating, but from the people I met.

I enjoy saying thank you, and after six years, the time has come at last. Christopher Byrnes, a student of Jack Kerouac before me, suggested this book. Henry Hays Crimmel, my St. Lawrence University professor of philosophy and the greatest teacher I have ever known, introduced me to the rigors of serious intellectual inquiry. His St. Lawrence colleagues Robert B. Carlisle, Jack Culpepper, Jonathan G. Rossie, and Robert S. Schwartz nourished my interest in the study of history.

At the University of Massachusetts, Mrs. Ann Langevin, the custodian of Herter Hall, fed me cake, tea, and sympathy, in the late and difficult hours of research. Mrs. Paula Mark made that university's library work for me. Philip Swenson, Jules Chametzky, and especially Bob Griffith read this manuscript and added considerably to it.

A book about a wanderer requires travel. On the road I encountered a plethora of generous people—friends of Kerouac even when they did not know him—who made my work possible. In Kerouac's hometown of Lowell, Greg Zahos introduced me to the world of Nicky's Café, and Jay Pendergast got me drunk enough to understand the vortex that is that eerie village. Above all, Tony Sampas made a thousand things possible, and I am endlessly indebted to him. Tony is a good person, one of the finest men I will ever know, and having his friendship is one of this project's greatest benisons.

In New York City I met Lucien Carr, another very special man, and Alfred G. Aronowitz, with whom I was to work for three years, in the process learning something of how to write. The Columbia University Archives are managed by Mimi Bowling and Henry Rosen, and I bless them. During my visits to the city, I stayed with four people who became friends: Ed D'Alessandro, John Hurley, Gerry Mooney, and Steve Buccieri. Their hospitality was gracious, unstinting, and crucial to this project. Last of all in Manhattan I found Marshall Clements, in many ways Kerouac's greatest guardian, and another man I am honored to call friend. In San Francisco I was made a guest of Travis and Bobbi Absher, truly kind hosts.

Two of Kerouac's most intimate comrades have enriched me beyond measure with loving fellowship, gentle criticism, and unfailing generosity: John Clellon Holmes and Carolyn Cassady. It is perhaps their love for Kerouac and their own beauty that taught me most of the man.

My extended family of friends and loved ones cherished me through the hard times and forced me to a higher and clearer perspective: Ed and Corinna Smith, who fed me and gave me refuge when I most needed it; my sister Maggie McNally, who loved me when I didn't deserve it; Jack Murphy, Suzanne Wilson, Kathy Berson, and Kate Carlson of Amherst; Georgie Feltz of Berkeley, who helped in the crunch; my road companion Jeff "Bear" Briss; my dear friends Sarah Grambs, Joe Poplaski, Meredith Manning, and Joe Cotter; Mary Carmen Driscoll, who taught me how to love; my brother Robert E. Stokes—no man ever had a finer one; my sister Eileen Geoghegan, who is an artist of life and perception.

Stephen B. Oates accepted an unusual topic with the encouragement I needed, endured my misplaced modifiers and multiple gerunds with charitable patience, gave me the freedom I needed, and made, all-in-all, this work possible. My agent Robert Lescher guided me and this work through the thickets of Manhattan commerce, and Kathy Matthews of Random House applied the last, crucial editing that has I hope focused my often prolix vision.

This book is dedicated to my three parents: my late mother, Mrs. Adeline Jacobson McNally, my late father, Reverend John FJ McNally Jr., and my mother, Mrs. Gertrude Homans McNally.

To all of you, living and dead: L'chaim.

Contents

	Preface	vii
I	In the Shadow of a Crucifix	3
II	Vanity Won and Lost	21
III	"Proud Cruel City"	32
IV	Myshkin at Sea	48
V	Visions in a World of Mushroom Clouds	62
VI	"A Western Kinsman of the Sun"	88
VII	Litrichuh and the Rolling Trucks	116
VIII	The Breakthrough	138
IX	Among the Fellaheen of Mexico and Manhattan	155
X	The Dharma Road	178
XI	A Revolution of Prophecy and Living Things	199
XII	The Angel Travels	221
XIII	Success, More or Less	240
XIV	*On the Road* in a Corvette Stingray	260
XV	Collapse	279
XVI	Waiting	292
XVII	The Village Idiot	311
XVIII	It's True: You Can't Go Home Again	324
XIX	Endgame	340
	Afterword	349
	Source Notes	353
	Index	395

Desolate Angel

I
In the Shadow
of a Crucifix

CAUGHT BETWEEN the plain and the hills, the Merrimack River bends to create a vortex at Lowell, Massachusetts, a swirling center that draws in human experience the way a crystal focuses light. The water rushing over the rocks generates simple physical energy, and factory-building Americans came to exploit that energy. But the great liquid arc inscribed below the falls made it a magic place long before the Yankee industrialists arrived. The falls are somehow a center, a place where human experience is intensified in ways beyond the ken of ordinary understanding. And it is a dark place. Near those falls, Henry David Thoreau was moved to exclaim, "If it is not a tragical life we live, then I know not what to call it." The river is the source, both of the subtleties of mood and perception, and the grosser realities of labor and commerce.

Francis Cabot Lowell understood the river's power, and cut its curve with a canal and a dam, creating the first industrial town in America, home to dozens of grimy red-brick shoe and textile mills. Long rows of cheap wooden boardinghouses surrounded the red-brick core, sheltering the thousands of workers who fled the boredom of their Vermont and New Hampshire farms for the opportunities of industry. But the tenements were houses, not homes, and that was one of the things that marked Lowell as different; from the beginning, it was a place for the alienated, those disjuncted from a rooted past.

First came Yankee farm women, then hungry refugees from Ireland, then late in the nineteenth century equally ravenous Greeks. But the largest group of immigrants came not by sea but by land, drifting from the frigidly hardscrabble farms of Quebec through the small towns above Lowell before reaching the factories on the Merrimack. One of those towns was Nashua, New Hampshire, and two of those immigrants were Leo Alcide and Gabrielle Levesque Kerouac.

Born in Canada, both Leo and Gabrielle grew up in Nashua, a town which down to its pink suspenders, straw boater hats, and popcorn stands, resembled nothing so much as a Norman Rockwell painting. Daughter of a mill worker who had prospered to the point of owning a small tavern, Gabrielle was orphaned at fourteen and forced into the lonely servitude of New England factory life. She went to work at the local shoe shop, earning along with her wages the permanently blackened fingertips of a skiving machine operator. Short and pudgy, she had rosy-red cheeks and glossy black hair that was usually caught back in a colorful ribbon. Though Mémère—Gabrielle's lifelong Quebecois nickname—maintained an attractive and serene presence, there was a bitter mass of hurt behind the constant smile and sunny disposition; marriage and family had rescued her from total dependence on the shop, but the long years of dreary work had left her with a gnawing, frustrated desire for higher social standing.

Leo was a squat but muscular man, stood five foot seven and weighed two hundred pounds. A soft beer belly falling over his belt marked him as a typical aging athlete. An insurance salesman, he was a card-playing, whiskey-drinking "man's man," jovial and virile, with a great booming laugh, huge gnarled hands, a thick and muscular neck, and a bulbous— and indubitably French—nose. He shared with his wife an easy disposition for both misty-eyed sentimentality and laughter, but his eyes, though the same bright blue as Gabrielle's, were more striking, perhaps because of his almost solid black bar of eyebrow. It was usually in motion, and when he was startled, it bounced in accent to his surprise, along with the Old Gold cigarette he tucked into one corner of his broad mouth.

It was a strong and happy marriage, and by 1922 they had two children: pretty three-year-old Caroline ("Nin"), and five-year-old Gerard, a pale, sickly victim of rheumatic fever.

On March 12, 1922, Gabrielle gave birth to her third and last child, Jean Louis Kerouac. It was a propitious day to begin a life. A thaw had mellowed the long Lowell winter; the air was soft, and the crusty snowdrifts were beginning to vanish. Secure in her experience, she elected to have this child at home, in their apartment at 9 Lupine Road. Throughout the afternoon she had twisted on the big brass bed underneath the crucifix; at 5 P.M., as a red sun set and the factories emptied out, Gabrielle gave birth to a fat baby boy.

By the time Jean was three, 9 Lupine Road was not big enough for the Kerouacs. It was only the bottom floor of a traditional shingled New England wooden double-decker, and the porches looked straight out on the street, for there was no yard. Besides, Leo was prospering; the year after the birth of his second son, he had opened his own business, a print shop that did job work and published *The Lowell Spotlight,* a small circular which featured theatrical and political news.

They moved first to a small white cottage at 35 Burnaby Street. Quiet and shady, it was a good place to raise children, but problems with the landlord forced another move that year, this time to 34 Beaulieu Street. While not so bucolic, the new location did eliminate the long walk to school Nin and Gerard had faced. St. Louis parochial school was now only one block away, and in fact they could see the rear of the new school building from their upstairs window.

Beaulieu Street was a rich setting for Jack's childhood. Though open space was minimal, and the identical two-story frame houses loomed straight out on the street, it was a lively block, a true neighborhood full of talkative people. Sitting on his front steps, Jean could turn left and see the Greenalgh Public School at the end of the block. To his right lay West 6th Street, with stores, bars, a lumberyard, and a firehouse. St. Louis Parish covered the next block over with its school buildings, convent, rectory, and the church itself. Beyond lay fields and a brook.

Centered around warm family suppers, the uproarious entertainment of Papa Leo's animal noises, and Mémère's bedtime stories, Jean's early years were affectionate and secure. But the peace of the Kerouacs was not to last. Always frail, Gerard began to die a slow, painful death from rheumatic fever.

Now nine, he had weakened dramatically, staying home from school more and more. Years later, Jean remembered his own satisfaction at this turn of events, for now his heroic big brother was free to perch in his sickbed and entertain Jean with animal sketches and Erector set toys. Gerard was more than a young Leonardo da Vinci to his disciple; he was St. Francis of Assisi as well, gifted with an almost supernaturally tender love for all living creatures. Jean's memory of the time that Gerard saved a mouse from a trap by the local fish store was like a saint's lesson to the younger boy, an epiphany of virtue that exposed the crude insensitivity of the men spitting and talking on the corner. When St. Gerard followed in St. Francis' path by spreading crumbs on the window sill and calling to the sparrows, Jean pressed closer to his brother, idolizing him.

But saints are difficult to live next to, day by day. Forced into docile sweetness by his health, Gerard set an impossible standard of behavior for his normal and rambunctious younger brother. Jean could worship his senior as a saint, but he was much too energetically healthy to emulate him, as Mémère regularly pointed out. Gerard wasted away, his body growing pale and light, almost ghostly; Jean's robust vitality seemed nearly criminal in contrast.

The house grew quiet. Nin no longer brought her friends home, and their parents' spirited parties ceased. The family drew together, watching the child suffer. In December of 1925, Gerard came home for the last time. He stayed in bed with swollen legs and tortured lungs. Increasingly, as Jean lay in the big crib on his side of the room, haunting sounds would cut through the darkness. First the sound of Gerard's breathing; the rasp would grow louder into panting gurgles that ended in a frightening choke. Then Gerard would awaken, and Jean could hear the tears of a Catholic boy who had absolved himself before God. "Why do I hurt?" Gerard whimpered. "I confessed." As the months passed, the whimpers became shrieks, the sobs screams of agony. Always, Mémère would scurry in, clad in her old brown bathrobe, and hold her child to her body.

Nothing helped. Jean borrowed Nin's holy pictures and spread them around Gerard's bed, but it did no good. The constant visits of the parish priest and Gerard's teacher-nuns gave authority to Jean's private certainty that his brother was a saint, but the visits could not save him, and after all the pain, on July 8, 1926, Gerard finally died. Jean was happy, for he knew that "my brother's gone away to heaven now."

The little boy was wrong; Gerard never really left at all. It was far more than his portrait on the mantel that haunted the Kerouacs. Their shared misery had been too intense, the blade had cut too deeply, had left wounds that would never truly heal. Leo stopped going to Mass, and took a special pleasure in the scandalous habit of eating hamburgers on Friday. The nervous strain had robbed him of his faith; it snatched the very teeth out of Mémère's mouth, and every clack of her dentures served to remind her of their loss. Her desperate frustration spilled over acidlike onto her remaining son. For the rest of Jean's childhood, tales of Gerard's goodness would be the staple of Mémère's lessons in behavior, lessons that reminded him endlessly of his inferiority and suggested that he was somehow responsible for his brother's death. Gerard the first-born, Gerard the hero, Gerard the saint; Jean and his family could never forget him. Thirty years later, Jean would write, "there's no doubt in my mind that my mother loves Gerard more than she loves me."

From this time on, Jean, later Jacky, then Jack, could never quite see pragmatic adult gradations of gray but only black and white, absolutes of good and evil born of deepest psychic hurt. His glimpse into the abyss that was Gerard's grave had filled his mind with an apocalyptic sense of life and death, and especially of good and evil. Somehow he felt torn between the moral poles. He tried to be his pure brother, and acquired a neighborhood reputation as an eccentric when he prevented his friends from torturing animals, especially kittens, which in his mind had become reminders of Gerard. His imitation failed to quiet his fears. Night after night, the darkness overcame Jean and he fell into the comforting brown warmth of Mémère's bathrobe as Gerard had, but it was mental rather than physical pain that drove him.

The Kerouacs soon moved to 320 Hildreth Street. Ironically, their nearest neighbors included a funeral home on one side and a cemetery on the other. There the first edge of grief dulled; Papa came home in the evening and roared, Mémère told her stories. Bereft of his brother's entertainment, Jean was forced to play alone. Through most of his childhood, he would create his own games and his own world.

As he grew a little older, he emerged into the excitement of his father's world. He and Nin even went out to the movies at the Royal Theater. Leo's Spotlight Press printed the Royal's tickets, and some of them went free to Leo Kerouac's children. Armed with their passes, Nin and Jean would leave their home in Centralville on the east bank of the river, cross the Merrimack into "Little Canada," and walk down the town's main avenue into a pink-and-gilt neo-Moorish crystal palace.

In the darkness of the theater, Jean found a reality of the imagination that was free of the strictures of Lowell. Sagebrush and sand, white hats and Colt .45's, tin lizzies, telephones, and raging stallions; they had passed through the screen into the wonderful world of Hoot Gibson, where Tom Mix incarnated virtue and always emerged victorious. For years Jean stalked his neighborhood mentally armed and ready for Bad Bart or any other desperado.

Sometimes the whole family would benefit from another Spotlight customer, and visit B. F. Keith's vaudeville theater. Backstage Leo played poker and swigged illegal whiskey with W. C. Fields and other glamorous showpeople, while Jean sat in the audience and fell in love with silent Harpo Marx.

Halfway between the two theaters on Merrimack Street lay the Lowell Public Library. Though its limestone steps and dark mahogany woodwork were not as entrancing as the magic lights and curtains of the shows, the library rapidly assumed equal importance to him. Downstairs the children's room held delights like *Rebecca of Sunnybrook Farm, The Bobbsey Twins,* and for more serious moments, *The Little Shepherd of Kingdom Come.* It would always be one of his homes.

Though movies and the library stimulated his mind, he had encountered something richer still—the terrible holy majesty of the Roman Catholic Church. Born under the sorrow of the crucifix, his earliest memories the black rustling skirts of the nuns visiting Gerard, Jean was destined to be an initiate of the Church's mysteries. Extraordinarily sensitized by Gerard's death, Jean approached the Church with an intensity unusual in his time and place. As he described it twenty-five years later, he had had a vision.

Glowing with some horrible phosphorescent light, Christ or the Virgin Mary had pushed at the foot of his bed one otherwise calm Saturday night. There was no sound; the words froze in his throat. Later that evening he saw a more pleasant spirit, a Santa Claus elf, slam his door. There was no wind, and this time he was able to call out to Mémère, *"Qui a farmé ma porte?* (Who slammed my door?)" Peacefully scrubbing Nin's back in the tub, Mémère answered with cheery ignorance, *"Parsonnes voyons donc."* He told no one. It became merely another twist of guilty confusion turning in his brain, a powerful reminder, as he later put it, that "I was haunted."

The Sisters of the Assumption of the Blessed Virgin Mary did not serve the Lord in so dramatic a fashion. In September 1928, Jean had followed in Gerard's footsteps and begun to attend St. Louis parochial school. Loving as she may have been, the Sister, like the later Brothers, looked to the nervous Jean like a "great big black angel with huge fluttering wings." Pale and almost wrinkle-free, she was as distant as the chalice upon the altar, as untouchable as the Communion wafers offered by the priest.

A good and happy student who never missed a day, Jean quickly learned the first lesson of the nuns: obedience to authority. Submission was exacted by inexorably swift and painful raps on the knuckles with heavy metal-edged rulers. Hovering about their charges in their flowing habits, the nuns reinforced Jean's morbid self-accusations of sinfulness with grim lectures on purgatory and an infinity of sins. In so doing, they initiated him into the ancient cult of the virgin-whore, the notion that women were either good—like Mémêre, like the Sisters—or evil. In later years, the cult would entrap him; any woman who could associate with so sinful a man as he must indeed be a whore.

All of this seemed ordinary enough to young Jean, and neither the discipline nor the work differed very greatly from the program at the Greenalgh Public School around the corner. One book and one hour of the day made the crucial difference. At the daily religious hour, the Sister handed Jean the most important book of his young life, *The Baltimore Catechism.*

Jean's eyes fell first on the "lamby gray strangeness" of Boucher's engravings, but soon enough he began to memorize the words, absorbing the meaning without conscious effort. He learned of God, sin, and penance, and of the magnificent crashing rhythm of the Apostle's Creed, the poetic summing up of the Christian faith.

Complex, terrifying, and fulfilling, the Church's sacraments embraced the whole of life, from Baptism at birth and Confirmation in childhood to the rite of Marriage and the Extreme Unction of death. Of all the sacraments, however, none was more important than the Eucharist, when the body of Christ was present during the holy sacrifice of the Mass. Sunday after Sunday for fourteen years, he listened to the priest and joined the parish in the whispered replies. Like rolling thunder, the refrains of the Mass swept him out of his body and into his soul. For they celebrated a mystery, fueled by the majesty of Latin.

At seven Jack was ready for First Communion. Leo and Gabrielle bought him his white suit, and an aunt gave him his Communion set, the rosary beads with a beautiful golden crucifix. Jean knelt at the altar, hands locked with his classmates, and shivered as the sacred Communion wafer melted on his tongue. They had confessed and received cleansing absolution the day before, and now they were junior soldiers in the Army of the Lord. Living in St. Gerard's eternal shadow, Jack took the Church and its authority more seriously than did his fellow students. They knew they might be bad at times; in a confused way, he was often sure that he was evil, unfit to be a true member of the Holy Mother Church.

Transcending the impact of his first Communion, he received another and final visionary sign, this time from St. Teresa-of-the-Child Jesus. A late nineteenth-century Carmelite nun, Teresa of Lisieux preached the "little way" of simplicity and perfection in the ordinary tasks of life, "of spiritual childhood, the way of trust, and absolute self-surrender." She had inspired an enthusiastic cult among bourgeois French and French Canadian people and was canonized much more rapidly than the Church customarily permitted. One day after seeing a film at school that depicted Teresa's vision of a statue of the Virgin turning its head toward her, Jean went home to encounter, bathed in red light, a statue of St. Teresa turning toward him. Again he told no one; his mind divided, the child could hardly explain what he did not himself understand.

Though he remained torn between spiritual and worldly dualities—the two pictures in his bedroom were of Jesus Christ and the race horse Man o' War—Jean bridged the gap with a special sensitivity to the picturesque and dramatic. In joy and in sorrow, Jean's attention was directed inward, to a private realm created by his imagination. Even something so mundanely sociable as visiting Rockingham Park race track with Papa Leo led Jean to search out every shred of wonder, then bring the images home to be reviewed in solitude. Though Jean enjoyed the days of "masculine" adventure at the track—breakfast at the Waldorf Cafeteria downtown, a morning studying the *Morning Telegraph* at the small table next to Papa's desk at the print shop, the graceful rhythm of charging horseflesh—his personal genius flowered when he returned home to recreate the races with marbles and an inclined board.

Alone in his room, Jean imagined himself as chairman of the board, chief steward, chief handicapper, boss trainer, star jockey, and owner of the greatest horse of all time, a giant ball bearing named "Repulsion." No conceivable detail was overlooked; the linoleum swept, a "trumpet" sounded the call to the races, "Dardanella" came over the Victrola as the horses paraded and, held by a ruler on the top of a Parcheesi Board, the horses werrre offandrunning! Carefully "trained" (chipped so that they would roll randomly), each marble went off at proper odds, for their past performances were exactly documented in Jean's track newspaper and diaries; each race had its proper name and appropriate value, each horse a trainer, jockey, colors, weight allowance, and stable. It was a tour de force of childhood fantasy whose rich sophistication would forever separate Jean from his more placid mates. The conventional world of marbles, of boys in a circle of competition, was never part of Jean's reality. His marbles were not agates or glassies, but thoroughbred horses.

St. Louis school remained the center of his life. The long days in the classroom fell away in dependable measure, and little changed but the name of the Sister in front. Generally Jean was a good student, but one part of the week was torture. Confession every Friday afternoon was a rite that picked at the unhealed scabs of his conscience, reminding him anew of his "corruptness." For some of the children, Confession was a casual experience. However, all the "Our Father's" and "Hail Mary's" in the world could not exterminate the guilt worm gnawing within Jean. Again and again he had to admit in a whisper to the unseen Father on the other side of the screen that *"Oui, mon père,* I played with *mon gidigne."*

Sexuality above all could not stand comparison with Gerard, and masturbation became another bar in Jean's prison of conscience. He had a lifelong pattern of "jacking off," even as it seemed ultimate blasphemy to him. Since he felt at heart that he was already unspeakably vile, it was easy to give up and indulge in the aching pleasure of orgasm. His resolve to be good would vanish, and he would stealthily slip into the bathroom, unbutton his pants, and enter the dream world of satisfied desire. As the pleasure faded and he scrambled about wiping up semen with a tissue, he would shudder with disgust at his gross carnality, and once again vow to be like his vision of good—Gerard, the Church, Easter lilies, kittens, and lambs.

Rather than becoming either a prude or a degenerate, Jean—and later Jack—hung suspended between the ethical boundaries, fascinated by the perverse as well as the holy, unable to wholly commit himself to either, and ultimately tolerant of both.

As he grew older, he discovered the Dracut Woods, lurking just a few blocks north of his house. Something delicious and low lay there, he was sure. His private vision of enticing evil touched not only the shadows of dark forest, but the faces of Lowell's bizarre lurching characters. Down on the garbage dump old Jean Fourchette hissed idiotlike between broken filthy teeth and out his snotty nose—"zzoo, zzzzoooooo"—and became ZouZou. Luxy Smith, an alcoholic hermit, inhabited a crumbling mansion in Pawtucketville (the neighborhood between Jean's Centralville and the Dracut Woods). Young as he was, Jean had an empathy that drew him, fascinated, to the poignant symbols of his era, lost and lonely people, zombies full of what he would later call "despair, raw gricky hopelessness [the], cold and chapped sorrow of Lowell." Hard times they called it: the Great Depression.

Lowell had been stagnant since the mills began to go South after World War I, but by 1930 it was dead and all but rotting. Two out of three workers, unemployed, cursed on street corners, and the only good business bet in town was charity; 40 percent of Lowell was on some form of welfare. Jean never missed any meals, but he saw the collapse in the frightened eyes of men sitting on the stairways of Little Canada, staring at silent factories. The Depression was inescapable, as real as the pain caught in the pictures of WPA workers in the town newspaper, the Lowell *Sun*. In the early thirties the *Sun* featured closer coverage of Al Capone and Billy Rose than it did of economics, but conservative Catholic Lowell shivered as it regularly splashed headlines like TEAR GAS AND NIGHT STICKS USED BY LOS ANGELES POLICE IN REPELLING COMMUNISTS across the front page. Just twenty years earlier, Joe Ettor of the IWW had failed miserably trying to organize the local mill workers, and antiradical paranoia remained thick.

Even Jean's special joy, the movies, had to respond to the disaster by lowering their admission charge, and soon he could spend an entire Saturday afternoon in the comfort of the Rialto, seeing a double feature, a chapter from a serial, a cartoon, and the newsreels for a dime. Jean found the newsreels a bothersome interruption; he had to watch the breadlines and apple sellers, learn new words and phrases like Republic Steel, Harlan County, and Okie, and become all too familiar with the pinched look of hunger.

Humor developed an edge in the thirties, and the *Sun*'s funnies adapted. Dick Tracy leaped off the page, first of the superheroes who were vicariously to solve the problems of a paralyzed America. Tracy's message was harder and more aggressive than either of Jean's old favorites, like "Wash Tubbs" (later "Cap'n Easy") and "Freckles and His Friends," or his all-time permanent favorite, Major Hoople's own "Out Our Way." Leo's spiritual brother, the major recalled earlier times with his gently raffish roguery. Poised over his billiard cue at the Owl's Club or lecturing the boarders at the Hoople Manor fireplace, Amos B. Hoople always had a scheme—or at least an explanation. "Just one of the guys" despite his pomposity, Hoople was a fixture in the masculine realm of cigars and sports, the brotherhood whose gods were Ruth and Gehrig, Knute Rockne and the "Gipper," whose myths . . .? But that is where things became gritty once again, for the Depression's primal male dream was wrought in hunger and pain.

Ultimately, there was only one stage for the dream, the square canvas ring at the center of Madison Square Garden, 50th Street and Eighth Avenue in New York City. A man in an incongruous dinner jacket would stand and announce a "bout for the champeenship of the woild," and some hungry kid named Sullivan or Goldberg or even Louis would stalk out of his corner and grab *all* the marbles with a crushing left hook. They dreamed those dreams at the small gym Leo ran at night, and Jean watched local hopefuls pound the bags, but it was the part about Madison Square Garden that attracted him. The center, the source . . . the City. When Jean turned on the radio with its brown-paper speakers, the shows he loved—Jack Benny, Rudy Vallée, *The Hit Parade, Amos 'n Andy*— all came from the City. "In New York" was also the title of a *Sun* column, and after dinner Jean could absorb gossip from the glittering world of Tex Rickard, El Morocco, and "Hizzoner," the inimitable Jimmy Walker.

Everything that was bright and interesting in his life, the worldly dreams and golden fantasies of the media, issued from somewhere near Times Square. As the years passed, the vision of New York, the world outside Lowell, the road of adventure, would become one in his heart with the notion of enticing evil, the dangerous world he desired so much. Lowell had its virtues, but the City . . . even if he would remain a townsman all his life, the City was part of his future. Once or twice the Kerouacs even journeyed to New York, visiting Gabrielle's stepmother in Brooklyn. Despite the Depression, they were pretty well-off; Leo, who acquired a driver's license only later that year of 1932, was able to buy his first car, a 1928 Model A Ford, and then hire a local man, Armand Gauthier, as his driver.

Prosperity moved them all the way out of the blank box that had been their home for the past four years, to Pawtucketville, where they settled first on Phebe Avenue and later on Sarah Avenue. With neighbors named Laflamme, Payette, and Houde, the new block was as French as all the blocks before it, and though the new location created changes in Jean's life, most of them were welcome.

That fall of 1932 at St. Joseph's his new teachers were not delicate nuns but roaring Jesuit brothers, and they forced him to make up for the deficiencies of St. Louis' curriculum. Jean had two major achievements in fifth grade: his scholarship improved so much that he was able to skip the sixth grade, and he became an altar boy at the religious center of French Lowell, St. Jean Baptiste Cathedral.

Eyeing their students with much the same intensity Leo did horses, the Brothers contemplated serious, dedicated Jean as a potential priest. Though a decade older, a young seminarian named Armand "Spike" Morrisette became a close friend of Jean's. Jean impressed Spike as a great worrier, a moody and thoughtful young man often given to reading the Sermon on the Mount. The elder Brother thought Jean would make a good priest, for in truth he seemed too unworldly to cope with the crudities of Lowell. Political and ethnic turbulence had intensified in

Lowell in the election year 1932, when the Democratic candidate arrived
to campaign there. Franklin Roosevelt's golden smile warmed Jean—set
free from school for the event—as his motorcade glided through town a
week before Election Day, but that was the only harmony in the struggle.
Excluded from the Democratic Party's largesse by the Irish first-comers,
the French and Greeks were Republicans, and while Lowell gave FDR
a 10,000-vote plurality, it elected Republican Albert Bourgeois to the
legislature. The Irish boycott was not an abstract issue to Leo, who ranted
sourly in his easy chair about the "gahdam Micks" at City Hall who
refused to give the Spotlight Press any business.

Lowell was no melting pot; perhaps that was why it tolerated eccentricity so well, and certainly why the war of clans was not confined
"gentlemanlike" to the ballot boxes. North Common in the neighborhood
called the Acre was the main Coliseum, and the gladiators were named
the Acre Pirates, the Warriors, the Blackhawks, and the Riverside Gang,
as the Irish played King-of-the-Mountain with the French and Greeks.

Jean was no warrior, but he was even less a saint, and in September
1933 he entered the Bartlett Junior High School, a public institution set
in the middle of the Greeks and Irish of the Acre. Leaving St. Joseph's
meant more than just not going to Mass every day; for the first time in
his life, Jean Kerouac no longer lived in an exclusively French world. He
had learned English in the Royal at the age of six, but French had been
the language of school and home, and he retained his accent until high
school. At Bartlett, Kokinas and Tsotakis, Gallagher and McNally replaced the French names. Jean Louis became Jacky.

It was a liberation. In 1933 most Franco-American schoolboys were
merely counting time until they could enter the mills, but Jacky had a
book hunger in common with the local Greeks, whose drive for education
was often compared locally to that of the stereotypical Jews of Brooklyn.
Having crossed the Textile Bridge, Jacky walked past the funeral homes
that had once been mill-owners' mansions, past the Franco-American
Orphanage, down Wannalancit Street, and into the bookish sanctuary of
Helen Mansfield's classroom.

Miss Mansfield was a sort of secular nun, an aging spinster whose life
was directed toward her pupils. But where the Sisters offered thorns and
a crucifix, she shared dreams, spells, and enchantment. Jacky had always
been a reader. Now Miss Mansfield, sensing his quickness and raging joy
in books, pressed great writers on him, and more. During that year, she
stoked his enthusiasm to the point where he turned a corner and began
to travel a new road; he discovered that he could write as well as read, that

in the unfettered world of the written word, he could act as well as be part of the audience.

Diaries, novels, newspapers, the form did not matter. He emulated the *Morning Telegraph* with a tabloid covering his own private athletic world, his race track of marbles and the equally detailed baseball and football games he played with cards. He gave Miss Mansfield a short story about the Irish cop on the beat which so pleased her she read it to the class. Set free by her approval, Jacky began to scribble into his back-pocket nickel notebook a novel he called *Jack Kerouac Explores the Merrimack*.

Those who come to write soon discover that isolation is an occupational hazard. French-Canadian Lowell was not a literate place. Save for the newspapers—*L'Etoile, Le Citoyen, Le Clarion,* the *Sun*—the town's French were uninterested in reading, and Jacky's parents were no exception. As Leo's fortunes began to dribble away, their hopes came to focus ever more intensely on their only living son, weighty expectations of a job in a brokerage firm, silk suits, a nice home in the suburbs.

Leo would counsel, "Forget this writing stuff, Jean, it'll *never* pay. You're such a good student—sure you'll go to college, get a good job. Stop dreaming!"

Mémère was harsher. Watching her baby slip away from her control, disappointed with his romantic fantasies of belles-lettres, she finally grew vicious. And although Jean already felt in some awful way what she said, it must have been crushing to hear his own mother spit out, "You should have died, not Gerard."

Sometimes the house grew stifling to Jacky, the enormous overstuffed leather-and-wood couches weighing down his spirits, and then it was time to escape out the door, down to the street, and join the gang: mournful, doomtragic George "GJ" Apostolakis, the lone Greek in the circle; Roland Salvas, the sunken-chested superspitter; silent Scotcho Boldieu and "crackbrained angel joy" Fred Bertrand. Beneath the eerie shadows of Pawtucketville the Dracut Tigers talked, wrestled, sang, sinned, got into trouble and out of it, grew up together. Almost every young teenage boy in the town was in one of the gangs, and they competed on North Common, blood often flowing. Several blocks away from the Acre, the Tigers usually left the fighting to others. Mostly they played football.

Saturday announcers had filled Jacky's ears with Red Grange and the Gipper; at six he had watched his cousins Armand and Hervé go one-on-one in the backyard. Faith and ambition took him on to the field.

Football was the chance—one of very few—to *be* somebody, not only in the hometown-hero-for-a-day sense, but because there was only one escape out of the mills for a Canuck boy from Lowell, and that was a college athletic scholarship. College, as symbolized by a complex fantasy of the Sweetheart of Sigma Chi being serenaded by Bing Crosby, was the way to the American dream, and it was worth every bruise and ache.

Jacky wrote the simple entry in the *Sun* sports page column of October 1935: "The Dracut Tigers, age 13–15, challenge any football team age 13–15 to a game in Dracut Tigers field or any field Saturday morning." With Leo howling out victory cheers for his son, Jacky sliced the Rosemont Tigers' defense for nine touchdowns, and walked home, as he said years later in a fictional setting, "goaded on by all the fantastic and fabulous triumphs that he [saw] possible in the world."

The Tigers' second game was down and dirty. Leo managed the Pawtucketville Social Club at night, and the older boys he regularly ousted for being broke figured to shut up the old man's bragging with one fast smack in the mouth of his son, "that little Christ of a Kerouac." Rising from a pileup swallowing blood, the curse hurting more than the punch, Jacky left cleat tracks across the offender's backside on the next play.

Home from the games, the boys listened to the radio programs— *Flash Gordon, Jack Armstrong, Dick Tracy, Buck Rogers*—that clustered around suppertime, or passed copies of pulp magazines from hand to hand until they were worn and shredded. Except for encouraging him to write and stimulating his interest in heroic fantasy, most of the pulps were too thin to seriously affect Jacky. Tom Mix metamorphosed into *Star Western*, one of over thirty cowboy magazines. *Operator 5*, only one of dozens of detective publications, established the character of the honorable "hardboiled" private eye that was later perfected by one of its contributors, Dashiell Hammett. Soaring further out on the vectors of imagination, golden Doc Savage rose and fell in popularity with the boys, but there was only one champion—The Shadow.

As one story put it:

> From thin, straight lips came a low, sinister laugh. It was a tone of knowing mirth—a foreboding mockery that carried an uncanny spell. It was a laugh that had brought terror to the underworld; a laugh that taunted friends of crime; a laugh that had marked the ending of insidious schemes, and had sounded the death knell to doomed evildoers.

The author of that laugh was a mysterious being who remained invisible at night, and who disguised himself by day. He was a personage who could seemingly be everywhere; the possessor of a master mind who could frustrate the deepest schemes of crime.

Only one pair of lips could utter that weird mockery that left no doubt of identity. The laugh of Lamont Cranston was the laugh of The Shadow!

Desjardins' candy store on Moody Street was a fitting place to pick up the new magazines every other Friday; the old man who lurched behind the counter was a reputed pederast, and the store seemed enveloped in an atmosphere of dissipation. By the time Jacky was out of the store, he was already attuned to the weird mysticism of Lamont Cranston, the Emperor of the Invisible. Home, Jacky was always near a speaker as the eerie notes of the theme song, "Omphale's Spinning Wheel," floated gently out into the night. Master of the mysterious, a friend of the devil even as he destroyed evil, The Shadow penetrated to the core of Jacky's turbulent and guilty dream world, a fictional character precisely in tune with Jacky's own thoughts. Though Pawtucketville could never be quite so perfectly pitch-dark as a Mott Street opium den, Jacky became the local Shadow for a while, spooking about in slouch hat and cape, swiping small items and stealthily leaving behind tin cans with the message "The Silver Tin Can Will Visit You Tomorrow," until everyone on Sarah Avenue wondered who it was. Incapable of imagining *her* son as anything but publicly virtuous, Mémêre was certain that it was GJ, until a lady down the block caught Jacky silverhanded, and he was forced to retire.

Now thirteen, Jacky was mature enough to hitchhike alone to Boston and stroll along the docks daydreaming of stowing away to Europe, but he was still fragile enough to flee to Mémêre's bed obsessed afresh with St. Teresa and Gerard after witnessing a stranger's death in the moonlight atop Moody Street Bridge. Adolescence brought Jacky's old guilts to a new intensity, a morbid concern with sin and death that bothered him as never before.

He needed some sort of impure savior, a hero who could reassure him that even sinners might still be good. Once again, his imagination rescued him. If he could not be a superhero, he could be a superhero's friend. And so he created an imaginary companion, a legendary hero named Dr. Sax, who had come to Lowell to join with Jacky and destroy the World Snake of Evil in the Dracut Woods.

Seventeen years later Jack would write down the tale of *Dr. Sax,*

Faust Part III, embellishing it with Spengler and Jung and many further details generated by an adult mind. But the core was there in his adolescence. Sax's complex lineage lay in a thousand fragments in Jacky's subconscious. Sax was deaths and funeral shrouds, the rain and the mist, musty cellars and spiderwebs in your face in the dark, the glitter of a phosphorescent crucifix. Sax was The Shadow's bastard child as well, with his hat, cape and invisibility, and the "mwee hee hee hee hee hee haaaaaaa" laugh that ripped through the skin and chilled you to the bone. Formed of the flickering images of the Royal, Dr. Sax's "brothers" were Bela Lugosi in *Dracula,* Lon Chaney in *The Phantom of the Opera,* and all the hidden truths in the Tibetan valley of *Lost Horizons.*

The fantasy of Dr. Sax sprang partly from lewd sexuality, from his guilty fascination at watching ZouZou the idiot masturbate himself and his dogs in a shack at the junkyard, in Jacky's voyeuristic raids on the privacy of couples humping in the funky summer warmth by the river, in Jacky's own adolescent homosexual fondlings and gropings. Though in the later written legend Jacky placed Sax in a burrow deep in the Dracut Woods, his true home was by the river, in the shadows of the sandbanks where he had first appeared in Jacky's imagination. Solitary walks along the Merrimack that frozen spring of 1936 were not tranquil strolls but encounters with his sense of self. For Jacky, the fantasy was palliative, soothing his fears about sin, but it wasn't enough; with the spring came the massive catharsis he needed.

Friday the thirteenth, March 1936: Bruno Hauptmann awaited the electric chair that week, Adolph Hitler—about to invade the Rhineland —was the favorite subject of political cartoonists, *Modern Times* was the new movie in town; and to an already overwrought teenager, the flood that threatened Lowell with destruction intimated not merely tragedy but the end of the world.

Winter had been cold and snowy, and the spring warmth felt especially good that year. By noon of March 13, the Merrimack had crested at 8 feet above the dam, only a thick slab of ice protecting Lowell from absolute catastrophe. As night fell, 50,000 cubic feet of water per second were smashing through Rosemont Terrace, the lowest part of town, damaging Fred Bertrand's and Miss Mansfield's houses, and the Spotlight Print. As Jack put it long after, the river was a raging snake, "an unforgettable flow of evil and of wrath and of Satan barging through my hometown."

Satan almost got Jacky, as he would later say. Foolishly, he and a friend named Billy Chandler were playing on giant piles of ice near the sandbanks, when at 5 P.M. that Friday afternoon the ice above the dam let go, and only his strong young legs saved his life. Lowell was relieved to see the Army Corps of Engineers troop in to protect them the next day, along with 2,500 WPA sandbag-filling workers.

For the next six days the river was moderately well-behaved, but by Thursday the nineteenth it was two feet higher than before and still rising; every mill in Lowell shut down, and Lakeview Avenue, only four feet lower than Jacky's home on Sarah Avenue, was swamped. The city was panicking, and by the next day, downtown Lowell—including all of Little Canada—was under two feet of water, a thousand families were refugees in the Armory, and Governor James Michael Curley had called in the National Guard to prevent looting.

Nursing an arm aching from diphtheria shots and a conscience troubled by his recurrent problems with sin, Jacky had connected the rage visited upon his town with his own guilts, and confusedly wondered if the catastrophe were about to consume them all. In some mysterious fashion, the roaring brown flood at his doorstep had crested with his childhood failures so that Lowell's fate was intertwined with his own. As he put it later in his adult myth, a poetically elaborated recapitulation, all of Sax's potions and amulets had failed, and the World Snake of Evil under Dracut Hill lived on.

But apocalypse was not yet.

And Doctor Sax, standing there with his hands in his pockets, his mouth dropped open, uptilted his searching profile into the enigmatic sky —made a fool of—

"I'll be damned," he said with amazement. "The Universe disposes of its own evil!"

That bloody worm was ousted from his hole, the neck of the world was free—

On Saturday the twentieth, the river's rise halted, drawing back from Lowell with only one victim, an elderly man. When it receded, as the book *Dr. Sax* made clear, Jacky's own morbid fears had somehow receded as well, leaving him less obsessed with filth and darkness, almost as if the river, blue once again after spring silt, had cleansed him, left him regenerated and released. As the sun came out and the waters eased into summer normality, Jacky's crisis passed too, for reasons as imponderable—and natural—as why a flood stops. He was not completely at peace, but he had "fought through the fear and guilt of Catholicism," as a close friend would later write, "to acceptance of the befuddled, complex loneliness of pre-adult life . . ."

He was not Gerard nor was he evil; he was Jacky, who stopped going to Mass about that time. It was not God but the Universe that disposed of its own evil. He had reached a delicate balance.

Two months later, Jacky graduated from Bartlett Junior High, and after a summer spotting bowling pins at the Pawtucketville Social Club for his father, he was ready to walk all the way downtown to Lowell High School.

Ahead lay football and romance and adulthood. The glee and guilts of childhood had assumed their proper proportion.

II
Vanity Won
and Lost

As SEEN from the river, the ugly yellow-brick building called Lowell
High School was unmistakably a product of the Sing Sing school of
architecture. In front of the school on Merrimack Street sat St. Anne's
Church, a perfect plot of English Episcopalian heaven seemingly transplanted, stone and ivy, from some Shropshire common. Actually, it was
built by a local factory, as was the canal on one side of the school and the
perfect red-brick Mason's Hall on the other. The walk through Little
Canada to and from classes fixed forever the giant capitalist power of the
mills in Jacky's mind; in three blocks he could see not only the architec-
tural evidence, but the people whose sacrifice had helped build them, sorry
black-shawled women off to Mass in the morning, old dead-eyed men
lurching drunk to their homes at night.

They were the lost, and Jack could not hurry past them sympathetic
but detached, for failure had struck home. Late in 1937, Jack's junior year
in high school, Leo had fallen prey to slow horses, low cards, and poor
business judgment, and was forced to sell out the Spotlight to his former
customers.

Heart and soul a worker, a meticulous print shop craftsman, Leo had
an enduring faith in the American notion of success. He'd been proud of
the word "estate" by his name in the City Personal Property Book. In
1936 it stood at $2,900, though it did not mention the $3,000 starter loan
that his friends Scoopie Dionne and Ed Dastou had made him years
before, nor could it foretell that a year later it would show a $2,000 loss.
Leo was a citizen of the old school, a reactionary workingman who detested FDR's liberalism, and it was more than just humiliating to end up

carrying water buckets for the WPA. Soured and brooding, Leo would rant on about the liberals, and Jack would defend them, though he rapidly lost interest in the subject.

After a while, Leo began to find printing work, sometimes in Lowell, more often out of town. With his family center shattered, Leo was, as Jack would later say, "a man of mournful vision." Faced only with missed opportunity and wasted potential, Leo craved better for his son, and was aghast at Jack's persistence in rejecting solid respectable work for the idle fancies of "literachoor."

"I wanta write, I'm an artist," Jack said.

"Artist shmartist, ya can't be supported all ya life," Leo replied.

Tortured by her impoverished childhood, Gabrielle was even more concerned with status seeking, to the point of snubbing Jack's friend Fred Bertrand—so Fred felt—because of his lower-class manner. Her husband a failure and her first-born son dead, Mémère reached out to her remaining son, flawed though he might be; if Leo could not gratify her frustrated social needs, perhaps in the future her bright young Jack could. Even as she reminded him of his failings, Mémère protected and doted on her boy, constantly urging him to study and rise in the world. Struggling to measure up to Gerard's example, Jack came to seem a bit of a "momma's boy" to his friends, for both his studiousness and the richness of his fantasy world served to separate him slightly from the "gang." They acknowledged his extraordinary recall with the nickname "Memory Babe." Fred Bertrand, the crazy skinny one, mostly played hooky in the brief period before he quit school entirely, as had Scotty Boldieu after his father died. Only Roland Salvas and George Apostolakis—GJ—went all the way down Merrimack Street to high school every day. Once there, Roland took the shop course, GJ—with a widowed mother to support—the commercial, and only Jack was college prep.

It was no surprise that Jack's friends, who had little academic motivation in the first place, would dislike Lowell High. Bigoted and traditional, the Irish ran the school and Headmaster Sullivan was not a fount of experimentation or creativity. Miss Mansfield had no worthy successor, and even English class was only a lazy blend of spitballs, notes, giggles, E. A. Robinson and Robert Frost to Jack; only the inspiration of Emily Dickinson justified his time there.

But Jack, as GJ later commented, made a religion out of whatever he was doing. He approached literature with a worshipful intensity, and the tepid rote of the classroom never satisfied him. So he began to skip some of his classes and get an education, half a block away at the library. He pored through the Harvard Classics, the eleventh edition of the *Encyclopaedia Britannica,* H. G. Wells's *Outline of History,* William Penn's *Maxims,* Hugo, and Goethe. More important, the young artist discovered two masters, William Saroyan and Ernest Hemingway.

It was a time in which popular fiction—the short stories in the *Saturday Evening Post, Collier's,* or *Liberty*—was almost totally populated by people named Jones or Lewis, the sort of WASP's Jack hardly knew. Saroyan, the dark-eyed Armenian from Fresno, was living proof that someone who wasn't an "American" could be a successful writer. Following Aram's wild misadventures with his cousin Moorad and the white horse or the Indian and his Cadillac, Jack loved the funny tone and the poetic charm of the tales. Too, Jack sensed in them—and argued ferociously with his father—the tragic depths below the chuckles, the dues paid by all of America's immigrants, the suffering that it took to be an American.

Beyond charm or even tragedy lay Hemingway. Clinging above the abyss of *nada,* saved only by the pure and terrible act of writing one real sentence, and then yet another, Hemingway was a worthy master for a young pilgrim like Jack. For the boy, Jake Barnes and Robert Jordan were *truly* alone; paying no attention to the macho code later epitomized in the Gregory Peck–white hunter–bullfighter–professional image, Jack saw only "pearls of words on a white page giving you an exact picture," as he remarked much later.

Though his artistic fantasies and labors made him an unusual Dracut Tiger, Jack was superficially a normal teenager, especially after Leo's financial collapse moved them from their small private home on Sarah Avenue to a fourth-floor tenement flat one block over at 736 Moody Street. Home from school, Jack would gobble a snack, then spring back down to the street to join the guys for a game or just some street-corner talk. He had an eye for the comic and absurd that lent ordinary events something extra. GJ's Lefty Grove–inspired windup amused Jack, but it was his own grandiose sideline descriptions that had the same effect on everyone else. He'd always told them "I'm gonna be a writer," and from the beginning he practiced with his mouth.

Late one Saturday night, Jack and his friends discovered the inebriated body of Luxy Smith, Pawtucketville's most distinguished drunk, and took it upon themselves to aid the old gent home. Accompanied by Jack's sepulchral commentary, they got him home and into bed and seemed to be doing fine until, to a muttered chorus of invective, Luxy fell out of bed, landing gracelessly on his skull. Hastily stuffing him back in, the boys raced home down the hill, with Jack melodramatically predicting their imminent arrest on "Moidah One, gentlemen. Moidah One. We're all gonna FRY!" By the bottom of the hill, GJ had to smack one youngster out of his panic, and every one of them breathed easier when the days passed and Luxy's grizzled visage failed to appear on the *Sun*'s obituary page.

Jack and the gang found the stuff of their dreams in many places, but especially at the movies. GJ was an usher at the Rialto, and escorted by the extra thrill of something for nothing, they watched Jekyll become Hyde, and then crossed the street to the Moosehead Café, where Jack leaped the railing and became the tragilunatic Hyde himself. Shabby, harshly lit cafés were part of both worlds; the Moosehead could well have been a set stark enough for *Little Caesar* or *The Petrified Forest* where, as one critic later put it, the "night diner [was] established as the stopping post for all the outriders of American society."

And the years of growing up passed with talk, the serious talk of men on street corners mulling over the Red Sox's chances and Beacon Hill's machinations, or the crazy talk of boys contemplating the secrets of girls. But Jack was painfully sensitive, aware that he was somehow different from the other guys in the gang, too conscious of the "buffoonery," the "brutality," the "carelessness," of what he saw around him, as he described it fictionally a decade later. Lost in the belief that he was "the only mortal soul in the town who [had] frighteningly understood the meaning of life and death," his true friends were Anna Karenina and Jean Valjean, Garbo, Byron and Tristan, Hedda Gabler. GJ and Fred and Scotty and Roland were good companions, but they saw only the surface of his personality. In the depths of his romantic adolescent imagination, Jack was certain that life had grander possibilities than his friends could ever conceive. What he needed was another brother-saint, a soul partner who could comprehend his devotion to Art and the wonder of his fantasies.

Then one day in the spring of 1938 he met a young man named Sebastian "Sammy" Sampas.

Sammy was a gloomy-poetic product of an enormous Greek home noisy with love and emotions and tears, tantrums, laughter, and music. Sharing Gerard's idealism and Jacky's own sensitivity to guilt, he was, Jack thought, "different from anyone else in the businesslike town."

Hunched over a cup of coffee at the White Tower in Kearney

Square, his delicate hands gesturing over the glories of Keats, Byron, and Rupert Brooke, Sammy challenged the mundaneness of Lowell with an imagination that was the equal of Jack's. Their dreams swept them off Merrimack Street and around the world; they grew extraordinarily close.

Not everyone was so enthused about Jack's new friend. Lowell's Greeks mocked dumb, mill-bound Canucks, and Sammy made Roland nervous with his cultured voice, his educated polish. When Jack wrote plays and Sammy acted them out, Fred thought they were both a little nuts.

Sammy was—in an extroverted way that Jack admired but could not duplicate—everything that materialistic, submissive Lowell was not. Exuberantly uninterested in Lowell's ideas of dress or behavior, he was a precociously intelligent man who could break into tears at the sight of a cripple. Though his artistic side set him off from the gang, Sammy had a political conscience that kept his poetry focused on Lowell and its common people, as in a poem called "Summertime in a Mill City," in which the noon heat swept through a factory, and

> Soon the red building
> Is an oven
> The workers,
> The French
> The Greeks
> The Poles
> Swear as they stand
> And pull the wet cloth
> From the vats of dye— . . .

Captured by John Reed's vision of comradely equality in the first blooming of the Russian Revolution, Sam and Jack solemnly formed a radical study group to enlighten humanity, calling it Prometheus, after the Greek god who brought down fire. With a few other friends they read *Das Kapital* and the *New Masses*, argued the theory and reality of social change, and consecrated themselves to their task. They ignored the dogmatic and factionalized U.S. Communist Party, for they were more seekers after "the light which passeth all understanding" than revolutionaries. Their quest flowed out of ethics and not economics; they sought a surrogate for the God their teenage atheism had momentarily displaced.

Jack never felt that vision with Sammy's all-consuming intensity, in part because he had another dream, one more in keeping with the American way: football. The lure of football success was a strong one, a rich myth of grace, power, and public acclaim caught in the image of a leaping end, pigskin tucked under arm, poised above the goal line. Football was also the freedom tunnel out of the mills, to a campus with ivy-covered libraries and flirtatious sorority women. Athletics compensated for more than Leo's thin wallet; they replenished a tarnished ego. Papa's pride overflowed with a star son to brag about.

Jacky went out for the team his sophomore year, and knew the anguish of being too small, too light, of being so tired the first day of practice that he missed the bus home, of walking back in a stupor and falling asleep at the supper table, his face resting limply in his plate. Junior year he returned, stubborn and intense, pushing beyond exhaustion to run yet once more through a leg-wearying series of tires laid on the ground. Summer heat gave way to fall rains, but Jack never played that year, and ran out the cold dregs of the season like all scrubs, working hard to avoid getting his hands and feet stepped on in the dark freezing practices of November. Raging away as usual, Leo claimed the coaches had been bought, typical of "this gahdam shittown on the Merrimack. This is the crummiest town anyway," he'd say, mashing his cigar into an ashtray.

Jack was a senior in the fall of 1938, and his name began to pop up occasionally in the *Sun.* Kerouac didn't start the first few games; though he was a gifted ball carrier, he played poor defense, and substitution was then uncommon.

Just as with his local gang before, Jack was never entirely part of the team. After their fifth game—at which point the "Red and Gray" were undefeated, untied, and unscored upon—the Boston *Herald* appropriately headlined a story, "Kerouac Is the 12th Man on the Lowell High School 11"; in some of the games he had played only a minute or two, and in two he had starred, scoring three touchdowns against Worcester Classical, and two against Lowell's crosstown rival, Keith Academy.

The second half of the season was less pleasant, as Lowell tied and then lost three games. But it was the final game against archrival Lawrence that counted. November 24, 1938, was a cold and miserable day, and with just a few minutes left, Lowell led by the thin score of 2–0. Lawrence could score at any time, and the Lowell fans shifted restlessly, praying for the clock to run out. Quarterback Art Coughlin took the ball, dropped back, and flipped a wobbling pass toward Jack; a giant Lawrence defensive end reached out and ticked the ball so that it sailed wide, and there seemed no possible way that Jack could catch it. Flying down the field, Jack looked back, stretched, plucked the ball out of the air inches from the ground, spun around and sprinted. At the five-yard line, two defenders swarmed up, but Jack dropped low and smashed into them, and as in some wholly improbable dream, he found himself inches over the goal line as the referee's arms shot straight up to signal a touchdown. The Lowell fans went crazy.

No matter that one of his teammates would sit cursing in the locker room because he had not scored, nor that Leo would carp and grumble about the quality of press coverage for his boy; for one golden day, Jack Kerouac was a hero.

Extract the essence of Lowell's lifeblood, and you will find alcohol. 'Gansett, Metaxa, Jameson's Irish—the label does not matter; the water of life deadens the pain, gives working people strength to get out of bed and through the door to work, destroys them. Jack was old enough that winter to take up his heritage. The barkeep at Moody Street's Silver Star Tavern was tolerant of underage drinkers, and charged only a nickel for an enormous glass of Pickwick Beer. Initiated into the brotherhood of booze, flushed, witty and profound—or so he thought—Jack weaved among the ancient barflies, tugging at their sleeves and urgently proclaiming, "Don't you know that you're God?"

Pleasantly muddled, Jack and the gang laughed and argued and reminisced. "Remember the time, GJ?" Jack asked. "We went into the Fox and Hounds Club in Boston, and asked that ritzy clerk to page Mr. Lamont Cranston, and he did!"

Whatever the topic, their deliberations progressed to the background of music—Tommy Dorsey, Artie Shaw, and Benny Goodman; along with most of their generation, they were the children of Swing. One night in 1935 in Los Angeles' Palomar Ballroom, Goodman's band had discovered the song "Sing, Sing, Sing," and within weeks it was enough to twitch the feet of every high school student in the land. Other white swing bands swiftly emerged, trying for New York's Paramount Theater and radio shows of their own.

Jack knew the band lineups and songs perfectly. He and Fred would sit up all night and listen to the *Milkman's Matinee* from Boston, or any of several other programs. The whole gang went to Lowell's City Auditorium to hear Harry James, bought *Metronome* with the gravity of stockbrokers purchasing the *Wall Street Journal*, and disputed fine points with the subtlety of diplomats. Captivated by white swing's union of sweet background and hot solos, Jack was as yet largely ignorant of the original creative source of the magic—black musicians like Fletcher Henderson, who had written the orchestration charts that made Goodman a millionaire, and the royal performers known as the Duke and the Count. From the beginning of his lifelong affair with jazz, Jack had a strong sense of discrimination, rejecting Tommy Dorsey as "too classical," digging the harder-edged sound of Gene Krupa. He loved the drums and constantly played around with an old pair of sticks, and when he listened to Krupa with Roland Salvas, he would pound along on the wall commenting, "Oh, listen to that man swing, he knows, he knows, he's got that beat!"

Though he was a handsome and appealing young man, Jack was shy around women, and his social life had been limited. The woman he met in the winter of his senior year changed all that. Her name was Mary Carney, and she attracted him in the special way that is the blessing of first love, the love that rages and trembles, explodes inside and washes away everything you once were, exalts and grieves you at the same time. A beautiful young woman with dark hair and a pale Celtic complexion, Mary was a year older than he, more socially adept, and their romance would create an indelible image in Jack's mind of what a woman should be.

They met at the Rex Ballroom on New Year's Eve 1938, introduced by a mutual friend. More sophisticated than he, she took him by the hand and led the nervous opening conversation, maternally fussing with his tie and hair, asking him if he had a girlfriend. He was gauche enough to say yes, but his dates with Peggy Coffey that fall had been merely pleasant, and this was something altogether new.

And so he spent the winter of 1939 running from his home in Pawtucketville to school to track practice to dinner to her home in South Lowell. They danced, went to the movies, shared ice cream and secrets. Alone at the kitchen table after her parents had gone to bed, they kissed with the eager, clumsy, nervous passion of youth. Jack's imagination had always endowed the events of his life with a mythic quality, and now he saw his lover as an angel, as the ideal.

Jack turned seventeen on March 12, 1939, and though Nin's husband Charlie Morrisette had slipped and revealed the secret, the surprise birthday party Nin and Mary threw for him was a very special night indeed. His girlfriend, his family, and his friends all plowed through a raging blizzard to Nin's house, gathering to celebrate. Handsome in his heavy letter sweater with the big "L" across the chest, Jack even had to pose with Mémère, Leo, Mary, Roland, and Nin for the *Sun* and *Citizen-Leader* photographers. A little dazed by the attention, he wandered from noisy conversations with GJ and Roland to whispered intimacy with Mary.

Life should have been perfect then, but he had discovered that romance was a two-sided blade that could create as much pain as it did joy. Jack and Mary were young and impatient, their personalities like quicksilver. They wanted everything, *now,* and often bruised each other in their mutual hurry. Many nights Jack trudged homeward over the bridge savoring Mémère's pithy homily *"On essaye à s'y prendre, pi sa travaille pas."* ("We try to manage," he translated, "and it turns out shit"). Restless and uneasy within the narrow patterns of her Irish working-class life, Mary was jealous—of Jack's former girlfriend Peggy Coffey, who was so good a singer that her friends had taken to calling her the white Billie (Holiday), of the track team that stole Jack away from the dance floor, of the ambition that was inevitably tearing him out of Lowell to college. Intuitively, she knew that Jack could not be an ordinary mate.

She was no sunny laughing lassie, but an Irish woman cut with Spanish darkness, a shadow behind her eyes that gave them depth—and pain. He could not cope with "her rippling mysterious moods, philosophic, faintly bestial like the torture of skulls and breasts of cats," and his joy could swirl dizzily into fury, his tenderness transmuted into cruelty, and "I'd want to rip her mouth out and murder her," as he later wrote. The warmth of her full body pressed soft against him, the dizzying odor of sweat and perfume, were not enough. However much he desired her, his hands stayed on her back, away from her breasts, away from between her legs. Armored in her slip and girdle, Mary was a Good Girl, and Jack knew it, and he trapped himself in his frustrations, and he suffered.

Marriage was their only solution. But when he proposed, Mary knew that he was unready, wanted him to be older, for then "You'd know more what to do with me," and she refused him. Jack had no trade, no future yet in Lowell. It was a lovely fantasy he conjured up— he would come tiredly home from work on the railroad to a white-picket-fenced house by the tracks and sit down on red kitchen chairs to dinner from her hands—but it was thin and insubstantial, and as the gray winter trees exploded into green that spring, he stepped back to reconsider. Now Mary was ready to say yes, and suddenly honeymoons looked deathly, and the thought of moving out and going to work had him panting childlike in fear. He paid close attention when Mémêre lectured him about the value of a college degree, and equivocated with Mary. Exasperated by his ambivalence, she shifted her affections to a new young man, and by May dates were difficult to get. His sorrow at losing her was cut with relief; at the time he was looking at the offers of two men, Frank Leahy and Lou Little, which were even more attractive, though nearly as disturbing.

Leahy was then football coach at Boston College, and that glorious week after Thanksgiving and the Lawrence game he had offered Jack a scholarship. B.C. was a comfortable Jesuit school only thirty-five miles from Lowell, and Joe Sullivan, Leo and Nin's boss at Sullivan Brothers Printing Company, was a school trustee; Leo argued loudly for the home squad. Unfortunately for Papa, during the previous season he himself had initiated events that would lead other ways. In between cheers for Jack at the Worcester game, Leo had met Elmer Rynne, a national tennis champ as a younger man, and still a well-known Lowell sportsman. Leo had importuned Rynne: "That's my boy out there. Why don't you be a good fellow and help him get into a school." Elmer was unimpressed until the next play, when Jack twisted loose for a touchdown. Then he began to make telephone calls, and ended up with Lou Little, the football coach at Columbia University. Little was a star himself, and to Jack and his generation he was, as one writer later put it, "the symbol of a man who breathed the very fire of immortality into one, a man who, as though with putty, molded All-Americans."

Mémêre was enthralled with the thought of her son's succeeding in the big city. Torn between his parents, Jack talked with Sam's big brother Charley. Jack had decided that he could balance the demands of art and money with a career in journalism, and Charley had not only the credentials of a *Sun* columnist but Leo's personal respect, earned years before when they were coworkers on *L'Etoile*. Speaking to a prospective writer and fellow lover of New York, Charley rhapsodized on the glories of Manhattan to Jack.

Not that it was ever really a contest. Disappointing his father was cause for many an orgy of self-punishment over the ensuing years—as Jack would later tell the story, Leo lost his job on account of his decision. It wasn't real people that led him to Manhattan, but images—Edward G. Robinson waving his cigar around Chinatown, or Don Ameche strolling down Fifth Avenue, or Hedy Lamarr languishing in a suite at the Ritz. Quite simply, New York was the City.

Following his lost love and his athletic success, the last months of high school were a boring anticlimax. With Mary gone, Jack returned to the gang, but that was beginning to crumble. Scotty was working in an airplane base up the road and Billy Chandler was planning to join the Army, harbingers of the war that would come increasingly to dominate the news.

Though the ominous news of Hitler's Reich might overshadow it, high school graduation was still a special moment for the class of 1939. On June 28, 1939, Jack and his classmates sat in the City Auditorium, agonized through the chorus' songs, the salutatory, the valedictory, and the awarding of prizes (Jack received none), then seized their diplomas from Mayor Archambault's hands and were gone.

Columbia had decided to hide Jack in Horace Mann Prep School for a year to give him a chance to gain weight and improve his scholarship from L.H.S. to Ivy League standards, and in September he boarded a New York–bound bus. As it pulled out of the depot, WPA workmen were tearing down the tenements at the heart of Lowell's Acre to build a modern housing project.

III
"Proud Cruel City"

A slow, lumpseated bus was an ignoble way to enter the sleekest, fastest city on earth, but the contradiction served to emphasize the overwhelming size of New York. Down the Boston Post Road—Route 1—Jack had traveled, rolling through the peripheral towns like New Rochelle, past the "infinite pueblo" of Bronx apartment houses, tenements and streets endlessly looming up and dropping behind. He was amazed to realize that there were still more than 200 blocks to go to the Battery, at the southern tip of the island. Finally the bus crossed a bridge, past black people crowding the sidewalks of Harlem, down Columbus Avenue, then east until sweeping out of the narrow tenement corridors at 110th Street, its passengers could look down the three miles of green Central Park flanked by the grand apartment houses of Central Park West, the other end of the Park framing the skyscrapers that erupted in midtown Manhattan. The bus shifted to Ninth Avenue, and the endless stores and shoppers were like dozens of Kearney Squares end to end, finishing only in the furious rush of Broadway and many more people and lights and action.

The Big Apple. Fiorello La Guardia was its mayor, Tom Dewey its virtuous district attorney, and Walter Winchell its prophet. Its sound was an exhilarating, nervewracking blend of the pushcart vendors who still filled the Lower East Side, the squawking blind newsies who sold its seven dailies, the bells of St. Patrick's Cathedral, and the swing music that leaked out of the stage door at the Paramount Theater. Jack explored it as once he'd prowled the Dracut Woods, roaming from Battery Park and the Bowery to the ice-skating rink at Rockefeller Center, the Museum of Natural History and the Central Park Zoo, from the intimacy of Greenwich Village to Park Avenue's august splendor. In his heart he was a hard-drinking Spencer Tracy reporter-hero, with a white scarf, a topcoat, and a wife who looked like a movie star waiting for him beside a Park Avenue penthouse fireplace.

Actually, Jack stayed with Mémère's stepmother in Brooklyn, where his reality was lace doilies, stickball on the stoop, bead curtains, and the sound of Father Coughlin's rants on the radio. Not that he saw much of his new home; Horace Mann School was in the northern Bronx, over an hour away by subway, and he was up at 6:00 A.M. to catch the train at the Fulton Street IRT station. By 34th Street in Manhattan, he'd usually be able to sit down, doing his homework to the rhythm of the D-train rails. Then he walked up a steep hill to the school. Horace Mann was right out of "Tom Brown at Rugby," replete with ivy-covered gray-stone classroom buildings, a rose-covered headmaster's cottage and crisp green playing fields, all set in a prosperous German neighborhood perched on a hill overlooking the pastoral expanse of Van Cortlandt Park. Once a laboratory for Columbia Teachers College, the school retained enough of a connection to the university to fill out its largely Jewish and Irish upper-middle-class student body with a few of Lou Little's choicest cuts of football flesh, and Jack was one of five such prospects.

On the evening of September 21, 1939, the night before classes began, Jack sat in Brooklyn making the first entry in his new journal. He was terrified. Lowell was one thing, but Horace Mann was the big leagues, and his self-confidence wavered. Unsure of his readiness for this elite new world, he was utterly certain of the tremendous pressure that his parents' ambitions had created. When she'd visited the school in August, Mémère had been so thrilled by her son's gigantic step upward that Jack felt momentarily absolved of all his old guilts about her expectations. Years later he compared the way he felt to the purity of his first confession. Now he trembled before the specter of failure.

As he made his journal entry of September 21, his ambition burst forth in a pompous, rococo frenzy of writing. He paid homage to Thackeray, Samuel Johnson, and Dickens, concluding with "Stay! I am not suggesting that I be included in their fold . . ." In the hour or so between his return home and bedtime, he planned to devote himself to Latin, mythology, Spanish, literature, history, and the musings of his eminent journal. He gave up those particular ambitions by September 25. The intellectual realm would have to wait: his first challenge was to make the football team.

The first weeks of practice were the purest hell. His legs worked fine, but his imagination made All-Americans of his teammates and assured him of certain failure. By the second game, against the Columbia Frosh, he had resurrected his confidence enough to overlook being knocked out; he scored a touchdown, and Lou Little's staff watched as Jack led Horace Mann to a 20–0 victory. Leo came down for the Garden City game and was rewarded with Jack's three touchdowns and a 27–0 Horace Mann sweep. In the flush of success, Jack was proud of himself and his funny Papa, who visited the locker room and had all the guys on the team laughing. They closed their season against Tome, and the Kerouacian ace of fortune came up a second time. Late in the fourth quarter, with the score tied 0–0, Jack ran back a punt 72 yards for a touchdown, giving Horace Mann a 6–0 win and the unofficial New York City prep-school championship.

The academic side of Horace Mann he found tolerable, particularly when he discovered that he was just as smart as all those rich kids. But the way he exercised his intelligence was disturbing. He wrote English papers for his wealthier and lazier classmates at two dollars a throw—free to fellow out-of-town football team members. The money was nice, and it was obvious that he was sharp, but the rich kids still had the advantage on him, the price of the easy way out. And those lunches. Every time his tongue slowly worked the peanut butter down off the roof of his mouth, he looked across the table at the others with their turkey sandwiches and expensive pastries and chocolate milk, and he knew that he didn't quite fit in. He liked Dick Sheresky and Eddie Gilbert, but his occasional visits to elegant Fifth Avenue thick-rug apartments, his encounters with Negro butlers and silver spoons and *real* mahogany furniture were discomforting and somehow threatening. More often, going it alone was easier, and as fall wore on, the subway sometimes ran north from Times Square without him.

Exotic and entertaining but democratically anonymous, Times Square was the perfect haunt for a restless loner. French as it was, Lowell could not offer movies from Paris the way Times Square did, and Jack slipped into the midtown Apollo theater to watch his proletarian hero Jean Gabin in *The Lower Depths*. Blinking back into the sunshine, he'd munch a hot dog and stand watching the pulse of America as it registered in the crowds at Broadway and 42nd Street. The beat was quickening, that fall of 1939. The economy had been flat and the birthrate dropping until the Nazis had swept over Poland in August; now the American workers who boiled out of the subways and toward the lofts and offices knew that the tragedy of Europe promised a renewed American prosperity.

Among those respectable workers slid the gaudy whores and dizzy junkies, the pimps, numbers runners and sleazy "others" who were the area's true residents. One street woman in particular caught Jack's eye shortly after he began to visit the neighborhood. Having written a few extra papers at school and skipped several lunches, he gathered his change together, took a number of deep breaths to calm himself, and approached a redheaded lady on the street. He put down his money in one of the hooker hotels, and lost his virginity on a fall day. It would always be a pleasant memory.

Horace Mann had neither sleaze nor flash, but it did have wit, and though Jack was an innocent Massachusetts jock who couldn't keep up with the droll ribaldry of Sheresky, Gilbert, Morty Maxwell, and Henry Cru, he made a satisfactory audience. Dick or Henry would screw their voices into a simpering British Veddy-good-*rah* thuh accent, "like very high smotche smaz" as Jack later described it. Wizards of the private lewd humor of horny boys, their characters "Duke Douche," "Wanda Want-it," and "Flogg Itt" needed only to whisper the "in" word "Flazm" for yuks from their rustic friend. Cru, a mad-eyed giant with a fantastic laugh and a profitable sideline selling daggers to the younger boys in the toilet, was especially good at mixing an edge of insult into his humor. Goofing along, he would intone, "Kerouac is a victim, a *vic*tim of his own ima-*ghina*tion."

Since his mouth could not keep up with these nascent Park Avenue Grouchos, he attempted to do so with his pen. That fall the *Horace Mann Quarterly* published his first story. "The Brothers" wasn't very good. Seduced by his surroundings, he had crafted a detective story that rang of Henry James and was riddled with clichés—"millions of myriad stars swimming in my brain," "the stygian darkness." Moreover, its closing Sherlockian plot explanation was shamelessly looted from the chronicles of Dr. John Watson. For an incipient Grantland Rice, his sports articles in the school paper that winter were also fairly clumsy. But his second story, "Une Veille de Noël," reflected a much subtler appreciation of self. He placed it in familiar surroundings—a bar at Christmas Eve—and the barkeep's hockey talk, the foolish college students, and the grimly brooding main character Mike were all authentic, even if the visiting angel smacked a little of O. Henry.

When he returned home to Lowell for Thanksgiving, his triumph was complete. Mémêre was overjoyed with his descriptions of his friends, "such nice, well-bred boys," and even Mary, who had written him that fall, greeted him with happy kisses.

It was a strange and ugly winter that joined 1939 and 1940, as if a fog of impending disaster had permeated the atmosphere. The newsreels flickered images of corpses: white-clad Finns locked frozen with dark Russians. At home the mood was sour, three of every four Americans cheering on Martin Dies' HUAC as it joined with J. Edgar Hoover in harassing Jack's working-class radical hero, Harry Bridges, as well as such "dangerous" subversives as the Jehovah's Witnesses. Organized liberalism entered the new decade nearly hysterical about radicals, as the ACLU purged Elizabeth Gurley Flynn, while Van Wyck Brooks, one of those who had voted against her, condemned modernist artists as "rattle-snakes." Most liberals did not see fit to protest the repressive (if techni-cally constitutional) Smith Act, which required aliens to register, and which established political tests for citizenship.

In the first half of that year, 1940, six black citizens of the United States of America had been lynched.

Not all of Jack's friends were jokesters. Seymour Wyse was a bright English boy of esoteric interests, and he helped lead Jack from penthouses to basements, from the East 60's to 125th Street. Together they wandered Harlem, past Father Divine's 15 restaurants—"Chicken or Chops, 15¢"—and the churches he called "Heavens," the Mt. Olivet Baptist Church and all the hundreds of others, the record stores and beauty parlors, Jack developing his eye and tuning his ear; looking, listening. Seymour had an even more specific destination in mind for them, and one fantastic night, he and Jack approached the cultural heart of black New York City—the Apollo Theater. High in the balcony, Jack heard a black musician, Jimmy Lunceford, live for the first time, and was instantly swept up in the whirlwind known as American race relations, and especially the odd di-mension occupied by alienated whites who at least verbally reject racism and become respectfully interested, sometimes obsessed with, Afro-American culture.

Jack had been intently listening to music for years, but segregation applied to music as well as to lunch counters; few had a chance to buy black records, for in those hard times, few enough records at all were being produced, and mostly they were by white swing bands. In one *Billboard*

Top Ten of that period, Bing Crosby had the only record not by a regulation big band. With a superficial formula that mixed clarinets and saxophones for a sweet-smooth dancing sound, Glenn Miller had three of those songs, including "Imagination." The Dorsey Brothers together matched him.

The record companies were only one aspect of a business riddled with racism. Café Society, the first integrated night club in America, had opened in Greenwich Village only a year before, in December of 1938. That same year, the Benny Goodman Band had stunned the jazz world with a Carnegie Hall concert featuring Johnny Hodges and others from the Duke Ellington group, and Lester Young and Count Basie. Artie Shaw had hired Billie Holiday as a singer and Goodman featured Teddy Hill and Lionel Hampton, but basically the jazz world was as Jim Crow as Tupelo, Mississippi.

Digging into jazz lore inevitably forced one to take sides in the U.S. "race problem," and Jack's affinity for Afro-American music would affect his and his friends' cultural sympathies throughout his adulthood. George Avakian was a jazz critic and a Horace Mann graduate whose brother was a classmate of Jack's. Armed with those connections and a press card, Jack managed to interview Avakian in a Village night club called Nick's. He learned a lot that night, and one of the first things was that Avakian couldn't select one All-Star Band; there had to be two—one white, one black. Black Baby Dodds had to be matched by white Dave Tough on drums, Louis Armstrong by Muggsy Spanier on trumpet, and so forth. Avakian's real interest was in the old-time gutbucket "Dixieland" jazz played by a group of whites from Chicago nicknamed the "Austin High Gang." Records of that style were hard to find, and Jack was immensely pleased—and said so in a school newspaper article—when George Avakian produced the *Decca Chicago Style Album,* featuring Eddie Condon, Pee Wee Russell, and the other veterans of white Dixie. Jack was becoming part of the jazz cult, a little snotty and superior toward jitterbugging Harry James fans. In a word, he was Hip.

So in his review of the Decca Chicago album, he wrote that "most of today's swing is a sensationalized carbon-copy of jazz! It lacks both purity and sincerity." Listening to Austin High took him back to the black creators, Kid Ory and Louis Armstrong, and then back again to what Avakian had told him: "[Duke] Ellington stands alone." He studied Fletcher Henderson's black band, perhaps the best of them all in the early thirties, and came away with the sounds of Roy Eldridge on trumpet, Coleman Hawkins on tenor, and later Chu Berry on tenor.

Compared with these new black heroes, Glenn Miller's music seemed flabby, although when Jack got a chance to talk to the most popular musician in America, he grabbed it. The article Jack wrote on the interview was a straightforward account of their conversation about fame, though there was perhaps a touch of acid in his description of Glenn as "clean-cut," after being shocked at hearing him yell "shit" at one of his employees.

Actually, clean-cut shit was about what he thought of "Moonlight Serenade" and the rest of the most popular swing. With the guidance of Seymour Wyse, Jack had developed an understanding of "real jazz" that was profoundly unconcerned with dancing and entertainment values. For him, it was rather "music which has not been prearranged—free-for-all ad lib. It is the outburst of passionate musicians, who pour all their energy into their instruments in the quest for soulful expression and super-improvisation."

When he came to write about the best band in the land, Jack's taste unerringly passed over the more popular Miller and Goodman and Harry James groups, and led him to select the black Count Basie Band. Time proved him right; he said that "Count Basie's swing arrangements are not blaring, but they contain more drive, more power, and more thrill than the loudest gang of corn artists can acquire by blowing their horns apart." In fact, Basie's arrangements were not written but played by ear, instinct, and long experience, giving this very large band the intimacy of a quartet. The entire band was superb, but it was Lester Young who added the last touch of genius.

Billie Holiday had tagged Young as "Prez"; "We've already got a Duke and a Count," she said, "and besides, the most important cat in America is the Prez anyway." He was not only a surpassingly gifted performer, but a radical innovator whose tenor style would tremendously alter the course of Afro-American music. Jack's former model on the saxophone, Coleman "Bean" Hawkins, used a huge fat tone and a fairly ornate style to compete with the swing era's shrieking brass. With all of Basie's band swinging fine behind him, Prez was able to stand for his solos with a tighter, more laconic, yet more expressive sound. Moody and introspective, Prez's horn cut deep, back to the roots, back to the source and soul of Jazz. He played the blues.

"The blues is a thing," said W. C. Handy, "deeper than what you'd call a mood today." It is the freedom sound, the call of those displaced from Mother Africa, the cry of the people who can't go home again. The blues were inspired not by an abstract ideal but by the sound of the human voice, choked with tears or ripped by rage, but always the voice. "Blues truth," as a critic later wrote, "runs counter to hysterical confidence in progress, machines, and human power. It is a darker, more fateful, though ultimately more relaxed and humorous truth that has its own sober and sensual comfort." As Memphis Slim once remarked, when it all comes down, "you gotta go back to Mother Earth."

Blues truth seized Jack, ripped him out of the white world, made him companion to Ishmael and Huck Finn, thrust him into the twilight land between the races. Displaced from Lowell by desire, from Horace Mann by his roots, he found refuge in the blues—a music that didn't entirely fit the classical tradition either. Afro-American music was not exactly related to what Bach and Beethoven had to say; Bessie Smith was only the greatest of the musicians who discovered the uncharted areas between European notions of pitch, and jazz further liberated singers from the symphonic ideas of precise pitch and rhythm toward the more natural pace and melody of human speech. The blues made Jack colored, if not black, gave identity to a soulful, sensual-mystic eighteen-year-old whose commitment to art was as nebulously defined as it was serious. The sound, the beat, and the rhythm of the human voice and experience would obsess him always.

Spring came, but this year of 1940 it was dreadful, pocked with the shrapnel of the onrushing Wehrmacht, which easily conquered Norway and Denmark in April. Americans shivered and tried to escape this reality with a return to old pastimes. The World's Fair reopened for its second season totally altered; gone was 1939's faith and confidence in progress as symbolized by the Perisphere, an enormous steel globe representing the infinite, and the finite 700-foot-pillar called the Trylon. The monument to twentieth-century technology had reverted to a folksy county fair, though even that was no real escape; nervous visitors demanded that war news be piped over the loudspeaker system.

Jack reached back as well, tried to fuse Lowelltown with the City, and invited Mary Carney to the Spring Formal. It was a disaster. Eddie Gilbert and Morty Maxwell imported dates from the likes of Miss Power's Finishing School; Mary came on a free railroad pass, courtesy of her father. All the glories of a swank weekend in New York City—a visit to the fair, hearing Frank Sinatra with Harry James at Carnegie Hall, sipping crème de menthe at the Plaza Hotel—merely accentuated the distance between them. Driven apart by their different realities, they ignored the fact that Jack's white tie and tails were a gift, and that he went to the dance red-faced from his naïve use of a sunlamp; he was at least partly a citizen of Manhattan, and by the end of the evening, Mary was crying, begging him to come back to Lowell with her. "No" was all he could say.

New York City was his adopted environment, and thanks to his literary and athletic distinctions, he had achieved a reasonably comfortable standing for a latecomer to the hermetic world of Horace Mann. The yearbook said of him, "Brains and brawn found a happy combination in Jack." Graduation came in June 1940, and once again he remained largely aloof and alone. Without the money for a white suit, he lay reading on the grass behind the gymnasium, and escaped the torturous commencement addresses that told the class, "You must remember that you were born at a fortunate time. You can always remember the world as it was before 1940." Only days before, on June 4, the last battered ship had pulled out of Dunkirk, fleeing dive bombers and tanks, the horror of the blitzkrieg. Sticking a leaf of grass in his mouth, Jack paged through Walt Whitman until the talk was over, came out and shook his teachers' and headmaster's hands, and walked back down the hill for the train ride home to Lowell.

It had come along at the perfect time in his life, that deceptively simple book *Leaves of Grass;* all that summer Jack and Sammy Sampas, his dearest friend, walked beside Walt, listening to his "barbaric yawp," to the crashing thunder of his visionary prophecy. Jack also read Thoreau and Thomas Hardy and Emily Dickinson, and even had a fling with Jack London. The Nietzschean beast raked over his dreams, made him literally hear "the call of the wild," taught him of the free ones, the hobos, the bums, left him with a vision of freedom—and the open road. London gave him a taste for high adventure, and his romantic vision was ever more colorful as a result. But it was Whitman, a creature of the cosmos, who truly fed Jack's dreams.

In a country that was reading about plans for a Nazi invasion of the United States, Jack listened to the prophet of a roughnecked, reverent, free America. Perhaps never again in Jack's life would he have the faith and confidence to be totally in tune with Walt's swirling vision. For the young man who wandered meditating by the river, Walt saw eternity in a leaf of grass as well as a star, and felt that

Each is not for its own sake,
I say the whole earth and all the stars in the sky
are for religion's sake.

The water's babble became the sound of the cosmos to Jack as he
pondered the meaning of life, death, rebirth. He killed a moth and lay
it on his desk, lamented it with a written elegy, saw the easy snuffing out
of its life as a key to understanding eternity. There was no smile on his
face when Sammy turned to him one day that summer and said, "Don't
think me insane, but I know, I *know* that I shall die young." They read
intently as Walt informed that wisdom is not a product of schools, but
that "Wisdom is of the soul, is not susceptible of proof, is its own proof."
But Walt was more than a metaphysician to them; he was an American.
Whitman was the bard who sang for the soul of a great country, who
exalted the common working people, who would not exclude a prostitute,
who howled of righteous freedom. A fiercely patriotic hyphenated American, Jack nodded when Walt said, "These States are the amplest poem,"
and took it personally when he read, "Who are you indeed who would
talk or sing to America?/Have you studied out the land, its idioms and
men?" In the pause before the war, as he listened to the sounds of Lowell
voices, the town was never more alive to Jack, might well have seemed
the source for Walt's cosmically democratic thought, "A great city is that
which has the greatest men and women." The political impulses of their
Promethean radical study club had not entirely faded; along with the great
poet, Jack and Sammy felt a strong empathy with the downtrodden, a
cosmic sense of democracy. Jack and Sammy were illuminated with a
sunny vision of the plain-dressed common citizens of America—Boston
Irish dock workers, Alabama tenant farmers, Texans, New Yorkers—
standing healthy, beautiful, and grand in their liberty.

As friends on their way to the World's Fair drove Jack to his freshman year at Columbia in September of 1940, freedom was on almost every
American's mind. The entire country had erupted into a red-white-and-
blue frenzy of flags set to the sound of Kate Smith's "God Bless America."
Every flat blank space in the city, from walls to the sides of subway cars,
was plastered with posters demanding that New Yorkers "Help Holland,"
"Aid Norway," or contribute to the "Paderewski Fund for Polish Relief"
and "Bundles for Britain." As Jack stood by the sundial at the center of
the Columbia campus, he might have read the names Goethe, Herodotus,
and Plato he saw etched on the library frieze and thought that Morningside Heights was a sanctuary; Columbia President Nicholas Murray But-

ler, one of the leading members of the Committee to Defend America by Aiding the Allies, made sure that it wasn't so. Whatever illusions Jack had nurtured about the tranquil scholastic dignity of college must have vanished at least by the time he began to wash dishes at the student union for his room and board.

He arrived at Hartley Dormitory on September 17, and was immediately disappointed with a room that overlooked noisy, smelly Amsterdam Avenue and came equipped with an obnoxious roommate complete with glasses and a beanie. A quick move to Livingston Hall and a room set on the interior courtyard eliminated the roommate, but he had to wear the blue-and-white beanie like the rest of his 500 classmates, or suffer the hazing of the worldly sophomores, as Columbia tradition demanded.

They passed through the various placement examinations, bought the "Blue Book," the guide to campus life, paid their $3.50 dues to the student association, and listened to President Butler's homily, replete with a line from Longfellow, about "The Joy of Work." Compared to the panic of the previous year, football practice seemed routine to Jack, down to the fact that once again he didn't appear to be a starter. Academically, though, things were interesting. Science, in the form of chemistry, was alien to him as usual, a confusing babble about specific density and molals, but Professor Mark Van Doren's Shakespeare class had the sense of wisdom and insight Jack had shared with Sammy, and the man's meditations on the Bard sent Jack's imagination flying out the window, over the pigeon shit on the sill, into the freer reaches of contemplation and musing.

By eight o'clock in the evening he would be seated at his desk, fiddling with his collegiate pipe, the radio tuned to the classical music on WQXR, burrowing into the ponderous literature Columbia offered first-year students in those days—Aeschylus, Plato, John Stuart Mill, and of course Homer. In the golden lamplight of freshman year, he settled into the university, put on coat and tie and visited a suitably ancient and fusty dean for dinner and a look at the old gentleman's dinosaur egg. Jack even joined a fraternity. Kerouac was part of the elite fifth of his class who did so—one of his fellow pledges at Phi Gamma Delta was named Courtney Rockefeller—but he didn't last. Years later he said it was because he wouldn't wear a beanie, though money and breeding might also have entered into his decision to quit.

But 116th Street and Broadway was not an ivory-tower environment for an idealistic scholar-athlete in the fall of 1940. President Butler wanted warriors. In cooperation with the National Defense Research Committee headed by Harvard President James Conant, Butler had enrolled the "Blue and White's" men of science in the war effort, and established a Military Engineering course, a Civil Aeronautics Administration unit, and a Marine Corps ROTC unit on campus. No one objected aloud to all this until Butler told the campus newspaper, the *Spectator*, that "those in conflict with the University's goals [which meant Butler's pro-war views] should resign." Then the faculty growled. Pressure from heavyweights like Franz Boas, Wesley Mitchell, and Robert Lynd forced the president to back down, but the affair created community division and bitterness.

The oncoming war began to touch Jack more personally. On October 16, 1940, classes at Columbia were suspended for the day, and Jack joined his out-of-town classmates in registering for the nation's first "peacetime draft." He couldn't listen only to WQXR, either. Since August, WCBS had been broadcasting a voice like death belonging to a human cloud of cigarette smoke named Edward R. Murrow, each show beginning with the fateful words, "This . . . is London." The newsstand across the street from Livingston Hall was crowded with aerial pictures of London pimpled with puffs of smoke and orange erupting fire. The gallant "Cloud Cavalry"—the RAF—was fighting the Battle of Britain. In American minds, all Britons were involved in the war, from the Trafalgar Square flower vendor warming her hands at an incendiary bomb to the old man lighting a cigarette from it. One popular poster depicted a skull, one eye of which was an American flag, with the caption "Defend America by Aiding Britain." The British plight was vivid in Jack's mind.

It wasn't *all* serious, of course. Columbia was still a college in an age when the sorority of one school regulated the skirt lengths of campus flirts and paddled offenders, and coeds at another university taught their sisters not to smoke if their date didn't, since it would make him feel ineffectual. War or no war, life went on; on October 16, after Jack registered for the draft, he got on the subway as usual to go to football practice.

The Columbia frosh had lost 18–7 to Rutgers on the previous Saturday, and while Jack had only gotten into the second half, the *Spectator* said that the team had a "fairly good running attack at times, with Jack Kerouac showing up well." He started the second game, against St. Benedict's Prep, and ran the opening kickoff back 90 yards, but couldn't quite score. He was flying, looking great, but three plays later he planted his foot one way, his leg went the other, and he felt the terrible grinding pop of a broken leg. Far worse, Coach Furey didn't believe it was serious, called him a softy. "Run it off," he grunted, "it's just a sprain." Jack limped around for ten days, cursing the coach and his luck, before the X-ray revealed the break and he swapped his uniform for a pair of crutches and clippings in the *Spectator* that called him a "star back," a "fleetfooted backfield ace," and mourned his loss to the team in a headline article.

Jack enjoyed being a noble wounded hero dragging himself about campus on his crutches, and spent the rest of the fall sitting near the fireplace of the Lion's Den, a Columbia student hangout, eating filet mignon and hot fudge sundaes. Injury had its compensations; if he could no longer be a gridiron star, he now had time to think and relax, catch a movie or have a beer at the West End Café, another favorite student spot. His class attendance continued to be erratic, and by the end of the year he had gotten an A from Van Doren and flunked chemistry. But he was more interested in alchemistry than its modern successor, and for that he went beyond the laboratory to the American Faust, Thomas Wolfe, whom he started reading in the Lion's Den.

His leg propped on a pillow, he tuned out the cup-rattling background of the Den and began with *Look Homeward, Angel,* then rapidly devoured the entire canon. His reading must have seemed eerie at first, for Eugene Gant's young life in *Look Homeward, Angel* read like a précis before the fact of Jack's own. Here was a sensual loner, a "stranger who had come to life, fed by the lost communications of eternity, his own ghost, haunter of his own house, lonely to himself and the world. O lost." Saddled with a ravenously ambitious mother, a wailing, gloomy father, a dead younger brother, and the ignorance of their hometowns, Eugene and Jack were fellow "outsiders" enthralled by the majesty of the American dream. Both suffered from religious upbringings that distorted their natural sensuality, each had been blessed with a schoolteacher who had set him on the track of letters, and both were permanent inhabitants of the land of fantasy, though an Oz rather than a Lilliput, for they were *American* dreamers.

As Wolfe wrote of Gant, "He was not a child when he reflected, but when he dreamt . . . he belonged with the Mythmakers." Jack drew back from Eugene Gant and felt that Wolfe's writing was "a torrent of American heaven and hell that opened my eyes to America as a subject in itself." In Whitman's footsteps, Wolfe had sought to craft an epic of America, of his own gargantuan consciousness colliding with the nation and its common people, its sights, sounds, smells, and geography. Above all, the book was a rush of sound, the surreal noise of blended American accents and idiom, the sound of the voice, or perhaps the magic sound of perfect poetic beauty:

> Deep womb, dark flower. The Hidden. The secret fruit, heart-red, fed by rich Indian blood. Womb night brooding darkness flowering secretly into life.

Like Lester Young, Wolfe taught Jack to listen; like Whitman, he gave Jack America as a subject. There were other lessons, though it would be years before they took root. By the time Jack read Wolfe, he had already written nearly a million words of prose, and was committed to the idea of stylistic craft. Though he would have agreed that Wolfe's work was nothing but *confession,* he followed his master's style literally rather than making his *own* confession. Second, Wolfe made him want to move, to see Asheville—and Fresno San Francisco Nome Dallas Cheyenne Denver and all the rest. That would have to wait for a while.

Once his leg healed, Jack resumed his New York wanderings, especially when Sammy Sampas would visit him. Together they'd drink beer in waterfront bars, walk along the docks and warehouses, hold vigil on the Brooklyn Bridge, go to museums and theaters, or scream Byron's poetry at dawn to the Statue of Liberty from the deck of the Staten Island ferry. They grew close in those brief visits, and Jack was glad to rejoin him for the summer in Lowell. Though he'd flunked chemistry and would have to make it up, he deserved to feel satisfied with his first year in college. Spring football practice had drawn several favorable comments from Lou Little to the *Spectator* about Jack's bright future, and since many juniors and seniors were leaving to join the military, his chances of playing—and being a star—were good.

The summer of 1941 should have been just like its predecessor, but little differences subtly combined to make it unusual. Jack still played baseball and swam and guzzled beer with the gang, but now GJ was away in the Civilian Conservation Corps, and another old friend, Billy Chandler, was in the Army. Even their old haunts on Moody Street had been altered by the conflict, the old black-clad Greek ladies of the Acre now displaced by the dozens of prostitutes who worked the trade from nearby Fort Devens, which had increased enormously in size. Even the music on the radio had changed, and the hit tune of the season was not by Glenn Miller or Harry James, but Beethoven. No one knew who had first taken the opening four notes of the Fifth Symphony to go with the Morse code

. . .—"V," though a BBC announcer called it "fate knocking on Hitler's door." But "V" became the common symbol of the Allies, and though two thirds of America—especially college students—wanted to stay out of the war, their sympathies were clearly with England.

Jack and Sammy spent time in Lowell, of course, reading Wolfe now rather than Whitman, literally in tears over Gant's artistic agonies. They once got drunk together, or pretended to, and went over to Sam's brother Charley's house to tease the newly wedded couple late one night. They'd often cut out of town and hitchhike to Boston, where Sammy made anti-Fascist, Marxist-Leninist speeches on the Common. His audiences were now more respectful, because Communism, as equated with the Soviet Union, had been refurbished by Hitler's recent attack on Russia on June 22, 1941. Now the Communists were England's allies. All that spring Americans had watched the Battle of the Atlantic, and the mushrooming might of America's own developing war machine. Everyone became involved, from baseball star Hank Greenberg, drafted in May, to Walt Disney, whose studio designed military insignia. In August *Life* readers even saw their first pictures of American troops practicing a beachhead assault.

The harbingers of war were everywhere that summer, pervasive enough to infect Jack even in happy moments. After years of itineracy, Leo had gotten a steady job, and in August of 1941 the Kerouacs moved to New Haven, Connecticut. Jack was empty and nervous as he felt his roots being ripped out of the ground, something like the way he felt as a boy seeing Lowell threatened by the flood. But now it was he who would endure the changes, and without Lowell, he didn't know who he was anymore. Sitting on the front steps as Mémère and a cousin packed, he stared up at the stars and entered the security of a fantasy world. As he described it many years later, he imagined himself triumphantly leading Columbia to the Rose Bowl, scoring an A in chemistry, running a four-minute mile, hitting uncountable home runs for the baseball team and turning down a Yankee contract, writing the greatest play Broadway ever saw, stunning Madison Avenue with a perfect book, knocking out Joe Louis at the Garden for the championship of the world. Jack's vanities, however ordinary, gripped his imagination; they seemed to him suitably crazy dreams for a mad time.

He returned to Columbia in the fall of 1941, but studying and practicing seemed trivial exercises in an apocalyptic world. Far worse was the weakness Leo had shown as Jack had left the cottage in New Haven for school, pleading with Jack to save the "family honor," be a good boy and get ahead. His family's expectations created a pressure on Jack that added to the distortions of a brave new world at war, and the result was a quagmire of indecision.

FDR was on the radio that September 11, 1941, and he was declaring naval war on Germany. Responding to an attack on the U.S.S. *Greer*, he compared the Nazis to pirates and rattlesnakes and told America that henceforth German ships in American defensive zone waters would be shot at on sight. At Columbia, Jack couldn't take the absurdity of it all anymore. "I was getting very poetic by that time," he recalled later. "And I'd get black and broody and everything. Packed my suitcase and walked right out in front of Lou Little. He said, 'Where you going?' I said, 'Oh, this suitcase is empty. I'm going to my grandmother's house to get some clothes.' I walked out with a full suitcase."

He took his suitcase and got on a southbound bus and was gone. On September 26, the *New York Times* printed an announcement that "Jack Kerouac, Sophomore wingback, will not be available this fall." It took tremendous will to leave Columbia and hurt his parents the way he did, to burn down his whole athletic career—in fact, to cut himself off from traditional achievement forever. Sunk in confusion, Jack had little idea of what or why intellectually. But his intuition was sure: wherever his future lay, it was more likely to come with diesel smoke and a lonely bus seat on the road than gymnasiums, dormitories, and the cheers of the multitude.

IV
Myshkin at
Sea

AND SO he wandered, "joyed like a maniac" to Washington D.C.,
slept a night or two in a hot and buggy room, returned to New Haven,
got a job in a rubber plant and quit at noon of the first day, sat and
watched children at play and thought of himself as a "sad young man like
Saroyan." Leo was disgusted, growling at Jack, "Why don't you [young]
people ever do right?" An old Lowell buddy got Jack a job as a grease
monkey in Hartford, Connecticut; his rented room there was shabby
enough, but it was his own—he was independent at last. Nights after
work, he labored at a collection of short stories called "Atop an Underwood," studiously imitating Saroyan, Hemingway, and Wolfe. It was a
melancholy autumn, as American soldiers maneuvered in Louisiana, and
the U.S.S. *Kearney* was sunk near Iceland. Thanksgiving 1941 would have
been thoroughly lonesome, but Sammy knocked on his door that morning,
and his presence made their blue-plate turkey specials at the local lunch
cart quite tolerable. They shared their writing, and Sammy urged him to
return to Lowell and work on the *Sun;* two weeks later, when Leo wrote
that he and Mémêre were going home, Jack was only too pleased to follow
them to Crawford Street in Pawtucketville.

Home it was, even if he was a failure and not a returning hero, even
if the red brick seemed drab compared to Manhattan glitter. The *Sun*
listed track meets he'd not compete in, and mentioned that Hank Mazur
—a teammate whom Jack had disliked his sophomore year in high school
—was now captain of the West Point football team.

One Sunday he saw *Citizen Kane*. He was astounded by it, by
Welles's poetry in film, the fantastic chilling castle dissolving into the

lightning flashes of "News on the March"; one day, he vowed, he'd write that way. Kerouac lunged into the cold streets ready to go home and try his hand at script writing, and learned that 10,000 miles away the Japanese had bombed Pearl Harbor; his gloomy ponderings on the future had been replaced with the flat certainty of war.

At first he planned to enter the Navy V-2 program to train as a flier, and while he waited for his application to be processed he put on a tie and got a job writing sports for the *Sun*. By noon he'd have his copy filed, and his editor Frank Moran would watch him speed-write his own story, stream-of-consciousness style, which he called "Vanity of Duluoz." (Many years later he would publish a totally different book with that title.) His days were full, working out at the Y after work, studying H. G. Wells after dinner, talking with Sammy. His old friend Peggy Coffey was around, and occasionally the two would meet in the afternoon at his parents' house. With Leo and Gabrielle off to work, they enjoyed the privacy horizontally. Their high school morals had long since vanished, worn away by the grim realities of war. A hundred miles east of Lowell, German submarine packs preyed on American merchant ships. With U.S. troops as yet uninvolved in fighting, the focus was on the war machine and its component workers—Willow Run in Michigan, the Brooklyn Navy Yard, where 35,000 men worked 24 hours seven days a week and where pictures of a rat with a swastika captioned "Starve Him with Silence" stared out at the laborers.

For Jack, there was another war—between himself and Leo. Enraged by his own failures, jealous of Jack's potential and worried over his son's stagnation in Lowell "Shittown," the elder Kerouac yelled and carried on, demanding, "Do you think you can do what you feel like all your life?" But career and financial achievement were not important to Jack; ultimately, even the war itself was insignificant. Years later he said of himself at this time, "Mighty world events meant virtually nothing to him, they were not real enough, and he was certain that his wonderful joyous visions of super spiritual existence and great poetry were realer than all." Inside a nation rapidly transforming itself into a superb war machine, Jack turned away and immersed himself in "visions of super spiritual existence." He went to the library and checked out three volumes, and entered a mystic world occupied by Goethe's Faust, Job, and above all else, Fyodor Mikhailovich Dostoyevsky.

It was not an escape into some simple-minded refuge, but a confrontation with reality that was as frightening as the headlines. Faust's desire for absolute experience and expression was resonant to Jack as a young artist, and he would surely have sympathized when Faust wagered his soul with Mephistopheles for absolute knowledge. Eventually, Faust was saved by divine intervention. It was another wager that forced Jack to peer into the abyss, for the Book of Job was not merely a tale for the faithful, but a mind trap. Satan told God that Job, "the greatest" of His subjects, was faithful only because he had been well rewarded: "But put forth thine hand now, and touch all that he hath, and he will curse thee to thy face."

Stripped of all but his life, Job endured. At last God appeared, told Job that his limited human idea of justice was inconsequential before the mystery of His will, received obeisance, and rewarded Job with an even fuller life.

Jack was in no mood to accept a benevolent-parish-priest's ending to the story, and the obvious counter possibility must surely have occurred to him as he read it, he said later, "down to its tiniest detail in its entirety." What if? What if justice was nothing more than a heavenly crap game and one's deeds and one's rewards were unrelated? Or as the victim himself asked, *"Why is light given* to a man whose way is hid, and whom God hath hedged in?" Job scoured Jack's intellectual world clean, made fate and the cosmos into a pure reality of tumbling dice, and left him ready for the gambler named Dostoyevsky.

Over the next two years, Jack would read all of Dostoyevsky's major works. He began his study with the gloomy nameless voice of *Notes from the Underground.* The narrative opened with the words "I'm a sick man . . . a mean man." He was a totally alienated bureaucrat—spiteful, perverse, and depraved. He was a mouse, a denizen of the underground, a midget Hamlet frozen in futility. Sunk in despair, he dictated a philosophical monologue and a memoir.

Notes from Underground was a frightening, naked confession, truth in all loathsome detail. It was classic prophecy, raging at the foul corruption of the world, but it was consciously apolitical, since Dostoyevsky had nearly faced the firing squad and had spent years in Siberia for being involved in "revolution." If Dostoyevsky was a mystic Christian nationalist, he was also unsure of his faith in God, and his ambivalence was reflected in his narrator, who was not merely a dummy for the Lord to smite, but an authentic louse. For at the end of the story he cruelly mistreated a sad nameless whore, then told himself, "My insult will elevate her, purify her through . . . through hatred . . . well . . . maybe through forgiveness." "What's better," he mused, "cheap happiness or lofty suffering?"

Jack felt that Dostoyevsky was right, that suffering was the only cause of awareness. And because suffering is *not* intellectual, Dostoyevsky and all of the major experiences of his life told him that modern liberal progress—"civilization"—was not the omega of human existence. For it was based on reason, and "reason is only reason, and it only satisfies man's rational requirements," wrote Dostoyevsky. "Desire, on the other hand, is the manifestation of life itself—of all of life—and it encompasses everything from reason down to scratching oneself. And although, when we are guided by our desires, life may often turn into a messy affair, it's still life and not a series of extractions of square roots." Only the independent, creative free will meant anything to Dostoyevsky—or Jack—and the bloodthirsty "civilized" society around both of them seemed absurd at best—possibly mad.

Jack felt that prophecy deep inside. Billy Chandler, a close childhood friend, had been stationed in the Philippines, and was even then taking the long walk that led to Bataan. As the war engulfed America, Jack would contemplate the new reality of a mystical perspective, trying to make a mournful Dostoyevskian sense out of his times and his nation's changes.

Lowell, Papa, the *Sun* all became insufferable; in March 1942 he caught a bus to Washington, where GJ Apostolakis had a job and a place to stay waiting for him. His buddy knew Jack had changed. As GJ remembered it, "I was asleep and all of a sudden there was a light in my eyes and a gun in my face and a guy talking Cagney, 'You squealed, you dirty rat, and I'm gonna murderlize yah.' Jack would *never* have messed with guns before. He was real worried about hurting his parents . . . Mémêre didn't understand that he just *had* to be a writer . . . she didn't *want* to understand. Washington was crazy."

For the young poet who would study his native land, the Capital was the perfect subject, an augury of the American future. Erected on the rational, progressive, liberal ideology of the New Deal, integrated with the erupting military-industrial establishment, the American government had become a Technocracy, a system where party labels and values were subsumed to the demands of technical bureaucrats; all of it was caught in the image of the Pentagon, the largest office building in the world. Jack worked on a Pentagon construction crew for a few days, and it affected him deeply. Arlington, Virginia, seemed like a deathtrap to him, and in his mind the Pentagon was "Gethsemane," where Christ died.

The government itself was growing so unbelievably that Civil Service tests were held two and three times a day while Jack was in Washington.

Agencies of social change like the Federal Writers Project and the rest of the WPA, the CCC, the Farm Security Administration, and the NYA all vanished, while the Army and allied offices mushroomed. The war altered the nation's economic structure; though nearly two thirds of the prewar GNP and virtually all of its manufacturing was the work of small business, the Revenue Act of 1940 and the appointment of Donald Nelson, Chief Buyer for Sears, Roebuck, as head of the War Production Board all signaled the accession of big business to power. The war redrew the very face of the land, pouring the bulk of its expenditures into the South, Southwest, and the Pacific Coast—the "Southern Rim"—creating standardized boom towns that would serve as models for postwar suburbia.

For his part, Jack did not analyze Revenue Acts, but knew only that Washington was enormous, crowded, busy, "crazy." Intuitively he was aware of a different change; every time he screwed a willing lady on newspapers laid down in a park it was clear that his old moral code, aside from his enduring worship of marriage, had all but disappeared. Twenty years old, he even let himself be "kept" by a waitress girlfriend for a brief period, and after quitting the Pentagon job and later a job as short-order cook and soda jerk, he went back to Lowell thinking about getting laid in ways that would have made no sense to him a few years before. Easy "pussy" was not just sex to his mournful Gerardian soul, but a symbol of an America lost and mysteriously changed, as unfamiliar as his own new personality.

He touched down in Lowell only briefly before hitching to Boston with Sammy to get Coast Guard papers for shipping out as a merchant seaman. Sammy had lost his scholarship at Emerson College in Boston, his railroad job was uninspiring, and he wanted to join Jack and travel. Jack was actually relieved when his papers came through first, telling Sammy, "I just wanta be away from you and Lowell and New York and Columbia for a long while and be alone and think about the sea." He hitched to Boston with another buddy and began the process of joining the Marine Corps. Released in the afternoon to set his affairs in order, he elected to forget them in Scollay Square, Boston's sleazy equivalent of Times Square, and, "serious even in his dissipations," he ended up so drunk that he slept that night hugging a toilet, absorbing the effluvia of America's sailors. The next morning he woke up, dove into the harbor and cleaned off, and went to the local National Maritime Union hall and signed up as a scullion on the S.S. *Dorchester*, sailing the following day, July 22, 1942, for Greenland. Saying goodbye to a tearful Sammy on the docks was hard; each saw death in the other's eyes. They weren't silly romantics; it was the last time they would ever see each other.

Jack did not choose to be a sailor out of cowardice. As his ship steamed out of Boston Harbor, the Army had lost 1,400 dead, the Navy 3,420; the NMU, with one tenth the men of the Navy, had lost nearly 2,000, and two NMU ships a day were sinking into the Atlantic. He chose it because it was a looser, hipper organization. The Merchant Marine was the only integrated service in America, and the NMU was a militantly left-wing group, many of whose members were veterans of the Spanish Civil War. Its negotiators had won the seamen time to themselves on board, with an eight-hour day for a hundred dollars a month and a hundred-dollar monthly war bonus. The bag he carried on the ship, filled with clothing and a load of classical literature, caused him trouble by marking him as a punk college football player, but he felt that "being misunderstood [was] like being the hero in the movies." He was a silent, moody, romantic youth preoccupied by death, scribbling into his journal, "Death hovers over my pencil," and writing of the nonstop poker games that "the stake is money and the stake is life." He was curiously unafraid. Death seemed a "joyful, even pleasant thought at times," to him, as he would later write, "full of dark heroism and wonder, a magnificent thought."

He felt cleansed and free out on the ocean, and he stood on deck for hours staring at the flanking destroyers on the horizon as the green breakers crashed over the bow. Wallowing in the greasy slop of scullion-hood was less pleasant. Old Glory, the six-foot six-inch black boss cook, was outrageous enough to be entertaining as he laid out an unendingly cynical monologue on the ways of mankind. The homosexual pastry cook who jacked off into the cake mix, the Abraham Lincoln Brigade steward, and the dagger-carrying Moro (Filipino) deckhands all made for interesting breaks in the routine, but it was a largely meditative trip. Poker and rumors were the crew's main pastime on the *Dorchester,* and since Jack was broke, his only companions were his dreamy thoughts of death, his writing, a novel he called *The Sea Is My Brother,* and the sea itself. The ship was ferrying construction workers to a base in Greenland, and the icebergs floating in cold seas under the thin ice-blue sky were nothing like the Polynesian fantasies he'd enjoyed in Boston. He had few illusions about combat, either. When their destroyer escort sank a German submarine one morning as Jack fried bacon for a thousand men, his thoughts were with his blond German Billy Budd scullion counterpart; far below

decks himself, he felt like a slave deep in the hold of the ship, and took
to carrying a razor blade for suicide should they sink. Six years later in a
fictional setting he would comment that "the world was mad with war and
history, and he could not understand it at all. It made great steel ships
that could plow the sea, and then made greater torpedoes to sink the self
same struggling ships. He suddenly believed in God somehow, in goodness
and loneliness." Losing their partner ship, the U.S.S. *Chatham,* to
torpedoes on the return run intensified that sense of madness, and the run
ended with the gross and appropriate absurdity of an enormous, feather-
blizzarding pillow fight among the crew.

In October 1942 the *Dorchester* docked in Boston, and Jack strode
off the ship overjoyed at being back. Lowell was a pleasure to visit this
time, for he was a man of some experience now, could look Leo in the
eye and talk about his work on the ship. Jack didn't stay long in his
hometown, however, for a day or two after his arrival he received a
telegram from Lou Little that read "You can come back on the team if
you want to take the bull by the horns." And so just three days off his
ship he was washing dishes—this time for Columbia—reading *Hamlet,*
and trying to get ready for the West Point game. Army was still captained
by Hank Mazur, a Lowell High senior when Jack was an underclassman,
and Jack wanted revenge on the haughty boy who had, as Jack recalled
it, once harassed him. Crouched on the sidelines at Baker Field, Jack
pleaded with Little: "Get in there now, Coach?" Lou wouldn't put him
in. "You lost too much weight at sea," he said, and ignored Jack's vows
to smear Mazur. Robbed of a confrontation with his past, football seemed
trivial, bloodless, a film whose colors had been leached away. A week later,
Jack sat in his room as the snow dropped, thinking about scrimmaging in
the mud and snow, as the radio began to play Beethoven. "Dum dum dum
dummmmmmmmmmmmmmmm." *"I'm going to be an artist,"* he said.
"I'm not going to be a football player." He never played again. Instead
of suiting up, he left Columbia and returned to Lowell to read, sip coffee,
and stare into the blank future.

Waiting for the draft in Lowell was no better that winter than the
one before, and Jack's only useful occupation was printing out by hand
the novel he had written on the *Dorchester, The Sea Is My Brother.* Drunk
one night, feeling the weight of his travel and experience, he tried to strike
back at his past once more before leaving for the Navy, and vowed to
screw Mary Carney. She laughed at his futile, fumbling efforts to pene-

trate her thick rubber girdle-shield, and he went home with his head hanging out the bus window, sick and cursing.

In February 1943 he entered the Navy, and his service rapidly became a disaster. He was nearly twenty-one, while his comrades were mostly eighteen. Boot camp's disciplinary methods—the seemingly useless labor of washing garbage cans, the petty rules about cigarette smoking, close-order drill—were designed to mold individuals into obedient and cohesive team members, and Jack was incapable of being a team member or even of understanding the program's rationale; he wanted the commandant at Newport Naval Station to hire "shits" to wash the cans. Taking his model from fiction, he tried to adopt the attitude of Melville's little man Bartleby, who had said, "I would prefer not to."

Sammy Sampas also dominated Jack's thoughts. Sam had enlisted in the Army, and was at this time a guard at the Camp Lee stockade. His letters meditated on Spengler and spontaneity in art, and on the artist's, and the citizen's, duty. He told of a prisoner who pointed at him and repeated Thoreau's classic comment to Emerson, *"You* are the real prisoner."* A few months later, Sam wrote another friend, "Somehow out of all this catastrophe and chaos, I've . . . found a religious sustenance to see me through the darkest days." In a letter to Jack, he could only pray that God really did exist. He encouraged Jack with the pledge "I have kept faith," but his brotherly message was not enough to sustain Jack.

One day at drill he simply opted out, laid down his gun, and went to the library to read in quiet. He played the jailhouse game with his warders and demanded aspirin for nonexistent headaches, and entered the psychiatric ward, there to be terrified by some of his more wild-eyed fellow inmates. As he watched frustrated guards beat patients, he was troubled with the age-old question "Who is really insane around here?" Eventually, the guards caught him and a buddy named Big Slim pocketing butter knives and sent them straitjacketed to Bethesda Naval Hospital. Leo came to the hospital and ranted to the doctors about the Jewish-Marxist conspiracy and how the "Germans should not be our enemies but our allies," but that didn't free Jack. It took a liberal Jewish psychiatrist, who believed Jack when he likened himself to Samuel Johnson, and said, "I'm too much of a nut and a man of letters" to be in the Navy, that he couldn't submit to military discipline. In May 1943 he received an honorable discharge for "indifferent character," but what he called his "boot camp madhouse dreams of regimented life I hated so much" would recur for a decade.

Once again Jack couldn't fit in. He was at a crux in his life, and he chose or was compelled to follow an anarchistic path away from the American mainstream. At the moment he only knew he wasn't cut out to wear a regular uniform. In a bitter moment twenty-five years later, Kerouac regretfully wrote that the experience at Bethesda came to represent his "lost dream of being a real American man."

In a historical sense he was quite right; a man who could not submit to discipline was not a normal American by the middle of the twentieth century. World War II was the most powerful collective experience in American history, completing a realignment of American culture: it very nearly seemed that those who did not accept large-scale organized life patterns like big business or suburbia *were* misfits. The war's primary lesson was that the nation with the most sophisticated scientific and industrial structure would prevail. Jets, missiles, radar, silicone, new plastics, DDT, sulfa drugs, and the atomic bomb became facts of life. America's largest magazine, *Life,* gave regular and dramatic coverage of scientific war-waging with pieces on "Industrial Chemistry—It Meets the Demands of War," "Rockets," "Plastics," and "Mechanical Brains." Progressive education at American colleges almost vanished, to be replaced with a more ordered, scientific approach. In the years following the war, academic disciplines like economics, political science, and sociology were all swept with a rage for quantification and scientific models; American philosophy was almost totally Positivist, the philosophy of science. Off-campus, science fiction replaced the pulp magazines of Jack's day as young American boys' reading matter, and within sci-fi itself, *Astounding Stories'* sophisticated use of hard technical data killed off old-time "John Carter on Mars" fantasy and substituted spaceships flying mathematically accurate orbits.

Science assumed its cultural influence in more subtle ways than the powerful but obvious image of the white lab coat. The unstated ideological girder for the entire process of large-scale bureaucratic wartime (and postwar) organization was that it was neutral, dispassionate, "scientific." That it was not neutral but subservient to the needs of large business made it no less dominant.

Jack had flunked chemistry and he did not think much about science, but he had come to perceive the soulless, antihuman mood of his native land through his own method: direct personal experience. He felt, saw, experienced the dismemberment of the American family.

Processed out of the Navy in June 1943, Jack headed home, not to Lowell but to a dull apartment above a drugstore on busy Cross-Bay

Boulevard in Ozone Park, Queens. Leo and Gabrielle had joined the flood of American migrants searching for work, and now Papa labored in a Canal Street print shop, while Mémère assumed her usual position behind a skiving machine in Brooklyn. It was their new jobs that had originally brought them to the city, and now New York was also a central meeting place for their wandering children: Nin was in the WAC's and Jack was planning to ship out as a merchant seaman. Leo and Gabrielle were among millions who had escaped dead small towns to cluster in boom towns— and stayed, far away from other generations, in-laws, roots. Sixteen million men moved at least temporarily away from home to enter the service, and many millions of women moved after them, following their husbands and leaving behind a lasting image of haggard, exhausted young ladies in bus or train station chairs, waiting, waiting. Children paid a war tax as well. Their mothers made up one third of the work force, and with their fathers gone and no supervision, often living in new and unfamiliar neighborhoods, American children were lost and disturbed. In New York City at the time Jack was waiting at the hiring hall for a ship out, vagrancy and sex charges against teenage women had nearly doubled in the past year; "Victory Girls," they were called.

Jack could see the war in his father's eyes, too, in the frightened look of a lonely townsman stunned by the exotic sight of rabbis or wealthy women, by a city that overwhelmed him. Once while walking in the Lower East Side with Gabrielle, some rabbis walking arm in arm would not part for them, and Leo knocked one into the gutter with his broad belly. Not only was Jack a transient, but Nin had left the Church to divorce Charles Morrisette, her first husband, before joining the WAC's and moving thousands of miles away. Leo's ordered life had been swept away, and his son's eyes measured a man far away from the glory days at Rockingham Park.

Many people were as confused and upset as Leo, and Americans nursed their wounds with sentimentality. A gentle sigh for old, gracious ways lurked even in Hollywood or Broadway's most passionately patriotic events. James Cagney's *Yankee Doodle Dandy* and Irving Berlin's *This Is the Army* were actually moderate compared to *The Sullivans*. On its next run after Jack left the ship, the *Dorchester* had sunk with terrible losses, and its four chaplains had captured the nation's imagination by giving away their life jackets. Hollywood's version of it focused on five brothers named Sullivan in the crew, and ended as the youngest raced off to join his brothers in the clouds of heaven, calling out, "Hey, wait for me!"

Vaudeville enjoyed a revival, and the rage of 1943 was "Pistol Packin' Mama," which joined Bing Crosby's "White Christmas" in the war-song hall of fame. "Praise the Lord and Pass the Ammunition" was another popular song. Traditional religion revived as well, most notably in Bing Crosby and Barry Fitzgerald's classic film *Going My Way* and *The Song of Bernadette*.

But Bing was middle-aged and Jack was young, and for him and his generation, there was ultimately only one sentimental artist during World War II. It was a hollow-cheeked skinny kid with jughandle ears, a golfball Adam's apple, and a voice that slid up your spine and made you cry, and his name was Frank Sinatra. Jack went to see him at the Paramount, the only male, as he later recalled, in a line of 2,000 screaming teenage girls, but when Frank sang "Mighty Like a Rose" and "Without a song . . . the road would never end," Jack sighed too. Tender, wistful, vulnerable, Sinatra was the first superstar of youth, and he stood artless before his swooning fans as the eternal adolescent in an adult world gone amok. Best of all, Sinatra was music for romance, and Jack was in love with a young woman, an attractive art student named Edie Parker.

Henry Cru had showed her off to him the previous fall in the West End Café, and shortly thereafter they began going out. Just before shipping out in June, Jack went to see Edie in Asbury Park, New Jersey. Though he was glad to be out of the Navy, he was disturbed by a health problem; warts had sprouted on his penis, and he spent hours in toilets examining them. Edie soothed his worries. Relieved, Jack left for sea; they planned to live together when he returned from his voyage.

On a sweltering day in late June 1943, Jack boarded the S.S. *George Weems* and it set sail for Liverpool, flying the red dynamite flag for its cargo, 500-pound bombs. As it slipped past the Statue of Liberty, dimmed for the duration, the situation was very different from the year-past departure of the *Dorchester*. The three airplanes painted on the *Weems*'s smokestack told the story; now the United States was not retreating, but fighting and winning. Midway, the Coral Sea, Guadalcanal and North Africa were all history, as was the German surrender at Stalingrad. While the *Weems* was at sea, the Allies would assault Sicily, and Italy would surrender. Jack kept writing.

He was able to use the purser's typewriter, and he continued to labor on *The Sea Is My Brother*. Awkward and violet though the prose was, those who read it felt the emotional rush of his experience. No more a scullion-in-the-bowels-of-hell, he was an ordinary seaman this run, a deck hand standing watches and listening for hours to the hypnotic *ssshh* of the bow break, lost in the magic liquid world that happens when it rains at sea and sky and ocean seem to blend. Once again he was a silent loner, slipping through the ship at sunset to check the blackout curtains, while doing his best, off duty, to sleep all the way to England. When awake, he stayed in his bunk and devoured John Galsworthy's *Forsyte Saga*, which gave him a taste of England, and also, he said, an idea "about sagas, or legends, novels connecting into one grand tale."

London, during his brief leave there, was everything he'd dreamed of, Shakespeare and Sherlock combined. He wore a "uniform," a black leather jacket, khaki shirt, and Merchant Marine brass hat, and looked the proper man of the sea as he paid homage at Lord Nelson's statue. Hyde Park struck him instantly with a vision of Dr. Jekyll, though he probably hadn't expected to see Americans playing softball there. He attended a performance of Tchaikovsky compositions at the Royal Albert Hall, refused to be impressed by a seatmate who displayed a copy of T. S. Eliot's *Four Quartets,* and emerged into the utter darkness of blacked-out London to find the bars of Piccadilly Circus and a fur coat named Lillian who performed her services and possibly lifted his wallet—he was never quite sure—with equal ease. Empty, the *Weems* passed the Irish cottages that made him think of Joyce and bounced through a rough trip home, reaching the Brooklyn docks in October of 1943. But just before it left Liverpool, Jack had a sudden burst of illumination, as his literary task crystallized within him, and his amorphous commitment to art focused into a duty, a "lifetime of writing about what I'd seen with my own eyes," as he wrote years later, in whatever style he chose, all of it put together as a "contemporary history record for future times to see what really happened." He vowed that he would be a divine scribe, capturing on paper the life in front of him, even as the special angel of death perched on his shoulder gave his visionary record a transcendent power.

Paid off and drunk, Kerouac got on a subway that reeked of cinnamon to him and headed uptown to see his love, Edie Parker, who was sharing an apartment with her friend Joan Vollmer. It was pouring rain as he cut through the Columbia campus from the Broadway subway stop to apartment 15 at 421 West 118th Street near Amsterdam Avenue, and he didn't feel a drop. His black leather jacket plopped into a chair, and Edie's arms encircled his neck. After a snack of cold asparagus and olives in mayonnaise, they fell into bed for his sailor's welcome home.

It was a particularly pretty fall in New York, if only because some two million chrysanthemums, donated by a philanthropist, bloomed for weeks in Central Park and Rockefeller Plaza, and for a time Jack even got along tolerably well with Mémêre and Leo. One night in October, the four of them went out for beers at a German tavern on Cross-Bay Boulevard, and life was reasonably mellow. Jack worked the winter away with odd jobs like switchboard operator, read and wrote and enjoyed his love life.

The war ground on, limned in maps on the front pages of newspapers, black for the Nazis, red for the Soviets; a quarter-inch of color shift meant another thousand human beings had been consumed. Sam was now a corpsman at the Anzio front, writing letters home that spoke of freedom and democracy, that identified their struggle in the mud with his own past, the golden age of Athenian democracy. He continued to write poems and published them in the service paper, the *Stars and Stripes*. One, "Côte d'Or," prophesied a future where another youth might stand at Anzio, "But he shall be a freeman's son, intelligent and strong/Nurtured in faith, and worthy of heroic song." Sam's passionate love of life endured even the savage misery of the war in Italy, and he wrote another poem, which he called "Rhapsody in Red."

> Last night was hell,
> Pack't upon hell.
> And luddies blasted in the black
> As Stukas strafed our posts again.
> Oh! Mars was in a vaunted glory,
> Extolling us,
> Extolling them,
> Gaily he dashed around and around and around
> Last night he wore a carmine gown!
> Last night he blazed with scarlet glory
> You know that kind of red
> Like when you cut your hand in winter
> And you watch the valentine-shaped drops warm blood
> Falling softly on the satin softened snow . . .

His blood, his heart, his faith were intact.

And Sammy's richly gallant beauty became transmuted into a symbol of love and sharing, but a symbol without physical reality nonetheless. Jack was only Sam's spiritual brother, not his parent, and so he never received the telegram that read "The War Department regrets to inform you . . . ," but early in February 1944 he learned that Sam was dead. Pacing the cold and windy streets of New York City that night, Jack could only know that death had cursed him again, that the madness of war had reached out to consume what was good on the earth. Happy as he was with Edie his lover, he was alone, robbed of his true and loyal friend, shivering like a four-year-old whose brother has just gone away to heaven, exiled from camaraderie once more.

V
Visions in a World of Mushroom Clouds

TWELVE YEARS had passed in Jack's life between Gerard and Sammy, but it was not his destiny to wait very long for his third brother; Edie kept talking about an amazing kid who was hanging out at the West End Café. Short, thin, and attractive, Edie had what Jack thought of as a "birdlike intelligence," coming on slightly dumb to mask her perceptiveness and very real good taste in people. So he listened to her, and one night in June 1944 he went out to the bar. At first, he thought the kid—a mere nineteen to his twenty-two—was a "mischievous little prick," but soon enough Jack knew there was more to him than that.

Lucien Carr was quite simply the most beautiful man he'd ever seen, electric, with blond hair and slanting green cat's-eyes, a small but wiry build, and a sneer that gave his angel face a devilish quality, and hinted at the punk beneath, the attitude that was unafraid of rules, uninterested in conventions, that "played at intellectual putdowns out of sheer high spirits," a friend later said, "out of a healthy sense of self." For Lucien was wholly unlike Jack; he was the product of an upper-class St. Louis family. Had he been coarser, perhaps a little stupid, he could have qualified as an authentic Regency rake, the wastrel younger son of some provincial family dispatched to London to swill champagne, pinch maids, and run up gambling debts. In wartime New York City, Lucien was a Columbia freshman, having already been evicted from Bowdoin College and the University of Chicago, and instead of being an oafish squire, he seemed to friends more like Rimbaud, whose portrait in his edition of *Fleurs du Mal* he eerily resembled.

Immediately they began carousing together as brothers in spirit, floating out of the West End in liquefied bliss until Lucien had Jack jump into an empty barrel and then rolled him down the empty sidewalks of late-night upper Broadway. A few nights later they anointed each other with bottles of black ink as they sat in the gutter in a pouring rain singing foolish songs, especially the summer's hit, "You Always Hurt the One You Love." Lucien was "wild," and his way with Jack wholly lacked Sam's tenderness; he was stunned to find in Jack "No resentment . . . no rancor at all," and he loved him. Still, his cynical side reacted scornfully to Jack's serious peasant virtue; Lucien called him a "mean old tightfisted shitass no good Canuck . . . Indian no good bully." "I'm no bully," Jack would reply to the mockery, and Lucien always had a topper. "Well, bully for you. Give me a drink."

Lucien's style and class kept Jack off-balance and amazed—once Jack became angry and protested that it was unfair when three men attacked Lucien, and Carr sneered, "Oh, let's have more of those splendid Lowell mill-worker remarks!" Yet strikingly different as the two men were, art and affection bound them securely together. Lucien danced on the tightrope of his sensibilities not as an entertaining pose but because he—and Jack—sought more from life than the present rules implied was available; they were serious if obstreperous pilgrims in search of what they called the "New Vision." Their comrades in the quest were equally provocative, and in the week following Jack's first encounter with Lucien, three more men would step into the apartment on 118th Street and have a profound impact on his life, as important as anything that had happened to him since Gerard.

One of them was Allen Ginsberg.

Jack was sitting in the apartment eating breakfast early one afternoon when Ginsberg walked in, a skinny seventeen-year-old boy with stick-out ears. He noticed the boy's horn-rim glasses, so much a part of the costume of "nice Jewish boy from Jersey," but he also noticed the intensely burning black eyes behind them. They began to talk about Dostoyevsky. Jack soon felt that Allen was "exalted" like Sammy, and adopted him as a very-much-younger brother. Later he would see Allen's notebook, across whose cover were the words "Now, from the cracked and bleeding heart, triumphantly, I fashion—Art!" He was never ordinary, this child who had at age ten staved off bullies with an unending string of polysyllabic words, and declared at fourteen that "I'll be a genius of some kind or other, probably in literature . . . Either I'm a genius, I'm egocentric, or I'm slightly schitsophrenic [*sic*]. Probably the first two." Wounded by a mother who shuttled in and out of mental hospitals, Allen felt he was a "lost child, a wandering child, in search of the womb of love." He had arrived at the Union Seminary dormitory he shared with Lucien incandescent with political idealism. He'd vowed as he went to take the college entrance examination that, should he pass, he would never betray his ideal, "to help the misery of the masses." His vow withered under Lucien's cynical tongue, but his idealistic sensitivity remained. A few weeks after Jack and Allen met, Jack helped him move out of the dorm, and watched respectfully as Allen said goodbye to his room, to Lucien's room down the hall, to the door, to the seven flights of steps. "Why, that's what I do!" exclaimed Jack, and what Allen thought of as a "transmission of real feeling" passed between them, solidifying their intellectual affinity.

Lucien sent two other men to the apartment, men who with Ginsberg and Lucien himself formed the quartet that would redefine Jack to himself. The first was William S. Burroughs, in one critic's words the "most highly enervated, hyperaesthetic specimen of humankind" that Jack would ever meet. Though he received a small sum of money from his family every month, Bill was not a direct heir to the Burroughs Adding Machine fortune; still, his family was socially prominent in St. Louis. In 1944, Burroughs was thirty, a Harvard '36 graduate and former medical student in Vienna who had worked as an adman, a detective, a bartender, and an insect exterminator.

Sitting in the apartment in his seersucker jacket and wire-rim glasses, he was tall, spare, and seemed to Jack "patrician thinlipped" and "inscrutable because ordinary looking." He bore a slight resemblance to the deadpan Protestant Buster Keaton. A decade later, the street boys of Tangiers called him "El Hombre Invisible."

Nothing about Burroughs caught the eye at first. Even his voice was ordinary, dry to the point of satire, a slight Midwestern drawl flattened through the nose. Yet more than his subtle brilliance or his homosexual preference marked Burroughs as unusual. As a friend wrote of him much later, "All of us who failed to participate in the war effort owing to one form of unclubbability or another have, I think, felt the necessity to conduct private wars of our own." Jack probably noticed that the first joint of Bill's right little finger was missing; only later would he discover that Burroughs had himself cut it off with kitchen shears to impress someone as a "Van Gogh kick." Ostensibly he was there to pump Jack for information on shipping out in the Merchant Marine, but as Jack blah-blah-blahed his way through the details, he acquired an important friend who would teach him ideas that focused his intuitive feelings.

Burroughs was accompanied by his old St. Louis friend David Kammerer, the tall red-bearded man who had already met Jack through Lucien at the West End, and who had brought Burroughs around to the apartment to make introductions. His was perhaps the strangest story of all. Kammerer was in love with Lucien Carr, so obsessed with the gorgeous young man who had once been in his charge during school sports that he had chased him from St. Louis to Massachusetts to Maine to Illinois to New York, in the process contributing to Lucien's being thrown out of several schools. He was a Doppelgänger whose sexual desires Lucien would not gratify; their connection was an intertwined mass of frustration that hinted ominously of trouble.

Blood scent was an appropriate choice for their "New Vision"; the inspired art that Lucien desired could hardly settle for anything but the absolute scent of life. Along with Celine Young, Lucien's blondly sensual, aristocratic and slightly dreamy girlfriend, the group circulated about the apartment on 118th Street, Lucien's room in Warren Hall, Burroughs' apartment on Bedford Street in Greenwich Village, and George's Bar in Sheridan Square. Valeska Gert's, a thirties Berlin-style bar on West Fourth Street, was another regular set for their random inquisitions into the state of the culture, and through an immense energy created by what Jack felt was self-hatred, Lucien took center stage, going deeper and further into the idea of the New Vision than the others cared to. Jack and Allen shared something different, for Allen was silently in love with the Jack he saw as "romantic, moody, dark-eyed Dostoyevskian," and they joined in a more affable partnership concerned not only with identity in the midst of an overwhelming, chaotic world, but also the ancient rules of unity and literature. Their hero was the human Faust of Goethe. Lucien, driven by his disgust at the trap of life, sought even more than Nietzsche; he wanted to go beyond personality or intellect or the soul to . . . ? Buried in *Finnegans Wake* or *Ulysses* or *The Magic Mountain*, Jack was certain that art was his proper path, without the mystical self-destruction Lucien advocated; nonetheless, he recognized in Lucien's lectures a path for himself.

"Know these words," wrote Ginsberg, "and you speak the Carr language: fruit, phallus, clitoris, cacoëthes, feces, foetus, womb, Rimbaud." "Prurience" was another favorite; Lucien and Celine clutched and pawed at each other, but kept their underwear on, Allen was as yet a virgin, and Jack remained a compulsive masturbator as always, so that their discussions were flavored with the mysto-decadent excitement of voyeurs.

Hunched over their worn copies of Rimbaud's *A Season in Hell*, they were living Flaubert's words: "When the exterior world is disgusting, enervating, corruptive, and brutalizing, honest and sensitive people are forced to seek somewhere within themselves a more suitable place to live." They had rejected, as Rimbaud had put it, "Science, the new nobility! Progress. The world moves on! Why shouldn't it revolve? This is the vision of numbers. We are on our way to the *spirit.*" Lucien, in a red shirt, gulped Pernod and arrogantly proclaimed, as Allen put it in a fictionalized re-creation at the time, "I tell you that I repudiate your little loves, your little derivative morality, your hypocritical altruism, your foolish humanity obsessions, all the loves and penalties of your expedient little modern bourgeois culture." The prurience, the Pernod and beer, the all-night coffee-and-cigarette talk sessions fueled their romance with Rimbaud's last and most potent question: "When will we go, beyond the beaches and the mountains, to greet the birth of the new task, the new wisdom, the flight of tyrants and demons, the end of superstition; to adore—the first ones!—Christmas on Earth?"

For what they found in the bars, the streets, the lost corners of Manhattan was "Christmas on Earth," a religious sensitivity to mortality, the cycle of generations, to the poignancy of moment and the passage of time. Oh, conventional religion was dead all right. Allen was a Jew by birth only, and when Jack talked of the Church it was in a melancholy tone, chuckling sadly over the time he confessed to playing with another boy, and the priest asked him, "How long was it?"

Rather showily, Allen announced in his journal that the "New Vision lies in a highly conscious comprehension of universal motives, and in a realistic acceptance of an unromantic universe of flat meaninglessness." Their tutors—the renegades of high culture like Yeats, Rimbaud, and Baudelaire—had abandoned politics and religion for beauty, a beauty unrelated to nature, since God its creator was dead and since nature was not "real"; we know only what we perceive, and art determines what we perceive. But the New Vision celebrated the transcendental *act* of making art more than beauty the product, and Jack took from Nietzsche the phrase, "Art seducing me to a continuation of life." He did not see any rational justification for art; it was merely what gave meaning to his life

—and what reminded them all that life is transient, illusory, "such stuff /As dreams are made on . . . ," as another of their favorite writers put it.

Not that it was a morbid summer for Jack. He found Lucien a rainbow flash of color coming on top of the darkness of sea, and the more Jack saw of Burroughs the more interesting he became. Lucien was fond of what Gide called *actes gratuits*, absurd and spontaneous displays that shattered middle-class conventions, and Bill could top him with such macabre, unblinking coolness that he seemed almost devilish. Once at Bill's apartment, Lucien stunned Jack by chewing on a glass. Ever the gracious host, Burroughs offered them a snack, disappearing into the kitchen to rummage a minute before returning with his "mother's delicacies"—a plate of razor blades and light bulbs. Sitting in the park a few days later, Bill asked Jack why he refused to wear his Merchant Marine uniform and get an easy serviceman's wartime entry into movies and clubs. Clad in his T-shirt and chino pants, Jack virtuously replied that it was a "finkish" thing to do. Bill twitched, blinked, and observed that "It's a finkish world."

Yet Jack was not naïve, for he was often possessed of what he called a "materialistic Canuck taciturn cold skepticism"; it was Allen who was the butt of the mockery. Lucien took the future labor organizer in hand and showed him a working-class bar at 125th Street and Broadway, snickering, "You've never worked in your life. You'd feel like a self-conscious idiot if you went in there." Rather quickly, Allen's interests shifted from pre-law to literature. Social class was, however, part of the group's dynamic; Jack had an enormous social inferiority complex around someone like Lucien, particularly when Lucien met Leo, and Papa made remarks about rich punks. Jack was a "working man proletarian Jack London redneck," thought Allen, verbally pugnacious when pressed and always, Lucien later noted, "emotionally aware of class." Actually, politics was not a major interest for any of them, although they agreed on a vaguely anarchistic disdain for bureaucracy and the welfare state, a reactionary working-class perspective they shared with Leo.

Despite the steamy heat, New Yorkers were enjoying the summer of 1944. Shortwave, on-the-scene reporters, and wire recordings had brought D-Day—the long-awaited second front—as close as the radios blaring out open windows into 118th Street, and as the Allies punched through the hedgerows on their drive to Paris, it seemed as if this would be the last summer of war. Rationing regulations had eased, money loosened, and party life revived. Jack was restless. Edie kept talking about getting married, and he was broke anyway, so August seemed like an opportune moment to ship out, this time for real. In May he had taken a bus to New Orleans to catch a ship, but the trip had ended in drunken letters back to New York that pleaded for travel money home; later it had seemed foolish, merely an excuse for seeing the South, and the only memory worth preserving was an afternoon stop in Asheville where he got drunk with Thomas Wolfe's older brother, the two of them sitting in the parlor listening to the Kentucky Derby as they stared at a melancholy picture of Wolfe's beloved oldest brother Ben. Fleeing the August heat, Jack and Lucien lay on the grass of Riverside Park at 116th Street, contemplated their situation, and decided to escape New York.

Lucien had his own reasons; David Kammerer was becoming too intense, too weird. He had begun to slip into Lucien's apartment in the middle of the night, there to stand and stare at him as he slept. Tense and fretful, Lucien had spotted a hole in Burroughs' vintage seersucker jacket the night before their day by the river, inserted his finger and shredded the sleeve before Kammerer joined in to dismember it entirely. David had also tried to hang Jack's cat, though Burroughs had saved it. Gerard had once said that "God gives us kittens to teach us how to pity," and for Jack the idea of maiming such a love symbol was monstrous. Even though he didn't find out about David's attempt until much later, uneasiness hung palpably heavy in the still late-summer air.

Gazing fitfully at the gray Hudson River from beneath the trees of Riverside Park, Jack and Lucien conjured up an adventure. They'd jump ship in Le Havre, and with Jack's rustic French and Lucien as a deaf-mute, they'd walk to Paris and beat the Army to liberation day for the moment of a lifetime. Their dream closely resembled the movie they'd seen with Edie and Celine the previous week, Renoir's *Grand Illusion*. Appropriately, it was an antiwar film that involved a Jew escaping from a military prison, along with a peasant type, played by Jack's old hero Jean Gabin, and an aristocrat. Lucien wanted to walk Montmartre like Rimbaud, "find symbols saturated in the gutters." He felt "like I'm in a pond that's drying out and I'm about to suffocate."

After several days of waiting, Jack and Lucien finally found berths through the NMU on the S.S. *Robert Hayes,* departing from New York for France on Sunday, August 13, 1944. Saturday night they cadged a last free meal from Burroughs and then joined Edie and Celine at Minetta's

Tavern in the Village before winding up in an artist's loft on MacDougal Street for a final party. Incredibly, Kammerer interrupted their celebration; he had somehow succeeded in tracking them down and then had climbed onto a night-club marquee and crawled in the loft's window. His relentless tenacity was unnerving.

After sleeping late the next morning, Jack and Lucien rushed out and chased their ship down, first to Hoboken and at last to Brooklyn. Gleefully singing "What'll you do with the drunken sailor?" and trying to ignore the thick pall of smoke from a burning freighter that shrouded the docks, they were met by a union delegate who warned them not to sign on because the first mate was a "Fascist." Ignoring this, they stowed their gear and then hit the food locker, gorging on roast beef and cold milk, loudly planning their walk from Le Havre—and exulting in the absence of Kammerer.

Suddenly, their new first mate materialized screaming curses before them, an enormous wraith who looked frighteningly like a beardless David. He had overheard their plans to jump ship and roared, "You didn't sign on. Fine. Now get the *fuck* off this ship you cocksucking no good little pearly-assed punks." The man was much too big to argue with, and with a parting "Fuck you," they disconsolately stumbled back out into the Brooklyn heat and returned to 118th Street to endure Edie and Celine's teasing.

As Jack described it many years afterward, they moped around the apartment, dully furious at their luck, fighting the intransigent sizzle of August in Manhattan with cold showers. As night fell and the streets cooled, they went to the West End for a beer. Jack left at midnight, ready to assault the NMU hiring line first thing in the morning. As he cut through the Columbia campus past St. Paul's Chapel, he met David Kammerer, who wanted—as always—to know Lucien's whereabouts. Jack told him and then went home to sleep. It was so hot that he and Edie couldn't even lie close, but slept in the living room, exposed to any stray breeze the window might produce.

Swimming out of the cloud of sleep at dawn, Jack became aware of Lucien shaking his arm. "Well," Lucien said, "I disposed of the old man last night." Jack knew instantly what he meant: David Kammerer was dead. Lucien was shaken but dry-eyed, gathering courage to give himself up to the police and the "hot seat"; before doing so, he wanted Jack to help him dispose of Kammerer's glasses and the murder weapon, and to share with him one last drunk. Though Jack might attack many of the technocracy's laws, he was still enough of an altar boy to obey most of them. Yet he went with Lucien because Carr was his brother, because loyalty mattered. Jack showered and dressed, kissed Edie goodbye, and began to pump Lucien for information.

"What'd you really do?"

"I stabbed him," Lucien said.

David Kammerer had caught up with Lucien for the last time at the West End, and when it closed they ended up at Riverside Park, quite near where Lucien and Jack had plotted their trip to Paris. What passed between them can never be properly known, but Lucien killed David, bound his hands and feet with shoelaces, then tied rocks to the body with pieces of his shirt. He pushed it out into the Hudson River, but the rocks were too light and it floated downstream, where the Coast Guard would later find it.

Lucien first ran to Burroughs for advice. Summoning up his last theatrics, he greeted Bill at the door by offering him a smoke from a package of Lucky Strikes. Inside, he kept repeating his fear of the "hot seat," the enormous grim electric chair at Sing Sing Prison. Bill didn't let him down, but calmly questioned him, then told him to go home, get a lawyer through his mother, and plead self-defense against rape, what the *Daily News* would later tag an "honor slaying."

Lucien went next to Jack, filling him in on the story as they walked down 118th Street to Morningside Park, where Jack drew attention by pretending to take a leak and Lucien buried the glasses. Later he dropped the knife into a sewer grating on 125th Street. They headed for a bar, Lucien mumbling repeatedly over beers about the murder. He muttered, "He died in my arms," and thought of himself as the white-gloved aristocrat in *Grand Illusion,* recalled their missed ship in Brooklyn, thought of the chair, the chair, the chair. Eventually they took a cab to Park Avenue, where Lucien borrowed five dollars from his psychiatrist, then found a cool dark theater playing the movie *Four Feathers,* which featured an endless Technicolor succession of Sudanese rebels butchering English soldiers and vice-versa. One of the characters was named Burroughs, which made them wince. Hot dogs, Times Square, a visit to the Museum of Modern Art, another bar—the afternoon passed somehow. At last Lucien stripped off his imaginary white gloves of aristocracy, handed them to Jack, and went to turn himself in to the police. Jack wearily got on the subway and returned to Edie and 118th Street.

Edie found out about David's death only when two plainclothesmen arrived the next night to arrest Jack as a material witness. After a night in a cell at the local precinct, Jack spent the next day in the D.A.'s office downtown, where he convinced his arresting officer, James O'Brien, that he was a heterosexual "swordsman," that the *Daily News* tag on the murder was true because Lucien wasn't a homo. "If he was," Jack said, "he'd have tried to make me." His tearfully passionate meeting with Edie reminded him of a Cagney picture, but his cell was boring. Only the newspapers, where the death had temporarily eclipsed news of George Patton's tanks smashing across France, were entertaining; the *News* featured a picture of Lucien on the riverbank at 79th Street, where the body had landed, and the *Journal-American* reported that Lucien's jail reading included Rimbaud and "A Vision," by William Butler Keats (*sic*).

As an invasion of cold rain thundered down on the city on Thursday, August 17, Jack and Lucien came together to be arraigned. As Jack sat unconsciously whistling "You Always Hurt the One You Love," the judge set his bail at $5,000 and ordered him sent to the Bronx City Jail, the "Opera House" where the (stool) pigeons sing. Before he could go uptown, he had to go down, to East 21st Street, and the city morgue, deep in the bowels of Bellevue Hospital. A fat attendant munching on a sandwich, cheese stuck in his teeth, whipped open Drawer 169 to reveal Kammerer. To Jack, he looked like a tormented patriarch, his beard jutting out, his corpse blue and bloated after two days in the river. It was his cock that really caught Jack's eye; it hadn't rotted yet.

Aside from the cold, ugly weather, the Opera House wasn't too awful. Reading Somerset Maugham's *Cakes and Ale* and Aldous Huxley's *Brave New World*, Jack passed up the card games, but did spend some time conversing with various employees of Murder, Inc. (the underworld execution gang), all of whom found an excuse to stop by his cell and get the inside word on whether or not Lucien was a "queer." Things improved further on Saturday, August 19, when Jack found out that he could post a hundred dollars and get out on bail. But the conversation with Leo was short and horrible, and as Jack hung up the phone he felt weak and deserted, his father's outraged words echoing in his brain: "No Kerouac ever got involved in a murder . . . I'm not going to lend you no hundred dollars and you can go to hell and I've got work to do, Good*bye!*" Another guilt, another failure. Writing about that summer three years later, Jack moaned, "Something's happened to me! . . . I ought to be a real son. Why does it always have to be *ought?*"

Desperate and alone, Jack called up Edie and proposed marriage, the plan being that she'd borrow the money from her family to bail him out, which he would repay by going to work in a Detroit factory before shipping out again in the Merchant Marine. On Tuesday, August 22, the district attorney released Jack for the afternoon, and he and a burly Irish cop rode a subway down to City Hall. With Celine as the maid of honor and the cop as best man, Jack and Edie zipped through a Justice of the Peace service, then proceeded to the nearest bar. Bemused by his role as best man, Jack's guard picked up the tab for an afternoon of pleasant drinking until Jack kissed Edie and returned to his cell and the lewd snickers of his cellmates. It took a while for the money to arrive from Michigan, and Jack read Gogol's *Dead Souls* while Lucien was indicted on second-degree murder charges. On August 30 the judge reduced Jack's bail to $2,500, Edie posted bond, and he walked out. As the newly wedded couple prepared to leave for Edie's home in Grosse Pointe, Lucien remained in jail, reading *Jude the Obscure* and sympathizing with the "dark and hopeless" suicidal ending of Hardy's book. Burroughs, the other material witness, had already been bailed out by his family and returned to St. Louis. In mid-September Lucien pleaded guilty to manslaughter charges, and on October 6 he was sentenced to one to twenty years in Elmira Reformatory, of which he was to serve slightly more than two years before parole.

Only Allen remained near campus, "faithful to the past," sickened with hepatitis and musing on a world he considered "neurotic and perverted." As he wrote his brother Eugene, much of the episode could be traced to the decline of the West; the circle of friends that had created the New Vision had fallen prey to the poisons of a dying culture.

September 1944: Americans were ecstatic at the liberation of Paris, and New York as well became a City of Light, as the blackout ended after eighteen months. Technical gadgets like RDX plastic explosives and robot bombs made the news, as well as the shiniest new toy of them all—television. "The next great development in radio is now ready for its enormous market," *Life* told America. Jack was in the nation's tool center, Detroit, counting ball bearings from midnight to eight in the morning and industriously applying himself to the study of American literary criticism. He was uncomfortable living in a Grosse Pointe home with silver, linen, and chandeliers, but although Mémêre and Leo had visited him in jail and all was forgiven, the ball-bearing job was the only way to pay off his bond, so he persevered. Even Edie's mother, whose knowledge of the literary world extended no further than Pearl Buck, was impressed with his dedication and seriousness. By early October he had paid his debt, and Edie's father arranged a ride to New York and the docks for him.

Waiting for his ship to sail, Kerouac went to the West End to hang out with Celine and Allen. Beautiful Celine was causing him problems. In the process of "dumping" Lucien, whom she felt was "messianic" about ridding the world of Kammerer, she was flirting with Jack, and though he managed to feel guilty about his disloyalty to Lucien and Edie, he spent the night making out with her and was disappointed when it went no further. One night in the West End, she attracted a couple of Navy student officers, who began to heckle Jack and Allen. After a couple of practice punches on the men's-room wall, Jack came back to the table and in traditional fashion invited the officers outside. He gave as good as he got, but was on the ground, with Ginsberg trying to pull one of the students aside, when the bartender stopped the brawl as unequal. It was no trivial event; violence disgusted Kerouac, and even a sidewalk dust-up impressed him as a grave act. It was very possibly the last time Jack Kerouac ever hit another person; there were any number of stories later of his being hit and refusing to respond in kind.

The judge who had set his bail had joked that the sailor was safer at sea, but long before his ship reached Norfolk, Jack was angry and afraid. His new bosun kept riding him, calling him "handsome" and "sweetie-pie," and this sexual manipulation forced Jack to jump ship in Norfolk and return to New York.

He was almost totally alone. His wife and family thought he was at sea, Burroughs had left town, and only Celine and Allen, who had gotten him a room in a campus dormitory and some books from the Columbia Library, knew of his whereabouts. Convulsed by Lucien's pain and the shattered state of his own life, Jack hurled himself at art on both emotional and intellectual levels—"Self-Ultimacy," he called it. It was a spasm of romantic artistic purity so intense that, caring nothing for the written product of his labors, he burned almost all that he wrote. In the flickering light of a candle, he gouged himself and in his own blood wrote "The Blood of a Poet" on a card, then pinned it up on the wall, along with Rimbaud's "Christmas on Earth" quotation and Nietzsche's statement "Art is the highest task and the proper metaphysical activity of this life." Though abstract ideas were never his main interest, he filled reams of paper with speculations on a host of European thinkers, ranging from Gide to Thomas Mann to Yeats and Joyce. He sought to fuse Huxley's idea of ceaseless growth with Freud, comprehend the artistic spirit of Dionysus and "sexual neoplatonism" while rejecting bourgeois culture and political liberalism. More powerful than thought, however, was the profound impact of sheer experience, the emotional rush, as Allen recorded Jack's comments in his journal, of being "In that far city and to feel the smothering pain of the unrecognized ego." What Jack termed Self-Ultimacy was a serious effort at self-purification, so that art would become a holy duty that transcended all intellectual concepts. Ideally, phoenix-like out of the ashes of his old self would come a new personality capable of an extraordinary perception.

Biweekly sojourns with Allen Ginsberg were his sole diversion, and Jack was gaunt and wasted when Burroughs returned to New York in early December and came to visit. Bill sniffed and snorted at the blood and candles, then said, "My God, Jack, stop this nonsense and let's go out and have a drink." Kerouac lurched up out of his chair, and though he realized it only later, the walk to the nearest bar conceded the futility of Self-Ultimacy; he needed his models in the flesh, and Burroughs, the skinny near-ghost walking in front of him, was going to be his prophet for the next year.

A man once sang, "To live outside the law, you must be honest," and the line fit Jack's new teacher. Burroughs had long since intellectually exiled himself from America and its cultural precepts, but he was a very special sort of outlaw, something of a hybrid of Jesse James and Ralph Waldo Emerson. He had deeply impressed Jack and Allen with his compassionate treatment of Lucien in August. Dispassionate, as well; David Kammerer had been Burroughs' lifelong friend, and what struck the younger men most, aside from Bill's fearlessness in dealing with the police, was that he didn't seem to make moral judgments in personal situations, only perceptive observations. And so, mostly in an apartment they shared on West 115th Street, Jack followed Bill into what he later called "a year of low, evil decadence" fashioned from amphetamine, cigarettes, coffee, and endless dark consideration of the corruption of the postwar world. The 115th Street apartment was a very special place, a Magic Theater of sorts; surely few places in 1945 America balanced so harmoniously Times Square hustlers, drugs, and a bookshelf with Yeats, Céline, Rimbaud, Blake, Spengler, Kafka, and Korzybski. The apartment began its portentous career with Joan Vollmer, once Edie's roommate. Joan was a dark, attractive woman, humorously cynical, intelligent and cool, something of a female counterpart to Burroughs. A widow with one child, she also had a strongly developed taste for the sweet rush of Benzedrine, which in those days involved buying nasal inhalers, removing the small pads of soaked paper from the split-open case, then swallowing the paper with coffee for all-day highs.

Around Christmas 1944, Edie returned from Detroit, and she and Jack moved in with Joan. The reconciliation quickly failed; by mid-January Edie was back in Detroit, writing strange letters to Allen. Edie had never been entirely comfortable with Jack's aesthetic intellectualism, and her letter to Allen was a petition for tutoring. "I want you to form a private education for me such as books to read like the ones you first read. Give me questions on them. Then when you think you [sic] understand the book thoroughly why give me another and so on . . ." She went so far to threaten to expose Allen's "secret"—his homosexuality—if he failed her. It was not merely that she lacked the background to talk for hours with people whose favorite phrase was "supreme reality"; her letter came on the stationery of the Michigan Social Register, which alone suggested her incompatibility with the 115th Street den. From all accounts, she and Jack would have no contact for several years. Though she was the wife of his youth, Edie left few traces on Jack's life, remaining a cloudy figure in the decades to come.

January 1945 was an eventful month for the circle of friends. Despite his unhidden predilection for male sex partners, Burroughs married Joan Vollmer on January 17, and moved into the apartment. Allen also moved in, but under different circumstances: He was expelled from Columbia in an escapade that was sad, funny, bizarre, and revealing.

Superficially, Allen was a model student—an editor of the humor magazine the *Jester*, a member of the literary society Philoxean, a History pre-law major. But he didn't fit in. As Diana Trilling, wife of Allen's mentor Lionel, later put it, "He made life too messy." Incapable of understanding his experiments in consciousness, she and the rest of the Columbia establishment categorized him as a status seeker and a careerist. Off-campus, Johnny the bartender at the West End had complained to the dean, and the dean to Allen's father Louis, about Allen's late hours there. But it was a dusty window that finally nailed Allen. He didn't get along very well with his maid, so out of a giggling curiosity as to how long the filth might remain in peace, he sketched some slogans into the soot:

"[Columbia President] Butler has no balls" and "Fuck the Jews." He also drew a cartoon of cock and balls, and a skull and crossbones.

Early one morning a few days later, Dean Ralph Furey appeared in Allen's room to find him in bed in his underwear sleeping back to back with a nonstudent named Jack Kerouac. It was a perverse encounter; in the fall of 1940, Dean Furey had been the freshman football coach who called Jack a pansy and hounded him because he didn't enjoy running on a broken leg. The truly wretched part of the scandal was that it was nonexistent; much to Allen's disappointment, there hadn't been any sex, and Allen's roommate Bill Lancaster confirmed it. Jack looked up to see Furey erupting, got out of bed, and without saying a word went across the hall to Lancaster's room, dove under the covers, and went back to sleep. The next day he was banned from campus. Allen's fate was harsher. "Mr. Ginsberg," puffed Dean of Students McKnight, "I hope you understand the enormity of what you've done." Allen was ordered to stay away from campus for a year, get a job, and see a psychiatrist, all of which he did, more or less. Burroughs was his informal and unaccredited psychiatrist, however, and Burroughsian values did not harmonize with those of the good dean.

The intellectual barrenness of the Academy was virtually complete, and in that period the only faculty member to contribute much to Jack and Allen aside from Van Doren's friendly presence was Raymond Weaver, who taught a course in communications at Columbia. His rich past included friendship with the great harpsichordist Wanda Landowska and years of residence in Japan; Weaver brought to his classes a touch of Zen and a vision of Gnostic wisdom that was unique. That spring, Allen brought Weaver a copy of Jack's first (and never published) book, *The Sea Is My Brother*, and the professor recognized in it a kindred spiritual approach. Weaver responded with a reading list of ancient Gnostics, including Plotinus and the Egyptians. Campus was irrelevant; the real classroom was 42nd Street, a bar, Joan's big double bed sprawled with bodies; wherever Bill was, the talk was likely to be intriguing.

With the Western value system fragmented by the enormity of the war, Burroughs searched through the shards of Manhattan culture for an understanding of the times like the detective he had once been. But he was no Sherlock Holmes, whose evidence had been hard, physical, certain; his approach resembled more closely that of a popular American fictional contemporary, Nero Wolfe, who probed intellectual and verbal facts so subtle as to be nearly mystical, "Tenuous," as Wolfe said of his work, "to the point of nullity." Times had changed, and Burroughs and Jack first collaborated on a detective story modeled on another contemporary, Dashiell Hammett.

A few days after Bill had "stolen" Jack away from Self-Ultimacy, they were sitting in Riordan's, a bar on Columbus Circle. The radio news ended with the startling story of a flash fire at the London Zoo; the reporter concluded his tale with the phrase, "and the hippos were boiled in their tanks." The phrase became the title of a Hammett-style novel Jack and Bill coauthored which fictionalized Kammerer's death. Writing alternate chapters, they put together an occasionally slow but generally straightforward narrative that recounted the past summer's events but set them mostly in the Village. Cynical and humorous, Bill ("Will Dennison") described things from behind the bar where he worked—Lesbians, soldiers, cops, and fights. As "Mike Royko," Jack focused on the NMU hiring hall, old ship's tales, and Kammerer's death. The dark iron taste of Dashiell Hammett permeated the book's style, down to a gratuitous piece of violence Jack attributed to himself.

Hammett's world was like theirs, a place of black and white and gray, anything but "clean, orderly, and sane." His greatest character, Sam Spade, was an "existential knight" who sliced through the fraud, the phoniness, the corruption, the lies, to the bonehard facts. Spade had little respect for society's rules, but he worked with a sense of honor: "Listen. When a man's partner is killed he's supposed to do something about it. It doesn't make any difference what you thought of him. He was your partner and you're supposed to do something about it." The quality of loyalty remained important.

There were other authors to study. One day Bill handed Oswald Spengler's *Decline of the West* to Jack with the comment, "Eddify yer mind, me boy." The German's heavy tome was sneered at by the members of the American Historical Association, which was perhaps why their parochial histories made no impression on Jack, Bill, or Allen. But Spengler's attempt to transcend chauvinism and picture the world *as* history, a dynamic portrait of "things-becoming," fulfilled them. Seeking a logic of history that could answer questions of *being* and justify prophecy of future development, Spengler had arrived at a cyclical-organic view of life. Fusing him with Nietzsche and Yeats, his three readers elaborated the beginnings of a cyclical theory of history that included seven categories. The theory began with a natural, idealistic stage, moved through a logical Apollonian stage, lost itself in puritanical

Protestantism, moved through iconoclasm to artistic recovery, and ended in nihilism and hedonism.

Spengler's recommendation to his readers at the end of his introduction was the key: "And I can only hope that men of the new generation may be moved by this book to devote themselves to technics instead of lyrics, the sea instead of the paint-brush, and politics instead of epistemology. Better they could not do." Each man reacting as his personality dictated, Burroughs came away from Spengler with an apocalyptic vision of collapse. Years before, he and a friend at Harvard had written a lampoon of the *Titanic* called "So Proudly We Hail," which featured an orchestra playing "The Star-Spangled Banner," a captain in drag looting the safe, and a spastic paretic who chopped off the fingers of all the victims trying to get into his boat: the sinking of America. Sailor Jack, still a disciple of the roughnecked working class, interpreted Spengler's call as a retrenchment to his roots, to the plain people, to what Spengler called the fellaheen. Though Kerouac was an urban intellectual by circumstance, his soul was not in it.

Nor was he ever entirely committed to psychiatry, one of the other primary concerns at the 115th Street apartment. Years later he told a friend that rational psychotherapy was for him only another superstition, and he preferred the richer, deeper, sad peasant mysticism of Quebec Catholics. Or perhaps he rejected psychiatry because Bill, acting as the psychiatrist, got too close to his innermost fears. Allen had the first hour with Burroughs, and Jack the second. Lying on the couch while Bill took a chair, they'd stare vaguely at the rising column of his cigarette smoke and free-associate in the usual way. It was not Freudian analysis but Burroughsian, the impersonal, benevolent indifference of a friend. One day, after a long period of "analysis," Bill stirred in his chair, and in his gray nasal snort-thunk voice began to prophesy to Jack the future of his guilty attitudes toward Gerard's death and Mémêre. He spoke at length, building a detailed, frightening picture of Gabrielle's starched white apron strings turned snake, guilt worms coiled ever tighter, ever tighter around him. Jack was no fool; he understood his attitudes toward his mother. Allen and other friends had heard him analyze himself incisively and in copious detail; it was not a lack of intellectual comprehension that forced him to accept the mythology of his guilts toward Mémêre and his virgin-whore complex, but the passive nature of his personality. He was an observer, and when he acted it was to describe a scene, not to change it. He was a dreamer, and one cannot control dreams. Part filial piety and

part homage to Gerard, Jack's stubborn loyalty to his parents—and particularly Mémère—was unshakable, even when they quarreled, as they frequently did. After all, it was the division between Lowell and the City,
light and dark, family and sin that had generated his vision. Even when
it hurt, he would straddle both poles. Jack was moved and astounded at
Burroughs' perception, and he was astonished, too, that Bill should make
the effort to take notice of his life, but it remained a difficult balancing
act.

There was a subtlety to life at 115th Street such that even charades
became a "conscious travesty," as Allen said, of their personalities and
America. Straw-hatted Jack became a bumptious hayseed, Allen in a
bowler a sly Hungarian hustler, and a fright-wigged Burroughs Allen's
female partner in a confidence game. "Gee, I never seen no culture like
this," burbled Jack, as they showed him "valuable heirlooms" for sale.
"Yes, my dear," Allen would reply, "we haff ferry much culture. You vill
stay here and learn." Occasionally, Jack and Allen would ride the subway,
while Allen would peer through a hole ripped in his newspaper waiting
for someone to notice him noticing them: "We were conscious of them,
and it was an opportunity for them to be conscious of us being conscious
of them . . . to provoke some sort of human consciousness, to bring
eternity into the subway." "Supreme reality" was their watchword, but
widening consciousness involved risks. The "Atomic Disease" was Allen's
phrase for the zombielike quality of contemporary reality, and also for the
Benzedrine-induced paranoia that was beginning to consume Joan
Vollmer Burroughs.

As spring turned into summer, the American and Russian armies met
on the banks of the Elbe River, Mussolini and Clara Petacci ended up
hanging by their heels, and 500,000 New Yorkers surged into Times
Square to celebrate the end of war in Europe. In mid-June Allen received
his draft notice, Burroughs drifted to St. Louis for a while, and Jack spent
more and more time in Ozone Park with Leo and Gabrielle; the form of
the 115th Street family had changed.

It was a weird and frustrating summer for Jack, compounded of
emotional, financial, and artistic problems. A story he'd written about life
at sea had failed to sell, and some other quickie magazine pieces were also
rejected. He decided to ship out for Europe in July, decided against it,
then elected to work in a summer camp, only to become disgusted at the
idea of scrubbing toilets for $30 a week, and quit. Broke and floundering,

he returned to Ozone Park. If all his problems had been monetary, though, he probably could have stuck out the ship or camp; what threatened him was much worse.

That summer Jack was driven half frantic by the split in his life between two worlds, the clean Lowell–Ozone Park axis of jobs and family and security, and the drug-hustler-homosexual scene of Allen, Bill, and Times Square. Though Jack was basically an enthusiastic heterosexual who lusted after whores and worshiped virgins, he moved on the fringes of a shadowy sexual ghetto that disturbed him even though he barely participated in it.

Allen had "come out" to Jack the previous fall, thrust out of the closet by the shock of Lucien's imprisonment. Sitting in Hartley Hall, he had told Jack, "You know, I love you, and I want to sleep with you, and I really like men." Jack sighed, covered his face with his hands, and half-smiled, half-moaned, "Oooooh, noooo." Yet because of what Allen saw as his "mellow, trustful, tolerance and sensitivity," Jack didn't reject Allen, and he was, months later, still willing to share a bed—clothed— with his spiritual brother. Allen conceded that his approach had been crude and a bit selfish, "with all my harlequinade and conscious manipulation of your pity." It was a measure of the repression of the times and Jack's own uncertainty about the double life of Ozone Park kitchen table and Manhattan back streets that he could only be vague and oblique even in his letters to Allen.

Ginsberg had been rejected by the draft after claiming homosexuality, and he landed that July of 1945 in the Maritime Service Training Center in Sheepshead Bay. He wrote Burroughs at the time, "I feel more guilty and inferior by reason of faggishness than intellectualization will admit is proper." For Allen, the "mountains of homosexuality, Matterhorns of Cock, Grand Canyons of asshole" were a "weight on my melancholy head."

Allen established, and Jack accepted, a dichotomy between them. "We are of different kinds," Allen said. "Jean, you are an American more completely than I, more fully a child of Nature and all that is of the grace of the earth." As a Jew, Ginsberg was "alien to your natural grace, to the spirit which you would know as a participater [sic] in America. . . . I am not a cosmic exile such as Wolfe (or yourself), for I am an exile from myself . . . I wish to escape from myself, I wish to obliterate my consciousness and my knowledge of independent existence, my guilts, my secretiveness."

Trapped in Ozone Park reading *The Maxims of the Duc de la Rochefoucauld*, Aquinas, Boethius, Rabelais, Pascal, and the Bible, Jack the "child of nature" had mostly concrete under his feet, dreams about Lucien and self-hatred for his attraction to the drug-sex netherworld inside his head. And, as he told Allen, he disliked the psychological self-centeredness, the repetitious analyses of sex, that seemed to preoccupy everyone. For Jack, the endless stories he was writing were more important than anything. Back came letters from Allen accusing him of rationalization, of pretending to be something he was not, of denying "your double nature." Allen was correct; so was Jack when he argued that until he could express and reveal his divided psyche in a specific technique of art, nothing about him would make sense. At the age of twenty-three, Jack was quite positive that he had the vision necessary to write, but he needed to discover the method that could translate ethereal clouds of thought into written words. As August passed, no resolution appeared, either in his writing or his emotional state.

While Jack fidgeted in Ozone Park, the nuclear sword cracked down on Hiroshima and Nagasaki, and in the hideous light of atomic fire, World War II ended. At 7 P.M., August 14, Harry Truman told America that he had received from Japan a message "I deem . . . full acceptance of . . . unconditional surrender." Two million hysterical New Yorkers surged into Times Square drunk with joy. Picking their way through the 5,000 tons of ticker tape that filled the streets, Jack and Bill were as liquored as the rest, but were outsiders; it was a serviceman's night. Burroughs came as Beelzebub in a crimson-lined coat and Panama hat, and Jack walked silent beside him, savoring the ironies of companionhood with a satanic messenger on this day of deliverance. Seen in the blinding glare of a mushroom cloud, this new nation *was* hell as far as he was concerned. The war had left the federal government tripled in size and corporate assets doubled, with an accompanying increase in "efficiency" and a decrease in the visionary and human qualities that Jack prized.

Yet sorrow was not the war's only bequest. In some mysterious process of balance, certain American artists had taken from the war the elements of a rich new art. Ten blocks north of Jack on 52nd Street, dozens of black Americans, soon to be followed by thousands of whites, were creating a new music inspired by the frustrations and insights that Jack shared. More, black musicians were starting a cultural revolution that would replace white big-band music with a new beat called Bop.

Bop began innocently enough. The war had destroyed the big bands with entertainment taxes on dance floors, gasoline rationing, which ended bus travel, and shellac rationing, which made recording virtually impossible. Things were changing even more rapidly within the Afro-American culture; coming north en masse to enter the industrial system, more and more talented young blacks demanded to know why jazz, the black art, was putting money only in white pockets. In 1941 Minton's, a reasonably priced, out-of-the-way club on 118th Street in Harlem, hired pianist Teddy Hill to organize a house band. Especially on Monday, the Apollo Theater's off-night, young musicians began to drop by and jam, including Kenny "Klook" Clarke on drums, John Birks "Dizzy" Gillespie on trumpet, and Bud Powell on piano. By 1942 two more men had sat down to stay, a mystic goateed and shaded genius on piano named Thelonious Sphere Monk, and a smiling extrovert named Charles "Bird" Parker on saxophone. Later additions included Max Roach and Miles Davis. With no white publicity, they had space to think, and the stage at Minton's became a scene of extraordinary creative experimentation; the jams weren't competitive, but shared attempts to make music more than entertainment, to make it express what the times were about. Bop was Afro-American music doubled in speed, intensified in emotion, and made far more subtle in its treatment of the roots—rhythm. As Max Roach would later comment, "We kept reading about rockets and jets and radar, and you can't play 4/4 music in times like that."

Bop reflected the technical changes of World War II—greater speed and magnified complication—with perfect precision, but the music's social aspects were equally important. For the first time, black musicians saw themselves as artists to be respected, as artists in revolt. As protection from American racism in general and the crudities of audiences in particular, the Boppers developed a whole culture of restrained coolness that enraged bourgeois critics and older musicians but entranced Jack and many of his peers. Their language was distant and oblique. Their dress—berets, goatees, and glasses—seemed affected. And their drugs, usually marijuana, sometimes heroin, enraged all the squares. Above all else, it was their withdrawn, somnambulistic intensity onstage, their refusal to talk or smile or shuffle, that made the usually generous Louis Armstrong accuse them of malice and the leading magazine of jazz, Downbeat, attack them as fanatics. As one student of Bop later wrote, "Jazz had broken itself free of the middle-class world's social conception of what it should be."

Bop's audience, the "hipsters," was at one with the music's contempt for the old style. John C. Holmes, a writer and later a close friend of Jack's, would come to argue that a Bop fan was "a different sort of person than a fan of swing or Dixie—with Bird you had to *dig* to know; your consciousness had to be at a different level of evolution . . . If a person dug Bop, we knew something about his sex life, his kick in literature and the arts, his attitudes towards joy, violence, Negroes, and the very processes of awareness." Jack had been hearing about Minton's since 1941, when his school buddy Seymour Wyse had let him in on what was happening, but he became involved with the music somewhat later, when the Boppers moved downtown to 52nd Street. Jack was only outwardly restrained and cool, but he was naturally hip, and he got along well enough with the hipsters to blend in.

Listening to Bird, their heads nodding yes, yes, the hipsters looked "like criminals" to Jack, but "they kept talking about the same things I liked, long outlines of personal experience and vision, night-long confessions full of hope that had become illicit and repressed by War."

Criminal or not, bohemia had become Kerouac's chosen nightworld. Here Jack followed Burroughs, who had made a new friend in a man named Herbert Huncke, and found a new experience in morphine. Sometime in the fall of 1945, Bill acquired several gross of morphine Syrettes and a submachine gun. He mentioned this to a soda-jerk friend of his who had a few underworld connections, and asked the friend if he knew anyone interested in buying the stuff. Around nine one night that week, the friend took Burroughs to a strange apartment located on Henry Street on the Lower East Side, which was occupied by Herbert Huncke and Phil "Sailor" White, both of whom were interested in narcotics.

It was a bizarre place, with black walls, a red ceiling, heavy drapes, and Aztec mosaics, all of which reminded Burroughs of a vulgar "chop suey joint." Huncke, a small, ferret-quick man with enormous dark-brown Arab eyes that were always on the lookout for a hustle or the cops, wasn't too impressed with Burroughs, either. Herbert quickly dragged his friend aside, hissing, "Hey man, this looks like heat to me, get rid of him." After reassurances, Huncke and the sailor sampled the merchandise. Having cooked up, tied up, and shot up, they helped Burroughs, who had never done "hard" opiates before, to do the same. Morphine hit Burroughs in the "back of the legs first, then the back of the neck, a spreading wave of relaxation slackening the muscles away from the bones so that you seem to float without outlines, like lying in warm salt water."

There was nothing in Bill's life at that point to stand in its way, and "by default," he said, junk soon became the entirety of his existence. He soon learned that a certain doctor on 102nd Street sold morphine script, that certain drugstores were easy for needles and droppers, that with the right connections anything at all could be purchased at the Angler Bar on 43rd and Broadway. Briefly Burroughs "worked the hole"—that is, picked subway drunks' pockets—with the Sailor. Their night would begin at eleven, when they'd roll uptown from Times Square looking for victims; Bill would read the *Times* next to the drunk while Phil reached behind to lift the wallet. One night they had to blackjack a light sleeper, and when his cut turned out to be three dollars, Bill quit. Marijuana dealing was too bothersome, so he settled on selling junk in partnership with an addict friend named Bill Garver.

Jack watched it all, absorbing every detail, eating Benzedrine until his hairline receded and his body became flabby, until he became so pale that Vicki Russell, a friend of Huncke's, had to apply pancake make-up to his face so that he wouldn't feel conspicuous in the subway. Sick-carnival Times Square had been a haunt of Kerouac's for five years now, but he never appreciated it until he began to follow Huncke and Burroughs on their rounds, often wide-eyed with fear and excitement. Huncke was an authentic Professor of Hip, a street cat to the bone; there was little meanness in him, but neither was there the slightest regard for anything resembling middle-class ethics. "Creep" was what the cops called him, the lowest of the low, and though there seemed no more unlikely a person to learn from, Jack, trembling with nerves, would follow Huncke into the Angler Bar for his lessons. When Dr. Kinsey looked for homosexual hangouts in New York, he went there and chose Bill and Huncke as two of the interviewees. But the Angler was no teacup-elegant gay bar. Across the street was the Times Square Bar, aka "The Bucket of Blood." The Angler wasn't a great deal gentler.

For its component junkies, fags, hookers, cops, and observant fledgling writers, the Square was bounded on the north and south by 50th and 42nd streets, and east-west by Eighth Avenue and Broadway. Grant's hot-dog palace on 42nd Street offered nickel hamburgers and huge dime hot dogs. Bus stations were major stalking grounds; the Greyhound at 51st Street, the All-America Bus Terminal between 42nd and 41st, and the Dixie Station on 42nd. Huncke introduced Kerouac to the notorious Whelan's Drugstore on Seventh and 47th, pointed out the cheap prostitute hotels that linked 46th and 47th streets, and spent hundreds of hours with his eyes on the street from a booth at Chase's all-night cafeteria, sipping coffee and stealing overcoats—and anything else available. Though Jack struck him as an "All-American boy" and Allen as a "starry-eyed" idealist, Huncke didn't mind performing for such an attentive audience.

Bent over a beer at the Angler, he talked about one of his old friends, Elsie-John, a bizarre character who was a penny arcade hermaphrodite in Chicago. Elsie was six feet, six inches tall, with long henna-red hair lying on an egg-shaped head. She, or he, had enormous deep-blue eyes, green or blue eyelids, silver nails, a red-painted mouth usually set in a slightly idiotic smile, a distinguished taste for heroin and cocaine, and generally appeared in the company of three Pekinese dogs. Even in Times Square there weren't many people quite so outré, but Elsie's kindred spirits were legion, and Jack roamed appreciatively among the furtive dropouts of the Square.

Jack's reading suited the atmosphere; that summer of 1945 he had gotten drunk and stolen a copy of Louis-Ferdinand Céline's *Journey to the End of the Night.* Floating on a wave of Benzedrine, Jack transcended 42nd Street and entered, in his mind's eye, a horrifying world whose main ingredients sometimes seemed to be shit, piss, vomit, mucus, boils, pus, and maggots. Céline's world, the life of Dr. Destouches, was all schemes and failure, charlatanism and guilt and death. Yet out of the odious corruption of that world came a peculiar vision which exposed the lies of modern life with Destouches' kindly compassion for his sad dying patients. Some of Céline resonated with Jack's own life—a socially ambitious mother, sour working-class father, a gloomy, suspicious view of life. Yet it was the style that impressed Kerouac the most. Trotsky said of Céline that he "writes like a man who has stumbled across human language for the first time." He wrote as people talked, putting spoken language into print with his famous ellipses. His style was not linear but rather circular, detail building on detail in conversational, seemingly random order, the words elastic, slippery, almost diaphanous.

It was all too much for Jack, the Benzedrine and talk and intense reading and horror. In December 1945 his legs swelled with thrombophlebitis. Confined to bed in the Queens VA Hospital and surrounded by returned veterans, he had an opportunity to reflect on the chasm between his hip urban life and the values represented by the shabby apartment in Ozone Park where Leo and Gabrielle resided. Leo had stomach cancer, and around this time had to quit work. He and Gabrielle could not understand their son's almost neutral curiosity about the street, were appalled at the drugs and his "foreign ideas." They demanded to know why Jack couldn't get a good job, and were sure that Bill and Allen were going to get him into further trouble.

A refugee from the nineteenth century, Leo was wholly unable to comprehend this rushing new world of "Electro-Mechanical Brains" and atomic bombs. The labor struggles led by John L. Lewis in the spring of 1946 were an abomination to him as an honest workingman. No one else understood the nation's changes, either. A February 1946 issue of *Life* featured horrifying pictures of suicided Nazi war criminal Dr. Robert Ley's brain being dissected in the interests of science. No answers there. Lying in the white hospital bed, Jack found himself thinking, as he wrote many years later, that "the city intellectuals of the world were divorced from the folk body blood of the land, were just rootless fools." He "began to get a new vision of my own of a truer darkness which just overshadowed all this overlaid mental garbage of 'existentialism' and 'hipsterism' and 'bourgeois decadence.' " When Jack got out of the hospital, he went home to Ozone Park to nurse Leo.

There is something especially cruel about watching your father die. How can the big strong man who once threw you around with such power wither and waste before your very eyes? It was his seed that helped make you. It is the flesh that helped create your flesh that is being consumed. Jack now had the true disillusionment forced upon him. His father's death taught him that nothing ultimately mattered but the angel of death perched on his shoulder.

All the winter and spring of 1946 Leo grew gaunt and haggard, pounds melting off his face and chest, cirrhosis spots blossoming on his hands. Around him was the stench of stomach cancer, the foul miasma of rotting, festering flesh. His belly bloated with fluid, and every two weeks a doctor came to drain him. Sometimes he'd be cheerful, sit up and talk, sip coffee and listen to the radio to find out how the Red Sox did. Sometimes he just sat and cried. He slept worse and worse, rising in the middle of the night to sit in his chair and hold communion with his parents, and God, and himself, asking them all why the world was so wretched. "Life is too long," he said. Repeatedly he made his son pledge to take care of Mémère when he died, and Jack swore that he would.

One morning as Jack sat writing, he heard Leo snoring from the next room. The snores were his papa's death rattle, and when Jack left the table it was to find Leo's corpse and to note with wonder the printer's ink that still stained his father's hands. It was May 1946, and now two of the Kerouacs were dead. They took Leo Alcide Kerouac home to Nashua, New Hampshire, and they buried him.

Jack returned to Ozone Park, slipped a blank piece of paper into his typewriter, and set out to write his tale in pain and glory, to redeem his life from death.

VI
"A Western Kinsman of the Sun"

FOR MOST of America, 1946 was a year of ongoing postwar catharsis during which the Puritan strictures of wartime gave way to billboards advertising the film *The Outlaw* with the lecherous question, "What two things are responsible for Jane Russell's success?" Pensive in Ozone Park, Jack roamed from room to room mournfully singing Gershwin's "Why Was I Born?" Mémêre raised futile objections to his choice of songs, but continued to work at her shoe-factory job, supporting Jack while he wrote an idealized autobiographical novel that he called *The Town and the City*. The work reflected his return to his family, replacing the New Vision aura of symbolic decadence with the style of his first love, Thomas Wolfe. Culled from notebooks that were already several years old, the work was underlaid not only with his new insight into death but with the idealism of Goethe's autobiography *Dichtung und Wahrheit (Poetry and Truth)*, Kerouac's main reading matter that summer and fall. A dignified, gentle work, *Poetry and Truth* fit precisely the somber quiet of Jack's mood. Goethe had taken nine hundred pages to detail his first twenty-four years of life, and his charming tales of a romantic, fairytale childhood soothed Jack's soul. Goethe calmly rejected satire and preached an affirmative love of life, and more, told Jack that all of his work was merely "fragments of a great confession."

Seated at the kitchen table, oblivious to the wash flapping on the lines outside, Jack worked at his own confession whenever he was in Ozone Park. He would do so for two years, grimly struggling from morning until late at night to recite the history of the Kerouacs and America. Concentration was easy, for distractions were few. Burroughs had fled

New York after a narcotics arrest, and following a brief career as salesman for Death County Bill's Tooth Tablets, he had settled on a farm in New Waverly, Texas, to raise marijuana for the New York market. Joan turned up in Manhattan that fall, but too much amphetamine sent her to Bellevue Hospital Psychiatric Wing. Allen reentered Columbia in September, and even had a publication to his credit; he had reviewed William Carlos Williams' poem "Paterson I" for the Passaic Valley *Examiner*, snidely urging the unwashed masses to put aside their crossword puzzles and read it. But that fall Allen was also heavily involved in drug experimentation, and because of that and Leo's deathbed injunction against Ginsberg, "that cockroach," Jack did not invite him for Thanksgiving dinner. Lucien's release from prison was the best news of the season, and he and Jack ended 1946 together with Vicki Russell and Celine, seeing the movie *Crime and Punishment* before they hit a series of Horace Mann socialite parties where they disappeared under the piano with purloined drinks and talked in the New Year.

The calm was only temporary; around that time Hal Chase, a Columbia friend of Kerouac's who had lived in the 115th Street apartment, brought news that a young Denver friend of his was in town. The friend, a former inmate at the New Mexico State Reformatory who read Schopenhauer and wrote letters demanding to be taught about Nietzsche, had come to New York hoping to enter Columbia. Jack had seen the letters, and as he and Hal rode the subway to the apartment in Spanish Harlem he pictured a frail and poetic saint of the cells.

The door burst open and Neal Cassady stood naked before them, his well-muscled athlete's body radiating energy, a Nietzschean "sideburned hero of the snowy West," Jack thought. As they talked, Kerouac's eyes fixed on Cassady's bobbing, pumping head, with its broken, soft-ended nose, smooth high cheekbones and blue flirtatious eyes. In pictures, they sometimes resembled each other enough to be brothers, and almost immediately they were spiritual partners, as Jack latched on to this "young jailkid all hung up on the wonderful possibilities of becoming a real intellectual." After seven years of cynical East Coast sophistication, Jack had endured enough. Twenty-year-old Neal swept into his life like a West Wind siren singing freedom, excitement, kicks, a "wild yea-saying overburst of American joy," as Jack characterized him, enthusiastically flying after food and sex like a holy primitive, a "natural man"; he was the embodiment of Jack's American dream.

Neal's fantastic talk took Jack back to the excitement of Pawtucketville street corners, punctuating Kerouac's shy mumbles with "Yes!" and "That's right!" Cassady ordered his wife LuAnne out of bed and into the kitchen with an unceasing flow of electric verbal persuasion: "In other words we've got to get on the ball, darling, what I'm saying, otherwise it'll be fluctuating and lack true knowledge or crystallization of our plans." A sixteen-year-old with curly auburn hair and a voluptuous body, LuAnne also caught Jack's eye. But it was Neal who captured Kerouac's mind, his imagination, and his heart, this young man whose ragged clothes fit perfectly, made by the "natural tailor of natural joy," who could throw a football seventy yards, run a hundred yards in less than ten seconds, broad jump twenty-three feet, and masturbate five or six times a day, every day.

Indeed. For Neal, as Jack said, sex "was the one and only holy and important thing in his life, although he had to sweat and curse to make a living and so on," and Cassady, the man with more energy than anyone, devoted most of it to what he called "that thing 'tween them li'l ole gals' legs." Though his demonic sexuality was so frenzied that it was hardly pleasurable, Neal was a seemingly fearless man who had been stealing cars and getting laid at the age Jack played Shadow and jerked off. A hero whose energy and spirit seemed full worthy of emulation had finally arrived in Jack's life.

Yet Jack did not simply romanticize Cassady, and over the ensuing weeks as they held all-night beer-and-cigarette talks, he knew him as a brother-sufferer—as *the* brother, Gerard. Neal, whom Jack thought was born at about the same time as his elder brother's death, seemed to fill the empty spot in Jack's heart; as Gerard echoed in his misty Lowell dreams, Neal focused the excitement of a wider world. Cassady, with all the intuitive insight of the con man, asked Jack to teach him how to write, and although Kerouac denied that he could, Neal's blurted coax swept him away. "Yes, of course, I know exactly what you mean," gushed Cassady, "and in fact all these problems have occurred to me, but the thing that I want is the realization of those factors that should one depend on Schopenhauer's dichotomy for any inwardly realized . . ." Neal was like the true cowboy of Western mythology, generous and antimaterialistic, romantic yet misogynous at core, whose life had thus far rolled along opposed to the dread middle-class words "responsibility" and "maturity." And oh how he suffered for his cowboy freedom, for his energy and drive were the product of deep self-hatred, of a childhood wrought, as Jack later put it, of "a million disorderly images of damnation and strangulation in a world too unbearably disgusting to stand." Over the coming years, the two brothers would share their histories, and piece by fragmented piece, Jack would puzzle over his brother's sad and lunatic past.

In *The First Third,* his fascinating memoir of a few years later, Neal called himself the "unnatural son of a few score beaten men," because after a young childhood spent watching his older half-brothers systematically pound living hell out of his father, Neal Sr., for coming home drunk, at age six he went with Neal Sr. to live in Denver's skid-row bum hotel, the Metropolitan. The elder Cassady was a totally ineffectual meek slug of a wino, a sad doormat for whom his son begged nickels for a bottle, pleaded for mercy from judges, and painfully helped home after Saturday-night drunks. They shared their room with a legless misfit named "Shorty," who was usually gone when Neal awoke to go to school. As a first-grader, Neal got himself off to class alone, his father still unconscious from the night before.

The seven-year-old boy washed up in a common bathroom stinking of vomit and filth, elbow-to-elbow with sad old derelicts trying to spruce up for downtown "high class" begging. For the Cassadys, breakfast and dinner were taken at the local mission, and they spent their midweek evenings kibitzing cards at the Metropolitan's lounge. On Saturday Neal Sr. usually managed to find work as a barber, while Neal lived in the movie theater next door, delighted with *The Count of Monte Cristo, The Invisible Man,* and *King Kong.* Life with father was weird but free, and Neal was unhappy when he had to return to his family in later school years— summers to be spent with Pop.

His "normal" family life included a year as a model altar boy, a special link with Jack that involved not only their mutual veneration of the Church but their traditional Roman Catholic sexual guilts. While with his mother, he was regularly tortured by his brother Jimmy, whose favorite hobby was crushing the skulls of cats; Neal he merely imprisoned inside a fold-in-the-wall bed, or forced to fight with other boys.

There was only one solution, and that was to run; at age fourteen, Neal Cassady discovered holy sanctuary behind the wheel of a stolen car. Along with sex, the speed and freedom of a moving car became his avenue of growth, giving him one place at least to breathe. *Go.* It didn't matter where. *Just go.* Night after night he'd steal a car or pick up a woman. Or better still, he'd organize a whole party and rush off into the mountains above Denver. By the age of twenty-one, he'd stolen 500 cars, been arrested ten times, convicted six times, and spent fifteen months in jail.

During one of his reformatory stretches, Neal was tormented by dreams of being like his father, so he began to read philosophy, and when he was released from the sentence at the age of fifteen, he spent as much time in the library as in his other main haunt, Peterson's Pool Room. Peterson's gave him the first of his benefactors, a young man named Jim Holmes, the hunchbacked wizard of rotation pool, a suffering patron who listened silently when Neal madly propositioned him with an offer to teach Jim philosophy if Holmes would tutor him in the finer points of eight-ball and the like. The lonely boy's attempted con worked, and Jimmy took him home, fed him, gave him a suit, and introduced him to his gang; in a few days Neal was its star.

His second advocate was more worldly. Justin W. Brierly was a Denver high school teacher who, as Jack later told the story, once knocked on the door of one of his tenants and had it opened by a naked, very erect Neal, then in the midst of screwing the maid. Brierly, who played sponsor to many young men, chirped, "My dear fellow, your ears aren't washed," sent him home and later to school, and introduced him to other young Denver men he'd gotten into his alma mater Columbia, including Jack's friends Hal Chase and Ed White. Chase had impressed Neal with his conversation, especially his enticing stories of college life in New York. Even Neal's studies in philosophy altered when Hal remarked that "The poet is much more important than the philosopher." With his young bride LuAnne occupying one sphere of his life and Rimbaud another, Cassady stepped off the bus in New York City aflame with artistic and sensual curiosity, ready to devour new experience in any form.

One of the first things he learned was how to smoke grass. On January 10, Jack took one of his periodic breaks from the writing of *The Town and the City* and took him up to a studio apartment in the East Eighties to meet Vicki Russell. Coincidentally, Allen was also present. Allen and Neal had met at the West End the previous fall when Neal first arrived, but then Neal had been unsure how much of Allen's "dark brooding eyes" was a con. This time, Neal, "the holy conman with the shining mind," locked gazes with Allen, "the sorrowful poetic conman with the dark mind," and they plunged into an intense, supercharged dialogue.

With what Allen called his characteristic "energetic efficiency," Neal, then working at the Hotel New Yorker parking lot on 34th Street, planned to divide his nights three ways. Two evenings would be spent writing with Jack in Ozone Park, two nights in rapt intellectual conversation with Allen, "staring into each other's eyes," Allen later said, "finding out whether or not we bugged each other, what the limits were," and three nights rolling and tumbling with LuAnne. LuAnne soon decided that she had the lesser part of the bargain and returned to Denver in February 1947, but even before that something very special had happened.

Late one night in January the traveling party ended up at the tenement apartment of a friend of Allen's on 104th Street. There weren't enough beds, so Neal and Allen shared one. Trembling with desire, shame, and fear, Allen edged away to one side of the bed, only to have his mind spun upside down in merciful relief when Neal in tender compassion reached over and pulled him back. He was the same age as Allen, and his warm, generous lack of inhibitions overwhelmed the nervous Ginsberg. Allen fell in love with him. It seemed to Allen a "total accident," since Neal was basically interested in women; his sexual relationship with Allen, formalized with love vows a week later, came mostly out of a large compassion. Jack was "curious, envious, humorous, cutting . . . proud," of the liaison, and later compared it to Verlaine and Rimbaud—and to himself and Sammy Sampas.

The trio of young men talked in bars, the parking lot, at home; high on tea, drunk on beer or racing on amphetamine, all three of them stood emotionally naked and hungry for intimacy before each other. By March 1947, Neal told Jack that he had decided to write a life history, and through Allen had a two-page list of books and magazines that would have done credit to a very hip college's entire humanities program; the three most important books were Spengler's *Decline of the West,* Kardiner's *Psychological Frontiers of Society,* and Korzybski's *Science and Sanity,* while Neal chose as general reading Djuna Barnes, Camus, Céline, Kafka, Joyce, Mann, Proust, and Gide, among others. He felt he should be absolutely familiar with Baudelaire, Rimbaud, St. John Perse, Rilke, Hart Crane, T. S. Eliot, Auden, and Yeats.

On March 4, 1947, Neal got on a bus to return to Denver (though not to LuAnne), with Allen and Jack to follow when summer came. The trio was close; the previous evening Allen had talked, as he told his journal, "soberly (and severely) and straight to Jack à la Cassady—and it worked!" After sharing beans and hot dogs at Riker's cafeteria, they clowned around hiding their nervous love by taking pictures in a bus-station booth, then cut up and shared the prints. Dressed in a new secondhand charcoal pinstripe three-piece suit, Neal lugged his hot portable typewriter onto the bus with Chicago written on it and was off.

Their correspondence was as chaotic as their talk. Days after Cassady left, Jack was giggling over Neal's slaverous description of his seduction of a teacher, a fellow bus passenger, after four hours of overwhelming hustle. Jack called it "The Great Sex Letter" and was most impressed, though Neal scoffed at it as drunken ravings. Most of his letters, though, were encouraging, urging Jack to work on his novel *The Town and the City* and not give up, affectionately informing Kerouac that he felt whole and peaceful in his presence. By April, Neal was complaining that Jack wasn't interested in him because of his lack of verbal facility, that their relationship's cutting edge of frankness was being corroded by Jack's defensiveness. Still, the letter ended positively.

As befitted lovers, Neal and Allen were more stormy with each other. In the first month after he left, Cassady wrote five times, beginning with a tortured cry of dependency and compulsive need, expressing an "almost paranoid fear of losing you, Allen"; by the end of the month he had rationalized his sexual relationship with Allen as a simple compensation for the intellectual gifts Allen brought to their friendship. Now he wanted to live with both Allen and a woman. Crushed, Allen fumed that he was a "dirty, double-crossing, faithless bitch." Neal explained and explained, but it wasn't until June that he told Allen of Carolyn Robinson, a woman he'd met in March.

Carolyn was a Bennington graduate and University of Denver graduate student in Theatre Arts and Fine Arts, the product of a secure middle-class family ensconced in a restored ante-bellum Tennessee mansion; her father was a professor of biochemistry at Vanderbilt Medical School. Blond and beautiful too, she was everything Neal was not. Yet he impressed her with his dignity, even clad in a T-shirt and suit. "Closer to relating to people totally" than anyone she had ever met, he was so aware of her welfare, so "considerate, conscientious, unselfish," that he flabbergasted her into love. He didn't bother to mention that he was married, and she discovered only much later that the love poem he read to her was actually written by Allen for him.

At last it was July, and after a spring of reading books about the pioneers and mountainmen, of studying maps with infinite care as he traced the red line of Route 6 from Cape Cod to Nevada, Jack was ready to take a break from Ozone Park, Mémêre, and *The Town and the City,* to hit the road, to expose himself to the loneliness of vagabondage, to join Neal, to look for America. It was a strange land he crossed, a nation caught in change, relentlessly solidifying into a structure Jack would detest: America was on its way to becoming a solidly middle-class, increasingly suburban country. The transformation began in the Lowell-style industrial revolution but its immediate impetus was, of course, the war. Haunted by memories of the World War I bonus and concerned with a possible postwar depression, Congress had passed the GI Bill of Rights, which turned out to be an astoundingly successful welfare program. It was not, however, a dole for sullen failures but grants for upwardly mobile middle-class earners who came back from the war able to buy a home, set up a small business or go to college, learn a trade or get a respectable government job. The GI Bill was the crucible that formed the core of the postwar managerial and professional class. A general prosperity reached to the bottom, too, as the bottom-income fifth of the nation increased its earnings by nearly 70 percent, the second fifth by nearly 60 percent, while the top fifth increased at the rate of 20 percent. Four million, three hundred thousand veterans took out home loans, deserting Flatbush Avenue for the cookie boxes William Levitt was conjuring up on old potato fields in Long Island. Sales of Emily Post's etiquette book rocketed in the late 1940's, according to her, because "Money has changed hands."

But there was a price; prosperity brought with it social conformity, materialism, and a lock-step faith in "scientific progress." As in the previous postwar era, anxieties about change found a symbolic outlet—the extraordinary fear of Communism that characterized the Cold War decade. Rather than resist the American tide of materialism and conformity, many citizens found it easy to attribute these gloomy portents to the Soviet Union, so that Communism became a code word for the deadly modern world. The result was stasis. By 1947 every major magazine in America from the *Atlantic* to the *New Republic* to the *Partisan Review* was rabidly anti-Communist.

Hammer-and-sickle Stalinists or red-white-and-blue Americans; there seemed to be no middle ground. In fact, there was at least one alternative, and that was Dwight Macdonald's *Politics* magazine, one of Allen's favorites. Macdonald was radically democratic, pacifistic and in favor of decentralization, opposing the worship of science, the warfare state, and the febrile notion of historical progress. Jack and Allen were kindred spirits, but all of the readers of *Politics* together could have lived in one large Manhattan apartment building, and they went unheard.

Literary criticism conformed to the times, and the reigning authorities were the consciously reactionary members of the "Fugitive School," John Crowe Ransom and Allen Tate. T. S. Eliot expressed their view in this manner: "Poetry is not a turning loose of emotion, but an escape from emotion; it is not the expression of personality, but an escape from personality."

Four incidents made the headlines in the summer of 1947, each of them symbolic of enormously powerful currents in the society. Handsome Bugsy Siegel, organized crime's advance man in Las Vegas, was assassinated on June 20 by his erstwhile employers, but the investment of Syndicate money in "legitimate" enterprises went on apace. Industrialist Howard Hughes was embarrassed with fraud charges before a congressional committee in July; suave as ever, he rode out the scandal and continued to grow rich and corrupt government officials. Americans everywhere shivered when 4,000 motorcyclists converged on the small town of Hollister, California, for the July Fourth weekend. Bored, the cyclists terrorized the town by destroying windows and other property, earning the disgust of the middle class and the interest of the media, which seven years later put out the movie *The Wild Ones.* Jackie Robinson, first of a wave of publicized black athletes, kept on stealing bases at Ebbets Field.

Meanwhile, Jack was cold, wet, and discovering that the symmetric beauty of maps does not always harmonize with reality. Having decided to follow Route 6 because it ran so beautifully from Cape Cod to Nevada, he had taken the subway to 242nd Street and the trolley through Yonkers, then hitched to Bear Mountain, New York, and the highway west. It was no picnic; that area was astonishingly empty considering its proximity to New York, and he found himself standing in a chill rain with his new-for-the-trip open-weave huaraches soaked, night falling, and his westward progress nonexistent. "T'hell with it." He caught a ride back to New York and got on the Chicago bus. Hitching from Joliet, he passed the great stinking Mississippi, and crossed Iowa eating apple pie and ice cream in the company of truckers. For a while he had to listen to the truckers' talk of cops; "They can't put no flies on *my* ass!" one said. Soon, though, the darkness would close in and all that would remain was the hammering roar of the engine and the white noise of the wind that canceled out all else, leaving his eyes focused in the widening cone of the headlights that guided his musings forward, out into the great void that was the land.

After a confusing, disoriented night in a train hotel, he discovered the other side of hitching, the frustration of standing for hours in a place like Stuart, Iowa, greeting those few cars going your way with a forlorn smile and an interior monologue that went something like: "Hey lady, I'm okay, c'mon, pick me up. Ahh, I won't rape you . . . damn. Hey man, please, I'll tell funny stories, I'll do *anything*. Screw you, then. Well, at least I'm warm. [Car slows] Hey, great, thank God! [And speeds away] Ahhhhhhhh fuck."

Lonely, Jack hooked up with a guy named "Eddy" in Iowa, and having passed Council Bluffs (the old wagon-train jumpoff point now no more than "cute suburban cottages" to Jack), they went rolling down U.S. 30 into Nebraska. Stopping in cafés, Jack was elated to hear cowboys laugh and tease waitresses: "Maw, rustle me up some grub before I have to start eatin' myself raw or some damn silly idee like that."

Deserted by Eddy, Jack waited through what seemed an eternity and then got the ride of his life in the back of a truck driven by two blond grinning Minnesota bumpkins on their way to the West Coast. Careening along through the mean Wyoming wind in the back of their pickup, Jack found a thousand laughs, some warming shots of rye whiskey, and a man named Mississippi Gene, who turned out to be a friend of an old sailing buddy.

Cheyenne was a little depressing, for its "Wild West Week" struck Jack as a sad fraud, a shabby commercial con that was no replacement for the real thing. Drunkenly wandering the town after he left the truck, he tried and failed to pick up a woman, and ended up spending the night in a bus station that might have been in Newark, but "for the hugeness outside" that enraptured him—that clarity and enormousness of horizon that does make Wyoming "Big Sky Country," the essence of America, the sense of limitless possibilities for a free people. Hitching south to Denver, he kept telling himself, "Damn! damn! damn, I'm making it!" romantically imagining himself as "strange and ragged and like the Prophet who has walked across the land to bring the dark word, and the only word I had was 'Wow!' "

After two days in Denver, Jack finally caught up with Neal, who was then rather busily working all day, making love with LuAnne and Carolyn in the evening and talking and making love with Allen—who had arrived the month before—all night. Allen's basement room, a sweaty-walled crypt with a bed, a chair, a candle, and an ikon, was their meeting place.

As Jack charged in, Neal looked up and effusively sputtered out a greeting. "Why, Ja-ack, well now—ah—ahem—yes, of course. You've arrived—you old sonumbitch you finally got on that old road. Well, now —look here—we must—yes, yes at once—we must, we really must!" But in the rush and fury of the visit, they never got a chance to really talk. In fact, Kerouac spent most of his time with Hal Chase's gang, which was then involved in a small social war with Neal, whom they considered a bum. Chase's friends Bob and Beverly Burford were Jack's main play-mates, along with Chase and Ed White, and they partied all over Denver and then in Central City, a reconstructed mining town in the mountains west of the city. Burford was a tough guy, a budding Hemingway, and though he thought Neal was "a hood," he was impressed with Jack's journals. The visit to the Central City Opera was a great party, and while Jack missed Neal and Allen, who were in another rooming house with Justin Brierly, he figured they'd only have been out of place in the innocent celebration. They seemed suddenly like characters out of *Fidelio*, that night's opera, like "the man with the dungeon stone and the gloom," Jack wrote four years later, "rising from the underground, the sordid hipsters of America, a new beat generation that I was slowly joining."

Back in Denver, Jack spent some time with Cassady and Ginsberg, and despite the fact that he fell asleep when Allen tried to explain ambiguity and complexity to him, they were sweet and mellow with each other. For no particular reason they had been out of sorts all spring, but after Denver, Allen wrote him that "you redeemed yourself in my eyes." One lovely night, Jack went with Neal and Carolyn to a tavern and talked over the jazz on the jukebox. Carolyn liked Jack, was charmed by his laugh; as they danced together, he must have regretted his loyalty to Neal.

As it was, Cassady supplied him with a waitress friend for the eve-ning, but after Carolyn's grace she was only depressing. Restless, he decided to continue his journey, and sent to Mémêre for money to push on to San Francisco, where his old Horace Mann friend Henry Cru had a sailing berth for him. By this time, Allen had convinced Neal—who had already detached himself from LuAnne—to leave Carolyn and take a trip to visit Burroughs at his ranch in Texas. Carolyn, meantime, headed for Los Angeles to try for a career in costume design. After only two weeks in Denver, Jack was back on the road in a bus headed for the Pacific— and disappointment. San Francisco on his first visit was cold, foggy, and bleak, and when he arrived at Cru's place in suburban Marin City, no sailing job was available.

Jack's sharpest memory of Marin City would be laughter, for

Cru's screaming shout was unmatched in the world, except perhaps by that of Mr. Snow, an elderly Negro man who lived next door. The unceasing brawls between Cru and his lady were not funny, however, and when Jack wrote a movie script for Henry to sell in Hollywood, all that Jack could later recall about the work was that it came out hopelessly gloomy. Broke, he joined Cru and worked as a guard at a nearby complex that housed workers shipping to construction jobs in the South Pacific. Since most of his pay check went immediately to Mémêre for safekeeping his savings reassured him. But he abhorred his fellow workers, who had "cop souls," the sorts of fellows who delighted in shiny leather and buckles and in strolling about lasciviously fondling their night sticks. All Jack wanted to do was "sneak out into the night . . . and go and find out what everybody was doing all over the country," but he was stuck in Marin City with squabbles and the September rain.

The mail from Burroughs' ranch in New Waverly was tantalizing. A silvery gray cabin plunked down in the middle of the East Texas bayou country, draped with Spanish moss and passed regularly by an armadillo, it housed Bill, then doing three shots of heroin a day, Joan and Huncke, who devoured between them a gross of Benzedrine inhalers every two weeks, Joan's daughter Julie, Bill Jr., and their guests Neal and Allen. High on the drugs and the fast-ripening crop of grass, Bill would sit on the porch blindly firing off shots at a tree while Neal, Allen, and Huncke bemusedly roamed the swamps.

Allen had a problem. Though he had earlier written Jack that he would be a Lover, and not a "sad prophetic jew," Neal's inattentiveness was destroying Allen's hopes and his heart. By Labor Day he felt insane, his mind crumbling, his love for Neal now a weighty burden. "If you want to know my true nature," he wrote Jack, "I am at the moment one of those people who goes around showing his cock to juvenile delinquents." Neal's edging away from him had devastated Ginsberg. Allen even tried to build a bed to share with Cassady, but it collapsed like their relationship and he decided to take a leave of absence rather than return to Columbia and ship out to Dakar, Africa. Even Allen's parting from Neal was a frustration; having promised him a last orgiastic night in a Houston hotel room, Neal spent the early evening with a young retarded woman and Nembutals, and slept through the rest.

In Marin City, Jack's restlessness finally overcame his inertia in October and he decided to leave, first climbing Mount Tamalpais, the magnificent hill in the center of Marin County due north of San Francisco, at whose base lay Mill Valley and Marin City. Mount "Tam" was held sacred by the earliest Californians, the Indians. As the fog blew in off the ocean, he bowed his head in prayer, then went back down the hill and hitched to Saroyan's Fresno, where the free rides ran out. He caught a bus to Los Angeles. It was to be no ordinary ride.

At once excited, lonely, terrified, and eager, Jack was receptive to whatever his journey brought him. In a way wholly different from Neal's previous example, he found a lover in the next seat. Frail, slow, and a little dazed, Bea Franco was a Chicano. As broke and lonely as he was, she reached into his heart, not with words—she grew instantly nervous with his kinetic urban conversation—but with smiles and touches. Crooning "I love love" and harmonizing with the song "If You Can't Boogie I Know I'll Show You How," Bea joined Jack in a search for a cheap hotel room in bleak, awful Los Angeles, walking the streets with the blacks and the hipsters, the desert rats and the nature boys, smelling the grass and beer as they listened to the Bop that floated out of the bars.

Running out of money, they decided to hitch to New York, failed, then took the bus to Selma, California, a small town near Bakersfield, to work in the fields and to retrieve Bea's young son. The earth felt good to Jack as he picked cotton, a true fellaheen peasant at last, and though he was exhausted, there was a profound satisfaction in the idea of his little family, the land beneath them and the sky above. Hopelessly inexperienced, he could earn only a pittance—barely enough for food—and as the nights grew chillier, it seemed too cold for a baby to live in a tent. Perhaps he was tired of playing peasant. In any case, he sent mother and child back to her parents, hitched to Los Angeles, and armed with ten sandwiches, rode the bus to Pittsburgh, which was as far as his money would carry him.

Hitching again and dizzy with hunger, he met a wraithlike hobo whom he called the Ghost of the Susquehanna, a bearded old man continuously mad-babbling about food and headed to "Canady," until at long last a salesman picked Jack up and drove him to Times Square. Huncke was nowhere to be found, so he hit up a tourist for subway fare and went home to Ozone Park to discover that Neal, who had driven the marijuana harvest north from Texas, had gone to join Carolyn in San Francisco. Cassady and Kerouac had crossed paths somewhere in mid-America.

• • •

Off the road in New York, Jack retreated undisturbed into the privacy of his own world, to a town he called Galloway in his novel *The Town and the City*. He stayed with Mémère for the most part, living off his savings and her shoe-shop wages. Bitterly as she had protested when he had gone off to Denver and California—and would protest in the future over other journeys—Mémère was now content to supply her son's domestic needs, leaving him free to write. Jack's extraordinary dependence on his mother—she would always control his finances—would exact a grievous price in later years, but for the moment he was satisfied. The world of Galloway and his subject, the Martin family, the artistic ideal of *The Town and the City*, were more important than his inability to support himself. It was an inner reality that dominated his life almost totally during the winter of 1947 to '48.

Letters from Neal were rare; one in October exulted in his love for Carolyn and apologized at length for missing him in New York, one in November described attending a Thomas Mann lecture, and one at Christmas spoke of his intense comradely love for Jack. A long letter in early January, the last for several months, analyzed a dream of Jack's which mixed Dostoyevsky's idiot symbol, with which Jack identified, Faust, and death among other things. Then silence.

Except for a brief voluntary visit to the Lexington narcotics facility, Burroughs remained in Texas, while Allen spent most of the fall in his hometown of Paterson, New Jersey, and Lucien, adjusting to life out of prison, was hard for Jack to deal with. It was a tense time across the country, as the crusading rhetoric of anti-Communism used to defend the Marshall Plan that year had generated a poisonous atmosphere characterized by the Attorney General's list of subversive organizations, repressive new visa and passport laws, HUAC's attacks on Hollywood and labor, loyalty boards for all federal employees, and a wretched farce of a propaganda program called "Zeal for American Democracy."

It was better to stay in the world of his own artistic creation, in Galloway, a town "rooted in earth, in the ancient pulse of life and work and death," the home of the Martins, a family of bounty, of life and emotion, of love. After two years of struggle, Jack finally caught fire on his twenty-sixth birthday, March 12, 1948, with a 4,500-word day that exalted him. Seated at the Ozone Park kitchen table Kerouac celebrated the glee and honesty of the "wild self believing individuality" of his childhood Lowell America; more, he became Jeremiah, and sorrowfully depicted the family's collapse under the weight of war. *The Town and the City* was many things. It was of course autobiographical, recounting his own story: the trips to Rockingham Park, the romance with Mary Carney, the Lawrence football game, Columbia, Kammerer's death (suitably altered), and Leo's death. It fulfilled the fantasy of his childhood. He moved the Kerouacs to a fine home in a better neighborhood, gave himself three sisters—Rosie (patterned after Vicki Russell), Ruth, and Elizabeth—and created five Martin boys—Joe, Francis, Peter, Charley, and Micky—all elements of himself. Joe was a swaggering truck driver, Francis a snotty, brilliant intellectual, Peter a romantic young football player.

Yet transcending fantasy or autobiography was a vision of childhood, of Lowell, America, a reality centered on family solidarity and on women, for Mémêre as Earth Mother reigned over every sentence of his book. "The depth of a woman's heart is as unknowable as that of a man's," wrote Jack, "but nothing like restlessness and feverish rue ever abides there. A man may spend the night tracing the course of the stars above the earth, but the woman never has to worry her head about the course of the stars above the earth, because she lives on the earth and the earth is her home." In sweetly symphonic tones, Kerouac depicted children's follies—a broken window, a bully—and how big brothers and sisters rescue their younger siblings. Francis, the gloomy one, might see the night as "all merciless and hopeless, the one that kills you in the end," but his sour spirit bowed to more generous sentiments: "A child, a child, hiding in a corner, peeking infolded in veils, by swirling shrouds and mysteries, all hee-hee, all earnest and innocent with shining love, sweeter than a bird, pure, the child, unknowing, yet best known, godly all-knowing, the child crieth—'I see you.' "

And it all shattered. As Papa Martin watched his "family falling apart . . . they talk[ed] of war." Plucked fragment by fragment out of his own life, Jack's story told "the whole legend of wartime America itself, a picture upon which was written the great story of wandering, sadness, parting, farewell and war." Exhausted mothers with children in their arms waiting in train stations, Detroit factories, the Pentagon, boys in uniform, children sitting much too late in a big-city park; the images swelled and vanished. George Martin fell sick, and Peter nursed him. Charley died at Okinawa. Liz's baby was stillborn, and in her grief, Liz divorced her adoring husband.

In the end, life returned from the city to the land, and the living gathered in "Lacoshua," New Hampshire, for George's funeral, until only the closing image remained—of Peter leaping into a truck and going on the road. On September 9, 1948, the manuscript was done, all 380,000 words of it. It was two years of effort, of keeping meticulous records of word-count progress, of an afternoon's sleep and 5 and 10 and 16 hours a night of labor. He had given everything to his book, to the point one night that spring of going into the backyard, thumbing a hole in the dirt, dropping his pants, and trying to mate with the earth, to drive his penis into the ground, to truly know life from his head to his cock as it banged into the mushy cinders of Ozone Park. His first reaction to the book's completion was natural; he second-guessed himself, wondering if he should have worked the last paragraph differently, if . . . There was no need. He had written as brilliantly as his master Wolfe, but Jack's book was also informed with a historical consciousness keyed to the war that lent it additional weight.

Allen saw the manuscript first. He was "astounded by its depth," and in fact "felt that all the turmoil and frenzy of the last five years had been somehow justified: Because I saw expressed in his novel a peace and knowledge and solidity and—say, a whole recreated, true and eternal world—my world—finally given permanent form." Art had redeemed life. Jack's novel had come at a crucial time for Allen, perhaps saved him from a breakdown. Still pining for Neal, Ginsberg had spent a lonesome winter worried by thoughts of failure, with the feeling of being "the only eccentric dope in a world of mechanical supermen." He'd haunted gay bars in the Village, thinking about death yet afraid of suicide. On one of Jack's visits to his East Harlem apartment Allen had pressed Kerouac sexually, so hungry for love that he was more than willing to plead, to grovel. Wanting Jack's hand one way or another, he even followed him to the subway stop and begged him to "Beat me up. Do anything you like—anything!" Shaken, Jack escaped past the turnstile and left, despite the charity and patience Allen had attributed to him.

Jack knew too well the causes of Ginsberg's instability. Over the previous year, he had accompanied Allen on several visits to his mother Naomi, had talked at length with the woman whom the director of Pilgrim State Hospital wanted to give a prefrontal lobotomy, the haunted lady who wrote her son, "the wire is still on my head, and the sunshine is trying to help me. It has a wire department, but the wire that's outside my head, the sun doesn't touch."

Jack also sympathized with Allen's intellectual torments, for Ginsberg too was seeking a style and form that would express his art. Allen had written two poems in the past year—"Denver Doldrums and Dolours" and "Dakar Doldrums"—but dismissed them as "hallucinations" full of contradictions "disguised with apocalyptic statements." Cézanne and William Carlos Williams had cracked his head open with ideas about *"petites sensations"*—the mind's-eye gap between words—and the use of colloquial American language, plain speech. But he wanted to be a "great intellectual poet, like Auden, or Dante," and dreamed of writing perfect love sonnets. When Allen put down *The Town and the City* he picked up his pen and wrote what he later said was his first good poem, "Sonnet I." He also began to write letters plugging the book to Lionel Trilling and Mark Van Doren, his old Columbia professors, assuring Trilling that it was "monumental, magnificent, profound."

Van Doren, for whom Jack had great respect—he seemed moral, like Dickens—sent him to the distinguished critic Alfred Kazin, but a June meeting with the author of *On Native Grounds* was canceled when Jack had to go out of town. Nin, who had by then remarried, had just had a complicated Caesarean delivery of her son Paul, and Jack had accompanied Mémère to visit his sister in the hospital in North Carolina. Charles Scribner's Sons, Thomas Wolfe's publisher, got *The Town and the City* first, but rejected it. Scribner's was the first of many politely negative letters Jack was destined to receive about his work.

Jack's concentration on the last stages of his book was rocked in late June with a letter from Neal, the first in many months. Contrary to Jack's suspicions, Neal hadn't been in jail. Things were much worse than that. Neal began his letter by explaining that all of his previous attempts to write had resulted, by virtue of his madness, either in maudlin pleas for help or unadulterated lunacy. Sunk in agonized despair, he had ridden the near edge of suicide for months, zooming his car across busy intersections at fifty miles an hour hoping to be hit. On his twenty-second birthday, February 8, 1948, Neal sat for fourteen hours in the back seat of a car, dissolved in sweat and nausea, plagued with fear, unable to pull the trigger of the silver revolver he held at his temple. In March he drove to Denver, and tried to freeze to death at the Continental Divide, but grew too cold and quit. One of his major concerns was that although he was still married to LuAnne, Carolyn was now several months pregnant, his efforts to procure an abortion having failed. LuAnne's eighteenth birthday—after which it would be difficult or impossible to obtain a speedy annulment—was on March 31. On March 29 he drove straight to Denver, crossing the Donner Pass without chains, got an annulment for his marriage to LuAnne, and returned to San Francisco on March 31 after forty-six consecutive hours of driving. On April Fool's Day he and Carolyn were married; miraculously, he managed to be on time and even thought to bring a corsage.

Allen was hurt and bitchy. "The idea of you with a child and a settled center of affection—shit," he wrote his former lover. Angry, Neal wrote back suggesting that Allen congratulate him on his marriage, as he would, perhaps, on the purchase of a car. Allen wanted Neal to be a visionary artist, but to Neal artistic duty had nothing to do with him anymore, was "Bullshit . . . I can't realize or express [anything]." In July he even suggested that Allen not write, though both ignored the remark. Jack received a very different letter, for Neal told him that this child would be his fifth, and he would keep and raise it. Somehow the growing mound of life in Carolyn's belly renewed his faith, because the letter closed with an electric flash of old-time Cassady enthusiasm for a new idea—a ranch commune that would house the Cassadys, Jack and Mémère, Allen, Jim Holmes, GJ Apostalakis, Huncke, and more—nine family members with room for at least nine first-cousin visitors for a day or a week or a year.

By July, Neal was opening his letters with giggling doggerel, outlining how long it would take to collect the necessary funds, assuring Jack that it was all hard cold planning and not raving enthusiasm. Their goal was not some twenty-first-century commune. Both men revered the family; they simply wanted to expand the nucleus, return to the traditional extended family, share their lives and the land, because "I just don't like the idea of everyone living in separate houses," argued Neal, "and having to go somewhere to see a friend." Carolyn was dubious, but they began to save their money.

Years later, Jack would comment, "By 1948 it had taken shape—a year when we'd walk around yelling hello and talk to anybody who gave us a friendly look." That summer's July Fourth weekend was that sort of time.

Saturday, July 3, was hot and steamy, and those who could afford it had fled Manhattan to Fire Island or the Hamptons; those who could not escape the inferno simply partied. Taking a break from the *Town and City* writing ordeal (which would end in September), Jack joined Allen for a bash at the apartment of Russell Durgin, a Columbia student and Ginsberg's friend. It was a memorable affair, because Kerouac made a new and enduring friend, an angular young man named John Clellon Holmes. Holmes was four years younger than Jack, but seemed a bit older and more stable, perhaps because he was part of a conventional marriage. A cerebral, analytical Massachusetts Yankee, he was also a writer, and when he read Jack's book, which a mutual friend named Alan Harrington handed him packaged in a beat-up doctor's black bag, he was thrilled. Summoning up his critical rhetoric, he felt the book was "too lyrical," and "needed structure," but he gloried in the compassionate feeling that leaped off the page. Shortly after that he read some of Jack's journal notes and was at once exalted and shocked; they served as a major catalyst for him, warning of both "the potential and costs of the vocation" of writing. They were so terribly different, the Canuck and the Yankee. Holmes was consistent, even, a bit dry, while Jack was generally reconciled to his own contradictions, impulsive, seeking the goodness of individuals while believing—still a Catholic—that life was flawed. Holmes was a liberal, and saw the dark side of individuals even as he held to the faith that life could be made subject to progress.

As he stood on the sidewalk buying beer for the party, the T-shirted Kerouac struck Holmes as a younger brother to the workingmen clustered around the *bodega,* his heavily muscled thighs, neck and forearms, his excited sensitivity to the surrounding street scene, the uncool, unchic "purity of [Jack's] emotion" marking him off as different from the *New Yorker–Partisan Review* sort of writer; yet it was obvious to John that he was "going to *some* serious fate." Instantly they were friends, and Holmes's fourth-floor apartment at 681 Lexington Avenue between 56th and 57th streets became Jack's midtown headquarters on his visits from Ozone Park. It was the scene of all-night talk marathons, considerations of the lit-biz, of his heroes Dostoyevsky, Wolfe, and the rest, of Holmes's beloved D. H. Lawrence. John was a Dixie music fan, and when Jack heard about that he made John buy the "simple" Dizzy Gillespie's "I Can't Get Started" and Bird Parker's more advanced "Koko" as the first of his lessons in Bop. Months later he quixotically dragged John off for another lesson at a certain jukebox on 125th Street where he played Willis Jackson's "Gator Tail," a musical sex piece complete with semen squirt-notes at the end.

Their conversations ranged widely, Jack matching Holmes's "solemnly radical undergraduate" political discourse with stories of wild kids, junkies, musicians, sailors, con men, and teenage Raskolniks. He raved for hours about "New York migraine liberals and intellectuals," proclaiming ad nauseum that everyone should stand "naked on a plain" in natural beauty. Holmes mentally dubbed him the "tramp transcendentalist" when he'd excitedly point out a beautiful woman, crying, "Look at that hair! Now, that's the kind of girl you never find in New York. She's like one of those chicks working in a lunch cart on the highway, a real woman. Right?" Always Jack's talk returned to the idea of buying land. It was a frustrating paradox that this eternal wanderer, never happy where he was, wanted most desperately to sink new roots.

Jack wasn't the only new friend Holmes made at the July third party; bouncing around the gathering with a glass of beer in his hand, Allen looked to John like an "inquisitive dormouse with black-rimmed glasses," full of awareness and delight, asking the most preposterously direct questions—"Does your wife approve of you?"—with a laugh that assuaged the effrontery. Ginsberg liked Holmes, found him "sweet and generous," but a little too calm and sensible, a bit too rational, because around that time Allen experienced a catastrophic mystical visitation that would direct his life for the next fifteen years, hurling him as never before into a visionary quest whose message was "widen the area of consciousness." Lonely and depressed in his East Harlem apartment, Allen had been reading St. John of the Cross and William Blake, then jacked off. As he gazed out the window, he suddenly heard a voice—William Blake's voice—reciting the poem "Ah Sunflower."

> Ah, Sunflower! weary of time,
> Who countest the steps of the Sun,
> Seeking after that sweet golden clime
> Where the traveller's journey is done . . .

Shocked on his shabby bed, Allen thought at first, "This is what I was born for," then, "Never forget, never renege, never deny." His "body suddenly felt *light,* and a sense of cosmic consciousness, vibrations, understanding, awe, and wonder and surprise." For Allen, "It was a sudden awakening into a totally deeper real universe than I'd been existing in." "The Sick Rose" followed. "O rose, thou art sick!/The invisible worm/ That flies in the night,/In the howling storm,/Has found out thy bed/of crimson joy, And his dark secret love/Does thy life destroy." When he heard this, Allen felt that his old life was truly dissolved. Over the next few days, kindred experiences boiled up, and at last—too threatening— were repressed. But his way was set. "Dreamlike and white, arden-esque," "the other world"—the mystical world—had become for him the "only valuable thing, the only possession, the only thought, the only labor of worth or truth." As he wrote Neal, he was now truly a Myshkin, the sorrowful saintly idiot, since he had lost control of his mind, and "seen the Nightingale at last." He told Jack that "We are inexistent until we make an absolute decision to close the circle of individual thought and begin to exist in God."

Jack thought Allen was going insane, but that in itself was interesting, and as they all sat in John's apartment that fall of 1948, they listened as Ginsberg balefully lectured on visions, God emanations, and madness. Then Jack would counter with his own discourse—that life was a divine and beautiful and impossible mystery, something he occasionally hated but never rejected.

Regardless of their differences on these matters, what they *all* rejected was the shabby middle-class liberalism that was then running America. Harry Truman was short, tough, and honest, like Leo, and though Jack respected him as a man, Truman's Cold War politics disgusted him. In the wake of the war, a majority of liberals had replaced the New Deal notion of government as a force backing the public against business with a view of government as a consensus of organized interests that included conservative labor, and attempted reform through economic growth, not redistribution. Truman's amazing victory at the polls in November of that year was not personal, but the success of the New Deal coalition, a reflection of the basically liberal consensus that reigned. But the people were excluded from the decision-making and cheated; they cheered the Marshall Plan to feed starving Europeans, never knowing that the United States sent guns and not butter to Greece.

Truman's Communist-devil rhetoric fostered an "illusion of omnipotence" for the United States over the world, and when that bubble burst, the collapse of the illusion, as one historian put it, "fathered the myth of conspiracy." That summer of 1948, Elizabeth Bentley and Whittaker Chambers had joined Louis Budenz of Notre Dame in their cries of Communist infiltration in Washington. In December, Alger Hiss was indicted for perjury. Raging anti-Communism clawed at American culture and disemboweled, among other things, American films; nearly one third of them had dealt with serious social themes in 1947, but in 1952 it was one eleventh.

Jack and John responded by avoiding current films, getting stoned to sit in the Beverley Theater under the Third Avenue El and watch W.

C. Fields and Charlie Chaplin. They were too disaffected, however, to be able to use the out that most of their fellow citizens took. Shaken and nervous, Americans in 1948 clutched to their hearts the simple solutions of best sellers like Dale Carnegie's *How to Stop Worrying and Start Living,* and Norman Vincent Peale's *A Guide to Confident Living.*

In a beery conversation one night in November, John had railed at Jack for his lack of concern with politics, with the starving displaced persons of Europe or the exploited workers of the American South; in short, for not being a liberal. Jack went home, sobered up a bit, and then wrote a passionate postcard defense of his feelings, arguing that he could not vicariously agonize and sigh over the fates of D.P.'s through Max Lerner's column, for that was self-indulgence rather than a true grieving. He could accept the notion of political action, but not middle-class liberal sentimentality and verbal hand-wringing. Jack's personal politics were emotional and sprang from two sources.

He was obsessed, enraged, with a sense of America being debauched by the clanking, alienating horror called the new industrial state. Secondly, his rage was cut with a sense of Dostoyevskian suffering and guilt, for he felt that the American citizen's complicity in the exploiting modern state went far too deep to be "solved." Racism and violence were not issues— *"Issues,"* he'd say with a curling sneer, *"Fuck issues"*—but sins, and for that only penance was possible. Two years later he would be revolted by the exploitation of Hiroshima he saw in John Hersey's book by that name, and he told Holmes such exploitation happened because we had lost our humanity. His attitude bewitched John, who saw it as a kind of "American existentialism," capable, as with black culture, of great spiritual radicalism. Having crossed the United States with a mind thirsty for sensation and experience, Kerouac had an enormous sense of breadth, of the limitless possibilities of the children fortunate enough to be born in such an astonishing place. By 1948, the only people Jack saw that retained the light of life in their eyes were the beat—"beat" was a hip term Jack learned from Huncke that meant tired, burned out—slinking hipsters who *knew.*

Painfully trying to describe his cultural mind-set to John one night in November 1948, he said, "It's sort of furtiveness . . . with an inner knowledge there's no use flaunting on that level, the level of the public, a kind of beatness . . . a weariness with all the forms, all the conventions." Their conversation circled on, picked up on the idea of generations, something Jack's roots in old Lowell spoke to, as well as the "Lost Generation" literary concept. "You know," Kerouac said, then snickered and erupted into a Shadow "Mwee hee hee hee hee haaaa" laugh, "I guess you could call us a beat generation."

His casual remark—the first time anyone had bothered to join the two words—would have lasting consequences on the nation's vocabulary and Jack's life.

Jack's moods fluctuated all fall. The slow and humiliating process of selling his book disgusted him, and he saw himself as a sad Samuel Johnson buffeted by a crass publishing industry. Alfred Kazin read Jack's book in October, but nothing happened immediately. Kerouac took a few classes at the New School, including one from Kazin on the Transcendentalists, but the experience was fun largely because of the $75 a month GI benefits he got, as well as the glorious spending spree occasioned by each semester's book allowance; he and John would go and raid the Fourth Avenue used-book stores and fill cartons· with their loot.

Early in October, Neal wrote to tell of the birth of his and Carolyn's first child, Cathy. Cassady was mellowed by fatherhood, and the letter not only demanded that Jack come to California immediately, but related a vision of Neal's love for brother Kerouac, of how beautiful he felt his brother was. As Neal told Allen, he felt "pure" and wise. He'd also begun to learn to play the saxophone, since he was convinced that he could never really communicate with the written word.

Words were still Jack's medium, and in early November he attempted a new method of writing. Churning out 1,500 words a day about Neal and his experiences on the road, Jack looked for a method that would allow greater freedom than he'd had with *The Town and the City*, and by Thanksgiving he'd written 32,500 words. It was all very experimental —he saw it as first draft only—and it left him feeling hollow and uncertain, quite different from the reverent feeling he'd gotten from the first book. As December grew colder, his mood grew more depressed. Bottoming out in a postwriting letdown, he felt distorted and ugly, largely because Scribner's hadn't taken *The Town and the City*. The adrenalin rush of creativity had washed away to leave him flat. He told Holmes, "Well, I've decided I wrote it because I wanted fame and money and . . . love; not for any sterile artistries. I was just wooing the world with it, being coy." Almost embarrassed by his openness, Kerouac grew more abrupt and concluded, "Why should you fool yourself, John? I'm feeling geekish [warped] because the world isn't interested in my clumsy valentine." A sulfurous letter to Allen in mid-December focused on "geekish" as well. Jack accused Allen and Burroughs of making him geekish, of forcing him to walk the tightrope of modern consciousness. Jack grumbled at poor Allen that he loved and hated him, and would go mad, and give up, that all he had left to believe in was food, sex, and the charming joy of Dickens. Allen retorted that he'd never have become geek if he hadn't already been a *"fallen* angel," that "the *abyss* is more real than present flesh or future fancy"; after years of Allen's trying to match Jack's joy, it seemed as if Jack was coming to resemble Ginsberg as a twisted, tormented soul.

Both men also had their minds on Neal: Vague rumors—a cryptic note on a postcard—had reached them reporting that Cassady was coming east in what Jack assumed was a stolen car. As Christmas approached, Jack would relax from the agony of writing and think of the land, imagine it rolling west, think of Neal, because out there on the last edge of the continent Neal symbolized the American dream to Kerouac. Finally Jack gave up and fled the city, joining Mémêre in a trip to Nin's place in Kinston, North Carolina, for the holidays.

Christmas passed peacefully until, a few days later, there was a thump on the door. The incongruities were mind-boggling. Standing in Nin's doorway, her staid Southern in-laws peering over his shoulder, Jack beheld Neal Cassady. Neal grinned, rubbing his belly under the skimpy T-shirt—his only top in the cold, late-December weather—jumping around and *talk*ing endlessly about *E*verything. A new season had come. Neal had swept across country and back into Jack's life after a year and a half, and for the first time they would travel together, living by Blake's dictum: "The road of excess leads to the palace of wisdom." Jack knew that he needed more experience to make his art work, and with Rimbaud as an example, he allowed Neal to sweep him into dissipation on principle, into the systematic derangement of reason and the senses that would destroy the old patterns and leave him naked and reborn. Grass, speed, the roadhigh drug itself, the means didn't matter; it was time to get back on the road.

All fall Cassady had been a more-or-less model husband, working on the railroad, playing with the baby. But a negative November referendum on the "Full Crew Law" had cut his work hours and eliminated the ranch-commune dream. Carolyn had suggested painting to combat his depression, and he tried. But in his rigid attempts to stay straight with his family, all he could produce were bands of uniform colors, lines as precise as a coloring book. It was a car, of course, that snapped Neal's resolves of virtue, a beautiful dark-silver 1949 Hudson Hornet in a show-room on Larkin Street. Lusting after the auto, Neal talked his old buddy Al Hinkle into marrying his girlfriend Helen. With her money Neal could drive them to New York on their honeymoon and get Jack. His whirlwind energy pulled it off, and fleeing Carolyn's and the baby's tears, he whipped out onto the road only to discover by Arizona that Helen didn't have very much money, and wanted to spend what she had on motels. Motels! So they deserted Helen in Tucson, and plagued with lewd memories of LuAnne, they charged north to Denver and after a few hours of frantic persuasion captured her and took off for North Carolina.

Neal's scheme continued, reaching out to involve Jack's family. They'd move some furniture from Nin's place to Ozone Park for Mémère, leave Al and LuAnne there and return to North Carolina and bring Mémère back to the city. His flight from marriage had pitched Cassady over the edge into near-lunacy and Jack sat stoned and mind-blown, listening to Cassady's frantic jabber through the East Coast night, because according to Neal, "Everything is fine, God exists, we know time. Every-thing since the Greeks has been predicated wrong. You can't make it with geometry and geometrical systems of thinking. It's all this"—and Neal stuck a finger into his closed fist, creating a symbol of oneness—"Now!" He was right, they knew the sweet rush of life and Go! measured only by the flying beat and extraordinary musical conversation of Wardell Gray and Dexter Gordon's screaming new Bop song "The Hunt," their trip theme song, and "Now is the time and *we all know time!*" Covering around 1,500 miles in under thirty-six hours, they moved Mémère's furni-ture, returned for her, and arrived in New York to plunge into a New Year's Eve party that lasted three days, Neal greeting 1949 in a jockstrap and kimono, rolling joints and yelling "That's right, That's right!" before they floated quickly out the door to hear George Shearing wail at Birdland.

Not everyone approved. The deserted Helen Hinkle had wound up at Burroughs' place in Algiers, Louisiana (having come to find the Lone Star State "uncool," he had moved), and though Bill found her a perfect guest, he was angrily firing off letters and telegrams to New York that denounced Hinkle. In his mad way, Neal tried to do right by Carolyn, sending her fifteen dollars on January 10 and asking her to pick up the baby and come to New York. Allen was still disturbed, and greeted Neal with a slow, sad warmth. Ginsberg was a copy boy with AP, and had even managed to graduate from Columbia, though neither fact gave him pleas-ure; when he spoke to Neal, it was about his gloomy poem "Dakar

Doldrums" and Hart Crane, asking Cassady, "Whither goest thou?" There were cheerful moments, and the three of them did manage one friendly sharing. Together they concocted a poem called "Pull My Daisy," which reflected the surreal atmosphere: "Pull my daisy/tip my cup/Cut my thoughts/for coconuts . . ."

With Jack, Neal tried to be the perfect loving brother, to the extent of sharing LuAnne. But Jack couldn't screw with Neal present, and passed up the offer. "I didn't want to interfere," Jack wrote later, "I just wanted to follow," and follow he did. On January 19, 1949, they zoomed out of New York bound for New Orleans and San Francisco, flying through the Jersey mist, snickered at a dawn Washington astir with Truman's inaugural parade, Neal beating out the rhythm of the music on the radio until he had pounded a hole in the dash. Though Virginia brought them a speeding ticket and an ugly encounter with the police, they quickly forgot their hassles, got high on the warmth of the Georgia air, swept through Alabama listening to the full details of Neal's sexual history, and smiled to hear a black New Orleans disc jockey wailing "Don't worry 'bout *nothing!*" Considering Bill's anger, their stay in Algiers was pleasant. Al and Helen disappeared into a back room, ignoring LuAnne, who wanted to witness the consummation of their marriage; amazingly, they made up and remained married.

In between playing the horses, wandering the city, and watching Bill shoot Benny tubes off the mantel with an air gun, Jack listened to Bill lecture on philosophy. Burroughs had developed an attitude he called "Factualism," which, for instance, rejected the idea of crime: "Crime is simply human behavior outlawed by a given culture," he intoned. Bill disapproved of Neal, but not on abstract ethical grounds. In that dry tone of his, he later wrote Jack that "If [Neal] does not *feel* 'responsibility' toward others, he does not have any. Of course, he can not *claim* anything from others under the conditions he himself has created." Bill mentally shrugged and continued, "I do not believe he understands this. I suspect he feels that others are under some mysterious *obligation* to support him." Burroughs felt people should just do as they wanted to do—a right-wing anarchism buttressed by his reading of Wilhelm Reich and his studies of Mayan culture. The whole Mayan culture had been dependent on the priest-run ceremonial calendar, and as the years went by, Bill would come to see the modern media as an equivalent and controlling calendar, editors manipulating readers through layout, editorials, and ads. Burroughs was impressed with Jack and wrote Allen that "He seems much more sensible, more sure of himself than I ever remember him." Jack was also favorably inclined to Bill's views, particularly when one night, while walking by the Mississippi, he had a mystical flash of oneness with the river until he tried to reach the water's edge to meditate. He couldn't get near the water; the government had fenced it off.

Burroughs deprecated their journey because it seemed pointless; yet to view it as futile or, as did many critics later, as an insane parody of the mobility of automotive America or as an escape from "civilization" à la Huck Finn was to miss the point. There was no escape from the pervasive fog of the technocratic culture. Rather, a trip such as theirs was like stepping off a cliff—and flying; ultimately their road led within. Something mysterious took place in the twentieth—or fortieth—hour of continuous driving, a product of wind and exhaustion and a questioning mind. Somehow, things slowed down enough to be truly clear only when the observer traveled hardest.

By now, of course, their trip had assumed its own momentum. Though Bill refused to lend them money, they set out on January 28 anyway, pressing through the dark Louisiana swamps and across the frozen Texas plains: Neal, Jack, and LuAnne sat in the front seat, Neal talking, LuAnne flirting with both as they rolled through the warmer New Mexico desert. Thanks to some adroit thievery and a pawned watch, they managed to stay supplied with gas, food, and cigarettes until they reached Tucson, where another New York friend, Alan Harrington, was willing to advance them a small loan. Across the Mojave Desert and up through the Tehachapi Pass, they pushed into the inner valley of California, where Jack had once picked cotton; Neal wouldn't listen to his stories of Bea Franco, and Kerouac wound up dozing through the small-town scene of his love.

And suddenly it was over, in more ways than one. Neal dumped Jack and LuAnne, both utterly impoverished, on a sidewalk in downtown San Francisco and went off to find Carolyn. There followed two days of such exotically painful hunger as Jack had never before experienced. LuAnne managed to talk their way into a room, but they walked miles to look for food, all to no avail. Jack told her of a dream of his the previous fall, about a saint named Dr. Sax who would destroy the world snake of evil with alchemical herbs, and bring peace. But LuAnne was unimpressed and finally deserted him.

Sitting on a park bench lightheaded with hunger, Jack spied an old woman who eyed him suspiciously. Shaken, he conceived the notion that two hundred years before he'd been her thief son. Lost in this fantasy, his mind tripped over the edge. "And for just a moment I had reached the point of ecstasy I had always wanted to reach," he wrote two years later, "which was the complete step across chronological time into timeless shadows, and wonderment in the bleakness of the mortal realm, and the sensation of death kicking at my heels to move on . . . in the magic moth swarm of heaven." He had fallen down the same rabbit-hole as Allen, into a place where the steady roar in his ears was everywhere the true sound, where what he felt was a permanent sensation of death and rebirth, bliss perfectly balanced with the agony of dying. He scrounged some butts out of the gutter, took them back to his room and was smoking them in a pipe when Neal arrived to rescue him. Dutiful despite her complaints, Mémère sent Jack his VA check, and as soon as it arrived he got on a bus and returned to New York.

He arrived there in mid-February; in late March 1949, he received a belated birthday present in a letter from Robert Giroux, editor in chief of Harcourt Brace, accepting *The Town and the City* for publication; at long last, Mark Van Doren had made the crucial phone call. Giroux was young and sympathetic, and Jack's life and career seemed redeemed. That night in his journal he prayed for continued grace as a child of God and not the world. Mémère was overjoyed. A thousand-dollar advance nearly solved his money problems, allowing again for the possibility of a homestead and marriage. Christ, he thought, all he had to do for the rest of his life was to write books!

On the afternoon he had first spoken with Giroux, he sat in a cafeteria at Lexington and 60th Street in Manhattan, his face creased in a permanent grin and his mind teased with thoughts of trips to Paris; he was young, handsome, successful and gloriously alive. He called John Holmes and asked him to join him. By odd coincidence, John had recently finished his own first novel, and that very day it had been rejected for the first time. As Jack sat there tense with joy, he told Holmes "I'd like to lay every woman in sight." The bizarre dichotomy of their feelings was too much for Holmes, and he made his excuses and left. As he walked away, Jack had his notebook open, jotting down what it felt like to own the world, writing.

VII
Litrichuh and the Rolling Trucks

JOHN HOLMES threw a party on Wednesday, April 20, 1949, to celebrate *Town and City*'s sale, and Jack gloried in the role of sophisticated author and suave guest of honor, drinking excitedly yet still, Herbert Huncke noticed, "just provincial French enough to be shocked because he'd bought two suits and didn't know how to explain this to Mémère." Allen was bugging him as well, asking him to store some letters. It was something of a drag, but then Allen had been so intensely gloomy of late, writing poems about his "vision haunted mind," "the feeling of being closed in/and the sordidness of self." Ginsberg couldn't decide whether the Blake vision was a "north polar fixed point life experience," or as his psychiatrist kept insisting, a hallucination to be dismissed. There were more immediate reasons for Allen's tension; he was in a tight vise, the one that occurs when the people you love ask too much of you, begin to consume your life with their problems.

Late in January, Huncke had materialized at the doorway of Allen's York Avenue apartment almost at the point of total collapse, his feet bleeding in his shoes. Though Allen needed peace and quiet, it wasn't in his heart to turn away the man who he thought suffered more than anyone, "like a saint of old in the making." At first Huncke was no problem as a guest, since he slept twenty hours a day for weeks. But by March he was healthy enough to resume his career as a thief, stashing the loot at the apartment, then bringing over his friends Vicki Russell and Little Jack Melody, who quickly moved in. Vicki and Little Jack made a bizarre couple, an energetic six-foot redheaded strutter and a half-bald elf. In a scene lifted from *The Beggar's Opera*, Little Jack and Vicki would evaluate their stolen merchandise as they made plans to have a baby. Sinking deeper into the morass, Allen even accompanied them on a few raids on parked cars. The crime scene was too much for him, and rapidly losing his nerve and curiosity, he thought about splitting town to visit Bill Burroughs in New Orleans.

Bill wasn't all that supportive in his letters—he was dubious about Allen's Blake vision and dismissed Allen's quandary about how to treat Huncke with a stiff comment about Huncke's obvious lack of devotion to middle-class morality—but life seemed safer in Louisiana. Allen's hope for a refuge was shattered when Joan wrote that Bill had been arrested on April 5. Caught in a random shakedown while out in his car, Bill had agreed to cooperate if the police turned Joan loose; the police found half a pound of grass, a jarful of seeds, a few capsules of heroin, and some needles. Unfortunately, they also found a few letters from Allen to Bill that discussed marijuana deals. Blessed with a good lawyer, Bill was quickly out on bail. He ended up fleeing the state and later the country, and when Allen heard that federal narcotics agents had interrogated Burroughs, he decided to hide his incriminating letters and journals for a while. That evening at John Holmes's party, when Allen pressed his request about storing the letters, Jack refused on the grounds that his name was in the letters as well. "Besides," he sneered, "if you really wanted to get them out of the house you would have done it already yourself."

The day after the party Allen was so broke that he couldn't afford subway fare, and he accepted a ride from Little Jack to Long Island, so that on the way back he could stop at his brother Eugene's apartment and store the letters, and perhaps get a free meal from Melody's family in passing. There was to be no food and no luck at all. Driving the wrong way down a one-way street in Bayside, Queens, Little Jack panicked when a cop approached, tried to run around him, then took off and rounded a corner at 65 miles an hour, the car flipping over to create a blizzard of letters and papers, furs and radios.

Stumbling blindly from the car, his glasses lost in the shuffle, Allen first called Huncke and warned him to clean out the apartment, since its address was strewn throughout the upside-down turtle of a car behind him. After walking miles and borrowing subway fare, Allen ran into the flat to find Huncke carefully sweeping up the floor, the heroin stash and loot under his bed untouched. Frantically emptying the junk into the toilet, he angrily questioned Herbert, who placidly replied, "But really, why get hung-up? Look how clean everything is." Taking Allen by the arm the way one treats the not-quite-right-in-the-head, Huncke crooned, "Now, don't be angry. It's too late to do anything with all this furniture . . . We can't dump it out the window." The police knocked a few minutes later.

Jack Kerouac was at a party with Holmes when a phone call came, sending them shocked into the streets for the early editions of the next morning's *New York Times.* Emblazoned across the front page of the April 22, 1949, edition was the headline "Wrong Way Turn Clears Up Robbery." Their eyes fell quickly on the subheadline: "Copy Boy Joined Gang to Get 'Realism' for Story." Jack was sorry for Allen, extremely uptight about the police, and enraged with Huncke. Neal called him down for it, pointing out that he'd had his nose in a book for years, had never really experienced jail, the stuck-in-quicksand feeling of hard—unending —time in the slammer. There was of course nothing Jack could do. Louis Ginsberg hired a lawyer, a respected Columbia professor told Allen friendly stories of being arrested as a young man, and Allen became distracted with yet another problem: mad Naomi Ginsberg was temporarily free from the mental hospital and wanted him to move in with her.

Jack allowed none of the mess to interfere with his plans for a country life, and in mid-May 1949 he and Mémêre moved to a home he had leased for $75 a month in Westwood, Colorado, in the foothills west of Denver. Neal had little money saved and was far away, so there was no ranch commune, but Jack had taken the whole of his book money, minus the price of two suits, and bet it against the fates, trying to put down roots into the land, to flee modern America. Westwood was a pretty place, full of golden butterflies. Set on the Continental Divide, it was the directing source of water, of life, and it seemed a promising place to begin anew. Walking in fields of sunflowers in the shadow of the Rocky Mountains, Jack felt, he wrote Carolyn, like an American Rubens rooted to his own land, while his thoughts went back into the past, thinking of old Lowell days as he wrote long letters to Holmes about GJ and childhood boxing matches.

Kerouac was also writing madly on his book about Neal, which he called *On the Road.* There was another piece of work as well, a Spenglerian myth about the plain people of Lowell, the fellaheen masses of the earth, called "Rose of the Rainy Night." "Rose" was a poetic experiment, an attempt to capture the past with a Melvillean style, to develop the dream of St. Sax (Jack never differentiated between St. and Dr. Sax) and "The Myth of the Rainy Night" that he'd had the previous fall. Hitching or riding a horse around Westwood, Jack listened carefully to the local people, who made allusions to Roy Rogers and Trigger the way urban intellectuals like Holmes used Dostoyevsky or Whittaker Chambers; summering on Cape Cod, Holmes reported that he was studying "Yeats' Plotinus-inspired Unity of Being and Blake's Swedenborgian Visions of Correspondences." Jack went to see Tex Ritter movies. As far as he was concerned, society was insane, an evil mistake; he wanted to become a mountain Thoreau, left alone to gaze at the stars, ride, pray, and sleep.

Three things disturbed his idyll: Mémêre, his sexual desires, and Allen. From her love for storytelling to her fondness for drinking to her rootless, gloomy inability to be happy anywhere, Gabrielle was just like her son, and she had quickly decided that the country was not for her. On July 4, 1949, seven weeks after they had settled in Colorado forever, she left Jack in Denver and got on a bus back to the shoe factory in Brooklyn. As to his carnal desires, Jack had never planned on being celibate, and he reached four years into his past, renewed his relationship with Edie Parker by mail, and planned to collect her in Detroit as he returned to New York. Above all, Allen's letters disturbed him, for Ginsberg had taken Meyer Shapiro's advice and copped a plea on his arrest, arranging to spend time at the New York Psychiatric Institute instead of jail; his madhouse tales rekindled Jack's horrible memories of his own Navy days, when he thought he could see inside people's minds.

Carrying his copy of the Bhagavad-Gita under his arm, Allen entered the institute and immediately confronted a fat man named Carl Solomon, who had just emerged from shock treatment. Ginsberg was, as he told his journal, "confused and impotent in action and a prey to all suggestion," but responded humorously when Carl asked him who he was by saying "I'm Prince Myshkin [the saintly Idiot]." Solomon smiled and replied, "I'm Kirillov [the hard nihilist in *The Possessed*]." Though Allen wrote Jack about "The Myth of the Rainy Night," approving of the rain as a symbol for time as he gleefully announced that there was a real Snake Hill with a castle on it near New York City, most of his letters were asylum horror stories of patients at the mercy of insane attendants and thin-lipped bureaucratic doctors.

Allen didn't know whom to believe; his smart lawyer told him that he was crazy and Professor Van Doren demanded that he choose between Huncke and society, while Burroughs harangued him about being "herded around by a lot of old women" like his father and Van Doren. There wasn't any doubt Allen was disturbed. The week before he entered the institute, he had tried to write an application letter for a job, and by the second paragraph he had blown his top, screaming curses at himself for hours into his pillow, hammering his head with his fists as he wallowed in hatred. He felt Bill was afraid of being revealed as crazy himself, that Allen's "analysis" in 1945 had been a "tragic," rather than a silly, farce; meantime he read his friend Carl Solomon's books, like Jean Genet, and *To Be Done with the Judgment of God*, by Antonin Artaud.

Jack was kinder to Allen than Burroughs, almost respectful. He wrote Ginsberg that he admired the move to the bughouse, since it showed a true commitment to experience, to learning from people. Gently, he warned Allen that he was playing at madness to somehow justify Naomi against Louis's hateful sanity, but what Jack perceived most was loyalty to a mother—a quality he revered. It was a loving and encouraging letter.

With Mémère gone, all that kept Kerouac in Denver was Robert Giroux's arrival to complete the editing process and prepare the manuscript of *The Town and the City* for the printer. It was a friendly visit, and even Allen, who had distrusted Giroux, approved of the resulting edited work. Bob and Jack hitchhiked a bit as Jack tried to explain his new work *On the Road* to Giroux, and the editor discussed Yeats and T. S. Eliot with Jack; later they went to Central City for the opera. Jack had dreamed of going to Paris to write "The Myth of the Rainy Night," the story of Dr. Sax, as a masterpiece of poetic re-created life mystery along the lines of *Ulysses* or *Pierre*. But the homestead project had left his plans in financial wreckage, and life seemed irrational, an empty balloon, as Allen had said. Seeing Giroux off at the airport, the thrill of accomplishment vanished for Jack. He wandered back into Denver naïvely but nonetheless sincerely wishing he were black or brown, a true fellaheen un-hung-up on career and achievement and success. Two weeks before, he had gotten a letter from Neal, the first in several months, sorrowfully inviting him to San Francisco, warning him that he'd be disappointed, but begging for help; in July 1949, Jack got on a bus, and on the way he saw the clouds as God, and words rang in his ear: "Go thou, die hence, and of Neal report you well and truly."

Naked once again, Neal answered his door at two o'clock in the morning, saw who was standing there, and cried out, "Jack! I didn't think you'd actually do it. You've finally come to see *me.*" "Yep," Jack murmured, "everything fell apart in me." Shuddering and yessing Jack's every comment, Cassady was on fire—and the road vibrations began to pound anew. Upstairs, a newly pregnant Carolyn began to cry, unable to accept the fact that Neal could only be an impulsive "Holy Goof," as Jack called him, not a dependable husband, knowing that the craziness was going to start again.

"Entirely irresponsible to the point of wild example and purgation for us to learn," Neal reminded Jack of Groucho, both in spirit and because his enormous bandaged thumb lent a slapstick touch to his appearance. He had broken it on LuAnne's head in January, then infected it with soiled baby diapers until he contracted osteomyelitis; later the tip had to be amputated. It flew bandaged behind him like a white flag of anarchy as he and Jack raced around the city, stopping only to listen to a tenorman at Jackson's Nook play "Close Your Eyes." Helen Hinkle and Carolyn's other friends cursed Neal for his ineptitude, and Jack came to his defense: "But now he's alive and all of you want to know what he does next," he told them. "And that's because he's got the secret that we're all bursting to find and it's splitting his head wide open and if he goes mad don't worry, it won't be your faults but the fault of God." After two weeks of celebration Carolyn threw them out of the house, and Kerouac proposed that they go to New York and then Italy; Neal had been shocked and suspicious that Jack cared enough to invite him, but soon accepted.

Early in August 1949 Neal left a note for Carolyn that promised never to bother her again and climbed into the back seat of a Denver-bound Plymouth to begin a high-speed dialogue with Jack about "IT!" —the mystic place where time stopped. They talked so frantically, their bodies jerking and bouncing about, that they rocked the car, irritating the tourist-couple-and-salesman trio in the front seat. Four hours out on the road, the front seat contingent demanded an overnight stop in Sacramento, where the car's salesman owner coyly informed Neal that some men actually liked sex with other men. As Jack watched from the toilet, Neal tried to hustle "the fag" for money, then fucked him, gaining control of the wheel as compensation next morning. At dawn they flew out of Sacramento, slashing across the Sierra Nevada mountains talking about each other and Dr. Sax while the squares in the back seat radiated grim hostility all the way to Denver.

Neal's hometown was a drag. At one point Neal hurt Jack's feelings with his teasing and they quarreled. Cassady was out of control, stealing cars left and right, drinking too much, so uncool that he enraged some murderous local rednecks. Jack and Neal quickly decided it was time to depart town, and a drive-away service presented them with a 1947 gangster-style Cadillac limousine to drive to Chicago. Ignoring the two college-boy riders in the back seat, Jack put his feet up on the dash and watched the countryside whip past at 110 miles an hour until the speedometer broke and he blessedly didn't know how fast they were going. After a quick mealtime visit to Neal's Wyoming childhood foster father, Neal put them back on the road for the most remarkable ride of Jack's life.

Approaching, as Burroughs said later, "the ideal state of absolute impulsiveness," Neal looked like Ahab behind the wheel, his bloodshot eyes glowing, the radio screaming out Bop as they tore across 1,200 miles of America—Wyoming, Nebraska, Iowa, Illinois—along 1949 two-lane roads, passing through an infinity of small towns—Pine Bluff, Kimball, Ogallala, North Platte, Grand Island, Carroll, Ames, Sterling—berserkly forcing the car beyond its limits, 110 miles an hour after agonizing hour, too fast, till Jack hid in the back seat, wincing at dozens of near-accidents. But it was not Neal Cassady's fate to die in a car, and seventeen driving hours from Denver they delivered a half-crushed and muddy wreck to the gangster in Chicago before they took a bus to Grosse Pointe to see Edie. Her reception was less than warm, and leaving her behind, they spent the night exhausted in the 35-cent balcony of a Detroit movie theater, drowning in images of Sydney Greenstreet and Peter Lorre in Istanbul of the East, and of Eddie Dean, the singing cowboy of the West. Pulling out their last few dollars, they got a car ride home; soon they heard Symphony Sid once again, the sound of their Bop city, and knew they were there. That night, at Mémère's new place at 94–21 134th Street, Richmond Hill, Queens, they were so wired they had to walk around the block before they could sleep. They had packed an extraordinary world of experience into the past few days, and they were burnt out with each other. They shared a visit to Birdland to see saxophonist Sonny Stitt, but when, five days after their arrival, Jack introduced Neal to a model named Diane "Di" Hansen, Neal's new romance took him almost completely out of Jack's life for nearly a year, despite the fact that he remained in Manhattan.

After his debilitating summer, it was easy for Jack to mellow down into his usual fall and winter routine, writing during the week at Mémère's, going on occasional weekend sprees with Holmes, Allen, and Lucien in Manhattan. He continued to write a book called *On the Road* through the winter, but this novel centered not on Neal but on a Denver

businessman consumed—as Jack thought was true of all businessmen—
with guilt; it was completely imaginary. Life at Mémère's was comfortable, if restricted. When she returned from work at the shoe shop, there
would be stories and friendly chat mixed with her regular complaints
about his refusal to take a job and his periodic desertions of her for the
road. Their relationship had a peculiar balance, for unto her son, Gabrielle
was as fiercely loyal as she was hypercritical.

The only interesting mail in the winter of 1949–50 was a mixed
collection of sweet invitation and ironic political argument from Bill and
Joan, who now lived in Mexico City. Life there was cheap and pleasant,
they reported, with "every conceivable diversion" available, including
boys for Allen at 40 cents a throw, and tequila at the same price per quart
for Jack. Burroughs' sociopolitical commentaries were intriguing; he
jeered at Allen's renewed decision to be a labor leader, and compared his
own ideas of unions to those of Westbrook Pegler, "the only columnist,
in my opinion, who possesses a grain of integrity." To Burroughs, the
United States was sliding inevitably into a bureaucratic police state similar
to that in the Soviet Union, and one of the main reasons he liked Mexico
was that cops there were on the social level of streetcar conductors.
Liberalism was a "sniveling, mealy-mouthed tyranny of bureaucrats, social
workers, psychiatrists and union officials."

He also lectured Jack and Allen on Wilhelm Reich, dismissing his
social and political ideas but defending the theories of physical health and
sexuality. America's approach to sexuality was then defined by a scientist
named Alfred Kinsey, whose 3-pound, 800-page book *Sexual Behavior in
the Human Male,* issued the year before, had sold several hundred thousand copies and created a national sensation. Kinsey's scientific, statistical
approach informed the world that one twelfth of American males were
predominantly homosexual, that more than a third had had at least one
homoerotic experience, and that seven tenths of white males had visited
a prostitute in the past year. Reich's adventurous theories went beyond
mere clinical description in an attempt to destroy prurient American ideas
of normality, and through a mind-and-body therapy break down sexual
repressions to create liberated human beings.

A November 1 telegram from Giroux—PROOFS BOOK ONE HERE
COME IN COME IN WHEREVER YOU ARE—set off the countdown to his late
February publication date, and as 1950 rolled in, Jack was at peace with
himself. He felt so good that he spontaneously wrote to Allen expressing
his love and high esteem. Kerouac even began to think again about

marriage and children—at least in the abstract. Joking one day with Holmes, he dubbed the fifties a Decade of Parties, and they briefly considered renting a loft on Rose Street, under the Brooklyn Bridge, as a permanent site for celebration. He had come full circle, as he wrote Charley Sampas after Christmas in a publicity letter for his book *The Town and the City*, bringing "us by a commodious vicus of recirculation past river Eve and Adam back to the nights when we'd all bump on the Square." For him, Lowell was like Asheville or Fresno, "the place where the darkness of the trees by the river, on a starry night, gives hint of the inscrutable future Americans are always longing and longing for."

By March of 1950, the American future had arrived, and it seemed like 1984. Suspicion, paranoia, and dull fear settled down over the official land. Five weeks before, after fourteen months in two trials, Alger Hiss had been convicted in a judicial disposition that was more cultural war than trial, a clash of symbols—Hiss, the radical urban intellectual, versus Whittaker Chambers, the seedy, roughcut middle American—which gutted the country. The event particularly interested Jack because Lucien was among those who covered it for UPI. The Berlin blockade had ended the previous September, while the Smith Act trials effectively eliminated the organized American left with October convictions of twenty-one Communist Party officials. All of China was united under the red-star flag in December 1949. In West Virginia the succeeding February, the junior Senator from Wisconsin, Joseph R. McCarthy, made a speech in which he attacked the Truman administration with the assertion that he had documentary proof of the existence of 57 . . . or 83 . . . or 205 "known Communists" in the federal government. When Albert Einstein blinked his puppy-sad eyes and told an enormous television audience that the newly developed hydrogen bomb meant that "general annihilation beckons," it was hard to ignore him. As *The Town and the City* was published, Klaus Fuchs pleaded guilty to A-bomb espionage charges in London, implicating Ethel and Julius Rosenberg in America, and Judith Coplon and Valentin Gubichev were found guilty of espionage in New York.

The critical climate naturally reflected the tortured dissolution of stable values that intellectuals saw all around them. On the middlebrow level, Robert Spiller's *Literary History of the United States* established a benign, sterile consensus of what constituted American literature. With more sophistication, the New Critics who controlled the leading literary quarterlies continued their domination of high-culture values—the values of the men who reviewed Kerouac's book—as no group had ever before dominated American literary culture. Shaken by the death of old classical values, anxious about the howling existentialist wind of the postwar era, the New Critics had become priests. In a tradition that reached back to Matthew Arnold, who proposed that intellectuals control the rude anarchistic masses by selecting "the best which has been thought and said in the world," they cultivated an elitist aesthetic.

Valuing order (versus anarchy) and thus form in literature above all, the critics had elevated their work to the point where they thought the study of art was superior to its practice. They felt that they were not only holding back the scruffy masses and their comic books, but defending humanistic values from science, the awesome juggernaut that held sway over the Western world's value system. Of course the New Critics were not a single entity, and in fact reflected art in their contradictions and ambiguity. But cumulatively they developed a rationale for objective, moralistic, elitist art. They turned poems into "aesthetic objects" and gloried in studying the last eight lines of *The Waste Land,* which contained eight quotations in five languages, including Provençal and Sanskrit, and one and a half lines by the poet himself. As a working-class Canuck, Jack didn't emulate the WASP values these high priests of culture certified.

Dedicated to Bob Giroux, "Friend and Editor," *The Town and the City* appeared on March 1 and received mixed reviews. Each critic noted its vitality, but worried over its form and message. *Newsweek* called it "almost a major work," but said "the longwinded nonsense of its intellectuals is well-nigh unreadable," while the *New York Times* found it a "rough diamond of a book," but decided that its negative view of the city was "exaggerated." Howard Mumford Jones in *Saturday Review* labeled it "radically deficient in structure and style . . . time as development is not treated." *The New Yorker* was least kind, terming it "ponderous, shambling . . . tiresome."

The intellectual "family" of New York had spoken, as Norman Mailer later put it, "after midnight in voices like snakes and beetles and rats, hiss and titter, prick and sip," but Jack partied on, the handsome young author lionized by new acquaintances, meeting Gore Vidal at a party, making contacts, learning the right names. It was something of a relief to go to Lowell on a publicity visit that March, and his hometown treated him well. Charley Sampas filled the *Sun* with blurbs about *The Town and the City,* the newspaper bought it for serialization, and Jack enjoyed the ritual of autographing copies at the Bon Marché department store before he hit the Blue Moon Lounge for a riotous celebration with his old friends GJ, Roland Salvas, and yet another of Sammy's brothers, Jim Sampas.

But his return to the city made the chasm between the *Partisan Review* intellectuals and the natural hipsters all too obvious. He was sure that if he remained in the intellectual set he would become a hustler among the bourgeois, a fraud, as he told John Holmes. Even the hip intellectuals like Jay Landesman, publisher of *Neurotica,* a magazine devoted to describing a "neurotic society from the inside," didn't share his mystic sense of life, though he published "Pull My Daisy" (under the title "Fie my Fum"), the poem Jack had written with Allen and Neal. Jack's inspiration was someone like Cleophus, a black man he'd met in February, a drinking buddy who talked and gesticulated like Neal, had Allen's spirit, and greeted Jack with a spontaneous burst of affection, shouting that "Christ is at our shoulder, everything's fine . . . I want to dig *everybody.*"

Shuddering at a now-hideous atmosphere, Jack longed to see a biblical curse strike America, leaving behind a resurrected, truly great nation rooted not in the slick sickness of *Time,* but the spiritual power of a man like Cleophus. As for himself, he told John Holmes that he had to choose between "the drawing rooms full of Noel Cowards and the rattling trucks on the American highways." It wasn't a really difficult decision; his subject was the road, not an Upper East Side salon. There was more to his choice than that, of course. Despite a blurb in *Publisher's Weekly* that promised "heavy national advertising," the book had not sold, and he was broke, forced to hitchhike, live with Mémêre, and go Dutch treat on his infrequent dates. Once his redeemer, the book now seemed vulgar, only hinting big, a mere delusion; suddenly he realized that he had associated it with home and land and farm and mother, with a life-force, while he connected Neal and Allen and Bill and hitchhiking and sex with the part of life that was death. As summer came, he knew that it was once again time to run the edge.

Jack cut out for Denver in June 1950, planning to spend a week with old friends before taking a train to Mexico City and Burroughs. He had a pleasant bus ride out, rolling through the ethereally beautiful Shenandoah Valley and over the misty Blue Ridge Mountains, and Denver was just as nice; Ed White and Bev Burford, his friends from the summer of 1947, were there, and the drinks and sunshine were refreshing. Then the phone rang. It was Neal's one-time sponsor Justin Brierly, with the news that Neal, "like a burning shuddering frightful Angel, palpitating toward me across the road," as Jack later put it, had left New York in a '37 Ford intending to pick up Jack in Denver, then go to Mexico to divorce Carolyn so that he could marry Diane Hansen, who was pregnant. Jack and Neal had seen little of each other since the previous summer; Neal had worked a parking-lot job and lived with Diane in an East Eighties apartment, smoking grass and playing with his old pornographic deck of cards. Cassady had come to Jack's apartment in Richmond Hill once or twice, usually to watch baseball on the TV set Jack had given Mémêre—when Neal was there usually two radios were on, to catch the Dodgers and Giants as well as the Yanks. Once, after Neal quick-changed a customer for some extra money, they went to see mighty Lester Young at Birdland.

Cassady leaped back into Jack's life as of old, raving about plans and glittering sheer energy, accelerating the pace of life back into the realm occupied by saints and lunatics. They collected a third partner for gas money, a young kid named Frank Sheperd who kept yelling "Hot *damn!*" and "Son of a *bitch!*" at Neal's more extravagantly poetic outbursts. They drove swiftly south through Colorado, New Mexico, and into Texas, then over a hill and into the lush tropical heat of the Rio Grande Valley. Nervous and more than a little confused, Jack made Neal throw away his grass seeds before entering Mexico at Laredo. But their customs official proved to be "lazy and tender," changing their money into lovely fat rolls of pesos that seemed to buy so much that they immediately burst down the streets of Nuevo Laredo, bug-eyed at the white-shirted men lounging in doorways even though it was three in the morning, and into a bar where they enjoyed their first Mexican *cerveza*.

They had escaped America, and even seedy Nuevo Laredo seemed like Holy Lhasa to Jack, now free of the constricting atmosphere back home where he felt so out of place. When they bought grass in the hamlet of Gregoria from a kid named Victor, and his aged mother came out from behind the house with a fat cigar full of guaranteed superior brain-cell destroyer, they thought they'd found paradise: "There's no *suspicion* here," whispered a delightedly shocked Neal, barely able to comprehend the possibility. Stoned to the eyeballs, they indulged in an expensive but superb mini-orgy set to mambo in a whorehouse before pushing on down the road through the bugs and jungle to a second shock: a friendly cop. Too exhausted to continue, they parked by the side of the road, and with Frank in the car, Jack on top, and Neal in the road, they slept. A cop came by, and asked Jack if Neal was sleeping. Jack nodded, *"Sí, sí, dormiendo,"* and assured that the dirty vagrant was not injured, the peaceful guardian sauntered off without bothering them.

It was good to see Bill and Joan, and Mexico City and its Indians, monasteries, unmufflered cars and roaring street life was the end of the road for them. The city was at once the last stop of civilization and an outpost, as Jack later wrote, of "Fellaheen Eternal Country Life." To Jack it resembled Lowell in its "simplicity [and] straightforwardness," but unfortunately, by the time he got there he was vomiting and burning with the fever of dysentery. As Bill and Joan nursed him, Neal, whom Jack thought of as "completely and godlikely aware of every single little thing trembling like a drop of dew in the world," bought marijuana, ignored the divorce process, and after a quick, delirious goodbye, jumped back into the car and hurtled back down the road bound for New York. Brother Cassady reached his zenith in the next few days, driving his car until the engine fell out in Lake Charles, Louisiana, then flying to New York, where he bigamously married Diane Hansen on July 10; two hours later he used his Southern Pacific brakeman's pass to get on a train to return to San Francisco and Carolyn.

When his health returned, Jack settled into a satisfying routine that floated on a wave of powerful reefer, the sort of 15-joints-a-day regimen that will leave one mummified in marijuana fumes, time and space slowed down so that it seems one is passing through invisible quicksand, the textures of every object become entrancing, the music in the street almost painfully sweet. Stuffing himself with cheeseburgers at a lunchroom on Insurgentes Boulevard, Jack was bothered only by the "police action" in Korea, which had begun on June 24, 1950, about the time he had arrived in Mexico City. He didn't care who had started it, only that people were dying, and that the younger brothers of the friends with whom he'd faced World War II were now draft bait. It all seemed pointless somehow, as he sucked in some more smoke to set the pleasant little colored spots to dancing in front of his eyes. Between the cheating scandals at West Point and CCNY, the Kefauver committee's televised exposure of squalid corruption and the Mafia, and the ugly rumors about "five percenters" in the Truman administration, it was much, much better to get stoned, listen to Bill talk about drugs that transformed people into insects, read Bill Junior's fairy tales, eat mangoes, and stay stoned.

But of course he couldn't escape all the evil, and seeping up out of the grass fumes, his own sorrow at the world, and a visit to the bullfights came a vision that made him decide that Ernest Hemingway was a fool, that the violent, "macho," exploitative United States of America was lost, that the human race was doomed. Returning from the killing of the first bull at the Cuatro Caminos Ring, he meditated on the bull, the sword, and the gallons of blood splashed on the sand, until he saw a pile of bricks and imagined it as an altar. Staring at it from a crouch, he felt over-whelmed by a whole series of images, each representing a possibility for his life, until one took over and dominated, an image of the "Great Walking Saint of *On the Road.*" The Walking Saint would be a pilgrim who would traverse until his death America's streets and roads as penance for its sins, loving all its creature-inhabitants, asking the cars as they hurtled by, "Whither goest thou?" With the hot sun glaring overhead and the bricks in front of him, Jack was sure that "We are doomed. But the light educates the gloom."

Dope was somehow light-bringing, Jack was sure, a liberating solvent that could give him further access to his memories and private images. For his semipermanent stupefaction on cannabis, as with everything else, was directed toward his art. The Navy had rejected him, he later said, as schizophrenic, and perhaps there was a point to that; surely he knew that there was a screaming division in his life over the past years between what he had been writing—and how—and the way he had been living. *The Town and the City* had been a tribute to more gracious times, written for Mémêre and Leo, yet his daily life was fueled with Benzedrine and roared down the road on flying wheels.

He saw the road, felt it to his core, but although the images bubbled and floated in his brain, he was still shackled with the writing rules he had learned at Columbia, was still bound up, unable to put down the rush, the flow, the energy of Neal and the road on paper. Mexico City was too distracting, between the easily available whores and Bill's morphine, and early in the fall of 1950 he returned to Richmond Hill with a bagful of strong marijuana and returned to his labors at the kitchen table.

After dinner with Mémêre, he would slip into the bathroom, smoke two or three joints, and dizzily sit down at the kitchen table to celebrate the mystery that was Neal in long exfoliating sentences. He wrote 20,000 words about *one day* of Neal's life, the day he had met Jim Holmes in Peterson's Pool Hall. All the hours of Neal's flaming road monologues on his childhood became condensed and purified as Jack wrote, the grass a stimulant to his mind. Yet it was all so strange, so different. No one in the New York literary world was writing like that, and Kerouac was unsure of what he had created. He showed his work to Holmes one day in Glennon's Bar, their favorite tavern, and though John was enthusiastic, Jack still plunged into a deep depression, wandering Manhattan with Vicki Russell, listening to George Handy's "The Blues," preoccupied with dope and death.

When he began to rant to Allen about being in a godly state, even the Blakean mystic began to doubt his sanity. It was true that that summer Allen had begun his first deep relationship with a woman, sighing in relief to Jack, "I'm a man, I'm a man, I've got a cock," and had a job working for the New Jersey *Labor Herald*. Yet Ginsberg hadn't changed too dramatically. He counseled Jack "to destroy all in your nature that gives you feelings of lonely power and pride: which destruction is accomplished by a sort of Jewish skeptical humor in regard to one's own megalomania." He called Jack's attitude megalomania because Kerouac claimed that his piece on Neal's boyhood was his best work so far; as Neal told Allen, it was the solitary pride of marijuana talking; high, "the sheer ecstasy of utterly realizing each moment makes it more clear to one than ever how impossibly far one is from the others."

The experience of the grass was intense enough, but then a calamity surfaced that made life yet more strange: Jack's Village drinking companion Bill Cannastra died, and in such a strange way that the mind couldn't let it rest. Cannastra was a handsome graduate of Harvard Law School who worked in a bakery, and whose alcoholic dissipations and sometime cruelty were nearly legendary in that circle of friends. He was simply outrageous, walking into longshoremen's bars and wetly kissing the biggest brute in the place; as that particular maneuver made obvious, he seemed surrounded by what John Holmes called "a tantalizing aura of doom." Sometimes the doom was tangible, as when he'd teeter on the edge of a roof seventy feet from a fast splat on the asphalt, coyly asking Jack, "Do you want me to fall?"

Though Cannastra's loft on West 21st Street—a few doors from Lucien's place—was above a lampshade factory and stank of glue, it was a major party scene, and Jack even did what he called a "couple of collaborations" with Bill and some blond ladies there. Cannastra was wild and interesting to watch—one morning about three, he ran naked around the block in the rain, and Kerouac followed, though in his shorts. Cannastra usually preferred to do the watching; he'd had a peephole drilled so that he could observe people in his bathroom.

Cannastra's outrageousness cost him his life. As his train pulled out of the Bleecker Street subway station on the night of October 12, 1950, he suddenly got up and decided to go back to the San Remo bar for another beer, pulled down a window and climbed halfway out until his head snapped into the tunnel wall and his neck splintered and he was dead.

Shocked into a painful limbo, Jack left town for a while and then returned and moved into Cannastra's loft in early November, in the process meeting Joan Haverty, Cannastra's last girlfriend. She was tall, dark-haired, and model-attractive, the right kind of woman for Jack, thought John Holmes, "full of youth and eagerness, the kind of innocence that goes with being twenty." With hardly any warning to anyone, Jack and Joan gathered up a few close friends on November 17, went to a judge's apartment on Abingdon Square, and with Lucien as best man, got married. Afterward they returned to the loft on West 21st Street and threw a party—twenty were invited, two hundred showed—that went on all night and left dozens of cigarette butts on the floor, a clogged toilet, and an amazing quantity of unidentifiable but evil-smelling stuff in the crevice behind the refrigerator. The party resounded with Lucien and Allen's rendition of "Them Wedding Bells Is Breaking Up That Old Gang of Mine," but they sang without "real sadness," Allen explained, since they knew that "anyway we could break into each other's apartments still in the middle of the night."

Joan worked in a department store and Jack got a job synopsizing novels for possible script use at 20th Century-Fox, and through the end of the year, their married life passed in familial security. Only Neal and Lucien had reservations about the relationship; Lucien thought he'd married Joan because she was an upper-class bohemian. Neal wrote a long profile of Jack's character to Allen, calling him a "true peasant"—"like a potato," as Jack said of himself—gentle-natured and yet overwhelmingly emotional, contradictory, and possessed by a "morbid dread of Hassles." Given Jack's artistic and intellectual focus and Joan's complete lack of interest in such things, Cassady the man of many women felt "It all depends on how much she'll leave Jack alone, I fear she won't be bright enough to see this." His letter to Jack wished him the best as he congratulated him on the possibility that he had impregnated Joan on their wedding night, but warned Kerouac of his own somber nature combined with his deep and thus far frustrated desire for family. Neal was right; Jack worshiped the romantic marriage ideal in the abstract, but never had the ability to realize this ideal himself. There was only one god Jack could really worship, and it was inside a typewriter. After a couple of weeks of marriage he complained that too many friends came by the loft and he couldn't work, so they moved in with Mémère. Gabrielle's reaction went unrecorded, but she chose to exclude her daughter-in-law by speaking only French with Jack. Joan liked her mother-in-law anyway, but the utter lack of privacy in Richmond Hill drove her out of the house, and she moved into the ground floor of a brownstone on West 20th Street between Eighth and Ninth avenues, with Jack docilely following.

Things were confused, because originally they'd planned to move to San Francisco. Neal had been gigglingly teasing Jack to join the Cassadys and get out of "frosty fagtown New York" all fall, and in January 1951, Jack returned from a late-night walk to notice a funny smile on Joan's face and a battered copy of Proust on the radio; his Western kinsman had arrived. Unfortunately, Neal was five weeks early, the Kerouacs had saved none of the necessary money, and they couldn't go anywhere. Neal went to visit Di Hansen and their son Curtis, born the previous November, then exhaustedly lugged his pitiful cardboard suitcase onto a train back to San Francisco.

His letters continued, and they were powerful. Throughout that previous fall and well into the spring of 1951, Neal would write Allen and Jack to tell them that he was unable to write, that he had bought a tape recorder to avoid working—"SO HORRIBLY HORRIBLY SHITPOT HARD FOR ME"—on his autobiography, that he was emotionally paralyzed and unable to cover the necessities of life, like seeing the doctor about his nasal problems, foot problems, his thumb and hemorrhoids, see the dentist about his teeth, fix his car, and buy a railroad lantern. Yet in September he managed a superb letter to Jack about a conversation with a bum at work one day, and in November a wonderful eight-page description of a brief encounter with a bullshitting bore on a railroad trip, an infinitely detailed re-creation of how he had led the man on until he announced that he had written a clinical study, *The Confessions of a Dope Addict*. Neal depicted himself slowly destroying the man's pose with sharper and sharper questions until—in an extremely funny passage—he wholly ruined the phony's aplomb with a spasm of hysteria, snarling to his seatmate that he, Cassady, was a marijuana addict who had an extreme compulsion to strangle people. The fool didn't sleep for as long as he had to share the car with Neal.

Ten days later Neal sent a contemplation of the concept of soul to Allen that included thoughts like "At any particular time, therefore, the current image of the soul is a function of the current language and its inner symbolism. Scientific psychology . . . Like everything else that is no longer becoming but become, [has] put a mechanism in the place of an organism . . . And the soul remains what it was, something that can neither be thought nor represented; *the* Secret, *the* ever-becoming, *the* pure experience." On February 6 he wrote Jack to assure him of his love, but said that he was sunk in masturbation and terrible blood dreams, sleep pursuits that eternally ended with him caught, conning his way out—and waiting unto infinity for resolution.

In late February of 1951 Cassady sent a letter that convinced both Jack and Allen that he was the best writer among them, a reportedly 40,000-word masterful description of his relationship with a Denver woman named Joan Anderson that, said Allen, "reads with spew and rush, without halt, all unified and molten flow; no boring moments, everything significant and interesting, sometimes breathtaking in speed and brilliance." Neal shrugged off their praise, though he admitted it was the result of three solid Benzedrine-filled afternoons and evenings; to Jack, it was a godsend, a click of recognition in his inner ear that told him that *this* was the way to tell a story—just spontaneously tell it, allow it to flow out, to assume its own shape, to use the infinite accretion of details as a form itself.

Early in April 1951, Jack pulled up his chair to the kitchen table he had placed behind a screen in the apartment on West 20th Street and began to write the story of Neal and the road. Since he could type a hundred words a minute, he'd always been distracted by the repetitive task of replacing sheets of paper after quickly filling them, but this time he taped together long sheets of Chinese art paper to form a long roll that fed through his machine. Steaming on a small river of coffee, he sat down in the morning and got up late in the evening, devoting himself utterly to the story of meeting Neal and their various voyages since 1947.

The sentences were short and tight, clickety-pop word bursts that caught the rhythm of the high-speed road life as no author before him ever had. He was deliberately optimistic as he wrote, filling the new and final *On the Road* with exuberance and superlatives as a conscious counterargument to Burroughs' Spenglerian skepticism about life. Early on he wrote, "I shambled after as I've been doing all my life, after people who interested me, because the only people for me are the mad ones, the ones who are mad to live, mad to talk, mad to be saved, desirous of everything at the same time, the ones who never yawn or say a commonplace thing, but burn, burn, burn . . ."

On the Road was about being lost in America with Neal; the focus was tight and Jack usually kept himself more or less invisibly in the background. It was a mature work from a perspective that Allen called "rueful self appraisal," which left in his embarrassing day hitchhiking at Bear Mountain just because it was true. Some of the book even appropriated Neal's letters, transmuting sentences into book dialogue.

Kerouac had written *The Town and the City* to Jascha Heifetz; *On the Road* was set to the flying pound of Max Roach's Bop drums, the whole of the book bursting with energy, with a feeling of life struggling inside a deathly society, energy burning bright before the laws of entropy and the nation caught up. And he wrote it with wisdom, for his description of his San Francisco hunger satori in January of 1949 was not "the work of a wounded boy," as Allen later said, but "of a completely matured Bodhisattva prophet."

He had completed 34,000 words by April 9, and finished the book, around 175,000 words in all, on April 25, after twenty days of writing. "He didn't know if it was any good," recalled John Holmes, who saw it on April 27; "he hadn't read it yet." Holmes was excited and enthusiastic, and Allen wrote of it to Neal, "the writing is dewlike, everything happens as it really did, with the same juvenescent feel of spring." Like his future works, the book was usually accurate history, though at times it was rather the truth dredged from dreams and visions, the mythologization of a life.

Kerouac paid a heavy price for the book; immersed in the endless space of creativity, at once at the very peak of his artistic power and yet in such fresh territory that he was wholly vulnerable to criticism, he gave all of his attention to his typewriter and none to Joan. Sick of slaving at an ugly, boring job to support a distracted zombie who refused to get a job like other men, a newly married husband who wanted only to be left alone, Joan began to complain. One of the central myths of Jack's life was of Dostoyevsky's wife and her unflagging support of her husband, of the duty of the untalented to support the creative artist. Uninterested in reshaping American prose, Joan knew her feet hurt and she had a lazy bum for a husband; on May 5 she threw him out, and he went back to Mémère.

That lasted only a few days, before Kerouac moved into the loft

Lucien had on West 21st Street, where he typed for hours on a roll of teletype paper, then began to type the long roll into pages, changing and adding to it a little—the sentence about the "mad ones," for instance— as he typed. Then he submitted it to Giroux, and so began six years of frustration. He wanted to end *On the Road* with a prophecy, but as Allen told Neal, "He is afraid to foretell tragedy." Neal thought that he was too trivial a theme for a book, that Jack should, like Neal's favorite writer Proust, make *On the Road* merely the first book of many, and begin a second book on the Dr. Sax material. As for his own future, Neal predicted an early death from prostate cancer caused by excessive masturbation or possibly death in a chain gang after being sent to San Quentin for the rape of a teenager. Allen and Lucien both criticized the book for looseness and lack of focus, and it hurt Jack. He agreed with many of their overt literary criticisms, but saw his work as Blake's "crooked road of prophecy," and thought that his friends wanted him to take a straight and easy path. He began immediately to plan revisions, cuts as well as extensive insertions. One plan was to eliminate all the non-Neal material, expand Neal's childhood, and surround him with imaginary characters like the Walking Saint or "Pictorial Review Jackson," a young black North Carolinian who had originally been one of the characters in Jack's childhood baseball-card games.

In May catastrophe visited him twice. Giroux rejected the book, according to Jack because "the sales manager would not approve of it," though the editor also commented, "But Jack, it's just like Dostoyevsky." As Giroux later recalled it, it was because the book was too messy, and what he saw in manuscript was not what was later published as *On the Road.* Holmes gave the manuscript to his agent, Rae Everett, and she returned it with a great deal of carping criticism.

To make matters far, far worse, Joan told Jack that she was pregnant. A few weeks after they separated, she and Jack talked on Lucien's roof and almost reconciled, but the idea of eight-hour wage slavery in support of a child frightened Jack too much in his vulnerable state, and he wouldn't go through with a return to marriage. Instead he decided that it wasn't his child and ravingly denied paternity to his closest friends. His action stemmed partly from a selfish desire to devote himself to art rather than shit-labor, but it also sprang from a deep and basic horror of bringing life into the sorry world, a reflexive attitude that involved Gerard, Sammy Sampas, and Leo, that reflected his increasing distrust of life, and of women—both things inextricably wound together in his mind. Janet Michele Kerouac would be born on February 16, 1952, and Jack would not pay a penny for her support until she was ten years old.

His body reacted to the tension and removed him from the battle zone. Once again he was stricken with thrombophlebitis, which forced him to move in June of 1951 to Nin's place in Kinston, North Carolina, where Mémêre had moved to be with her daughter.

A classic bored invalid with his leg propped up on a chair, Jack could find excitement only in the long rushing letters that Neal sent from San Francisco, enticing Jack to come and live in his attic for free. He made an attractive invitation. Neal described the fine huge desk, lamps, dictionary, and radio in the attic, and promised free laundry, Dexedrine, use of the car; total freedom to write or not, get up or not, be grumpy or not. Cassady promised Valhalla and very nearly threw in Carolyn on the side, for in fact he needed Jack very badly. According to Neal, it would all be like an English country weekend that stretched into months. Later he sent a letter guaranteeing a brakeman's job at $500 a month until December, easy as anything, come Come COME!, assuring him that he should be on the road the day he received the letter. Jack accepted, but couldn't do it immediately; his leg kept him in Kinston till August, then put him into the Kingsbridge, Bronx, VA Hospital until early October. In the meantime he read voraciously—D. H. Lawrence's *The Rainbow*, Blake's *Marriage of Heaven and Hell*, Melville's *Encantanadas*, and more—and listened to baseball on the radio.

A piece of writing briefly occupied him, a piece of traditional fiction not vulnerable to the criticisms of the raw, spontaneous *Road*. He told Allen and John it would be called *Horn*, and would concern jazz. That was only a cover. The path he was following with *Road*'s spontaneous fluidity was undoubtedly the right direction; it was merely insufficient. Writing Holmes, Kerouac said, "I want deep form, poetic form, the way consciousness *really* digs everything that happens."

Sitting in his chair under the burning Carolina sun, a book in his lap and the radio on, his life a total shambles, Jack was strangely calm; after all, there was very little left to go wrong. With his marriage a failure, his health crumbling, and his art so strange that a respected editor had rejected it, all that remained for him was his identity as a writer. Between Cape Cod and the Golden Gate, few knew the land the way he did, had eaten so much road dirt, talked to so many wanderers, heard or felt or touched or smelled so much of the complicated inland sea called America;

if he could combine his sense of land, time, and space, and his awareness of temporality and death in some "deep form" fusion, he would be redeemed, and he was sure of it.

He sat and thought, writing occasionally in his nickel notebook, waiting for illumination, for the fire to come down.

VIII
The
Breakthrough

TRAPPED BENEATH a thin white hospital sheet, Jack was tense with excitement, his books and pen for once ignored as he listened to Mel Allen, the New York Giants' radio announcer, describing the final National League pennant playoff game between the Giants and the Brooklyn Dodgers. It was October, and the mad season of 1951 was about to end. Ralph Branca, pitching for a classic Dodger team that included Roy Campanella, Duke Snyder, Jackie Robinson, Pee Wee Reese, and Gil Hodges, looked down the sixty feet six inches to the plate, eyeing third baseman Bobby Thomson, the Giants' batter. Branca's Dodgers led 4–2, but there were men on second and third base, and every Dodger fan in America was wondering whether the never-say-die nobodies on the Giants were going to work some terrible hoodoo.

Finally, in one of those divine moments that give sport its place in human affairs, Bobby Thomson belted Branca's pitch into the Polo Grounds bleachers for a 5–4 Giant win and Jack, as he later put it, "trembled with joy and couldn't get over it for days and wrote poems about how it is possible for the human spirit to win after all!"

As if his joy had lifted him above all roadblocks, Jack began to understand crucial new elements of his art in October, his favorite month, the time when the cleansing fall winds blew away the cobwebs and molds and diseases that he associated with summer. Nearly two months of uninterrupted contemplation while staring at the VA Hospital ceiling had forced him to some basic conclusions about his career as a writer. The most painful realization was that his new material was probably too different ever to be published, so that he would consequently never be respectable, never be able to support Mémêre. But somewhere within he found the courage to humiliate himself, to live off his mother and devote everything to his art. It was a terribly damaging sacrifice of self-respect, for Jack was not so much a careless bohemian as a working-class Canuck who believed in family loyalty and filial piety. In the years to come he continued to consider his failure to support his mother a sin—Gabrielle's regular and bitter complaints about her worthless son insured his remembering in any case.

Yet his shame hardly counted; he was an artist and had no choice. His writing had become a sacred obligation to him, and he chose to disregard the social stigma of being supported. In an ironic twist, his utterly dependent financial situation somehow made him more free than ever before, and this liberation showed in his new style, which disregarded the current conventions of form. He had decided to ignore everything but completeness of detail, with telling the truth in all its delicate and hideous glory. Walking in the October winds in Richmond Hill, he was about to be struck by two bolts of creative lightning that would point him in a new stylistic direction.

In the middle of the month he went to hear the great alto saxophonist Lee Konitz at Birdland. Konitz slipped with awesome subtlety into the middle of "I Remember April" and swam through chorus after chorus of a solo, crystallizing for an entranced Jack the spontaneous, improvisatory nature of his *own* art; he wrote in his ever-present nickel notebook, "Blow As Deep As You Want to Blow." A week later, on October 25, 1951, he sat in a Chinese restaurant near Columbia, and when his friend Ed White suggested that he try sketching like a painter, but with words, Jack instantly knew he was on to something. He ran home that night from the subway station, then stopped in front of a bakery window and began to "sketch" its contents into his notebook, down to the last cherry on the coconut cake, until his fingers grew too numb from the cold. Then he raced home to the kitchen table to complete the sketch from memory.

Many experiences contributed to Kerouac's conception of spontaneous sketching: Neal's letters, the idea of unrestricted orgasm in Reich, his childhood Catholic confessional, Goethe, Yeats's trance writing, even the movies. After staring for hours at movie screens—not the story lines, but the abstract electrical particles that were pieces of the whole—he wanted to invent a book movie that was not a scenario but an actual sensual movie on the page. The seed of sketching was as old as the panoramic consciousness of the football scenes in *Town and City*, an extended style that was now about to achieve fruition. Yet his primary desire was to write with total honesty and shamelessness, capturing in words the segment of time —"Time is of the essence"—and space that he envisioned. Honesty alone, it seemed to him, could revitalize the arts and human relations in the sickly atmosphere of the Cold War. He was of course completely beyond the literary field of the New Critics, whose elder statesman John Crowe Ransom warned that "the direct approach is perilous to the artist, and may be fatal . . . an art is usually, and probably of necessity, a kind of obliquity." R. P. Blackmur, another leading New Critic, added that "When you depend entirely upon the demon of inspiration, the inner voice, the inner light, you deprive yourself of any external criterion."

External criteria were all the rage for most young Americans, who shared a pronounced distaste for both the war in Korea and pacifism, whose ambitions focused solely on career and marriage and mortgage. In the words of one contemporary observer, it was a generation "pathetic, laconic, no great loves, no profound hates, and pitifully few enthusiasms," a beaten generation that generally scorned Jack's deadly intensity, often perceiving him as an egocentric goof.

Kerouac worked alone that November, sketching a diner, a movie theater, and the Elevated station at Third Avenue and 47th Street, re-creating the diner, detail after detail coalescing into a portrait so real that a later reader could dream that he'd been there, been to a 1940's diner that was not white tile and aluminum but wood and marble, the home of Edward Hopper and Little Caesar, the theater scruffy, a B-movie dump. The description of the dull-brown El station opened in the urine-yellow men's room, Jack contemplating the difficulties of masturbating while seated before going out to watch the bums who haunted the place, seeing the "flash of their mouths, like the mouths of minstrels." He went into St. Patrick's Cathedral but fled in disgust at stylish tourists and a grotesquely patriotic sermon on Douglas MacArthur. As he sat in a Sixth Avenue cafeteria window later, he noticed the play of lights across a car fender outside, mirrors and neon and windows psychedelically combining to form a magic theater from which he observed. He wrote, "I dig jazz, a thousand things in America, even the rubbish in the weeds of an empty lot, I make notes about it, I know the secrets . . . and I dig *you* as we together dig the lostness and the fact that of course nothing's ever to be gained but death."

The agonies of the road and mournful memories of Lowell had opened him up and refined him into an observing anima, a "recording angel" as he later called himself, and after nearly twenty years of constant writing, he had achieved a facility with language that turned words into fluid notes, ready to help him sing the tale of his age, to be, as he described himself, "a great rememberer redeeming life from darkness."

By December of 1951 his leg had fully healed, and it was again time to roam. Even more to the point, Mémère was closing their flat; she had once more decided to accept Nin's offer to move to North Carolina. Though he wanted to join Neal in San Francisco, Jack was too broke—until salvation arrived in the rotund form of his prep school friend Henry Cru, who once again promised him a sailing job, this time on the S.S. *President Adams.* As he read the fascinating destinations—Manila, Kobe, Singapore—inscribed on the *Adams'* cargo stacked on the Hoboken docks, Jack was even prepared to work as a deck hand to get on the steamer, which was on a round-the-world cruise.

Unfortunately the job never quite came through. But Henry persuaded him—and lent him the money—to take a bus to San Pedro, California, to join the ship there. Jack packed his seaman's bag with crepe-sole shoes, blue Eversharp pencils, a tiny Bible he'd stolen somewhere, dark glasses, his rag ends of clothing, and the growing stack of manuscript he'd created that year. He took the bus to San Francisco, worked the Christmas rush at the railroad baggage room there, then rode free to Los Angeles with a pass Neal had given him. Wasted by a cold, he slumped wearily on the San Pedro docks, choking and snuffling through the stench of oil, rubber, and a cat-food factory. Behind him he sensed the raw bulk of his own America, but ahead were new lands to explore and record.

There was, of course, no job; Jack had no union seniority. So he returned to 29 Russell Street, San Francisco, and moved into the spare, half-finished attic room the Cassadys had offered him so that he could teach Neal how to devote himself to writing—actually, he expected to learn infinitely more from his brother than vice versa. In fact, over the next six months he would write some of the best material of his life there. At first he was shy and formal with Carolyn, because the last time he'd seen her she was evicting them. But since Neal had returned to her from Diane Hansen and New York, their romance had evolved into a ripe and loving union. She encouraged Jack to talk about the breakup of his marriage, and he told her about Joan. "You see," he said, "she was an only child, raised by women, a mother and aunts. They all hated men and they taught her to, too." Then he began a bitter rant, shocking Carolyn, who'd always heard him speak with the utmost sentimental regard for women. With Neal often away at work, the two of them grew close, strolling together through Chinatown and North Beach.

Twenty-nine Russell Street was a tiny house on a miniature block, nestled on the side of elegant Russian Hill and cheered by the sound of cable-car bells, and life in the attic was all that Neal had promised. The low bed with its paisley spread, the burlap curtains and huge desk made it homey and a perfect work place for Jack, except that he had to pass through Neal and Carolyn's bedroom to get to the bathroom. Often he urinated out his window rather than take the chance of seeing or being seen nude.

He enjoyed being uncle to the children, telling stories to four-year-old Cathy and cuddling his special love, two-year-old Jamie, for hours on end, although he was nervous about holding baby John. In five months there was only one mishap. On February 8, 1952—Neal's birthday—Carolyn contracted Bell's Palsy, a temporary facial paralysis, and Neal stayed in to care for her. Late that night, a drunken Kerouac called Neal from a bar and told him he'd been "arrested," and to come and "bail me out." The ploy worked, but their escapade was dull—they picked up a couple of Neal's women friends, played some strip poker, and ended up aimlessly but obstinately driving around all night. The next morning they roared into the house and Jack tried to smuggle his lady up to his room, scandalizing Carolyn, who protested at the foot of the stairs with a patch over her eye and her mouth propped up with a paperclip, her hair in curlers, as Jack's guest cursed her loudly and thoroughly. Neal and Jack stood embarrassed and silent until finally they took the guest home.

When Carolyn returned from the doctor's later that day, she found that the title page of her copy of *The Town and the City* had an addition from the author, a humble apology and a plea for forgiveness lumped with a promise that such a thing would never recur.

It didn't. The attic was satisfying and secure; he felt happy and his work went well. After a hard day's writing, Jack would descend to the kitchen to sip a small bottle of Tokay or Muscatel and talk companionably with Carolyn about Mémère, Nin's contemptuous attitude toward his writing, and his current work, a massive and experimental tome on Neal that he would call *Visions of Cody*.

Jack and Carolyn were destined to become even closer. One day as Neal was on his way out on a two-week work trip, he stopped at the door, smiled, and in a tone Carolyn thought was full of meaning said, "My best gal and my best pal," and sped away. The two of them edgily skirted each other during the next two weeks, but when her husband returned Carolyn pounced on him, demanding to know whether he had really meant that she and Jack should become lovers. "Well, ahem, ah-yes-ahh," burbled Cassady, "I thought it would be nice." At first Carolyn was insulted, but after a while she decided to do it—partly out of affection for Jack, mostly to spite Neal. On Neal's next absence she fixed pizza and wine, put the kids to bed early, and sat in the twilight talking with Jack about his coming summer's trip to Mexico and the strange mind of Burroughs. As "My Funny Valentine" came on the phonograph, Carolyn sat near Jack on the couch.

"Remember when we danced in Denver?" she murmured, with a fond smile of recollection.

"Yeah," grinned Jack. "I wanted to take you away from Neal."

"Maybe you should have" was her reply.

Jack did not pass up the opportunity to share Carolyn's remarkably graceful love, and they began an intermittent affair that lasted several years. Carolyn found him a "tender and considerate lover," though she still wanted Neal; certainly nothing they were doing was intended to break up the marriage. In fact, their affair brought the three of them peacefully close, the men competing for Carolyn's attention as they sat in the kitchen reading aloud from Proust or Shakespeare or *Visions of Cody* while she cooked.

The trio's closeness filled a dead space in Jack's life, but fundamentally he was in San Francisco to listen to his stoned brother Neal, whose mind, as Carolyn later observed, "would add extra dimensions to the enjoyment, swooping and soaring on wings of fancy, relating even small features or minor observations to a whole set of corresponding ideas in other areas of life, literature or the arts . . . comic strips, movie actors, fictional or historical figures came out of his mental file to be exposed in satire, humor or scorn, or to be given some relationship to the immediate scene."

Seated at his typewriter, Neal found himself "engulfed in ideas," paralyzed and drowning in a wave of possible words, but when he talked he was an authentic genius. Switching on his Ekotape recorder, the two men sat stoned and jabbering for hours, listening to the music of Lady Day or the Bird as they swapped stories about the summer of 1947 in New

Waverly or contemplated Jack's writing or perhaps shared a letter from Neal's father. Their pet words "mellow," "cool," and "energy" bespoke the pulse of their moods as they cherished each other's thoughts and affection. The recording tape was like a kaleidoscope as it reflected the personality of the author and his subject discussing work in progress. As Neal strained to express himself, Jack struggled to grasp his brother absolutely, and their parallel efforts reached a penultimate logic when they analyzed Jack's transcription of the previous day's conversation. His choice of the word "demure" to describe Neal's expression catalyzed an exhaustive, spiraling dialogue. Though they hardly knew it, they expressed the guiding spirit of Jack's attempt when they sighed:

"You're not gonna get hardly any of this recorded, you know," Neal said.

"Well," Jack replied, "that's the sadness of it all."

Sad or not, Jack strove to leave behind a true record of his times. In an attempt to document his *Visions of Cody*, he placed their taped conversations, dull as they sometimes were, at the work's center, an honest slice of life to ground his rhapsodies, for their talk was art too, communication, the intimacy of shared souls. As Allen later said, "the *art* lies in the consciousness of doing the thing, in the attention to the beginning in the sacramentalization of every-day reality, the God-worship in the present conversation, no matter what."

The previous summer, Neal had mischievously predicted that future historians would have an intriguing time as they researched the period when Kerouac lived with Cassady and did his best work in the attic on Russell Street. Cassady's bravado in comparing the possibilities to Gauguin and Van Gogh was perhaps a bit much, but he was right about Jack's work. With the all-night sound of his favorite Bop disc jockey, Pat Henry, pouring out of the radio behind him, Jack slaved away on *Visions of Cody* at the enormous desk, a "crazy dumbsaint of the mind," as he later described spontaneous writers. Having shed his "literary, grammatical and syntactical inhibition[s]," he sat "in tranced fixation dreaming" upon his subject, relating "the true story of the world in interior monologue." The freedom and the trance and the agony yielded what Jack neatly described as "the unspeakable visions of the individual."

Visions of Cody was a passionate commitment to artistic truth, an attempt, as he later said, to "begin not from preconceived idea of what to say about image but from jewel center of interest in subject of image at *moment of* writing and write outwards swimming in sea of language."

Nineteen years after he began, he was writing out of his deepest self in a sinuous, unbroken flow of spontaneous prose, which took its own shape, organically, an evolved shape rather than an imposed form.

Visions of Cody was an American monologue, something "like Bop," thought Jack, "we're getting to it indirectly and too late, but completely from every angle except the angle we all don't know." As he remarked to a friend four years later, he had shed the nervous Hammett-Burroughs staccato of *On the Road* for a natural speech pattern that suited the rhythm of his imagination and was "not so much concerned with events," wrote a friend, as "with consciousness, in which the *ultimate* events are images." He was free. Exultantly he wrote Holmes: "What I'm beginning to discover now is something beyond the novel and beyond the arbitrary confines of the story . . . into the realms of revealed picture . . . wild form, man, wild form . . . my mind is exploding to say something about every image and every memory . . . at this time in my life I'm making myself seek to find the wild form, that can grow with my wild heart . . . because now I know MY HEART DOES GROW."

A child again, pure, he wrote out his name and grade, "Jacky Kerouac, 6-B, Composition," and metaphorically tugged on Neal's sleeve—"now you're going to listen to me now, and let me tell the Story." He had before him the sketches of the Elevated station, the theater, and the cafeteria window, the transcribed conversations with Neal, and the section on Neal's childhood he'd written stoned in 1950. Now he added the final piece, entitled "Imitation of the Tape." It was a fragmented, volatile portrait of a fragmented, volatile man. And it was a picture of America, too, for in Jack's mind Cassady and America were one. The "Imitation" was a surreal exposition of American culture with a B-movie motif—but "dream golden," Jack said, "not Technicolor"—that included Bud Powell floating past Herman Melville, Moon Mullins and Papa Leo, baseball, and Saroyan. Quite simply, it was "about the wonders of the world as it continually flashes up in retrospect," Jack thought, like Proust in that, but since Kerouac floated on waves of sound, dialect and puns, he tried to create images that surpassed "words with true instinctive communication."

Intellectually his message was the same as in *The Town and the City*, but now he expressed his intuitive understanding of the American loss of community not in plot but in the perfect fused image of "the red brick wall behind the neons," the despair of solid wall behind the city's pleasantly inviting red lights, the grim reality of factory exploitation like Lowell's red-brick mile of mills that underlaid the modern glow of false optimism and cheer. The only form was the shape of Jack's mind; as Allen wrote later, "Mind is shapely, Art is shapely." The "Imitation" ranged from the literary history of New Orleans to playful games with American dialect, smoothly changing accents with a shift of word choice and pattern, modernizing Twain by inserting a joint in Huck's mouth to make the trip down the river all the more sweetly peaceful.

One night Jack relaxed and sauntered about the steeply gracious streets of Russian Hill, and encountered a different sort of artist; a few blocks from Russell Street, RKO Pictures was filming the movie *Sudden Fear*. Joan Crawford's repeated rehearsals of her scene meant only artifice and "form" to Jack, and he longed to tell her, as he put it in *Visions of Cody*, "you muster up a falsehood for money." The technicians who lounged outside the massive circle of lights made him see the film as "the Death of Hollywood . . . upon us," a clanking mechanical abomination of technique rather than inspiration, a machine that could produce only fraud. *Sudden Fear* was a bomb as a movie, but Jack's description of it —"Joan Rawshanks in the Fog" in *Visions of Cody*—was remarkable, possibly the best thing he ever wrote, re-creating a panoramic consciousness of the fog swirling through the floodlight beams, Joan and her mink coat, the director, the crew, the wealthy tenants of the overlooking exclusive apartment building, the police as they held back the giddy teenage girls who stared at the show, everything in fact, until the description became a separate but equal reality, as close to an actual experience on paper as humanly possible, down to the director's red lollipop. "Joan Rawshanks" was the "New Journalism" fifteen years early.

And then *Visions* returned to Neal, simultaneously a "Homeric warrior" and a member of the Three Stooges in his shredded pants stained with "baby food, come, ice cream, gasoline, ashes," one with Stooge Moe, "the leader, mopish, mowbry, mope-muffled, mealy-mad, hanking." Images of Jack's life floated to the surface of his mind, were depicted, pinned like a butterfly to the page, and succeeded by the next; memory to Jack was thought, creation, meditation and nostalgic self-knowledge all in one. As the manuscript progressed, Kerouac retold the tales of the *On the Road* voyages of 1947–1950, and of his Neal, the "empty minded, vacant, bourgeois Irish proletarian would-be Proust tire recapper."

In March of 1952 it seemed as though Cassady was settling down to be a family man, and Jack mourned the world's loss of a psychic warrior, celebrating the rare vision and energy that he loved so much—and that ordinary American mores found so distasteful in Cassady and Kerouac both. There were beautiful prose poems, as in "great spindly tin-like crane towers of the transterritorial electrical power wires standing in serried gloom . . ." Closing, he sang Neal home from Mexico City in 1950 with a paean to his large nature that compared him to Lester Young, the hippest cat of all, and then blew dirge for his encroaching bourgeois-ness, and America's, muted drum taps for Jack's loss, and the nation's. The last words were a hail and farewell for Neal, a blessing and an elegy: "Adios, King."

Kerouac had reached a state in which his writing was very nearly a biological act, an experience of sensorium functioning, a meditation that operated through both the conscious and subconscious levels but was controlled by neither; as friend Michael McClure later wrote, he was

> . . . an athlete
> of sense
> modalities
> and clarities
> and their inter-
> combinations.

Significantly, he was not alone. At roughly the same time and place and in response to the same stimuli—a world at once accelerating and constricting—the painter Jackson Pollock and the musician Charlie Parker had accomplished similar revolutions in their own art forms. The direct parallels of their lives were astonishing. All three men were working-class sons of matrifocal families who refused to "adjust" to the conformist society of mid-century or the accepted styles of their disciplines, and for their efforts were labeled psychopaths and falsely associated with violence. Each ignored the critical authorities in their field and stood emotionally naked before their audiences, spewing words, notes, or paintdrops that were like the fiery rain of a volcano: The rain captured the passing moment in a luminous veil of particulars that depicted the universal as an expression of the artist's own self.

Jack's link with Charles "Bird" Parker was obvious, since he consciously modeled his writing after Parker's magnificent music. As technically sophisticated as his tunes like "Ornithology" or "Groovin' High" were, Bird played with the raw energy of a high-power line, and it was that stabbing electricity that Jack had attempted to put into *On the Road*, that mortal sense that the candle *must* burn furiously, else the times will surely snuff it out. Parker blew from the roots of Afro-American music, from rhythm, and from rhythm, speed, improvising an ever more fluid melody with faster and faster notes until the front row of his audience was awash in the sounds that expressed what a later critic called his "naked passion and hurtling, uninhibited romanticism."

The tunes themselves were spontaneous improvisations on old pop tunes, worn fragments plucked from the commercial popular culture and reenergized. Parker's art had affinity for Jack's not only in their transmutation of the old culture, but in their concern for the human voice and breath. When Bird blew he sang, the man and his horn were one, the reed and keys and chamber of his saxophone only an extension—like a typewriter—of his voice and mind, sounding out a style that was like speech in its inflection and phrasing. Listening to Bird—and he did so constantly —Jack felt myriad connections of subject, style, and approach, and tried to reflect that aural perfection in his own prose.

Privately, Bird resembled Neal, for he was surely one of the few drug addicts in history who retained an insatiable appetite for sex, food, and drink. Spontaneity was Bird's conscious goal as well, for America was a "down trip, man," and he wanted to break the psychic bonds both for himself as an individual, and because "the style was not a style, but the man himself," for his art. Hurtling deep out of his consciousness came a deluge of sounds—human sounds—that he used to try to crack America apart.

The third member of this creative trio was the rogue king of American painting, Jackson Pollock. Shortly before Pollock made his breakthrough to "drip" painting, which involved resting the canvas on the floor and the use of a hardened brush held just above the canvas to spatter the paint, he put into note form the general idea of what he was attempting.

> Technic is the result of a need--
> new needs demand new technics----------
> total control-----denial of
> the accident----------------
> states of order------
> organic intensity---------
> energy and motion
> made visible-----------------

memories arrested in space,
human needs and motives----------
acceptance-----

Though the visual arts were never one of Jack's major preoccupa-
tions, he recognized Pollock as an "artist of genius" in an article written
several years later; had he discovered these notes in 1952, he would have
recognized a close brother who shared a virtually identical aesthetic.
Pollock was another artist who wanted to stand in his work totally naked
and confessional, romantically expressing his self and, as the painter put
it in a later note, the "Experience of our age in terms of painting—not
an illustration of—(but *the equivalent.*)" Like Jack, he sought not outward
form but a way to explore his emotional and sensual universe; "deep
form," as Jack had once put it. His wife, the painter Lee Krassner, wrote
that "He sensed rhythm rather than order." The canvases, the records,
the growing stack of manuscript pages were merely captured moments
that revealed a *process,* a rendering of an artistic consciousness spontaneously at work.

Pollock too had recoiled from the new order defined by the war—
or for him, by Picasso's "Guernica"—and conceived of spontaneous approaches that accepted "accident" as part of the whole and organically
depicted energy, rhythm, and motion, "memories arrested in space." Like
Jack he was a shy man who often hid behind alcohol, appeared at the most
proper occasions in the most bedraggled dress, said of jazz that it was "the
only creative thing happening in this century," and was essentially a
sensuous Puritan fascinated by the perverse.

All three of their approaches were as much of the senses as of the
mind, and each performed with a savage physical intensity. Pollock spoke
of being *"in* the painting," and Jack and Bird sometimes lost ten pounds
after a spectacular night of creation. All three were labeled undisciplined,
explosive; it seemed to the critical mentality that their stormy spontaneity
was somehow too easy. Each artist had concluded that in the limbo of war
and Cold War, only the most risky commitment to personal creativity and
intuition could allow them to transcend the times. "Mind is shapely,"
Allen had said—and spontaneous words or notes or paintdrops could
become great art when twenty years of experience shortened the arc
separating mind and medium to nothingness.

So Pollock stood at the center of the canvas dappling himself down;
Bird blew high, higher, into the smoky night; and Jack wrote on. At a time

of hydrogen bombs, missiles, and biological warfare, their models were not scientists but sorcerers, their approach not intellectual but sensual, their goals aesthetic and religious. Those who sank deeply enough into the vortex of "Groovin' High" or "Blue Poles" or *Visions of Cody* found themselves finally in awareness of an infinite universe, joyously wordless and silent.

In March Jack completed his unpublishable masterpiece *Visions of Cody* and put it away in his duffel bag. Three months later he reached his aesthetic peak in a new book, the story of the "Myth of the Rainy Night" and Dr. Sax, which he came to call *Dr. Sax.* *"Dr. Sax,"* Allen said, was the attainment of the "perfect executive conjunction of archetypal memorial images articulating present observation of detail and childhood epiphany fact." When Jack completed *Dr. Sax* in June 1952, he was with Burroughs in Mexico, but his physical location hardly mattered. In the three weeks he spent on *Dr. Sax*—he had taped a one-hour précis in San Francisco, but wrote it in Mexico City—he was in a timeless zone of recall where he muttered and exclaimed over the shards of his childhood.

The tale was a meld of several elements: the 1948 dream of his boyhood imitation "Shadow" companion Dr. Sax, who visited Lowell to destroy the "world snake of evil"; a satire on New York intellectuals in the characters Amadeus Baroque and Count Condu; and Jack's immediate atmosphere in the snake and eagle symbols of modern Mexico. Above all, it was a transcendent Faustian recapitulation of childhood, the summation of what Sax had told his boyhood alter ego: "You'll come to death, civilization, sociology, solitude, nightmares, old age, maturity, but you'll never be as happy as you are now in your quietish innocent book-devouring boyhood immortal night."

The seed of the vision was a dream of a certain "wrinkly tar" street corner in Pawtucketville, and as Jack said, "memory and dream are intermixed in this mad universe." Kerouac passed from a second version of the opening description of the Merrimack River—so much more sensitive now to the dark currents of time than in *The Town and the City*—to his own birth: "I was born. Bloody rooftop. Strange deed." He peeled through the layers of memory—GJ, Desjardins the dissipated candy man, drunken priests, child funerals, cartoons and coal ("now it's atom-bomb bins in the cellar communist dope rings"), the flood of 1936, Mémère and Leo, and then the myth of the rainy night. High above his birthplace on Lupine Road "sat" a castle inhabited by one Count Condu, an improvisation on Bela Lugosi and "part of a general movement of evil." Up the road to

Lowell trudged Dr. Sax, pool partner to "Old Bull Balloon"—W. C. Fields—gleeful alchemist and river pilot, seeking "the enigma of the New World—the snake of evil." *Sax* was about "something secretively wild and baleful in the glares of the child soul, the masturbatory surging triumph of the knowledge of reality," about the sounds of eternity Jack sought to replicate, gibberish on the surface, yet a madly sensible gibberish.

Neal's beloved Proust affected it stylistically, Melville's *Confidence Man* and *Finnegans Wake* as well, and even the wild dancing finish of Disney's 1950 *Alice in Wonderland,* which Jack had seen the night before he began to write.

Jacky and Sax slipped invisibly through Lowell's silent dream streets, past Mayan spiders and Chimu centipedes, into the Pit; in a preposterously thrilling climax, Sax invoked his powers and charms, and failed. Evil endured. Glum amid the hellish smokeclouds, Sax sat ordinary again, having discovered that "nothing works in the end . . . the universe doesn't care what happens to mankind." Spawned of Freudian symbolism, Aztec mythology, and Kerouac's own vision, a giant eagle escorted by white doves swept out of the sky, seized the snake, and carried it off: Jack and Sax realized that "the universe disposes of its own evil."

Sax was also about America, as Sax said, "a dense Balzacian hive in a jewel point," and at the center of that jewel there was a horrible flaw. "Something that can't possibly come back again in America and history," Jack wrote, "the gloom of the unaccomplished mud heap civilization when it gets caught with its pants down from a source it long ago lost contact with—[nature]."

When he completed *Dr. Sax* in Mexico in June 1952, Jack had wrung his soul for his vision. There would be no more artistic developments for him that he could truly control, only variations and changes, "losses and exasperations," as John Holmes would later say, further choruses. *Sax* was the exorcism, the legend of Lowell. Kerouac had burned, burned, burned . . . and now he had to wait.

Before he left Russell Street for Mexico and Bill Burroughs in May 1952, Jack had to endure a spring filled with the delicious agony of possibly selling *On the Road.* Allen's old madhouse friend Carl Solomon was an editor—his uncle, A. A. Wynn, was owner—of the New York paperback publisher Ace Books, and Ginsberg had become everyone's agent. Allen had already sold Burroughs' narcotic autobiography *Junkie,* and was encouraging Neal to work on his own autobiography, *The First Third*. Most of Ginsberg's energy was devoted to selling *On the Road* and the 20,000 words on young Neal in the pool hall, which at the time was lumped with it. (Later it would be part of *Visions of Cody*.) But in addition to being a rather prickly character, Carl Solomon had fixed ideas about literary style, thought *Cody* was unpublishable, and bluntly said so. Allen blamed the rejection on office politics, and wrote in his April journal, "I think Jack is the greatest writer alive in America of our own age—yet Harcourt (Giroux) rejected his first as being too personal and subjective . . . and now this second version seems to them a garble of unrelated free associations. I think I'll stick with Jack."

In hungering to see his friend recognized, Allen resembled Holmes, who wrote, "so passionately did I long for his work to be given the recognition it deserved, that sometimes I caught myself wishing he would blunt the edge of it a little toward that end"; Allen tried to mollify Carl and urged Jack to be more cooperative. Utterly certain that he had attained his peak, that in future years he would be astonished and regretful that he could not continue at such a level, Jack wondered jokingly if he might be headed for a breakdown, and refused to consider changing a single word.

Literary news invaded the tranquillity of his Russian Hill attic and sickened him with envy. Holmes had finished his "beat" novel *Go* and sold it to Charles Scribner's Sons. Though he conceded Holmes had treated himself no better than anyone else in the book, Allen felt the editor—a "Whore! Whore! Whore!"—had debauched the book. Jealous and frustrated, Jack condemned Holmes as an interloper and exploiter of their legitimate literary movement (composed of Jack, Allen, Neal, Bill, and Huncke).

His other correspondence from New York reported that Mémère was being plagued with visits from police and the Brooklyn District Attorney's Uniform Support of Dependents Bureau; Joan had sued for child support, and Jack's anger was mixed with his terror of police and the court system. His unseen child named Janet was haunting the Kerouacs. Holmes had separated from his wife Marian. Their marriage had been a great symbol of stability to the circle of friends, and everyone was disturbed by the divorce. Jack urged John to try to patch it up, and to hit the road if he couldn't. Even more upsetting than divorce was the suicide of Phil "Sailor" White, Burroughs' old subway pal. White had informed on former accomplices to get off a murder charge, and while imprisoned in the Tombs he was exposed as a traitor. Convinced that he'd never live through his sentence at Riker's Island prison, he had hanged himself.

The only pleasant news concerned Allen. Then nearing the age of twenty-six, he continued to lurk among the subterraneans of New York, even as he felt that he "should be more *connected* to outside things, like $ and society." He dreamed of marrying his new woman friend Dusty Morland, though he lacked the love or money. But his poetry (later published as *Empty Mirror*) was budding, and in late February he received a wonderful letter from William Carlos Williams, the master poet of Rutherford, New Jersey, assuring him that he would be the center of the new *Paterson Poem,* and that "You *must* have a book. I shall see that you get it." The poems, "eavesdroppings on my consciousness," were brief, humorously gloomy introspections on his spiritual odyssey; the title was a symbol of the futility of the inward voyage. Jack was proud of Allen's success, even though the optimism proved false, and the book was not published for almost a decade. Though he'd never read much of Dr. Williams, Kerouac used his theories on spoken prose in poetry as a springboard for advancing his theory of spontaneous writing to Allen, the first of a series of many lectures Ginsberg was to hear about the virtue of the "wild" first thought.

All the friends had grown closer that spring, as Jack had encouraged Carolyn to overcome the bruised feelings of their conflict over Neal's attentions and write to Allen. Their new correspondence mellowed both of them, Carolyn assuring Ginsberg, "You are the wisest of men—in truth, as Jack says, a mystic genius." Neal also wrote Allen, inviting him to the attic to "make love to wife and me."

All told, his passage with the Cassadys had been a good one. Jack had even spent some time as a yard clerk for the Southern Pacific Railroad, learning about switches and boxcars, making a little money as he acquired a valuable skill. The high point of the spring came when a friend of Neal's, a poet named Philip Lamantia, had given them some peyote. Allen was particularly thrilled to hear about it, because he'd read Lamantia's surrealist poetry—written at the age of fourteen—in André Breton's magazine *View.* Though they later boasted to him of their new experiences in the alteration of consciousness, it had been an unimpressive trip; perhaps they hadn't eaten enough.

To be sure, Jack had a few worries in the Russell Street house. The Cassadys wanted a suburban home in which to raise their children, and as Neal worked double shifts and they pinched pennies for a mortgage down payment, hobo-artist Kerouac felt estranged from their plans. His creative fantasyland was far distant from marriage and stability, and at times he felt isolated and patronized by his brother.

In May 1952 the Cassadys dropped Jack off in Nogales on their way to Tennessee to visit Carolyn's family and show off the children to their grandparents. Jack's wallet was limp but his bag was beginning to fill with more and more of what he knew was his best writing. While in Mexico, he wanted to portray Burroughs as he'd just portrayed Neal. After returning to New York he would write a book on "The Mysteries of America" that focused on Lester Young, who with the Mississippi River seemed to epitomize the nation's spiritual greatness.

Otherwise, it was good to be temporarily free from his native land. More and more, it was beginning to choke up, to calcify, as Neal seemed to be doing with his familial responsibilities. Modern concrete superhighways, like the just-opened New Jersey Turnpike, were starting to replace the cracked-tar two-laners that Jack had known. The past Christmas, America had seemed "so big, so sad, so bleak" to him, "like the leafs of a dry summer that go crinkly ere August found its end, [it's] hopeless . . ." Swaying on the bus to Mexico City, Jack had pencil and paper, and was anything but hopeless; he had trapped visions on paper and created an indelibly fine art. He was a writer.

IX
Among the Fellaheen of Mexico and Manhattan

"**M**Y NAME is Enrique," said the brown young man sitting next to Kerouac on the Mexico City–bound bus. "And this is my brother Gerardo." Jack was a little lonely; the Russell Street attic had been a haven of peace and security for him, and now he was adrift again. He reached out gratefully for the proffered friendship, and their conversation warmed. Enrique shifted in his seat, then showed him the radio sitting in his lap. It was hollowed out, its tubes and circuits replaced by half a pound of ripe green marijuana. "You wanna get high?" Enrique whispered, with the demure, inquiring look of nonviolent hipsters when they identify a fellow member of their underground. Jack was delighted to share the wealth, and the three of them spent an afternoon bus layover in Sinaloa with Indian friends of Enrique's.

They smoked grass and opium until Kerouac sat transfixed, listening to their Indian host lecture on revolution—a mad, mystic revolution that the political types back in Union Square New York could never comprehend. "We'll take the snake out of the woods!" their host exclaimed. "We'll tear the wings off the great bird! We shall live in the iron houses overturned in fields of rags!" For they were—as Jack realized in a sudden insight that cut through the warm drug haze that swirled about him— all Roman Catholics, and that link was a strong one, deeper and more binding than any political dogma. He squatted barefoot on the dirt floor of the hut in Sinaloa, thinking that "the earth is an Indian thing," and that he was one of Oswald Spengler's "world citizens, world pacifists, world reconcilers," a metropolitan man of the north come to listen to the peasants, to experience what he called "that timeless gaiety of people not involved in great cultural and civilization issues." To Jack, the Indians in front of his bedazzled eyes were the people of the pure land.

He approached the *campesinos* with affection and respect, saw them not as clownish "Panchos" but as people in touch with elemental truths filtered out of American life by the technocracy. Like the Afro-American culture he had studied for twenty years, there was something ancient and enduring in the Indian lifestyle. On his previous expedition to Mexico he had watched people silently lust after Neal's beat-up old car, and had mourned their materialism. They did not know of the atomic bomb that obsessed him, the nuclear demon that could destroy all of the toys of America-Babylon, so that, he thought, "we would be as poor as they someday, and stretching out our hands in the same, same way." In Jack's eyes, Enrique and Gerardo and their host were part of "the essential strain of the basic primitive wailing humanity that stretches in a belt around the equatorial belly of the world." As Neal told Allen, Jack was "with the Indians permanent."

As he listened to the village's "African world Fellaheen sound" or bounced on the bus among the chickens and goats, singing Bop tunes like "Scrapple from the Apple," Jack saw the United States as something far away, an ugly, insubstantial cloud above the Rio Grande. But the cloud was mushroom shaped. As Jack left for Mexico City, the Atomic Energy Commission demonstrated a nuclear explosion in Yucca Flat, Nevada, thrilling some 35 million Americans who watched it on television at home. The other prominent scientific news featured the product chlorophyll, which was sweeping the U.S. deodorant market in the ongoing American war against body odor. Control was the essence of America, but it was a subtle, invisible control. On the political level, the Republicans chose the blandly optimistic Dwight Eisenhower before millions of Americans in the first widely televised presidential nominating convention. If only in memory of Leo, Jack liked Taft; Allen backed his fellow New York Democrat Averell Harriman. Neal's comment was "It makes not one whit of difference."

The political system had reached a quiescent, placid consensus, and party labels in the new technocracy were as irrelevant as buggy whips. After twenty long years "out," the Republicans brayed loudly of change, but altered nothing when they assumed power. No less than the "liberal" bureaucratic Democrats, they were locked into a control system of large-scale unions, mature corporations with a monopoly on money and expertise, supervised education and the increasingly well-planned organization of almost everything. Senator Joseph McCarthy flailed about silencing dissent and debate, eight tenths of American aid to Western Europe was military in nature, the Cold War turned the 1952 Helsinki Olympics into an athletic battlefield, and the war in Korea ground on. Negotiations had dragged through a year by 1952, but the only use served by the little hut marked with a spotlight at Panmunjon was to give a border reference point to night reconnaissance patrols.

Organization was the American reference point, and even something as shiny-new as rock and roll was subject to it. That summer of 1952, a Cleveland disc jockey named Alan Freed had invented the term "rock and roll," but the music was then under the technical and commercial domination of Atlantic Records producer Jesse Stone, who had conceived the fundamental chord changes that made rock out of rhythm and blues. Teamwork was everything, and though Americans wistfully cherished the lone gallantry of Gary Cooper in *High Noon,* they knew better than to try anything like it in real life; after twenty years of depression, war, and atomic Cold War terror, Americans were realists.

As Jack saw it, the United States was only laws *against,* not laws *for,* and his long-anticipated visit to Mexico was as exhilarating as playing hooky. His bus slowly crunched two thousand miles down the spine of the continent, past red plains dotted with wild burros and horses. Kerouac sat by his dozing *compadres* and nursed his worries. Terrified at somehow being pursued by the New York police over the divorce and Joan Haverty's demands for child support, he was also unsure of how Burroughs had survived Joan Vollmer Burroughs' recent death.

Nine months before, on a hot and drunken day in September of 1951, Joan and Bill had entertained two GI's from Florida—Edwin Woods and Lewis Marker—in their Mexico City apartment. Supposedly Joan teased Bill into shooting a glass of gin off her head William Tell–style. Certainly Bill was obsessed with handguns, and Joan's death wish was legendary. The month before, Allen and Lucien had visited Mexico (Jack's phlebitis attack had prevented him from going along), and Allen had been terrified at Lucien's and Joan's suicidal drunken driving. In any case, there was a gun, a .38 revolver. Bill fired it, and it killed Joan.

The newspapers were pleased with a juicy story; the *Daily News* blared "Heir's Pistol Kills His Wife: He Denies Playing William Tell" and presented Burroughs as a "wealthy Texas cotton grower" held on murder charges. Given the Mexican system of justice, it was no surprise that Bill managed to avoid prison, but he was temporarily confined to the country.

Shortly before Jack arrived, Bill's spirits plummeted further. Burroughs' sexuality was no simple thing. He had once boastfully written to Allen that "I have been laying women for the past 15 years and haven't heard any complaints from the women either," and Joan had graced the letter's margin with the word "correct." Allen's agonized plaints about gay life elicited Burroughs' comment that "the problems and difficulties you complain of in queer relationships are social rather than inherent resulting from the social environment (to my mind one of the worst in Space-Time) of middle class U.S.A." In the backwash of Joan's death, though, Bill had taken up with a young man and fallen in love with him. The object of his affections was unmoved. Jack had once written of Bill that he had left his "sexuality back somewhere in the opium road"; certainly his dry, intellectualized vision of Bill ignored the fleshly realities. When the young man grew to dislike Mexico and returned to the United States, Bill suffered, writing him multiple, unanswered letters. He tried to salvage the pain with a new work, to be called *Queer*.

Burroughs had begun to write two years before, in 1950, because there had been "nothing else to do," but in time he had become engulfed by his art. His first book, *Junkie*, was a generally straightforward description of his drug life; Allen had sold it to Ace Books that March. Bill's letters were increasingly devoted to prose techniques, and his comments on *Visions of Cody* were perceptive and precise. He wrote in April that "the excerpts from your novel sound mighty fine. Of course, the *Finnegans Wake* kind of thing can be fully appreciated only in context of the whole work, which in the case of this kind of writing more than any other is an actual amoeba like organism." With that sort of encouragement, Jack arrived in Mexico City in late May 1952, anticipating stimulation and another book, having warned Allen not to tell Bill and make him self-conscious about being a subject.

Kerouac hurried to Burroughs' place at 212 Orizaba Street. Jack was mildly upset when Bill swiftly steered him away from Enrique, his companion on the ride down, but since he was broke and Burroughs was supporting him, Jack said goodbye to Enrique. It had been seven years since Bill had been Jack's mentor, but the younger man still listened attentively to the subtleties expressed in Bill's dry flat tones. The previous year Jack had assured Allen that he still regarded himself as a Burroughsian Factualist, in the spirit of clarity and lack of preconceptions, and in a world view defined by the overreaching fact of death; dying—the end of time—was of the essence. Kerouac's occasional querulous moodiness Burroughs dismissed. When Jack complained of John Holmes's recent financial success with his novel *Go*, Burroughs replied, as he had once written a similarly disposed Allen, that "Envy or resentment is only possible when you can not see your own space-time location."

Bill was equally impressed with Jack and the new book, informing Allen that "He has developed unbelievably. He really has a tremendous talent." Enjoying Bill's sourly witty, outrageously misogynist harangues, Jack smoked grass and typed up—revising as he went—*Visions of Cody*, then sent it off to Allen, his "agent." Stoned and peaceful, he joined Bill at the ballet, and also indulged himself sexually with a "splendid" Mexican whore and an expatriate American woman. Drugs were one attraction of his stay at Orizaba Street. Morphine, Bill's current kick, was freely available; Burroughs had a Board of Health permit that allowed him seven grams a month for $30. Despite his seven years' experience with hard drugs, Bill was still astonishingly subject to bum trips with junk. "I got the horrors," he wrote, hallucinating a face corrupted with disease that led "to the final place where the human road ends, where the human form can no longer contain the crustacean horror that has grown inside it."

When he and Jack ate peyote a couple of times early in June, Bill launched into a monologue about being a prisoner: "Ah, I feel awful, I feel worse than if I was suddenly a prisoner in the High Andes, a penalist . . ." The Mexico City hip scene's atmosphere began to come unglued. An old Harvard friend of Bill's named Kells Elvins had been set up and arrested on drug charges, and local paranoia was sufficient for Bill to order Jack not to smoke marijuana in the house. More discreet drugs retained their popularity, and the Orizaba Street flat was a popular scene for refugee American hipsters like "Wig," a Bop bassist who had played with some of the best California jazzmen, including Art Pepper, Hampton Hawes, and Shelly Manne. Wig was one of Bill's customers, and brought not only dope money but a present, a small but rich stack of the best jazz records around.

Between visits to the bullfights or Lola's Bar, Jack plunked himself down in the only private place, Bill's toilet, took out his nickel notebook, and in three weeks spilled onto paper his vision of his marble-playing childhood as seen from the shroud, *Dr. Sax*. It was not only ancient memory but present reality; Burroughs' dry, waspish humor tinged much of the book. The story reeked as well of a pungent sexuality—while his money lasted, Jack was actively making the rounds of Oregano Street's brothels, where a "date" cost him 36 cents. Returning to the cool tile cell of his meditations, he would envelop himself in clouds of marijuana and begin to write. Though it was only the second time he'd seriously attempted to write while high, he was somehow in enough control to make of *Dr. Sax* his masterpiece, his language rolling subtle and loose, his guilts and glee transmuted into a wonderful prose study of the magic space between shadow and light.

Despite the fact that *Sax*, because of its surreal style, was as unpublishable as *Cody*, Jack was euphoric with his victory and bursting with ideas for new books. He planned a series of sketches on Bill Burroughs and the Mexican Indians, then thought he might do a Civil War novel, though it would have to await a better library. Somewhat more realistically, he warned John Holmes not to do a novel about jazz, and outlined his ideas for a book to be entitled *Hold Your Horn High*. Part One, "Afternoon of a Tenorman," would focus on Lester Young, Jack's Horace Mann friend Seymour Wyse, and the Swing Era, while Part Two would feature Neal and Slim Gaillard. The third section centered on Al Sublette, a black student and sailor drinking buddy from Jack's previous stay in San Francisco, whose favorite expression was "Blow, baby, blow!" Jack told John that he would close the book with a chapter about "The Heroine of the Hip Generation"—Billie Holiday, Lady Day.

Through mid-June he was ecstatic, aglow with post-creative plans, anticipating a South American quest after drugs and mystery with Bill, then a merchant voyage or two to earn enough to buy a trailer so that Mémère, who was then nearing retirement age, could settle in Nin's backyard in North Carolina. Then, pronouncing the most paradisaical image of life in any locale since William Jennings Bryan sold Florida, he and the Cassadys would settle together in Mexico City, where life was cheap and wonderful. In four months, Jack promised, Neal could earn enough on the Southern Pacific Railroad to support his family for a year below the border, with filet mignon at 60 cents a pound, rent for a nice home with garden and fireplace at $27 monthly, cigarettes at 6 cents a pack, and bus fare from the border to Mexico City at $6.

Toward the end of his last stay in San Francisco, Jack had run "into a blank wall" in Neal, seen him as indifferent, like a patronizing elder brother who would no longer answer his younger brother's questions. Now Jack cheered up quickly when Carolyn assured him of Neal's sustained concern for him, shrugged off their lapse in communication as mere posturing on Cassady's part, and continued his selling job, trying to soothe the Cassadys' marital problems by offering Neal the whores, fruit, weather, good and high times of Mexico City. Neal was jealous, albeit very confusedly, of Jack's recent affair with Carolyn, but Kerouac counseled him from the long perspective of his own anticipated death. Seen from the grave, jealousy was an empty abstraction, wrote Jack. He had philosophically confronted death, and though he cherished his friends, he warned the Cassadys that all relationships were finite and limited before what his favorite humorist, W. C. Fields, called "the fellow in the bright nightgown." Better, he urged Neal, to stay high and accept eternity in the warm beauty of Mexico City, and for them all to love each other the way human beings could.

In late June 1952, though, Jack's vibrant mood collapsed after a series of souring events. First there was a letter from Allen Ginsberg, who was toiling in the New York fields of commerce, trying to sell books while all of his friends roamed free. Allen desperately wanted to escape the city, but was "terrified of going into the night again, toward death maybe, or an oblivion beyond the pale tenderness of New York daily life," and was sure that "all would die . . . if I weren't around to clean up messes." From New York he wrote Jack his own opinion of *Visions of Cody.* "I don't see how it will ever be published," Allen groaned, "it's so personal, it's so full of sex language, so full of our local mythological references." He went on: "The language is great, the blowing is mostly great," the sketches were "the best that is written in America," but "It's crazy. (not merely inspired crazy) but unrelated crazy." Ginsberg felt that Jack still hadn't caught Neal, only himself, and mixed the chronology too much, so that the surreal end sections were "juss crappin around . . . just a hangup." Allen even challenged Jack's motives: "What are you trying to put down, man?"

To Neal in San Francisco he was even more explicit. *"Visions of Cody,"* he wrote Cassady, was "a holy mess—it's great all right, but he did everything he could to fuck it up with a lot of meaningless bullshit I think, page after page of surrealist free association that don't make sense to anybody except someone who has blown Jack." Frustrated by his "business" role, Allen wondered, "why is he tempting rejection and fate? fucking spoiled child . . . it ain't *right* to take on so paranoic just to challenge and see how far you can go."

Allen was caught in an awkward situation; the year before, 1951, he had wangled a small advance from Ace Books based on the style of the young Neal in the pool-hall segment, and the rest of *Visions of Cody* was radically different. Not only had his star author pulled an aesthetic tantrum, Allen reflected, but Carl Solomon—Ginsberg's only connection to the publishing world—was at present incapable of confident literary or business judgment, due to a spectacular nervous breakdown.

Solomon had left his wife, attacked books with knives, stopped traffic by hurling his brief case and shoes at cars, flooded his apartment and smeared its walls with paint, and landed in Bellevue Hospital's psychiatric wing. Carl, who wrote of himself, "I have not been mad/But merely a prophet, without profit motive," also announced, "I wasn't sure which it was, this reality or the other one, and there are so many realities . . ." He used that sort of shifting psychic gears in his business letters as well as his poetry, rendering commerce difficult.

His first letter to Kerouac, written in the fall of 1951, began with a fascinating lecture on the cosmic meaning of the zinc penny, "loss of respect for authority, the second war, demonism, the atomization of the American petit bourgeois," progressed to a discourse on American writers as gays—"Here writers are trade and editors are aunties"—dismissed *The Town and the City* as repressed homosexuality, brusquely informed Jack that he was acting like an "undertipped head waiter" and thoroughly dressed him down for the crass philistinism of hiring an agent. Early in 1952 he suggested Jack do a picture book on Bop, but the idea never bloomed. While Jack was in the Russell Street attic, Solomon's letters concerning the possible sale of *On the Road* were usually abusive, calling Jack a "jackass" for offering to produce a book in a month when A. A. Wynn had offered a two-year contract. The original twenty-one-day *On the Road* was "work shirking" to Carl, and Jack's personality with publishers was a "nasty, stupid, worthless, idiot-brat son of a royal house" pose.

Kerouac's art was so revealing in its stark intimacy that there was almost no distinction between art and artist; to him, an attack on his work translated as a devastatingly absolute rejection. Yet his reply to Allen's criticisms was gentle, a murmur about some Blake dreams he'd just had, a quiet, wry suggestion that he might very well be going insane, but was closer to salvation for it. Nevertheless, he thought *Visions of Cody* a work of genius comparable to *Ulysses,* and he refused to consider the remotest possibility of cuts or revisions.

Life pitched downward. By late June 1952, Jack was deeply depressed, awash in what he perceived as his failures; he was thirty years old, had 60 cents to his name, a wife who wanted to jail him for non-payment of child support for a never-to-be-seen daughter, a mother still working, three books no one would publish, and the sad mushy feeling of holes in his shoes. Thieves had stolen his raincoat and ten dollars Mémêre had sent him. Worst of all, his poverty had generated a war with Bill regarding the division of food in the Mexico City apartment. Burroughs' money was committed to his legal expenses—his advance from Ace was only $180 anyway—and he couldn't support Jack, who had developed a habit, when two rolls remained on the table, of immediately gobbling both.

Frantic, Kerouac wrote to Carolyn begging for a loan, but received no reply; the letter had been delayed. According to Bill, he was "usually surly and ill-tempered," "insufferable," and "paranoid," and persisted in smoking grass in the flat, an undiplomatic gesture for the guest of a man negotiating his way out of murder charges. Actually, Bill was fed up with Mexico, and had decided to go to Panama, then Peru, looking for a new drug called "yage," an "uncut kick that opens out instead of narrowing down like junk"; perhaps it was, Bill hoped, "the final fix."

Desolate and bone-tired, his energy sapped by the grim futility of his struggle with the publishing world, his responsibilities as a son to support his mother in retirement unfulfilled, and his friends having apparently deserted him, Jack fled to holy sanctuary in a little church. Contemplating the Catholic crucifix in an Aztec land of blood rites and savagery, he begged Christ and the Blessed Virgin and Leo and Gerard for help, screamed supplication for some blessing. The penitents who inched on their knees toward the altar reassured him, affirming patience and forti- tude as he tried to convince himself that life was but a dream and death, that things didn't matter so much as he was allowing them to. Bit by bit, the quiet dignity of the church calmed him and left him a measure of faith, and he walked out of the cool shadows and into the harsh sun a more tranquil man. Bill grumbled and groaned when Jack asked to borrow $20 for bus fare, but later conceded to Allen, "We are good friends . . . so I guess I have to forgive him," and Jack rode the bus back to North Carolina and family.

After a few of Mémêre's meals he grew bored with North Carolina and briefly visited New York; on July 18, 1952, he and Allen stood talking on the corner of 14th Street and Eighth Avenue. Jack was tanned, in good physical shape, and even well dressed. But he struck Allen as tired, vacant, his attention straying. Both of them were frustrated. Their conversation wandered; Jack was planning, he told Allen, to watch the Republican

Convention on TV the next day, though it was a bit meaningless to him; "We are but poor people." Idly scratching his mosquito bites, Jack gloomily agreed with his "little brother" that there was "no hope" in their lives, that they were empty of all but the physical appetites, and their crucial desire—for love—was unfulfilled. "No," Jack said, shrugging as he headed toward the subway stop, "we thought we were alive but we weren't ever."

The feeling of emptiness stayed with him on his bus ride back to his family's home in Rocky Mount, North Carolina. Rocky Mount proved even more depressing than usual, as Nin bitched at him to get a job and Mémère grumbled about his choice of friends, especially his black sailing buddy from San Francisco, Al Sublette. Gabrielle clipped articles on rape and shoved them at him, hissing about "his niggers." So poor and so blank that he could hardly conceive of a positive destination, Jack might well have come dangerously close to unraveling but for a late summer letter from the Cassadys. Their relationship had foundered without Kerouac as balance wheel, and Neal enticed him to return with the promise of a railroad brakeman's job, enclosing an S.P. brakeman's button and some old receipts that would permit him to ride the rails west; unfortunately the passes were useless and he had to take the bus.

For the first few weeks, California was grand. Carolyn and Neal met the freight train he'd taken from San Francisco to San Jose—the Cassadys had moved to there, fifty miles south of San Francisco, and their huge new house included a room especially reserved for Jack—before Neal caught one of the trains to go to work. Carolyn welcomed him with a memorably passionate necking session in the car before she drove him to the threshold of his new home. Home. The children dragged him about their nice big yard, Carolyn served pizza and wine and occasionally shared her bed with him, and he and Neal would read Proust or *Dr. Sax* to each other, pleasantly arguing about Nietzsche or child rearing or even high school football.

But October 1952 was no clean, healing month in Jack's life; he sank into his most ferocious despair yet, strangled on the bile of his impotent rage at the publishing world. Radiating hostility like a dark star, he was a victim of his own gift for empathy. Yet, even as he asserted his art, he sometimes agreed with Mémère or Carl Solomon's criticisms of him as a ne'er-do-well, and wondered if he should go on writing. He regarded Goethe as his hero and he had faith in his work, but time was dribbling away, and his patience with it. To further complicate matters, his feelings for Carolyn Cassady had gotten out of hand. Neither of them had intended their affair as a challenge to the Cassady marriage, but Jack's love became soured by his gloomy mood, and he grew jealous and troubled. Neal, he had decided, was a philistine interested in bills and not literature; when Cassady offered him some grass he had been growing, Jack morosely declined. They had an absurd argument about the cost of the food Jack was eating that culminated in his threat to buy a hot plate. Lost in his depression, Jack finally fled to a San Francisco skid-row hotel called the Cameo, where he lived while continuing to work as a brakeman for the Southern Pacific.

In October he exercised his spite on Allen, his long-suffering agent, in the ugliest letter Jack ever sent. Ginsberg was already quite vulnerable; the day before the letter arrived he had noted in his journal that he felt kin to the warped Caliban of *The Tempest,* that "quite a few people have given up on me and I have myself." Jack snarled and grumbled that the failure of his career was purely the result of everyone's parasitic jealousy. He professed not to understand why even with its popular sex-and-drugs plot *On the Road* had failed to find a publisher, while Holmes's *Go,* which Jack reviled, had just earned a large paperback advance. Wallowing in the gratifying despair of martyrdom, he saw himself as an eternal victim, a Li'l Abner swindled by the city folks. Holmes had no talent, Allen's book of poems was mediocre, and *Road,* though fantastic, would never be published. He told Holmes at the same time that Allen had somehow betrayed himself to Carl Solomon's big-city sophistication, while Kerouac remained a superstitious Celtic peasant. With all the rhetorical force he could muster, Jack closed his blast at Allen by telling him to go away and leave him alone, slamming shut an imaginary door and stalking haughtily away. That he would—as Allen and he both knew—edge blushing back into the same figurative room a little while later made his torment no less real.

The wretchedness of his mood was intensified by the fact that he did nothing but work as a brakeman and put his earnings in the bank. At $600 a month, his railroad wages were the highest of his life, and he became a miser, fanatically saving every penny while he kept meticulous records of his expenses. He stole chicken wire from a junkyard rather than buy a piece for his hot plate, and waited patiently to find a replacement when he lost a single glove. Room rent at the Cameo Hotel was only $4.20 a week, and when he splurged he went to an eatery called the Public Restaurant, where three eggs cost 26 cents, and the décor included the sight of crumbling winos who often proved unable to keep down what was probably their first meal of the week.

Kerouac was one of the lost now, among derelicts as wasted and useless as he felt himself to be. A year before he had encountered a dead bum on the sidewalk, but only now, he thought, could he understand the awfulness of it. The Cameo was a creepy flophouse at 3rd and Howard streets, a home for toothless old men, its curtains stiff with dust, its sheets gray with the rubbing of too many scabrous bodies. It was ordinarily quiet, but Jack spent most of his time elsewhere, generally at work.

Life on the railroad was an exercise in nostalgia, reminding Jack of the rails that had spread over inner Lowell like a spiderweb. His schedule was erratic, and sometimes the work call would come from the S.P. office about 4:30 A.M., forcing the Cameo's potbellied, white-haired desk clerk to slip up the stairs to rouse him. Breakfast consisted of raisin toast, eggs, and coffee, along with another childhood favorite, lettuce and peanut butter. His "energy for sex changing to pain at the portals of work," he would shrug into jeans, workshirt, heavy shoes, fur-collared jacket and baseball cap, pick up his lantern, keys, timetable, knife, and handkerchief, and run for the station. Usually late, Jack needed every bit of his remaining football speed and moves to fly across the station floor and catch his train. Being a brakeman was not overly difficult; mostly he set brakes under the cars and served as flagman and switchman on the runs from San Francisco south into the coastal farm country around Watsonville.

Writing about his experiences in a superb, slightly drunken barroom soliloquy of a piece he called "October in the Railroad Earth," Kerouac focused on the life at the side of the tracks—hobo encampments, the Pomo Indian sectionhands, *braceros* "working to pluck from the earth that which this America with its vast iron wages no longer thinks feasible as an activity yet eats, yet goes on eating," the urbane "commuters of America and steel civilization," and lovers wandering into the lush fields to have sex. His workday ended as the return train rumbled past the rose neon West Coast Bethlehem Steel sign in South San Francisco, near the meat-packing lots where he faked boxcar numbers rather than descend to the rat-infested mud flats to inspect the train properly. Off duty, Jack thought San Francisco was but "end of land sadness," and his only pleasures were a bottle of Tokay, his extensive writing, and the free show of people in the skid-row streets.

He worked into November, but his spirits remained foul with lonely frustration; he was a writer, not a brakeman, and physical labor galled him.

Holmes caught the brunt of his spleen, at least in part because Jack had once accepted charity from the man he now regarded as his creative inferior. Before his pay checks began to come through in October, he had received $50 from John Holmes. A friend of John's had lent Holmes a crucial $50 early in the year, and when John received an $8,000 payment for *Go*'s paperback rights in late September, he sent along $50 and the story to Jack, in an effort to keep the good karma flowing. Jack wrote a gracious thank you in accepting the blessing, but in private he succumbed to bitter envy.

Go was a basically accurate retelling of the gang's life around 1948, with Jack as Gene Pasternak, Neal as Harte Kennedy, Allen as David Stofsky, and John as Paul Hobbes. As Jack had suggested, the story focused chronologically on Neal's visit at New Year's 1948–49, and reached out to include Cannastra's death. Written without hope about "the lost children of the night," *Go* was stylistically more traditional than Jack's experimentations. More important, a tinge of square moralism sometimes impinged on Holmes's consideration of various exotic sexual and narcotic subjects, giving the book an occasional touch of unintended breathless sensationalism. It was the honest work of an intellectual trying to make sense of aliens, and Holmes succeeded as well as anyone not wholly of a scene could. Two years before, Jack had told John that he liked almost all of the characters except himself, and that he thought it was a sincere and righteous work. At present he avoided saying anything to Holmes.

A *New York Times Magazine* editor named Gilbert Millstein had spotted the phrase "beat generation" in *Go* and asked Holmes for an article, which was published as "This Is the Beat Generation." Like the novel, it was sound and intellectual. John wrote that "beat" was a "nakedness of mind, ultimately of soul," the "feeling of being reduced to the bedrock of consciousness." To be beat was to be obsessed with the need for faith in the world, with the need for values and a home place: "A man is beat when he wagers the sum of his resources on a single number." Holmes mentioned Jack in connection with the term, and Jack wrote back thanking him politely, making gracious noises about the piece and its impact in San Francisco.

The fact of the matter was that Jack—though the creator of the term and as beat as any man alive—was quite unlike the Greenwich Village bohemians with whom the media would associate the phrase. Where the Villagers read Sartre and Beckett, he still revered St. Teresa; where they were often politically cynical and antagonistic to middle-class mores, he was patriotic and frequently resided with his mother. Most importantly, the Villagers practiced "cool" as an art form, but when Jack came into Manhattan to be sociable, he was drunkenly "hot," emotional and intense. In time, the relevant distinction would be that while too many of the bohemians were merely conforming to a different drummer, Kerouac followed nothing but his instincts.

In 1952 Kerouac and the bohemians were united by a sense of the emotional, aesthetic, and spiritual deficiencies of the nation, and Holmes's book and article were the first public reflections of that attitude, the first signal of a process that would turn alienation into a fad. "This Is the Beat Generation" struck a responsive nerve, and the magazine received an extraordinary 400 letters about the piece, running them for three weeks after. A few people lost in America were interested in semicriminal dropout sub-cults.

Always seasonal, work on the railroad dwindled away with winter and in early December Jack was laid off. Heading for Mexico after a conciliatory visit with the Cassadys, he took his heart in his hands and invited Carolyn to join him; Neal stood on his equanimity and said yes, but thought no. Marriage and the children were of prime value to Carolyn, and so it was Neal alone who drove Jack to Mexico as part of a speedy dope run. Having partially rebounded from his gloom, Jack had already made up with Allen, writing that Ginsberg had honored him by understanding his work. He pledged his affection for his younger brother, but warned him that his New York–style criticism was not meaningful for a spontaneous writer. Kerouac wanted to tap the preliterate sources of art.

Just as he and Neal arrived in Mexico, Bill departed for Florida and later Panama. Neal bought his grass and returned home; alone, Jack moved into a small adobe room on the roof of 212 Orizaba Street, a little cubicle open to the sun and moon and stars, the perfect location to attempt the novel he thought of as his last possibility for success. It didn't work; he had regained his normal pleasure in people after October's depths, and now he was so tremendously lonely that before Christmas he returned to New York, where Mémêre had resumed living. New Year's Eve he spent with Allen, at a party at Horace Mann classmate Jerry Newman's Bop recording studio. It was a lousy party for him. Though he had admitted his need for company, Jack was still too devastated to communicate. As a result, he was, Allen noticed, "all hung up on noise, music, bands . . . artificial excitement," and unable to be a simple companion. As the first dawn of 1953 broke, Jack maudlinly lamented Mémère's cruel fate in being cursed with a wastrel son such as he, shedding the tears of booze and pot in a cab on the way home, "older," Ginsberg thought, "and (no?) wiser." Allen was pudgy and a bore to him, Holmes seemed to be eating in expensive restaurants and hailing cabs; the only thing left for Jack to do was write another book.

Originally called *Springtime Mary* and finally *Maggie Cassidy*, the book was Jack's first telling of a love story in Proustian terms, as he put it, a mournful recounting of his romance with Mary Carney. It opened on New Year's Eve 1938, "before the war, before everyone knew the intentions of the world to America," when no one had any idea "that the world would turn mad." Hung down with his loneliness and the impossibility of his love for Carolyn Cassady, Jack loaded up on pot and goofballs, typed the first chapter, then wrote the rest by hand, "with just a touch of the Canuck-half Indian doubt and suspicion of all things non-Canuck non-half Indian."

Though it was about the joys of the first love one never quite recovers from, *Maggie Cassidy* concluded that "love is bitter, death is sweet." Death would at least be a release for his loathsome self, the guilty persona destined to be thrown "in a hole already eaten by the dogs of dolor like a sick Pope who's played with too many young girls." Though it was often quite graceful, the writing reflected the melancholy sensation of lostness from the era of American community, the era when Jack himself was young and full of potential. Loneliness debilitated him, and the support of his art paled at the desperation of his need for love, or at least attention. Somehow, he was being beaten to death with the short end of the stick; Holmes made $20,000 for *Go*, Jack reported to Carolyn, while he had been offered only $250 for an option on an unnamed book.

The publishing world stirred up further bile in Jack. Ace Books had brought out Burroughs' *Junkie* in January, written under the pseudonym William Lee, replete with a cover of a sleazily voluptuous blonde being beaten as a syringe fell off the table at her side; there was no such scene in the book. In late February Allen asked Jack for a blurb to go into David Dempsey's *New York Times Book Review* column, and Kerouac replied the next day with a petty, spiteful tantrum, whining that Bill was protected by the pseudonym and Holmes's blurb seemed to come from a disinterested observer. Indignant, he referred Allen to his new (and only briefly retained) agent, Phyllis Jackson of MCA. Ginsberg replied, as he said, "most respectfully and in the spirit of strictest commerce," and dropped the subject for the moment. Jack was far nastier to Holmes, dismissing their relationship as a flimsy and meaningless New York connection between a "rich" man and a member of the laboring class. Furthermore, Jack huffed, his own suffering was real, but Holmes had to dig his out of Dostoyevsky. A suspicious fury had so engulfed Kerouac that he raised ugly questions about John's motives for sending him the present of $50. It would be two years before Jack wrote another letter to Holmes, though in April he contributed a blurb for *Junkie* to Allen: "A learned, vicious Goering-like uninhibited sophisticate makes the first intelligent modern confession on drugs . . . stands classic and alone."

Trapped in the corners of the claustrophobic little apartment the two Kerouacs occupied in Richmond Hill, Jack wrote to Carolyn of feeling emasculated at not being able to support Mémère, and toyed with the idea of working on the Canadian railroad. That notion vanished quickly, and in mid-April 1953 he returned to the Southern Pacific Railroad, working out of San Luis Obispo, California, about 250 miles south of San Francisco. Bored and miserable, he worried that his mind was being sucked down into the narrowing center of a whirlpool, and his only comfort was a vague but developing fantasy of going into the wilderness that summer to learn, Thoreau-like, how to survive independently on the land. He tried to break the drowning sensation by leaving the railroad, and after a ghastly San Francisco drunk with Al Sublette he shipped out on the S. S. *William Carruth* in early June, bound through the Panama Canal for New Orleans.

Liquor drowned the "loneliness Angel" on his shoulder, produced what he called a "sparkle glow" in his belly, "turning the world from a place of ash serious absorption in the details of struggle and complaint, into a gigantic gut joy." Flavored with Tokay, the world was too sweet in fact, and he drank so much on the *Carruth* that he became frightened at his inability to hold a job. Having talked himself into a job as officers' waiter, Jack fell nervously silent, dispensing only a slight superior smile to his crewmates; what he later observed was his "inability to be gracious and in fact human and like an ordinary guy" infuriated his shipmates and officers, and when the *Carruth* docked in New Orleans in July 1953, he quit the ship and returned to New York.

From the mighty to the ephemeral, very little about 1953 appealed to a troubled Jack. *Victory at Sea*, the Cold War epic retelling of the naval battles of World War II, had been the winter's television hit, but Kerouac was disgusted with the technical colossus it celebrated, unleavened by any sensitivity to human suffering. Little about the era enriched him; "I Believe" was the hit song of 1953, and though the thought was sentimentally attractive, its turgid lyrics and weary melody were unappealing. Just after he hit New York the war in Korea ended, but his mild relief was washed away by the horror of so many uselessly dead. A month before, the American government had executed Julius and Ethel Rosenberg at Sing Sing. Allen had telegraphed President Eisenhower that the "Rosenbergs are pathetic Government Will sordid execution obscene America caught in crucifixion machine only barbarians want them burned I say stop it before we fill our souls with death house horror." Idealistic prophecy did not suit the times; 1953 was synonymous with the barbarism embodied by G. David Schine and Roy Cohn, then rampaging through USIA libraries putting the torch to books.

Jack's only desire was to be published, and at long last he had a bit of hope; in March 1953 he had lunch with Malcolm Cowley, the well-known Viking Press editorial advisor. In July Cowley wrote to Allen, whom Jack had just given full power of attorney for his writing. "You are right in thinking that I am interested in Kerouac and his work," Cowley said. "He seems to me the most interesting writer who is not being published today." Cowley thought that *On the Road* stood a good chance of immediate publication, although *Visions of Cody* and *Dr. Sax* (much to his regret, as he would later observe) were much too experimental for regular publishers. But everything took time. The post office misplaced one manuscript, Jack was, despite his periodic complaints, too timid with both Allen and the publishers, and the months slipped by and nothing happened.

Except that Jack fell in love.

Her name was Mardou Fox and she was half American Indian and half black, a strikingly beautiful woman whose rich mahogany skin was stretched over high, elegant cheekbones, her black eyes glittering out at Jack with an energy he had never before seen in a woman. It was her voice that was unique, a hoarse blend of Saks Fifth Avenue class, black street hip, and Village-Columbia intellectualism that left him enthralled. She was perched on a car fender in front of the San Remo Bar when Jack saw her. That evening he approached her, in good Village fashion, with the line "What are you reading?" Their coming together was somewhat odd; Jack was of course no "subterranean," as Allen called the Villagers. The bohemians who clustered at the San Remo, Jack thought, were "hip without being slick . . . intelligent without being corny . . . intellectual as hell and know all about Pound without big pretensions . . . they are very christlike." Jack was not cool but hot, a "big paranoic bum of ships and railroads," as he described himself, dressed in an uncouth Hawaiian shirt half-unbuttoned à la Harry Belafonte, not at all the "thin ascetic strange intellectual" that Jack thought Mardou would want.

After a week in Richmond Hill reveling in fantasies of her, Kerouac arranged with Allen for the three of them to meet at Allen's place on 206 East 7th Street before going to see Charlie Parker at Birdland. At midnight Allen gracefully disappeared. Jack and Mardou returned to her apartment on Paradise Alley, on the Lower East Side. Surrounded by the air-well babble of Puerto Rican *mamacitas* calling down to their children as the radio roared about "che-puh *cerveza*" (Schaefer Beer), they danced in the dark, and made love, and in the morning Jack rushed back to Richmond Hill's order and peace and quiet.

It was only a few days later, when Jack spent a night at Allen's and Mardou came in unexpectedly to borrow bus fare, that they talked deeply for the first time, lifted the veil and told their life stories. Mardou's husky hip voice told a tale of madness and painful despair that resembled in spirit Jack's own life. She had been living with various cool hipsters— which meant she was living alone—and had flipped out. Jack thought they'd treated her badly. "Yeah, well, they never treat anyone . . ." she muttered, eyes lost and faraway, "like they never do anything—you take care of yourself, I'll take care of me." Jack spat out the word "existentialism" in sarcastic agreement and she nodded and added, "But American worse cool existentialism of junkies man."

As Jack later recalled their talk in his story "The Subterraneans," Mardou snuggled against Jack in a chair at Allen's and whispered of losing her sense of self entirely, of walking naked out into the Village night propelled by some deeply felt and uncontrollable symbolic necessity that made her crouch catlike in the mist on a back-alley wood fence, utterly paralyzed of will, until at last she passed through some private apocalypse and came down off the fence to borrow some clothes and some money and go "buy this brooch I'd seen that afternoon at some place with old seawood in the window, in the Village . . . it was the first symbol I was going to allow myself." When she confessed her paranoia about someone injecting her, Jack recalled a similar hallucination of his own eight years before while eating Benzedrine with Vicki Russell. He listened intently as Mardou described an early-morning encounter with a man in a wheelchair. "A great electrical current of real understanding passed between us and I could feel the other levels, the infinite number of them of every intonation in his speech," she whispered. "I'd never realized before how much is *happening* all the time." As her story unwound to include a stay at Bellevue at the end of that day, Jack sat overwhelmed by the first spontaneous soulful talk he'd heard in years; this black-Indian woman was a true American, another sufferer like Neal, and she bedazzled him.

They made love and that night went to a friend's apartment. Jack was a drunken boor, freeloading booze, looking at homosexual pornography and listening to Marlene Dietrich until three in the morning, oblivious to Mardou's desire to go home. But at last he relented. To him, she was "so hip, so cool, so beautiful, so modern, so new," and Jack's self-confidence swelled as they cruised along the Village streets on their way to the Five Spot Café for music, the San Remo for drinks, or Allen's apartment for a party. Yet she was too hip, too cool, and it made him nervous, so that he often drank too much. He wanted to get her away from the city to Mexico, or perhaps a hut in the woods, but Mardou had no "eyes for that hysterical poverty deal." Too, he distrusted her "city decadent intellectual dead-ended in cause-and-effect analyses and solutions" mentality, her sloppiness and intensity, her closeness to his soul, her blackness. The first time they'd gone to bed, he later told her, "I thought I saw some kind of black thing I've never seen before, hanging [from her body], like it *scared* me."

Ultimately, their real enemy was Gabrielle Kerouac, whom Jack described as "sweetly but nonetheless really tyrannical." Though he was disgusted by her racism and understood that her interference in his life was unhealthy for a man of thirty-one, Jack permitted his disapproval to be swept away by his absolute commitment to loyalty, to supporting this good Catholic mother emotionally if he could not do so financially. Mémêre's bigotry was oppressive, but she really needed him, and Mardou did not. His rarefied and extended consciousness was a superb recording instrument, but its focus was sometimes too tight to allow for any action but the pushing of a pen. A camera eye was his joy and curse, and even rushing orgasms never displaced it; he could feel but never give wholly, could never achieve one-ness with a lover. Jack made a slight fetish of black panties and demon lust, but even his fantasy world only demonstrated the virgin-whore stereotype that trapped him. Though garter belts and black stockings were a thrill, they were no foundation for a balanced love.

Jack and Mardou's relationship spun and yanked like a set of works with an unbalanced center wheel. Then Gregory Corso appeared and Jack's jealousy cooked their romance to a dry crisp. Twenty-two at the time, Corso was a strange young poet, "a refinement of beauty out of a destructive atmosphere," as Allen would say of his work, a prophet of the gutters. After giving birth to Gregory on Greenwich Village's Bleecker Street in 1930, Corso's mother deserted him and returned to Italy while he was an infant, leaving him to be raised first in an orphanage and then by several sets of foster parents, who seemed to him a "parental hydra, as it were." Teacher-nuns pulled his ears and frightened him; sent to live with his father at the age of eleven, he fled and was confined three months for observation at Bellevue, later for five months in the Tombs. At age sixteen his bedroom was the subway—he took the A train, since it had the longest run—and at seventeen he was caught in a mad scheme to heist a Household Finance office and was sent to Clinton State Prison. An old con there gave him, as he later told the story, copies of *The Brothers Karamazov, The Red and the Black,* and *Les Misérables,* and by his 1950 release, Shelley and his own poetry were the center of Corso's life. Enthusiastic as always, Corso was sitting one night in the Pony Stable Bar as Allen walked in, and they began to talk.

A cheerfully excited time later, Gregory offered to share his greatest treasure with Allen, the voyeuristic gem of a certain young woman who danced nude before her window every night. Ginsberg recognized the scene. "Why, I know her!" laughed Allen, and he took Gregory up to meet his old girlfriend, instantly sealing their budding friendship. Somehow, Gregory and Jack were never in town together, and their first meeting was in connection with Mardou Fox.

Even before Gregory's arrival on the scene, Jack and Mardou's relationship was deteriorating. Jack was usually drunk and frequently late, so consumed by his own fears that he could not recognize Mardou's own insecurities. He found her "little girl-like fear so cute, so edible." Self-conscious and mumbling, their talk wasn't stimulating any more. Once he'd plotted to get rid of Mardou, but Gregory's presence made Jack realize how much he wanted her. She and Gregory seemed so young to Jack, and sitting in the Five Spot listening to Thelonious Monk and Art Blakey, he was remote, heartsick to think that he'd failed once again as a lover.

When Allen threw a party honoring John Holmes, Jack fell apart trying to cope with his twin jealousies, John and Mardou, ran away and got sickeningly drunk with Lucien. Crying with the pain, Jack imagined a picture at the bottom of his glass, an image of Mémère's grasping-but-nurturing love for him, his sole support in the muddle of a stupid-drunk-ard-self-hating life. Later he tried to work things out with Mardou, but when he learned that she'd slept with Gregory, it was all over.

No matter what his pain, there was always his writing to give meaning to life, though for his personality it might well be as debilitating as Mémère. He doubted his act even as he performed it, interjecting that "a Baudelaire's poem is not worth his grief," but he seized his art like a crucifix against the vampire of sorrow. Swallowing some Benzedrine, he sat down at a typewriter with a teletype roll and in "three full moon nights" wrote his confession of the affair, a story he called *The Subterraneans*.

Modeled after Dostoyevsky's *Notes from the Underground*, *The Subterraneans* was a sacramental revelation interpolating his conscious memories and unconscious feelings with a wonderful replication of Mardou's syntax and diction, her private sound. Recording his tragedy did not relieve the pain, it only justified it, "redeemed" it, and for such high purpose he told his tale in full-blown honesty, admitting—as few men in 1953 would—that he feared her vagina as a vise, that he was afraid. *The Subterraneans* ended with fateful words that caught the essence of his life, reflecting the consciousness that left him one step removed from the present reality: "And I go home, having lost her love, and write this book."

Pale and shaken—he'd lost some fifteen pounds in three days of writing—Jack got on the subway and went to Allen's apartment for the ongoing party created by Bill Burroughs' visit en route to North Africa. They enjoyed a pleasant and creative reunion. Allen had a job, an apartment, and enough money to play host, and with nine years of intimacy already among them, they gossiped and became reacquainted. The fact that Bill was in love with Allen sharpened the atmosphere, and Jack was, Allen thought, "astounded, horrified, and pruriently interested" in this new twist in their lives. Allen had just completed a fine poem about Neal entitled "The Green Automobile," Jack was at his peak, and Bill was exploring what he called "routines," word-sketches about an imagined place called Interzone.

Bill and Allen were also editing together a book of their recent correspondence, to be called *The Yage Letters*. Burroughs had left Mexico in search of the psychedelic plant yage in an odyssey as bizarre as Homer's.

His astringent pen recorded encounters with Circean "whores and pimps and hustlers" in Panama, and the Scylla and Charybdis of the Canal Zone Civil Service. "He does not have a receiving set," thought Bill of one specimen, "and he gives out like a dead battery. There must be a special low frequency Civil Service brain wave." To Burroughs, policemen looked like "the end result of atomic radiation," but he saved his most exquisite loathing for one priest, who "sat there in his black uniform nakedly revealed as the advocate of death. A business man without the motivation of avarice, cancerous." He was conned by a jungle medicine man and proved vulnerable to the blandishments of local boy hustlers. "Trouble is," as Bill said of himself, "I share with the late Father Flanigan—he of Boy's Town—the deep conviction that there is no such thing as a bad boy." Bill had finally located the yage through a friendly German in a most un-remarkable shop, and brought a few samples to Allen's.

Impressed by *The Subterraneans*, Bill and Allen asked Jack to draw up a checklist of how he wrote spontaneously, which he called "The Essentials of Spontaneous Prose." Bill's visit gave them an enormous number of new things to consider, and their conversations encompassed nostalgic wartime memories, the Mayan and Egyptian art they saw at the Metropolitan Museum, their writing, and their generation in America.

As November 1953 passed, things got a little out of hand. In some horrific replay of his time in the jungle, Bill kept insisting that he and Allen "were ultimately going to schlup together," Allen recalled later, "sort of shlup and absorb each other, a kind of monstrous junkie-organic-protoplasmic schlup of two beings." Jack was not an entirely disinterested observer of their sexual plight. Late in November, he commenced to write a letter to Bill and Allen, both of whom were about to leave New York. Junked out on dolophines, his brain roiled with wine and goofballs, he figuratively staggered to a podium to bestow his after-dinner blessings on his departing friends, to smoke a fine cigar and express his love for them. Too befuddled to deliver his post-banquet enconium, Jack instead slid into a tirade against homosexual writers, deprecating the work of Paul Bowles, Carson McCullers, and especially Gore Vidal.

Three years younger than Jack and the author of four published novels, Vidal was a symbol of literary business success, an elegant, criti-cally acclaimed writer gracefully at home in a world that spit out Jack like an unwanted seed. One night in the San Remo Bar with Burroughs, Jack recognized Vidal and gushingly brought him over to introduce Bill, gid-dily trying to create an historic meeting of authors. The night wore on to the sound of clinking glasses. Drunk, Jack began to flatter Vidal grotesquely, fawning over him. "Boastfully queerlike," as Allen said, Jack grabbed Vidal's hand and offered himself for the night; they went to Gore's room at the Chelsea Hotel and Jack proved impotent, slipping away to sleep in the bathtub.

At that juncture failure on every plane had destroyed his patience, and his inner reserves were almost gone. He needed something in his life to give him a measure of solace, something that could defend him from frustration and booze and Mémêre and the rest of his tattered life.

X
The
Dharma Road

THE LIVES of the remaining New York members of the circle changed once more, scattering down new paths, both geographic and spiritual. In July 1953, Allen and John Holmes had thrown the Chinese coins of divination called the *I Ching* as they pondered leaving the city. Both interpreted their answers as yes, and Holmes left New York to renovate a house and settle in Old Saybrook, Connecticut. After all his years of dull Manhattan grief, Allen was at last ready in December to leave New York and accept Neal and Carolyn's invitation to join them. In celebration of his long-delayed release, Allen planned no simple bus trip but a vast pilgrimage to delights that would nurture his city-stunted soul. There would be stops to see Florida, Havana, Yucatán and its Mayan ruins—"as Byron saw ruins of Athens and Rome," Allen put it—and the rest of Mexico, so that when he saw Neal he would "be able to talk for hours about not only NYC intellectual beauties but also manly savage solitude of jungles." Neal had a parking-lot job waiting for Allen, with Jack to hold it down until he arrived. Jack planned to work the Penn Station baggage room through Christmas and leave for San Francisco on the twenty-sixth, arriving in time to celebrate New Year's Eve 1953 with the Cassadys. When Allen set off on December 19, Jack collapsed into another frozen depression.

His guilts over Mémêre had flayed him raw, and his dreams tortured him with images of Leo endlessly returning to Lowell in search of a job. Struggling awake, Jack would be certain that *he* was Leo, that they shared the same dying soul. Riven by his sadness, he felt he was a "sheepish . . . idiot turning out rejectable unpublishable wildprose madhouse enormities." A madman clown to the publishers who lived by the code of business lunches and legal contracts, Jack worried that his devoutly prophetic writing—prophecy in the sense of truth—was being debauched.

At Christmas he enthusiastically wrote Neal and Carolyn that he'd be on his way as soon as his pay check came through in early January, hitching through the south to buy marijuana in Mexico. Yet his underlying weary disgust with his life kept him in Richmond Hill until another pleading-encouraging message from San Jose put him on a bus that arrived in California early in February of 1954.

But in the middle of the forlorn chaos of his life there was a hint of hope. It came in the form of Buddhism. Distraught over Mardou, Jack had sought refuge in Thoreau's *Walden.* He felt an affinity with Thoreau's fellaheen rejection of "civilization," and more important, he was intrigued by Thoreau's tantalizing references to Eastern philosophies. Shortly before Jack left for California, he went to the library and checked out Ashvagosha's biography, *The Life of the Buddha.* One phrase— "Repose Beyond Fate"—caught his eye and seized his imagination.

Buddhism promised peace, freedom from Mémère's bitter tongue and the publishing world's vagaries, personal as well as aesthetic fulfillment. Jack began to meditate. At his first attempt to seek Buddha, he closed his eyes "and saw golden swarms of nothing, the true thing, the thusness of creation." Searching further, he came upon the four noble truths of Gautama Buddha, which made sense to him in a way Christianity never had, resonating in his soul the way Bird, Diz, and Monk could fuse a perfect harmony in his ears. The first truth was incredibly simple, yet defined Jack's life as he saw it. "All Existence is suffering." The second truth said that "The cause of suffering is desire and ignorance." Third, "There is a possible end of suffering." Last, "This end may be achieved by the eight-fold path." The eight-fold way demanded right knowledge, aspiration, speech, conduct, labor, endeavor, mindfulness, and meditation.

Some aspects of this new practice resembled his old Catholicism; there were five commandments, which banned killing, theft, adultery, lying, and drinking alcohol. All but the last harmonized with Jack's natural impulses. Over the next year he would practice Hinayana chastity and focus on developing compassion toward all life. He learned the *Gatha of Impermanence,* that "All composite things are impermanent,/they are subject to birth and death;/Put an end to birth and death,/And there is a blissful tranquillity."

And as far as a lone student could, he tried to

> Pursue not the outer entanglements,
> Dwell not in the inner void.
> Be serene in the oneness of things,
> And [dualism] vanishes by itself.

Buddhism was symbolized by a wheel which depicts the various gati, the six realms of existence. A blind woman represented ignorance, a house the senses; desire showed in a drunkard, and life was captured in a man carrying a corpse. Classic Mahayana Buddhism denoted six worlds of Gods, men, demons, asuras, animals and Pretas (Ghosts), and its complex mythology was appealing to a child of saints, martyrs, and popes. Jack's Buddhism was fervent and pious, full of the "hearts and flowers sentimentality" of his Catholic childhood. Zen student Philip Whalen, later a close friend of Jack's, thought that he was sensitive to the "imaginative part, the spaces and times and giganticism" of Buddhism, but his "Edgar Guest sensibilities" bound him close to the religious sentimentality of St. Teresa of Lisieux, the bourgeois saint.

No one could doubt his sincerity or his courage. Americans in those days knew as little of the Way as they did of the far side of the moon; in the decade before Jack discovered Buddhism, there had been only eleven articles on the subject in all of the nation's general magazines. In them, Buddhism was either exotically cute, as in a *House and Garden* story on temple gardens, or faintly ludicrous, as in *Life*'s coverage of a Brooklyn man who had assumed the robes of a monk in Ceylon. Allen had discovered the beauty of Chinese paintings a year before at the New York Public Library. But his was an intellectual interest; Jack had no intellectual interests, only passions, and for the time being the aesthetic pleasures of Asian art remained abstract and distant to him.

Now, with the sureness of a true believer, Jack arrived in San Jose convinced that he had found the solution to living in the modern world, and anxious to proselytize Neal and Carolyn. Incredibly, Neal beat him to the punch: *He* had found a prophet and was ready, with all of his energy and charm, to convert Jack! Some months before, Neal had come upon a copy of Gina Cerminara's *Many Mansions* in the back seat of an automobile he was parking. He began the book idly, then excited, he zipped through the book and brought it home for Carolyn to read before he carefully replaced it. *Many Mansions* was the saga of Edgar Cayce, a mystic American healer who identified people's past lives by entering into a trance, and his preachings were an extended version of modern Christianity which incorporated belief in reincarnation, clairvoyance, Atlantis, and especially karma.

Confronted with this new doctrine, Jack retreated to the San Jose Public Library and read about Buddhism, primarily in Dwight Goddard's *Buddhist Bible* and particularly in the classic *Diamond Sutra.* The Sutra, a dialogue between Buddha and his disciple Subhuti, was an interminable cycle of negation that spun wisdom into Jack's mind, repeating over and over that life meant suffering because humans failed to recognize that it was illusory: Recognize the illusion, and the suffering pilgrim would escape the cycle of birth and death and enter the infinite and unchanging void. As the Buddha poetically concluded,

> All composite things
> Are like a dream, a phantasm, a bubble and a shadow,
> Are like a dew-drop and a flash of lightning;
> They are thus to be regarded.

At the Cassadys' kitchen table Jack read the Buddha to Neal and Carolyn in the urgent voice of the faithful, but their faith in Cayce was unshaken.

"But a *soul,* man, you *are* a soul; the soul is *you,* individual, special," Neal would preach. "The You you've been building from dozens of lives . . . makin' it and blowin' it, see?" Matching Jack's beatific certainty with a glittering self-confidence, Neal summed up, "What you sow, so shall you reap."

Jack shrugged in frustration, grimaced; "Pah! All life is suffering and pain . . . the cause is *desire.* The world is all illusion . . . nothin' means nothin' . . . period!"

As Neal pressed his argument, Jack would be too frustrated to do anything but bellow "WORDS!" and their arguments took on the contemptuous edge of fanaticism. Later Jack would understand that "The sound of silence is all the instruction you'll get," but while he lived with Neal and Carolyn he continued to try to convert them. In a mellow moment, Jack conceded that it was all a superficial difference in choices, a matter of cosmic style. Often his imagination was more acidulous; Neal had taken to preaching Cayce to the Italians and bohemians of San Francisco's North Beach district, and Jack likened him to Billy Graham.

Cayce struck Jack as a cross between Jesus of Nazareth and a redneck mountain hick. The Cassadys thought Jack used Buddhism as a nihilistic evasion—"nothin' means nothin' "—and Jack retorted that Neal was a typical egotistical American, proud of his suffering and unwilling to accept the universal reality of the First Truth of Buddha. On that point, Carolyn agreed. Neal wanted a powerful God to stop him from committing his "sins," and Caycean karmic retribution fulfilled this need. Jack thought it was all a Christian-authoritarian dualistic fraud; he lectured Carolyn that Jesus should have gone to Asia, where Buddha would have saved him from his messiah complex, emphasizing to Carolyn that Buddha was no God, but the enlightened one, a state available to all.

After two months of spiritual argument, in March of 1954 their mutual certainties and Jack's gloomy poverty made them irritate each other. They quarreled over who would pay for some pork chops, and Jack moved back to the grimy comfort of the Cameo Hotel. Gazing out his window at the winos, whores, and police cars, he wrote little sketch poems he called the "San Francisco Blues." In between his writing, he debated whether or not to sit under a tree and meditate, to find Allen in Mexico, or perhaps visit Mexico with his West Coast drinking pal, Al Sublette. But Sublette was too much a devotee of wine and the ladies, and Jack wanted a chastely spiritual expedition. It was a cruel irony that as Buddhism estranged him from his old friends, it was almost as painful as the private agonies meditation had begun to heal.

Allen's journey had indeed been astounding, but Jack recognized it as essentially private, and chose not to interfere. Allen hadn't been impressed with Florida and Cuba, but once free of the United States and its colonies, he found the Mexican jungle a fantasyland of adventure that exceeded his wildest dreams. He settled briefly at an archeological dig near Chichén Itzá, wandering among giant Mayan ruins which he described as "stone cocks a thousand years old grown over with moss." Then he visited the forests of Quintana Roo and plantations that housed exiles taken straight from the pages of *The Treasure of the Sierra Madre*. Karen Shields, an American woman whose family once owned the Palenque archeological site, invited him to stay at her cocoa finca for a week or two, and it stretched into months. Using the farm as a base camp, he explored the back-country scene of an earthquake. The local people were impressed with the intent young man and permitted him to see their sacred cave, which they called "Acavalna" (House of Night); Allen was equally struck by their primitive Christian church, with its drums and "long sinister pagan candles." Prowling about the jungle on air, horse, foot, and mule trips, Allen grew physically attractive, with a dapper beard, while his poetry reflected a new dimension as well; he emerged from Mexico with his radiantly sensitive new poem "Siesta in Xbalba."

Meanwhile, broke and bored with the Cameo Hotel, Jack drifted back to New York in April, just missing Allen's solitary arrival in California. Yet he felt a glowing affection for Allen, if only because his younger brother had enjoined him to begin a private correspondence course in Buddhism. Jack's nervous beginner's grasp made him pompous—his letter demanded that Allen give him the same concentration that he would give Einstein as he lectured on relativity. Jack confined his first lesson to a book list that excluded the Bhagavad-Gita as too worldly and included Goddard, Ashvagosha, *The Gospel of Buddha* by Paul Carus, *Buddhist Legends* by E. W. Burlingame, and *Buddhism in Translation* by Henry Clarke Warren, among others. Having typed up his San Jose Library research as a manuscript he called *Some of the Dharma* (it would turn into a lifetime project), he offered to send it on request, though he warned that some of it was mistaken or written while high. His poem "How to Meditate" was in the same vein: "—lights out—/fall, hands clasped into instantaneous/ecstasy like a shot of heroin," for the goal was "deadstop trance."

The tone of Jack's letters to Allen was one of dreamy calm and patronizing, mysterious certainty. Having reached what he believed to be the center of tranquillity within, Jack murmured like a character out of Shangri-la, he need suffer no more. It was unfortunate that life was not so directed. Jack needed a Thoreauvian hut, but instead had a querulous mother, a crowded flat in Richmond Hill, and an aching desire for a literary career. Though he wanted to abandon the licentious outward manifestations of life for the noble essence of enlightenment, on Saturday night he still hopped the subway for boozy communion with the subterraneans of the San Remo bar in Greenwich Village.

He had a brief fling with a woman who happened to be an addict, but heroin and alcohol produced different personalities, and the affair soon proved much too emotionally draining for him. As a consequence, Jack swore that it was too late for him to love, though he still desperately wanted to. Mardou Fox was around for a while; although they held hands and he vowed that he loved her, nothing came of their brief moment of renewed romance. There was another quarrel with Holmes—Jack became enraged when John was forty-five minutes late for a concert, and didn't speak to him for nearly a year. Henry Cru, his prep-school friend and fellow sailor, was fat and boring, and in all New York that spring of 1954, Jack could tolerate only Jerry Newman, another Horace Mann classmate and jazz fan, then setting up the Esoteric Record Company, and Lucien, his eternal drinking partner and much-admired language man. Mémêre was so disgusted with his paganism that he became convinced she was going to throw him out, and he planned to live as a pilgrim in Mexico, eating bean stews and reading the *Buddhist Bible.*

His anxieties, as always, focused on his writing. Seymour Lawrence at Little, Brown had just rejected *On the Road,* which Jack had retitled *The Beat Generation* after the publicity generated by John Holmes's *New York Times* article. Lawrence had the usual complaints about lack of craftsmanship. Mark Van Doren, for whom Jack had such deep respect, had dismissed *Dr. Sax* as "monotonous and probably without meaning in the end." Allen had stopped acting as his agent when he'd left for Mexico, and now Jack alone sent manuscripts out all over New York, and all they did was gather dust. He continued to write, he told Carolyn, only because it seemed wasteful not to use his experience. Plagued with ugly dreams, he slept wretchedly.

From late April through June 1954, the nation sat transfixed before the TV and watched a blue-white flickering duel for power between Senator Joseph McCarthy and the United States Army. Later, most American intellectuals blamed McCarthyism on the seedy masses, pontificating that it was a traditional Midwestern populism out to devour the symbols of the cosmopolitan East. The historians were wrong; their fear of McCarthy had made them accept the elitist contempt for the masses that had created McCarthyism in the first place. Despite his personal genius for creating disorder, McCarthy came to power as a product of the Republican right wing, the foot dragging of the Southern Democrats, and what one historian called "the fear of honorable men" in the rest of America's leaders. In 1952 America had chosen the moderate Eisenhower, not the right-winger Taft; they may have been uncomfortable with Stevenson the "egghead," but there was no evidence that McCarthy ever significantly influenced their votes. Rather, he survived by manipulating the Senate, so terrifying such leading Senate progressives as Hubert Humphrey that they tried to outdo him with neofascist bills like the "Communist Control Act." His senatorial collapse was due to his lack of manners, as much as anything else. In the public opinion polls he lost because he had become a bore.

While Jack had begun to write gentle, meditative Buddhist poetry, Americans in 1954 put two kinds of books on the best-seller lists. They purchased religious material like the Revised Standard Version of the Bible and Norman Vincent Peale's *Power of Positive Thinking*. They also wallowed in the bloody adventures of Mickey Spillane's Mike Hammer. Brutalized by Buchenwald, Hiroshima, and Korea's Pork Chop Hill, half convinced that the Cold War ugliness would never end, Americans readily embraced this violent, anti-Communist superhero, and in the process made Spillane one of the best-selling authors in American history. Never before could an American hero have said, "I snapped the side of the rod across his jaw and laid the flesh to the bone . . . [a scream] cut off in the middle as I pounded his teeth back into his mouth with the end of the barrel . . . For laughs I gave him a taste of his own sap on the back of his hand and felt the bones go into splinters." Spillane's New York was filled with vermin, and Hammer, friend of blind newsies and the little guy, was the exterminator. Jack thought Spillane was a moron.

The "defense of freedom" that Mike Hammer's crusade represented was not limited to the popular culture; uptown intellectuals had their own methods as well. Early in the 1950's American writers and critics like Sidney Hook, Arthur Schlesinger, Jr., James T. Farrell, and Diana Trilling had founded the American Committee for Cultural Freedom. It was part of the world-wide Congress of Cultural Freedom, whose house organ was the journal *Encounter*, which was edited by men as renowned as Irving Kristol and Stephen Spender. The magazine projected a tone of sophistication and learning in the inarguably virtuous name of defending free inquiry. It was also a CIA front, its managing editor Melvin Lasky a CIA agent and CCF director Michael Josselman another.

Reading *Encounter*, the U.S. intellectual elite absorbed a basic CIA perspective predicated on a ferocious anti-communism that defined "freedom" as the defense of the United States and Western Europe from the Soviet Union and canonized the U.S. federal government as the ultimate arbiter of all significant debate. The invisible and pervasive CIA–*Encounter* mentality would define any divergence from the norm as sick; in the years to come the magazine would label Albert Einstein a Communist, and Jack Kerouac a lunatic.

Jack was fascinated with the theatrical qualities of Joseph McCarthy's TV program—"Point of Order, Mr. Chairman, Point of

Order," Roy Cohn's lizard eyes, the Beacon Hill folksiness of Joseph Welch—and came away from his television with several different reactions. Jack kept yelling at Lucien that "McCarthy's got the real dope on the Jews and fairies," and about that time he himself began to denounce Jews, fairies, and Commies. As Jews and homosexuals were emblematic of the publishing world to Jack, his rhetorical attacks were simply a new and more ugly side to an old frustration. Ignorant of national affairs (and fiercely anti-authoritarian), Jack discovered that politics was an area where he could easily propitiate his parental guilts by adopting Leo's traditional Roman Catholic anti-Communism. When Neal's friend Al Hinkle became enamored of radical politics, Jack castigated him as a fool who represented not sturdy American dissent but treason. Yet his nightmares kept bothering him. Around that time Jack dreamed of a mass prison breakout in the Mississippi River Valley, the heart of the nation. As he transcribed his night visions, he added, "I feel sickened by the cowardice and hysteria of America become so blind as to misrecognize the freedom needs of imprisoned men 'Communists' or not."

He revealed his feelings about the times in a story he wrote during the hearings called "cityCityCITY." A science fiction tale that owed much to Aldous Huxley and William Burroughs, "City" was set on a future earth totally covered by steel plates and apartments several miles deep. All babies were born at Central Deactivator, where a Deactivator disk was riveted in their breastbone, permanently linking them to the Computer of Infinite Merit, which controlled everything on Earth from Master Center Love. Women controlled the computer, but were generous with their inferiors, men and children. All citizens had access to a TV called a "Brow Vision Set," a rubber disk on the forehead that produced total sensation. There was also 17-JX, a delightful somalike drug.

Two things disturbed the somnambulistic serenity of the City. The extraordinary population pressure required the occasional extinction by mass electrocution of those blocks whose deportment grades and 17-JX consumption were lowest. And there were subversives, wraiths called "Actors" who penetrated the electronic barrier that enshrouded the planet and left fumes that hipsters trapped and sniffed, fumes which blocked the soma and allowed people to think again.

M-80 was a goofy thirteen-year-old boy whose father, T-3, was administrator for his block. The story began with M-80's astonished discovery of a puddle of water: In the land of machines, water was controlled by pipes, and M-80 had never seen water except from a faucet. Being different in the City was a punishable offense, and the mechanical aberration cost M-80's block its life. T-3 went to the council to defend his community, but his enemy G-92, who had "carefully cultivated for years, to advertise himself as a tireless champion of some kind, for some cause, whatever cause they wanted," blocked any humanity, prevented even a farewell speech, and sent T-3 back to die in his home, Zone 38383939383–338373.

Hip and funny, "cityCityCITY" neatly expressed Jack's disgust at the technocracy that smothered him, and G-92 was a precisely inscribed portrait of "Tail-Gunner Joe McCarthy." To Jack, freedom was a spiritual rather than economic or political quality. One should free oneself of attachment, see all as illusion, and enter the void.

So Jack tended a little garden in his backyard, fought with Mémère in the crudely friendly manner of "buddies" that they had fashioned from their mutual needs—Lucien came to dinner and was shocked to hear him call her "you dirty whore"—and tried to get by. He worked two days as a brakeman for the New York Dock Railway, but his arm swelled and he had to quit.

It was at this low moment that his frustrated professional life began to move toward success. In May he found his first—and only—serious agent, Sterling Lord. Lord was a sophisticated man with a genuine love of literature, a fine taste in wines, and a French wife, all of which endeared him to Jack and Mémère. "Trust in the Lord" became their slogan. If in the end Jack's closest friends thought Lord a businessman more interested in sensation than literature, his presence was reassuring in 1954. At the same time, Malcolm Cowley sent Jack's work to Arabelle Porter of *New World Writing*, who bought an excerpt Cowley had taken from *On the Road* called "Jazz of the Beat Generation," which was published the following year. "Invitation to Innovators," Cowley's August 21 article in *Saturday Review*, singled out Jack as the man who invented the phrase "beat generation," whose "unpublished narrative 'On the Road' is the best record of their lives." It was a beginning.

In Richmond Hill, Jack continued with his Buddhist studies, although he began to equivocate. He concluded that he was more a flexible Taoist than a Buddhist ascetic, because the character flaws that prevented him from holding a normal job also made asceticism too difficult. Too weak, too sensual, and too sensitive to cope, he withdrew one step from normal reality through alcohol and Buddhism into a private and internal sanctuary, as he later wrote, "to see the world from the viewpoint of solitude and to meditate upon [it] without being embroiglio'd [sic] in its actions, which by now have become famous for their horror and abomination . . . a man of Tao, who watches the clouds and lets history rage beneath." He showed his manuscript of *The Subterraneans* to Mardou and Gregory Corso, who had settled in the Village. Years later Corso would say of the book that it "was very straight, it wasn't fiction, and that's what I say is so good about it." Now Jack thought Gregory was "contemptuous," and before Mardou would return the manuscript Jack almost had to break her door down. Jack fled his confused pain again, getting drunk with Lucien and also writing two pieces on Buddhism. The first defined life as "A Dream Already Ended," and replicated the *Diamond Sutra* in Jack's own language, a new solo on an ancient riff. "The Little Sutra" condemned Allen's cherished concept of twinkly-eyed Chaplinesque love as nothing but hypocritical Western lust, and repeated the commandments to suffer and be kind.

Jack's thriving faith was evident in his West Coast correspondence. In April he had written a snide note to the Cassadys informing them that the world—including the pork chops they had quarreled about—was all dancing illusion painted on the water. Given a little time to overcome his anger, Jack was soon writing friendly love notes to Carolyn, interspersed with lectures that life was a dream, that only Dharmakaya, the Truth Essence, was real. Carolyn should endure suffering and practice pity toward poor, tortured Neal, whose anxious self-hatred was merely the product of non-enlightenment, of not having seen beyond the transitory. Neal had taken a Rorschach Test, and the psychiatrists had classified him as prepsychotic, anxiety prone, sadistic, and generally sick. Jack advised Carolyn that she *knew* how wild her man was, while the doctors only measured it. In Jack's view, Neal mostly needed love.

When Carolyn caught Neal and Allen having sex together in August and evicted Allen in a manner that reminded Ginsberg of his mother's paranoia, Jack shrugged benevolently and tried to soothe everyone's feelings from three thousand miles away. A month after the incident, Carolyn wrote to Allen and invited him to visit. By then Allen had a suit and tie, a market research job, a hip and pretty girlfriend named Sheila, a developing network of San Francisco poet friends that included Kenneth Rexroth and Robert Duncan, and another problem. Bill was still ravenously in love with him and had left Tangiers in September 1954 to join Allen in San Francisco. Burroughs' romantic technique employed the cruel strength of the dependent lover—"You don't love me anymore!"—to seduce the now temporarily straightened out Allen. Neal was of no use in this crisis, since he spent his time off the railroad either in bed masturbating, lecturing on Cayce, or playing chess.

When Bill stopped in Richmond Hill on his way west to San Francisco, Jack was begrudgingly involved in the affair. Jack watched Bill write love letters to Allen and pondered what a mysterious, terrifying man Burroughs was, remembering what the demon of junk and boys had written to him earlier in the year: "I say we are here in *human form* to learn by the human hieroglyphs of love and suffering . . . it is a duty to take this risk, to love and feel without defense or reserve." Trying to reassure his former teacher, Jack lied that Allen still wanted to be with Burroughs or he would not have written; actually, he thought Allen had ditched Bill because he was too bizarre. Gilding the truth produced several letters of accusation, denial, explanation, and argument among the three of them, with Jack serving as a foil for other people's pain. He had pain enough of his own, and grew further aggravated by the way Burroughs totally ignored his Buddhism. Infuriated, Jack denounced the way Allen had involved him in the love problems of homosexuals— about which he vowed he knew nothing—and accused Allen of being the devil, although he conceded that he might be insulting an angel as well. The lovers, Jack said, would have to face each other in mutual confession, while he planned to be celibate and break the wheel of birth and death by relinquishing lust.

It was October, Jack's month of breezy absolution and cleansing. He was working on a piece about Lowell when the autumn leaf smell blew down from New England and across the industrial wasteland of Richmond Hill, teasing his nose and memories; he got on the subway to Port Authority terminal and caught a bus to his hometown. Too ghostlike and mysterious and mentally far away to stay with GJ or the Sampas family, Jack slept at the skid-row Depot Chambers Hotel and walked mile after mile around town, recognizing old friends as he passed unnoticed. His Japanese plaid shirt, white crepe-sole shoes, blue jacket and brown corduroy trousers felt effeminate in Lowell, but he chomped on crisp red apples, puffed on a corncob pipe, and tried to transcend his fears and comprehend the town and his life there. Mary Carney was the only old friend whom he approached, but their silent parlor visit in front of the television was stiff, and he was glad to flee after a couple of hours.

In Lowell the only appropriate place for a sorrowful mystic was in church, and there he came alive. Immersed in the light of the stained-glass windows and the odors of incense and candle flame, he had a mystical experience, his first in twenty-eight years. It seemed as if the statue of the Virgin Mary had turned to bless him. More deeply than ever before, the term "beat" made sense to Jack, signified "beatific," holy, compassionate, the ungrasping affection of the downtrodden. As he knelt before the candles and crucifix, only the quality of his feeling mattered, and his devotion to Buddha was renewed and strengthened, his seeking after salvation confirmed in a moment of profound catharsis.

Walking down 52nd Street back in New York City, Jack saw Norman Mailer with his new wife, Jack's one-time girlfriend Adele Morales, and Manhattan seemed like a carnival; rather than go to Richmond Hill, he headed down to his new hangout, the Montmartre Bar, where he met the gifted young pianist Cecil Taylor and had a memorable evening. Better still, Allen came east for his brother Eugene's wedding in mid-December 1954, and their meeting at the San Remo was sweet. Allen felt beautiful in a good tweed suit and close-cropped head, and listened respectfully to Jack's lectures on his religious discoveries. Late in November, Jack had said that he had decided to stop letter writing, drinking, and all nondisciple friendships in a final effort to break his dualism and enter the light. The simple act of eating cornflakes and sugar made him consider that taste itself was only an arbitrary conception.

With Allen once again seated across from him, he continued his teaching in a more humble mood, acknowledging that he was too drunken and ignorant to be a teacher; they were fellow seekers before the awesome Way. Thumping his manuscripts of poems, *Book of Dreams* (his own recorded dreams), and *Some of the Dharma,* he described his horror at the ignorance of the modern world, and his fear that creative but uncommitted poseurs—possibly including himself—might misappropriate Buddhism and use its images and wisdom for aesthetic reasons instead of to further the Way. Allen related his own recent experiences, especially the peyote trip he'd taken with his lady friend Sheila and Al Sublette, a journey in which the Drake Hotel's two Starlite Roof bathroom windows became the eyes in a "Golgotha-robot-eternal-smoking-machine-crowned visage." Later Allen would call it "Moloch."

Starved for a responsive audience, Jack dominated their talk with his analysis of Buddhism as a fellaheen thing, not of Lowell the town or megalopolitan New York, but of the desert and the mountains. While in Lowell he'd dreamed of visiting Thoreau's hut at Walden Pond and finding a small box full of marijuana, and he was sure that it meant that his faith needed to live in the wilderness to survive. Surely it could never bloom in New York, where he drank and took Benzedrine and goofballs and dope, where hard-headed Catholic Mémère scorned his faith in Buddhism, the publishers ridiculed him, and the police investigated his income. Joan Haverty still wanted child support, and the whole subject panicked him. On December 19, 1954, he wrote in his journal that he was "AT THE LOWEST BEATEST EBB OF MY LIFE . . . CONSIDERED A CRIMINAL AND INSANE AND AN IMBECILE, MY SELF SELF-DISAPPOINTED AND ENDLESSLY SAD BECAUSE I'M NOT DOING WHAT I KNEW SHOULD BE DONE A WHOLE YEAR AGO." In the desperate rote of a man on the edge of an abyss, he repeated that he must hew to the Way, walking calmly, practicing charity and sympathy to all "the hedgings and cavils of the world," so as to enter the bright holiness through his mind essence. With no attachments, no sense-dependencies like drugs or false emotions, no fame, he might yet "free himself and release his own mind."

In mid-January of 1955, Jack went to court to contest Joan's paternity suit and demand for child support, and saw Joan for the first time in four years. She had converted to Catholicism, which intrigued him, and she scoffed a little at the material on Buddhism he packed about in a large manila envelope. The real shock came when she showed him a snapshot of four-year-old Janet Michele; after years of noisy denial, Jack privately acknowledged to Joan that she was probably his daughter. Though he revered the abstract idea of the family, Jack knew that he could not live a nine-to-five life; if he could not support Mémère, he could not support a daughter. He maintained his public denial of paternity and produced a letter from a VA doctor that documented his phlebitis and inability to work, and the judge set aside Joan's warrant. So long as Jack avoided riches or fame, he was free of his monetary obligations to Janet. So long as he and Mémère stayed totally out of her daughter's life, Joan wrote several years later, she didn't much care.

Relieved but disoriented by a sense of impending death after this brush with the world of social responsibility, Jack got on the subway to go home, his fellow passengers unseen as he repeated that they were not real, that only mind essence was real. At home he redoubled his efforts in meditation, memorizing the Great Dharma of Lord Buddha's Crown Samadhi, reciting it on his knees, even though the pain and swelling required him to tape his legs. Though he still drank wine, popped amphetamines and smoked cigarettes, he felt sufficiently committed to the Way—and revolted by the commercialism of the publishing business—to order his agent Sterling Lord to pull back his manuscripts and cancel his "career," because from now on his writing would be strictly Buddhist. Mercurial as always, he allowed Lord to dissuade him, but focused on his meditations, one long dhayana (meditation) a day, since it took him at least twenty minutes to quiet his mind. In the ache of his chastity he realized suddenly that his practices involved mind *and* body, that his football-trained muscles could help him to reach Nirvana. As a form of piety he translated Tibetan sutras from the French and read secondary scholars, though he always preferred the emotional brilliance of the sutras themselves.

By February he was peaceable and satisfied. He told Allen that he had had a "dhyana of complete understanding," and while he was perhaps not so advanced as that, he had come to understand physically that life was but a flickering dream, breaking into a plane of tranquillity that was altogether new to him. Later that month he moved to North Carolina to help build Nin's new home and babysit for his nephew Paul, and his serenity did not dissipate immediately. In fact, he tried to build on it, reaching out to the Cassadys. Wry, gentle, and compassionate, he confessed his guilt at their last quarrels, assuming full responsibility but reminding Neal that they were brothers, and there should be no crap between them.

Jack wrote at his most vulnerable and hungover, because he had lost a god the week before. Charlie Parker died in New York City on his birthday, March 12, 1955, one year older to the day than Jack. Although Jack tried to be flippant about it, his jokes were the defensive wit of a battered man.

Having already urged Allen to publish Neal's wild prose piece from 1951, the "Joan Anderson Letter," Jack exhorted Cassady to continue writing, assuring him that he was the best writer in America, a peer of Proust, blessed with an ear for the speech origins of language that far surpassed his own gifts in *On the Road.* Jack assumed that Carolyn disapproved of Neal's work because it was so sexual—a Cayce "sin"—but Jack defended it as a holy confession, and offered to type Neal's scribbles and send them back via the railroad. Chortling gently over the previous fall's crisis between Allen and Carolyn, Jack compared them to the "Three Stooges," and dismissed all their conflicts as foolish. Even Cayce and reincarnation received his homage when he speculated that Neal, who he (incorrectly) thought had been born nine months after Gerard died, might through reincarnation be his brother in flesh as well as spirit.

Though harassed by loneliness and poverty in North Carolina, Jack was beatific as he tended a huge vegetable garden, typed up his latest book *Buddha Tells Us,* an American version of the *Surangama Sutra,* and worked on a biography of the Buddha to be called *Wake Up.* Buddhism had not extinguished his ego: He told Allen that he would still be the best writer in the world, but his achievement would be measured by the thousands he might convert to the Way. Rocky Mount was like a Nether-lands landscape to him, and he felt like Cézanne—sad, deep, and serene —as he walked into the piny woods to meditate under the stars. In lighter moments he sipped a concoction of moonshine, orange juice, and ginger ale, satisfied with the companionship of his brother-in-law's two hound dogs. Mémère was Nin's housekeeper and so happy to be retired from the Blakean hell of the Brooklyn shoeshops that she was easier to get along with.

Most important, Jack's literary tensions were at least temporarily abated by the pleasure of holding the latest issue of *New World Writing* in his hands, even though his fear of Joan Haverty had led him to publish "Jazz of the Beat Generation" under the pseudonym Jean Louis. He was in good company; one of the other pieces in the volume, "Catch 18," was by another unknown writer, Joseph Heller. Later that spring the *Paris Review* would publish a section from *On the Road* called "The Mexican Girl," mellowing Jack so much that when E. P. Dutton rejected *Road* he still had enough perspective on his professional life to see it as flowers of illusion. He kept on with equanimity, particularly since Allen had been showing his manuscripts about San Francisco. Kenneth Rexroth, the reigning experimental critic in the Bay Area, had focused on Jack in a radio show about that issue of *New World Writing,* and compared him favorably with Céline and Genet.

Nothing happened. *New World Writing* had reactivated Jack's hopes for publication, and all through May he waited for news from Lord; insensitive to Jack's excitement and an undependable correspondent in any case, Lord often allowed weeks to pass without a word. Allen com-forted Jack with the thought that "I guess you're going mad in a way, as the termination of the process of consciousness of vision . . . but as Carl [Solomon] said, Everything that's going to happen has happened already, so DON'T FLIP." Jack, in his turn, replied sympathetically to Allen's struggles as a poet. Jewish writers had achieved national importance, he wrote, but overlooked their own best bard, Ginsberg, who would one day, Jack promised, be acknowledged as a hero. Jack's letters mixed occasional inanity with compassion, as when he assured Allen that he had progressed past enlightenment, past Buddhism because it too was an arbitrary conception.

It was a lonely spring in Rocky Mount. His phlebitis was acting up, and Nin kept harassing him about his drinking and meditations—"You think you're God." More, he missed New York, its baseball games on bar TV's, the Village, waterfront walks, and French movies. In mid-June he borrowed ten dollars from Mémère and went to the city for a brief drunk that included long talks with Lucien Carr about death, huge orgies with Gregory Corso, an enormous new blood clot on his left ankle, and a jangling set of business news.

Though Jack felt it was light-bringing and magical, *Buddha Tells Us* had been rejected by Malcolm Cowley and Robert Giroux, and Viking had turned down Jack's request of $25 a month to finish a new, Buddhist, "epic" *Road*. More positively, he sold "cityCityCITY" to *New American Reader* and offered *New World Writing* a few more stories. Cowley and another editor at Viking named Keith Jennison continued to be interested in the original *Road*, and on July 19, 1955, Cowley wrote to assure him of its publication, promising to write a foreword for the book, which was to be entitled *The Beat Generation*. In addition, Cowley had secured a $300 loan for Jack from the National Institute of Arts and Letters. Even though there was still no contract, Jack felt glorious.

Reassured by the news, a beautiful pleading invitation from Allen, and a gift of $25 from Allen's brother Eugene Brooks, Jack took off to summer in Mexico. In September he would visit San Francisco before returning to live—like his heroes Thoreau, Dickinson, Blake—in a cottage somewhere in the country; as Al Sublette had once said, all Jack really wanted was a "thatched hut in Lowell," and he was getting closer.

Two hundred and twelve Orizaba Street, Mexico City, presented a stoned and creative atmosphere after too much North Carolina boredom. Jack had the little adobe hut on the roof, with Burroughs' old junkie friend Bill Garver down on the first floor for company, Burroughs himself having landed in North Africa. Though his abode had no water or electricity and the door was fastened by a flimsy padlock, its candlelight was a good atmosphere for his continuing studies. On Sunday he read the sutra called Dana (Charity); on Monday, Sila (Kindness); Tuesday, Ashanti (Patience); Wednesday, Vyra (Zeal); Thursday, Dyana (Tranquillity); Friday, Prajna (Wisdom); and Saturday the conclusion; the *Diamond Sutra* came every day. Sad and empty feeling, Jack daily plunked himself down in the rocking chair near Garver's own chair and listened to the old man. Garver was a twenty-year addict, the probable thief of half the overcoats stolen in Manhattan in the 1940's; by 1955 he rarely left his room, preferring to sit in purple pajamas and mutter unceasingly about Mallarmé, politics, his past, or Minoan civilization. Tall, wizard-thin and tender, Garver intrigued Jack as much as he had bored Burroughs.

Continuously stoned on marijuana and occasionally floating on a gift shot of morphine from Garver, Jack was rather sedentary during this passage in Mexico City, lost in a never-never land sealed off from the smells of the crumbling building and the gay screams of the children who played all too close to the unprotected roof edge. Wriggling into a comfortable position on Garver's bed as the soft drawl of his host's voice droned on about him, Jack began to write spontaneous poems, meditations, mind-transcriptions which he later called *Mexico City Blues.*

He was, he said, a "jazz poet blowing a long blues in an afternoon jam session on Sunday. I take 242 choruses, ideas vary, roll from chorus to chorus." A chorus was defined only by the size of his notebook page, and otherwise he simply tried to direct the flow of his mind onto paper, its twists and turns, sketching his senses, sometimes dictating pure sound. Some of the choruses were parody and three— numbers 52 through 54—were Garver's own junked-out talk. Jack's mind coursed over images of Corso, Burroughs, maps, and rivers, and belief, "in Jesus, Buddha, St. Francis, Avalokitesvara." He touched on Gerard and doves, baptism and the path of the spiritual seeker: "No direction to go/(but) (in) ward."

Garver's choruses told of his fixation on suicide by an overdose of Sodium Amytal, "Blue Heavens." Then Jack soloed on reality; "Dharma law/Say/All things is made/of the same thing/which is a nothing." A demand to Joe McCarthy to "remove my name/from the list/And Buddha's, too," followed memories of Lowell days, Papa and his cigars. *Mexico City Blues* sang the blues for real, because "I get tired/of waiting in pain/in a situation/where I ain't sure." Near the end, his nakedness of mind complete, Jack spun off a desolate expression of his spiritual odyssey:

The wheel of the quivering meat conception
Turns in the void expelling human beings,

Pigs, turtles . . .
Poor! I wish I was free
of that slaving meat wheel and safe in heaven dead.

Mexico City Blues was a playfully serious word game, an eavesdropping on his Buddhist meditations, and his land; America, Jack concluded, "is a permissible dream."

Jack continued to write after he finished the *Blues,* this time about Esperanza Villanueva, Garver's dope connection and a goddess of the slums whom Jack romantically and chastely adored. A Catholic Indian with heavy Lady Day eyes and a trembling sexuality, Esperanza was also strung out on ten grams of morphine a month. Writing in pencil by what he saw as the sacramental light of a candle, Jack transcribed her tale, changing her name from Esperanza (Hope) to Tristessa (sadness); hope did not express her junk truth, that she was, as the subtitle proclaimed, "Born to Die."

Tristessa was a religious meditation on pain as much as anything else, a tale whose cramped and knotted narrative line was wholly synchronous with its tortured subject. Following her around the slums, past the hobo Indians in shawls, the fruit stands, the pathetic displays of walnuts spread on towels on the sidewalk, Jack would go to her apartment with its kitten and dove and see the Buddha in her grim life. "I am sad because *la vida es dolorosa,"* he would say in his pidgin Spanish. She understood intuitively. When she sold her morphine on credit, Tristessa looked upward, clasped her hands, and said, "My Lord, he pay me back, *more."* Junked out himself, Jack reached to light a cigarette off the candle on her little altar, and then realized his error, begging Esperanza's pardon in French: *"Excuse mué, ma Dame."* Later it occurred to him that he had meant "Dame" as in Damema, the "mother of Buddhas." Then he recalled that Esperanza was sterile, and bemusedly wondered why he had seen motherhood in her tortured soul.

Mexico City was gentle and pleasant, but by mid-September it was time to leave for San Francisco. Jack had received the most remarkable invitation of his life, for Allen had sent him a copy of a new poem, a poem so good, so stupendously creative, that Jack's curiosity demanded he investigate what his old friend was up to in this new scene. Though Allen was planning to enter graduate school at Berkeley—Jack thought it was his natural milieu, though it would teach him nothing about writing—this new work bore Jack's jazzy-spontaneous swing, not the careful precision of academic poesy.

Jack dubbed the as-yet-untitled poem "Howl," and in terms of literary quality and social influence, it was undoubtedly the most important poem of postwar America. After years of what he now conceded was "resenting and resisting" Jack's theories, Allen had taken a deep breath and let out a Whitman "Hebraic-Melvillian bardic" shout of ecstatic rage in the midst of the twisted nation he called Moloch. Beginning with his Drake Hotel peyote vision, he wrote what he called "a lament for the Lamb in America with instances of remarkable lamblike youths":

> I saw the best minds of my generation,
> starving hysterical naked,
> dragging themselves through the negro streets
> at dawn looking for an angry fix,
> angelheaded hipsters burning for the ancient
> heavenly connection . . .

In Part II he named the villain:

> Moloch whose love is endless oil and stone! Moloch
> whose soul is electricity and banks! Moloch
> whose poverty is the specter of genius!
> Moloch whose fate is a cloud of sexless
> hydrogen . . .

In Part III Allen answered Moloch with a call addressed to his madhouse companion Carl Solomon, a cry to resist, an ideology of solidarity that brought the lament full circle into a gentle sharing: "Carl, I'm with you."

The child of sorrow and humiliations, the victim with the ashy taste of loss and self-hatred in his mouth, the nice Jewish boy from Jersey had become a prophet.

After making sure that "Howl" hadn't been rewritten—he told Allen he wanted spontaneous work or nothing—Jack was thoroughly knocked out. Traveling up the coast toward the U.S.A., he must have sensed that something profound was about to occur. His own work was edging toward publication, Burroughs was developing his writing, and this new poem— along with Allen's gossip about the exciting atmosphere in literary San

Francisco—signaled a breakthrough. The subterraneans were about to crawl blinking into the public light.

Crossing the border, Jack was something like a lyric guerrilla come to aid the poetic revolution. "LET'S SHOUT OUR POEMS IN SAN FRANCISCO STREETS" he wrote Allen. "PREDICT EARTH-QUAKES."

XI
A Revolution of Prophecy and Living Things

T HE WIND was howling and it was terribly cold in the gondola car of the train Jack was riding up the California coast toward Santa Barbara. To stay warm, he jumped around and flapped his arms and meditated on the warmth of God; his companion, a shadowy, shrunken old hobo, sat hunched in a corner with the patience of the ages. After a while, Jack pulled out some bread and cheese and wine; prompted by memories of the Charity section of the *Diamond Sutra,* he shared it with his comrade. Warmed by the wine, the old man also had a gift: He pulled out a slip of paper and shoved it gently over. Tugging it from dirty fingers, Jack read the prayer of his childhood patron, St. Teresa, and of her promise that she would someday return to earth by showering roses over all living creatures.

Jack's affection for bums was one of the fundamental ways he differed from middle-class America; he and his friends "were about transcending class," as the satirist Paul Krassner later said. "When you do this you don't feel superior to anybody," Krassner explained, "you learn from them all—the panhandlers and the hustlers. So your education is a product of experience rather than somebody else's distortion of experience."

This commitment to direct experience in all its sometime grubbiness was a particularly unusual attitude in mid-fifties America, for this was the benign and passively prosperous nation led by a Republican President who was, one critic thought, a "Truman Democrat with the arms race as WPA." The Department of the Army was far more successful than the New Deal; the U.S.A. was the fastest-growing country in history. Its GNP was $318 billion in 1950, nearly $400 billion in 1955. Its 200 largest manufacturers earned profits of $3.8 billion in 1954 and $5.2 billion in 1955. It was a consumer nation as no one had ever remotely dreamed was possible. By the middle of the decade Americans had become familiar with TV, four-engine airplanes, supermarkets, ranch homes, sophisticated food packaging, automatic transmission, power steering and brakes for their cars, air conditioners, freezers, dishwashers, garbage disposals, FM radios, power boats and tranquilizers. They played Perry Como and Patti Page on their hi-fi's, or listened to the watered-down "cool jazz" of Dave Brubeck (whom Jack disliked).

TV Guide was the major new U.S. periodical, along with *Playboy*, which had begun publication in 1953 but achieved popularity only in the prosperity of 1955. There the middle-class male could find easily digestible lessons in the right consumer goods—wine, clothing, cars, women—along with titillation. One of *Playboy*'s favorite subjects was Jayne Mansfield. Totally artificial in her bleached hair, heavy make-up, tight clothing, and phony little-girl voice, Mansfield was, as her biographer later noted, the "perfect model of the moral and sexual dishonesty of the fifties." Perhaps the symbolic moment of the era took place on July 18, 1955, when the first clean, safe, homogenized amusement park opened under the name of Disneyland.

About the time that Jack pulled into San Francisco, *Life* issued a plea: "Wanted: An American Novel." According to *Life,* most American literature was seemingly "written by an unemployed homosexual living in a packing-box shanty on the city dump while awaiting admission to the county poor house." Yet *Life* had already discovered its tough-but-affirmative voice in the aging Papa Hemingway, who had contributed fifteen pieces in as many years to the magazine. What *Life* objected to was only the style, the querulous, nose-sniffing tone of American poets and high-culture critics. As one critic pointed out, there seemed to be no artistic heresy anymore, as comfort, security, and peace of mind became the primary values of writers for the *Partisan Review,* the *Kenyon Review,* or the *Hudson Review.*

Most literary intellectuals did not adopt *Life*'s ponderous Babbittry, but too often confined themselves to writing ironic, ambiguous, remote but technically sophisticated pieces. "Thus, the arriving poet, university trained to begin with," wrote John Ciardi, critic for *Saturday Review* and Princeton faculty member, "joins a university faculty, publishes primarily in university subsidy under university editorship, reads primarily the poetry and criticism that the universities sanction or have themselves developed, and when he publishes his own slim volume (quite possibly in a university press imprint) finds it reviewed for praise or damnation by university men in university magazines."

The various "reviews" of fall 1955 included Flannery O'Connor's "The Artificial Nigger," John Crowe Ransom on critical theory, Irving Howe on Dostoyevsky, and poetry by Delmore Schwartz in the *Kenyon Review*. Though current mythology identified a massive chasm between the conservative literary aesthetes of Kenyon or Sewanee colleges and New York's hyperpolitical radical intellectuals, the *Partisan Review* ran poetry by Ransom's fellow member of the Tennessee "Fugitive" school of criticism, Robert Penn Warren, and an essay on "The Intellectuals and the Discontented Classes" by Harvard's Riesman and Glazer. It was as if American high culture were a repertory theater that had only a handful of shows, and those by playwrights of remarkably similar values and background. The shows were all too often exercises in incestuous trivia.

In fact, there were only a very few threads in any level of the culture that were not part of the gray flannel weave. One was James Dean. An intuitive, high-energy, nonintellectual and supraemotional actor not interested in pretense or theatricality, Dean was a moody bisexual devoted to drums and fast cars. He had died in a car crash on Highway 101 a day or two before Jack hitched past the same spot. Another thread was San Francisco itself; it was the end of the land, and for many reasons it was different from the rest of the country. The beauty of the setting and the Mediterranean *dolce far niente* relaxedness of the climate helped. Too, San Francisco had not experienced the Stalinist/Capitalist New York political split of the Cold War, because from World War II on it had an active Anarchist Circle that welcomed draft resisters from the Waldport, Oregon, camp and never succumbed to the rigidity characteristic of the East Coast. Perhaps the atmosphere dated all the way back to the 1840's, when the city was settled, as Kenneth Rexroth liked to point out, not by Protestant farmers and merchants like the rest of the nation, but by lunatic miners, whores, pirates, Latinos, and Asians, scarcely a WASP child of virtue among them. Maybe it was just because it was three thousand miles and two enormous mountain ranges away from New York City. But it was freer, as Allen had already discovered.

After a peaceful night on the beach at Santa Barbara under a dark and diamond universe of stars, Jack caught a ride from a gorgeous half-clad blonde driving a Mercury convertible, and very quickly ended up striding down the walk to Allen's cottage at 1624 Milvia Street in Berkeley. Allen was not the same morbid gloom monger Jack had known in New York; he was like a picture brought into tight focus for the first time, a *mensh* with a poem, a love, and a much more solid identity.

His love was named Peter Orlovsky, a dreamy refugee from a childhood spent in a Dickensian tie-making loft, a man who compared himself and his brothers—Lafcadio, Julius, Amiel, and Nicky—to the Karamazovs, a "big strange dumbbell saint," Jack thought, who guarded the gates of heaven like his namesake but was "so goofy he lets everybody in." In December 1954, nine months before Jack would arrive in Berkeley, Allen had met painter Robert La Vigne in the San Francisco artists' headquarters, Foster's Cafeteria at Polk and Sutter streets. In between Allen's stories of Willem de Kooning, Franz Kline, and the San Remo bar, he went to La Vigne's apartment, where he was transfixed by an enormous painting of a "naked boy with his legs spread," as he later described it, "and some onions at his feet, with a little Greek embroidery on the couch. He had a nice, clean-looking pecker, yellow hair, a youthful teeny little face, and a beautiful frank expression." A minute later the model, Peter, walked in. He had been La Vigne's lover, but that was about to end, and La Vigne suggested that Allen replace him. Allen was too eager, and the affair began with a period of longing and bruised feelings.

Eventually, Peter and Allen sat in Foster's and vowed mutual interpossession as Allen offered his intellect and Peter his body and love. They exchanged their pledge: "I do, I do, you promise? Yes, I do." As Allen later recalled, "at that instant we looked in each other's eyes and there was a kind of celestial cold fire that crept over us and blazed up and illuminated the entire cafeteria and made it an eternal place." Jack wrote offering his approval from Mexico City, and then Allen took another major step. After months of tortuous psychoanalysis, his psychiatrist deprecated his self-doubts and said, "Why don't you do what you want?" Since Allen was afraid of being free to write poems, get high, and live with Peter, he raised various "square" objections. In a moment of common sensitivity, the psychiatrist smiled and replied, "Oh, you're a nice person; there's always people who will like you." Shortly thereafter Allen wrote a report at work that led to his job's being replaced by a computer, began to collect unemployment, and made the changes in his life that two months later in the summer of 1955 had allowed him to write "Howl."

•   •   •

Allen's Milvia Street garden cottage was a simple room and kitchen-ette furnished with pillows, floor mats, a bookcase with Catullus and Pound and a Webcor phonograph stocked with Bach and Ella Fitzgerald. Charmed by the scent of mint and tomatoes, Jack felt comfortable there. After he and Allen had shared their news, Allen told him of the upcoming big event. He had organized a poetry reading at the Six Gallery in San Francisco; in two weeks he would read in public for the first time.

Neal showed up in one of his usual junky cars and zoomed them over the Bay Bridge, first to Vesuvio's, a North Beach bohemian bar, and then to the Six Gallery, an old garage with white walls, a dirt floor, one toilet whose door didn't lock—an audience and a stage. They were amazed to discover on their arrival that the Gallery was packed with well over a hundred people. Kenneth Rexroth, the M.C. and Papa-critic of avant-garde San Francisco, greeted them with his gurgling half growl, half smile; in honor of the event he'd gone to Goodwill that day and come away with a spiffy gangster-pinstripe suit.

Allen's talent for organization had surfaced when another poet had asked him to organize a reading at the Six Gallery. Bustling about in his role as producer, Allen selected as readers himself, a young poet named Michael McClure, whom he'd met at a party for W.H. Auden, and Jack and Neal's old friend Philip Lamantia. Rexroth had suggested he see a young student of Oriental languages named Gary Snyder. Just back from a summer of work in the high Sierras, Snyder was fixing his bicycle in the yard of his Berkeley cabin when he saw "a cat with a flannel suit and tie and glasses . . . kind of sneaking around the corner." They shared some tea, talked of their mutual interest in William Carlos Williams, and Allen read some of Snyder's poems with the comment "Well, this is all right." Gary suggested his Reed College classmate Philip Whalen, and "Six Poets [the five readers plus Rexroth] at the Six Gallery" was born. Its birth announcement was a postcard Allen sent out: "Six poets at Six Gallery. Remarkable collection of angels . . . serious poetry, free satori . . . charming event."

The crowd warmed to the poetry immediately and discarded the usual silent decorum of poetry audiences when Jack collected money and brought back giant jugs of Burgundy, wandering about the room to offer everyone a healthy slug while cheerfully murmuring in chorus with Neal a running series of "Wow!" and "Yes!" Lamantia—whom Jack found a bit too delicate—read the poems of his late friend John Hoffman. Then came McClure, at twenty-three the youngest reader, a poet influenced by abstract expressionist painters and biology whose aim was "a new and truly wild and noble chivalry of blood fire and meat. No bullshit, the spirit finally and totally, violently freed." He read his elegy "For the Death of 100 Whales." By then Jack was leading a chorus of "Go!" "Go!" cheers to the rhythm of his thumping jug, and the room was starting to rock. Philip Whalen took the reading to a 10:45 P.M. break with poems like the hilarious yet deadly serious "Plus Ça Change."

Then came Allen. Few but Jack had ever read "Howl" before. Allen began slowly: "I saw the best minds of my generation,/starving hysterical naked,/dragging themselves through the negro streets at dawn . . ." But by the time he had reached the Part II declamation of Moloch he was rhapsodic in prophecy, swaying on his planted feet, a cantor wailing out doom, crying with brothers and sisters who were momentarily as caught up as he. It was, as Lamantia later said, "like bringing two ends of an electric wire together." Visible in the fire of that arc was the fact that inside the Six Gallery was a community radically different from the America outside.

These few pilgrims were mystics who rejected materialism and rationalism as the highest level of reality in a nation that went to church but believed in a mechanical universe, a nation that felt man was nature's master and was capable of perfection, a people who celebrated optimism, consumerism, and conformity. One tenth of all college students wanted a job that was particularly creative, and two thirds of all adults believed that Communist-written books should be banned. Three quarters of all high school students felt that obedience was the single most important virtue. As one of the few radical periodicals, *Liberation*, put it six months after the Six Gallery reading, "Power is everywhere openly or secretly idolized . . . those who should furnish vision and direction are silent or echoing old ideas in which they scarcely believe themselves." The language of the time was of euphemism: police action, coexistence, pinko.

"Howl" had rent the muffling cloak of euphemism with a burst of creative inspiration, and suddenly the poets were aware that the desire and talent for readings, for poetry itself, still existed. Snyder and Whalen had all thought of themselves as essentially solitary, and only Lamantia had ever read in public before; now they knew that they weren't the only freaks, but rather members of a tribe, of a poetic resistance. Allen roared on, and the tribe was dumfounded. There was magic in the Six Gallery that night.

It could not have been easy for Gary Snyder to follow all that with his poem about the Indian myth figure Coyote, "The Berry Feast," but he did, and Jack was particularly impressed. Later he wrote that Snyder's "voice was deep and resonant and somehow brave, like the voice of old time American heroes and orators." Jack went along with the poets to Sam Wo for a post-reading Chinese supper, and as Snyder showed him how to order and use chopsticks, all the while telling humorous Zen anecdotes, Jack became more and more intrigued with him.

The reading night of October 13, 1955, had been significant for Jack, for in its course he made several friends and a later enemy. Rexroth was the man he would eventually antagonize. At a jolly planning meeting a week before the reading, Jack had pulled his mustache and kissed him, but Rexroth was a man with a passionate and constantly shifting "shit list," and he would swiftly place Jack the non–San Franciscan on it. Born in 1905, Rexroth had been a late member of the 1920's "Chicago Renaissance" with Carl Sandburg, Theodore Dreiser, and Vachel Lindsay, and had then moved on to San Francisco. An authentic and independent radical, Rexroth had taken part in the wartime "Libertarian Circle," and through his KPFA radio program—itself a mark of San Francisco's unique freedom—he encouraged poetry in an anti-academic atmosphere that reflected his work in the woods and the longshoreman Harry Bridges more than any academic scene.

A second major figure for Jack's future (though not till a few years later) was Lawrence Ferlinghetti, who also attended the reading. With a background that included a B.A. from the University of North Carolina, the rank of lieutenant commander after nearly five years in the U.S. Navy, a Columbia M.A., a Ph.D. from the Sorbonne, and his present occupation as a merchant, Ferlinghetti should have been out of place. He wasn't. Later he would insist that his dissertation title was *The History of the Pissoir in French Literature;* his business was in fact the hippest bookstore in America. Graduate school on the Boulevard St. Michel had made him an aesthete with a taste for Parisian life. Early in the fifties Ferlinghetti had left New York for San Francisco—"the only place I knew of," he said, "where you could get decent wine cheap"—and in 1953 he was a partner in the City Lights Bookstore, probably the first paperback bookstore in the country.

The original idea was for the shop to support a magazine of the same name. The magazine soon folded and Ferlinghetti's partner sold out, but they never could get the store doors closed. A coffeehouse without the coffee, City Lights' late hours and relaxed ambience made it an instant and ongoing success. In the French tradition, Ferlinghetti decided to open a publishing house over his store, and so he created the Pocket Poets series—inexpensive, democratic, one of literary America's finer traditions. By 1955 he had published his own *Pictures of the Gone World*, and for 1956 he'd scheduled books by Kenneth Rexroth and Kenneth Patchen. A day after the Six reading he telegraphed Allen offering to publish "Howl."

Philip Whalen, "180 pounds of poet meat" as Jack described him, Jack had immediately liked when they met at the reading. Later he swore to Phil that meeting him and Snyder had been the secret, unfathomable reason that had drawn him back to California against his will. Imperturbably puffing on his pipe, Phil always seemed a touchstone of calm wisdom to Jack, and though his background—rural Oregon, the Army, Reed College—was quite unlike Jack's, they got on well. Whalen had eaten peyote that summer of 1955, and it had loosened him tremendously, so when Gary had written about the reading he had come to San Francisco. A student of Buddhism, he felt alien in America, and was charmed by Jack, who had such deep ethnic roots, from the way he ate to the authors —Balzac, Proust, Rabelais—with whom he identified.

But it was Gary Snyder who was Jack's new hero. He seemed like Walt Whitman—

> Me imperturbe, standing at ease in Nature,
> Master of all or mistress of all, aplomb in
>   the midst of irrational things,
> Imbued as they, passive, receptive, silent as they,
> Me wherever my life is lived, o to be self-balanced
>   for contingencies . . .

Like a piece of oak he was, close-grained, balanced, strong and beautiful, his "peace and purposefulness" wondrous to Jack. Here at last was a hip, energetic man hung up neither on Ginsbergian intellectualities nor the aimless frenzy of Neal. Just before the reading Jack had come off a ruinous binge that left him wrung out, tortured with dream premonitions of his own death that somehow evoked Gerard as well; he had been hanging out with Neal at the racetrack, caught up in Cassady's driving and constant get-high. Worse still, Neal now lived in Los Gatos, a suburb sixty miles south of San Francisco, in a new house without a guest bedroom. There were no peaceful dinners with Carolyn on this visit, only hurtling flights over the San Francisco hills and bejabbering Cayce monologues.

Jack had first met Snyder on his way to the pre-Reading meeting with Rexroth. As Jack and Allen had waited for the other poets on a street corner in North Beach, Jack noticed a small, tough man, "wiry, suntanned, vigorous, open," toting a rucksack stuffed with books. Except for expensive hiking boots, Snyder wore the durable working-class corduroy and flannel Jack favored, and the sharp contrast between Snyder's work shirt and Allen's suit formed Jack's first impression of the man. Later, when Jack told him of his experience with the St. Teresa–prayer-carrying hobo, Gary pronounced the old man a Bodhisattva, a Buddhist "saint," and the harmony of their class and religious sensitivities led them swiftly into intimacy.

A few nights later, Jack strolled over to Gary's cottage to be charmed by its functional beauty and by Gary himself. The Zen-simple place on Berkeley's Hillegass Street was furnished with straw mats and orange crates stuffed with books of poetry and on Oriental religion, and bespoke an ordered, contemplative life. They talked late into the night about the poems of Han Shan that Gary was translating. After two years of talk about a solitary mountain shack, Jack had found the guide who could lead him there. Like his master the Chinese spiritual pioneer and hermit Han Shan, Gary was a "poet, mountain man, Buddhist man of solitude" able to live, Jack thought, "purely and true to himself." His poetry—about campfires, bear shit, work and trees and Coyote—was a "rip rap (steps) on the slick rock of Metaphysics," Snyder said. He wrote short, tough, simple words whose goal, in the words of one critic, was to "enable the traveler to ascend—to ascend on earth, not to slide back nor to fly." His poems re-created the wilderness in the mind, not a flowers-and-Bambi fantasy but the real thing: "the city's not so big, the/hills surround it." Gary had eaten of the bear of solitude, had experienced the confrontation with one's soul of a lone traveler in the wilderness. It was a lesson that sociable, gregarious Jack desperately needed to learn if he was to be a full-fledged bhikku, a true religious pilgrim. More, Snyder had what he called his "greatly enjoyed tricks of living on nothing" to cope with the economic realities of the city.

Gary was twenty-five when he met Jack, having grown up on a scratch farm in Washington. A childhood burn had made him bedfast for several months and opened his mind to books, especially the glorious

Indian studies of Ernest Thompson Seton; throughout his youth Indian lore and old I.W.W. anarchist stories were his companions as he roamed, whenever possible, in the woods. Zen Buddhism captured his imagination and became the core of his life. After graduating from Reed College in 1951, he went to Indiana University to study anthropology but left after a semester to pursue Asian languages at Berkeley. At the time he met Jack he was preparing to enter a Zen monastery in Japan. I.W.W. anarchist, student of American Indians, Zen student, Gary was first of all a woods child, an initiate of the path Jack sought. Snyder had had his troubles. Once married, now divorced, he had also been blacklisted out of the Forestry Service as a radical; Jack the rabid anti-Communist thought he'd probably espoused anarchism at some meeting, and dismissed the charge as foolish.

Jack and Gary's relationship wasn't simple adoration on Jack's part. Gary had already read "Jazz of the Beat Generation" in *New World Writing* and was much interested in its author. A few nights after the Han Shan talk, Allen, Philip, and Jack visited him with wine and manuscripts, and he read *Mexico City Blues,* which he later called "the greatest piece of religious poetry I've ever seen." The four of them had a wonderful evening of poetic communion, Gary and Allen arguing about Ezra Pound, whom Jack had discovered only a year before. Late that night the three visitors returned to their homes, walking through the peaceful autumn college-town streets singing and laughing. It was perhaps the best October Jack had ever known.

Jack differed from Gary in his practice of Buddhism, for he thought of himself as a "dreamy" Mahayana Buddhist, concerned only with mitigating the first truth of suffering with compassion, and felt that Gary's Zen studies were rather intellectual. A few years later he would say that "Zen ideas are only technical explanations without tears and truth," and in a bitter moment still later, that Zen was "the invention of [the Hindu God] Mara the Tempter . . . The Devil's personal war against the essential teaching of Buddha." In truth, it was as Snyder said, "a split that didn't exist." Zen was part of Mahayana, differing from it in practice and style, most notably in the use of koans, mind-cracking questions flung at a student by his or her Roshi (teacher), as the student had to "spit forth truth or perish." Koans were designed to derail the mind from its ordinary sequential thought pattern and release it into an extended realm of spontaneous nonconceptual perception. Though it was a highly organized system of meditation based on an intricate philosophy, this form of Zen

—Rinzai Zen—operated in so subtle a region of the mind that few Westerners could appreciate it, except in association with certain practices subsidiary to the koans and sitting meditation, such as archery, flower arranging, painting, or haiku. There the student labored over an art form until the technique became transcended into artlessness, the art and the artist one. In such a state of clarity, the action attained the pure preconceptual élan of spontaneity—freedom after total discipline. Then the bowman aims not at his target but at himself; the mind gone, the enlightened one is aimless, egoless, purposeless, "childlike" and uncalculating, and wholly alive.

The first koan was said to date from the time that Sakayamuni, the Buddha, gave a discourse by silently sitting in front of his disciples with a flower in his hand; only Maha Kasyapa smiled, and he would inherit the teachings. Obsessed with death and sin, Jack could follow Buddha's truths in an emotional and ethical way, but could not step off into the no-zone terrors of Zen where everything—intellect, emotion, spirit—was discarded. His approach to Buddhism was more prayer than meditation, and where Zen was of the present, Jack was fascinated by the pageant of *Lotus Sutra* eschatology and legend. The Master Bo Shan argued that the koans and stories were designed to generate the "I chin," the doubt sensation. Already consumed in doubts, Jack preferred to contemplate his and Gary's favorite saint, Avalokitesvara, the Kwannon Bosatsu, the Bodhisattva of Compassion, the Buddha of the human voice. Part of the *Surangama Sutra* said of him, "His body of love he keeps under control like thunder that shakes the world; his thought of compassion resembles a great mass of cloud from which a rain of the Dharma comes down like nectar, destroying the flames of evil passions. [His is] a most exquisite voice, a voice that surveys the world . . . that excels all the voices of the world."

Like any student whose ideal Roshi happened to be Han Shan, Jack had to go into the mountains. Late in October he went climbing for a weekend with Gary and a friend named John Montgomery, a wilderness sojourn that would focus his feelings on Buddhism, nature, and himself into an epiphany that may well have been the most tranquilly happy moment of his life.

John was an odd duck, a librarian whose witty stream of surreal babble entertained them as they drove toward the Matterhorn, in the country east of Yosemite Park. Jack made them stop at a bar that night for a drink—wine was too heavy to carry in their rucksacks—and though he grew disgusted with the mighty hunter oafs lurching about, the Christian Brothers Port did its mellow duty, and they were pacific as they went to sleep.

After a fine country breakfast, for good luck, Gary drew the first mandala Jack had ever seen, and they set out. Floating on the rhythm of the trail, Jack crowed with the joy of a new convert, enthusing over the superiority of nature to boozing in North Beach's The Place, his new San Francisco hangout. Snyder reproved him with a stern voice and a twinkling eye. "Comparisons are odious," he said. "It's all the same old void." Montgomery's flood of chatter might have proven distracting to them, but early on John realized that he would have to return and put antifreeze in the car, and catch up with them later. Quieted by the sorcery of the Matterhorn, they hiked through fields tinged with the red of low-bush huckleberries as past lives flashed through Jack's mind. Moving higher, they had to clamber up a boulder field, dancing from rock to rock in a stark world of wind and water and stone until they reached a ledge and camped for the night.

Words were impotent, and Jack described the moment simply: "Here now, the earth was a splenderous thing." Gary's most exquisite lesson was the harmony Jack felt at that moment, not a "harmony *with* nature," as a critic said of Gary's poetry, "but an inner human harmony that was equivalent to the natural external harmony." Through Gary, Jack had dredged out of his intuition the philosophical meaning of the word ecology, and he revealed it in his description, two years later in a book he called *The Dharma Bums,* of two speck-humans and a universe of stone called the Matterhorn.

This was six years before Rachel Carson's *Silent Spring;* Jack had no understanding of a scientific ecological view. But "as in most other things," Gary said, "he had a strong natural intuitive sense of interconnection, Karma." All is one. Having rejected the path of Aristotelian yes/no logic, Jack sensed the indivisibility, the interdependence of life, the true subject of ecology. Or as Gary put it in a poem written at this time, homo sapiens was not an ideal, not a creation apart, but

> A skin bound bundle of clutchings
> unborn and with no place to go
> Balanced on the boundless compassion
> Of diatoms, lava, and chipmunks.

Snyder's love for the American Indian culture stemmed in part from a recognition that theirs was the only ecologically sane model available in postwar America, sane in the sense of preserving earth's life cycle, and sane in nurturing the full potential of humans as well. "As poet," he wrote, "I hold the most archaic values on earth. They go back to the late Paleolithic: the fertility of the soil, the magic of animals, the power-vision in solitude, the terrifying initiation and rebirth, the love and ecstasy of the dance, the common work of the tribe. I try to hold both history and wilderness in mind, that my poems may approach the true measure of things and stand against the unbalance and ignorance of our times." History may well demonstrate Snyder's poetic vision to be the most significant and enduring of all those produced by the San Francisco poetry renaissance.

As Gary had predicted, there was no need for wine in the clean thin air of their ledge, the mountain looming above them and the roar of silence in their ears. They had tea and talked a bit. Jack captivated Gary when he told him of his special prayer, which listed people—friends, enemies—"so and so equally empty, equally to be loved, equally a coming Buddha." Then they meditated, Jack in turn impressed that Gary did so with his eyes open, the two of them poised on the lip of space as night fell. They passed an hour after dinner as Gary pointed out constellations. Just before they slept, he gave Jack his prayer beads— in return, he said, for the special prayer. Impressed with Gary's sense of charity, Jack slipped off to sleep remorseful about his boozy, wastrel life, but vowing to do better. He had no nightmares that night.

In the morning John joined them, and they pushed on, Gary leading the way up the scree; the path grew steeper and steeper, the wind began to howl like the authentic wrath of God, and Jack's legs turned to lead. John quit, but Jack pushed on, his lungs on fire with faster and faster gasps. Disturbing déjà-vu sensations disoriented him, and he pondered the Zen saying, "When you get to the top of the mountain, keep climbing." He heard Gary's shout of triumph from the top, but couldn't respond, depleted by fear and exhaustion. Suddenly Gary whizzed by, almost running down the mountainside, and Jack divined that *"it's impossible to fall off mountains you fool"* and leaped after him into the void, yelling with joy as he grasped, satori-like, that "you just have to *do* it."

As they cut along a deer trace back to the car, for the moment Jack felt he was a dharma bum, a member of those "who refuse," as Gary said, "to subscribe to consumption," a commando in the "rucksack revolution of drop outs." Gary was a sophisticated political thinker who sought a "hopefully decentralized anarcho-syndicalism as ultimate goal," and Jack couldn't accept his entire message. Essentially apolitical, Jack tried to follow Confucius and "avoid the authorities," but he was happy, back in town, to outfit himself at the Army–Navy store with a good sleeping bag of his own, a fine nylon poncho, cook pots, and a rucksack—all that he needed for self-sufficiency.

November passed pleasantly, sweetened by an encouraging letter from Malcolm Cowley, who continued to promise publication of *On the Road*, though there was still no contract. It was enough, however, to make Jack dream of a film version of *Road* that would star Marlon Brando as Neal and Montgomery Clift as himself. His buoyant mood received a further boost from a visit to Carolyn in Los Gatos. Neal had moved into the city to live with his new love, Natalie Jackson. After years of effort Carolyn was heeding the Caycean advice to "keep still," and Neal visited her regularly. While Jack was at their home, the Cassadys also entertained the local bishop of the Unification Church. A slight young man with a puttylike face, the reverend had dropped by with his mother and aunt at the Cassadys' invitation, and had collided with Jack, who drunkenly quoted the *Diamond Sutra*, Neal, who lectured on Cayce, and Allen, who wanted to know about sex. Electrified by a good argument, the bishop changed from an effete milquetoast into a man possessed, and held his own and then some during the evening's dialogue; Jack thought he was secretly a stud, and a few years later he would utilize the evening as the inspiration for a play and movie called *Pull My Daisy.*

On November 30, 1955, Jack stopped by Neal and Natalie Jackson's apartment in San Francisco to say goodbye for a while. The city had grown too cloying for him, and he was ready to search for a clean, quiet place in the wilderness. What he found at Natalie's convinced him that he should avoid cities in the future. Neal's romance with Natalie had been special among his affairs, but it had had no effect on his massive addiction to racetrack gambling; in order to prove his betting "system," he had convinced her to forge Carolyn's signature on a $10,000 check. It had tripped her over the edge of sanity and she was paying the price. Natalie had always been thin, but now she was wasted, her eyes wild and terrified, the razor-blade scars on her wrists still livid. Riding the edge of paranoia, she kept hissing at Jack, "Now they know *everything* about you."

Neal had to go to work, and asked Jack to keep an eye on her. He was reluctant, but a quote from the Bible convinced him. Infected by her fear during the long wait for Neal's return, Jack lost his patience the way he always did in trying to explain Buddhism to his family or Allen or his girlfriends, who felt, Jack was sure, that he was a slightly daft dreamer in a serious world. "It's nothing but bullshit!" he yelled at Natalie, "God is *you*, you fool!" Later he brought a small party back to the apartment, and she quieted down. But after Neal returned and fell asleep, she went up on the roof and cut her throat. Neighbors called the police and when one policeman approached her, she backed over the edge.

Sickened with death and the city, Jack left San Francisco a few days later. In Los Gatos, he tried to comfort Neal, who had returned to Carolyn while praying for Natalie to survive the horrible karma of suicide that Cayce taught. After a short stay, Jack caught the Midnight Zipper to Los Angeles and met another hobo, who advised Jack to stand on his head every day for his phlebitis. It worked. He took a bus to Calexico, where a lonely trucker violated the rules that prohibited riders and carried Jack all the way to snowy Ohio, where another bus brought him across barren cottonfields to Rocky Mount, North Carolina, home for Christmas. A warm cat in his lap, he read St. Paul and grew nauseated at the bishop's rich vestments on the televised St. Patrick's Cathedral Christmas Eve Mass, preferring his own little meditation spot in the piny woods in back of the house. Nin and her family were gone for Christmas, as was Mémêre, who had left for Brooklyn to attend her stepmother's funeral.

With no one to talk with, Jack focused all his attention on writing a new book. Three months before, *Mexico City Blues* had, due to the grass and morphine he used when writing it, sent him deep into his past, and thoughts of one funeral took him back to his first one. Obsessed as well with the mystic death—and potential rebirth—of his contemplations, Jack was somber. One day after his visit to the woods he fell to the ground and screamed, "I'm gonna die." That certainty was more powerful than any philosophy, and his new book reflected it. "Death is the only decent subject," he wrote, "since it marks the end of illusion and delusion." So he told of the most important death in his life, that of Gerard's, in a tale first called *St. Gerard the Child* and finally *Visions of Gerard*.

On January 1, 1956, he sat down at the kitchen table and for twelve nights wrote steadily by hand—it was no subject for a "rackety typewriter," he said—from midnight to dawn. Whizzing along on benny and tea, he continued to write spontaneously, although he did reject all of one night's work. The language was windblown and Shakespearean, and especially sensitive to nature in a voluptuously swirling description of spring.

Visions of Gerard asked, "Who will be the human being who will ever be able to deliver the world from its idea of itself that it actually exists in this crystal ball of mind?"

Though a beautiful composition, the story was too lachrymose for most readers when it was later published; it was less a novel than a passionate elegy. Much of its detail came from the letters Papa Leo had written Jack during college, although he also re-created his childhood by eating peanut butter on Ritz crackers and playing his card baseball game. Jack recounted his memories of Gerard and the sparrows, the visits of the nuns, and the freeing of the mouse. Who would deliver the world from illusion? "One meek little Gerard with his childish ponderings shall certainly come closer than Caesarean bust provokers with quills and signatures—and cabinets and vestal dreary laceries—I say."

As if to balance the purity of his prayer in Gerard's memory, Jack visited New York in late January 1956 and hit the bars, only to feel old and burned out amongst a blithe new generation, flinching as he watched Mardou kiss another man at the Montmartre Bar. Worse still, he also discovered that Cowley was not in New York, where Jack had supposed that they were to do the editorial work on *On the Road* that would make it suitable for a contract, but at Stanford University, which Jack had just left. The confused delay set back *Road*'s publication by six months. The fact that Lucien—hard-drinking, cynical reporter Lucien—liked *Visions of Gerard* was the only bright spot in his visit to New York, but somehow Jack didn't plunge into his usual quagmire of depression.

Back in North Carolina with his family, he found a letter offering him a job as lookout on Desolation Mountain in Washington State's Mount Baker National Forest; he would follow as bhikku in Gary Snyder and Phil Whalen's path. Now his life had a linchpin, and he planned it out—summers in the wilderness, fall and spring in Mexico, Christmas and winter in North Carolina with Nin and Mémère—a rich and full cycle that he felt would nurture him. With his $500 summer wages, he even daydreamed in a letter to Whalen about founding a monastery for what he called "Pure Essence Buddhism" near Mexico City.

Safe now in his North Carolina piny woods and prayer arbor until he left for Washington, he meditated for long hours and felt increasingly at peace. A springlike day in February followed by a moonlit, frog-croaking night put him near ecstasy, and he worked in perfect contentment on his translations of the sutras and other Buddhist materials, which he called *Book of Prayers*. Aside from his tranquil mood, two psychic experiences convinced him that he was entering a state of grace. The whole family had been interested when Nin had brought home the current best seller on reincarnation, *The Search for Bridey Murphy*, though the Cassadys had long ago introduced Jack to the notion of past lives. Deep in renewed meditation, he had encountered seven prior selves, and claimed to Carolyn that he had once been Avalokitesvara, Asvaghosha, a monk, a pot-boy, Shakespeare, an eighteenth-century English footpad-thief, and Balzac. On the earthly plane, Mémère had come down with a sneeze and cough that struck Jack as unnatural. He went to bed and meditated and "saw" a Heet liniment bottle, a brandy bottle, and the white flowers on her bedside table. Going into Mémère's room, he put the Heet on her throat and took the flowers away. Later a doctor confirmed that she had an allergy to flowers. Jack warned himself against a messiah complex, but felt that he was a channel of God, "dealing in outblowness, cut-off-ness, snipped, blownoutness, putoutness, turned-off-ness . . . gone-ness, gone out-ness, the snapped link, nir, link, vana, snap!"

A dharma bum was welcome at the Zen Center in San Francisco, but didn't fit in socially with the "good ole boys" who were Nin's neighbors in Rocky Mount. No one had taken to following him down the road with a shotgun, but any man who didn't comb his hair or shave and went about barefoot in overalls like a child was a lunatic in the eyes of the locals. When Jack occasionally tried to explain that all was empty illusion, they looked to one side and told him to stick to the religion he was born with. More than ever before, Jack was the odd man out, the patronized "goof" who had no one's respect. Not a soul in Rocky Mount could communicate with him about his writing or his religion—and that was virtually all he had. Often he would pout in his frustration. His dreams reflected his agitation with his disbelieving family as when he dreamed of appearing on the Dinah Shore TV show, until his gauche Canuck autograph hound mother and sister would appear and embarrass him.

Late in March Jack learned that Gary Snyder had a place for them to spend the spring in Mill Valley, near San Francisco, before Jack left for his Desolation Mountain job and Gary boarded a freighter to Japan and his initiation into the Daitoku monastery. Jack quickly hit the road in a desperate attempt to catch Malcolm Cowley at Stanford, but Cowley was already gone, and the trip was a nightmare. He fried in the roadside South Carolina heat, and finally took a bus he could not afford to El Paso. Crossing the river, he ended up drunk and frightened by his hipster dope connection in Mexico. He took the Southern Pacific to San Francisco, and late one afternoon he hiked up the hill in Mill Valley to Gary's hut, "Marin-An."

Their neighbors down the hill at 348 Montford Avenue were the McCorckles, fellow refugees from American consumerism. Locke was a bearded, part-time carpenter whose only significant possessions were a guitar and his hi-fi set, and he and his family thrived on vegetable soups, homemade bread, and simple entertainments. Some years later Locke would write a beautiful meditation on sex called *How to Make Love*. The atmosphere on Montford Avenue was hospitably creative.

Gary's cabin was cozy, with burlap wallpaper, wildflowers in clay jars, *goza* mats, Chinese prints and maps on the wall. Jack had some supper cooked when Gary came in from work, and after three months of good ole boys, it was nice to be with someone who took Buddhism seriously. It would be a rich and peaceful spring for Jack, and he would come to prize his days with Snyder. Their lives on the hill were insulated from the conventional world, and though they listened to jazz at the McCorckles' and entertained visitors, they had no newspapers, magazines, or TV. They chopped wood, talked of masters and koans, Kasyapa's flower sermon and Coyote. Much of their time was spent in meditation, though Jack mostly ambled and dreamed while Gary was more rigorous.

Four different writing projects absorbed most of Jack's energy. Two —the *Duluoz Legend* and a film script called "The Book"— were short-lived. The "Legend" was an autobiography incorporating past lives, and ancient religiosity was at the center of "The Book." Its chief character was a Bodhisattva called The Attainer, whose family had names like Rock Silence, Dawn Bird, and Star Pity, served by merchants, servants, slaves, courtesans and scavengers inhabiting an enormous city on a North Atlantis river long, long ago. Jack's major—and later published—pieces were a meditation called *The Scripture of the Golden Eternity* and a poem first called "Lucien Midnight" until Lucien objected, later "Old Angel Midnight."

In "Old Angel Midnight" (OAM) Jack tried to catch the sound of all tongues, the infinite sound of the universe as it floated into his window late at night, and for the first time he permitted himself absolute freedom to write anything that came into his head. The poem was extremely long and devoid of meaning in the common sense, a high argument between Jack and God in a universe of hurricane winds that swept his words around like confetti. St. Benedict conversed with Danny and the Juniors, while Carolyn and Burroughs made love in the midst of Buddhist lore. In fact,

Jack's trance was so deep that much of "OAM" was written in an illegible scribble most unlike his usual neat printing.

The last piece Jack wrote that spring, *The Scripture of the Golden Eternity*, required encouragement. "All right, Kerouac," announced Gary, "it's about time for you to write a sutra." The *Scripture* was a development of the *Diamond Sutra*, substituting the phrase "Golden Eternity" for "emptiness." While smelling flowers in the yard, Jack had stood up to take a deep breath and passed out. He was unconscious for a minute, a neighbor said. "During that timeless moment of unconsciousness I saw the Golden Eternity," Jack wrote in the *Scripture*, "the rapturous ring of silence abiding perfectly."

> Did I create the sky? Yes, for if it was
> Anything other than a conception in my mind
> I wouldn't have said "sky"—that is why I am the
> Golden Eternity. There are but two of us here,
> reader and writer but one . . .

Because it was scripture, Jack said, he wouldn't allow himself to be spontaneous, and polished it in the conventional fashion.

Montford Avenue was not entirely a retreat. As Gary's May 15 departure to Japan drew near, Jack enjoyed various parties, picnics that he thought were the D. H. Lawrence sexual revolution in action. Still chaste, he cooked or sat talking in a corner, his eyes averted from the occasional nude lady who passed by. Gary's going-away party starred the naked trio of Allen, Peter, and Gary, with John Montgomery reading *MAD* magazine, Kenneth Rexroth lecturing on poetry, and Neal on Cayce. Allen was luxuriating in the imminent publication of "Howl" and letters of congratulation from Mark Van Doren and William Carlos Williams, having already planned to send copies to Ezra Pound, William Faulkner, and T. S. Eliot, among others. Leavened by a fertile pinch of success, Allen no longer seemed evil to Jack. In fact, Jack reported to John Holmes, he was beginning to suspect that his younger brother was a saint.

For Jack, the spring had peaked a few weeks earlier, when he and Gary quietly hiked over Mount Tamalpais—Jack's first time there since 1947—arguing about Christianity all the while. Jack tried to be ecumenical, and thought Jesus was Maitreya, the Buddha who was to come after Sakayamuni. Mount Tam was easier hiking than it was on their previous jaunt, and they sat near the peak bathed in the sweet odor of pine and wet logs while they discussed Gary's trip to Japan and Jack's to Desolation Mountain. After a simple meal, they slept high among the mountain spirits, swam at Stinson Beach, and came home. Gary presented Jack with a Hershey Bar, and in return Jack gave him a slip of paper on which he'd printed "MAY YOU USE THE DIAMONDCUTTER OF MERCY."

On May 15, 1956, they shared a final hug on the docks, and said goodbye. Though they had known each other only a few months, Jack's pure brotherly love for Gary was profound, and he missed him terribly over the coming years.

Lost without Snyder's steadying presence, Jack immediately got drunk. The night Gary left he met a suitable drinking companion, a poet and editor named Robert Creeley. Dark, restless, and lonely, Creeley had separated from his wife and wandered to San Francisco to visit Ed Dorn, his old student from Black Mountain College. In something more like karma than coincidence, Dorn's successor at the Greyhound Bus Terminal baggage room was Allen Ginsberg, and in a moment that was portentous for the future publication of the San Francisco poetry, Creeley and Allen soon met. The "Black Mountain poets" had a deep affinity for the Beats like Allen and Gregory and the San Franciscans like McClure, Snyder, and Whalen—they too, as one critic noted, searched "for the personal voice, for the immediate impulse and its energy, for the recognition of (even surrender to) process, to the elements of randomness, whimsy, play." Though it had a faculty that included the finest avant-garde artists in America—John Cage, Merce Cunningham, Willem de Kooning, Buckminster Fuller—Black Mountain was mired in financial difficulties, and chose Creeley to edit a magazine that would advertise it to the world. The *Black Mountain Review* had already distinguished itself by publishing Charles Olson, Kenneth Rexroth, and Paul Goodman when Creeley came to San Francisco to gather material for the seventh issue. He chose Allen as contributing editor, and the spring 1957 issue became a Beat–San Franciscan showcase, publishing Allen's poem "America," Jack's "October in the Railroad Earth," sections from Burroughs' *Naked Lunch* and poems by Whalen, McClure, and Snyder.

The night that Gary left, Creeley became extraordinarily drunk, smashed enough to pick a fight with the bouncer at the Cellar Bar. Jack helped him to a friend's home in South San Francisco, then walked home alone fifteen miles across the Golden Gate Bridge to Mill Valley. In the course of the evening's excitement, Creeley was also arrested for vagrancy, and Jack invited him and his lover Martha to cool off at the Montford

Avenue cottage until June, when he would leave for his lookout job on Desolation Mountain. Martha's last name was Rexroth, and her estrangement from her critic husband sowed the seeds of much subsequent conflict.

After hitching from San Francisco to the ranger station at Marblemount, Washington—itself thirty-five miles from the nearest significant town and a hundred miles from Seattle—Jack climbed into a boat on Ross Lake for a long ride to the foot of the mountain. From there he and two rangers packed in his supplies by horseback six steep miles to the mountaintop. Desolation Mountain was in deep wilderness, as isolated as any part of the continental United States, and as Jack hitched up the coast to his job he thought that when "I'm alone I will come face to face with God or that light and find out once and for all what is the meaning of all this existence and suffering and going to and fro . . ."

In two months on the mountaintop he grappled with true solitude; he never went up on the mountain again.

Shrouded in fog and filthy from the previous tenant, his "little shadowy peaked shack" depressed him when he arrived on July 5, but with the cabin cleaned and the fog gone two days later, its setting was magnificent. Jack relaxed into a routine, reading Shakespeare and vintage cowboy pulp magazines, singing Sinatra songs out over the cliffs, the gnarled trees, and the lake a mile below. Generally he became silent and prayerful. Although he listened to his colleagues banter with each other on the shortwave radio, he rarely joined in. On his knees he asked "What is the meaning of the void?" of the "mad raging sunsets pouring in sea foams of cloud through unimaginable crags," of the deer that ate his leftover potatoes, of all the aspects of the Dharma.

Soon boredom set in. He pictured his return to the city in total detail, played card baseball games with the absolutely detailed verisimilitude of his childhood days, thought of Mémère and how old she was getting, prayed to Avalokitesvara. On August 7, exquisitely lonely after thirty-three days of perfect solitude, he sank into horrible old nightmares of his failure to support Mémère, worry, self-hatred, and grief intermixed. The next day he was briefly hysterical and killed a mouse—no trivial thing for this Buddhist—and tried to kill another. His patience snapped: "Just *be*," he told himself, "Just *flow*," *pass through* all these dreams, and he relaxed a little. "Wait, breathe, eat, sleep, cook, wash, pace, watch, never any forest fires" was his summation.

He stared at Mount Hozomeen, whose naked face loomed in front of his little window like the void, and kept on keeping on. Sixty-two days into his struggle on the mountain, he opened a bag of peanut-raisin dessert, and the smell triggered memories of Gary, who'd given him the pouch, and Gary's "rucksack revolution." Desolation Mountain's solitude had been too much for a sociable urban man like Jack. He wanted fat luscious Mexican whores calling for *agua caliente* (hot water), chocolate bars, furry rugs, and comfort. Around him was only silence, rock, the void, and himself.

At last the fall rains made his vigil unnecessary, and he hiked down the mountain, rode the boat back to Marblemount, ate some ice cream, grew nearly sick from the suddenly unfamiliar smell of fresh printer's ink on a newspaper, and set off to hitch back to civilization, down the highway to Seattle, his first stop.

Even as he went down the road, America was changing; while he'd been in Marblemount, President Eisenhower had signed the Federal Highway Act of 1956, which would transform two-lane roads into the four-lane cross-country controlled access interstate routes of the 1960's, apt symbols for a giant concrete Moloch that was increasingly more evocative of the nation than Jack's mournful, tender vision.

XII
The
Angel Travels

SEATTLE WAS a mélange of dreary skid-row shops and totem poles and a bar with the Friday night TV fights, where Carmen Basilio was hammering Johnny Saxton's face into the canvas. Jack bought the *Sporting News* and learned that Mickey Mantle was hitting home runs near Babe Ruth's pace. The September 17, 1956, issue of *Time* informed him that there had been desegregation riots in Clinton, Tennessee, and political violence in Algeria, Cyprus and Egypt. The Republican Party had just renominated Eisenhower and Nixon, and though Jack wasn't registered to vote, he told a flabbergasted poet friend later that he would have cast his ballot for Papa Ike, because his opponent Stevenson was "so elegant so snide so proud."

As his first evening in "civilization" wore on, Jack bought some Italian Swiss Colony Port, put it in his canteen, and went off to indulge himself in lush fantasy at a burlesque theater, one of many men with hats in their laps. He was only thirty-four, but as he described it in a book he would write three months later, when he ogled a waitress in a Chinese restaurant afterward he felt too much of a bum, too lost and scabrous ever to be attractive again.

The rugged hike off the mountain had blistered his feet, so he took a bus rather than hitch to San Francisco, where he arrived on a Sunday afternoon in mid-September. Very shortly thereafter Jack was to conclude that his "vision of the freedom of eternity" was "of little use in cities and warring societies." He had passed from the lonely purity of a mountaintop into a gangbanging frenzy of rivalries, the creative friendship he had left in June contaminated by envy. Fame and success—in the form of a photographer from *Mademoiselle* magazine sent to do a story on the booming local poetry scene—was in the air.

At first his stay in San Francisco was just traditional city kicks; he got a hotel room and frantically rushed to the Cellar for the Sunday afternoon jam session, then to The Place for beer, then back to the heartbeat jazz, feeding dimes into pay phones to try and catch Allen and get some action started. The next day he located Neal and snatched up Allen on the way; they found Cassady in his conductor's blue pants and vest, starched white shirt, and trainman's hat. "Jackson, me boy-y-y," drawled Neal in greeting, and they set off for Mill Valley with the newly arrived Gregory Corso to pick up some of Jack's manuscripts. Corso and Cassady did not get on well, and their bad feelings colored the philosophical argument they carried on between Neal's Edgar Cayce and Corso's hero Shelley.

Allen and his lover Peter Orlovsky came over to Gregory's later in the day, and in between raving about love!, orgies, nakedness, and love!, they began to fondle Corso's girlfriend, which aggravated him greatly. Serene, Jack tried to calm everyone by reading his paraphrase of the *Diamond Sutra*, and diplomatically managed to include Gregory when Neal made plans to go to Golden Gate Fields racetrack the next day.

Race day was wild, from the moment Jack awoke at Peter and Allen's apartment to greet a young lady named Penny who'd come to visit. Penny didn't think Jack was quite so decrepit as he imagined, and Jack's year-long Buddhist chastity melted like cotton candy at the touch of her lips. Neal bounced in a moment later with some grass and began to advise Peter's silent younger brother Lafcadio on astral bodies. Jack thought his spiel was merely "words," but was soon too stoned to argue very much. Then Cassady led them off to the track, where they had a grand and lucky day; Gregory picked mystically and came home even, Neal won playing his mad system, and Jack got peacefully drunk.

Two days later the poets came together for the *Mademoiselle* article on the "San Francisco Poetry Renaissance." In the flash of the strobe lights Jack envisioned them as a "Million Dollar Outfield"; Allen was the "serious Lou Gehrig," Gregory the graceful DiMaggio, and Phil Whalen the "pillar of strength" catcher. Jack depicted his personal dichotomy of aesthetic ego and private doubt in his own archetype; he was the gifted but unlovable, murderously intense Ty Cobb. Physically Kerouac was striking. Tanned and healthily lean from the mountains, his hair slightly tousled because Gregory wouldn't allow him to comb it, a crucifix Gregory had given him at his throat, Jack was Lochinvar, James Dean, and Merlin all in one. But it wasn't a true team photo session. Robert Duncan and Michael McClure had their pictures taken at a different time, and Rexroth had reservations about carpetbagging New Yorkers.

Despite the publicity, Jack had hardly any reason to be happy with his career. He would publish nothing in 1956, and he still had no contract for *On the Road,* although in July he'd threatened to withdraw it if Viking didn't formally sign with him. Jack's frustration had been so bitter the previous winter that he had accused Allen of plagiarism in "Howl," and although they had tried to resolve their differences, their conversations were often stilted and uncomfortable. Jealousy made Allen frantic, and he yelled, "Hand in *hand* it's got to be!" McClure saw it differently. To him, Allen the organizer was pushing a "comrades and lovers," "join or die" campaign on the poets, and such neopolitical abstractions had no appeal for Mike. Besides, Corso kept taunting, "You hate me, McClure." He would reply, "I don't hate you, who says I hate you?" The daisy chain of squabbling went around and around. Corso's provocations didn't help matters, and McClure dismissed the whole argument with the comment, "None of you know anything of *language*—with the exception of Jack." In later years, McClure remarked that the poets' "competitions were not nearly so strong as their bonds of mutual support and camaraderie, though in fact it was the intensity of both the competition and [the bonds]" that created the new poetics. Still, the present squabbles made Jack nervous.

Now that the national media had begun to take notice of the emerging poetry renaissance, too many egos were pushing and shoving for the limelight; a second major reading in early May 1956 had included Robert Creeley, and City Lights Bookstore had become a literary Lourdes. On September 2, 1956, the *New York Times Book Review* heralded the San Francisco poetry scene with a piece by critic Richard Eberhart entitled "West Coast Rhythms." Eberhart had attended the May reading, which had its own postcard invitation: "Celebrated Good Time Poetry Night. Either you go home bugged or completely enlightened. Allen Ginsberg blowing hot; Snyder blowing cool; Phil Whalen puffing the laconic tuba . . . One and only final appearance of this apocalypse." Eberhart was an older and accepted poet. He wrote in a positive—if tentative—fashion that the Bay Area poets had "a young will to kick down the doors of older consciousness and established practice in favor of what they think is vital and new." Unsure of its significance but gratified to be present at the birth of an aesthetic revolution, Eberhart concluded: "Poetry here has become a tangible social force, moving and unifying the auditors, releasing the energy of the audience through spoken, even shouted verse, in a way at present unique to this region." The word had gone forth from the *New York Times.*

In October 1956, City Lights Press published *Howl and Other Poems,* dedicated among others to Jack, "New Buddha of American Prose," and with an introduction by William Carlos Williams: "Hold back the edges of your gowns, ladies, we are going through hell." The graphic certitude of publication fulfilled Allen and also added to his apprehensions about fame and the San Francisco scene, and he made plans to tour Europe with Jack and visit Burroughs in Tangiers. Ginsberg had earned money by shipping out to the Arctic Circle and inherited some more. Though the circumstances of his bequest were painful, he was free to travel. On June 9, 1956, he had received the telegram NAOMI GINSBERG DIED SUDDENLY SATURDAY AFTERNOON . . . Later his brother Eugene wrote and described her pitiable funeral, where the functionary who was to speak didn't know her name, asked, and couldn't get it right; since there were not enough men present to constitute a *minyan* (the quorum of ten necessary for formal prayer), there was no Jewish prayer for the dead. No one said Kaddish for Naomi Ginsberg.

Before they left San Francisco, Jack and Allen's increasing notoriety brought them some enjoyable times as well. Ruth Witt-Diamont, Director of the San Francisco State University Poetry Center, gave a dinner for Randall Jarrell, the Library of Congress poetry consultant, and *New Yorker* poetry critic Louise Bogan. She also invited Allen, Gregory, Jack and Phil. It was a relaxed evening, even after what Jack thought of as his gaffe.

Jack: "I ride freight trains."

Gregory: "So what!"

Jack: "But it's a first-class freight train!"

In the amused chuckling around the table, Jack mentally shrugged and determined to be the Bodhisattva who enlightened through laughter, rather than try to explain that the California Midnight Zipper was indeed a first-class train. The stately and charming Bogan picked up the conversation again by asking the poets if they believed in God. "Every once in a while I feel I have to have a white talk with God, myself," she said. She was shocked, Philip later recalled, when Allen and Phil said no. Jack, though, said yes.

The attention was pleasant, but Jack generally preferred the company of his brothers, as at a later party, this time a dull affair in an elegant mansion where the most interesting guest was Peter's brother Lafcadio, who spent the evening staring into a mirror. The "gang" exited the mansion singing rowdy harmony, only to confront the police. Jack advised them to "avoid the authorities," and they passed quietly on, as Jack recalled it, "walking talking poetry in the streets, walking talking God in the streets. (and at one point a strange gang of hoodlums got mad and said 'what right does he have to wear that [Jack's crucifix]?' And my own gang of musicians and poets told them to cool it)."

Wrung out by the social scene, Jack left Allen to catch up with him a month or so later in Mexico City, and rode down to Los Gatos with Neal and Gregory, arriving late at night to sleep in the yard and be awakened by the Cassady children's chorus of Cathy, Jamie, and John. Corso was bored and said it was "bullshit" when Neal played his usual TV roulette, spinning continuously between *Queen for a Day* and *Oral Roberts,* bowing his head in prayer for Oral's cripples and the game show's sad contestants. When Jack was about to leave he took the children on a long walk in the local orchards, weaving a fairy tale of kings and monkeys. He hugged Carolyn goodbye, and got into Neal's battered jalopy. Worried because Jack was drunk, Neal was full of "instructions and care" as he drove to the station. Jack managed not to get too tripped up in the unnecessary details of how to jump a train, swung onto the Zipper and was gone for Mexico City.

The world was "growing narrower in its views about eccentricity every day," Jack later commented in his book *Desolation Angels,* and he felt like a Rembrandt who painted until dawn as his subject-burghers snoozed in bourgeois quiet. Hiking in the desert near Tucson, he found himself surrounded by police cars, their searchlight beams illuminating his jeans, work shirt and rucksack. The officers wanted to know where he was going, why he didn't sleep in a hotel. "I'm studying hobo," he said. Eventually they gave him up as a dimwit and turned him loose.

Mexico was a return to solitude, "to dream all day," as he later wrote, "and work out chapters in forgotten reveries that emerge years later in book form." Once again he had his marijuana, his rooftop adobe room with Garver downstairs for company, and his work, the completion of his book on Esperanza, the drug connection, *Tristessa.* Esperanza Villanueva had written him several times since he'd left her, and Jack had often pondered her ravaged beauty. He was aghast when they met; no beauty remained, only the bruised remnants of a body and mind that had endured a river of morphine and endless goofballs. By the time of this second meeting in the fall of 1956, she was so far gone that she nodded off and fell in the street, battering herself in the dirt. She lost control and attacked Garver, driving him in a tremble to sleep with Jack on the roof. Drooling with the same goofballs as Esperanza, Garver had a tendency to wet Jack's bed. Cherishing memories of nursing Papa Leo ten years before, Jack ran errands to the store for his guest's magazines, candy, and cigarettes. The thought that he should have stayed in Mexico with Esperanza tore at Jack's conscience, and he silenced his guilt with a vicious combination of wine and tequila that left him ready one night, as he drunkenly boasted a decade later, to "nail her." She said, "Shhh the landlord will hear. Remember, I'm weak and sick." In one of the bizarre moments of Jack's life when his roles as participant and recorder spun in confusion, he whispered back, "I know, I've been writing how you're weak and sick." Soon he ran away from her.

Garver's lectures on Alexander the Great, Crete, and Gilgamesh continued in the background, and with *Tristessa*— one of the "long sad tales about people in the legend of my life"—completed in mid-October, Jack lit another candle in his hut, brewed some cocoa, and began the manuscript he called *Desolation Angels,* the story of his summer on Desolation Mountain and in San Francisco. *Desolation Angels* was no quickie transcription of his journal notes, nor was it stylistically like what he called the "ingrown toenail-packed mysticism" of *Tristessa.* It had a more direct narrative than *Tristessa,* but went far beyond travelogue as Jack's memory roved to Lowell, wartime Greenland, and Desolation. Philosophically, *Desolation Angels* was all its title hinted, the tale of a desolate man, a pilgrim who had given up on Buddhism, as on all systems. He prophesied that the final prayer would be "I don't know, I don't care, and it doesn't matter." There was no further need to tell stories, no need for anything. But life remained, "an aching mystery." His writing was controlled and powerful, his subjects ranging from Mount Hozomeen in the wilderness—"like a tiger sometimes with stripes"—to a goaty lust song for a Seattle stripper and a forlorn soliloquy for America. Above all, Jack wrote of angels of desolation, of death . . . "and I will die, and you will die, and we will all die, and even the stars will fade out one after another in time."

Jack's month in Mexico City before his friends joined him stretched out in gloom. Allen, Peter, Lafcadio, and Gregory arrived in Mexico City in October 1956 to find Jack sullen and morose. They gathered with Garver, who immediately flashed his catlike smile and gave Allen a shot of morphine. As was his custom, Peter began to scrub the floors and woodwork, while Lafcadio slumped inscrutably into a corner. Corso had been writing brilliantly at the time—Ferlinghetti would soon publish him—and was full of energy, jumping about, as Jack described it, to "dramatize the way he felt." Cheerfully grandiose, he identified with Garver's ramble about Alexander the Great, thinking of himself as a future poet-conqueror. Jack was still Buddhist enough for the talk of past heroics to trigger mental images of the trail of corpses left in Alexander's wake.

Often nervous, Jack was frightened one day when the street boys whistled at them, until Allen explained that their whistles were not a mocking commentary on Peter and Allen, but excited admiration. Later they visited the pyramids of Teotihuacán, Peter and Allen and Jack in the lead as Gregory mused off to the side and Lafcadio stepped along machinelike behind them. Smoking pot at the top of the pyramid, they blinked at the sun and tried to comprehend the minds of the ancient Aztec priests whose shades drifted about them. Gory sacrifice seemed so very strange in such a beautiful place, and when they spent an hour examining a giant ant colony below, they took great care not to crush any of the insects.

Oregano, the avenue of whores that Jack dubbed the "street of nausea," was another of their haunts. Braving the stench of fried sausage, brick, muddy garbage, and banana peels, they went to the Club Bombay, its tawdry mariachi singers reeking of sweat in seedy costumes. Peter and Jack visited the brothel in back. Jack chose a fourteen-year-old child— "nobody *cares*, " he told himself—while Peter returned six times and acquired a painful case of gonorrhea. Gregory avoided the orgy with a massive spell of depression that brought him home early. Revolted by the sham Americanized Pepsi-taco culture of the slums, Corso thought Mexico City was "poor, sick, and nowhere." After five days of sluicing late-November rain, he flew to Washington; having been charmed by him and his poetry at Ruth Witt-Diamont's dinner, Randall Jarrell and his wife had invited him to stay in their home.

After Gregory left, Jack and Allen visited the famous floating gardens of Xochimilco. Allen was gleeful, anticipating a triumphant return to New York and then a long sojourn in Europe with Jack. Dazed by drugs and beauty, utterly devoid of ideas about his future, Jack flopped down in the boat, lugubriously deaf to Allen's energetic vision of their possibilities.

Though he was pleased that the newly begun *Evergreen Review* wanted to purchase *The Subterraneans* at a penny a word, Jack was worried about editorial meddling with his prose, and still had no formal word from Viking about *Road.* The continuing uncertainty bled his energy away.

Too, he was made uneasy by the direct social criticism of Allen's poetry, although he'd enjoyed it when Allen had described how he'd squelched a heckler at a reading in Los Angeles. The man querulously asked Allen what Corso's poetry meant, and demurred at the answer "Nakedness," demanding to know "What's that?" Allen made his point directly, taking off his clothes, then putting them back on as Gregory continued to read. But Jack was wholly unable to cope with any sort of conflict. His sense of the future had turned dull and blank, futile roads to nowhere merging in an empty gray horizon.

As Jack described it five years later, Allen wriggled in their boat at the gardens as once he had squirmed on Times Square cafeteria seats, and urged him to come to New York: "It's time for you to *make* it! After all!" Jack carped and moaned, and Allen raised his finger and berated him. "Where's your old Dostoyevsky curiosity? You've become so whiny! You're coming on like an old sick junkie sitting in a room in nowhere." His eyes flashing, Allen shouted, "It's time for the poets to *influence* American civilization!"

Jack saw an opening, and laughed. "Allen, if you'd really seen a vision of eternity, you wouldn't care about influencing American civilization."

Delighted with a response at last, Ginsberg slammed home his riposte, and teased Jack's curiosity enough for him to join the pilgrimage to New York, Tangiers, and Europe. "I have a Blakean message for the Iron Hound of America," Allen whispered. "How can the East have any respect for a country that has no prophetic poets?"

Their journey to New York was grueling, with six men (Jack, Allen, Peter, Lafcadio, two others) and their baggage crammed into a too-small car. Back in Greenwich Village, they emerged from the car into a bleak early December morning, coughing and spitting from too many cigarettes as they shivered in the chill. Jack was gaunt at 155 pounds, his lowest weight in years. A woman friend of Allen's put them up and even shared her bed with Jack, but after a week he moved to Lucien's, where he watched old Clark Gable films—Gregory had said that he had hands like Gable's—and hid from the present by reading Mallarmé, Proust, and Corbière in the original.

It was well that Jack was surrounded by friends when he finally heard from Viking Press; he might have exploded without compatriots to share his joy. In mid-December 1956, almost six years after composition, *On the Road* was officially accepted by Viking for publication the following September. Jack's long vigil was over, but it was perhaps too late for festivities. The six-year wait to publish again had demanded too much of Jack, had stripped him of every personal resource but his work itself. Truth be told, he'd even sacrificed full spontaneity; working from Cowley's general suggestions, he'd edited the manuscript in a professional—though not extensive—manner, pruning away a sentence here, a three-word phrase there, adding nothing but cutting out his loose blowing asides to keep the narrative focused on Neal and the Road. For the moment he was delirious with joy. He raced about town getting libel clearances signed, caught Cecil Taylor at the Five Spot Café, enjoyed an orgy with a budding poet and admirer of Allen's named Diane DiPrima, and went to the Russian Tea Room to meet Salvador Dali, who said that he was more beautiful than Marlon Brando.

On his way to Orlando, Florida, to join Mémère and Nin for Christmas in their new home, he stopped in Washington to see Corso. Caged in Randall Jarrell's dignified home, Gregory reminded Jack of a prize Pekinese, a tiny black-haired bundle of pethood, stroked, spoiled, and patronized. Jack still liked Gary Snyder's idea of eccentric dharma bum poets, and out of principle he liberated some of Jarrell's Jack Daniel's whiskey, smoked marijuana in the basement, and started giant arguments over spontaneity in poetry with Jarrell, asking, "How can you confess your crafty soul in craft?" It had been Gregory's sheer outrageousness that had given him meaning in Jack's eyes, and his current discretion—no drugs, no swearing—was dull. Corso wouldn't be a "good boy" for long, but his current phase made Jack foresee something dreary in literary success. As he waited for the bus to Florida later, Jack became tearfully drunk, not on Tokay but on the drink of prosperity, his new delight, Jack Daniel's.

In Orlando, Mémère was less ambivalent about her son's achievement. She was sixty-one now and happily retired, and enjoyed having Jack to fix her martinis as she watched the St. Patrick's Cathedral Midnight Mass, or serving him a fine fat turkey for New Year's 1957. Even more, Gabrielle Kerouac relished her son's New Year's pledge to her—the long-awaited resolution of his guilts as her wastrel son; *On the Road*'s proceeds would buy her a house of her own, in repayment for all the years she'd supported him.

Returning to New York early in January to complete his business with Viking, Jack plunged into a cauldron of attention. He began to date a young woman named Joyce Glassman, an editorial assistant who resembled his second wife, Joan Haverty, in her mannered upper-middle-classness. Lucien called Joyce "Ecstasy Pie," and her affair with Jack would endure for an erratic year and a half. Allen led the poets on a pilgrimage to Rutherford, New Jersey, to meet his spiritual father, William Carlos Williams. Dr. Williams encouraged Jack's writing, and Jack spent most of the afternoon with Mrs. Williams, speculating about his upcoming trip to see Burroughs while she reminisced about her young womanhood in Europe. The old doctor had advice for the poets: "Lotsa bastards out there," he warned them, pointing out the window.

They rushed back to Paterson and Louis Ginsberg's sun room, where they spent a day gloating as they typed up poems and wrote letters to the first of what became a flood of mimeographed poetry magazines, *Combustion* of Toronto. The "Beat united poetry front" had functioned, if only briefly. As they returned to New York City, Jack refused when Gregory asked him to pay his bus fare. Jerking up and down on his seat in a spasm of anger at this miserliness, Gregory yelped, "All you do is hide money in your beauty. It makes you ugly! You'll die with money in your hand and wonder why the angels won't lift you up." Jack burst into tears; far from being wealthy, he'd sent his *Road* advance to Mémère, and had borrowed his boat fare to Tangiers from Allen.

In an imposing flurry of appointments, Jack signed his *On the Road* contract with Viking, had his picture taken (hair combed) by *Life*, and signed a contract with Grove Press to publish *The Subterraneans* in the May *Evergreen Review*. He, Peter, and Allen enjoyed the weekend of January 19 at John Holmes's place in Old Saybrook, Connecticut, joyously playing football in knee-deep snow and ice-skating on the frozen cove. Jack impressed Holmes as lean, sober and meticulous, still very much affected by Buddhism, somewhat withdrawn but happy. John caught up with the Kerouac legend by reading *Desolation Angels* and *Tristessa*, and their long cheery talks before the fireplace in Holmes's fine New England home renewed their nearly decade-long friendship.

As Jack discoursed before the fire, the signs of his oncoming fame began to accumulate, like the first clicks on a Geiger counter that registers the approach of a nuclear cloud. Jack and his friends were new and different, and so the amorally sensation-hungry popular magazines covered them. But that did not mean it took them seriously; *Mademoiselle's*

February 1957 issue hit the newsstands with Michael Grieg's "The Lively Arts in San Francisco" surrounded by advertisements for Peck & Peck blouses, Neet hair-removing cream, Bonne Bell pimple lotion, Jantzen bras, Mamselle shoes, and advice on "How To Be More Perfect." The text was scant, but the pictures—a striking Jack, bearded Allen, McClure, and Ferlinghetti at City Lights—attracted immediate attention. One swift reaction came from Jack's first wife, Edie Parker. Having somehow managed to track him down in New York, she called Jack late one night and volunteered to pay her own fare if he would include her on his European "tour." Jack's reaction went unmentioned. British publishers were negotiating for *On the Road.* Jack had dinner with a Warner Brothers story editor.

The media began to react. A *Village Voice* reporter named Dan Balaban interviewed Jack, Allen and Gregory. Though Norman Mailer had contributed an ostentatiously hip column to it only the year before, the *Voice* was interested in high rather than bohemian culture, and in middle-class Village politics; one of its most popular features was a sports-car column. Balaban's article, "Three 'Witless Madcaps' Come Home to Roost," focused on the trio's most exotic one-liners—"Don't shoot the wart hog" was Gregory's contribution—and emphasized the exploitative cuteness of its title when it buried Allen's point that "we want everyone to know that we had to leave the Village to find fulfillment and recognition." Jack thought New York was "too big, too multiple, too jaded." He continued, "We're saints and Villagers and we're beautiful. And we went to San Francisco and did beauty there." Deadly serious and without a hope of being understood, Jack admonished *Voice* readers to "Pity dogs and forgive men."

Jack's girlfriend Joyce Glassman and other friends sent Jack off with an exhilarating bon voyage party in honor of his first trip as a ship passenger, and he sailed for Tangiers in February on the freighter S.S. *Slovenia*, with Allen and Peter to follow as soon as they cleaned up some legal business.

Foretelling many of his future travels, Jack's celebratory African-European journey began in high anticipation and eventually—in this case a few months later—collapsed into a weary and still-restless return.

Feeling "light and gay," Jack enjoyed his first days aboard ship. He savored his lone occupancy of a double stateroom and indulged in fancies about the Communist Yugoslavian crew and his red-white-and-blue self, nearly convincing himself that the only other passenger, a Russian woman, was a spy.

Halfway out, a monstrous storm washed over them like Prospero's tempest, and his feeble notions of politics and even his Buddhism vanished. Later he'd agree with the *Lankavantara Sutra* that "There's nothing but Mind," but when the green seas began to break over the bow, all his faith in the void evaporated as he sagged loose-boweled in panic over the toilet. He told Holmes later that he'd seen a glow of light on the dark holocaust of the ocean, a godly affirmation of some sort, but his stormy gloom was so deep that when he read a history book over the next few days, all it communicated was misery and awfulness.

At last the tan smudge on the horizon filled and came into focus as Africa, and Jack went ashore to meet a changed Bill. After a year of doing almost nothing except shoot junk and stare at his big toe, Bill had fled to London in 1956 for a course of treatment that involved apomorphine, morphine boiled in hydrochloric acid. The ghostly junkie had been partly transmuted into a "tanned, muscular and vigorous" man with enough energy to play tourist guide, delighting Jack with Tangiers' exotic architecture, veiled women, and cafés filled with men smoking hashish and sipping mint tea. Below the city the brilliant blue Straits of Gibraltar were flecked with bright-sailed fishing boats. Jack took a room on Burroughs' roof, where he could entertain an occasional veiled prostitute while Bill dallied below with boys and opium.

Though he had at last controlled his morphine habit, Burroughs was no dewy repentant lamb, but a scintillatingly mad genius who reminded Jack of the evil science fiction character Dr. Mabuse and Robert Louis Stevenson's Mr. Hyde. "I'm just a hidden agent from another planet," Burroughs told Jack one day as they walked above the city, "and the trouble is, I don't know why they sent me, I've forgotten the God damn message, dearies." Bound in sweet compassion, Jack interpreted Bill's comment agreeably. "I'm a messenger from heaven too," he said. When Jack gushed over the precious sight of a shepherd carrying a newborn lamb, Bill sniffed and defined the chasm between them by cackling, "Oh well, the little pricks are always rushing around carrying lambs."

Burroughs' persona as a word-sorcerer had developed extraordinarily in the twilight of his drug life. He was, he said, "trying to arrive at some absolutely direct transmission of fact on all levels," and had adopted Jack's sketch method to reproduce his own visions. The result was a manuscript Jack thought so apocalyptically true that when its original title *Word Hoard* proved already taken, he dubbed it *The Naked Lunch*. The book was a record of agony, a twisting of the life source in all ways, especially the sexual.

At the age of forty-three, Burroughs was attempting to exorcise a lifetime of homosexuality, which he had come to regard as "a horrible sickness." At the same time, he burst into tears as he begged for any news Jack could provide about Allen or Peter. All of the pain came out in *Naked Lunch*, about which Bill told Jack, "I am shitting out my educated Middlewest background for once and for all. It's a matter of catharsis where I say the most horrible thing I can think of—realize that, the most *horrible* dirty slimy niggardliest posture possible."

Jack began to type up the manuscript and thought it was wonderful, superseding Genet, De Sade, and Aleister Crowley, and simultaneously revolting, a progression of ghastly scenes based on the fact that men have erections and orgasms when hanged. With the slime of a cosmic cesspool on his mind, Jack began to have terrifying dreams of endless bolognas coming out of his mouth, materialized out of his intestines the way a magician might produce a scarf. *Majoun* (hashish and honey candy) had something to do with his nightmares, as well as his visits to the sleaziest dive in Tangiers, the Dancing Boy Bar, and the amphetamines and barbiturates which were freely available at the corner drugstore. Then he received the proofs of *The Subterraneans* from Grove Press in New York and went berserk, arguing in letters to Lord that editor Don Allen had castrated it with cuts and defiled the sacred, personal sound that was his work. Lord forced the substitution of another of his pieces, "October in the Railroad Earth," in *Evergreen*, while *The Subterraneans* would come out as a book a year later, unretouched.

It was a narrow escape, and Jack was tense and preoccupied when Bill offered him some opium. Eating the magic little ball was like standing knee-deep in water and clamping down with both hands on a 10,000-volt electric cable: His mind shook, crackled, snapped, he retched and puked and vomited some more, then stared at the ceiling for thirty-six hours while his eyes refused to close and his vision melted and swirled out of control. Boiling up came the sorrowful thought in the midst of dreamy chaos that all he wanted was his childhood back, his Wheaties and sunshine and health—and that was far away and long, long ago. The pictures a friend took of him one day on the beach revealed a Jack who looked like an aging middleweight boxer, his face annealed and without the suppleness of youth, his hair limp and thinning, his eyes distracted and tired.

When Peter and Allen landed in Tangiers, Jack was sitting on his rooftop patio reading the American critic Van Wyck Brooks. He was peaceably high on hashish but not at all ready for the strain between the ex-lovers Allen and Bill. When Allen and Peter called to him from the street, he took them to explore Tangiers, and bought prostitutes for himself and Peter. Out one day with Allen, they met a master checker player named Mohammed Mayé. Another natural man, Mayé reminded them of Neal, down to his affection for marijuana, which he sold to them at the rate of twenty joints for 5 cents American.

Sickened by the opium, his publishing anxieties, and his eternal restlessness, Jack could not remain in Tangiers. Only two weeks after Allen and Peter arrived, he was off for Paris in early April, riding a rotten fourth-class ferry to Marseilles. He met some American diplomats and swiftly grew irritated with them, "stiff officious squares with contempt even for their own Americans who happened not to wear neckties . . . an endless phony rejection in the name of 'democracy' of all that's of pith and moment of every land." But Jack was even more bothered by what he saw as the shallow fraud of the late-fifties hipsters he encountered in Europe. Fools who dismissed Bird as undisciplined, latter-day hipsters had no Dostoyevskian rage or joy or love or even curiosity, Jack concluded, but a "postured, actually secretly *rigid* coolness that covers up the fact that the character is unable to convey anything of force or interest, a kind of sociological coolness." Yet cool hipsterism was becoming a fad and, most frightening to the shy drunken Bodhisattva Jack, would "be attributed in part to my doing."

Jack delighted in France, especially Paris, where he walked for miles with a flask of cognac, particularly in the neighborhood of Montmartre and Sacré-Coeur, the natural home for his rococo religious taste. He went to the Pantheon and had soup in a student restaurant, saw Van Gogh, Rembrandt, Rubens, and Breughel at the Louvre, but was "too fucking professionally morose" for Gregory Corso, who had come to France alone, and with whom he bar-crawled across the Left Bank. In London he saw his old Horace Mann buddy Seymour Wyse, hunted for Sherlock's 221B Baker Street, saw St. Paul's Choir perform *The St. Matthew Passion* on Good Friday, and visited the British Museum to research his genealogy. The crest of the Kerouacs was a stripe of gold on a blue shield, with three silver nails and the motto *"Aimer, Travailler, et Souffrir"* (Love, Work and Suffer). Jack was happily perplexed by the thought that the motto could well have been a synopsis of *The Town and the City*.

His ship home, the *Nieuw Amsterdam*, was too elegant, and his jeans and flannel shirt stood out in the silk and crystal dining room. Mostly he read in his bunk, walked the upper decks at night, and tried to stuff in enough extra helpings at meals to justify the high fare as he returned in May 1957 to an America that was a strange mix of superficial unity and underlying doubt, an atmosphere epitomized in the nation's popular book, soon to be the best-selling piece of fiction in American history until then: *Peyton Place*.

Grace Metalious' epic sold so well because of its prurient sexuality —"Is it up, Rod?," said one "tramp." "Is it up good and hard?"—but for deeper reasons as well. In her labored style of writing, Metalious took well-established social patterns from the Southern mill town and transplanted them to picturesque New England: the mill owner and his rotten son, the kindly doctor, the closet homosexual, and the sensitive outsider. Metalious' puppets were designed to reassure her audience that such archetypes, such a notion of stability, still existed. She created an illusory tension by salting the characters with secrets, then concluded with her most brilliant sales stroke, the meting out of strict Puritan justice to each.

Peyton Place's sexuality was a trivial lure that disguised the rigidly traditional virtue at its core. In reality, it was as pious as the nation's most popular entertainer, Lawrence Welk, whose two weekly TV shows had an audience of nearly 50 million people. Yet if the small cluster of citizens who had heard "Howl" at the Six Gallery and their kin were in revolt against the literary establishment, American youth en masse had already dispatched Welk, Doris Day, and watered-down jazz. When Jack toyed briefly that May with the idea of calling his book *Rock and Roll Road*, he may have been momentarily foggy in his taste, but not in his sense of what appealed to America's youth. Jack loved Chuck Berry and then Elvis, and respected rock and roll as another black music form that emphasized vitality over slickness. Sadly, in a few years the best rock and rollers, Chuck Berry and Jerry Lee Lewis, were in jail, Elvis Presley was in the Army, Little Richard had quit for the church, and Buddy Holly, Ritchie Valens, and the Big Bopper were dead. The first wave of the new music was all too brief.

While in Tangiers, Jack had conceived of yet another attempt to make Mémère and himself happy; he decided to move her to Berkeley so that he could live with her yet be around the scene, close to Neal, Phil Whalen, and later Allen (though Gary Snyder remained in Japan). Still hoping for a refuge, Jack also planned eventually to build a Thoreau-style shack in Marin County, north of San Francisco. When the *Nieuw Amsterdam* docked in New York in May 1957, he spent a little time with Joyce Glassman, sped to Orlando, packed up his manuscripts and Mémère's "silk bloomers, rosaries, tin cans full of buttons, rolls of ribbon, needles, powder puffs, old berets, and boxes of cotton wads from old medicine bottles," and joined her on a bus headed west. Suitably fortified with aspirins and Coca-Cola, Mémère enjoyed eating oysters in New Orleans as she flirted with old men in the bars, and was moved at the sight of the crawling penitents in a Juarez peasant church. But when they arrived in mid-May, Gabrielle wasn't so sure about 1943 Berkeley Way, Berkeley, California. Earthquakes and fog made her nervous, and she had no close company but Jack, who was speeding on Tangierian Benzedrine and found it difficult to work on his poem "Old Angel Midnight" with her in the house all day. The Berkeley police slapped him with several jaywalking tickets, which exasperated him, and there were more serious troubles.

Edie Parker wasn't the only ex-wife who'd seen his name in the media; though she thought he was still in Tangiers, Joan Haverty had a warrant out for his arrest for nonsupport. Jack corresponded with her through Burroughs, and avoided trouble for the time being. He was reminded of the sage Milarepa, who commented, "Keep low and poor and no litigation will arise." Phil Whalen was close to the Kerouacs, in part because Mémère adored him, called him "Old Gran'pa" and made him welcome. Neal was hardly to be seen, and Jack's feelings were hurt. He'd come to California for a big two-family scene at last, and Cassady was cold, Jack thought, and afraid of being chiseled on. Heavily preoccupied with a dance recital, Carolyn did not learn of their presence immediately, and before she had a chance, the Kerouacs were gone.

Wearied by the problems of managing his money, half-listening when Mémère shrewishly warned him that everyone was out to rob him, sick of her nagging him every time he went into San Francisco to drink, his work completely blocked, Jack conceded after six weeks in their "final home" that he'd been a fool; try as he might to sink roots, there was no home anywhere for the displaced Kerouacs, no place to rest and be nurtured. Early in July he and Mémère rode the bus back to Orlando and Nin's home, but just before he left, he had a strange epiphany.

Standing in the Berkeley Way apartment, Jack had just ripped open the carton that contained his advance copies of *On the Road* and had a precious, as-yet-unopened volume in his hand when the door flew open and in burst the book's characters Dean Moriarity, Marylou, and Ed Dunkel (Neal, LuAnne and Al Hinkle). The visitation from the past collided in an eerie way with the artistic present. Jack grinned shyly and handed the copy to Neal, but worried that Cassady had looked away "shifty-like" as they parted. Success had added a new guilt to his catalogue of insecurities; the potentially awful consequences of using friends in his art. Actually, though he did not approve of his own lifestyle, Neal enjoyed being the star of a book, and advertised all through San Francisco that he was Dean Moriarity.

Once he and Mémêre climbed off the bus in Orlando, Jack found a bungalow complete with citrus trees that Mémêre thought was "cute," and after a couple of weeks of Florida heat he lit out for Mexico City to write a magazine article on the "Beat Generation" at Viking Press's suggestion. Badly frightened by an earthquake just after his arrival, he soon developed a massive fever that made him sweat so much it rotted out the lining of his sleeping bag. Underlying that misery was the sad news that his old friend Garver was dead. Jack presumed that he'd run out of dope, and as foretold in *Mexico City Blues,* had committed suicide by swallowing forty Sodium Amytal tablets. Somehow Jack managed to complete the publicity article (which was never published), rereading Spengler as he likened the Beats to Tao, Dionysism, and Buddhism as an essentially religious movement that in the twentieth century was rooted in the Gothic style as it strove to supplant the decadence of the technocracy.

Late in August 1957, he returned to Orlando and troubles. He was working on a never-to-be-published book about Burroughs called *Secret Mullings About Bill* and planning for a *Visions of Gary,* because Snyder was the only man since Cassady to have engaged him emotionally. But the local newspaper sent reporters to interview him and the neighbors stared when he tried to sunbathe or read in the yard. The autograph fiend was about to engulf him, and he was alone. Allen had knocked on hundreds of publishers' doors as an agent, so was better equipped to cope with literary success, but he was enjoying himself in Spain and Italy, where he infuriated Mémêre by denouncing the Catholic Church as a "bunch of hard up, fig leaving, psychotic Politicians." Jack could not handle the publicity, and the deluge was just beginning to build. There were two more major stories that summer—the *Howl* censorship case and the *Evergreen Review.*

The overwhelmingly European first issue of the *Review* led with

Sartre, Beckett, and Henri Michaux; an article on old-time jazz drummer Baby Dodds was the only significant concession to Americana. The editor had friends in the Bay Area who had alerted him to the San Francisco poetic earthquake, and when Allen, Gregory, and Jack had passed through New York in December 1956, they'd helped him put together the second issue of the *Review,* an encyclopedic catalogue of "Beat" and San Franciscan writing.

The San Francisco Renaissance issue of the *Review* was instantly and astonishingly popular—its first printing was double the first issue's, and it was reprinted several times—and remarkably prescient as well, running nearly every San Francisco artist destined to endure. It opened with a letter from Rexroth, and included older poets William Everson (Brother Antoninus), Josephine Miles, James Broughton, and Jack Spicer. From the younger poets came Michael McClure's "Night Words," selections from Ferlinghetti's "A Coney Island of the Mind," Gary Snyder's "A Berry Feast," and Philip Whalen's "The Road Runner." Dore Ashton on painting, Henry Miller on Big Sur, and San Francisco *Chronicle* columnist Ralph Gleason on jazz rounded out the perspective with intelligent sidebar pieces.

The issue closed with Jack's "October in the Railroad Earth" and Allen's "Howl." Only Corso was absent from the cornucopia; there had been so much material that his poems had to await the third issue. Rexroth had already informed *Nation* readers in February about "San Francisco's Mature Bohemians," comparing Jack to Henry Miller, Céline, Durrell, Beckett, and Algren—"only a good deal more so . . . this is the literature of disengagement, but it is a wildly passionate disengagement . . . a smashing indictment." Publication of the *Review* brought respectful notices in Louise Bogan's *New Yorker* column, an article—"Avant Garde at the Golden Gate"—in *Saturday Review,* and a photo essay on New York bohemia in *Esquire.*

Even more than the *Review,* Captain William Hanrahan of the San Francisco Police Department Juvenile Division brought national attention to the esoteric subject of poetry; after customs officials tried and failed to stop the book, in June 1957 he put art on the front page by arresting Ferlinghetti and clerk Shig Murao of City Lights Bookstore for selling obscene material like Ginsberg's *Howl.* Embarrassed by the arrests, San Francisco's newspapers sneered at the police with headlines like "Making a Clown of San Francisco" and "Cops Don't Allow No Renaissance Here," and mocked Prosecutor Ralph McIntosh's inept attempts to discuss prosody with defense witnesses Mark Schorer of Berkeley, Kenneth Rexroth, and *Chronicle* critics Vincent McHugh and Luther Nichols.

Judge Clayton Horn taught church school on Sundays, but Defense Counsel Jake "The Master" Ehrlich's presentation led Horn to issue a decision thumpingly on the side of literary freedom. At first Jack had been amused by the trial, imagining what lawyers would do with lines like "and sweetened the cunts of a thousand girls in the sunset." Soon he was thoroughly intimidated by police and politics, and though Horn's decision pleased him, he pledged to remain a quiet Buddhist pilgrim. In the course of the arrest and trial, *Howl* sales had risen enormously, never to slow down.

Late in August, Jack left Florida for New York to enjoy his September publication. Out on Cape Cod, a young *New York Times* editor named Gilbert Millstein—the man who had solicited Holmes's 1952 Beat Generation article—was writing *On the Road's* first review. It was singular good fortune that brought the book to Millstein, only a fill-in on the daily *Times* reviewing staff. Orville Prescott, nicknamed "Prissy," the dean of the *Times* reviewers, was providentially on vacation. Had he written the review, it would surely have been as negative as the Sunday piece that followed Millstein's article by three days.

At the same time as Jack headed north, Joe Gould, comrade of Maxwell Bodenheim and the last survivor of the pre–World War I New York bohemian generation of Mabel Dodge, John Reed, the Province-town Players, and *Seven Arts*, died a penniless bum at Pilgrim State Mental Hospital.

XIII
Success, More or Less

READING Gilbert Millstein's review in a newspaper hastily plucked from a newsstand late in the night, Jack must have felt like Bobby Thomson as he watched his home run drop over the fence, or an actor who'd just heard his name read off at the Oscars; the review confirmed his unequivocal triumph, certified by the good gray *Times*. Millstein hailed *On the Road*'s publication as an "historic occasion," and compared it with *The Sun Also Rises* as a generational testament. "The most beautifully executed, the clearest and most important utterance yet made by the generation Kerouac himself named 'beat' . . . *On the Road* is a major novel."

On Sunday the *Times Book Review* waffled, first praising the book as "enormously readable and entertaining," then dismissing it as "a sideshow—the freaks are fascinating although they are hardly part of our lives." To understand *On the Road* one somehow needed an affinity for the intuitive and the sensual, for the romantic quest as opposed to the generally analytic realm of the critics. Since most critics had never experienced anything like the *Road*, they denied its existence as art and proclaimed it a "Beat Generation" tract of rebellion, then pilloried it as immoral.

It was "verbal goofballs" to *Saturday Review*, "infantile, perversely negative" to the *Herald Tribune*, "lack[ed] . . . seriousness" to *Commonweal*, "like a slob running a temperature" to the *Hudson Review*, and a "series of Neanderthal grunts" to *Encounter*. The New Yorker labeled Dean Moriarty "a wild and incomprehensible ex-convict"; the *Atlantic* thought him "more convincing as an eccentric than as a representative of any segment of humanity," and *Time* diagnosed him a victim of the Ganser Syndrome, whereby people weren't really mad—they only seemed to be.

Herbert Gold, an old Columbia acquaintance of Ginsberg's and a man who considered himself hip, wrote the most overtly hostile piece for the *Nation*. His review first incorrectly identified Jack as a cool hipster—a pose Jack had never suggested of himself—then sneered that he cared too much to be a hipster. "Kerouac has appointed himself prose celebrant to a pack of unleashed zazous who like to describe themselves as Zen Hipsters," Gold wrote. *On the Road* "is proof of illness rather than a creation of art, a novel." Gold saved his worst spleen for his old friend Allen (Carlo Marx in the novel), who was a "perenially perverse bar mitzvah boy, proudly announcing, 'Today I am a madman. Now give me the fountain pen.' "

Paul Goodman's review for *Midstream* thoughtfully suggested that the *Road* rebellion was too narrow, and only the *Village Voice* offered a positive assessment, lauding Jack as "not just a writer, not just a talent, but a *voice* . . . a rallying point for the elusive spirit of rebellion of these times, that silent scornful sit-down strike of the disaffiliated."

Just as the prose critics finished, the slow-moving poetry reviews caught up with *Howl*. They were as harsh as their colleagues. John Ciardi wrote in *Saturday Review* that the work had "a kind of tireless arrogance at least as refreshing as it is shallow," *Poetry* mumbled dimly about its "celebration of the intellectual outlaw," and James Dickey gave the *Sewanee Review* a piece that attacked *Howl* as an "exhibitionist welter of unrelated associations, wish-fulfillment fantasies, and self-righteous maudlinness." Perhaps the most damning review came from a Columbia classmate named John Hollander in the *Partisan Review;* he conceded that Ginsberg had talent and an ear, but yawned that *Howl* was a "dreadful little volume . . . very short and very tiresome." Later Allen replied: "Poetry has been attacked by an ignorant and frightened bunch of bores who don't understand how it's made, and the trouble with these creeps is they wouldn't know poetry if it came up and buggered them in broad daylight." However sure Jack and Allen were of their art, the arrogant hostility of the establishment was debilitating.

Over the course of the fall, "Beat" articles appeared in magazines from *Life* to *Commentary*, and there were several pieces in *Saturday Review*'s popular "Tradewinds" column. *Life*'s "Big Day for Bards at Bay" concentrated on jazz-poetry readings, with pictures of Allen,

McClure, Brother Antoninus, Rexroth, and Ferlinghetti. Norman Podhoretz disparaged the San Francisco Renaissance as "a product of Rexroth's publicistic impulses," and momentarily the issue rested.

Though *On the Road* made the best-seller lists for five weeks and reached the Number Eleven spot, that fall American critics chose another best seller for their approval, James Gould Cozzens' *By Love Possessed,* which displaced *Peyton Place* as Number One, while at the same time winning tremendously favorable reviews. Rather than embrace the sprawling, often-slapdash energy and vision of the *Road,* the critics preferred what Dwight Macdonald called a "novel of resignation," a latinate, polysyllabic story of a reasoning, moralistic man—a prig, in fact—who snuffed out his emotions and senses that he might be a more servile citizen.

The day after *On the Road* was published, Jack dreamed of having his head bandaged from a wound while the police chased him. He ducked into hiding inside a parade of children chanting his name, which shielded him as they all walked into Mongolian exile. No exile nor children's crusade could block his fate now, no matter what the future cost. His long trial was about to pay off in a certain kind of success. Warner Brothers Films offered $100,000 for movie rights, Jack told Cassady, and Sterling Lord smiled and asked for more; Marlon Brando was rumored to be interested in the project. Lillian Hellman solicited a play from Jack, and Lord closed quick money deals with *Esquire, Pageant,* and *Playboy.* Success meant more than an end to rejection slips. For Jack, the adulation of the New York hip scene was like a hit of good heroin straight in the arm. Just as the subterraneans had fondled Jackson Pollock, they began to rub against Jack for luck.

What horrified Jack was that his fans weren't really groping him, but "JackKerouacauthorofOntheRoad," and the private person inside him began to crumble. Abuse he could comprehend, but not the blankness of an image-blinded fan. For a quarter-century he had been an observer, a voyeur who could not always go through doors but who took pictures through his special keyhole. Now he was strapped to a chair with what seemed like all of New York City peering through the hole at him. The terms of fame were impossible. Even immersed in his booze, "my liquid suit of armor, my shield which not even Flash Gordon's super ray gun could penetrate," it was difficult for him to talk with people. Hungover and trembling, he groaned to John Holmes, "I can't stand to meet anybody anymore. They talk to me like I wasn't me." The fans wanted Jack to be Dean Moriarity, the free American cowboy, the limitless man who lived on life's mental frontiers. What no one beyond friends knew was that *On the Road* was six years old and superseded by a body of work Jack considered superior. Worse still, the Great God Public had condemned Jack to the easy-to-catalogue stereotype role of the bohemian novelist; evermore, he would be the King of the Beats.

In the week after publication, John Holmes received thirty-five phone calls asking to be introduced to Kerouac. Joyce Glassman's telephone rang with women screeching, "You're young. I'm twenty-nine, and I've got to fuck him now!" On at least one occasion, Jack was mobbed on the street by a crowd of young female fans who tore at his clothing until his friends were able to drag him into their car. Shaken by such perverse affection, he could never learn Gore Vidal's lesson, that "in an age of total publicity personality is all that matters," and when he went on John Wingate's popular TV program *Nightbeat*, he "clammed up almost totally," as a reporter later remarked to him, "looking like nothing so much as a scared rabbit."

"Yeah man," Jack said. "I was plenty scared. One of my friends told me don't say anything, nothing that'll get you into trouble. So I just kept saying no, like a kid dragged in by a cop. That's the way I thought of it —a kid dragged up before the cops."

His success had spun into a kaleidoscope of greedy faces, all feeding on him to steal a little of his new power, too much whiskey and attention, too many photographers and autograph seekers and excited nights. "You know what I'm thinking when I'm in the midst of all that—the uproar, the booze, the wildness?" Jack asked John Holmes in a still moment later. "I'm always thinking: What am I doing here? Is this the way I'm supposed to feel?"

In October he retreated to Orlando, where he caught up on his sleep and cleared up some business. Though he generally detested blurbs as artificial, Jack was happy to send one to Ferlinghetti for Corso's new Pocket Poets volume *Gasoline:* "A tough young kid from the Lower East Side who rose like an angel over the rooftops and sang Italian songs as sweet as Caruso and Sinatra, but *in words.*" As earlier he'd plugged John Holmes at Random House, he sent Ferlinghetti some samples of Burroughs' *Naked Lunch* and also tried to interest City Lights in "Old Angel Midnight" or *Mexico City Blues* as a Pocket Poets book to fulfill the Corso-Ginsberg-Kerouac triumvirate. As Allen had imagined, "God knows the revolution that would take place in American poetry if you as well as Gregory and me were published by Ferlinghetti."

Jack wrote a play about the "Beat Generation" for Lillian Hellman —she rejected it but later he salvaged the third act for the movie *Pull My Daisy*—then sat down at his typewriter early in November and in ten sittings wrote *The Dharma Bums*. It was an unmystical, tightly knit narrative, not, as a few critics suggested, because Viking was salivating for a commercial duplication of *On the Road*, but because it was Gary's portrait. Tempered by his experience with *On the Road*, Jack grew a bit discreet, altering the sequence of events to create a fictionalized archetype rather than a literal but privacy-invading record. The form flowed from the subject, and *The Dharma Bums* was superlative reportage that created a portrait of Snyder in the tough, supple material of his own speech and poetry.

Philip Whalen read it later and was impressed; it was not a simple recording of events, he thought, but "as complicated as Flaubert" in its selection. Recalling the events of two years past, Whalen realized that it "could have been four times as sensational," for Jack had said much by what he failed to say, deleting Neal and the racy blonde who drove him up the coast from this religious chronicle of bhikkus and mountaintops and the void in a drop of dew. "He went," Snyder later said, "for the simple, interesting, paradoxical bones of things."

One sentence, later excised by Malcolm Cowley, concerned an argument with Gary, who mock-sputtered, "You old son of a bitch, you're going to end up asking for the Catholic rites on your death bed." Jack leered, "How did you know, my dear? Didn't you know I was a lay Jesuit?" Totally absorbed in Gary's personality for ten nights, Jack even allowed overt politics in the book: "Colleges being nothing but grooming schools for the middle class non-identity . . . rows of well-to-do houses with lawns and TV sets in each living room with everybody looking at the same thing . . . while the Garys of the world prowl the wilderness to find the ecstasy of the stars." There were not many books, reflected Whalen as he put it away on his shelf, that remind people "that there are other things to do besides getting out of Yale and going into Kidder and Peabody in Wall Street."

The book finished, Jack went to New York the week before Christmas to make a reading appearance at the Village Vanguard jazz club, and initiated a series of critical exchanges that kept him uselessly trying to explain mystical poetry to pragmatic reporters who wanted nothing from him but hot copy. He was like a sweaty-faced political candidate in a losing race, always responding, never relaxed. No one would really listen to him at the Vanguard, he felt, so he got extremely drunk. Dan Wakefield sniped in the *Nation* that his reading was a sordid attempt to boost *On the Road*'s sale to Hollywood; still, performing onstage was a considerable gesture for a man so shy, especially after the police harassed him about registering as a performer and owner Max Gordon forced him to read accompanied by musicians. Kids slogged in off the road and stacked their rucksacks in the Vanguard's cloakroom to hear him read from Ginsberg, Burroughs, and "October in the Railroad Earth." Wobbling all the way, he stayed sufficiently innoculated by Jack Daniels to finish, then assured one reporter that he'd never do it again. "I'm no Jackie Gleason," he grimaced, "I'm a poet."

Fame was a "bad bit," he said, and only a certain sense of irony could have extracted some amusement from the fact that Mémêre adored Jack's success, since it had made her the recipient of a fat stack of letters from long-lost relatives who now invited them to visit. The music critics were as bilious as their literary confreres, and even the usually generous Nat Hentoff attacked him.

Jazz truth was the putative subject of Jack's December *Playboy* article about a Negro hobo, "The Rumbling Rambling Blues." Pure fiction and one of his flimsiest pieces, the *Playboy* story, along with the passage in *On the Road* about "wishing to be a Negro" left him open to critical bleats of "Crow Jim"—reverse racism. Kenneth Rexroth weighed in with the comment, "Now, there are two things Jack knows nothing about—Jazz and Negroes," to be contradicted by Anaïs Nin, Ralph Gleason, and David Amram, who had higher opinions of Kerouac. The avant-garde essayist Nin included Jack in her estimate that America's most important writing derived from jazz, and though the San Francisco *Chronicle*'s distinguished jazz columnist Ralph Gleason acknowledged the "Crow Jim" label, he also opined that "Kerouac leaves you with no feeling of despair, but rather of exaltation . . . meanwhile writers like Kerouac and music like jazz are [the present generation's] voice."

An even more professional opinion came from the composer and musician David Amram, who accompanied on French horn as Jack read poetry at the Brata Art Gallery on East 10th Street in December, and again at the Circle in the Square Theater in February 1958. Jack had "a phenomenal ear," Amram said. When Jack improvised words like notes to go with David's horn, "it was like playing duets with a great musician."

Amram also came along when Jack went to Brooklyn College to give a lecture. He was "not there to promote his books," wrote Amram, "but to share a state of mind and a way of being." His way completely befuddled the students. Warmed with Thunderbird wine, Jack performed as a Zen master, first telling his audience that he wrote because he was bored, and published to make money. "I'm a story-teller and a preacher like Dostoyevsky," Jack proclaimed.

After a few stories, he opened the floor to questions that he tried to answer Roshi-style, turning the question back on the questioner. When a proto-writer asked about the influence of Céline, Jack solemnly replied, "You've got the answer in your question, and it's a beautiful answer." Brooklynites were unready to accept either Jack's style or his running argument that to add to his writing would be dishonest, and the atmosphere grew mildly hostile. At last a blue-eyed, curly-headed young man who resembled Harpo Marx rose up and asked Jack, "When you take all those trips . . . to Mexico and the desert and all, doesn't your mother ever get worried?" The house broke up in such noisy laughter that Jack never had to shock them by saying yes.

Jack's wild-eyed mystical talk usually left his pragmatic audiences bemused and bewildered; since they had little or no intellectual background in mysticism, most Americans assumed he was slightly crazy. Late in January Jack finished typing up *The Dharma Bums* and returned to New York to have a dourly skeptical Mike Wallace take him step by step through his beliefs on CBS television news. Often what read well in the *Diamond Sutra* failed to communicate over the screen.

To Wallace, Jack's vision of golden light on drugs sounded "like a self-destructive way to seek God." "Oh, it was tremendous," replied Jack. "I woke up sick about the fact that I had come back to myself, to the flesh of life."

Wallace: "You mean that the Beat people want to lose themselves?"

Kerouac: "Yeah. You know, Jesus said to see the Kingdom of Heaven you must lose yourself . . ."

Wallace: "Then the Beat Generation loves death?"

Kerouac: "Yeah. They're not afraid of death."

Wallace: "Aren't you afraid?"

Kerouac: "Naw . . . what I believe is that nothing is happening."

Wallace: "What do you mean?"

Kerouac: "Well, you're not sitting here. That's what you *think*. Actually, we are great empty space . . . an empty vision in one mind."

Though Jack was utterly serious when he spoke of death and emptiness, the hard-nosed reporters whom he lectured heard it only as absurd-ity, and were convinced that he was a fool or a madman. When he told *Saturday Review*'s "Tradewinds" column that "We love everything, Billy Graham, the Big 10, rock and roll, Zen, apple pie, Eisenhower—we dig it all. We're in the Vanguard of the new religion," the *Review*'s editors chuckled indulgently; *Time* magazine's first "Beat" article covered the Wallace interview, but there probably wasn't a soul in the Time-Life building who really wanted to understand what Jack was trying—however confusedly—to communicate.

Coping with the media's misunderstanding of his spiritual mono-logues was difficult, but far worse were the outrageously false assumptions made about him. Kerouac had waited seven long years with an idealization of Art as his main support; he had not endured to pose as a cynical nihilist vomiting out America, but to affirm comradely communication and spiritual search. "The Beat Generation *believes,*" he wrote in *Pageant* magazine, "that there will be some justification for all the horror of life." Beatific in the tradition of St. Francis, the Beats were "sweating for affirmation" in a "search for gnosticism, absolute belief in a Divinity of Rapture." Jack concluded, "I believe God is Ecstasy in His Natural Immanence." True humanity was possible only when one was nakedly honest and free to rave unashamed. The mystical and rhapsodic "Beatific" tradition was as ancient as the Alchemical Brotherhood of medieval times, and was related to the nineteenth-century's Diggers, Romantic poets, and American Transcendentalists. But the line had been interrupted in the United States, and the postwar critics held very different basic beliefs. They generally assumed that their own pragmatic, middle-class values were absolute, and assumed ex cathedra that Jack's work—often any work, in fact, that disagreed with their fundamental assumptions about contem-porary life—was an act of rejection and hostility. The havoc Jack had wreaked on the contemporary rules of form they interpreted as madness, and although there hadn't been so much as a fistfight in *On the Road,* the critics ascribed to it the usual quality of maniacal documents: violence.

His association with violence Jack could blame primarily on recent history, Norman Mailer, and his old friend John Clellon Holmes. In the placid consensus of the fifties, the only visible dissidents to middle-class morality prior to the Beats had been violent juvenile delinquents, homici-dal maniacs like Charles Starkweather and Carol Fugate, or the intellectu-alized hipsters propounded by Norman Mailer's widely publicized 1957 essay, "The White Negro."

In a search for existential authenticity, Mailer had proposed in his article that the only way to resist the "psychic havoc of the concentration camps and the atom bomb" was to "accept the terms of death" and "encourage the psychopath in oneself." Identifying this gut-level, orgasm-oriented lifestyle with the street wit of the urban black man, Mailer vowed that "the psychopath murders—if he has the courage—out of the necessity to purge his violence, for if he cannot empty his hatred then he cannot live, his being is frozen with implacable self-hatred for his cowardice."

In an article in the February 1958 issue of *Esquire,* a piece called "The Philosophy of the Beat Generation," John Holmes recalled Jack's TV desire to have "God . . . show me His face," but ultimately Holmes was closer to Mailer in spirit. Holmes described a grotesquely meaningless murder as a "specifically moral . . . crime, which the cruel absence of God (De Sade) made obligatory if a man were to prove that he was a man and not a blot of matter." Much of "The Philosophy of the Beat Generation" was brilliant, analyzing the values of tribe—"inviolability of comradeship, respect for confidences, and an almost mystical regard for courage"—and the relationship of James Dean and Charlie Parker to Beat.

The media had quickly stereotyped Dean Moriarity as a juvenile delinquent or Maileresque hipster capable of absolute depravity. Of course, Holmes's and Mailer's theories of the psychic need for violence answered their own needs and came from a universe that excluded Jack Kerouac. Jack craved authenticity as well, but he was the man who'd grown disgusted at a bullfight, the man who told TV viewers that every night he prayed to "my little brother, who died, and to my father, and to Buddha, to Jesus Christ, and to the Virgin Mary . . . I pray to those five people." Kerouac's bohemians he described as "ragged, beatific, beautiful in an ugly graceful new way . . . characters of a special spirituality who didn't gang up but were solitary Bartlebies staring out at the dead wall window of our civilization." They bore bells and candles, not switchblades, were "high, ecstatic, saved," not murderous.

With this ongoing critical argument about violence as a background, Grove Press brought out *The Subterraneans* in March of 1958. The reviews were predictably hostile. "Latrine laureate of Hobohemia . . . ambisextrous and hipsterical" cried *Time;* Kerouac "celebrates the self as something irresponsible, without ever identifying it with a world of objective, relevant values" was the analysis of the *Times Book Review.* Perhaps the most perceptive comment was offered many years later by Mardou Fox, heroine of the book; she suggested that it was written from a petit-bourgeois perspective that put down the upper-class Lucien and glorified the working-class Neal. Only Allen acclaimed Jack's "American actual speech—and thought—reproduction," and among the famous, only Henry Miller was publicly positive. When *The Subterraneans* came out in paperback, Miller wrote in the introduction: "Believe me, there's nothing clean, nothing healthy, nothing promising about this age of wonders—except the telling. And the Kerouacs will probably have the last word."

Early in April of 1958, Jack completed the purchase of a home on the North Shore of Long Island and headed for Florida to collect Mémère, his cats, and a suitcase full of manuscripts. Photograher Robert Frank accompanied him because *Life* had given them expenses for a provisional photo-article on the road; as once he'd listened to Neal, Jack now studied Frank's constantly scanning eye, and the way he'd seize his camera for a shot out the window as he drove. They prowled decrepit old bus stations and a dusty South Carolina barbershop, and fell over themselves grabbing camera and pencil at the sight of an Iowa woman on a Florida beach, "come 1500 miles," noted Jack, "to turn her back on the very ocean and sit behind the open trunk of her husband's car, bored among blankets and tires."

Though *Life* never published the essay, Jack enjoyed Frank's company greatly, and missed him when he and Mémère moved to New York. There in April 1958, they settled in their new home at 34 Gilbert Street, Northport, and Jack took cover in a yard full of flowers, writing in the shade of a grape arbor. Good and bad, recent events had overwhelmed him. He had appeared on several TV shows, including the Wingate *Nightbeat* program and Jack Paar's, and recorded two poetry albums, one backed by Steve Allen on piano. Kerouac also had the living hell beaten out of him one night at the Kettle of Fish Bar in the Village, when he drunkenly offended three local characters. Dripping blood and badly dazed, he managed to stumble to Joyce Glassman's East 13th Street apartment. She took him to the hospital, where he begged the doctors to "Cauterize my wounds, cauterize my wounds," as if cleansing fire were his only salvation.

Chastened by too much drinking and the swirling undertow of fame, Jack pledged to spend an ordered summer at his home in Northport. Through June he avoided the city, meditating at night under the arbor before losing himself in Dracula, Clark Gable, and Marlon Brando on Mémère's eternal TV. Agent Sterling Lord sold *The Subterraneans* to

MGM for $15,000, and although Jack had promised a month of prayer to Buddha if *On the Road* made him financially secure, it was only a small-time production company that picked up *Road's* film option, with Mort Sahl cast as Neal. Sahl was hardly Marlon Brando, but the check was no less real for that. Sipping iced white port, Jack began work on a new novel about his childhood. He entitled it with his boyhood nickname *Memory Babe*, and briefly contemplated going to Lowell for research. Viking Press had purchased *The Dharma Bums*, and Jack was momentarily so confident that he boasted of converting the publishing world to the Way before commercialism besmirched him. He gardened barefoot and in overalls like a child, worked up a sweat shooting baskets at the high school next door, and kept his focus and a sense of pace.

By July it was clear that there was no sanctuary anywhere. College kids came roaring up to the house to get him—and Mémère—drunk, and Jack found it impossible to say no to anyone. He was inundated with letters from money grubbers and crackpots and men who desired him sexually, and these disembodied admirers so disturbed him that he decided to forgo a visit to Phil Whalen and Gary Snyder in San Francisco that summer, worried that he might be entrapped by a phony narcotics arrest. *Memory Babe* wouldn't gel, and he had to fight with Viking over editorial changes of *The Dharma Bums* manuscript.

And then there was Rexroth. The maestro had returned to the United States from an extended stay in France to discover that his rule as king of the bohemian literary scene had been eclipsed by New Yorkers Allen, Gregory, and Jack. His review of *The Subterraneans* read in part, "Herbert Gold is right: Jack is a square, a Columbia boy who went slumming on Minetta Alley 10 years ago and got hooked." In an April *Nation* article, "Revolt: True or False," Rexroth implied that Jack was a puppet of New York publishing houses, and in the May 3 *New Yorker* he snarled, "I've *lived* in the kind of world that Jack Kerouac *imagines* he has lived in." When Jack wrote him, Rexroth refused to answer. Jack tried to shrug off Rexroth's venom, but he couldn't understand why the man who was supposed to understand and help the cause of new literature had become so hostile.

In July, Jack was relieved of his unintended role as spokesman for the Beat Generation by the arrival of Allen Ginsberg in New York. Though Allen was reluctant to "face all them aroused evil forces," as he put it, "for fear I'll close up and try making sense and then really sound horrible," his presence rescued Jack; at last the real impresario–manifesto-writer was back. Allen understood why the critics detected revolution in *On the Road*, and calmly explained to his father that "actually it only seems to be so to people who have accepted standard American values as permanent." As Allen wrote to Jack in this period, the media Beat image "is among the hep a fake and among the mass Evil and among the liberal intellectuals a mess—but that is weirdly good I dig, that we are still so purely Obscure to philistines that it's inevitable that it be misunderstood —since how can a whole Nation perceive the Illusion of Life in one year?" "The poets and writers will ultimately have to be priests," he told the press, "sexy illuminated priests who will stand up . . . and take the responsibility for spiritual guidance in this country."

In the fifteen months since Jack had left him in Tangiers, Allen had wandered Europe from Spain to Dachau to Amsterdam, where he had written Jack, "now you don't have to worry about existing only in my dedication and I will have to weep in your great shadow." Allen had spent most of that winter at 9 Rue Git-le-Coeur, Paris, in the "Beat Hotel," a little Latin Quarter hostelry run by Madame Rachou, who oddly enough preferred young—even troublesome—Americans to dull Frenchmen, and was concièrge to Burroughs, Allen, Peter, and Gregory.

Impoverished, Allen had been forced to dun Jack for the money he'd loaned him a year and a half before, and Kerouac replied with a drunkenly abusive airgram. But Ginsberg attributed Kerouac's guilty outburst to bad American karma "due to loss of comradely vision," and tried to reassure his harassed brother on the need for patience: "Those who have doubts have doubts, what can you do? Undoubt the whole civilization in one year?" Ginsberg's long sojourn outside his native land had further sharpened his political perspective, and his long letters to his father were perceptive and prescient analyses of Algeria and Korea, and of colonialism in general. He advocated a "revolution of consciousness in America" that rejected the "war psychosis on both sides."

In March Jack had tenderly written how much he missed Allen, yet by July his relief at Ginsberg's return was obliterated by his terror at the political atmosphere. His fear was not empty paranoia. Shortly before Allen arrived, they had both learned that in April Neal had been arrested for possession of marijuana, convicted, and sentenced to five years to life in San Quentin Prison. According to the police, Cassady had smuggled many pounds of Mexican marijuana on the train, but court testimony was confined to two joints he admitted offering two men—who proved to be undercover agents—in exchange for a ride to work. The publicity of *On the Road* had not created his problems, but rather Neal's boasts in every North Beach bar and coffeehouse that he was "Johnny Potseed," the man who was turning on the whole of San Francisco; Allen mournfully thought Neal "uncool . . . heroic, but uncool." Neal had been distraught ever since Natalie Jackson's death. Try as he might to be a family man, he was so miserable at home that he could only sleep or watch TV, and on the street he pressed his luck with outrageous legal risks, trying to provoke the fates into delivering him up for the punishment he so abjectly desired.

Prosecution testimony alleged that he had taken $40 from two men. Later he supposedly suspected that they were agents, and kept the money. The police arrived in the morning after the children had left for school, but never bothered to search the house, leaving Carolyn to speedily find Neal's home supply and burn it. The grand jury concluded that there was insufficient evidence, and released him.

One day later he was rearrested and recharged before the grand jury, with bail set at $23,000. He had been calm and philosophically patient during the first arrest, but now he was furious, raging at everyone: at Carolyn, who refused to second-mortgage the house for his bail, even though he told her that he could get $100,000 "easy"; at the incompetent public defender who botched his case; at the judge who pressed him to testify against his fellow defendants.

When his sentencing came, Neal stood frozen, his expression rigid and dignified as the judge bellowed about Cassady's "double life" and sentenced him to two counts of five years to life with the comment, "I'm sorry about his wife and kids, but I don't like his attitude." After a stop at Vacaville State Prison for psychiatric testing, Neal packed his books— the Bible, and *The Third Classic,* St. Teresa's own guide—and moved to a tiny cell at San Quentin. There he swept cotton in the textile mill, screamed prayers to drown out the looms, and glared at the walls and the thirteen tan bars of his cell. On clear days he could sit on his bed and see dust rising off the flying hooves of his beloved thoroughbreds at the race track directly across San Francisco Bay.

In one of Neal's saddest moments, Jack now deserted his friend and did nothing for him during his legal problems. He hadn't written the Cassadys in many months, and Carolyn had assumed that he feared for his money. Guilty about having possibly contributed to the arrest with *On the Road,* Jack described the scene to Phil Whalen with a burst of saccharine optimism that outdid Candide. In Jack's view, Carolyn was painting, Neal was learning and meditating in jail, and both were blooming, beatific contributors to society. Mémêre intercepted Allen's letters with the news about Neal and threatened to call the FBI if Ginsberg ever came near the house. Burroughs cursed all the way from Paris in a scathing commentary on Mémêre's lack of generosity and Jack's feeble kowtowing to her interference. Bill thought Mémêre's threats to Allen about the FBI were insane, and Jack agreed with him, then resolutely closed his ears, unfocused his eyes, and babbled that Mémêre was indeed a little goofy about Allen and really it had nothing at all to do with him anyway.

Sick with kidney stones, Allen stayed away from Northport and accepted Jack's behavior in silence. His absence relieved Jack mightily, for he was wallowing in fears of political repression that summer, and they focused on Ginsberg and his polemics. Ironically, Allen's libertarian radicalism was virtually unique. Left-wing critics generally disliked both Kerouac and Ginsberg; though David McReynolds defended them in the radical magazine *Liberation*, conventional Socialists like Michael Harrington condemned the Beats as "protest without program."

In August of 1958, *Look* magazine published an unsigned article entitled "The Bored, the Bearded and the Beat," leading with a picture of North Beach character Hube "the Cube" Leslie. With his goatee, shades, and tattoo—"Blessed, blessed oblivion"—up front like a used-car salesman's smile, Hube was the archetypal "beatnik," the ripest symbol of the commercialization of *On the Road* that Jack loathed. San Francisco *Chronicle* columnist Herb Caen had invented the term beatnik in the wake of Sputnik, since "Beat" and sputnik were "equally far out" to him. The faintly ludicrous ring of the fusion made instant sense to a nation whose lingua franca was epitomized in the complacency of its best-selling books: *"Kids Say the Darndest Things, Don't Eat the Daisies,* Pat Boone's *'Twixt Twelve and Twenty,* Harry Golden's *Only in America,* and the collected *Dear Abby.*

Beatnikdom had begun in February of 1958, when *Playboy* ran a trio of articles—"Cool Swinging in New York," "A Frigid Frolic in Frisco," and another of Herbert Gold's essays. Each article painted an absurd picture of cool zombies who bordered on catatonia. *Playboy*'s puppets bore not the slightest resemblance to Allen, Jack, or Neal. New York's beatniks were figments of the writer's imagination; they were rich, spoke *only* in bizarre slang, went topless if female, and salted hamburgers with ground glass before serving them to a messenger boy in rhapsodies of lobotomized joy. *Playboy*'s San Francisco beatniks were nearly as nonsensical, and were also a hallucination of the author. Gold's *Playboy* article lashed out at Maileresque hipster coolness, "sick refrigerator[s]" in flight from emotion, "sex without passion, religion without faith."

A revolutionary later wrote that "The power to define is the power to control": The press had created the astoundingly fraudulent beatnik image of what one article called "The Innocent Nihilists Adrift in Squaresville." The sad and frightening part of the fraud was that an undoubted majority of Americans accepted it as reality. First *The Nation* and then *Saturday Review* rushed to bury the phenomenon with hasty obituaries. Sales of *Howl* and *On the Road* remained steady.

Despite the fears that the ugly publicity and Neal's arrest had generated, Jack continued to see Allen whenever he visited Manhattan. Allen sometimes disturbed him, but nothing kept them apart for very long, and on October 15, 1958, they met in the Village, anticipating that evening's publication party for *The Dharma Bums*. Ginsberg had reverted to his agent role, advising Jack to ignore Viking's requests for further travelogues and put out something wildly experimental like *Dr. Sax*, perhaps through Grove. "Don't let Madison Avenue try water you down and make you palatable to reviewer mentality," Allen warned. Ginsberg was also attempting to sell Snyder and Whalen and *Mexico City Blues* either to Grove or James Laughlin's New Directions Press. In a *Voice* interview that week, he had championed Gregory with the comment, "I'm too literary, you know, but Corso can write about moth balls or atom bombs," and went on to list no fewer than twenty worthy young poets across the land, thoroughly impressing the reporter. In a respectful, meditative conclusion, the reporter conceded that he could grasp only part of what Allen was saying; few of his colleagues shared his frankness, as their ridiculously twisted reports made clear. The poetry propaganda business rapidly became a cancer to Allen, and he wanted out, although some of his encounters were enjoyable. He had presented a copy of *Howl* to Thelonious Monk, and a week later saw him outside the Five Spot and asked if he'd read it. The silent genius of the piano said, "Yeah, I'm almost through." "Well?" cried Allen. Monk nodded impassively: "It makes sense."

Access to well-known people was part of Jack's and Allen's new fame. They learned that D. T. Suzuki, America's foremost interpreter of Zen, wanted to see them. The afternoon of October 15, Jack jumped into a phone booth outside Allen and Peter's Lower East Side apartment and rang up the sage. When Dr. Suzuki's secretary asked "When?" Jack shouted "Right now!" and the three of them caught a cab uptown to his West 94th Street home. It was a nasty irony that as Jack prepared to meet his first Zen patriarch he was incapable of profiting from the experience. The year's permanent rampage of drunken uninvited visitors to his Northport home had left him shattered, his hands shaking too badly to type, his Buddhist meditations a thing of the past. In fact, he had begun to write Catholic poems for the church magazine *Jubilee*.

Still, he was to pass a charming afternoon with Dr. Suzuki, then eighty-seven and a lecturer at Columbia, who as a writer had influenced Toynbee, Huxley, Heidegger, Jung, John Cage, and Dizzy Gillespie among others. Suzuki, a bald little man with prodigious eyebrows, sat them down in chairs and plopped behind his desk. Their talk wandered into koans, and Jack nervously showed the Roshi his own: "When the Buddha was about to speak a horse spoke instead." Suzuki sighed that it was typically Western and overcomplicated. "After all," the old man said, "the Buddha and the horse had some kind of understanding there."

The philosopher fixed green tea while his visitors wrote haiku, and they sipped and talked about old Chinese prints and religion. In an embarrassing excess, Jack volunteered that he'd had samadhis (satori, bursts of enlightenment) that had lasted up to half an hour, and lapsed into silence when Dr. Suzuki gently remarked that a true samadhi had no time and all time. Impatient to get to the Viking cocktails, Jack thought to leave, then indulged one of his quicksilver bursts of enthusiasm and decided that Suzuki was his father. He told the elder, "I would like to spend the rest of my life with you, sir." Suzuki giggled and said, "Sometime," then came down to the steps with them, waving goodbye with the comment, "Remember the green tea."

As they rode toward the publication party, their thoughts turned to Jack's book. Evaluating *The Dharma Bums*, Allen had smiled as he told Jack, "This time it should be funny. You'll get attacked for being enlightened." Ginsberg's prescience was straight on, for the critics had typed Jack, in John Holmes's trenchant phrase, as the "poet of the pad and the bard of bebop," and were uncomfortable when he wrote about religion. The literati had ignored the mystical aspects of *On the Road* and *The Subterraneans* to sell Jack as a dope-smoking jazzhound, and they were unaware of the six-year time span among the three books. They assumed Jack was cashing in on the Zen fad, and labeled him "naïve" *(Hudson Review)*, "juvenile" *(New York Times)*, and "adolescent" *(New Yorker)*. *Time* subtitled its review "How the Campfire Boys Discovered Buddhism." *Newsweek* preferred Japhy Rider (Gary's pseudonym) to the "vicious, animal-like" Dean Moriarity, but Jack's only good prestigious review came in Nancy Wilson Ross's essay in *The New York Sunday Times*. She had already contributed a necessarily superficial but intelligent piece on Zen to *Mademoiselle*, and her article on *The Dharma Bums* was sound and respectful.

Ginsberg, however, hailed it in the *Village Voice* as an "extraordinary mystic testament," a "record of various inner sign posts on the road to understanding of the Illusion of Being," and a review in the *American Buddhist* was also laudatory. If nothing else, the "Beat" influence, of which *The Dharma Bums* was the best example, had helped to stimulate a serious interest in Buddhism. In 1957 and 1958 alone there were seven articles on Zen in the mass media, and though the best statement on Beat religion and vision-seeking would not appear until Gary Snyder's "Notes on the Religious Tendencies," several of the Zen articles were quite informative.

Though Jack had moved to Northport in the hope of finding a quiet retreat distant from Manhattan excitements, it had become a prison; no matter where he slept, his dreams had become carnivals of torment, theaters whose curtain rose as he sat naked in a field and Jack Paar popped up in front of him with a microphone and camera. Young Jean tried to fend him off with a flabby-futile punch—and then he was in an unspeakably loathsome maze, or had to dance on a thin high wavering ladder hanging sick in space off the Empire State Building. There were Technicolor atom bombs and executions by strangulation. Birds pecked at his brain. Fame had become Moloch and pulverized Jack. The nearly violent attention of curiosity seekers and his own crippling self-doubts had drained him, but the shrill antagonism of America's critical establishment was the final blow. The fall and winter of 1958–59 brought three more severe attacks, as New York's intellectual community disparaged Kerouac and his work in pieces by John Updike, Robert Brustein, and Norman Podhoretz.

Slick and urbane as always, *The New Yorker* presented its attack in the form of a John Updike satire entitled "On the Sidewalk." Young Lee (Jack) threw a fond backward glance at his mom standing in "pearly mystical United States home light" and leaped onto his trike to join mad, scooter riding Gogi (Neal), an imbecile saint with a Band-Aid flapping off his thumb, to go "contemplate those holy hydrants." At last Gogi tore off to gogogo, deserting Lee, who wasn't allowed to cross the street. Lee mourned, "I'm thirty-nine now, and felt sad."

Jack had committed a lifetime to his art; shrugging off hard-edged satire was not in him.

Columbia lecturer Robert Brustein fired the second round. A graduate of Amherst, Yale, and Columbia, Brustein produced two essentially identical essays—"America's New Culture Hero" and "The Cult of Unthink"—that were essentially expressions of middle-class fear of the "masses." In both pieces, Brustein hypothesized a new American "inarticulate hero," a composite of Marlon Brando in *The Wild Ones* and *On the Waterfront*, James Dean, and Dean Moriarity. Of medium height and lower-class birth, with a "surly and discontented expression," beetling brows, and uncombed hair, the new hero was muscular and slouchy and scratched himself a lot. "Self indulgent and inwardly conformist," the hero was usually "cool," which Brustein likened to the death aspects of Jack's and Allen's religious vows toward transcendence.

Primarily, the hero was "inarticulate," unequipped with middle-class verbal facility. His portentous silence frightened the intellectuals, bespoke reservoirs of physical strength, grace, and sexual power. As it had with black men, the intellectual class flinched at its own fantasies of macho strength in the Beats. Caught up in their own traditional verbal violence, the critics concluded that these stupid, muscle-rippling hoodlums must certainly be physically violent. "Kerouac, McClure, and the others [Jackson Pollock, for one] fling words on a page not as an act of communication but as an act of aggression"; Brustein warned his colleagues to be "prepared for violence in every page."

Agitated beyond his patience, Jack wrote a reply to the characterization at the request of a reporter, although it was never published. He reminded the public that there had not been the least suggestion of violence in *On the Road*. Rather, it was about tenderness among wild young hell-raisers; giggling Dean Moriarity was not a knife-wielding hoodlum but "spiteless."

In the spring of 1958, the *Partisan Review* published what was undoubtedly the most extreme attack of them all, Norman Podhoretz' "The Know-Nothing Bohemians." Podhoretz informed his readers that Jack and his friends were "hostile to civilization; [they] worship primitivism, instinct, energy, 'blood.' " Jack's intellectual interests were reported to run to "mystical doctrines, irrationalist philosophies," and, "left-wing Reichianism." Jack supposedly used Bop slang—although he rarely did—

to demonstrate "solidarity with the primitive vitality and spontaneity they feel in jazz or of expressing contempt for coherent rational discourse." When Podhoretz accused Jack of "an anti-intellectualism so bitter that it makes the ordinary American's hatred of eggheads seem positively benign," Jack plaintively asked a reporter if any critic had ever read Goethe's idealistic biography, *Dichtung und Wahrheit.*

Podhoretz had already created a portrait of Jack that was hysterically false, yet his frenzy knew no bounds: "Even the relatively mild ethos of Kerouac's books can spill over easily into brutality, for there is a suppressed cry in these books: Kill the intellectuals who can talk coherently, kill the people who can sit still for five minutes at a time, kill those incomprehensible characters who are capable of getting seriously involved with a woman, a job, a cause."

Allen thought Podhoretz' problem lay partly in the fact that when Ginsberg had been a literary editor at Columbia he had rejected Norman's poetry. Partly it was, as John Holmes thought, that Podhoretz could not "comprehend the nature of awe and wonder," and "want[ed] things firmly in their places." He was a man uncomfortable with anything nonverbal or sensual. Secure with the ideas of a rational technocratic liberal, Podhoretz could not begin to appreciate the Beats. The critics generally were disturbed and confused by artists who ignored John Crowe Ransom's tortuous rules, and they were probably also troubled by the knowledge that more and more copies of *Howl* and *On the Road* were going out to Des Moines and Pocatello and El Paso, where few people indeed bought the *Partisan Review.*

On November 8, 1958, Jack made another public attempt to respond to all the criticism he had received. He agreed to participate in the Brandeis Forum with Professor Ashley Montagu, New York *Post* editor James E. Wechsler, and English writer Kingsley Amis. Their subject was "Is There a Beat Generation?"

Kerouac was misled by his hosts as to the ground rules—he had prepared a lengthy essay at their request—and unnerved by the evening. By all the rules of literary debate, he'd lost when he walked in drunk to read his address (later published intact as "The Origins of the Beat Generation" in *Playboy*). Swaying slightly over the podium, he outlined a mystical interpretation of recent history that entranced the student audience and confused his co-panelists. "It is because I am Beat, that is, I believe in beatitude," Jack said, "and that God so loved the world that he gave his only begotten Son to it." "Who knows," he continued, his speech still clear, "but that the universe is not one vast sea of compassion actually, the veritable holy honey, beneath all this show of personality and cruelty?" He traced the Beat Generation's roots to "the glee of America, the honesty of America," its "wild self-believing individuality." Harpo, Lamont Cranston, Krazy Kat, Popeye and Lester Young were the immediate progenitors of this "revolution of manners," and Jack swore "Woe unto those who don't realize that America must, will, is changing now, for the better I think . . . Woe unto those who would spit on the Beat Generation—the wind will blow it back."

His checkered shirt, black jeans, and ankle boots marked him off from the suited men on the panel; his closing poem, a mystic chorus of love and death from *Mexico City Blues,* was from another world. Amis was erudite and polished as he briskly denied the existence of the "angry young men" of England. Wechsler proudly asserted that he was "one of the few un-reconstructed radicals of my generation," and came off as the most vigorous philistine since the hero of *Front Page.* "Life is complicated enough," he grumped, "without trying to make it a poem." The Beats, thought Ashley Montagu, were the "ultimate expression of a civilization whose moral values had broken down."

Jack clowned. Impolitely roaming the stage, he giggled and shouted interruptions of Wechsler's profundities. He thought of himself as a "Zen Lunatic," but conceded to Buddhist Phil Whalen in a sober moment later that he'd become corrupt somehow, empty, and tired. "Live your lives out" said the Wechsler mentality. "Nay, love your lives out," Jack bellowed as the evening came to a close. When critics reproached him for his lack of dignity, he explained that writing was not a gloomy profession but an experience of the moment. Drunk or sober, crabby or expansive, Jack was one with his art, never crafted or polished for presentation.

As Jack later recalled it, Allen and Gregory were in high glee as they sat around after the forum. In the silly hours after midnight, Allen leaned over and said, "Look, we've done all this, we've made great literature. Why don't we do something REAL great and take over the WORLD!"

Tugging at Jack's sleeve, Gregory added, "I'll be your HENCH-MAN!"

Jack liked the joke, but intruded a note of reality; he shrugged and sighed, "Awww, I just want to be Cervantes alone by moonlight."

XIV
On the Road
in a Corvette
Stingray

J ACK CELEBRATED New Year's Eve 1959 with Lucien in a traveling Manhattan drunk that left him still befuddled by a nightmarish hangover on January 2: He slumped in front of the TV in Northport and tried to ignore the telegrams from *Newsweek* and the phone calls from *Life* that clamored for his attention. Worse still, Mémêre missed Nin and unmercifully needled him about it. An Old Crow highball in his hand, Jack brooded over how much he owed Mémêre for the years she'd supported his art, and exactly what price she was exacting from him now. She hadn't approved of the way Joyce Glassman washed dishes on her few visits to Northport, and for various other reasons Joyce had drifted away from Jack in the past summer.

That fall of 1958 he had found a new lover named Dody Müller, and she was a very special woman. Dody was the widow of the painter Jan Müller, a creative and independent artist in her own right, and she and Jack got on extremely well. As a worried Peter Orlovsky had noted, Jack was "calm and peaceful in Northport but it's when he comes to the city that too much commotion flies around [and] he gets drunk too fast." Now Jack had in Dody a loving companion in the city, and Peter hoped that she might be his salvation. At thirty-two, Dody was an exciting, vibrant woman, a hard-drinking rocker with long, beautiful dark hair, a husky-sensual voice, and a tremendous laugh. Her husband had died only the previous year, and that fall Jack had helped considerably to ease her grief and renew her life. She thought he was "sweet and kind," and when he asked her to marry him and go to Paris she would have said yes, she recalled later, but for Mémêre.

Sitting in her vibrator chair on Sunday morning, Mémêre would sip cheap whiskey and lo-cal ginger ale as she said her rosary with TV's Fulton Sheen. She was "despicable and obscene" to Dody, an evil ghoul who had Jack in her clutches and would never release him. She controlled her son's finances through their joint bank account, and manipulated his social life by her refusal to permit him to sleep with women in his home. Mémêre had lost her husband and her first-born son, and now Jack was everything to her but a sex partner; when they fought, Dody said, "it was a lover's quarrel." Mémêre had given Jack the structure of support, the hot dinners and clean laundry, from which to write, and he felt he owed her tribute. Further, Jack had largely relinquished responsibility over his finances and normal "adult" life, and become so purely a perceptual instrument that he refused to consider the emotional cost of their mutual dependence. When Dody entered his life it was too late; he could not separate himself from his mother.

Though he blanched at his mother's voracious anti-Semitism, Jack allowed her to ban Allen from his home, and so became lonely and drank more. As he grew more thoroughly besotted, Jack was less and less able to communicate with Allen and his other friends when he did venture into New York. He became ever more completely reliant on Mémêre for his most basic views and moods. "Immaculately-sick-clean," Gabrielle would grow furious when Dody came into the kitchen without a hair net, and after Dody washed the dishes, Mémêre would redo them—and get them cleaner. Mrs. Kerouac called Dody "La Sauvage" for her bare feet, long black hair, and Indian ancestry, but one night she decided Dody was worse than barbaric. They'd had a wonderful candlelit roast beef dinner, and in the dreamy sated reverie after, Dody had played with the soft dripping candle wax. Early the next morning Mémêre cornered Jack in the kitchen and hissed at him that his lady was a "witch" making a voodoo doll to steal him away from her. Jack knew his mother was sick, but only shrugged; he saw his fate, but could not act.

Northport was quite pleasant when Mémêre visited Nin in Florida. Jack and Dody took long peaceful walks, went ice-skating, or read *Macbeth,* and Dody gave Jack painting lessons. He had a perceptive eye and was rather good, splashing enthusiastically away in an expressionist style that resembled his writing. All of his subjects were Roman Catholic, most often the newly anointed Pope John, whom he loved. At Dody's Village studio, Jack watched her paint and talked about Paris, Neal, and Gerard, or Shakespeare and Proust, the only authors he read anymore.

The couple haunted the Five Spot Café, listening raptly to Ornette Coleman and Don Cherry before they hit Jack's favorite drinking bars, the White Rose taverns. A seedy Bowery-style chain, the White Roses were frequented by the working-class men with whom Jack felt really comfortable. At the very least, they accepted his alcoholism. As a rule, Jack was a noisily emotional drunk, and loved Dody for not chiding him about his exploits.

Jack spent most of early 1959 in the Village with Dody, because he'd become involved in a new project, a film called *Pull My Daisy*. Eventually, director Alfred Leslie begged Jack to stay off the "set"—Leslie's Fourth Avenue loft—because his Bowery bum guests disrupted filming. Jack must have been outrageous to be noticeable in a scene where the cast and its visitors smoked grass in the wings while making jokes to break up the cameraman, Jack's photographer friend, Robert Frank. The occasionally unclothed "stars," Allen, Peter, and Gregory, regularly threatened either to jump out the window or douse passers-by with water.

The director was a well-known Village artist who'd given up film as a teenager to concentrate on his painting. Disgusted by the emotionless surrealists, Leslie wanted to make non-Hollywood but popular narrative movies, and in the mid-1950's he had joined with Robert Frank. *On the Road* and Frank convinced Leslie that they should film something of Jack's, but there seemed to be too many possibilities after he read all the manuscripts that Jack showed him. Then he visited Northport, and sat in Kerouac's spare, tiny bedroom, its dressers filled with notebooks and typescripts, a crucifix over the bed. Jack had reread the third act of *The Beat Generation*, the play he'd written for Lillian Hellman, and then spontaneously recited a new version of it onto tape, a fanciful rendering of the evening the bishop visited at Neal and Carolyn Cassady's home. When Leslie heard the tape, he concluded—unaware that there was a slim basis of reality in the tale—that all the characters were aspects of Jack, like Vittorio De Sica's *The Bicycle Thief.*

They inveigled Walter Guttman, a stockbroker and aesthete, into bankrolling them with funds he had charmed mostly out of Jack Dreyfus of the Dreyfus Fund. Leslie and Frank wanted actors whose pasts would be authentic for the roles, so they cast Allen and Peter as themselves, Larry Rivers the painter and saxophonist as Milo (Neal), Mooney Peebles as the bishop, composer David Amram as Mezz McGillicuddy the "hip-tape man," and Gregory Corso as Jack.

The only professional in the cast was Delphine Seyrig as Carolyn, and she did not appreciate the spontaneous chaos unleashed in the loft. Alfred would rehearse the scene and Frank would set his camera angles, but all that followed was in the lap of the gods. When Delphine objected to the disorder, Gregory snapped, "This is supposed to be real and poetic, beautiful and soulful, not that show business bullshit." Leslie's oft-repeated, slightly bemused comment was "That's terrific, terrific, terrific . . . I've never seen anything like this. It's alive and spontaneous!" After Leslie and Frank had edited the film, they collected a very stoned but still lucid Jack from Central Park, took him to his old friend Jerry Newman's Esoteric Studios, and showed him *Daisy* twice. Listening to Amram's piano for his rhythm, Jack spontaneously recited a narrative that sewed the film together. Amram's music was excellent, both the instrumental background and the song "Pull My Daisy"—Jack and Allen and Neal's 1949 poem, which Amram had scored for Anita Ellis to sing. Over it all, Jack laid down a superb narrative line.

He began in a warm and gentle tone with the phrase "Early morning in the universe," and described the room, Carolyn, Milo's "poor tortured socks," Allen and Peter and their beer, and then Milo and the bishop. Gregory as Jack posed questions about Buddhism, while Peter asked the bishop if baseball was holy; the film ended as the boys dragged Milo off to a party. Jack's supple voice neatly caught the quixotic, episodic nature of the film, depicting a reality that was more stoned than surreal, and was of a piece with Frank's observant, natural camera work.

Though *Daisy* shared the common fate of experimental films and died with few bookings after its June 1959 opening, several reviewers were impressed. Peter Bogdanovich called it "brilliant" and *Village Voice* film columnist Jonas Mekas thought it a "signpost . . . of purity, innocence, humor, truth and simplicity." Film critic Dwight MacDonald found it "refreshing," and singled out "the narrative by Jack Kerouac, which kept things rolling along on a tide of laughter and poetry, showing an unexpected virtuosity at the Great American Art of kidding."

Aside from the fact that Leslie had offended his sense of spontaneity by asking for two complete narratives to be spliced together, Jack's only question about the film had concerned a moment when Milo made a pistol of his finger and pointed it at Corso, which introduced a note of violence that Jack thought "played into the hands of literary snobs." His call for self-censorship was overly emotional but not without foundation. The American establishment had not succeeded in laughing the Beats away, and in a sporadic and unorganized manner, its police and educational leaders began to apply direct repression to the arts.

The major case of early 1959 was the suppression of the *Chicago Review*, and since Jack's and William Burroughs' "dirty words" had triggered the situation, Jack could not ignore it. The *Chicago Review* was a traditional student-run literary quarterly at the University of Chicago that published faculty and student poetry and short fiction. Though in 1956 it had run "Disaffiliation and the Art of Poetry," by Los Angeles bohemian Lawrence Lipton, the *Review* became a showcase for the Beats only when Irving Rosenthal assumed the editorship in 1958. Rosenthal filled the Spring 1958 issue with poetry by Ferlinghetti, Ginsberg, Duncan, Lamantia, McClure, and Whalen, an essay by Kerouac ("The Origins of Joy in Poetry"), and an excerpt from Burroughs' *Naked Lunch* manuscript. The Summer issue centered on Zen, with essays by Alan Watts, D. T. Suzuki, and Gary Snyder, and the Autumn issue included a second selection from *Naked Lunch*.

Chicago *Daily News* columnist Jack Mabley didn't approve of William Burroughs, and his October 1958 column, "Filthy Writing on the Midway," panicked the university administration. With the tacit support of the faculty, the university blocked publication of the spring 1959 issue, which would have featured Jack's "Old Angel Midnight," more of *Naked Lunch*, and Gregory Corso's poems "Army," "Power," and "Police." Led by Rosenthal, all but one member of the *Review* editorial board resigned to form the magazine *Big Table* (Jack had suggested the name after seeing a note he'd made to himself about his need for a larger work space), then sent out a plea for financial help that was answered by Allen, Gregory, and Peter. The poets agreed to interrupt the filming of *Daisy* and come to Chicago for a January 29, 1959, benefit reading under the ultrarespectable auspices of the George Bernard Shaw Society.

At this time Allen was at his poetic peak, and after a year and a half of preparation, he had just completed his brilliant elegy and lament for his mother, "Kaddish." Her death, to Allen "that remedy all singers dream of," had closed a circle in his life. "Kaddish" was an exorcism of the memories that had scarred him for life. Now he cherished her—and himself. "There, rest. No more suffering for you," he sang, "I know where you've gone, it's good." "Kaddish" ended in a stillness graced by the cawcawcaw of crows over her Long Island grave.

"Mescaline," "Laughing Gas," and "Lysergic Acid," Allen's other contemporary poems, recorded his consciousness-expanding drug experiments; though he was taking enormous psychological risks with the drugs, he was on Promethean fire for the moment. The Chicago reading was a huge success, as an overflow crowd of seven hundred jammed the ballroom cheering in ecstatic welcome. Not one of the Chicago newspapers mentioned the audience the next day in their unanimous revulsion at the "beatnik invasion." *Time* magazine's account—entitled "Fried Shoes"— was equally damning, a review that ignored the reading to focus on a one-minute exchange between Corso and a Northwestern University professor at the postreading party.

Corso: "You don't know about the hollyhocks."

Professor: "If you're going to be irrelevant, you might as well be irrelevant about hollyhocks."

Corso: "Man, this is a drag."

The "Fried Shoes" article did not mention the suppression of the *Review,* and instead "spat on the appearance of the soul of Poetry in America," wrote the poets in a letter to the editor, "at a time when America needs that soul most . . . You are an instrument of the Devil and you crucify America with your lies: You are the war creating whore of Babylon and would be damned were you not mercifully destined to be swallowed by oblivion with all created things."

Repression was not merely the result of a weak university or a manipulative press. The post office refused the *Big Table* a mailing permit in April, and although Judge Julius "The Just" Hoffman ordered it mailed in July, it had been labeled as obscene and somehow subversive. Even with its exciting contents and a circulation of ten thousand, the *Big Table* was unable to attract financial support, and it died two years later. Over the coming years, obscenity trials would devour the time and money of authors Michael McClure (*The Beard,* 1966), Lenore Kandel (*The Love Book,* 1968), and William Burroughs (*Naked Lunch,* 1962). In June of 1959, New York City authorities required Beat poets to register with the police in order to read—unpaid—in coffeehouses. In Los Angeles that September, a noisy bohemian bar in the Venice neighborhood drew repeated arrests and citations. Distracted by the furor, Jack hid in Northport.

One of Jack's few visitors at his Long Island home was New York *Post* reporter Alfred G. Aronowitz, who somehow managed to charm his skittish subject into an interview. *Post* editor James E. Wechsler's son was reading *On the Road* and smoking marijuana with beatniks, so Wechsler had dispatched his star feature writer to do a hatchet job. Somehow Jack intuited that the glib, materialistic, middle-class Jew on his doorstep was sympathetic, and his instincts proved correct. In fact, Kerouac would utterly alter Aronowitz' life.

The Kerouac who revealed himself to Aronowitz and the New York *Post* readers was a man obsessed with money and bitter about his treatment as a literary figure. In between his memories of the week at the Village Vanguard, school, the Navy, the "St. Louis clique" of 1945 (Lucien and Burroughs) and the creation of the term "Beat Generation," Jack assured Aronowitz that he'd "only paid *fourteen*" for his house. When he spoke of money, Jack dropped his voice into the same tone of emphatic awe that he used when he mentioned his home's previous owner, Mona Kent Eddy, the *"very famous"* author of the radio serial *Portia Faces Life*. An hour later Jack returned to the subject of the house and detailed how he'd paid for it. He denounced Hollywood, which had paid little for *The Subterraneans,* while *On the Road's* option had lapsed, and was unsold. Popping down beer after beer, Jack explained that he'd only earned about $20,000 since he'd become famous.

The struggle between his loyalty to Mémêre and his aesthetic needs was never so evident as when she joined the conversation and complained in the *Post* article, "Everybody says, 'Beat Generation!—He's a juvenile delinquent!' But he's a good boy . . . a good son. He was never any juvenile delinquent. I know, I'm his mother."

"Yeah," Jack said. "We're Middle Class, we've always been Middle Class. We're Middle Class just like you."

"Oh, I was making good money," she continued later. "We're Middle Class—we've always been that way."

"We're bourgeois," Jack said.

Aronowitz gave Jack a ride into Manhattan that night; Jack left Northport wearing a nice bow tie, as Mémêre had instructed, and took it off in the first bar.

Whatever Wechsler's implied instructions had been, Aronowitz found himself growing obsessed with his subject, and his original one month's research grew to three. Later he took six months off to write a book about the Beats, but his fanatic commitment to his subjects made him at first unwilling and later morally incapable of producing a cheap "quickie." He never managed to get it to a publisher.

Aronowitz was not always in touch with his subjects. He wanted to talk sex when he interviewed Neal in prison, and Cassady inundated him with Caycean mystical talk about Kundalini yoga and the pineal gland, then dismissed him as a "pagan." Aronowitz also served as a messenger when Neal asked Jack to send him a typewriter. Jack supplied the money, and Allen delivered it to San Quentin; Neal enjoyed the new machine, and wrote his first letter to Kerouac in many years. He was bitter: "Giving those three offbrand cigarettes to that cop . . . did finally free me from that ludicrous lifetime job and the even funnier family it supported so I could concentrate entirely on really important things like at which wall to stare in this——cell I share with a gunman."

Though Neal thought he was an ignorant pagan, Aronowitz included the metaphysical Cayce lecture and Neal's defense of marijuana in his New York *Post* series, the most sensitive of all the journalistic treatments of the Beats. Eighteen years later, "The Beat Book" would still be the center of Aronowitz' life. He had become a link in a chain; Jack had introduced him to marijuana, and later he and Bob Dylan would do the same for the Beatles. The Beat aesthetic vision turned him inside out for life.

Despite Aronowitz' sympathetic treatment, the majority of Jack's critics remained hostile. Truman Capote got off the most memorable one-line Kerouac zinger on David Susskind's *Open End* program when he squeaked, "That's not writing, that's *type*writing." Trivial, sensationalized articles in his hometown Long Island *Newsday* depressed Jack just as he had to absorb the sickening impact of the *Dr. Sax* reviews: "Bad taste," "incoherent," "psychopathic fantasy," "stupefying in its unreadability," "Barefoot Boy with Dreams of Zen." Lawrence Lipton, Los Angeles' answer to Rexroth, cashed in on the scene with his corny, egotistical tome, *The Holy Barbarians*.

Jack struck back. Muttering threats to flee the abuse and move to Florida, he began in the spring of 1959 to write a column for the men's magazine *Escapade*, and accepted the editorship of a three-times-yearly Beat anthology for the Avon Press. Keeping busy, he read the *Diamond Sutra* and Casanova, typed up his "Book of Sketches," wrote dozens of letters soliciting everyone's most fantastic and unpublishable material for his anthology, and read an enormous stack of galleys for the flood of his books that would be published in the next fifteen months: *Maggie Cassidy, Tristessa, Mexico City Blues, The Scripture of the Golden Eternity*, and part of *Visions of Cody*. Sterling Lord had grabbed quickly at $7,500 paperback advances for *Tristessa* and *Maggie Cassidy* from Avon. There was no order and little dignity to the sluice of publications, and Jack suffered in the end for it, particularly as he constantly complained that Lord always wanted his "latest adventures." That spring *Holiday* magazine paid Jack $2,000 for two articles—"The Vanishing American Hobo" and "The Roaming Beatniks"—which he in fact wrote in collaboration with Gregory, Allen, and Peter, splitting the proceeds with them so that they could travel again.

The pace was too hectic for Jack, and his drinking accelerated to a quart of whiskey a day. Prudish Jack was unhinged enough to drop his trousers and expose himself at a party on one of his New York binges. Much of his self-loathing stemmed from Lowell, where his relatives, he told Phil Whalen, had disowned him as a disgrace to the name of Kerouac. Jack wrote a letter to the Lowell *Sun* about *Dr. Sax*, conceding that it might well be banned, but that "It's wild . . . It is the completion of the Faust legend, and also a gothic New England with roots in Melville and Hawthorne . . . After *Sax*, I will never dare to visit Lowell again, but it is my deepest vision of the world, which to me was and still is Lowell."

Just as his emotional life lay more tattered than ever before, his publishing career had peaked. "Old Angel Midnight" was in the editorial works at Ferlinghetti's City Lights Press and *Pull My Daisy* premièred at the Museum of Modern Art, sparking a bar crawl that Jack began with Willem de Kooning and ended by being ousted from Birdland in the company of jazz drummer Elvin Jones. Jack even went with Gregory Corso to read at Wesleyan University, and enjoyed the personal atmosphere.

Part of the reason Lowell condemned Jack was his column in *Escapade*. Yet it was no surprise that his work appeared in the "girlie magazines." Thanks to two enlightened editors—A. C. Spectorsky at *Playboy* and Seymour Krim at *Nugget* and later *Swank*—many experimental works were published surrounded by a garden of languorous smiles and smooth flesh. Since they had no reputation to lose, the sinful hoydens of the publishing business were quite tolerant. Jack's contributions to *Escapade* were eccentric, often charming, and always spontaneous. Entitled "The Last Word," Jack's column began in April of 1959 with an expert if surreal history of "The Beginning of Bop" to test the water. Then in June, Jack published a piece on his "position in the current American literary scene," boosting Burroughs, Corso, Ginsberg, and his own unpublished work.

In succeeding columns he defended Ted Williams and attacked baseball's Boudreau shift (which put virtually the entire team on one side of the field to stop Ted) as "unnatural," taught Buddhism and the Four Noble Truths, berated bullfight fans for their insensitivity to agony, and sorrowfully described the history of the world as "bloody and sad and mad." He pondered foreign policy and sounded like Dean Acheson, and then quirkily and from his heart defended Nikita Khrushchev for wearing a hat while Eisenhower gave a speech, because the sun had been hot. Jack grew used to the column form, and his best columns were his last two, before he quit over the low pay and lack of prestige. The last piece, a segment of *Visions of Cody* that began "The mad road, lovely," was excellent. The article on the future of jazz was best of all, accurately prophesying the ascension of Ornette Coleman, Don Cherry, and John Coltrane; for the present, Max Roach was the best percussionist and Thelonious Monk the "greatest composer who ever lived."

Jack was certainly correct in writing off the column as an ineffectual method for answering the critics. *Escapade's* readers didn't care what *Partisan Review* critics said, and *Partisan Review's* audience confined its interest in *Escapade* to nervous rifflings at the newsstand. Still trying to help Neal in San Francisco, Allen had nearly given up, emotionally torn by the "joyless ambitions" he saw in the local poets and the unrelenting barrage of criticism. New York's intelligentsia continued to dismiss the upstart Beats as insignificant unruly brats. Alfred Kazin's article in *Harper's,* Irving Howe's highly publicized "Mass Society and Modern Fiction" in the *Partisan Review,* and John Ciardi's "Epitaph for the Dead Beats" in *Saturday Review* each deprecated the "Beat rebellion" as a "naked and unashamed plea for 'love.'" The Beats themselves were anti-intellectuals indulging in "unwashed eccentricity."

Critical snobbery reached its apex in Diana Trilling's *Partisan Review* article, "The Other Night at Columbia," a report on Allen, Peter and Gregory's February 1959 reading at the University's McMillin Theater. Earlier, she had described Edith Wharton as "the aristocrat that all literary artists are, and must be, in spirit," and wrote her attack on Ginsberg from that perspective. Professing astonishment that the audience and poets smelled clean, she dispatched the crowd as "without the promise of masculinity," and the readers as "miserable children trying desperately to manage." The smell of revenge on her oddly impersonal prose, she informed her readers as an insider that Allen had been disturbed since college days, and that he adored her husband Lionel as a father figure, dedicating a "passionate love poem" called "Lion in the Room" to Trilling at the reading. Actually, it was called "A Lion for Real" and was about God, death, and the alteration of consciousness, not romantic love.

Mrs. Trilling's sentiments were shared by most of the intellectual press, including *Encounter*, whose "Portrait of the Beatnik" was a fantasy of hipsters lighting up on "muggles" (marijuana) culled from the pages of *Look* and *Playboy*. The American right wing was even more graphic in its contempt; to the *National Review*, Beat poetry was "a combination of nausea and the stirrings of the urino-genital tract" produced by mass culture weaklings rather than virile individualists. Even the *"Playboy Philosophy"* dismissed Jack and Allen as irresponsible profligates.

Represented by Professors Richard Hofstadter and Leo Marx, the academic world denounced Kerouac and company as "adolescent," and Doctors Francis Rigney and L. Douglas Smith of the American Orthopsychiatric Association diagnosed the typical beatnik as "a sad, mentally sick individual, who needs the professional help of the psychiatrist." Rigney and Smith's later book, *The Real Bohemia*, was a classic specimen of statistical flimflam that divided their tiny sample of fifty North Beach resident "Beats" into seven improbably neat categories: Men were "Tormented Rebels" or "Lonely Ones," women were "Angry" or "Beat Madonnas"; both were either "Earnest Artists" or "Passive Prophets," or "Atypical." *Newsweek* and the *New York Times* ran ponderously impressive articles based on *The Real Bohemia*.

In fact, the only writers in America who half-defended the new art were Catholic intellectuals. Father Donachie at St. Patrick's Cathedral might attack the Beats for their failure to accept the Church, but articles in *America*, *Cithera*, and *Catholic World* applauded Beat antimaterialism and its sense of morality, although they cringed at its actual application.

Allen and Gregory each had a reply. In "Poetry, Violence, and the Trembling Lambs," published that summer of 1959 in the *Village Voice*, Allen argued that "recent history is the record of a vast conspiracy to impose one level of mechanical consciousness on mankind and exterminate all manifestations of that unique part of human sentience, identical in all men, which the individual shares with his Creator. The suppression of contemplative humanity is nearly complete." The new poetry was a "crack in the mass consciousness of America" that illuminated a "nether world of nerve gases, death bombs, bureaucrats, secret police systems . . ." Gregory wrote in his "Variations on a Generation":

The Beat Generation is youth quarrels vexation
American disappointment of a cherished hope, an
enlightenment, a testimonial of honor and distinction.
The Beat Generation is high, is good omen, is
like frog.

Though it was perhaps a good omen for the future, as Corso said, the Beat Generation still had to cope with the present-day United States, a nation that in 1959 was led by men firmly convinced of their own rectitude and obsessed with the sins of others. That year the U.S. media made an overnight hero of an Army corporal who refused to allow Soviet guards to inspect a convoy traveling from West Berlin to West Germany, and grew nervous about the Cuban revolution ninety miles from its shores. When Nikita Khrushchev made his fall visit, American citizens lined the streets to stare blankly at the Soviet monster. On the whole, Americans preferred to cheer, to salute the seven crew-cut pilots who that fall were selected as astronauts, to glory in the astounding prosperity that had made the American good life possible. Still, there was something wistfully reactionary in the TV networks' decision to retreat to the golden age of cowboys; thirty-two of that year's prime-time programs were Westerns.

Few Americans read the *Partisan Review, Howl,* or *On the Road,* but virtually all of them knew what a beatnik was. The small New York intellectual family had established an image for the beatnik, but cartoonists and television script writers made the image common knowledge. In the fall of 1959, America's best-known beatnik was not Allen or Jack, but an inept if good-hearted waif named Maynard G. Krebs, the costar of the *Dobie Gillis* show. A Los Angeles critic of the beatniks had announced, "We're not criticizing their clothing and beards or their way of life, except when it becomes immoral," and Maynard satisfied that sort of mentality perfectly. He was instantly identifiable as a beatnik, since he played bongos, prefaced every sentence with "Like," and wore sneakers, blue jeans, a sweat shirt, and a goatee.

Since *Dobie Gillis* was a situation comedy, Maynard was as threatening as a lamb. With his shy smile and failures with women, he was the expression of the childlike image of the beatnik (versus the threatening evil hipster). He was a dopey goof who became convulsed with a spasm of eye-bulging fear whenever the idea of labor was mentioned. He was illiterate, stupid, incapable of doing anything of significance, and accident-prone. Yet Maynard was also given a child's virtues: truthfulness, loyalty, generosity, and love. Young viewers adored him.

Dobie Gillis had been a popular series of short stories by Max Shulman, but Maynard was created expressly for TV. In one typical program, Maynard met "Eddie," a girl who looked and thought exactly like him. Mocking their friends' boring conventionality, they amused themselves with visits to a stockyard and a bridge building site. When their friends persuaded them to go to a dance, Eddie dressed up for the event and turned into Cinderella, deserting beatdom in a flash. Secure in her new popularity, she assured Maynard that he would soon straighten up and join society as well; unmoved, Maynard continued on his eccentric, solitary path.

A few years later, in 1962, television dipped again into the Beats to create a new program by the simple expedient of sanitizing *On the Road.* Trading in a muddy 1949 Hudson for a gleaming Corvette Stingray, producer Stirling Silliphant took the archetypal freedom image from Jack's book and added George Maharis, an actor who eerily resembled Kerouac, to produce *Route 66.* Appalled by the show's violence, Jack asked two different lawyers to sue Silliphant for plagiarism, but both concluded that there was insufficient evidence.

Most TV beatniks were criminals, as the villains on detective shows like *San Francisco Beat* rapidly sprouted goatees. In real-life 1959, the *New York Times* headlined "beatnik" drug arrests, although the drug dealers were caught in a "lavish" Central Park West apartment. At the same time, producer Albert Zugsmith unveiled his new film, *The Beat Generation,* a sleazy B-grade opus of rape and assault. The film was patently a standard plot dressed in goatees and sunglasses for quick publicity, but Zugsmith assured reporters that he'd written a book by that title two years before, "And we don't actually show them smoking tea, but they act like the typical beatniks." Music was by the advanced modern trumpeter Louis Armstrong, and the cast included Charles Chaplin, Jr., as the lover-boy beatnik, Maxie Rosenbloom as the boxing beatnik, Jackie Coogan as the nutty beatnik, Ray Danton as the rapist beatnik, and Mamie Van Doren as the victim.

Inexhaustibly creative in its methods of exploiting a fad, the American economy repackaged the Beat image in a thousand ways. *Playboy's* "Beat Playmate" ate health food, read Dylan Thomas, and drove a Jaguar. Even Northport bookstores sprouted porno paperbacks like Jerry Weil's *A Real Cool Cat.* There were Beat Generation drinking sweat shirts and

Halloween masks. A pop song called "Beatnik Fly" vanished with merciful haste, but 1961's number-one song was "Sugar Shack," about the espresso joint where Jimmy Gilmer found a beat chick in leotards to marry. *Playboy* ran a beat variation on "The Night Before Christmas." *Mad* magazine, America's most popular satirical publication, thought the Beats too "esoteric" to spoof, though *Mad* did dress Alfred E. Neuman in cool-daddy goatee, beret, and horn-rims for one of its paperback collections. Beat cartoons were everywhere. One showed a beatnik sitting disconsolate while his friend groaned to another poet, "Clifton Fadiman called him witty and urbane." The comic strip "Pogo" had Churchey La Femme, the turtle, read a poem from the Dead Beat Generation accompanied by Pogo on bass drum, and beatniks appeared in the soap opera *Helen Trent* and the comic strips "Gordo" and "Popeye."

Beat art had passed through the media crucible and emerged to a mass reception that was defined by two special pictures, the first a *Saturday Evening Post* cover and the second a *Life* photograph. That summer of 1959 the *Saturday Evening Post* ran a short story called "Beauty and the Beatnik," a silly tale of a hard-working young woman so shocked at the sight of a young man sunbathing on a Monday morning that she proceeded to fall in love with the lazy beatnik. "James Jones. Jack Kerouac," sniffed the bohemian. "They're Dun and Bradstreet compared to me. I'm a real bum!" Of course, the young man was swiftly revealed as a vacationing district attorney, and everyone lived happily ever after. That issue's cover painting depicted midsummer-night lovers under an apple tree, romantically painting sky castles of their future—in the form of washing machines, stoves, and two-car garages.

As a sidebar to Paul O'Neill's late 1959 piece on the Beats, "The Only Rebellion Around," *Life* printed a staged photo of the "typical Beatnik pad." The furnishings consisted of a "beat chick" in black leotards and a turtleneck, a naked light-bulb, a hot plate, a (phony) marijuana plant, some books in fruit crates, a hi-fi, a typewriter and poem, a Charlie Parker record, a wine bottle with candle, a guitar and bongos. In an issue that turned verbal backsprings for the Marine Corps, O'Neill's "Rebellion" essay assailed the "hairiest, scrawniest and most discontented specimens of all time: the improbable rebels of the Beat Generation . . . talkers, loafers, passive little con men, lonely eccentrics, mom-haters, cop haters, exhibitionists . . . writers who cannot write, painters who cannot paint."

O'Neill turned San Francisco poet Michael McClure, then working as a gymnasium manager, into a "towel boy," and retold an apocryphal anecdote in which Allen Ginsberg had encouraged Dame Edith Sitwell to shoot heroin. The harangue sourly concluded, "What have we done to deserve this?" Kerouac, McClure, and the rest asked the same question, especially when the article was reprinted for millions in *Reader's Digest.*

Long before O'Neill had completed his diatribe, Jack was numb, too battered by the word and picture storm to focus. His greatest gift had come to betray him. His innocent eye could never develop a saving shield of cynicism, and when his creation—the term "Beat Generation"—was defiled in the service of violence or corrupt profit, he could only cry, or curse, or get drunk enough so that the images blurred and softened; there was no forgetting what was happening to him.

The fraudulent media image mocked the public as well. Three young ladies from Kansas wrote to Lawrence Lipton and asked him to visit their town of Hutchinson and "cool us in." When Lipton accepted the invitation, the town fathers gibbered and withdrew the welcome, forcing one of the three girls to tell a reporter, "All we did was send a letter. We know beatniks aren't good, but we thought they just dressed sloppy and talked funny. Now we know that they get married without licenses and things like that."

For Jack, the fall of 1959 was gruelingly alcoholic but commercially productive. He sold a section of *Visions of Cody* for December publication in *Playboy,* convinced Allen to relieve him of the energy-absorbing Avon anthology, and saw *Mexico City Blues* published by Grove in November. Though later Robert Creeley and Anthony Hecht reviewed it favorably, the *Blues's* first notice was an essay by Kenneth Rexroth, which appeared in November in the *New York Times Book Review.* After associating Jack's views on jazz and Negroes with those of the Ku Klux Klan, Rexroth delivered a closing assault: "I've always wondered what ever happened to those wax work figures in the old rubberneck dives in Chinatown. Now we know; one of them at least writes books."

Under the impact of such critical fury, Jack further increased his drinking, which became so uncontrolled that in mid-November 1959 he and an equally besotted Mémère lay unconscious in the living room while a visiting Phil Whalen rapped on their door but could not rouse them from their stupor. A week later, Jack was still drunk when he flew to Los Angeles to appear on *The Steve Allen Show.* Sweating and nervous, he cut down to wine for the show itself, and although the Lowell *Sun* would run indignant columns on his galvanic behavior, he played a subtle, mischievous trick that revealed how he felt about his fame and his public. When Steve asked him to read from *On the Road,* Jack pulled out a copy and began. Only Allen Ginsberg and John Holmes knew that instead of *On the Road* he was reciting the moving passage of farewell that closed *Visions of Cody* with the words, "Adios, King."

After touring the *Subterraneans* set at the MGM studio, Jack joined *Pull My Daisy* director Alfred Leslie and drove to San Francisco, where *Daisy* was entered in the International Film Festival. Clad in a red-and-black hunting shirt, Jack cut an odd figure at the snobbishly elegant postfestival party, and was unable to find a seat until David Niven made him welcome at his own table. Jack responded to the general air of contempt with drunken obstinacy, and staggered through the remainder of the festival—at one point he fell off the stage—until he reeled off to a North Beach long since debauched by publicity and commercialism.

As had Gary and Allen before him, Jack planned to lecture Neal's San Quentin prison class on Comparative Religions. But at the last moment, he collapsed in guilt and liquor, refused to go, and escaped into the bars with Al Sublette. When things began to go blank on him, he sought out his dependable comrade Phil Whalen. Whalen was still on the East Coast, and Jack fell in with two of Phil's roommates, Lew Welch and Albert Saijo. A college classmate of Whalen's, Welch was a mad, hard-drinking Irish poet who'd only recently fled a "career" in a Chicago insurance office. With this charismatic new road partner matching him drink for drink, Jack began to gulp down whiskey with an intensity that convinced Saijo his love affair with the bottle was a deadly form of penance.

In the midst of their spectacular San Francisco binge, Jack talked an agreeable Welch into driving him home to Northport in Lew's jeep "Willy," and the road madness flared back into reality, cushioned this time by a substantial bankroll for motels, an occasional restaurant, and a transcontinental vista of bars. After stopping in Chinatown for Jack to buy Mémêre a present, Lew, Albert, and Jack rolled through the night to the Mojave Desert, Lew at the wheel and in charge of the conversation, spouting as relentlessly as Neal in the old days about American dialects and literature, sports, logging and ladies.

They skipped the Grand Canyon but took in a Las Vegas replica of George Washington's Mount Vernon, then drove on, interrupting their songs to argue lightly about "politics and politicians, intricate crimes, wars and panics, food, drink, hometowns, travel, movies and movie stars, ghost stories," until the darkness silenced them. Cruising across the Arizona desert, Jack brought them to a sudden halt with a yell from his shotgun seat, then ran back to pull up a small white roadside cross that marked the site of a fatal accident. They agreed that the marker should go to Allen. Their journey careened in and out of bars, and crested when Jack dragged Lew and Albert into an East St. Louis strip show, scattering money like confetti.

In New York, they ate in Chinatown and visited with Jack's old Times Square friend Herbert Huncke, then posed for Village photographer Fred McDarrah's picture book *The Beat Scene*. They paid a final tribute to their odyssey at the Cedar Bar and the Five Spot, and came to rest in Northport, where Jack tried to convert Welch to spontaneous prose by showing him how to hook up a paper roll to a typewriter.

As the New Year 1960 began, Jack tried to break the downhill slide of his life with a new book; he'd had nothing but false starts since *The Dharma Bums*, two years before. He avoided the city and trained hard with long walks and plenty of sleep, then retired to his newly finished attic to begin "Beat Traveler," the story of his life from 1956 to 1959. On this attempt he was confident of success, because for the first time in years, he had an ample supply of his ever-dependable Benzedrine. The speed crackled through his veins and he paced the attic, his mind crawling with half-memories that did not fuse into a story. Spring flowered, and he continued to pace in a closed and futile circle. The damp attic aggravated the phlebitis in his leg and the neuritis that had developed in his hands; he'd also smashed his elbow during a binge. Lost in tedious depression, he wrote nothing.

He dreamed of a refuge from the publishing business, and planned trips into the Adirondacks or New England to find land on which to build a hermitage. When literary business did intrude on Northport, it brought more politics and division. When Peter Orlovsky sent him Kenneth Tynan's petition for a "Sane Nuclear Policy," Jack scowled that Tynan was a publicity seeker and possibly a Communist, and returned it unsigned. Ferlinghetti visited him in April, and they decided that City Lights would publish *Book of Dreams* rather than "Old Angel Midnight." Soon after Ferlinghetti left, a Long Island State Representative attacked a portion of his poem "A Coney Island of the Mind" as "anti-Christian." Jack told Larry that the poem was an honest portrayal of Christ as the true hipster, but he squirmed and twisted and mumbled that just for the hell of it—and to silence Jack's police-state fears—he should placate the middle class and capitalize "Jesus."

In June 1960, New York firemen shut down two Village coffeehouses and were picketed by the erstwhile customers, who were then swept into a small social war when the Village's old-time Italian residents began to drop water bags and sometimes rocks on passing interracial couples. By the fall of 1960, Actors Equity and the police had forced poetry out of the remaining coffeehouses, which turned to presenting the more genteel mode of folk music. Beats began to move into the cheaper Lower East Side to avoid the tourists and police of the Village proper.

Gutted by what critic Ralph Gleason identified as "too much publicity and too many amateurs," North Beach had also become a cheap tourist trap. The Place was an art goods shop. Vesuvio's was a tourist bar, and its owner Henri Lenoir had added an extra attraction; he hired Hube "the Cube" Leslie to sit in the window for the tourists to stare at.

North Beach had been destroyed as a hip community by commerce and by the police, who in January carried out mass marijuana raids. The authorities were spearheaded by Officer William Bigarini, who harassed interracial couples and systematically provoked poet Bob Kauffman, a black man and old friend of Jack's, until Kauffman had to flee the city. So did many poets and much of the audience. The only good news that spring was that Neal Cassady got out of jail. Cheered by his release and relieved that Carolyn wasn't going to divorce him, Jack wrote the Cassadys for the first time in a long while.

In New York the sign of the times was a classified advertisement in the *Village Voice:* "Rent a Genuine Beatnik." Guaranteed to come equipped with beard, bongos, shades, turtleneck and acceptably raffish manners at $25 a crack, the human puppets were a brief vogue at Long Island society parties.

In June, Jack sat wincing at the première of the movie *The Subterraneans.* The sound of André Previn's strings macerating the jazz of Gerry Mulligan and Art Pepper opened the film and served to warn Jack instantly that something was terribly wrong with this cinematic reproduction of his work. Jack was portrayed by a WASPish George Peppard, whose performance was as colorful as a diet of white bread and mayonnaise.

Life, it was understood, was sought in North Beach, where Peppard drove his convertible until it was surrounded at a street corner by a gaggle of wild-eyed subterraneans led by Gregory, played by Roddy McDowall.

Kidnapped to a bar called "Daddy's Catacombs," Peppard met Mardou Fox, a role improbably filled by Leslie Caron. In Caron's previous film she had been the gamine Gigi, and she somehow managed to transport Gay Nineties coquetry into North Beach.

Five minutes after meeting her, Peppard was busily defending her honor with a beer bottle in his hand, and that suggested act of violence was utterly repugnant to Jack. In a plot device invented for the film, Peppard began to flirt with Roxanne, an exotic dancer. Caron reacted with a traditional fit of jealousy, sweeping him off to her posh pad, where they danced with the passion of skim milk and awoke fully clothed the next morning.

As in real life, the cinematic Jack romanced Mardou in between her visits to the psychiatrist, but compared with Mardou's cataclysmic personality, Caron's neuroses were the peccadilloes of a spoiled child. Falling into Peppard's arms after he told her, "You cook, I'll write," Caron recounted in a bowdlerized fashion the story of her naked walk on the fence, ending it for the film not in high epiphany but at the local mission. Jealous of Caron and Roddy McDowall (Gregory), Peppard fell apart in Hollywood's time-tested, fists-and-whiskey manner; he got drunk and threatened to break McDowall's arm. Confused, Peppard tried to take up with Roxanne, only to be rejected with the explanation, "You're a whirlpool, [Jack], and I don't want to drown."

Retracing the trite pathways of Hollywood's favorite plot, Peppard returned to Caron, dodged when she threw a knife at him, and melted her with words of love that allowed them to slide into the obligatory clinch as the credits rolled by.

The Subterraneans had been a pure, naked confession, and this trivializing film was almost too ugly to grasp; Jack cringed in revulsion. Afterward he returned to Northport and reached for the comfort of a bottle of wine. Presently the depression lifted, the critics and Mémère and Gerard and all his terrors momentarily far away. He drank on. The wine made him free and funny for a while, his body sweetly alive, the rich liquid running into his belly like an electric transfusion and a sedative all at once.

He drank and drank and drank.

XV
Collapse

TWO MONTHS after *The Subterraneans* opened, Jack's wine-soaked panic carried him all the way across the country to San Francisco's skid-row Mars Hotel, where he awoke one summer day to stare into a cloudy mirror at his face, a mask riven by anguish and corruscated by alcohol. Salvador Dali had once thought him more handsome than Marlon Brando, but now Jack saw himself as "so ugly, so lost." It was Monday, July 25, 1960, and he was a long way down the road from idealism or joy or anything worthy of pursuit.

As Jack had grown increasingly desperate that summer, Ferlinghetti had offered him a refuge at his cabin in Bixby Canyon, on the California coast near Big Sur. In the peace of the Sur woods, Jack figured, he could take a stand against the psychic nausea that threatened to destroy him, get back into physical shape by chopping wood, and ease his mind with the therapeutic rhythm of the waves. But instead of avoiding his public and meeting Ferlinghetti in secret for the ride to the cabin as they had planned, Jack made a drunkenly theatrical entrance into City Lights Bookstore on Saturday night, July 23, then whirled into a weekend drunk with Philip Whalen and painter Robert La Vigne. On the Monday after that weekend toot, he was excruciatingly hungover and without a ride, since Ferlinghetti had given up trying to awaken him and had gone ahead to the cabin. Jack moaned wordlessly as he turned away from his image in the foggy glass to survey a vista of empty white port bottles and cigarette butts, then thought, "One fast move or I'm gone."

He had been floundering all year, a lonesome mystic displaced in time, out of sync with the national atmosphere. Nineteen-sixty marked the gathering of a sophisticated and energetic mood in American youth that sloughed off Eisenhower for John F. Kennedy. Norman Mailer's metaphor was apt: "Kennedy has a jewel of a political machine. It is as good as a crack Notre Dame team, all discipline and savvy and go-go-go, sound, drilled, never dull, quick as a knife." In an era of go-go-go, Jack was, as Allen put it, a "shy drunken Catholic Bodhisattva," sensitive enough to perceive the winds of change, but far too disillusioned to adapt. John Kennedy's Ivy League technicians were about to accede to the White House, and the peculiarly youthful enthusiasm stilled by Republicanism had found a new champion. A few lonely idealists talked of Adlai Stevenson's intellect and honesty, but when Kennedy's crack team steamrollered Adlai Stevenson at the Democratic Party Convention in Los Angeles, American youth went wild for Jack and Jackie Kennedy. Though he had, on principle, never voted—"avoid the authorities"—had he done so Jack Kerouac would have chosen Richard Nixon.

Essentially, Jack had had nothing to do in the spring of 1960 but drink and quarrel with Mémère. Dody Müller had loved an all-out two-day bash, but Jack's binges easily stretched to a week. Bit by bit, her patient affection wore away, and by spring their affair was finished. In the wake of his loss, Jack's first reaction was an old one. Once again he set off to search for a wilderness hut, but when he visited one in Pennsylvania, his wallet was stolen and he found himself stranded penniless in the backwoods of the Pocono Mountains. His holy *Scripture of the Golden Eternity* was published that spring of 1960, but its pure message was so foreign to his profane mood that the event only accentuated his guilt over his sad condition. His other publications for the year were old—"October in the Railroad Earth" in *Evergreen*—or casual *Holiday* travel essays. In June he worked on the galleys for a collection of his travel articles to be called *Lonesome Traveler*, and that was the extent of his labor for the year. With no meaningful work to occupy his mind, the whipsaw tension between his perceptivity and his claustrophobic living situation that had cut him off from Dody and Allen sent him veering out of control, and he drank even harder.

Jack was now utterly disillusioned, stripped of the brave vanities of his ambitious youth. All that remained to him was a fierce loyalty to Mémère—"I don't want to throw my mother to the dogs of eternity like you did, Allen"—and his drinking. The glare of fame had consumed so much of his identity in the past two years that he needed these two final crutches.

He was stricken with his first attack of delirium tremens in May 1960, after a spectacular Manhattan bender that ended only when he had spent every cent, and had to borrow his train fare home from Peter Orlovsky. Once Dody had kept his return tickets for him, but no longer.

Jack felt as if he were being martyred, and he reached out to Allen, who was retracing Burroughs' expedition in search of *"yage,"* the South American psychedelic vine. On June 6 Allen replied with a letter that urged Jack to run down the street to the nearest airport and fly to Peru, where "I wish you were here and we could apocalypsize over jungles together and visit strange Indian tribes." That night Allen ate of the *yage* vine and felt "What I thought was the great Being, or some sense of It, approaching my mind like a big wet vagina . . . Then the whole fucking cosmos broke loose around me," Allen wrote Burroughs, "I think the strongest and worst I've ever had it nearly."

Waves of death fear and nausea tormented Allen; he saw snakes wiggling after him out of his own vomit, and felt like a "completely lost strayed soul." As he put it in his *yage* poem "Magic Psalm," "Drive me crazy, God I'm ready for disintegration of my mind,/disgrace me in the eye of the earth, attack my hairy heart with terror . . . devour my brain, One flow of endless consciousness, I'm scared." "The Reply" was the next poem in the sequence: "God answers with my doom. I am annulled . . . change[d] from Allen to a skull." His lifelong struggle for a cosmic identity had ended in the frightening visage of a skeleton, and Allen appealed in panic to Burroughs. Bill tried to calm him, but Allen's eyes had the look of a man who faced extinction. The *yage* death experience and his earlier Blake visions had established poles in his life he could not yet span, and it would be three years before he was again tranquil.

Indian shamans in the jungle were not Jack's idea of peace, and it turned out to be Ferlinghetti who was able to answer his plea for help, when early in July 1960, he had invited Jack to stay at his cabin in Bixby Canyon. The première of *The Subterraneans* and the publication of *Tristessa* had left Jack with stomach cramps, diarrhea, nightmares, and insomnia, and he scrambled to accept Ferlinghetti's kind offer. He swore that his sanity was on the line.

Once more Jack packed his rucksack with the St. Christopher medal on its flap, but this time his "road" was a private roomette on the crack Chicago–San Francisco express train, the California Zephyr. Watching the land roll past, Jack thought wistfully of all the kids who were sure that he was a laughing young man hitchin' on down the road. He was nearing forty, a little fat, and very tired.

When Jack awoke in the Mars Hotel on the Monday—July 25, 1960 —after his arrival in San Francisco, Phil Whalen lay asleep on the floor. Jack was close to Whalen, in part because Phil never criticized his drinking, and that morning while Jack was still clear they managed a few hours' peaceful conversation by the waterfront. Their tranquil afternoon made Phil hopeful that Jack might yet be all right. Sickened by the skid-row room and the state of his life, Jack thought otherwise, grabbed his rucksack, and headed for Bixby Canyon.

He rode a bus to Monterey, where he hired a cab that brought him at three in the morning to the canyon's entrance, a gate just off U.S. Highway 1 many hundred feet above the ocean. All of Jack's prior journeys along the California coast had been inland, and he'd never seen the awesome cliffs and narrow valleys of the Big Sur region, whose only road, Highway 1, was like a thin thread wriggling lightly against the mountainside, fragile somehow, occasionally running over a delicate bridge set above a chasm a thousand feet deep. The coastal mountain range acted as a barrier against the ocean wind, trapping its moisture in the fog that often enshrouded the highway. It was Druidic country, mysterious, beautiful, and sometimes ominously frightening. It was surely no place to first confront in the dead of night after anticipating a charming Eden.

Jack flashed his railroad lantern around, but the misty darkness swallowed up its light, and he became disoriented by what he wrote of as an "aerial roaring mystery in the dark." As he inched down the steep corkscrew road that ran from the highway to the canyon floor, Jack was confused by the roar of the surf, which seemed to come from the wrong direction. The shadows that played at the edge of his flashlight beam made him think of rattlesnakes, and his panic made the creek's merry babble sound like the roar of a holocaust. Safe at last on level earth at the bottom of the canyon, he unrolled his sleeping bag by the creek and dropped off into an uneasy doze.

Even in daylight, the canyon—a narrow crack in the coast range of mountains—was imposing. At one end a slight optical illusion made the ocean seem higher than the land, its giant black sentry rocks like the rotted teeth of a monster. The mountain at the land end reminded Jack of a dream he'd had in February, which he called "The Flying Horses of Mien Mo." The dream had been set in his peacefully creative Mexico, where he had stared at a gigantic mountain topped with palaces and temples and encircled by thousands of winged, caped, inexpressibly sinful horses. In his dream Jack failed to convince the local Indians of the evil nature of the mountain, but alone in California he needed no encouragement to sense Satan about him. Arching over the whole of Bixby Canyon was a bridge so far away that it seemed like a bird, a grim metal egg below it—a car that had driven off the highway and tumbled into a rusty wreck on the boulders at the foot of the cliff.

However nervous he was, Jack was now sober, alone at last in his bhikku cabin. For the next three weeks he settled into Ferlinghetti's shack, reading *Dr. Jekyll and Mr. Hyde* in the glow of a kerosene lamp. The cabin served him well as a haven, even on the night a bat blundered in as he sat mending his leaky old sleeping bag. The thick summer fog discouraged the other canyon landowners from visiting their property, and Jack was entirely alone. Night after night he took his railroad lantern and walked to the water's edge, where he sat cross-legged with a Camel cigarette in his mouth and worked on a poem called "Sea," trying as he had in "Old Angel Midnight" to record universal sound.

During the day he prayed for peace to the kettledrum and fife tunes of the creek, striving to transcend his fear, to "keep concentrated on the fact," as he later wrote, "that after all this whole surface of the world as we know it now will be covered with the silt of a billion years in time." Jack wound down now, stretched out by the creek in dreamy Proustian recall or building a millrace in the creek, like Nick Adams in Hemingway's "Big Two-Hearted River." He made friends with Alf, the local burro, and even began to laugh again. A satisfying hike brought him to a nearby valley that was an Arden of mighty redwood trees and lovely ferns, and he strolled in peace.

Periodically, his underlying feelings of pain and terrified depression would crack through, and the dry swirl of leaves gathered by the wind would make him think, "Oh my God, we're all being swept away to sea no matter what we say or do." Boredom plagued him, but he repeated Emerson's dictums on "Self Reliance," baked muffins, listened to the sea, cherished the butterflies and fed the raccoons, birds, and mice. Meditating on the superior utility of a 10-cent dish scrubber over the fancy trousers he'd bought for *The Steve Allen Show*, Jack persevered, grimly childlike, on the path of simplicity.

Three weeks into his retreat, he walked up to the highway to mail letters to Lucien and Mémêre. As he recalled it later, when he returned to the beach, he sucked in a huge breath of fresh ocean air, and inexplicably became clutched with panic, left vulnerable by a tidal wave of fear that dwarfed his life. Like some hideous crone, the sea seemed to shriek at him to end his struggles and die: "GO TO YOUR DESIRE DON'T HANG AROUND HERE." Devastated by a sense of utter meaninglessness, Jack gave up for the moment and set out for the safe ruin of the drunken sociable city. The journey to San Francisco was a 1960 road nightmare of station wagons filled with sanitized, Sanforized P.T.A. families who would never think to help out a woebegone hitchhiker.

Children screamed at him, and their mothers hid behind what he called "sneering dark glasses." Their potbellied, neatly dressed husbands, whom Jack suspected would rather be out getting dirty by a campfire somewhere, pretended not to see him as he shuffled along. America's most famous hitchhiker was forced to walk almost the whole of the fourteen miles from Bixby Canyon to Monterey, as the August-hot pavement cooked his feet into blisters. At last a kindly trucker took him to the Monterey bus station, and Jack rode back to San Francisco. After a night's sleep in a skid-row hotel, he strolled into City Lights Bookstore to be dealt a blow.

Sitting before Ferlinghetti's rolltop desk as once he'd perched at Leo's, he read a letter from Mémêre: "I really don't know how to tell you this but Brace up Honey. I'm going through hell myself. Little Tyke [their kitten] is *gone* . . . he started belching and throwing up. I went to him and tried to fix him up but to no *availe* [*sic*]. He was shivering like he was cold so I rapped [*sic*] him up in a Blanket then he started to throw up all over me. And that was the last of him." Jack was well aware that he was "a little dotty" about cats, that deep in his mind he'd connected them with Gerard, Mémêre, angels and purity, but his self-knowledge had never really affected his emotions.

Shaken, he left City Lights with Phil Whalen for a few beers at Mike's Pool Hall. They went to Washington Square Park and relaxed in the sun, gabbing easily about everything and nothing as Jack interjected speculations about the consciousness and futures of the passers-by. Sympathetic and firm, Whalen was a shy, blushing companion who comforted Jack.

The sun set and Jack's night fever bloomed. He went to Vesuvio's and began to throw down double bourbons, then called up Lew Welch, his wild drinking partner from the previous fall. Minutes later Lew swept up Columbus Avenue in Willy the Jeep, accompanied by an audience for

Jack, a young friend of his named Paul Smith. Cashing five hundred dollars in traveler's checks—later he would wave them before Carolyn with the comment, "That's all anybody loves me for"—Jack was once again party King of the Beats, Willy's swaying shotgun seat his throne, a bottle of Pernod his mace. They tore off on a crashing ride to Los Gatos, past the cookie-cutter tract homes that had sprouted on the prune fields of his brakeman days.

Drunk and rude, Jack pushed Carolyn away as he entered her home, his thoughts on Neal, who was at his tire-recapping job. Still worried about how *On the Road* might have affected his brother—they had not seen each other in three years—Jack encouraged himself when they did meet with the thought that Cassady seemed radiantly patient, not bitter. Desperately optimistic in his later account of their meeting, Jack even managed to convince himself that prison had benefited Neal by giving him an opportunity to grow spiritually. Jack tried to explain why he had failed to give the San Quentin religion lecture the previous December, and Neal was magnanimous, though this son of a wino disapproved of heavy drinking. Their conversation sputtered and fizzled, distracted by a noisily adoring audience, and Jack and Neal had no chance to be intimate.

After spending the night, Jack and the gang rushed back to San Francisco, where early the next morning Jack had to endure an imitation of an *On the Road* journey over the city's incredible hills; he had mentioned that Lew and Neal were the best drivers in the world, and one of Lew's neighbors set out to prove himself Dean Moriarity's equal. Dawn of the next day broke on a terrified Jack Kerouac trapped in the front seat of the speeding car.

During a quiet period in the week's lunacy, Jack and Lew drove to a TB sanitorium to visit Albert Saijo, their comrade of the previous fall. Albert was tired and gloomy, and though he clowned with Jack as they said goodbye, the visit was a disturbing experience that Jack swiftly exterminated with a drink. Jack already had more pain than he could handle, and illness in others unnerved him. The next morning, he picked up a copy of Boswell's *Johnson* to escape his hangover. Years before he'd told a Navy psychiatrist of his identification with the great man of letters, and since then he'd played Boswell to Neal's Dr. Sam; the book usually had a soothing effect on him. But all that he found in Boswell this day were reminders of death, and he began to tremble in a phantasmic attack of fear that was cut off by a telephone call from Neal, who had just lost his

job and needed to borrow a hundred dollars for the mortgage payment.
Jack promised to deliver the funds immediately, and asked Lew Welch
to drive him down to Los Gatos.

It was a weekend, and by the time they left San Francisco, they had
organized a giant party to be held in Bixby Canyon. On their way they
put Phil Whalen and Paul Smith in Willy's back seat and added a second
jeep with Ferlinghetti and his friend Victor Wong. They delivered the
mortgage money, and after a pizza feast in Los Gatos, first Neal and then
Michael McClure and his family joined them to form a four-car caravan
that wound down Highway 1 to Bixby. Everyone enjoyed the night's
party, which came alive in mad talk around a huge bonfire on the beach.
Jack had stopped eating, and kept a secure grip on his wine jug as he
shouted pleasantly with Neal, then read from his ocean poem "Sea," while
McClure recited his poem "Dark Brown" and Larry and Phil swapped
stories. Later Jack read aloud from *Dr. Jekyll and Mr. Hyde,* and McClure
was deeply moved. "It was at moments like that," McClure later said,
"that I began to understand his genius." Jack "eulogized" writers in his
conversation and denounced the poets when they began to play the game
of "Have you read such and such?" "This is intellectual mutual masturbation," Jack shouted, and urged them instead to *"Deliver* your information,
don't ask a putdown question."

Now that it was nearly fall, the prevailing winds blew offshore, out
of a clear and fogless sky. Jack had earlier taken comfort in Bixby's soft
gray cloak of fog, and he grew uneasy when the autumn wind roared down
the throat of the canyon so intensely that he could no longer hear the
creek. The noise and the wine kept Jack awake, and he spent most of the
night frantically jabbering with Ferlinghetti's friend Wong, somehow
afraid that he'd miss something if he slept. As he realized later, paranoia
was beginning to catch at his mind, and when the men visited the Big
Sur mineral baths the next day, Jack momentarily imagined that he saw
sperm floating in the water, wrigglers out to bite him.

Everyone returned home the next day except Paul Smith, who
begged to stay with his hero. Jack was too far gone to deny him, though
he wanted to be alone, and Paul's youthful enthusiasm depressed the
worn-out King of the Beats, reminding him of the boys who had once
visited him in Northport wearing high school letter jackets emblazoned
with THE DHARMA BUMS. His last bottle of white port safe in his grasp,
Jack managed for his admirer to produce one night's performance. But
Jack awoke to an empty bottle, and began to come unglued with the

torture of alcoholic withdrawal. The anguish was so fierce that he felt as if he'd betrayed his own birth and was now being crucified by cancers that dissolved his face, loathsome and unclean. At last he broke down and asked, *"O mon Dieu, pourquoi Tu m'laisse faire malade comme ça—Papa, Papa aide-mué* (Dear God, why do you torture me this way, Father, Father help me)," groaning exactly the way Leo had, fourteen long years before.

When Paul left Bixby to visit McClure in Santa Cruz, Jack was able to regain his self-control in domestic solitude: He chopped wood, sewed, and read an old *Evergreen*. In the moonlight the canyon looked like a beautiful Chinese scroll painting to him, and he celebrated it with a ditty that ran, "Man is a busy little animal, a wise little animal, his thoughts about everything don't amount to shit."

McClure visited him the next day, and they sat within the dark cabin talking about poetry and Michael's heroes Billy the Kid and Jean Harlow. Suddenly the door crashed open, flooding them with sunlight and the startlingly golden sight of the blond Cassady family, who had come to visit Uncle Jack. Peering at them out of the gloom, Jack yelped, "A band of angels, with St. Michael at the head!" Inexpressibly pleased with this treat, Jack shared a joint with Neal and later sat on the beach talking quietly with Carolyn. It was as if they hadn't seen each other in many years. She asked him if he still wrote, if he still carried his little pocket notebooks, and he had to admit that he hadn't written prose in years, and frequently forgot his pencil and paper. "I don't like *On the Road* or *Subterraneans,*" she continued, "they're not *like* you. Jack, remember that Dickensian Christmas story you wrote for me once? *That's* you."

"Yeah, well," Jack replied, "when we went to the hot springs, Neal and I were the only ones who weren't naked . . . the only modest ones in the bunch."

Carolyn tried to convince Jack to come and spend some quiet time in Los Gatos. He nodded "Yeah, yeah," and accompanied them to the town, but that night, when he and Neal were supposed to attend a play for which Carolyn had done the costumes and make-up, Jack was rowdily drunk and was soon ousted. Neal decided to take Jack to San Francisco, and soon they were hurtling down the road, brothers once more in a car about to leap into heaven, for a moment back in 1949 as a frantic Neal described his new girlfriend Jacky, whom he wanted to share with his brother Jack. Yet in 1960 Jack realized with a faint shock that each man had grown to resemble the other's father—Neal with his bluster and hurry and racing forms, Jack with his wine—and their old energy had vanished.

Jack had planned to return to Los Gatos after meeting Jacky, but her resemblance to Lucien and something in the sad catch of her voice entranced him. He plopped down into the center chair of her living room, took a sip of white port, and began to talk with her. After Neal left, they fell excitedly into bed, and Jack momentarily found his dead loneliness displaced by the nervous exaltation of a new affair. It wouldn't last long, since most of her conversation was California-Metaphysical, a revolving series of channels, evolution, planes, planets, and karma. Jack couldn't stomach that talk from Neal, much less anyone else, but he sat in her chair, sipped his wine, called her Lucien, and listened.

Absorbed in the broken-hearted timbre of Jacky's voice, Jack stayed in the chair for a week, leaving only rarely to go out with Neal and Jacky's weird strong-arm prison friends who hustled him for meals, or to Jacky's bed, where they made love as her seven-year-old son watched. Both activities began to chip Jack's mind into paranoid splinters. Things blurred and made less and less sense, and he began to think that only plots and schemes and intricate conspiracies could define this reality. Ferlinghetti, McClure, and Whalen came to visit, but Jack remained in the chair, pouring down endless quarts of wine as his money ran out and his bloodshot eyes began to signal the approach of something horrible.

Philip Whalen managed to drag him out for a quiet afternoon in Washington Square Park, where Jack dozed in the sunshine while Phil kept watch. After he awoke, Phil chided him for his fears of going crazy with the comment "You said that to me in 1955," and added, "Stop thinking about yourself, will ya, and float with the world." Trembling, Jack leaned on Whalen as they walked back toward Jacky's place. When he watched Phil saunter away while he waited for Jacky to return from work, his serenity vanished. He clutched at the window curtain like Lon Chaney in *The Phantom of the Opera*, unable to float as Whalen had suggested. Instead he raged at himself, guilty, he said, "for being a member of the human race," for being a foolish drunkard in a slimy world of crooked judges and a deathly war machine.

When Jacky cooked supper that night, Jack looked up and saw her son waiting, spoon in hand, for his dinner. Children and kitchens and domestic bliss were for someone else, he thought, someone normal and responsible, and the scene tripped off the soft interior adrenal explosions of panic. His fears momentarily rested on the little boy, and everything somehow made sense when he concluded that the child was actually

Satan. More to the point, Jack could feel Jacky pursuing him, hungry for more than he now wanted to give. That night Jack slumped heavily back into his chair after supper, and it collapsed into several pieces under him. As he picked them up, he noticed that the two goldfish in the bowl next to the chair were dead, strangled in a week's solid cloud of cigarette smoke. The omens piled up until Jack's fear overcame his dull sense of futility, and he suggested that they escape to Ferlinghetti's cabin. Call Lew Welch, get him to snatch up his woman friend Lenore, and the five of them would run away to peace and quiet. *Lez go Lez go Lez go!*

Singing "Home on the Range" and "Red River Valley," they flew down the road to Bixby Canyon, with a sad, stupid visit to Los Gatos; Jack had said that he wanted to pick up a shirt Carolyn had mended, but actually he'd plotted for Carolyn to meet Jacky, although at the last moment Carolyn had to invite her in. Carolyn wasn't too disturbed, but Neal was stiff with jealousy over Jack and Jacky's romance. Jack sobered enough to realize what an ass he'd been, and fell silent and lost, like a ghost, a stranger forever passing through but never fully in touch with anyone.

As his body, cell by cell, began to demand more alcohol the next morning in Bixby Canyon, September 3, 1960, Jack realized that the nearest wine was thirteen hard miles away and fell apart. The autumn wind was a prolonged scream that ripped the leaves off the trees to dance and fly and swirl, and his mind followed the wind. His hands trembled so badly that he couldn't light the fire. Jacky's son kept whining and asking questions that tried Jack's patience as he sat and shook, waiting for Lew's return with supplies. Sitting with his back to a boulder, Jack watched Jacky walk along the water and remembered the way that she'd deserted her son the night before to dive after him into his sleeping bag, gloomily pondered the fact that he didn't love her, and worried that he was leading her on. He briefly contemplated suicide. All he could be sure of was that he was exhausted, his eyes on fire. He and Jacky began to talk, but her calm attempts to help him had to filter through what he later acknowledged was a mental screen of paranoia. Jack decided that she was witching him. The boy kept crying and pulling at his mother, until she began to beat him, crying herself and horrifying Jack until all three of them sobbed in a hideous mess.

At dusk Jack and Jacky tried to make love, but the boy kept tugging at his mother's shoulder and it got on Jack's mind. Periodically Jack rushed to the creek to cleanse himself with a drink of water, but the clear skies had brought tourists. To Jack, the camera-toting visitors were there to harass him, and as the moon rose he began to mumble to himself that they had poured kerosene into the creek. Lew returned from fishing, and tried to divert Jack with a lecture on how to clean fish. But he was too cheerful, and only turned Jack back in on himself, a weary flop "devoid of human beingness." Caught up in self-hatred, Jack thought the idea of eating Lew's present seemed hypocritical, and began to talk about cutting off their planned week-long stay to return to San Francisco. Lew was disappointed, which further depressed Jack, failure folding in on failure until he was buried in self-abasement.

Reality slipped and Jack tipped over into a full, unhinged breakdown. While Lew cooked dinner Jack raced from the cabin to the creek and back, fearful in the shadows, wanting only to scream while Lew talked bravely on and Lenore tried to get Jack to eat a little something, a piece of tomato or an hors d'oeuvre. But he had decided it was poisoned, that his eyes were dilated as if drugged, and after picking at his food he bolted back to the creek in what he later described as an "automatic directionless circle of anxiety, back and forth, around and around."

As his friends huddled to talk about his bizarre behavior, his mind flowered with hallucinations—at Neal's instigation, they were plotting to poison him after he married Jacky, then share his money. He did not want to break down, and tried desperately to communicate with Lew and Lenore in the moments of lucid calm that regularly punctuated his frenzies. Moments after accusing Lenore of some horrible crime, he would acknowledge the absurdity of his words in an ultimate—and terribly damaging—demonstration of his mercurial nature.

His attention slid away, and the creek babble filled his head, swarmed over his mind, raped him, wouldn't stop, crushed his skull in a vise of noise, kept on, until he stood paralyzed under the menacing full moon and screamed at his mind to "STOP IT! STOP THAT BABBLING!" He tried to sleep with Jacky but the cot collapsed and the sleeping bag was too hot and a mosquito tortured him and his eyes bulged the way Humphrey Bogart's had as the mad Fred C. Dobbs in *The Treasure of the Sierra Madre*. He gave up and lay alone in a corner and cried out for Mémère and Tyke the cat, raved that Lew and the gang were Communists, and then sank into a series of internal voices that went on, unstoppable, for hours. In the hideously bright light of the moon he dreamed of angels and devils. Bathed in cold sweat, his body rigid with tension, he saw the Cross

. . . then devils, then the Cross, Saxian trolls in struggle with Gerard's true pure Cross until he fell into a half-awake nightmare of snow and ice, a God Monster Machine, fornicating vultures, dough-faced people, and a place of puke and slime and filth.

The morning's bright glare only made him feel worse, and Jack demanded that they return immediately to San Francisco, where he distressed even Whalen by abusing old friends in an ugly frenzy. He stayed at Ferlinghetti's for two days and dried out a little, ignored his publisher's advice to enter a sanitarium, and avoided Neal. On September 7 he jumped on a New York–bound jet and returned to his Northport monastery, the Reverend Mother Gabrielle presiding.

For the moment, he told Phil, his desperate panic was behind him and his breakdown seemed like a satori: He was only drinking burgundy now. In mid-September he received a letter from Allen, who reported that "I took a lot more [*yage*] and realized I AM that emptiness that's movie-projecting Kali monster on my mind screen . . . So not scared any more. But I still can't *stop* the appearance [of the monster] . . . I'll have to study yoga or something finally."

It was much too late for anything so creative for Jack. Good art and perceptiveness were in him yet, but no balance now, no peace: only thirst.

XVI
Waiting

Soon after his return to Northport, Jack made himself a present of the old eleventh edition of the *Encyclopaedia Britannica*, which he'd coveted since he'd plundered it in Neal's attic in 1952. The delicate antiquity of its articles on Rousseau and mysticism nurtured him through a quietly bittersweet fall. He continued to search for a country cabin, but what he really sought and could never find was an evanescent state of mind called security.

One of his desires was fulfilled in December, when City Lights published his dream journals. It had not been an easy process. When Ferlinghetti had produced a broadside of Jack's poem "Rimbaud" earlier in the year, Jack had complicated matters tremendously with a last-second demand that the lines of the poem conform to their original shape in his notebook. Dogmatic absolutism about his work was not new to him, but now he went further to explain that he was a channel of God, his writing a scripture; unfazed, Ferlinghetti was still eager to publish a full book.

Jack tried to include Phil Whalen as an editor, but finally had to select the dreams himself, and just before Christmas, *Book of Dreams* laid his naked subconscious before the public. It was a frightening work, Buddhistically perfect in its dreamy lack of intellectual discrimination, yet horrible in its portrait of the "selfhood of death—the fruits of self at last and the pain and terror of it." In the dead hours before dawn, Jack had visions of his own body rotting away, of his childhood baseball games turned into riots, of the mortal shame incurred by the imagined theft of $5 from his uncle's body. In his sleep he was a child chased endlessly by grownups through a world of yellow puke and bloody brawls, H-bombs, frustration, and despair. Jack's night world was permeated with the hovering presence of Mémêre, who always blocked him from sex and good times, and the demonic shadows of Lowell. He would wake up screaming, *"Jesus, pourquoi tu'm maitre des portraits comme ça?* (Jesus, why do you make me see images like this?)" Yet *Book of Dreams* was also an act of faith, a statement that dreaming "ties all mankind together," Jack thought, "in one unspoken Union and also proves that the world is really transcendental which the Communists do not believe."

Jack plunged further into his subconscious in January 1961, when he participated in Dr. Timothy Leary's Harvard psychedelic experiments. Intrigued with the idea of artists as research subjects, Leary had administered psilocybin to Allen Ginsberg in late November, and although Allen began with a roiling stomach and low spirits, he soared into ecstasy, ready to walk naked through the Cambridge streets preaching love and peace. Leary convinced him to stay indoors, so Allen decided to call up Khrushchev, Eisenhower, Kennedy, Mao, Mailer, and Burroughs, and solve the world's problems. He settled for Jack, demanding that Kerouac rush to Cambridge.

Jack's drug experience a few weeks later produced two bemused comments: "I think I'll take a shit out the window at the moon," and "Walking on water wasn't built in a day." Also, it briefly stopped his drinking. Impressed with the drug's therapeutic potential, Jack wrote a friendly report for Leary, whom he had nicknamed "Coach." When the doctor later evolved into a cult figure, Jack disavowed him and his magic pills.

The psilocybin experience blocked his alcohol cravings for only a week, and in the dregs of winter Jack consumed Christian Brothers Tawny Port and then whiskey until he was, he told Whalen, a warped and ugly demon. For the first time, viciousness became part of his character. Allen visited him and Mémêre early in February, and after a generally pleasant meal, they watched an old movie about Hitler on television. As the swastikas danced across the screen, Mémêre whined, "Oh, those Jews are still complaining. They can't ever forget it." Riding the leading edge of hysteria, Gabrielle, possibly recalling Leo's deathbed dictum against Allen, flicked a glance at him, and spat out, "Hitler should have finished off the job." Silent when Jack chorused in agreement, Allen was even more shocked when the Kerouacs began to argue with each other. Mémêre's darling baby boy was now a "filthy prick." Jack growled back that his mother was a "dirty old cunt."

A few days later Allen tried to combat Jack's anti-Semitism with a rational list of his Jewish friends—Lucien (partly), Seymour Wyse, Gilbert Millstein, Allen himself—to balance Brustein, Podhoretz, and the Hollywood producer Albert Zugsmith—but Jack was too soggily emotional to be reasonable. Around that time, he denounced Ferlinghetti for traveling to post-Castro Cuba. Jack was so wound up in garbled political abstractions that he wrote to Ferlinghetti that he hated him. Later he blamed his outburst on wine and Ferlinghetti's foolish political ideas, which Jack thought were the product of fear. In truth, the subject of political abstractions almost always made Jack stop thinking and confusedly mouth Leo's platitudes or Gabrielle's invective. This time he wrote Ferlinghetti that he should fear only death, then caught himself in mid-argument and admitted that death was a sweet and joyful reward. Politics was an octopus of argument that smothered him with two new arms when he'd ripped one away. Communists, he wrote Ferlinghetti, were violent and nasty and—when Jack was quite drunk—ruled by the Jewish Ukraine, but members of the John Birch Society were thugs as well. The reflexive patriotism of a child of immigrants made him denounce pacifists as anti-American, but at heart Jack wanted only to preach Dickensian kindness to Americans holding hands not in some political union, but in the name of poetry.

Jack had no political quarrel with the media, but that made him no less miserable. Cholly Knickerbocker's "Smart Set" column ran an item that described one "Jack Kerouac"—an impostor—buying an expensive necktie on Fifth Avenue to wear as a belt. He felt like a lonely orphan, he told one admirer, hounded by "jackals," the police, the hoodlums, and the critics. New York *Journal-American* columnist Louis Sobol was only joshing when he suggested that Jack succeed "the harassed Norman Mailer as the Existentialist Party's candidate for Mayor," but his wit wrenched from Jack a desperate plea for peace. "I am seriously devoted to my writing," he told Sobol, "someone who never was and never cared to be of the beatnik clan."

The fact was that he hadn't written since 1957, had killed off his *Escapade* column, and would publish nothing of consequence in 1961. President Kennedy had enriched the spy writer Ian Fleming with a plug for his *Casino Royale,* but the First Lady did not have the same effect on Jack when she told *Reader's Digest* that she read everything from "Colette to Kerouac." This tiny bit of publicity cheered Jack immensely, but his sales remained slow. A committee of Northport ladies raised a small ruckus and demanded the removal of his work from local book racks while ignoring, Jack told Whalen, the sleazy, prurient violence of Mickey Spillane and his ilk.

Far worse than all these distractions, Joan Haverty had come to New York to sue for child support, and served Jack with a warrant in March 1961. He hired Allen's brother Eugene Brooks as his counsel and began to rave about his wife and her lawyer's attempt to take Mémère's money and life. Gabrielle had supported his art, and deserved to share his money; in any case, Jack knew that he was much too ill to ever hold a job again. He planned to leave the country if he lost the case, but Eugene held things off and Jack hollowly insisted that a paternity test would vindicate him. The ponderous, awesome law drained Jack, bled off his energy. The bad publicity, the divorce, lonely-bitchy Mémère, and his writing block each contributed to a wasting depression. Even public events soured him. In April, Yuri Gagarin became the first human to orbit the earth, and sarcastically announced that he saw no heaven, which infuriated Jack as much as the Cuban Bay of Pigs invasion five days later scared him. His life empty but for foul dreams each night, Jack was, as a song later ran, "Buried alive in the blues." To Whalen he admitted that he was an incurable alcoholic, and except for his fifth, he didn't really give a damn about anything at all.

In May 1961 Gabrielle finally convinced Jack to join Nin in Orlando. Their subdivision bungalow bored him, but a happy Mémère made his life easier, and having Joan Haverty 1,500 miles away relaxed him enough to consider another summer trip to Bixby Canyon. Instead, in July he took a dismal, dusty room on Cerrida Medellion, Mexico City, looked once more into the mirror, and saw the results of a river of whiskey and a thousand interruptions: "I got to look like a Bourgeois, pot belly and all, that expression in my face of mistrust and affluence (they go hand in hand?)."

He stiffened his resolve, lit a candle, and wrote Part II of *Desolation Angels*, which carried his story from his fall 1956 visit to Mexico City through the ill-fated move to Berkeley. The writing was good but not nearly his best, and it was marred by an undercurrent of hostility: "I shall bullwhip the first bastard who makes fun of human hopelessness any way." A mournful man estranged from this "modern America of crew cuts and sullen faces in Pontiacs," Jack saw himself as "wondrous of contradictions (good enough, said Whitman)," and rambled to cover his every facet. He painted Gabrielle as a "suspicious paranoid" who was also "patient, believing, careful, bleak, self-protective, glad for little favors." In a gloomy funk, he echoed Allen and sent a message to "Mao, Arthur Schlesinger Jr. at Harvard and Herbert Hoover": "Eternity, and the Here-and-Now, are the same thing," and "for every Clark Gable . . . comes disease, decay, sorrow, lamentation, old age, death, decomposition—meaning, for every little sweet lump of baby born that women croon over, is one vast rotten meat burning slow worms in graves death."

Just before he left Mexico, his suitcase was stolen, and he became so toweringly furious that he returned to Florida and drank a fifth of Johnny Walker Red a day for weeks at a stretch. Even his sense of his own writing was colored by his mood, and he wrote to Carolyn Cassady that he'd use Part II later for notes. Though he'd change his mind in a month, for the moment all writing seemed meaningless, and he wanted to quit it, he announced to Ferlinghetti, as he'd quit football in 1940.

Fall in Florida lacked New England's cleansing breezes, but it was at least cooler now. In September he slowed his drinking to sips of Martell Cognac, read Balzac and Dostoyevsky, and lost weight pitching horseshoes. A month later he swallowed some Benzedrine and jumped to his typewriter, where in ten days he wrote *Big Sur,* one of his most remarkable books.

Big Sur was an account of the previous summer in Bixby Canyon, a detailed, oddly detached self-analysis of paranoia and madness that astonished Lenore Kandel with its literal truthfulness. If others might argue Jack had fictionalized in his other accounts, Lenore wondered rather how he'd been able to hear the words he'd accurately attributed to her. "Worth the telling," he said of his summer, "only if I dig deep into everything." *Big Sur*'s seed was the question of a modern Job, *"O why is God torturing me,"* and his Célinesque short-phrased text expressed perfectly his frenzied visions of Flying Horses and the Cross. Jack had always empathized with his subjects, but now he bridged his own agony and empathized with himself. The portrait was incisive, but cost him much; he had literally given himself to his art, and the man that remained behind was shrunken and lost, without the desire to carry on.

Expansive as always in the first thrill of work accomplished, he anticipated writing books on Allen, Peter Orlovsky, Corso, Burroughs, and GJ in Lowell. When the flush of artistic glory faded, he reached for Johnny Walker and stayed drunk for weeks, got fat again, and fell into deep depression. At the seat of his mood, he confessed in a letter to

Carolyn, was his shame at exploiting his friends, though he made an effort to conceal names and circumstances. Philosophical, he swore that in the future the mess of their lives would be perceived as a simple working out of karma. He anticipated the critics' hostility and rationalized that their certain rejection set him free to write as he wished. Partly as a result of that, he thought of *Big Sur* as a symbolic obituary for a "Beat Generation" whose publicity had eviscerated him.

As a public event, the "Beat Generation" was exhausted. The anthologies had come and gone, *Evergreen* now tended to emphasize exotically suggestive pictures over experimental writing, and the *Big Table* had ceased publication. Among the anthologies, Thomas Parkinson's *A Casebook on the Beat* and Donald Allen's *New American Poetry* had been excellent, while the rest were either limp or crass. Parkinson had made an interesting mix of the very best poems of Corso and Ginsberg, Kerouac's "October in the Railroad Earth" and other essays. To this he added an excellent selection of Ferlinghetti, Snyder, Whalen, and McClure, and the critics—Podhoretz, Herbert Gold, and the first intelligent article on Jack, Warren Tallman's "Kerouac's Sound." The *Casebook* was truly superior to the exploitative quickies like Gene Feldman and Max Gartenberg's *The Beat Generation and the Angry Young Men* or even Seymour Krim's *The Beats*, both of which roped in Anatole Broyard and Chandler Brossard to fill out generally thin contents. Krim's own "The Insanity Bit" was superb, and his inclusion of Gary Snyder's "Notes on the Religious Tendencies" marked a fine taste, but basically *The Beats* was weak.

The New American Poetry had no such problems. Though Donald Allen would later regret organizing it on a regional basis, the fact that it had been constructed out of a consensus of the poets themselves made it a powerful volume that encyclopedically included the best open-form poetics. The "Black Mountain" poets, the Beats, the San Franciscans and dozens of others from across the country were all represented. United only by a revulsion for technical craft for its own sake, they agreed with Charles Olson when he said, "one loves only form,/and form only comes/into existence when/the thing is born." The collection did not express a new, structured establishment, as Robert Duncan later commented, but a poetic community whose work was destined to endure. Hypercritical, Allen felt that the Creeley and Corso selections were off and that Jack was underrepresented, but he conceded the book's high value. About the same time, Donald Hall, Robert Pack, and Louis Simpson organized a "rival" collection of traditional young men, *The New Poets of England*

and America, without a single duplication of Donald Allen's book. Over the ensuing years, the "establishment" poets of Hall's book—Robert Bly, John Hollander, Robert Lowell—would alter their style to the looser, more personal mode of Donald Allen's rebels.

Although *Evergreen* continued to publish work by Ginsberg, Kerouac, Snyder, and McClure through the early 1960's, the era's most interesting periodical, of which only one volume was then published, was Michael McClure, Lawrence Ferlinghetti, and David Meltzer's *Journal for the Protection of All Beings.* Mixing Thomas Merton, Artaud, Corso, and Gary Snyder's "Buddhist Anarchism" with "The Surrender Speech of Chief Joseph [of the Nez Percé Indians]," the *Journal* further developed the earth consciousness implied by Jack's *The Dharma Bums,* which would later coalesce in related form in Gary Snyder's *Earth House Hold* and Stewart Brand's *The Whole Earth Catalogue.*

By 1961 the critics were through with the Beats. Allen and Gregory had left the country, while Jack had exiled himself to Florida, and the last few articles trickled out their insults without verve. Writing his way out of his own academic exile in a teaching post in Montana, New Yorker Leslie Fiedler informed *Partisan Review* readers that Allen Ginsberg had "invented" Jack through the 1957 media, transforming "the author of a dull and conventional Bildungsroman remembered by no one into a fantasy figure capable of moving the imagination of rebellious kids." Ginsberg himself, Fiedler declaimed, had been created by Lionel Trilling's short story "Of This Time, of That Place"—which turned out to have been written some three years before the professor met his student.

Ironically, in a time when Henry Miller's once-unpublishable *Tropic of Cancer* ranked next to Harold Robbins on the best-seller lists, many critics were at last able to stop cringing and respect Ginsberg's poetry. M. L. Rosenthal, once utterly revolted by Allen's explicitness, joined George Oppen in writing extremely respectful reviews of *Kaddish.* Fiedler had concluded, with a whistling-past-the-graveyard certainty, "Finally, the Beats have made no difference." Jack told a high school student who interviewed him that the Beats were "the young people who have transferred literature from the colleges and academies into the hands of the folk, in the same way that rock and roll young people have transferred music composition from Tin Pan Alley to the folk." High culture and popular culture slipped past each other, and there the issue rested.

In his contemporary "Pome on Dr. Sax," Jack replicated his own life, turning the dream hero of his childhood into a skid-row bum imprisoned in "this impossibly/hard life" with a bottle of rotgut Tokay for comfort. Kerouac felt sluggish, he told Carolyn, as if he were already entering senility. In November 1961 he left Florida for a month-long New York binge with painters Hugo Weber and Jacques Beckwith that crested when Jack was bounced from the Village Gate night club by the owner and welcomed back by the club's star performer, Stan Getz. Returning to Florida, Jack passed a lonely January and February while he typed up *Big Sur* in the company of Mémère and three cats, and it was almost a relief to flee them for his return to New York in March 1962 to settle in court with Joan Haverty. Still, family court was a nightmare.

That year he wrote, "I demand that the human race/cease multiplying its kind/and bow out/I advise it." Although Jack "lost" on the blood test and was forced to acknowledge paternity, Joan's lawyer presented a thin case and the Honorable Judge Sidney Fine awarded Joan the sum of $12 a week child support until Janet Michelle Kerouac was twenty-one. Eugene Brooks, Jack's lawyer, felt that Jack's denials of paternity were sincere, but since Jack had already lied to his counsel in an income history he'd prepared for the trial, his real convictions were open to question. Allen was convinced that the case might have been settled amicably but for Mémère's fearful nagging, and he was probably correct.

New York State Case #7275-1961 earned Jack one idiotic New York *Daily News* headline—BEAT BARD DENIES HE'S THE DADDY-O—and reunited him briefly in Manhattan with Gregory Corso, who had returned to the United States. Gregory was disgusted with Jack, who he thought "just cares about his self and demands I respect that self, but I can't if he just sits about babbling drunkenly how great he is and how bad who else is, so unreal, unrelated, that he truly bored me." A friend once wrote of Gregory that "I don't know anything that's going to keep Gregory from Angelism, of which heroin is perhaps a purer form than poetry." Corso was severely addicted to junk at that time, and their different drugged realities were in separate universes.

Florida was as boring as ever on Jack's return, a treeless subdivision slum noisily crammed with children, a lonely trap where Jack could only pass time, as he said, waiting. Nothing happened. Turning away from a bleak present, he entered the past and efficiently organized all of his letters and manuscripts in a shiny new filing cabinet. Only the mail mattered to him in the broiling heat, and it brought some gratifying news. Agent Sterling Lord had sold *Big Sur* and *Visions of Gerard* to Farrar, Straus and Cudahy, and the editor would be Jack's cherished friend Robert Giroux. Lord also sent a petition defending Barney Rosset in a Supreme

Court censorship case over Henry Miller's *Tropic of Cancer*, and Jack signed it, secure in his companionship with Edmund Wilson and the Fourth Amendment to the Constitution.

As the summer of 1962 passed, Allen's letters from Africa and Asia joined Nabokov's *Lolita* as Jack's main entertainment. The flimsy green air-mail squares contained huge messages of travels through India as well as weird news about Burroughs. Bill was "inhumanly independent of passions" and manipulative, a black magic "void preaching guru" who terrified an Allen still split by the metaphysical void between Blake and *yage* death. After a brief split-up, Allen and Peter had reunited in Israel, where Allen had consulted with the theologian Martin Buber, then journeyed to India via Kenya. In Bombay they had joined Gary Snyder and his wife, Joanne Kyger, and the four of them had wandered across the subcontinent, true dharma bums.

The letters Jack sent to his friends were not so enlivening. In fact, they were mostly drunken babble, the same stories repeated three letters in a row, and reached a nadir when he called Carolyn, the woman he revered, "Lady Cunt." As he confessed to Neal, he was wholly out of touch with reality and had been for a year. Drunk or sober, he told his brother, he was a dull blank who could barely pronounce his own name.

Jack had talked for two months about going to Paris, Cornwall, and Scandinavia, but as his weight touched two hundred pounds and his alcohol consumption was up to the quart-a-day level, he had the d.t.'s again, saw the devil and witches as in Bixby Canyon. Though she wanted to be near Nin, Mémêre had to acknowledge her son's desperation, and she demanded that he find a house in New England.

Instead of Paris, Jack flew to Maine. But he decided that the French-Canadian resort town of Old Orchard Beach was "dreary" and sped off to a depressingly crowded Cape Cod. There the black bouncers at a jazz joint became insulted by his "nigger" talk and beat him unconscious. He returned to Orlando to heal, and Mémêre sent him to the one dependable friend he had remaining in America—John Clellon Holmes.

One Sunday in early September 1962, a sober Kerouac arrived in Old Saybrook to begin house hunting, and Jack, John, and his wife Shirley spent a pleasant evening getting reacquainted, sharing literary chatter and storytelling. On Monday a pajama-clad Jack resumed his chair to read Balzac and guzzle his daily quart of Hennessy Cognac. As in Jacky's apartment, he literally did nothing else; as the work-week passed, this once-meticulous man did not bathe or shave, and would come to the dinner table only when Shirley poured a glass of wine. Friday night he could not climb the stairs and passed out on the sofa. Saturday he revived, cleaned up, and managed to spend a few hours looking for a home, but one beer in the afternoon sent him off again. Afterward he was guilt-stricken at having screwed up once more. Unable to face Holmes, he packed an enormous Mason jar full of ice cubes and brandy and fled, stumbling into a hastily rented limousine for a $60 ride, to Lowell, a destination at once unlikely and utterly logical.

The King of the Beats had returned to his hometown to receive homage, and never did Jack Kerouac put on a greater performance than in his twenty-day bar crawl of Lowell, an alcoholic jubilee before an audience of Lowellites come to see a king who was his own court jester. His court was a very special group of people, a mix of young college-educated working-class Greeks and Irish—Huck Finneral, Greg Zahos, Jay Pendergast, Danny Murphy—and the older Greek gamblers and bookies who habituated his stage, the Sac Club. Reaching back to his childhood, Jack called up his old comrade GJ Apostalakis, but GJ was a hustling insurance salesman who couldn't drink twenty-four hours a day, and after one uncomfortable night he avoided Jack. Mary Carney found Jack equally offensive, and their Sunday-afternoon visit was awkward and brief.

With two exceptions—James Curtis, a lawyer with literary interests, and a Lowell Tech English instructor named Charles Jarvis—Lowell's middle-class professional people wanted nothing to do with their town's most notorious citizen. Though Jack told Curtis that "someday they'll take down [the soldier's monument in front of City Hall] and put me up, just like Thomas Wolfe in Asheville," Lowell's elite ignored him then as ever. Curtis and Jarvis had a half-hour on the local radio station called *Dialogues in Great Books,* and they were thrilled at the opportunity to have a famous author on their program.

Well lubricated with beer and brandy, Jack gave them a performance they would never forget. Professor Jarvis opened the show with routine introductory remarks, and that was the final routine moment; when Jarvis spoke of "milestones" in Jack's career, Kerouac seized the microphone to proclaim, "I am Lewis Milestone, gallstone . . . death." In the next half-hour he raced through a rainbow of emotions that spanned the scale of human possibility, destroying his hosts' ideas of polite literary discussion with a display of consummate—if drunken—spontaneity. Irritated by the condescending way Curtis and Jarvis had treated their engineer, Jack

introduced the man, then interrupted every question with a surreal monologue on Gerard, the nuns, and their childhood visits to the Franco-
American Orphanage religious grotto. "And I have followed him ever
since," Jack said, "because I know he's up there guiding my every step."
An erratic encyclopedia, Jack discoursed on Buddha, yoga, the healthiness
of headstands, and Shakespeare, who had also written spontaneously and
died of drink in Avon. The just-published *Big Sur*, Jack advised them,
"went back to a vision I had of heaven—my job is to describe heaven, a
little bit." The style of *Big Sur* was like Proust's, "only fast," and still
resolutely spontaneous, because "Once God moves your hand—Go back
and revise, it's a sin!"

Jack spent most of his time in Lowell at the center table of the Sac
Club, a bar and bookie joint in the Greek neighborhood called the Acre.
The table was usually surrounded by a shifting audience that included
Manuel Nobriga, Voo the owner, Mousy, and Billy Koumantzelis, the
younger brother of a close friend of Jack's who hadn't come back from
World War II. A second ring pushed in around Jack's table and the crowd
grew to a dozen or more, with young college men like Huck Finneral and
Greg Zahos. The last member of the circle was Tony Sampas. Tony was
Sammy's younger brother, a gaunt and balding man who betrayed his
nerves with an unending stream of well-chewed Marlboro cigarettes and
a pained expression that masked his empathy for Jack. A remarkable blend
of a friendly Lowell working guy, a former OSS guerrilla, and a master's-
degree graduate in psychology, Tony was a man who liked to discuss
literature as well as swap stories. Of himself Tony would only say that "I
treat people good," but it was more than that. Over the next few years
he and his sister Stella would protect and cherish the bewildered Kerouac,
becoming the family he had so long missed.

The Sac Club crowd dubbed Jack "Jacques le Coque" and he ruled
the bar, calling for "more of the grape"—Courvoisier—as he drew pictures on the table in cigarette ash, "table thumping," the *Sun* reported,
"and jumping up to crow or bark or laugh." "Let's go," he shouted. "Let's
go to Paris and visit Cocteau . . . oh, but my favorite French writer is dead,
he's dead." Memories boiling through his mind like hashish smoke bub-
bles in a hookah, Jack raved on: "Once, I was in Morocco, and I saw a
shepherd boy carrying a little LAMB . . . I hate what France has done
to the French language. They've RUINED it. They've fancied it up
. . . where they really speak French is in QUEBEC."

He'd come to Lowell to see the river and its haunted sandbanks, the bridge, and Pawtucketville, but he never got out of the bar, too intent on the stories around him. He spilled drinks in his frantic excitement. His uncomfortable shyness was obscured by the roar of the binge, the secure noise of working-class Lowell, a "vast collection of Christians," as he put it. From near the Sac Club's front door he could see the golden dome of the Greek Orthodox Church in the Acre and the steeple of his childhood St. Jean Baptiste, and their vigil was a warm blessing of security that permitted him to indulge in boozy pleasure. He fended off seriousness except when one of his young proto-poet friends asked for advice about writing. Greg Zahos showed him some poems, and Jack tried to dissuade him from the road, from the quest: "The price is too high, kid. It'll kill you."

He was in Lowell when *Big Sur* was published. Some of the reviews were astonishingly positive. In *Saturday Review* Herbert Gold thought Jack was "on the right road at last . . . in focus, troubling and touching." The *New York Times Book Review* felt *Big Sur* had "a sense of structure and pacing . . . the scenes click and signify." But *Playboy* sneered at his habit of dropping the g's from gerunds, and the *Herald Tribune* thought his writing was like a "Vogue perfume ad." *Time* issued an all-out attack, labeling the author of *Dr. Sax* and *On the Road* a "confirmed one-vein literary miner," and mocked his breakdown by sniffing, "a child's first touch of cold mortality—even when it occurs in a man of 41—may seem ridiculous and is certainly pathetic."

Ralph Gleason suggested that Kerouac had "committed the worst crime of those who go against the traditional in literature; he has been read." Jack's explanation to Neal and Carolyn was simpler, if ugly; the critics hated him because he wasn't Saul Bellow or Bernard Malamud or J. D. Salinger or Herman Wouk—because he wasn't a Jew. He adopted a façade of megalomaniacal bravado, assuring the Cassadys—and anyone else who would listen—that he was the greatest American prose stylist since Melville, an equal of Joyce and Shakespeare.

In Jack's last week in Lowell he met a thirty-four-year-old barfly named Paul Bourgeois, who announced to the wobbly Kerouac that they were cousins. Further, Paul Bourgeois claimed that he was no Lowell bum but the "Moon Cloud Chief" of the Four Nations of the Iroquois, whose four families were named Kirouac, L'Evesque (Mémêre's maiden name), Sirois, and Bourgeois-Ogallag. Jack was entranced as Paul related the history of the Iroquois. Only three thousand remained in their home near the North Pole, Jack wrote Holmes and Ferlinghetti, because they were being wiped out by atomic submarine pollution which killed fish and polar bears. "Chief" Bourgeois wanted to move them south, Jack reported, and Secretary of State Rusk had suggested that they wait a while. Because Jack was a cousin of the tribe, in two years he would be allowed to visit its homeland, chopping wood to earn his share of strengthening Caribou blood. It was a magnificent fantasy, worthy of *Dr. Sax,* and Jack accepted every word of Bourgeois' rantings, recruited Paul as driver-companion, and promised to write a book to free his brethren when he sobered up. In Jack's letter to Ferlinghetti describing the Moon Cloud Folk, he mentioned everyone's Indian name and concluded, "I intend to find out my own name there in two years."

The *Sun* columns had flooded the Sac Club with too large an audience, and Jack tired rapidly. Taking refuge in Tony Sampas' home to dry out, Jack collected Paul Bourgeois and another Lowell man as the first edition of the Lowell traveling squad that would surround him in his wanderings for the next few years. They set out for New York, where they drank with Lucien before Jack and Paul flew to Orlando. Mémère did not approve of Bourgeois, and one morning while Jack was asleep she put Paul on a train for Lowell. Jack still couldn't stomach Florida, and after a few weeks of restful boredom he flew north to transfer his Florida mortgage to a new home in Northport.

Shortly before Christmas 1962, he and Mémère moved into a well-landscaped Long Island ranch house complete with a fireplace and the usual high fence for privacy. After a horrible year, Jack felt good enough to conceive of a new book, *Vanity of Duluoz,* which would cover 1939 to 1945—football, the war, and Leo's death. Duluoz was the name of the persona Jack had chosen for the legend of his life at least twenty years before in his war-time novel; he hoped to publish a uniform edition of his chronicles someday that would use Duluoz instead of the various earlier names he'd used for characters representing himself. *Vanity of Duluoz* would take him four years to complete.

A major source of Jack's writing difficulties was the minimal demand for his work. In part because of Jack himself, American youth culture had shifted. The romantic energy of *On the Road* had filled a need in the dull stasis of 1957, but the atmosphere of 1962 was permeated by the Cuban missile crisis. John Kennedy had thrilled the nation with his cool, super-masculine bravado in facing down the Soviet Union over the missile sites. Kennedy's stylish First Lady, his games of touch football, and his formation of the Peace Corps united with his undoubted courage to create the image of Camelot; most of the era's wave of youthful romantic energy became embodied in the style of "the Best and the Brightest."

Many of the dropouts who'd left the conventional world for North Beach and the Village ran home to careers, but in every American city and college town a few hardy subterraneans struggled on. The legal attacks and commercial exploitation of the "Beat Generation" had made them wary, and the mid-sixties underground culture reflected the times with a starkly aggressive style. In the wake of the Beats, three special voices added themselves to the chorus of visionary discontent, a trio of artists who encountered America and found it wanting: William Burroughs, Lenny Bruce, and Bob Dylan.

Despite the publication of *Junkie* and his work in the *Chicago Review*, William Burroughs achieved major attention in America only late in 1962. In 1958 Ferlinghetti had warned that the publication of *Naked Lunch* was "pure and unpremeditated legal lunacy," but in November 1962 Grove Press brought out what Norman Mailer would describe as "prose written in bone, etched by acid." *Naked Lunch* was a "frozen moment," Burroughs said, "when everyone sees what it is on the end of every fork." His knife-edge satire brought Jonathan Swift to Jack's mind with the hope that it might shock its readers into honesty. Bill thought it was a "modern inferno" whose chief character, Dr. Benway, resembled the Grand Inquisitor in *The Brothers Karamazov.*

Grove Press had published the most horrible book in American history, a series of withered, deadpan images of obscenity. The images coalesced to portray addiction not as a vice but as the given state of Americans enslaved by their need to be controlled, to repress their sexuality in material consumption. Addiction was something Burroughs knew well; morphine was, he realized, "the ideal product . . . the ultimate merchandise . . . the junk merchant does not sell his product to the consumer, he sells the consumer to his product." Junk created a biological totalitarianism, a manipulative addict-dealer structure that was a harsh and simplified replica of modern society's web of electronic and political controls. Junk was a virus of addiction, but the deceitful words of government agencies, advertisements and the mass media were a virus as well. *Naked Lunch* and Burroughs' succeeding volumes were designed to inoculate the reader against the virus with a silence of perfect awareness that canceled out the insidious desire to be controlled, the mainstay of the liberal technocratic ideology Burroughs despised. "Control," he wrote, "can never be a means to any practical end . . . It can never be a means to anything but more control . . . like junk."

Norman Mailer gave the book instant cachet when he told the Edinburgh Writers' Conference that Burroughs was "the only American novelist living today who may conceivably be possessed by genius," and Mary McCarthy's review in the powerful new *New York Review of Books* was sensible, intelligent, and positive. They were nearly unique. The *New Republic* thought it was "trash," *Time* dismissed it as "second growth Dada," and the *Partisan Review* only shuddered.

Curiously the book made sense in 1962, just as Jack's tender faith did not. It was a time when the United States tested nuclear weapons in the atmosphere, extended electronic communications with the Telstar satellite, and made best sellers of two realistic books about a potential nuclear war, *Fail-Safe* and *Seven Days in May*. Aside from President Kennedy, the hero of the age was James Bond, the cool English agent "007," who armed himself with flashy technical gadgets bearing the right brand names and went off to slay all threats to the Western hegemony. America's fantasy hero was racist, violent, and antiemotional.

Bond's diametric opposite was the second artistic successor to the Beats, a bitterly romantic hip "white Negro" named Lenny Bruce, who raised "standup comedy" to unprecedented levels of artistry along the lines of the Beats, and shared in their critical fate. Bruce lampooned everything from prison movies ("Father Flotsky") to race ("Colored Friends") to class ("White Collar Drunk"), but the razor style of his monologues made Jack detest him. Once Jack and some young buddies visited John Holmes, a bona-fide Lenny Bruce fanatic. The young men begged John to play one of Bruce's records, and Jack shrieked that Lenny was a "kike, dirty mouth, mean," and drowned out the rest of the record. Jack's muse was sadness, and he distrusted Lenny's enraged wit. It had been years since Jack defended the Church, but Lenny's blasphemous "Religions Incorporated" shocked him; no son of Mémère could laugh at "John Baby," the Pope.

Such narrowness was a grievous loss for Jack, because Lenny was his spiritual kin. Both suffered lonely childhoods, smothering mothers, and a distaste for regimentation, and shared as well an obsession with jazz and the carnival of Times Square. A critical difference between them was that Lenny's drugs of choice were usually stimulants like Methedrine or mescaline, while Jack remained loyal to alcohol.

In January of 1958 Bruce opened in a San Francisco club called

Ann's 440; the Beat liberation of culture allowed him to say things he'd never dared before, and in a few weeks his career exploded with the publicity of Herb Caen, Ralph Gleason, and Lawrence Ferlinghetti. Lenny's comedy rapidly surpassed the funny but packaged bits like "Father Flotsky" with *Visions of Cody*-style spontaneity and free association, a narrative based on orally dictated rhythm rather than any preset form. Lenny was as naked onstage as Allen had been at the Six Gallery, like Burroughs a shaman exorcising his and his generation's guilts, a Kerouacian truth-teller who improvised a tale from what a later writer called the viewpoint of an "alienated conservative."

Outraged by Bruce, the Catholic Church and the police set out to destroy him with a series of obscenity and narcotics arrests. In four years Lenny Bruce was broke, fat, and dissipated, though still madly confident that the courts would vindicate him. Tattered and torn, he yet had a message. Its allusion to Christ would have shocked Jack. Although Jack chose not to understand him, Lenny was like Jack when he told the nation: "Remember this, I'm dying for your sins. I'm dying, so—well, just *shape up!* That's all, I'm dying so that, in the future, things will be right, so you just realize what the values are. Good things—remember the good, remember that being born is an original sin."

The third Beat heir was a poet and singer from Hibbing, Minnesota. Kitten-fragile, spring-steel tough, almost decadently sensitive, Bob Dylan scoured a path of Rimbaudian fire and visionary prophecy across an America whose most popular music in the early 1960's was Bobby Vinton's "Roses are Red," the "Wah-wah Tusi," and "The Stripper." Though Dylan came to fame as a protégé of Woody Guthrie, he was never a regulation member of the folk crowd; sometime later he would acknowledge that "it was Ginsberg and Jack Kerouac who inspired me at first." His first recorded songs ranged from a folk saga of a larger-than-life character named "Rambling Gambling Willie" to a vignette of a wino called "Man on the Street" to a road blues called "Standing on the Highway."

In a blend of cultural traditions, the songs came out of his populist Guthrie heritage full of images that might have come from *Visions of Cody.* Dylan's alienation from his native land was far too deep to be satisfied by wearing blue jeans and celebrating "the folk." When he read *Time*'s "Fried Shoes" article on Allen and Gregory's Chicago reading and saw through the distortion, he realized that there were "other people out there like me!" A friend gave him a copy of *Mexico City Blues* and later

Dr. Sax and *Big Sur,* and Dylan grew with the knowledge that words could be free. By 1962 his rhythmically visionary indictment "A Hard Rain's a-Gonna Fall" was a clear successor to *Howl.* "Brecht of the Juke Box," the *Voice* called him, "The first poet of the mass media," said Ralph Gleason. "With God on Our Side" was a bitterly sarcastic review of patriotism that was estranged from Kerouac's faith, but as Dylan developed over the next few years, his songs assumed an autobiographical, visceral orientation much like that of *The Subterraneans.* In a creative breakthrough of style that earned him accusations of treason from the folk critics, Dylan affirmed a boyhood spent listening to Little Richard, picked up an electric guitar, and brought his life and art back home to the Afro-American beat of rock and roll.

Dylan lived on a frightening mental frontier, and his songs often expressed Rimbaud's "systematic derangement of the senses," the tortuous separation from structured America that Lucien and Jack had confronted twenty years before. Dylan's political epigrams were as anarchistically beat as *The Dharma Bums.* Death preoccupied the singer as it had his predecessors, hauntingly expressed in his song "It's All Right Ma (I'm only bleeding)."

Again Holmes tried to interest Jack in this new artist; Jack thought Dylan was "another fucking folk singer" at first, but after a while gruffly conceded, "Well, okay, he's good." A tired forty-year-old man, Jack had no desire left to digest anything new, especially when it issued from a youth culture that snickered at his potbelly.

Jack and Mémêre's new home at 7 Judy Ann Court, Northport, was the most elaborate that they had ever lived in. Jack was proud of the two baths, the fireplace, and the finished basement with its wood-paneled rumpus room. As he settled into it and the New Year 1963, it occurred to him that this was Mémêre's twenty-sixth home since his birth, and though it was nice to have a fancy home, it had somehow come too late. He'd wanted to be a bhikku, he told Whalen, but he also wanted a nice home for Mémêre. Now he had the house, but his feelings of solitary religiosity had been leached away in booze, and he was empty. A melancholy lassitude settled over him, and he paced gray January Northport out of touch, not even sure where Allen and Gary were anymore, certain only that his road life was from another world, another lifetime.

Having combed old newspaper clippings, family pictures and letters in preparation, he tried to begin *Vanity of Duluoz,* but a February 1963 letter from Carolyn disrupted his concentration. After Neal's probation ended in July, Carolyn informed him, they were getting a divorce. Perhaps because he could not achieve it, Jack worshiped the marriage pact, especially Neal and Carolyn's. As irregular as the Cassady marriage was, it had been a dependable factor in Jack's life for fifteen years, and now it was gone. The Cassady children were his especial concern, and he advised Carolyn not to bother her son with the nosy and foolish P.T.A., and to bless her daughters with the Sermon on the Mount rather than party dresses. Carolyn had wanted to free Neal to go his own way. Afterward she feared she'd destroyed him.

Neal took up with a woman named Anne, and bereft of his security in Carolyn, he swept into a purgatory of suffering that would endure to his death. Late in July of 1963, Cassady came east to Northport with two friends.

When they were alone, Jack found Neal graciously peaceful and illuminating, but one of his friends raided the refrigerator and Neal's other companion put his feet on the kitchen table. In Mémêre's house Jack observed the formalities, and he became grievously offended. The possibility that Neal's car was stolen unnerved him, and he quickly sent his visitors away, so shaken by the pathetic guttering out of his past that he stopped drinking for several weeks.

That summer John C. Holmes sent Jack a list of questions as part of the research that led to his book *Nothing More to Declare*, and Kerouac's answers were a reflection of his distaste for the mind-controlled, antiseptic world he inhabited. Life was so horrible, Jack felt, that children cried at birth because they did not want to be exiled from the bliss of the womb.

The summer of 1963 passed in quiet gloom, and in September, Farrar, Straus and Cudahy published *Visions of Gerard*. Jack's shy, sentimental memoir was oddly out of place in an optimistic society of 90,000 millionaires, a consumer's paradise of Barbie Dolls and Polaroid Color Pack cameras, a circus of football led by Jim Brown. The slow, easy rhythm of Jack's childhood baseball had been replaced as the national game by professional football, a gigantic, swift, and brutal sport that was emblematic of the times. Zip codes and direct dialing had further standardized living patterns, and that fall when President John Kennedy died in Dallas in the afternoon, seven of every ten Americans knew of it in half an hour, and 99.8 percent of them knew by dark. Such efficiency was the backdrop against which the critics adjudged *Visions of Gerard* as "self-indulgence" and "garrulous hipster yawping." The reviews, Jack thought, were like dirty gray cobwebs pulled over his eyes, and the worst was *Newsweek*, which called him a "tin-eared Canuck" and denied the essence of his work because "childhood is intrinsically a bore, and heartsy-flowery re-creations of it are intrinsically a fraud."

The past seemed to curve into the present, and bits of Jack's life began to wither and die. Allen returned to the United States in December, but Kerouac was uncomfortable with what he saw as Allen's white-robed messiah complex. After the Blake vision and *Howl*, after *Kaddish* and the *yage* death, Allen had relaxed within himself in an epochal metaphysical epiphany he called, simply, "The Change." "THE SNAKE'S ALL TOOK CARE OF," he had written Jack. "I renounce my Power: so that I do live and I will Die . . . *I am that I am* and no more mental universe arguments . . . and what exactly am I? Why I'm me, and me is my feelings . . . located to be exact in my belly trembling when eyes say yes."

In India, Ginsberg saw the dying riddled with fly-infested sores as they lay in the gutters of Calcutta, smoked *ganja*, and smelled the burning corpses on the pyres, prayed to "Kali, Durga, Ram, Hari, Krishna, Brahma, Buddha, Allah, Jaweh, Christ, Mazda, Coyote," sent Jack a leaf from the sacred Bo tree of Gautama Buddha and bathed in the holy Ganges. Stopping to see Gary and Joanne in Japan, he ended up in bed between them and felt secure lying between friends. A few days later, on a train ride to Tokyo, Allen was flooded by an inexplicable but wholly felt mystic resolution of his cosmic search. He burst into tears and came back to the present and to his self, released himself from his death vows of cosmic consciousness, gave up so that he could go on, became one with his body, came back.

Jack could not follow his younger brother in this pattern of spiritual growth, for it was far too late for that; he was tired, more deeply disillusioned, without the faith in life and search that made a cosmic odyssey possible.

As he told Carolyn, his present task was to sweat life out, to pass through the world patiently waiting for death to enfold him.

XVII
The
Village Idiot

LIFE PASSED as seen through the blur of a highball, and Jack took further refuge in the identity of a noisily wise fool; he could no longer effectively write, but he still had something to teach. As he'd put it in his journal, he'd become a "village idiot" to uplift and free his audience, and by 1964 his persona as boastfully silly barroom oracle was firmly established and often misunderstood. Though the butt of Jack's wretchedly scurrilous anti-Semitic attacks, Allen refused to take Jack seriously. "Once you gave it back to him, he'd laugh and back off," Allen recalled later. "He was teasing the *identity* as a Jew, for in the Buddhist sense there is no self . . . it was more a mocking of hypocrisy and timidity and liberal mealymouthedness, a red-neck jocularity that was aggressive but more xenophobic than anti-Semitic."

Kerouac could deal only with individuals, and though he delighted in abusing pretentious intellectuals face-to-face with a baseball-capped working-class harangue, he was usually within bounds. When he blithered of abstractions removed from his immediate reality, John Holmes pointed out, "he was full of shit." Much of the empty noise was the product of a man unsure of his identity, a man who could argue seriously for hours that he was the grandson of Pope Pius VI, who grasped eagerly for roots as a member of the "Moon Cloud Folk" or as a Cornishman. He had long cherished his Breton ancestry, but now his lectures on the ancient Celtic origins of the name Kerouac took on an obsessive quality, as if he were trying to find historic grounds for his existence. It was not only his spiritual and mental reality that had deteriorated, but his sexual self-image as well. Though Mémêre refused to take phone messages from Allen or allow him in the house—Jack by now conceded to Allen that she was as ill as Naomi had been—Jack would journey to the city to appeal to Ginsberg. "I'm old, ugly, red-faced," Jack blubbered, "I'm beer-bellied and a drunk and nobody loves me anymore. I can't get girls, come on and give me a blow job." After all his years of desire for the "romantic, handsome . . . dark, doomed" Kerouac, Allen couldn't respond, sexually revolted by the man before him who didn't look like Jack anymore, as Allen realized with a start, but Leo.

Jack's sullenness made their relationship sputter fitfully; he lived in the past now, alcoholically out of touch.

Allen was in an excitingly creative present. Set free by his psychological experience "The Change," he had moved into what might be called politics, his activities devoted to what a critic called "the expansion and generation of mutual consciousness." For the first time in many years, Allen's blend of cultural and political radicalism had acquired a responsive audience. Earlier, most bohemian dropouts had been apolitical, and most of the postwar era's few leftists had been aggressively middle-class in manner. In a strange marriage, the Beats and Kennedy liberalism had together given birth to the "Movement," a loose collection of antiwar, antipoverty, and civil rights groups composed largely of white college youth. As *Village Voice* reporter Jack Newfield later argued, the Movement was "an ethical revolt against the visible devils of centralized decision making, manipulative, impersonal bureaucracies, and the hypocrisy that divides America's ideals from its actions." This revolt derived quite as much from *Howl* and *On the Road* as Michael Harrington's poverty study *The Other America,* and called for a utopia more akin to that envisioned by William Blake than Mao Tse-tung.

It was certainly no coincidence that the Movement began at the time of liberalism's greatest triumph. Lyndon Johnson had harnessed the grief of a country desolated by the loss of a Prince to engineer a conservative version of the New Deal. The Job Corps, VISTA, and the Economic Opportunity Act attacked poverty, and in the next two years Congress dramatically increased federal aid to education. Medicare for the aged, rent supplements, Model Cities programs, a Voting Rights Bill and a Housing Rights and Civil Liberties Bill all erupted out of Congress to form the Great Society. Sure that the liberal technocratic mentality that fostered these solutions was the core of the problem, a few young radical activists wanted no part of it.

In 1964 alone, several events indicated the future. On August 4 the

United States strafed vessels of the North Vietnamese Navy in retaliation for an incident in the Gulf of Tonkin, and immediately after, Congress voted the President unlimited powers to pursue a war that would effectively eliminate the financing of wars on poverty and eventually destroy a generation's faith in liberalism. Young radicals lost their hopes early on when the Democratic Party excluded the integrated Mississippi Freedom Democratic Party delegation from the 1964 Atlantic City convention. In September student activists fresh from Southern voter-registration drives led the Free Speech Movement strike against the University of California at Berkeley in an explicit protest against President Clark Kerr's liberal technocratic style of education. The September release of the Warren Report was a final portentous event. Over the ensuing years the holes in the report would stimulate a cynical doubt of the government and a refusal to accept any account of John Kennedy's assassination—and increasingly of government in general—that did not include notions of conspiracy.

Against a backdrop of optimistic liberalism, Allen practiced an anarchistic resistance to a police state. He protested the arrest of Lenny Bruce and other forms of censorship, and devoted much of his energy to a scholarly research program into the history of drug laws in the United States, "Documents on Police Bureaucracies' Conspiracy Against Human Rights of Opiate Addicts . . ." Ginsberg's drug file soon dictated a complex set of conclusions that centered on the argument that the federal narcotics bureaucracy headed by Harry Anslinger had illegally wrested control of drugs from the medical to the police professions in the 1920's and '30's, and still exploited drug traffic.

The government tried to control drug research, but the accident of Dr. Albert Hoffman of Sandoz Pharmaceuticals—his finger touched a microscope slide containing some of his new drug, then his mouth—wrought high irony. As Allen later commented, "technology has produced a chemical which catalyzes a consciousness that finds the entire civilization leading up to that chemical pill absurd, because the consciousness was there all along with the animals in the forest."

Allen, Jack, Neal, McClure, Burroughs, Snyder, Whalen—all of them had taken organic peyote over the years, had overcome the bitter nausea and learned their various spiritual lessons. When Dr. Hoffman touched his finger to his mouth he ingested a compact, easily massproduced hallucinogenic with few physical side effects, called lysergic acid diethylamide, LSD-25; a whirling cosmic eternity now fit into a sugar cube. In the summer of 1964 several of the most creative students of LSD in the world were on their way to New York in a magical school bus driven by—who else?—the psychedelic chauffeur, Neal Cassady.

After his release from prison Neal had fallen in with a writer named Ken Kesey, a former University of Oregon wrestler then on a fellowship at Stanford University. Kesey had discovered LSD while employed as a drug-test subject, and when his book *One Flew Over the Cuckoo's Nest* put him financially ahead, he elected to spend his profit in financing a quest. His various friends, Cassady among them, gathered at Kesey's house in rural La Honda, south of San Francisco, and began to explore the new dimensions of reality visible when LSD wiped clean what William Blake had called "the doors of perception." Great visionary poets like Yeats, Blake, and Wordsworth had been able to see all reality trembling in a drop of dew, and with LSD that ecstasy was within everyone's reach.

At La Honda, Kesey recalled, "suddenly people were stripped before one another and behold; as we looked, and were looked on, we all made a great discovery; we were beautiful. Naked and helpless and sensitive as a snake after skinning, but far more human than that shining nightmare that had stood creaking in previous parade rest." Kesey went on, ". . . we were alive and life was us. We joined hands and danced barefoot amongst the rubble. We had been cleansed, liberated! We would never don the old armors again. But we reckoned without the guilt of this country."

They called themselves the Merry Pranksters, psychedelic warriors in Day-Glo paint, and they set out to free America. Their "biography," Tom Wolfe's *The Electric Kool-Aid Acid Test*, would focus on Kesey as a leader, but the essence of the LSD experience was that there were no leaders, only angels. They acquired an old school bus, suitably redecorated it with a music system, silks, and paint, and set out to visit the East Coast and consult with drug expert Timothy Leary. Neal drove the bus because . . . because Neal was the driver, the man nicknamed "Speed Limit," the voyager of inner space nearest to transcending the gap between thought and action. It seemed to Wolfe that Neal resented his role as "holy primitive, the holy beast, the Denver kid," that "people tuned him out when he tried to get thoughtful." Yet Neal was a teacher of perception, an expert on "subjects that haven't been identified yet," sensed Jerry Garcia, a gifted young guitarist whose band the Grateful Dead played for the Prankster parties, the "Acid Tests." Kesey said of Neal's path that it was "the yoga of a man driven to the cliff edge by the grassfire of an entire nation's burning material madness. Rather than be consumed by this he jumped, choosing to sort things out in the fast flying but smog free moments of a life with no retreat." Wrapped in the satori now of no retreat, Neal lived with an extraordinary sensitivity to his environment, an ongoing spontaneous monologue of observation punctuated by the phrase "You understand."

The Pranksters arrived in Manhattan, and Cassady raced off to Northport to corral his brother and bring him to the party. Jack had thought highly of *One Flew Over the Cuckoo's Nest*, and in turn Ken acknowledged a heavy literary debt to Kerouac; Neal ached to bring his old and new cohorts together in an epochal summit conference of literary hip. As they roared out of Northport, Jack blanched when Cassady gulped down amphetamines, and the ride became a wrenching ordeal for a sick, tired refugee trapped with a babbling Cassady, whom drugs had rocketed past the speed of sound.

The party made Jack equally uncomfortable. Nearly everyone but he had taken LSD that night, and the environment—floodlights, endless robot reechoing tapes, complex mirrors that distorted reality, an American flag as a couch cover—made no sense to him. Cavorting about for their movie camera, the young Pranksters were anarchically uninterested in a serious intellectual conversation. Any friend of Neal's, they thought, could adapt to LSD culture as easily as Allen had; Jack demurely walked over to the sofa, carefully folded the flag, and asked them if they were Communists. Conversation was impossible, and Jack left abruptly. Regretful, Kesey said that "we should have gone out to Northport quietly in the night," but it was too late.

Neal and Allen's participation in the early spread of LSD was not the only effect of the Beat circle on the growing youth culture of the 1960's. In fact, the Beat saga would influence millions of youth who might never read a word. Rock and roll produced at least two songs about Neal over the coming years, and both were superb. A duo called Aztec Two Step permanently enshrined his archetype with the lovely "Persecution and Restoration of Dean Moriarity." "Cassidy" (*sic*) was the second song, a beautiful ballad written by Bob Weir, a friend of Neal's and rhythm guitarist for the Grateful Dead.

Though Neal was the perfect hero, the other members of the Beat circle influenced the youth culture as well. William Burroughs' work contributed names to the rock groups Steely Dan and the Soft Machine, as well as phrases in several songs by the Rolling Stones. Another rocker, Boz Scaggs, had roamed Europe, as he put it, as a dharma bum, and *On the Road* decisively influenced two of the demigods of rock. David Bowie got his copy at age twelve, and was never the same again. Janis Joplin found hers in Texas and left for the West Coast, there to become queen of rock and roll. Years after, a leading rock critic lauded him with the simple confirmation, "Jack Kerouac was rock and roll." Yet perhaps the classic transmission of heritage came when a ragtag group in Liverpool took the term Beat, played the toughest Afro-American music it knew how, and became the Beatles.

Harassed beyond their endurance when local teenagers repeatedly peeked into their windows, the Kerouacs moved in August 1964, this time to St. Petersburg, Florida. Secure in the world's largest open-air mausoleum, Jack shot pool, ate Kentucky Fried Chicken, and visited with local sportswriters, but his few weeks of peace and quiet were canceled out by a shattering September: his sister Nin collapsed and died of a heart attack when her husband asked for a divorce. Mémêre was emotionally destroyed by the loss of her daughter, and Jack was left to sit alone night after night in his easy chair as memory storms flashed and crackled through his brain. Even as a child he had approached death with an appalled seriousness, but a funeral-parlor visit at the age of forty-two, a wake when he was slow and tired and fat and not at all sure that he could still write—those rituals ate him alive.

The winter after Nin's death was grim and sour. Jack corrected the galleys of *Desolation Angels,* tried again and failed to begin *Vanity of Duluoz,* was uplifted by reading a biography of James Joyce and made gloomy again when he spent a night in jail after drunkenly relieving himself in public. He worried about money and his lack of financial stature when he received royalty checks for $1.37 and $15.19, but *Playboy* ran "Good Blond" in January 1965 and *Horizon* bought a piece on his bus ride to Berkeley with Mémêre. As he read *Desolation Angels,* published in June of 1965, he was certain that his lifelong rendering of consciousness, *The Duluoz Legend,* was still the right literary choice. Still, it was a tender oddity in a period when best sellers almost unanimously concerned John Kennedy or war, either cold or hot—*The Spy Who Came in From the Cold, You Only Live Twice, The Looking-Glass War, The Green Berets, The Man with the Golden Gun.*

The critics of *Desolation Angels* were condescending. Kerouac was a "Bumbling Bunyan," *Time* said, who stood on his head not to relieve his phlebitis but "because that is his notion of how Buddhists behave."

To other critics, *Desolation Angels* had "a great deal to say about the time when he and his cohorts should have been coming of age"; it was "obsolete," a "disaster," an "inconsequential epic" of "exhibitionistic cults of coterie iconoclasts." One review was different. Dan Wakefield had disparaged Jack's Village Vanguard appearance, but now his response was positive. According to Wakefield, "Probably no other American writer—no, not even Norman Mailer—has been subjected to such a barrage of ridicule, venom, and cute social acumen as Kerouac . . . If the Pulitzer Prize in fiction were given for the book that is most representative of American life," Wakefield reported, "I would nominate *Desolation Angels,*" though the judges would doubtless be afraid. "We seldom recognize a real American dream when we see one," he added.

Dreams Jack had, and they were mostly nightmares. Fleeing the critics and the summer heat, he traveled to France in an attempt to break the writer's block that had plagued him for the four years since he had written *Big Sur.* Once more in search of his roots and sense of self, Jack flew to Paris in July 1965, planning to research the Kerouac genealogy with a visit to Brittany and perhaps add the sounds of the English Channel to his poem "Sea," which he had begun at Bixby Canyon.

Later Jack said he'd had some sort of satori on his trip to France, but he could never be certain where or when or even whether it had any effect. What was sure was that an icicle of loneliness stabbed him on his gray morning arrival at Orly Airport. Nervously locking his suitcase—there were no more rucksacks in his life—Jack pinned the key to his T-shirt, as Mémère had instructed, and went off to La Madeleine, the enormous revolutionary-era Greek temple of reason that was now a Catholic church. Soon he found a comfortable neighborhood in the Montparnasse district, the home of the Lost Generation of an earlier day. Though he had praised Gertrude Stein, Jack did not visit her nearby former home at Rue de Fleurus nor the lovely Luxembourg Gardens down the block, but located a bar. As it grew late he bought a woman as well, a soft denizen of the Paris night who reassured him that he was not impotent while hustling him for $120.

Headquartered in a new café in the St. Germain district, he drank cognac and reveled in being able to speak French to his barmates, tickled by memories of a Horace Mann teacher who'd mocked his accent as he lectured the entire café on the superiority of the Breton-Quebec pronunciation of the language. In a crippling swirl of lonely pathos, Jack wandered the red-light district of Pigalle, and became threatened by men who seemed to be following him; in self-defense he pulled out his Swiss Army knife and cut himself as he opened it.

After a few days in St. Germain bars, Jack struck out for the Bibliothèque Nationale and discovered that the records he needed had been burned by the Nazis, argued with a clerk at another library, and retreated to a bar where he tried to find a pool game as in St. Petersburg, and failed. Paris rejected him, or so it seemed, and he became perturbed by the truly murderous auto traffic, convinced that a gendarme had deliberately misled him, that every dark doorway harbored muggers. It seemed that even his French publisher Gallimard rebuffed him when he called his editor and was disconnected. Though he'd sneered at the American tourists who infested Paris even as they seemed to hate it, Jack was so lonely that he struck up an acquaintance with some fellow citizens and shared with them his only decent meal in France before going to see the film *Becket*.

Ever after, Paris would remind him of one awful embarrassment. He'd come in out of a misty night to the original namesake of his baptism church in Lowell, the chapel of St. Louis de France, and sat in peaceful reverie contemplating the candlelit statues and stained glass. As he listened spellbound to an organ and horn recital, Jack looked like a homeless vagrant, with his stubbly face and faraway look, and a pious woman who reminded him of Mémère passed by and dropped 20 centimes (4 cents) into the hat he held upside down in his lap.

A few days later he missed his flight to Brest, the capital of Brittany, because of an ill-timed visit to the men's room. He caught a train and grew drunk enough to lecture a priest on religion. On his arrival in a foggy Brest, he wandered forlorn, a distraught fugitive reeking of liquor, too nervous to speak to anyone until the police directed him to a boardinghouse. The next morning he cleaned up and put on a tie, then decided to return immediately to Paris. When Jack explained that he was Jean Louis Lebris de Kerouac, a friendly bookie-bartender in Brest persuaded him to call at least one person named Lebris before he left. Though Jack enjoyed his visit with Ulysse Lebris, and signed autographs for Monsieur Lebris' charming daughter, he went to catch the train anyway, missed it by three minutes, drank for eight hours, and caught the night train. In Paris he hired a taxi which whirled him fleetingly around the City of Light, past Sainte Chapelle, the perfect jewel of a chapel he'd planned only a week before to visit.

One place he'd never even planned to visit was the young vagabond headquarters of Paris, Chez Popoff. As *New York Times* headlines like

"Beatniks Flock to Nepal" and "A Baedeker of Beatnik Territory" indicated, the Beat Generation had sent people and a message out of America, to an often hostile reception. Rome police harassed students on the Spanish Steps, the Cuban government deported Allen Ginsberg for his sexual outspokenness, and the Czechs did the same after Prague students elected Allen "King of the May." Though inspired by *On the Road*, these early "hippies," long of hair, short of cash, but full of psychedelic joy, were to Jack never more than conformist stereotypes. The road was no longer his but theirs, and he gave it up for a plane at Orly Airport and a flight to St. Petersburg.

Just after he returned to Florida, Jack sat at the typewriter for a week with a bottle of cognac at his side and produced a new work, *Satori in Paris*. It was the first time he'd written while drinking, and it showed. *Satori in Paris* emerged out of a paroxysm of reflex, like a sad borscht-circuit comic telling the same joke for the seventeenth year. His old religious message of tenderness he now extended to himself as well—"have pity on us all, and don't get mad at me for writing." It was, Jack thought, a "tale that's told for no other reason but companionship, which is another (and my favorite) definition of literature."

Florida he tolerated with weeks of quiet sipping at home, interrupted by rowdy bar binges, and the month after his return he found new friends and a new bar. One was Cliff Anderson, a student at the University of South Florida (USF) in nearby Tampa, who had met Jack in a St. Pete bar and become a close beer buddy. The sort of unpredictable fellow who scraped through his courses and was often brighter than his teachers, Cliff swept Jack off to Tampa's Wild Boar Tavern on the night after its August 1, 1965, opening. The Wild Boar was a low-rent beer-and-wine joint owned by a recently fired USF speech teacher named Gerard Wagner. On the night of Jack's visit, the local sheriff raided the place and arrested Jack, although he was quietly asleep in Cliff's car out front. As Gerard soon realized, Jack was a man who "invested much commitment in simple acts," and was most gratified when Gerard bailed him out of the Hillsborough County Jail a few hours later.

In addition to his kind gesture and the coincidence of his name, Gerard was an exceptionally interesting man who stood 6' 4", had an imposing belly, and told wonderful stories in a charming Cajun accent.

Once a month Jack would find a ride to Tampa and spend four or five days in nonstop drinking at the Boar, accented by Jack's brilliant imitations of W. C. Fields's film *The Bank Dick* and bombastic put-ons of the young English professors who dropped by to debate him. Like Allen, Gerard discounted Jack's occasionally rascist maunderings because they were completely separate from his behavior; he was, Gerard felt, "the most democratic guy I ever knew," a classic good fellow and mate.

Perhaps because he feared them so much, Jack was cruel only to women. When a groupie approached him at the bar, he would turn on his still-enormous charm, lead her on, and at the moment where he might otherwise have said, "Your place or mine," he would assault her with insults like "Your cunt stinks." In his baggy hobo pants, flannel shirt, and Lowell Tech windbreaker, Jack was popular among the rowdy characters in the other local bars, where his outrageous crudity seemed colorfully normal, even as the English professors winced.

After the Boar closed at one in the morning, Jack usually spent the night—he rarely slept during a binge, and then only a cat nap—at Gerard's place on a lake outside town, and so came to dub his friend "Chevalier Gerard Alvin le Sanglier du Lac" (Sir Gerard Alvin the Wild Boar of the Lake). To the sonorous jug-a-rum of the croaking frogs, the two men would talk, of women—Jack said often that he'd loved only Mardou Fox and Mary Carney—and the music of his young manhood, for Jack owned every record Bird Parker had ever made. An interesting and creative man in his own right, Gerard was inspired by Jack, who "would lead you to thoughts, memories, you'd never otherwise know." One night they read Shakespeare's *Henry IV*, Gerard as Falstaff and Jack as Hal, and Gerard suddenly realized that Jack was not reading, but reciting his parts from memory.

Gerard asked about Jack's writing, and though Jack defended himself against the critics—"I'm not a spokesman for a bunch of hoods. I'm a novelist in the great French narrative tradition"—he never talked about his own work. Because of the massive emotional paralysis of his writer's block, Jack had turned from the solitary act of writing to the direct communication of talk. The two modes contradicted each other; a village idiot at center stage *was* the show and could not be the recording eye. Though Jack's wit taught those who might listen, it only depleted his writer's stock of images and sounds.

Memories had always been Jack's primary resource, and that fall of 1965 he received a letter that stirred them up most painfully. After camping in the Sierras with Gary Snyder, Allen had returned to the Bay Area to join Neal, Peter Orlovsky and his brother Julius, and Carolyn in

Los Gatos. In the nostalgic revelry of a party among old friends, they sat down and wrote a group letter to their missing family member Jack. Allen cheerfully reported Snyder's remark that "I finally got a climbing companion [in Allen]," Carolyn assured Jack that she'd loved *Desolation Angels* "best of all," but Neal's scribbles were disturbing. His handwriting had always been difficult to decipher, but now it careened jerkily over the page like the footprints of a drunk. Cassady pleaded for Jack to allow him to publish their letters, for "Carolyn and the kiddies." "If only you'll say yes I'll be overjoyed, if now you say no, well fuck it all then man, fuck it all." The day after the party ended, Jack phoned Neal at Carolyn's, oblivious to the Cassadys' divorce or the passage of time. "Who answered that phone," he growled at her. "I'll kill him—got my machete right here."

"That's [my son] John, Jack."

At last convinced that it was his namesake, Kerouac looked for his whiskey, couldn't find it and blamed Mémêre, "that damned ole alcoholic," then began to tell Carolyn in graphic sexual detail what he'd do if she were with him. "But I won't marry you as long as Neal's alive," Jack mumbled. "We gotta wait till the halls of Nirvana like I said in *Big Sur*. You're Neal's wife, an' you better not come knockin' on my do'," his voice assuming the "cracker" accent of his deepest drunkenness, "lessen you got that death certificate in yo' han', y'heah?" Carolyn said nothing, for she knew no possible response to these sad meanderings. After a while she made her excuses, said good night, and hung up.

Haunted by the way his past grew more and more far away, Jack had continued to travel, and although he couldn't afford it, he had visited Old Saybrook and Lowell in November. Holmes was shocked both by his drinking, which ceased only when he achieved unconsciousness, and with his gross lack of cleanliness, so unlike his old fastidious self. Bored and lackadaisical in Florida, Jack quietly gave in when Mémêre, bitterly lonely without Nin, demanded that they return north.

In May of 1966 they moved to 20 Bristol Avenue, Hyannis, on Cape Cod. The bars were no different there, and Tony Sampas periodically visited with friends from Lowell. One friend was a psychiatrist named Jacob Roseman, who stopped to visit that summer and was astonished when Jack wouldn't allow him and his wife to leave, but put up Mrs. Roseman in his own bed and sat up all night talking with the doctor. Though Mémêre grew disgusted when the talk turned to Ginsberg—"I doan like dem dere fags runnin' around de house

naked"—Jack spoke gently of Allen, agreeing that he envied Ginsberg's fame although he still rejected him as a "false prophet" and a
"show-off hung up on glory."

Later when Mémêre was asleep he admitted frankly that he'd had
sex with Allen once or twice, even as he threw a knife at the wall to irritate
his mother. Enveloped by a "larger than life character of astounding
erudition and honesty," Roseman left Hyannis a little saddened. As he
prepared to go the next morning, he asked Jack, "What is it you want out
of life most of all?"

"That God be justified," Jack replied, and snapped the cap off the
Anacin bottle that served as his whiskey flask to take another sip.

Late in the night Jack would call Holmes to urge him to visit—"we'll
bat out an article and make some bucks"—then launch into brilliant
orations, talking at John, not with him, wondering who Jack Kerouac was
anymore, and why his life had ended up the way it had. With a giggle,
he would hang up after first challenging John to call back, a little test to
see whether or not anyone still cared. Few besides Holmes did; Jack's
literary fame had gotten *Satori in Paris* printed in successive issues of
Evergreen that spring, but on the whole he was passé; when a Columbia
Ph.D. named Ann Charters offered to compile a bibliography of his work
for the Phoenix Book Shop he was grateful for the attention. Charters was
shocked by his flabbiness and drinking, but impressed with his memory
as she recorded the various editions of his books.

Disaster struck once more in September 1966, when Mémêre had
a stroke which left her paralyzed except, Jack said, for "her asshole and
her mouth." He tried to be flippant about it, but he was racked with grief
and worry, pacing about their dark little house only to fall into tears when
he saw his mother's dustily unused sewing basket. A broken-spirited orphan, Jack searched for help in his past, in Lowell and Stella Sampas, who
had long been the only woman with whom he could communicate.

Stella was a darkly attractive woman, and in addition to being
Sammy's sister, she was a steadfast and comforting influence in Jack's life.
He had known her for many years now, and as he lost contact with
Carolyn and Neal, Allen and Lucien, the duration of his life with the
Sampases became increasingly meaningful. Seventeen years before—prior
to his marriage to Joan Haverty—Jack had asked Stella to marry him, as
she recalled it, but she had had the youngest Sampas brothers and sisters
to help raise. Over the succeeding years she had read his books and stayed

in touch, and now when Jack asked, Stella said yes. On November 19, 1966, Jack and Stella were married by the Hyannis Justice of the Peace.

Twenty-two years after soul-brother Sammy had died at Anzio, Jack had become a member of the Sampas Family, united in the sacrament —even if it had been a civil ceremony—of marriage. An ancient dream of his life had been fulfilled.

XVIII
It's True:
You Can't Go
Home Again

PURSUED BY an eerie but blissful recurrent dream of returning to walk the "deserted twilight streets of Lowell," Jack came to rest in January of 1967 in his old hometown. After several drunk and disorderly arrests on the Cape, he, Mémère, and Stella had moved to the dreamy security of Lowell, settling in a comfortable suburban ranch home at 271 Sanders Avenue, a considerable distance from old Pawtucketville. When he wasn't at home, Jack lived at Nicky's on Gorham Street, where the owner Nick Sampas was one of his many brothers-in-law and the night manager was Tony Sampas. The jukebox had plenty of old jazz on it, and he could run a tab without questions. He was comfortable there; Gorham Street was Lowell's skid row, and Nicky's was flanked by a grimy diner straight out of *Little Caesar*, while across the block winos littered the stoop. As a new customer stepped into the bar, Jack would shout from the back of the room, frantic to start a conversation, to make some sort of human contact from the lonely universe of self that whirled about him.

The old friends with whom he had once shared his life—Allen, Gary Snyder, Phil Whalen, Michael McClure, Neal—were far away and involved in a creative cultural rebellion from which Jack excluded himself, although his work had helped to initiate it.

Three thousand miles from Jack in space and a million miles in spirit, tribes of flower-bedecked American pilgrims came together in San Francisco's Golden Gate Park. They traveled from Berkeley and Haight-Ashbury, Madison and Boulder and Taos, and on January 13, 1967, they gathered for the "Great Human Be-In," hippie angels celebrating life.

They were the direct heirs of *On the Road* and *The Dharma Bums* and *Howl.* Peter Berg, a member of the San Francisco Mime Troupe and one of the anarchist Diggers then spreading true communism in Haight-Ashbury, had journeyed to San Francisco after reading *Howl.* Steve Levine, editor of San Francisco's first psychedelic newspaper, the *Oracle,* had organized poetry readings at the Gaslight Café in New York with Ginsberg before he emigrated to the Bay Area. Digger Peter Cohon, Ron Thelin, the "hip capitalist" owner of the "Psychedelic Shop," Janis Joplin, Jerry Garcia—each acknowledged their roots in a prior Beat Generation. The Great Human Be-In was a celebration of self, a free-form human mandala in which the "audience" was the creator; the organized stimulus for the event came from the San Francisco poets. Allen Ginsberg, Lenore Kandel, and Gary Snyder met at Michael McClure's apartment to plan a celebration, and the result was the Be-In, in which a painted and beribboned and smiling crowd of psychic pioneers danced in the park.

Up on the stage, Gary Snyder bent and trilled through a conch shell, the symbol of disciplined Zen life, to call the tribes together. Gary had wandered far since Jack had last seen him in 1956. After a year in the Daitoku Monastery, he had worked on an oil tanker from the Pacific to Istanbul, spent 1958–59 in San Francisco, traveled with Allen in India, and returned to Japan to live in a commune on a rural island. He had been back in the United States only a short time in January 1967, but as he later told Philip Whalen, it seemed as if "the revolution has happened . . . it's already there, it's already alive . . . LSD has gotten into everyone's hands, everybody's free from all the old clap trap . . . the system is never going to get them back."

Though as yet a virtually unknown poet, Gary had already assumed his persona of revolutionary cultural prophet, guide to those free citizens who chose to listen. Over the next years he would publish magnificent poetry like *Regarding Wave* or the Pulitzer Prize–winning *Turtle Island,* as well as the seminal essays in *Earth House Hold.* His message was urgent yet simple: save life. Passing through New York before the Be-In, he cited Chief Joseph and the Dalai Lama as his heroes and suggested that New York City be leveled and made into a buffalo pasture. What he was after was a fusion of Western-style social revolution and Eastern "individual insight into the basic self/void." Wild free nature, coyote and chipmunk and algae, was still at the center of his prophecy:

> If civilization
> is the exploiter, the masses is nature.
> And the party
> is the poets.

Many poets—Ginsberg, McClure, Rexroth, Ferlinghetti—followed his lead into a new concern for the ecology; Allen's psychedelic poem "Wales Visitation" expressed the systematic unity of life, and Ferlinghetti sang the hope that the "new race of longhaired golden progeny descending from on high in Jefferson Airplanes" might yet save nature from the technocracy. Their most influential disciple was a poet of a different medium, a man named Stewart Brand. A former denizen of North Beach and a Merry Prankster, Brand reflected years later that "I owe everything to [the Beats] and still do." Brand tried to apply the prophecy by creating *The Whole Earth Catalogue* to give practical access to tools for the pilgrims of an ecologically sane lifestyle, then wheedled out of NASA for the catalogue's cover the first picture of the whole earth in space, blue and green and white and beautiful, a perfect image of what all the poetry meant: Life is one, the circle cannot be broken.

Not all the counterculture had forgotten Kerouac, and when Ray Mungo, a founder of Liberation News Service, passed through Lowell about this time, his musings made a poignant commentary: "Kerouac came back to Lowell after all those years making scenes, and that has scared me crazy," Mungo began. "Come back to Lowell even though nobody goes anywhere from there, he must have come back to die, that's the only thing makes sense . . . Stopped writing he did, just sat there in crummy Lowell with beer and idleness and the Lowell *Sun* at four in the afternoon, delivered by the local altar boy at Saint Ann's . . . Christ Kerouac, you're blowing my mind living in Lowell, will you never go back to Big Sur? . . . You stay here, you're as good as dead baby."

There were no trips to Big Sur, for Jack's life was now limited to Mémère and Stella, a bottle and a bar. He sat in Nicky's and ranted words he often didn't mean, the monologue of a dissociated consciousness that was a jumble of sporadic brilliance terribly out of focus. As he sat there, his finger constantly tracing a cross in a puddle of beer on his table, he'd try to pump old bums for information—"What's your story?"—or evaluate Bach and Beethoven with bartender Walter Full, Nick Sampas' German-born father-in-law. Sometimes Jack would ramble through a few mournful stories about the way the world was changing to John Mahoney, the bouncer. Mahoney was an ordinary working Lowellite, a tough—Jack liked tough guys because they were more honest—cop who liked Kerouac, thought "he stood for something," but never quite comprehended the writer's strangeness, and often wondered if anyone really knew his depths. Most Lowell opinions of Jack were less gentle; the consensus at Nicky's dismissed him as a "crazy asshole dreamer drunk." One typical young man was quietly sitting over a beer at Nicky's when he recognized Jack, who had approached him for a talk. "He was real drunk and was telling all sorts of stories. But they didn't mean much to me and I just sort of tried to get rid of him. After a while, I gave up and split." Flight was a common reaction.

When the barflies of Lowell ran away, Jack could turn to his relatives and old friends, but neither were very satisfactory as mates. Jack usually saw his relatives—cousin Hervé and his wife Doris and cousin Armand and his family—in the mornings when he was still essentially sober, and they would reminisce about childhood baseball games or talk gloomily of local politics. Hervé was a railroad man, and Armand was a butcher, and they had little in common with their notorious relative. Armand in particular was confused by Jack, and on one hand denounced his work—"No literature in his books, no grammar . . . I could do it"—while at the same time he defended Jack to reporters by swearing that "He was not a drunk." Family was Mémère's department in any case.

Jack's childhood friends avoided him. GJ Apostalakis felt that he was "a different person," Scotty Boldieu was enraged at what "those New York fellas did to him," and Fred Bertrand thought he was a failure. "He could have been a professional man," Fred said later, "but he missed the boat." Once when Fred met Jack on the street, Kerouac was so dazed by whiskey that he mistook Fred's son for Fred, and Bertrand turned away disgusted.

So Jack had mostly new friends, and besides Tony Sampas, the closest was Joe Chaput, a gentle, gravel-voiced man in his mid-thirties. Short and ruggedly stocky, Joe was a Merrimack College graduate who discussed Pascal and Kierkegaard, and a widower free to trek through the night as a drinking companion. One night in January 1967, Joe wandered into Nicky's, spotted the man whose books he'd read, and approached Jack. "Always glad to buy a starving author a drink," Joe cracked, and Jack accepted. As their conversation ripened, Joe inquired as to who "Maggie Cassidy" had been, and when Jack replied that it was Mary Carney, he smiled; "I went out with her." Jack chortled and leaped out of his chair, shouting, "Now I KNOW you're a bullshit specialist, come on let's go see her!" Mary turned them away at her door, so they went home to Sanders Avenue, where Stella was leery of a new drinking buddy but Mémère was charmed with a polite and gallant Frenchman, particularly when it turned out that Joe's cousin had once been her neighbor.

Even Stella, who had taken to hiding Jack's shoes in an effort to keep him home and moderately sober—he frequently went out barefoot—soon took a liking to Chaput, and he became one of the family. He and Jack would listen to Bird Parker on the tape recorder late at night or chat with Mémère of the old days, or make the rounds of the bars—Nicky's or the Blue Moon or the Peppermint Lounge—seeking that something, the anything, that would be meaningful.

In the bars Jack opened up his soul with Chaput, spoke of his life and his regrets, about how he should have completed Columbia, should have stayed in the Navy although "I couldn't take it." "Tell me about your bomber runs over Germany," Jack would wheedle, and they'd be lost in memories, only to surface in Vietnam. Though Jack detested the ragged, flag-burning "rabble" that opposed the war, he was appalled by the killing in Vietnam, and argued that it was caused by the machinations of "big money," a plot for Vietnam to grow rich on America. The two men would slam into the house at three in the morning, Jack bellowing out, "I'm home, Stella," and then sit drinking for hours as Jack contemplated his legend aloud.

He loved Lowell, he told Chaput, but had been estranged by his fear of becoming a "mill rat" like most of the other French young men. After forty-one years, he still missed his brother Gerard, and muttered tearfully, "You're my brother, Joe." As the nights passed he spoke of the critics who had never understood the beatific meaning of Beat, of his psychedelic experience with Tim Leary, a frightening descent into lostness that Kerouac now swore had ruined him. "I haven't been right since," he confided. Of his friends he was nasty only about Allen, who "stole my ideas," and what Joe called his "Jewish thing" popped up again and again. Burroughs' imagination still intrigued Jack, and he praised him to Joe with the recommendation, "Man, that guy can write some weird stuff."

Cruising around Lowell with Tony or Joe or Manuel "Chiefy" Nobriga, Kerouac would latch on to someone—anyone—and delve into their life, try to absorb and appreciate their passage through the years. When a member of a motorcycle gang complained that he and his friends were being harassed by the police, Jack recorded the conversation on Chiefy's tape machine and promised to write a publicity article for the "bikers." Everyone was fair game for his eye and tongue, although he said he liked Greeks especially, " 'cause they created Gods with weaknesses like people." Every person he encountered became an audience for Jack as he lampooned hypocrisy, pomposity and fraud as he saw it. He shared with Jackson Pollock the fate of colossal ambivalence, a mixture of soaring ego —Pollock said, "You know, there are only three painters; Picasso, Matisse, and Pollock"; Jack compared himself to Melville and Shakespeare—and colossal feelings of failure, artists who cried tears of abject unworthiness for their art and their world. For both men, fame had come too late, and with too many strings attached. Greg Zahos was one of Jack's young companions, and one thing about his hero disquieted him; Jack smiled often, but he rarely laughed anymore.

At home Jack drank quietly—he kept cases of Johnny Walker Red in the basement—still writing, although the results were never cohesive enough to satisfy him. His room was inviolate, a cell that he cleaned himself and from which he barred all visitors, even Stella. Old movies on TV fascinated him, particularly John Ford epics that made him cheer for the Indians. The Kerouacs owned a piano, and he plunked away on it; there was the Bible or Pascal to read. When the loneliness grew too painful he'd pick up the telephone and call Carolyn or John or Allen. Finally Stella had to disconnect it because the bills were too high.

When he did leave home, bars were not his only destination. Often at dusk he'd take a stroll and slip into a neighborhood church, light a candle, and pray. Though he urged his friend Billy Koumantzelis' son to go to parochial school, he had no formal contact with the Church, did not attend Mass and almost never spoke of churches or priests. But he was always aware of his life's spiritual realities, and nightly he prayed to Christ, to Gerard, to Leo, to all the passionate sufferers of the earth for an end to his own suffering, the extinction of his own nightmare.

In the spring of 1967 Jack overcame his writing block and wrote *Vanity of Duluoz*, a heartbreaking last effort as an author. He was tired now, and could write only eight thousand words at a sitting before he had to rest for a week, so it took from March until May to complete the 93-foot teletype roll. His prose had lost some of its elasticity, and the tone was often sour—"Insofar as nobody loves my dashes anyway," he wrote, "I'll use regular punctuation for the new illiterate generation."

But the essence of *Vanity of Duluoz* was shocking and gallant and at one with his lifelong devotion to his work at the expense of his personal happiness; he restated his young life from the perspective of the death angel, portrayed his life from the final curving facet of death and brought it to an end through his art. From a mental grave he dismissed his young adventures, from heroic football to his life at sea, as "Vanity." In the Buddhist sense he destroyed his early illusions, wreaked havoc on his own early romanticism with a combination of paranoia and humor that labeled himself a "wise guy" for messing up in the Navy, for "I could have gained a lot out of loyal membership to that outfit, learned a trade maybe, gotten out of the stupid 'literary' deadend I find myself trapped in now." When he left football in 1941, he "was telling everybody to go jump in the big fat ocean of their own folly. I was also telling myself to go jump in the big fat ocean of my own folly . . . what a bath!"

As Jack wrote *Vanity of Duluoz*, a Yaqui Indian shaman named Don Juan Matus told anthropologist Carlos Castaneda that "controlled folly" was the proper path of a warrior. Though Jack had little control over his life, he saw its folly, the emptiness of vanity and ambition. There was a still-too-ambitious shrillness in his voice when he defended his record and treatment as a football player, and a nostalgic mourning for old America as compared to the 1967 "potboiler of broken convictions, messes of rioters fighting in the streets, hoodlumism, cynical administration of cities and states, suits and neckties the only feasible subject, grandeur all gone into the mosaic mesh of Television." Worse, *Vanity* was cruel to Allen, a "lecher fondling legs," with an unflattering and apocryphal story about him. But his real subject was death, the systematic disillusionment of his life for his art, a lyric preparation for the end that left him drained and empty.

That fall three young men, his old hero William Saroyan's son Aram among them, came to interview Jack for the *Paris Review*. Sparring with their questions, Kerouac continued in a deprecatory vein to preach of simplicity and clarity, disparaging intellectualism: "God, man, I rode around this country free as a bee," he told Saroyan. Later in the year, critic Bruce Cook elicited the same anti-abstract reply when he tried to apply sociology to the Beats. "And I wasn't trying to create any kind of new consciousness or anything like that," Jack snorted to Cook, sitting in Nicky's. "We didn't have a whole lot of heavy abstract thoughts. We were just a bunch of guys who were out trying to get laid."

In both the *Paris Review* interview and his conversation with Cook, he goofed and wandered, momentarily serious on the role of the writer with Cook—"Let me tell you, a true writer should be an observer and not go around *being* observed, like Mailer and Ginsberg," Jack proclaimed. "Observing—that's the duty and oath of a writer." Intuition that transcended technique was still his way; "FEELING is what I like in art," he told Saroyan, "not CRAFTINESS and the hiding of feelings." When Saroyan asked him why he'd never written a book about Jesus, Jack exploded, "You insane phony . . . All I *write about* is Jesus. I am Everhard Mercurian, General of the Jesuit Army." He spoke at length to the *Paris Review* trio about the Iroquois and his Cornish roots, Buddhism, Kaspya, and the flower sermon, and was affectionate about Allen and Gregory as he complained of the distortion of "Beat" by West Coast leftists. Of himself he admitted to Saroyan that "Frankly, I do feel that my mind is going," and perhaps etched his own literary epitaph as well: "Notoriety and public confession in literary form is a frazzler of the heart you were born with, believe me."

Ironically, the very fact that he was being interviewed was not only a sign of pleasant literary respect but a mark of the ultimate success of his style; by the middle 1960's and after, the nakedly direct confessional interview had become a primary form of journalism. As well, the "New Journalism" had swept the literary world. As John Holmes argued, it directly paralleled Jack's style, for in it "the consciousness of a writer *is* the protagonist." While almost all fifties' magazine articles had been rigidly narrative in format, in the sixties writers increasingly accepted the Beat emphasis on the personal, confessional view, and became more subjective, more spontaneous in tone and approach. *Village Voice* columnist Jill Johnston had come to Manhattan to be a "beatnik," and replaced her formal dance criticism with a surrealistic subjective commentary on her own life, as did Charles Bukowski, whose Los Angeles *Free Press* column was a direct descendent of Kerouac.

In cultural realms far beyond writing styles, the Beats had been forerunners of a major American societal shift in the late 1960's and early 1970's that rejected traditional "masculinity." The resistance to the liberal-rational world view was embodied in the departure from private psychoanalysis to public, confessional, consciousness-raising and encounter groups, a turning away from "logic" in a mad world to values born of emotional openness and sensitivity in suprarational disciplines like Zen, yoga, meditation, astrology, and the occult. By the time it happened, it was too late for Jack, for nothing mattered greatly to a man who had mocked the most precious images of his early life to produce yet one more book.

Still searching for a past, Jack talked Joe Chaput into a summer vacation trip to the just-opened Expo '67 Fair in Montreal, with a stop at Rivière du Loup to examine some parish records on the Kerouac family. On the road once more in his customary shotgun seat, with a bottle of brandy in his hand, Jack sang old Bop songs with happy abandon, but his faith in the journey soon leaked away. Once in Rivière du Loup, Jack was so drunk and decrepit that Joe fretted about his going into the motel bar, and even after Jack cleaned up, he caused trouble when he launched into his tired lecture on the purity of Quebec French and how "the Jews have corrupted the language in France." A local Jewish citizen became angry enough that Joe had to shepherd Jack away.

Some of Jack's habits—his modesty for example—hadn't changed at all. Though he was in dire need of a bathroom, Jack could not bring himself to urinate in a country-store toilet screened only by a thin cloth curtain. When he began to relate an elaborate tale to two young women hitchhikers about his visit to the famous New Orleans brothel the House of the Rising Sun, Jack quoted the madam, who had told him, "Boy, I'm gonna teach you what lust is." Then he stopped, blushing at the idea of being sexually explicit in front of young women. He never reached the Rivière du Loup parish church, nor did he and Joe visit Montreal. After playing pool in a roadside bar with some sailors, they returned to Massachusetts and wound up in Boston's sex district, the "Combat Zone," for more drinks and more pool, Jack growing more abusive as their journey came to an end. The road always leads inward, and Jack could no longer respond to adventure.

As 1967 wore out, his money problems became grim. Sterling Lord had sold *Vanity of Duluoz* to Coward-McCann, one chapter on football from it to *Sports Illustrated* and the chapter on David Kammerer's death to the *Evergreen Review* (which ran it with essays by Fidel Castro, Che Guevara, and Regis Debray). Another short piece, "In the Ring," went to the *Atlantic.* But the Johnny Walker and the mortgage and Mémère's medical bills absorbed his advances, and Jack wanted desperately to accept when Professor Charles Jarvis offered him a position as writer-in-residence at Lowell Tech. There were emotional as well as financial considerations; the building he would teach in was part of *Dr. Sax,* just one block from his Sarah Avenue adolescence. Though one couldn't teach anyone how to write, Jack thought it possible to teach the relationship of great literature to its time. He got a haircut and assured the professor that he was ready to face the students. He wasn't. The day before he was to give a preliminary lecture, Stella called and begged Jarvis to release Jack from his pledge, for in his fear of performing, Kerouac had drunk himself into a stupor.

It was class values as well as a classroom that disturbed him. Jarvis was of upwardly mobile middle-class Lowell, a smoothly prosperous striver whom Jack regularly addressed as "You professor weirdo." Jack lectured on literature to those who would listen, like Jay Pendergast, a doctoral candidate in Irish literature at Trinity College in Dublin, who'd returned to Lowell to earn a stake for his research. But when Jarvis sauntered in and pompously asked Jack, "What was the influence of Joyce on your work?" Jack retorted, "Go fuck yourself." The one occasion Jack did enter a classroom in Lowell around that time, it was a disaster.

After an all-night binge with Greg Zahos, a young substitute teacher at Lowell High School, Jack decided to teach Greg's class in English literature. Chewing gum to cover his breath, he bought a cheap shirt and pair of pants to replace the rags of his debauched evening, but he still looked like a slob. Though he entranced the class with an uproarious performance of *Moby Dick,* afterward the high school football coach cornered him in the hall and ordered him to leave the premises. "I saved your school once against Lawrence," Jack volunteered, "don't you remember that?" Coach didn't care; thirty years had passed since that wonderful Thanksgiving of 1938, when Jack had been a hero.

The dreams of Jack's life winked out one by one. The crucial dream, the most important vision, had always been Neal. In February 1968 Cassady was nearing forty-two, and the weight of age was at his neck. "I get in a group," he told Carolyn, "and everyone just stares at me, expecting me to perform . . . and my nerves are so shot, I get high . . . and there I go again, I don't know what else to do." The previous December he'd been at Kesey's farm in Oregon in the midst of the usual ecstatic chaos, when terror suddenly swept over him; rushing into the cold night without cigarettes or a coat, he hitchhiked to San Francisco, where Carolyn picked him up and brought him home. There Cassady peered into his son John's empty room and panicked again, began to cry and screamed out, "My God, I've killed my son, I've killed my son," then hid in the shower and pounded on the walls until exhaustion put him to sleep.

In January 1968 he headed for Mexico to avoid several traffic warrants against him. One afternoon in San Miguel de Allende, Neal attended a wedding. The tequila flowed freely, and he swallowed a few Seconals as well, then took off to walk along the railroad tracks. He walked until he collapsed and lost consciousness, and died an hour after he arrived at the local hospital.

Carolyn called on February 4, 1968, to break the news to Jack, but Stella would not pass the message on. A day later she called again, and Jack answered, silencing a loud Stella with the comment "Shut up. Neal's dead." Sober and gentle, he comforted Carolyn, whispered all the right and beautiful things he could about her and Neal, but in the end he swore that "Neal's not dead you know, he couldn't be. Naw, he's hiding out somewhere, Africa maybe. He *can't* be dead."

As if to defy the fate that had snuffed out his brother, Jack set out on another voyage in March, this time to Portugal, Spain, and Germany. Unable to travel alone, Jack went with Tony and Nick Sampas and some other friends; Tony was a gentle bodyguard to keep him out of trouble, a large-spirited and compassionate man who did not get embarrassed when Jack behaved oafishly. At the airport Jack discovered that his friend Greg Zahos' fiancée Georgette and her two children by a previous marriage would accompany them on the flight to Spain.

During the monotonous transatlantic flight, Georgette grew irritated with her fretful children and brusquely ordered them to go to sleep. Jack tenderly remonstrated with her, murmuring, "Don't tell them, just love them." Gazing at the mother and children, he spoke in the wake of a recent scene with Mémêre that illustrated their relationship. In the middle of a shrieking argument with his mother, Jack had shrugged and snapped, "I don't want to fuck you, it's okay, relax." Mémêre had once pointed at the crucifix on her wall when friends of Jack's had visited her home and hissed, "Jesus is in my house, no sex here, no sex." Now she spat at him, "Don't use that word . . . you're just like your father," and continued bitterly, "He tried me and tried me." She added fiercely, "And he wasn't that good."

As if his love for his mother was genuine and *her* love had grown twisted and corrupt, Jack urged Georgette to be kind to her children— "Don't discipline them, talk *softly* to them . . . above all, don't be selfish with them, don't *use* them, because"—and he spoke with a tone of authority at that point—"you women have a special understanding about kids." Trapped in a web of love and guilt for the woman who had belabored and abused that love, Jack could not detach himself from

Mémêre, but only endure her desperate need for him. After asking permission, he gently kissed Georgette on her cheek and returned to his seat.

This vacation was an alcoholic duplication of the 1965 stay in Paris, but instead of buying sex from a prostitute Jack hired a woman in Portugal to stare into his eyes for an hour, as if to make a contact that was more real than the sexual gymnastics of a trick. The rest of his travels were equally bizarre. With his bankroll securely knotted in a handkerchief, he went out to talk with common people while his companions dined at fancy restaurants. The Germans depressed him with their stolid seriousness, and by the time Jack reached Stuttgart he was tired and ready to return to the United States, $900 in debt for a futile journey at a time when his income was around $60 a week.

When the Washington *Post* offered him a large advance that summer of 1968 for an essay on contemporary affairs, it was no surprise that he accepted with alacrity, and turned out a piece called "After Me, the Deluge." As he wrote, the war in Vietnam stormed on unabated. Jack's old school Columbia University had been torn apart by a student strike in May. Assassins had cut down Martin Luther King, Jr., in April and Bobby Kennedy in June. The feeling of apocalypse was in the air, and its near approximation was the frenzy of the Chicago Police Department riot during the Democratic Convention in late August. Caught in the ideological middle, Jack was frozen between the politicians and the demonstrators, more an outsider than ever before.

Denying that he was "the great white father and intellectual forebear who spawned a deluge of alienated radicals," he cried out in "After Me" that he was instead the "intellectual forebear of modern spontaneous prose," an artist, and that was all. Abbie Hoffman and Jerry Rubin and the Yippies were not spontaneous, he told Ginsberg, but egotistical and vainglorious, and served only as "new reasons for spitefulness." Eight years later Rubin would agree completely with that evaluation.

Yet Jack found the sleekly groomed upper class of American society equally unsympathetic to his private memories of grimy Depression breadlines and scruffy soldiers in foxholes. To Jack, every establishment smile or round of applause was "shiny hypocrisy," "political lust and concupiscence, a ninny's bray of melody backed by a ghastly neurological drone of money-glut." The dissidents were "quite understandably alienated nay disgusted by this scene," but had "no better plan to offer the grief stricken American citizens but fund raising dinners of their own." The students were barbaric McLuhanites who did not "believe in the written word which is the only way to keep the record straight," Learyite acidheads who could not address an envelope, Maoist "parasites" who manipulated people quite as much as the police. In a divided country, Jack dwelled in a chasm all his own.

Later in the fall of 1968 Jack again found himself lonely in the middle when he appeared on William F. Buckley's *Firing Line* television program flanked by a "hip" sociologist named Lewis Yablonsky and Ed Sanders, an East Village poet, publisher of *Fuck You/A Magazine of the Arts,* and member of the "Fugs," an interestingly perverse rock-and-roll band. Although he read William F. Buckley regularly—they were both graduates of Horace Mann School—Jack hadn't really wanted to do the show at all, but Mémêre thought it was a splendid idea, and Jack did want to see Sterling Lord. With Joe Chaput as driver and Billy Koumantzelis and Paul Bourgeois as outriders, Kerouac rode to New York and a strangely significant reunion. After some light drinking, Jack and his Lowell friends found themselves in William S. Burroughs' room at the Hotel Delmonico talking with Burroughs, Allen Ginsberg, and Lucien Carr. It was the first time since 1953 that the Beat circle of friends had been united.

Burroughs was still a teacher, but his audience and frame of reference had grown tremendously. In search of techniques to disrupt the manipulative nature of life in the Western world, he had investigated yoga, karate, and the use of sense withdrawal, stroboscopic lights, and sound manipulation to break the conventional lines of intellectual and sensual association. His own "cutups," randomly joined scissored pieces of manuscript, were designed to crack reality by creating a new reality in the space between the juxtaposed fragments. The world of *The Soft Machine* or *The Wild Boys* was nothing like the Aristotelian either-or mindset Americans took for granted. Misogynous and still bitterly witty, Burroughs was out, as he said, "to make people aware of the true criminality of our times, to wise up the marks," and to make them high, "high as the Zen master is high when his arrow hits a target in the dark . . . high as the karate master is high when he smashes a brick with his fist." The fulfilled student was weightless in space, and "this is the space age. Time to look beyond this run down radioactive cop rotten planet."

Wearing a tie beneath his dressing gown, Bill was his usual dryly dignified self as he warned Jack not to appear on Buckley's television program and corrected Jack's memory when they reminisced about events now a quarter of a century past. When it came time for everyone to leave for the television studio, he would not accompany them, but was content to say goodbye to Jack at the door of his room before he returned to his solitary work.

As Jack left for the studio to tape the Buckley program, he begged Allen Ginsberg to come along; gracious as always with his "older brother," Allen agreed. Carrying the harmonium he used to accompany himself when he chanted, Allen was a poet whose work, he thought, was "a kind of record of the times . . . useful in that it helps clarify the present." Allen's verse was a transcription of his naked mind, a form of meditation based on his understanding that "Mind is shapely, art is shapely." *Howl* had sold 260,000 copies by now, and Allen was preoccupied by a cultural revolution. His bedroom bulletin board was crowded with a poster from a Fellowship of Reconcilation rally, a "Fuck for Peace" banner, and a Zen flower scroll, and that variety only hinted at his interests.

The next year, in a *Playboy* interview, he would recommend as teachers Barry Commoner on ecology, Gregory Bateson on technical ideas, Paul Goodman on the reorganization of community, the Diggers on communes, Aldous Huxley on psychedelic drugs, Gary Snyder on the concept of tribe and Burroughs on educational systems—all of these perspectives designed to "include a larger consciousness in [the] revolution . . . and because of the ecological crisis, any effective revolution that will save the planet will have to include all sentient beings." Jack was wholly uninterested in such ideas, but their meeting was friendly and cheerfully affectionate; they had first met twenty-four years before, and since Allen could not pierce Stella's and Mémère's defenses in Lowell, they were acutely aware of how little time they would have to share with each other.

Before they reached the *Firing Line* studio, Jack stopped at Sterling Lord's Madison Avenue office, intent on ending their author-agent relationship, but Lord dissuaded him and he sped across town to the show. Though Stella had ordered Joe Chaput to stop his drinking, Jack picked up a pint of Teacher's Scotch on the way. They shared their elevator ride with Ed Sanders, who was excited to see his old hero Jack and wanted to talk. Nervous with the approaching ordeal of the television program, Jack was surly and told him to "Get the fuck off my back, kid." When he met Truman Capote—who was taping another *Firing Line* program after them—in the green room backstage, he was more gracious. "I don't care what you said about me," Jack said to Capote; "you're all right." Capote was unimpressed. It was ironic that *In Cold Blood,* the book that had established his mature reputation, bore no small debt to the "New Journalism" and the drunk who stood before him.

The red blinking cameras and floodlights and audience of Buckley's TV show frightened Jack, but made little difference; he behaved exactly as he had at Nicky's, a drunkenly honest, subtly funny man who grossly offended Buckley. His eyebrows bouncing like Yo-Yo's, Buckley condescended to Kerouac when he didn't ignore him. Pulling steadily at a coffee mug full of Scotch, Jack nodded off to sleep a couple of times, bored with the panel's intellectualized discussion of their putative topic, "The Hippies." Kerouac commented that it was "apparently some kind of Dionysian movement," and that the hippies were "good kids," then attacked Ferlinghetti for turning the pious and tender beatific idea into "the beat mutiny, the beat insurrection, words I never use, being a Catholic."

Rowdy and disorderly in the staid confines of a TV stage, Jack called sociologist Yablonsky "Abramowitz," and Sanders accused him of anti-Semitism, an accusation seconded by Buckley, who demanded that Jack apologize. "No, no. I thought . . . I forgot his name," said Jack. In a show that was largely windy rhetoric, he made one particularly perceptive observation. Kerouac's opinion of the Chicago riots—that "there are people who make a rule of creating chaos so that once the chaos is under way they can then be elected as the people who take care of the chaos"— would ring frighteningly true in succeeding years when the term *agent provocateur* entered the American political lexicon.

Jack's saddest moment came when Ed Sanders linked him with Allen. Even though Jack had begged Ginsberg to come to the studio, he growled back at Sanders, "I'm not connected with Ginsberg." As the camera panned over the crowd to settle on Allen, Jack blurted out, "And don't you put my name next to his." Paying no mind to his old friend's confused hostility, Allen bade Jack farewell on the street corner outside, touched him tenderly, and said with a smile, "Goodbye, drunken ghost." Allen never saw him alive again.

Once back in Lowell, Jack had to move his family yet again. Like a wailing, bedridden demon, Mémêre had worn her son down with a non-stop chorus on the joys of Florida sunshine. "I'll be able to walk if we go dere," she promised him, and although they lost an enormous amount of money on the unnecessarily hasty sale of their house, by November they were ready to head once more for St. Pete.

Perhaps there was a special reason for Jack's swift agreement with Mémère: he'd seen a ghost. Late in August yet another hippie woman of sixteen had turned up on Hervé Kerouac's doorstep, because he was the only Kerouac in the telephone directory. Hervé's wife Doris answered the door, and after she took a good look at the girl's face, she listened seriously to her story, dropped everything, and took her to Sanders Avenue.

The hippie's name was Janet Michelle Kerouac, and she was unmistakably Jack's daughter. On the road to Mexico, she had impulsively decided to see her father. Jack was shocked into silence, and said little except to ask her if she'd gotten the money, the $12-a-week child support he'd provided. There was no bravado or bluster or denial in him, only stolid acquiescence. Watching her leave, Jack might well have sensed his past—the dreamy memories that had always been the rich essence of his life—recede into the distance, as the sweep of his days curved in to an almost visible ending.

XIX
Endgame

HAVING SOLD his correspondence with Allen Ginsberg to Columbia University in order to finance a new Florida home, Jack climbed into the shotgun seat of a station wagon for yet another journey. Stella, Mémère, and the cats Pitou and Minette occupied the rear area, while Joe Chaput and a friend named Red were the drivers. As though he anticipated that he would soon be lonely in St. Petersburg, Jack talked almost continuously during their speedy twenty-four-hour ride, shouting and blowing on a harmonica as he reminisced about Joan Vollmer Burroughs' death, the time he passed out in a Scollay Square toilet, and his past adventures in Mexico and Tangiers. In St. Petersburg, the Kerouacs liked their new home, a cinderblock bungalow with a brick façade. As they settled in, Jack took out a library card and sat in the backyard reading Voltaire, Montaigne, Pascal, and William F. Buckley's *National Review*. This stay in Florida was unique. His visits to bars were few; Jack rarely left his home at all.

Lost in St. Pete, the city where the funeral notice list was always twice as long as the birth announcements, Kerouac seemed almost done for. As a commercial writer he was finished, and though he had well over a dozen published books to his credit, he could not get a decent advance on a new one. The last few reviews had been as bad as ever. *Satori in Paris* had been termed "credit card sensibility" by the *New York Times Book Review*; and *Vanity of Duluoz* was a "Road to Nowhere" to the daily *Times*, "infantile," a "banal plea for the Good Old Days" to the *Times Book Review*. *Time* thought *Vanity of Duluoz* was his "best book," but couched the review in qualifications that neutralized any pleasure in the opinion. John Holmes contributed a fine essay on the book to the *National Observer*, but the *Observer*'s title indicated Jack's bleak situation: "There's an Air of Finality to Kerouac's Latest."

Jack's utter lack of critical acclaim was made even more painful by the fact that poetry critics had grudgingly but finally capitulated to Allen Ginsberg, who used the methods and insights that Jack had taught him. The reviews of Allen's new book, *Planet News,* in the spring of 1969 were almost unanimously respectful. Ten years before, Allen had responded to a particularly nasty review by his former classmate John Hollander, "John, you've just got to drop it, and take me seriously, and listen to what I have to say." In 1968 the two men read together at Columbia and embraced, and positive articles on Allen ran in magazines from *Life* to *Commentary.* "The literary world has swung around to [Ginsberg's] way of thinking, not he to theirs," reported the *New York Times.* Allen had once told the poetry establishment that "we talk about our assholes, and we talk about our cocks, and we talk about who we fucked last night . . . so then—what happens if you make a distinction between what you tell your friends and what you tell your Muse? The problem is to break down that distinction." The *Nation* agreed: "What Ginsberg forced us to understand in *Howl* twelve years ago was that nothing is safe from poetry." Soon Allen would receive a National Book Award.

Allen's publisher, City Lights Press, had by 1969 published literally dozens of poets and essayists, and not only San Franciscans or Beats; William Carlos Williams, Andrei Voznesensky, Malcolm Lowry, Pablo Picasso, and James Joyce all graced the list, and Ferlinghetti himself was the subject of a *New York Times* article that acknowledged his significance.

Among many of the poets who had been in Donald Allen's *The New American Poetry,* Robert Creeley, Kenneth Rexroth, and Gregory Corso had all been hired to teach in universities, their demeanor and poetry untamed. As one poetry critic remarked, "It is not they but the academy that has changed." Perhaps the most amusing evidence of critical capitulation was an article by Louis Simpson, who in 1962 had condemned the Beats as "liars" who appealed only to a "certain devitalized, androgynous type—the male or female spinster." As the decade ended, Simpson figuratively stood up before the poetry world and conceded the accession of Allen Ginsberg; the new ancient Master was Allen's William Blake, not the New Critics' John Donne.

A student once asked Allen whether Kerouac was still important.

Ginsberg said, "Well, he was the first one to make a new crack in the consciousness." Writers like Pete Hamill and Jimmy Breslin honored Kerouac, but theirs were minority voices.

And so Jack remained at home in lonely obscurity, his unfocused eyes directed at the television set while the record player boomed out Bach or Handel. As the sun beat down with a withering glare, he stayed in his dimly quiet writing room and concentrated on a new book, oblivious to the tinkle of Mémère's bell that jerked Stella around like a puppet. Though he was desperately tired, Jack persevered on the new work because the specter of poverty demanded it; the Kerouacs were so poor that Stella had gone to work as a seamstress at $1.70 an hour. He did not have the emotional reserves to begin something new, so he decided to complete a tale he'd begun eighteen years earlier, just after finishing *On the Road*. It was called *Pic*, short for the name of his childhood card baseball game star "Pictorial Review Jackson." It was a simple, gentle tale of a black nine-year-old North Carolina boy, as much a dialect study of country Carolina speech as a novel.

An acquaintance of Jack's asked whether *Pic* was a story of prejudice, and Jack snorted, "Shit, it's a story of life, of people living." As Jack narrated the story, Pic's grandpa died in 1948, and Pic went to stay with his Aunt Gastonia, a righteous, God-fearing woman who spent much of her time praying in loud shrieks. She was "tedious" as far as Pic was concerned, and life was gloomy until a most unlikely figure slipped down their backwoods Carolina dirt road, a young man in zoot pants, beret, GI boots, red shirt, and goatee—Pic's older brother Slim. A saxophonist who lived in Harlem, Slim heroically spirited his younger brother out of Carolina, down roads with lines and guardrails that the youngun had never seen before, across the Mason-Dixon line and up to New York's 125th Street. When Slim's wife Sheila lost her job, the three of them—a true family —decided to strike out for California, Sheila by bus and the men by their thumbs.

There were two endings to *Pic*, and they revealed Jack's weary ambivalence about himself as a writer. Originally he had ended the tale by having Dean Moriarity and Sal Paradise of *On the Road* pick up the hitchhiking Slim and Pic, but Stella objected that the contexts did not meld. Irritated by her criticisms, Jack bolted in a huff to Mémère's room and produced a jumbled paste-up in which Slim and Pic encountered the "Ghost of the Susquehanna" from *On the Road*, then settled (at Mémère's suggestion) in a church. That he had taken to accepting literary advice from his mother made it clear that Jack's youthful sureness in his own powers of creativity had long since burned out.

In a rare foray out of his home, Jack visited a local black bar to celebrate the completion of *Pic.* When he began to talk "nigger," to boast of the fine book about Negroes that he'd just written, several of the customers in the bar took him into the parking lot and pounded him senseless.

To Jack, public events and the world around him were skewed somehow, not quite right. The underground event of the summer was a film about two men riding across America, but *Easy Rider* ended with their violent deaths, not Kerouacian satori. A Beat poet made the news again, but Hugh Romney helped run the music festival called Woodstock, and the monstrous crowd of 500,000 only disgusted Jack. Too antitechnological to take much pleasure in Neal Armstrong's and Buzz Aldrin's footsteps on the moon, Jack was also too gentle a patriot to relish Ho Chi Minh's death in September. The fall's best-selling books—Jacqueline Susann's *The Love Machine,* "Penelope Ashe's" *Naked Came the Stranger,* Philip Roth's *Portnoy's Complaint,* Harold Robbins' *The Inheritors* —offended Jack's prudish nature, and seemed to him symptomatic of a prurient, exploitative culture in turmoil.

President Nixon's Department of Justice began to prosecute the "Chicago Eight" for their involvement in the past year's Democratic Convention riot. The top-selling record album of the autumn, "Volunteers" by the Jefferson Airplane, was merely another signal of collapse. "We are forces of chaos and anarchy," screamed the Airplane's Marty Balin and Grace Slick. "Everything they say we are, we are. And we are very proud of ourselves . . . Up against the wall, motherfucker."

And always there was the war. Thirty-eight thousand, nine hundred and sixty-nine Americans had died in Vietnam as students across the nation demonstrated on October 15, 1969, Moratorium Day. Jack shuddered and tried to enjoy a televised miracle, as the New York Mets won a glorious victory in the World Series.

Aside from his television set, Jack lived by his telephone, which he'd had installed only late in September 1969. One person he no longer called was Carolyn Cassady, whom he had caught early in the morning just in from a party the previous Easter, too exhausted to talk. In the past year she had invited him to come and visit—"Carolyn," he groaned, "I can't hardly get myself to the bathroom to take a leak"—but on Easter she refused the call, and he didn't bother to try again. As October 1969 wore on, he called Greg Zahos and Jim Sampas, who weren't at home. Jim was a member of the Foreign Service and another of Sammy's brothers, and he was in Iceland when Jack called about building a cabin on some land he owned in Massachusetts.

Kerouac spoke with Bob Burford, his friend from the long-ago summer of 1947 in Denver. John Holmes received a typically drunken late-night message from Jack, who in the midst of shouting at Stella challenged him to "Call me back if you really love me." This time Holmes didn't call back. And of course Jack reached out to Tony Sampas, calling him at four in the morning on October 18 to tell him that he wanted to return to Lowell in the spring, and perhaps come back alone for a week or two in the near future.

Monday, October 20, was much like any other day. After a sleepless night, Jack went in to talk with Mémère about four in the morning. They reminisced about some old letters he'd found the night before, one of which mentioned Papa Leo and his shop, the Spotlight Print. At nine Stella fixed breakfast, and Jack tried to work on a new book about the years after the publication of *On the Road*, which he thought he might call *The Beat Spotlight* in homage to Leo. It was hot and boring and soon he quit to continue drinking and pass away his time with the TV program *The Galloping Gourmet*. Even in front of the television set he had his notebook open, and while munching a can of tuna fish he made another notation.

But the years of heavy drinking had weakened and consumed his body, and this morning they claimed the final price. A vein ruptured, and he began to bleed internally.

"Stella, help me," he moaned from the bathroom, and there was something in his voice that brought her running into the toilet just as he began to vomit blood; "I'm hemorrhaging, I'm hemorrhaging," he cried. She got him to St. Anthony's Hospital, and the doctors worked furiously, pumping thirty pints of blood into his body over the next twenty hours. He had wanted to die for a long time; suicide—except for the slow suicide of whiskey—was something he could not countenance, but now all he had to do was let go. At 5:30 A.M., October 21, 1969, Jack died. As an old friend noted in a later article title, he was "Gone in October," his cleansing, creative month.

•　　•　　•

John Holmes heard the news on the radio and was overwhelmed by a sense of his indebtedness to Jack, then wounded by a cold touch of his own mortality and loneliness. Allen and Peter and Gregory were at the farm Allen and Peter owned in upstate New York when the news reached them, and they walked into the woods and, "in the name of American poetry," carved Jack's initials into a tree. Holmes called, and they quickly agreed to meet at Allen's scheduled reading at Yale University the next night. It was a time when they wanted to be together.

Now that Kerouac was dead, the tributes rolled in. Though some obituaries were hostile, most were at least gentle. The *New York Times* was dignified and more accurate about him than usual, but it was the Boston *Globe* that ran an editorial which mourned him and attributed his pain and death to the fact that he had tried to tell the truth. Although Harvard was engulfed in political strife, and Kerouac was supposedly passé, the *Harvard Crimson* eulogized: "We should say a prayer for him: God give us the strength to be as alive as Kerouac was. Send us more to help burn away the bullshit." *Time* sneered and the *National Review* tried to exploit his death ideologically, but the youth culture's own *Rolling Stone* paid sincere tribute in "Elegy for a Desolation Angel."

Later, Ken Kesey would say, "I feel bad about Kerouac. He was a prophet and we let him die from us. He *did* know, and he *did* care, and the letters of praise that I composed in my head to him *would have* made a difference." Gregory Corso eulogized Jack in one of his greatest poems, proudly chanting through the tears:

> and as long as America shall
> live, though yee old Kerouac body hath died,
> Yet shall you live . . .
> Aye the America so embodied in thee, so
>   definitely
> therefrom, is the living embodiment
>   of all rooted
> humanity, young and free.

On Thursday the twenty-third, friends and family gathered in Lowell, the circle of life come full for Jack's wake. The ritual took place at the Archambault Funeral Home, a chillingly familiar scene from *Dr. Sax;* Jean Louis Kerouac had truly come home. He lay in the coffin in an incongruous black-and-white checked sport coat, white shirt and red bow-tie, rosary beads in his hands, the make-up on his face cold to the touch. Allen, Peter, Gregory, John, and Shirley arrived, and Jack's town and city friends greeted one another united in loss. There was no bitterness. Stella cried out, "All of you! Why didn't you come to Florida when he needed you?" But then she kissed and hugged everyone, for it was much too late for recriminations. Years later Allen even visited Mémère and Stella in Florida, slept in Jack's bed and sang Blake's "Lamb" to the ancient woman who'd hated him so long.

A reporter for the Boston underground newspaper the *Phoenix* saw the staid, well-dressed Sampases, who made up most of the mourners, and concluded that it was only the "Kerouac wake"; the farewell to the man of myth and dream and legend that was the "Duluoz wake" must have taken place long ago.

He was wrong. Most of the Sampases and the New York people went to bed that night after quiet talk and drink, but the Duluoz wake at Nicky's began at ten that evening and ran until dawn. The booze came off the top shelf, old Kerouac tapes replaced the jukebox, and Tony, Billy Koumantzelis, Paul Lekas, and Gerard Wagner swapped old stories and drained their glasses in memoriam. Two drag queens added a note of raunchy humor to the proceedings, particularly when a pair of salesmen wandered in by mistake and tried to pick up the "ladies." At gray dawn the mourners went to the Royal Grill, a funky Greek diner straight out of *Visions of Cody,* and breakfasted with the pimps and the hookers, the milkmen and the other fugitives of the dawn patrol.

Friday morning, Sterling Lord and Jimmy Breslin came from New York City, Robert Creeley from Buffalo, Edie Parker, Jack's first wife, from Detroit, the past re-forming yet once more in farewell. The funeral was at St. Jean Baptiste Cathedral, where Jack had been an altar boy thirty-five years before. Father "Spike" Morrisette, the young seminarian who had befriended him, eulogized Jack with a simple, righteous blessing.

They took the body to the Sampas family plot at Edson Cemetery, and they buried Jack Kerouac. Even though there would be no marker for several years, it became a site of pilgrimage, as dozens of wanderers would stop to commune with his spirit, perhaps say a prayer or leave a note. Later Bob Dylan and Allen would stand there and read from the "Wheel of the Quivering Meat Conception" chorus of *Mexico City Blues.* Eventually the stone would read "He Honored Life." A little corny, Allen thought —"He honored death, too."

Allen and John and Peter threw handfuls of dirt on the coffin, stared silently for long moments, then walked away. At long last Jack had joined Gerard and Leo and Nin in the New England earth.

The myths and dreams and the art remain, to disturb or inspire. Above all else, the road endures.

Afterword

I began this book as a twenty-two-year-old graduate student of history, convinced that Jack Kerouac was the ideal lens, a sensitive, perceptive witness whose personal story would trace his era, in particular the span from 1940 to 1960. My expectations were fulfilled, indeed surpassed. Looking at my work thirty years after beginning it and twenty-three years after publication, I remain convinced that Kerouac's life offers a profound insight into the metamorphosis of America in the years between the Great Depression and the war in Vietnam.

All that change is reflected in Kerouac's own transition from protégé of Thomas Wolfe to Jack Kerouac, author of *On the Road*. And a close examination of Kerouac's work and that of his chronological peers Jackson Pollock and Charlie Parker, as this study details, demonstrates a remarkable correspondence among three artists and their mutual reactions to their historical context. Each produced, in different media, great pieces of art that resonate with an eerie harmony to the underlying rhythms of their time. Even so long after the writing, I remain confident that this contribution remains not only valid but also valuable in understanding the '40s and '50s.

I began work in the summer of 1972 at the Odyssey Bookstore in South Hadley, Massachusetts, a wonderful place (not least because the owner, Romeo Grenier, advanced me books I could not immediately pay for), and found there most—but by no means all—of Kerouac's oeuvre. Jack was not chic in 1972. He'd died in 1969 as a result of his alcoholism, and his reflexive immigrant patriotism clashed with the young tastemakers of a nation mired in a war led by a president who'd already taken steps to steal that year's election.

My first interview was with Kerouac's friend Lucien Carr, in 2002 the last living member of Kerouac's New York scene in the 1940s, and in 1972 a hard-drinking editor at UPI. The writer who told me how to find Lucien warned me of his cranky ways and suggested I get him for lunch. When I called, Lucien affably said he'd be happy to talk with me, and we met after work at 6 P.M., strolling to the bar that was a second home to the UPI staff. As the evening passed we moved on to his home, and although I was not an experienced drinker, I managed until nearly 3 A.M. to take notes that, somehow, were legible the next day.

Lucien passed me on to John Clellon Holmes, and John to Allen Ginsberg, and I spent seven very happy years in pursuit of Kerouac's spirit. Eventually, thanks to Carolyn Cassady, I met a marvelous editor named Kathy Matthews and published *Desolate Angel* with Random House in 1979.

The tension between Lowell and the wider world that made Kerouac who he was—the immigrant boy absorbed by the most sentimental aspects of Roman Catholicism who would become a serious student of Buddhism, the wanderer who always came home, the spiritual seeker who would end his days in drink and bitter reactionary rant—went on within and without. He was the son of Lowell, and just as he didn't always know what to do with Lowell, for a very long time Lowell didn't know what to do with him and his legacy.

That was especially true for his wife Stella, who simply barricaded Kerouac's work in the decade after his death, refusing access or rights of quotation to scholars and preventing any previously unpublished manuscripts from seeing the light of day. But this ambivalence was not limited to Stella, as I found out most vividly in 1982, when I participated in a twenty-fifth anniversary celebration of *On the Road* at Naropa Institute. I found myself being asked about the source for a couple of quotes, including one particularly nasty remark attributed to Jack's mother—"You should have died, not [your elder brother] Gerard." At the time I couldn't recall the citations and suggested looking in the endnotes, but when I later realized that the references had been entered as "confidential," I was vexed. Trying to circumvent my desire to protect a source was only bothersome, but the attitudes it bespoke, the cliques within Lowell competing for the right to possess Kerouac, as well as similar rivalries among critics outside the town, left me feeling that I'd had enough.

I had a new subject to work on and felt I'd had my say about Jack. In any case, I felt no need to spend the rest of my life as part of the emerging Kerouac industry, and so I dropped out—no articles, no conferences, no disputatious letters. The industry, of course, got along quite well without me. Biographers, memoirists, and critics produced their work, as they will continue to do so for the foreseeable future. Seemingly as a result of Carolyn Cassady's pioneering *Heartbeat*, Jack's first wife Edie Parker became more accessible, lending Gerry Nicosia's *Memory Babe* some very valuable insights along with Gerry's own. Some of the other work—that of Ellis Amburn and Barry Miles, among others—seems less than generous, but the students of any significant figure can expect that. I expect Douglas Brinkley's estate-authorized work to bring insight, compassion, and breadth of understanding to the subject; it will be definitive. That one I'll read completely and with pleasure.

Recently, Douglas shared with me a glance at some copies of Kerouac journals that had been unavailable when I was researching, and that brings me to the second and perhaps most important point of Kerouac's legacy. Since the death of Stella Kerouac, control of Kerouac's papers has devolved to John Sampas, and that has meant the slow emergence of considerable significant material, most especially *Some of the Dharma*, for which all students of Kerouac and literature in general should be genuinely grateful. As I remarked earlier, I've had my say—but I do wonder, from time to time, what I might have done had I had a key to that legendary locked room in Lowell that was the de facto Kerouac archive in the '70s.

That accessibility nurtured the Kerouac boom of the early-to-mid-'90s, and boom or bust, will continue to do so. And everything else that can happen has, of course, happened—from legal squabbles (as far as I could ever tell, Stella's actions toward Jack's daughter Jan reflected Jack's own wishes, alas) to death. One by one, Kerouac's earliest associates—John Clellon Holmes in 1988, Herbert Huncke in 1996, Allen Ginsberg and William Burroughs in 1997—as well as Jan, in 1996, moved on to wherever their destinies led them, and the world is a poorer place for that.

Two facts stand out for me, or rather one outrageous fact and some deeply held opinions. The fact is the roughly $2.5 million

Indianapolis Colts owner Jim Irsay chose to lay out for the original scroll to *On the Road*. Since we live in a world that measures significance by the number of zeroes to the right of the dollar sign, this fact is an impressive (if ultimately tangential) testament to the enduring significance of Jack Kerouac.

My opinions, my conclusions about Kerouac, seem to me more important than money. Jack Kerouac consciously faced literary extinction; having published *The Town and the City* in a conventional style, he chose to 'light out for the territory,' to roam a stylistic literary frontier with no rules and no guaranteed reward, and having departed civilization he considered it quite likely that he might never publish again (suicide!). Having made his decision and endured his sojourn, he came back from the wilderness with a style that endured and with specific books like *On the Road* and *Visions of Cody* and many, many more. That brave declaration of freedom, that willingness to risk all, made him a hero in all the best senses of the word. He resisted Moloch by being himself.

As I write, early in the new millennium, the world seems to me ever grayer and more threatening as our environment, both social and biological, grows more polluted and less harmonious. The spiritual message that poor beat Ti Jean from Lowell brought to a smug '50s America seems even more valuable forty-five years after *On the Road* was published. I ended *Desolate Angel* by saying that the road endures. It would seem that now, metaphorically as well as literally, it's even less like Route 66 and more of a boring interstate than ever.

But our need to venture out, to look for the heart of the dream, to travel in Whitman's and Jack's and Neal Cassady's and all the other pilgrims' footsteps—that need is greater than ever. That is a faith worth cherishing, and that is why Jack, however desolate, was an angel. Twenty-three years after publishing *Desolate Angel*, I think this book still honors that faith.

San Francisco
October 2002

Source Notes

Initials frequently used in the notes:

W.S.B. William S. Burroughs
C.C. Carolyn Cassady
G.C. Gregory Corso
L.C. Lucien Carr
M.C. Malcolm Cowley
N.C. Neal Cassady
L.F. Lawrence Ferlinghetti
A.G. Allen Ginsberg
H.H. Herbert Huncke
J.C.H. John C. Holmes
J.K. Jack Kerouac
M.M. Michael McClure
P.O. Peter Orlovsky
G.S. Gary Snyder
P.W. Philip Whalen

PREFACE

"History is hard . . .": Hunter Thompson, *Fear and Loathing in Las Vegas* (New York: Popular Library, 1971), p. 67.

I IN THE SHADOW OF A CRUCIFIX

"If it is not . . .": Henry David Thoreau, *A Week on the Concord and Merrimack Rivers* (New York: Charles Scribner's Sons, 1921), p. 45. Early Lowell: Margaret Terrell Parker, *Lowell: A Study in Industrial Development* (New York: The Macmillan Company, 1940), Chapters I and II, passim. Boarding Houses: Richard P. Horwitz, "Architecture and Culture: The Meaning of the Lowell Boarding House," *American Quarterly* 11 (March 1973): pp. 65–82. Migration to Lowell: John Kerouac, *The Town and the City*

(New York: Harcourt, Brace and Company, 1950), p. 23; Interviews with Armand Kerouac and Armand Gauthier. Leo and Gabrielle Kerouac: Kerouac, *Town*, p. 6; Jack Kerouac, *Visions of Gerard* (New York: Farrar, Straus and Co., 1963), pp. 24, 94, 116; Interviews with Armand Kerouac and Armand Gauthier.

Birth of Kerouac: "Certificate of Birth" on file with City Clerk, City of Lowell; Jack Kerouac, *Dr. Sax* (New York: Grove Press, Inc., 1959), p. 17. Early homes of Kerouac: Personal observation of author; *Lowell City Directory* (Lowell: Sullivan Brothers Printing Co., 1922–1940), passim. Kerouac's childhood memories: Kerouac, *Gerard*, pp. 10, 21, 122, 79; Jack Kerouac, *Maggie Cassidy* (New York: Avon Books, 1959), p. 94.

Gerard Kerouac: Kerouac, *Gerard*, pp. 12, 7, 28, 24, 21, 16, 22, 8, 26, 14, 69, 83, 129; Kerouac, *Town*, p. 35; Interviews with Armand Kerouac and Armand Gauthier. "Why do I . . . confessed": Kerouac, *Gerard*, p. 83. "my brother's gone . . .": Ibid., p. 129.

Reactions to Gerard's death—Leo: Interviews with Lucien Desmarais, Will Desrosiers, and Elzear Dionne. Reaction of Mémère: Kerouac, *Gerard*, p. 92. Reaction of Jean Kerouac: Kerouac, *Sax*, p. 148; Kerouac, *Gerard*, p. 88; Kerouac, *Sax*, p. 38; Jack Kerouac, "The Origins of the Beat Generation," *Playboy*, June 1959, p. 42; Kerouac, *Maggie*, p. 90. Gerard's funeral: Kerouac, *Gerard*, p. 138; Interview with Armand Kerouac. "there's no doubt . . .": Kerouac, *Gerard*, p. 88.

Hildreth Street home: *Lowell City Directory, 1928*, p. 312; Personal observation. Private games of Kerouac: Kerouac, *Sax*, p. 102; Kerouac, *Gerard*, p. 50. Movies: Kerouac, *Sax*, p. 185; Kerouac, *Town*, p. 178. Hoot Gibson: Jon Tuska, "Powdersmoke Range," *Journal of Popular Culture* V (Summer 1971): pp. 65–78, passim. Vaudeville and B. F. Keith's: Kerouac, *Sax*, p. 110; Kerouac, *Gerard*, pp. 105–106; Interviews with Frank Moran and William Koumantzelis. Kerouac's early reading: Evelyn Byrne, O. Penzler, *Attacks of Taste* (New York: Gotham Book Mart, 1971), p. 79.

Kerouac's childhood visions: Interview with L. C.; Kerouac, *Sax*, p. 4. *"Qui a farmé . . . haunted"*: Kerouac, *Sax*, p. 4. Schooling: Kerouac, *Gerard*, p. 33; Kerouac, *Sax*, pp. 65–66; Charles Jarvis, *Visions of Kerouac* (Lowell: Ithaca Press, 1974), p. 19; Kerouac, *Gerard*, pp. 35, 40; Interview with Armand Kerouac; Benson Y. Landis, *The Roman Catholic Church in the U.S.* (New York: E. P. Dutton and Co., 1966), p. 12; L. J. Putz, *The Catholic Church U.S.A.* (Chicago: Fides Publishers Assoc., 1956), passim. "great big black . . .": Jarvis, *Visions of Kerouac*, p. 19.

Catechism: Kerouac, *Gerard*, p. 64; *The Baltimore Catechism* (no publisher, no date), passim. Church education: Joseph H. Fichter, S.J., *Parochial School* (South Bend, Indiana: University of Notre Dame Press, 1958), passim. "lamby gray strangeness": Kerouac, *Gerard*, p. 64. Church doctrine: Landis, *The Roman Catholic Church*, p. 16. Interviews with Father Fred Minnegan and Father Jean Martel. First Communion: Kerouac, *Maggie*, p. 170; Gerard Ellard, *Christian Life and Worship* (Milwaukee, Wisconsin: Bruce Publishing Co., 1956), pp. 77–87. St. Teresa: Kerouac, *Sax*, p. 4; Herbert Thurston, S.J., and Donald Atwater, *Butler's Lives of the Saints* (New York: P. J. Kenedy and Sons, 1903), pp. 412–417; Interviews with Father Armand "Spike" Morrisette and William Everson (Brother Antoninus). "little way . . . absolute self surrender": Thurston, *Butler's*, p. 15.

Horse races: Kerouac, *Town*, pp. 36, 101–110. Home marble races: Kerouac, *Sax*, pp. 80–90. St. Louis School: Kerouac, *Gerard*, pp. 39, 34; Interview with Armand Kerouac; Kerouac, *Maggie*, p. 43. *"Oui, mon père, I . . ."*: Kerouac, *Maggie*, p. 43.

"Zouzou": Interview with Tony Sampas. "despair, raw gricky . . .": Kerouac, *Gerard,* p. 13.

Depression Lowell: Parker, *Lowell: A Study,* pp. 2–5; Irving Bernstein, *The Lean Years* (Boston: Houghton-Mifflin Co., 1972), p. 255. Communism: Lowell *Sun,* February-March, 1930, passim. I.W.W.: Interview with Elzear Dionne. Depression movies: Advertisement, Lowell *Sun,* April 10, 1931, p. 10. Dick Tracy: William H. Young, "The Serious Funnies: Adventure Comics During the Depression, 1929–1938," *Journal of Popular Culture* III (Winter 1969): pp. 416. Major Hoople: Ned Polsky, *Hustlers, Beats and Others* (Chicago: Aldine Publishing Co., 1967), p. 31.

Boxing: Jack Kerouac, "In the Ring," *Atlantic,* March 1968, passim. Radio: Kerouac, *Sax,* p. 71; Kerouac, *Town,* p. 13; Interview with Fred Bertrand. Kerouac automobile: Interview with Armand Gauthier. Schooling: Kerouac, *Sax,* p. 72; Jack Kerouac, *Lonesome Traveler* (New York: McGraw-Hill Book Co., 1960), p. v; Interview with Armand Kerouac, Maureen Vigent, and Father Armand "Spike" Morrisette. Franklin Roosevelt: "Democratic Rallies On," Lowell *Sun,* November 1, 1932, p. 1. Leo Kerouac and City Hall: Interview with Armand Gauthier. "gahdam micks": Interview with George "GJ" Apostalakis. Ethnic wars in Lowell: Interviews with Father Armand "Spike" Morrisette, William Koumantzelis, and Danny Murphy.

Learning the English language: Jack Kerouac, *Vanity of Duluoz* (New York: Coward-McCann, Inc., 1967), p. 28. Reading material: Kerouac, *Town,* pp. 27, 120. Miss Helen Mansfield: Interview with "Duke" Chiungas as quoted in Jarvis, *Visions of Kerouac,* p. 44; Interview with George "GJ" Apostalakis. Jack Kerouac and beginning to write: Kerouac, *Lonesome,* p. v. Conflict within Kerouac family: Interviews with George "GJ" Apostalakis, Fred Bertrand, and Roland Salvas. "Forget this writing . . . stop dreaming!": Interview with George "GJ" Apostalakis. "You should have died . . .": Confidential interview. Kerouac's childhood gang: Kerouac, *Sax,* pp. 41–46; Interviews with George "GJ" Apostalakis, Fred Bertrand, Roland Salvas, Tony Sampas, William Koumantzelis. "crackbrained angel joy": Kerouac, *Sax,* p. 41. Childhood football: Interview with Armand Kerouac. American dream of college: Kerouac, *Vanity,* p. 15.

"The Dracut Tigers, age . . .": Kerouac, *Vanity,* p. 13. "goaded on by . . .": Kerouac, *Town,* p. 14. "that little Christ . . .": Kerouac, *Vanity,* p. 13. Radio programs: Interviews with William Koumantzelis, George "GJ" Apostalakis, Roland Salvas, and Fred Bertrand. Pulp magazine swapping: Kerouac, *Town,* p. 34. Pulp magazines: Ibid., p. 27; Richard Hill Wilkinson, "What Ever Happened to the Pulps?" *Saturday Review,* February 10, 1962, pp. 60–61, 67; Tony Goodstone, *The Pulps* (New York: Chelsea House, 1970), pp. 74–89; Allan R. Bosworth, "The Golden Age of Pulps, *Atlantic,* July 1961, pp. 57–60; Evelyn Byrne, *Attacks of Taste,* p. 79.

"From thin, straight lips . . .": Walter Gibson, *The Weird Adventures of the Shadow* (New York: Grosset and Dunlap, 1966), p. 24. "The Silver Tin Can . . .": Interview with George "GJ" Apostalakis. Hitchhiking to Boston: Jarvis, *Visions of Kerouac,* pp. 30–31. Dead man on Moody St. Bridge: Kerouac, *Sax,* pp. 125–127. Dr. Sax's heritage: Kerouac, *Sax,* pp. 4, 44, 47, 26, 69. "unforgettable flow of evil . . .": Kerouac, *Sax,* p. 108. Kerouac and flood: Kerouac, *Sax,* pp. 163–170. Flood and Lowell: Lowell *Sun,* March 12, 1936 to March 20, 1936, inclusive. "And Doctor Sax . . .": Kerouac, *Sax,* p. 245. "fought through the fear . . .": J. C. H. to J. K., May 1963. Summer work: Kerouac, *Maggie,* p. 27.

II　VANITY WON AND LOST

Lowell High School and its neighborhood: Personal observation; Parker, *Lowell: A Study*, p. 71; Kerouac, *Maggie*, p. 45. Leo's failure: Kerouac, *Town*, p. 37; Interview with Elzear Dionne; "City of Lowell Personal Property Book: 1936," (City Assessor's Office, Lowell, Massachusetts), p. 69; "City of Lowell Personal Property Book: 1937," p. 68; Kerouac, *Maggie*, pp. 82–83; Kerouac, *Lonesome*, p. v; Interviews with George "GJ" Apostalakis and Fred Bertrand. "mournful vision": Kerouac, *Gerard*, p. 95. "I wanta write . . . all ya life": Ibid., p. 62. Mémêre's social attitudes: Interview with Fred Bertrand. Kerouac as "momma's boy": Interviews with George "GJ" Apostalakis and Fred Bertrand. "Memory Babe": Ibid.

Lowell High School bigotry: Interviews with William Koumantzelis and James McNally. English class: Kerouac, *Maggie*, p. 56. Lowell Public Library: Kerouac, *Vanity*, p. 24. Popular fiction: Bernard Berelson and Patricia Salte, "Majority and Minority Americans: An Analysis of Magazine Fiction," in Bernard Rosenberg and David Manning White, *Mass Culture* (New York: The Free Press, 1957), pp. 236–247. Kerouac on Saroyan: "The Art of Fiction," *The Paris Review* 43 (September 1969), p. 82. "pearls of words . . .": Ibid. Kerouac and "the gang": Kerouac, *Maggie Cassidy*, pp. 8–26; Interviews with George "GJ" Apostalakis, Roland Salvas, and Fred Bertrand. "I'm gonna be . . .": Interview with George "GJ" Apostalakis. "Moidah One . . .": Ibid. Luxy Smith: Kerouac, *Maggie*, pp. 13–14. Movies: Jack Kerouac, "Origins of the Beat Generation," *Playboy*, June 1959, p. 31. Kerouac and "Dr. Jekyll": Interview with George "GJ" Apostalakis. "night diner became . . .": Andrew Bergman, *We're In the Money* (New York: Harper & Row, Inc., 1971), p. 11.

"buffoonery . . . brutality . . . life and death": Kerouac, *Town*, p. 54. Sebastian Sampas: Kerouac, *Gerard*, p. 13; Interviews with Charles Sampas, William Koumantzelis, and Tony Sampas; Kerouac, *Town*, pp. 180–181. "different from . . .": Kerouac, *Town*, p. 131. "Soon the red building . . .": Sebastian Sampas, "Summertime in a Mill City," (Manuscript in possession of Tony Sampas, Lowell, Massachusetts). Prometheus Club: Interviews with Tony Sampas and William Koumantzelis. Kerouac as atheist: Kerouac, *Maggie*, p. 127.

First years of football: Kerouac, *Town*, p. 55. "This gahdam shittown . . .": Ibid., p. 84. Football season of 1938: Interview with Arthur Coughlin; Lowell *Sun*, September 16, p. 17, September 1, p. 18, September 21, p. 9, September 23, p. 16, October 3, p. 13, October 6, p. 17, October 8, p. 1, October 14, p. 17, October 15, p. 1, October 22, p. 1, October 28, p. 16, October 31, p. 13, November 7, p. 17, November 12, p. 1, November 25, pp. 1, 15; Kerouac, *Vanity*, pp. 18–22. "Kerouac is the 12th . . .": Kerouac, *Vanity*, p. 20.

Silver Star Tavern: Interviews with Roland Salvas, George Apostalakis, and Tony Sampas. "Don't you know . . .": Kerouac, *Gerard*, pp. 137–138. "Remember that time . . . and he did!": Interview with George "GJ" Apostalakis. Swing music: Interview with Fred Bertrand; Kerouac, *Town*, p. 13; Interview with George "GJ" Apostalakis; Orrin Keepnews, *A Pictorial History of Jazz* (New York: Crown Publishers, Inc., 1955), pp. 103–155. "too classical . . . Listen to that man . . . that Beat": Interview with Roland Salvas. Mary Carney: Kerouac, *Maggie*, pp. 27–32; picture in Lowell *Sun*, March 13, 1939, p. 25. Peggy Coffey: Kerouac, *Maggie*, p. 39.

Kerouac's 17th birthday: Ibid., p. 122; Interviews with Roland Salvas and George "GJ" Apostalakis; Lowell *Sun*, March 13, 1939, p. 25. *"On essaye a s'y . . ."* Kerouac, *Maggie*, p. 113. "her rippling mysterious . . . murder her": Ibid., p. 91. Marriage: Ibid., pp. 73–75, 147, 150. "You'd know more . . .": Ibid., 147.

Leahy and Sullivan Brothers: Interviews with Fred Bertrand and Walter Bixby. Lou Little: Interview with Elmer Rynne. "That's my boy . . .": Ibid. "the symbol of a man . . .": Frederick Exley, *A Fan's Notes* (New York: Random House, Inc., 1968), p. 193. Mémère and New York City: Interview with George "GJ" Apostalakis. Kerouac's decision on college: Interviews with Father Armand "Spike" Morrisette, Charles Sampas; Charles Sampas, "Sampascoopies," Lowell *Sun*, March 16, 1939, p. 20. New York vision through films: Kerouac, *Vanity*, pp. 26, 39. Scotty Boldieu: Kerouac, *Maggie*, p. 51. Graduation: "953 Graduate," Lowell *Sun*, June 30, 1939, pp. 1, 20. WPA and the Acre: "Demolition Continues," Lowell *Sun*, September 7, 1939, p. 1.

III "PROUD CRUEL CITY"

"Proud, cruel, . . .": Thomas Wolfe, *Look Homeward, Angel* as quoted in Federal Writer's Project, *New York Panorama* (New York: Random House, Inc., 1938), p. 17. "infinite pueblo": Ibid., p. 9. Entrance to New York City: Ibid., passim; Kerouac, *Town*, pp. 354–357. Fantasy of being a reporter: Kerouac, *Maggie*, pp. 160–1. Description of Brooklyn and Horace Mann: Kerouac, *Vanity*, pp. 28–30; Kerouac, *Maggie*, p. 160; Interview with Dick Leonard. Mémère and Horace Mann: Kerouac, *Maggie*, p. 164. "Stay! I am not . . .": Kerouac, *Vanity*, p. 39. Football: Ibid., pp. 42–48; Kerouac, *Town*, p. 126.

Horace Mann life: Kerouac, *Vanity*, pp. 31–35, 40. French movies: Ibid., p. 41. U.S. economy: Geoffrey H. Perrott, *Days of Sadness, Years of Triumph* (Baltimore, Maryland: Penguin Books, Inc., 1973), pp. 23–24. Losing virginity: Kerouac, *Maggie*, p. 172. Horace Mann humor: Kerouac, *Vanity*, pp. 51–53; Jack Kerouac, "He Went on the Road," *Life*, June 29, 1962, p. 22. "like very high smotch . . .": Kerouac, *Vanity*, p. 52. "Kerouac is a victim . . .": Kerouac, *Lonesome*, p. 12. Horace Mann publications: Jack Kerouac, "The Brothers," *Horace Mann Quarterly*, Fall 1939, pp. 11–13; Jack Kerouac, "Une Veille de Noël," *Horace Mann Quarterly*, Summer 1940, pp. 16–19. "millions of myriad . . . darkness": Kerouac, "The Brothers," p. 12.

Mary Carney at a distance: Kerouac, *Maggie*, pp. 168–169, 172. American domestic politics: Perrott, *Days of Sadness*, pp. 90–101. Winter War: Picture, *Life*, January 29, 1940, p. 17. Seymour Wyse: Kerouac, *Vanity*, p. 35. Music in 1940: H. F. Mooney, "Popular Music Since the 1920's," *American Quarterly* XX (Spring 1968): pp. 67–85; Nat Shapiro and Nat Hentoff, *Hear Me Talkin' to Ya* (New York: Dover Publishers, Inc., 1955), pp. 314–320; Marshall Stearns, *The Story of Jazz* (New York: Oxford University Press, 1956), pp. 198–214; John S. Wilson, "The Cafe That Gave Us Chee-Chee and Boogie Woogie Too," *New York Sunday Times Magazine*, June 23, 1974, p. 9; George T. Simon, *The Swing Era* (New Rochelle, New York: Arlington House, 1973), passim. Billboard survey: Leo Walker, *The Wonderful Era of the Great Dance Bands* (New York: Doubleday and Co., 1972), p. 145.

Kerouac on jazz in Horace Mann publications: Jack Kerouac, "Swing Authority George Avakian," *Horace Mann Record*, December 8, 1939, p. 7; Jack Kerouac, "Glenn Miller Skipped School to Play," *Record*, March 15, 1940, p. 3; Jack Kerouac and Albert

Avakian, "Real Solid Drop Beat Riffs," *Record,* March 23, 1940, p. 4; Jack Kerouac, "Count Basie's Band Best in Land," *Record,* February 16, 1940, p. 3. "Most of today's swing . . . Ellington stands alone": Kerouac, "Real Solid," p. 4. "clean cut": Kerouac, "Glenn Miller," p. 3. "music which has not . . .": Kerouac, "Real Solid," p. 4. "Count Basie's Swing . . .": Kerouac, "Count Basie's Band," p. 3. "We've already got a . . .": Billie Holiday as quoted in Ralph Gleason, *Celebrating the Duke. . .* (New York: Dell Publishing Co., 1975), p. 72. "The blues is a thing . . .": W.C. Handy, as quoted in Shapiro and Hentoff, *Hear Me Talkin',* p. 252. "Blues truth runs counter . . .": Michael Lydon, *Rock Folk* (New York: Dial Press, 1971), p. 52. "You gotta go back . . .": as quoted in Ibid. Bessie Smith: Henry Pleasants, *The Great American Popular Singers* (New York: Simon and Schuster, 1974), p. 94.

World's Fair: Perrott, *Days of Sadness,* p. 129; Federal Writer's Project, *Manhattan Panorama,* Chapter 26, passim. Spring Prom: Kerouac, *Maggie,* pp. 174–176, 183. "Brains and brawn . . .": *Horace Mann Yearbook, 1940,* p. 44. "You must remember . . .": "What Americans Said and Did As Nazis Triumphed," *Life,* June 10, 1940, p. 26. Horace Mann graduation: Kerouac, *Vanity,* p. 59. Jack London: Ibid., p. 59. Plans for Invasion: "This is How the U.S. May Be Invaded," *Life,* June 24, 1940, pp. 16–17. "Each is not for . . .": Walt Whitman, "Starting from Paumonok," *Leaves of Grass* (New York: Holt, Rinehart & Winston, Inc., 1949), pp. 15–16. Kerouac and moth: J.K. to A.G., June 20, 1952. "Don't think me insane . . .": Kerouac, *Town,* p. 138. "Wisdom is . . . own proof." Whitman, "Song of the Open Road," *Leaves,* p. 127. "These states are . . .": Whitman, "By Blue Ontario's Shore," *Leaves,* p. 284. "Who are you indeed . . .": Ibid.

Flag waving and Kate Smith: Perrott, *Days of Sadness,* pp. 33–35. Posters: "Speaking of Pictures," *Life.* July 1, 1940, pp. 10–11. Kerouac's arrival at Hartley Dormitory: Kerouac, *Vanity,* p. 65. Daily routine: Ibid., pp. 68–69. Freshman rituals at Columbia: *Columbia Spectator,* September 12, 1940, to October 17, 1940, passim. Professor Van Doren: Kerouac, *Maggie,* p. 50; "Mark Van Doren, 78, Poet, Teacher, Dies," *New York Times,* December 12, 1972, pp. 1, 50. Kerouac joins fraternity: "Pledge List Includes 109 Freshman," *Spectator,* October 23, 1940, p. 1. Butler controversy: "Dr. Butler Announces War Policy," *Spectator,* October 4, 1940, p. 1; "Dr. Butler Defends Stand on Policy in World Crisis," *Spectator,* October 11, 1940, p. 1; "Dr. Butler Clarifies Stand in Reply to the *Spectator,"Spectator,* October 11, 1940, p. 1. "those in conflict with . . .": *Spectator,* October 4, 1940, p. 1.

Draft: "University Suspends Classes on October 16 for Draft Registration," *Spectator,* October 1, 1940, p. 1. Collegiate silliness: "Utah Sorority Regulates Leg Competition of Campus Flirts," *Life,* January 20, 1941, pp. 28–29. "fairly good running . . .": "Cubs Lose Debut," *Spectator,* October 14, 1940, p. 3. "Run it off . . . sprain": Kerouac, *Vanity,* p. 72. "star back . . . ace": "Kerouac Lost to Grid Team," *Spectator,* October 31, 1940, p. 3. Thomas Wolfe: Kerouac, *Vanity,* p. 78; Kerouac, *Lonesome,* p. v; Thomas Wolfe, *Look Homeward, Angel* (New York: Charles Scribner's Sons, 1929), passim; "stranger who had come to . . .": Wolfe, *Angel,* p. 66. "He was not a child . . .": Ibid., p. 325. "a torrent of American heaven . . .": Kerouac, "The Art of Fiction," p. 84. "Deep womb, dark flower . . .": Wolfe, *Angel,* p. 191.

Sam Sampas' visits: Interview with Charley Sampas. Lou Little: "Kerouac and Martin? Lou Says 'Wait Till Next Year," *Spectator,* April 2, 1941, p. 2; Herbert Mark, "Spring Football," *Spectator,* April 25, 1941, p. 3. Summer 1941: Kerouac, *Vanity,* p. 84; Interviews with Tony Sampas, Charley Sampas, and Fred Minnegan. "V" for victory: Perrott,

Days of Sadness, p. 130; "Picture of the Week," *Life,* July 28, 1941, p. 26. "fate knocking on Hitler's door": Perrott, *Days of Sadness,* p. 130. Move to New Haven, dreams: Kerouac, *Vanity,* pp. 86–89. Leo begging Jack: Kerouac, *Town,* p. 236. Franklin Roosevelt on radio: Kerouac, *Vanity,* p. 90; James McGregor Burnes, *Roosevelt, The Soldier of Freedom* (New York: Harcourt, Brace & Co., 1970), pp. 140–141. "I was getting very poetic . . . full suitcase": Jack Kerouac to Alfred G. Aronowitz, (Taped interview, 1959). *New York Times* announcement on Kerouac: "Grid News," *New York Times,* September 26, 1941, p. 31.

IV MYSHKIN AT SEA

"joyed like a maniac": Kerouac, *Vanity,* p. 95. "sad young man": Ibid., p. 97. "Why don't you . . .": Ibid. Sammy's visit, Kerouac's return to Lowell: Ibid., pp. 98–103. *Citizen Kane:* Jack Kerouac to Alfred G. Aronowitz, January 1959. Working for Lowell *Sun:* Kerouac, *Vanity,* pp. 107–110; Interview with Frank Moran.

Quarreling with Leo: Kerouac, *Vanity,* p. 112. "Do you think you . . .": Ibid. "Mighty world events meant . . .": Kerouac, *Town,* p. 274. Reading: Kerouac, *Vanity,* p. 110. "But put forth thine hand . . .": Job 1:7. "down to its tiniest detail . . .": Kerouac, *Vanity,* p. 112. *"Why is light given . . .":* Job 3:23. "I'm a sick man . . .": Fyodor Dostoyevsky, *Notes from Underground* (New York: New American Library, 1961), p. 3. "my insult will elevate her . . .": Ibid., p. 202. "reason is only reason . . .": Ibid., p. 114.

Visit to Washington: Interview with George "GJ" Apostalakis; Kerouac, *Vanity,* pp. 114–117. "I was asleep and . . . was crazy": Interview with George "GJ" Apostalakis. Domestic impact of World War II: Perrott, *Days of Sadness,* pp. 71–72, 251, 256, 260. "Gethsemane": Jack Kerouac, *Visions of Cody* (New York: McGraw-Hill, 1972), p. 264. Kerouac joins Marine Corps, NMU: Kerouac, *Vanity,* pp. 118–120. "I just wanta be . . .": Ibid., p. 119. "serious even in his dissipations": John Clellon Holmes, "Gone in October," *Playboy,* December 1969, p. 140. NMU losses: "NMU, It Is a Union Fighting a War," *Life,* August 24, 1942, pp. 77–80; Perrott, *Days of Sadness,* p. 318. "being misunderstood was like . . .": Kerouac, *Vanity,* p. 123. "death hovers over my . . .": Ibid. "the stake is money . . .": Ibid., p. 124. "deep, joyful, even pleasant . . .": Kerouac, *Town,* p. 299. Life aboard *Dorchester:* Ibid., pp. 300–310; Kerouac, *Vanity,* pp. 121–150. "The world was mad . . .": Kerouac, *Town,* p. 108.

"You can come back . . .": Jack Kerouac to Alfred G. Aronowitz, January 1959. "Get in there now . . . weight at sea": Jack Kerouac to Charles Sampas, October 4, 1969, published in Lowell *Sun,* October 23, 1969, p. 45. *"I'm going to be . . .* football player": Aronowitz interview. Printing "The Sea Is My Brother": Kerouac, *Vanity,* p. 152. Mary Carney: Kerouac, *Maggie,* pp. 185–189. Navy life: Jarvis, *Visions of Kerouac,* p. 98; Kerouac, *Town,* pp. 310–325; Kerouac, "The Art of Fiction," p. 72; Kerouac, *Vanity,* pp. 155–168. "I would prefer not to": Jarvis, *Visions of Kerouac,* p. 98. "You are the real . . .": Sammy Sampas to Jack Kerouac, undated (1943), in possession of Tony Sampas, Lowell. "Somehow out of all . . .": Sammy Sampas to Margerie Semonian, October 2, 1943, printed in Emerson College (Boston, Massachusetts) *Yearbook,* 1944, p. 77. "I have kept faith": Kerouac, *Vanity,* p. 163. "Germans should not be . . .": Kerouac, "The Art of Fiction," p. 72. "I'm too much of a nut . . .": Kerouac, *Vanity,* p. 167. "bootcamp madhouse dreams . . .": Kerouac, *Dreams,* p. 45. "lost dream of being . . .": Kerouac, *Vanity,* p. 173. "Industrial Chemistry . . .": *Life,* March 23, 1942, pp. 68–81. "Rockets": *Life,* January 17, 1944, pp. 71–75. "Mechanical Brains": *Life,* January 24, 1944, pp. 66–72. "Plastics": *Life,* May 3, 1943, pp. 70–79. Science Fiction: Brian Aldiss, *Billion*

Year Spree (New York: Schocken Books, 1973), Chapter 9, passim. Liberal ideology: Theodore Roszak, *The Making of a Counter Culture* (New York: Doubleday Books, 1969), Chapters 1 and 7, passim.

Ozone Park: Kerouac, *Vanity*, p. 173. War-caused migration: Perrott, *Days of Sadness*, pp. 325–333. Leo Kerouac and war: Kerouac, *Town*, p. 352; Kerouac, "The Art of Fiction," p. 73; Interview with L. C. *The Sullivans:* Larry King, "The Battle of Popcorn Bay," *Harper's*, May 1967, pp. 50–54. Wartime reading: Perrott, *Days of Sadness*, p. 380; *Life*, April-July, 1943, passim. Frank Sinatra: Pleasants, *Singers*, pp. 181–195; Kerouac, *Vanity*, p. 177. Edie Parker: Jack Kerouac, *On the Road* (New York: Viking Press, 1957), p. 51; Kerouac, *Cody*, pp. 186–187.

Life on the *Weems:* Kerouac, *Vanity*, pp. 173–181. "about sagas, or legends . . .": Ibid., pp. 181–182. London: Ibid., pp. 183–194. "I saw it . . . what really happened": Ibid., p. 195. Return to Edie Parker: Ibid., p. 196. "But he shall be . . . satin softened snow . . .": Sammy Sampas, "Côte D'Or" and "Rhapsody in Red," Lt. Ed Hill, ed., *Puptent Poets of the Stars and Stripes* (Italy: *Stars and Stripes*, 1945), no pagination.

V   VISIONS IN A WORLD OF MUSHROOM CLOUDS

Description of Edie: Interviews with L. C. and A. G. "birdlike intelligence": Interview with A. G. "mischievous little prick": Kerouac, *Vanity*, p. 200. Lucien Carr, appearance and activities with Kerouac: Pictures at Columbia University; Interviews with A. G., L. C., and W. S. B.; Kerouac, *Vanity*, pp. 200–201. "played at intellectual putdowns . . .": Interview with A.G. "no resentment, no rancor at all": Interview with L. C. "mean old tightfisted . . . Give me a drink": Kerouac, *Vanity*, p. 203. "Oh, let's have more . . .": Kerouac, *Town*, p. 386.

Allen Ginsberg: Kerouac, *Vanity*, p. 217; Kerouac, "The Art of Fiction," p. 97; Interviews with A. G., L. C., and W. S. B. "exalted": Kerouac, *Town*, p. 364. "Now from the cracked . . .": A. G. Journal, 1936–1944. "I'll be a genius of . . .": A. G. Journal, May 22, 1941. "lost child, a wandering . . .": A. G. Journal, August 3, 1944. "to help the misery . . .": A. G. to Howard Schulman, October 16, 1961, in Arthur and Glee Knight, *the unspeakable visions of the individual* 4 (*The Beat Book*, 1973), p. 74. Kerouac helps Ginsberg to move: Interview with A. G.; Allen Ginsberg, *Allen Verbatim*, p. 103. "Why, that's what I do . . . transmission of real feeling": Ibid. "the most highly enervated . . .": Craig Karpel, "Face to Face with the Goat God," *Oui*, August 1973, p. 70. "patrician thinlipped . . . ordinary looking": Kerouac, *Vanity*, p. 221. Background of William Burroughs: Interviews with A. G., W. S. B., and L. C., William Burroughs in Arthur and Kit Knight, *the unspeakable visions of the individual* 5 (*The Beat Diary*, 1976), p. 77. "All of us who . . .": Allen Anson, "William Lee, A Paen," manuscript at Columbia. "Van Gogh kick": Interview with L. C.

Atmosphere of the group, bars and talk: Interviews with A. G., L. C., and W. S. B. "Romantic, moody, darkeyed . . .": Interview with A. G. "New Vision": Interviews with L. C., A. G., and W. S. B. "Know these words . . .": A. G. Journal, undated. "prurience": Interview with A. G. "When the exterior world . . .": Gustave Flaubert, Introduction to *A Season in Hell*, by Arthur Rimbaud (Norwalk, Connecticut: New Directions Press, 1939), p. 11. "Science, the new nobility . . . to the spirit": Arthur Rimbaud, *A Season in Hell* (Norwalk, Connecticut: New Directions Press, 1939), p. 23. "I tell you that . . .": A. G., "A Dialogue in Morality," undated notebook. "When will we go . . .": Rimbaud, *Hell,* p. 95. Background on Rimbaud: Peter Michelson, "Beardsley, Burroughs, Decadence and the Poetics of Obscenity," *Tri-Quarterly* 12 (undated): pp. 139–155.

"How long was it?": Interview with A. G. Transience of life: Ibid. "New Vision lies in . . .": A. G. Journal, April 1945. "Art seducing me to . . .": J. K. note on undated A. G. Journal, "such stuff . . .": William Shakespeare, *The Tempest* (New York: Henry Holt & Co., 1903), Act IV, line 140. "mother's delicacies": Kerouac, *Vanity,* p. 208. "finkish . . . finkish world." Ibid., pp. 210–211. "materialistic Canuck taciturn . . .": Ibid., p. 207. Kerouac and class feelings: Interviews with L. C., A. G., and W. S. B. "You've never . . . working man proletarian . . .": Interview with A. G. "emotionally aware . . .": Interview with L. C. Visit to Asheville: Kerouac, *Vanity,* p. 199; J. K. to L. F., October 6, 1962. Escape to Paris: Kerouac, *Vanity,* p. 219; Interview with L. C. "God gives us kittens . . .": Kerouac, *Gerard,* p. 124.

David Kammerer's death: Interviews with L. C., A. G., and W. S. B.; Kerouac, *Vanity,* pp. 220–260; *New York Times,* August 17, 1945, p. 1, August 18, p. 14, August 25, p. 15, August 31, p. 19, September 16, p. 15, October 7, p. 15. "find symbols saturated . . . to suffocate": Kerouac, *Vanity,* p. 220. "You didn't sign on . . . Fuck you": Interview with L. C.; Kerouac, *Vanity,* p. 223. "Well; I disposed of . . .": Ibid., p. 229. "What'd you really . . . He died in my . . . If he was . . . No Kerouac ever . . .": Ibid, pp. 229–243. "Something's happened to me . . .": Kerouac, *Town,* p. 383. "dark and hopeless": L. C. to A. G., October 1944, "Faithful to the . . . perverted": A. G. to Eugene Brooks, October 1944.

Detroit: Kerouac, *Vanity,* pp. 255–257. "The Next Great Development . . .": *Life,* September 4, 1944, p. 85. Celine Young and the fight: Kerouac, *Vanity,* pp. 257–265; Interview with A. G. "messianic": Celine Young to J. K., October 15, 1944, (Columbia). "Handsome . . . Sweetie Pie": Kerouac, *Vanity,* p. 264. "Self Ultimacy": Ibid., pp. 265–266; A. G., "Excerpts From the Novel," notebook dated October 1944; A. G., "Self Ultimacy in Minetta's," A. G. Journal, October 18, 1944; A. G. to Eugene Brooks, October 1944. "Art is the highest task . . .": Kerouac, *Vanity,* p. 266. "In that for city . . .": Jack Kerouac, as quoted in A. G., "Self Ultimacy in Minetta's." "My God, Jack . . .": Kerouac, *Vanity,* p. 267. "to live outside the . . .": Bob Dylan, "Absolutely Sweet Marie," copyright 1966, Dwarf Music. Impressions of William Burroughs: Interview with A. G. "a year of low, evil . . .": Kerouac, *Vanity,* p. 269. 115th St. apartment: Interviews with A. G., W. S. B., and H.H., Joan Vollmer: Ibid.

"I want you to form . . .": Edie Parker to A. G., January 17, 1945. Allen Ginsberg's ouster from Columbia: Diana Trilling, "The Other Night at Columbia," *Claremont Essays* (New York: Harcourt Brace and World, 1964), p. 154; Jane Kramer, *Allen Ginsberg in America* (New York: Random House, 1968), p. 118; Allen Ginsberg in Allen Young, ed., "The Gay Sunshine Interview" (privately circulated transcript), p. 17; Interview with A. G. "He made life too . . .": Trilling, *Essays,* p. 154. "Butler has no . . . Mr. Ginsberg . . . you've done": Interview with A. G. Raymond Weaver: Ibid. Holmes and Wolfe: D. F. Rauber, "Sherlock Holmes and Nero Wolfe," *Journal of Popular Culture* 6 (Spring 1973): pp. 483–495. "Tenuous to the point . . .": as quoted in Ibid., p. 487. "And the Hippos . . .": Kerouac, "The Art of Fiction," p. 73; Interviews with W. S. B. and A. G. "clean, orderly, sane": Dashiell Hammett, *The Maltese Falcon* (New York: Vintage Books, 1972), p. 53. "Listen, when a man's . . .": Ibid., p. 197.

"Eddify yer mind . . .": Interview with A. G. Spenglerian theories: "The Beginning of the Cyclical Theory," A. G. Journal, February 1945; Interviews with A. G. and W. S.

B. "And I can only hope that . . .": Oswald Spengler, *The Decline of the West* (New York: Alfred A Knopf, 1932), p. 50. "So Proudly We Hail": A. G. in Alfred Kazin, *Writers At Work: The Paris Review Interviews* (New York: Viking Press, 1967), p. 285. Kerouac on psychotherapy: J. K. to J. C. H., June 1963. Psychoanalysis and charades: Interview with A. G. "Gee, I never . . . and learn": Ibid. "Atomic Disease": Ibid.; Kerouac, *Town*, p. 371. "We were conscious of . . .": Interview with A. G.

Kerouac in summer, 1945: J. K. to A. G., July 17, August 10, September 6, 1945. "You know, I love . . . Ohhh nooo": Ginsberg, "Sunshine Interview," p. 13. "mellow, trustful": Ibid. "with all my harlequinade . . ." A. G. to J. K., no date (Summer 1945). "I feel more guilty . . .": A. G. to W. S. B., no date (Summer 1945). "mountains of homosexuality . . .": Allen Ginsberg, *Kaddish* (San Francisco: City Lights Press, 1961), p. 16. "We are of different kinds . . . my secretiveness": A. G. to J. K., no date (Summer 1945). "Your double nature": A. G. to J. K., September 8, 1945.

"I deem . . . unconditional surrender": President Harry S Truman, as quoted in Eric Goldman, *The Crucial Decade* (New York: Random House, Inc., 1960), p. 1. Kerouac and Burroughs on surrender night: J. K. to A. G., August 17, 1945. Bop: Ross Russell, *Bird Lives!* (New York: Charterhouse, 1973), pp. 127, 130–134; Frank Kofsky, *Black Nationalism and the Revolution in Music* (New York: Pathfinder Press, 1969), p. 163. "We kept reading about . . .": Interview with Max Roach. "Jazz has broken itself . . .": Gilbert Sorrentino, "Remembrances of Bop in New York, 1945–50," *Kulchur* 3 (Summer 1963): p. 72. "A different sort of person than a fan . . .": Holmes, *Declare*, p. 105. "looked like criminals . . . by War": Kerouac, "Origins of Beat," p. 42.

Herbert Huncke and William Burroughs: William Burroughs, *Junkie* (New York: Ace Books, 1953), pp. 20–25; Interviews with H. H. and W. S. B.; in *Beat Diary*, p. 27. "chop suey joint": Burroughs, *Junkie*, p. 29. "Hey man, this looks . . .": Interview with H. H. "the back of the legs first . . .": Burroughs, *Junkie*, pp. 22–23. "by default": Ibid., p. 24. Angler Bar and Times Square scene: Kerouac, *Town and City*, pp. 363–364; Interviews with H. H. and W. S. B. Kerouac and scene: Interviews with H. H., W. S. B., and A. G. "All American boy . . . starry eyed": Interview with H. H. Elsie John: H. H., untitled manuscript dated 1959 (Columbia). Louis Ferdinand Céline: J. K. to A. G., August 23, 1945; Louis Ferdinand Céline, *Death on the Installment Plan* (New York: Signet Books, 1966), passim. "Writes like a man who . . .": Leon Trotsky, as quoted in Introduction, Ibid., p. 12. Kerouac in hospital: Kerouac, *Vanity*, p. 272. Kerouac's relationship with his father: Interviews with L. C. and A. G.; Kerouac, *Town*, pp. 422, 470–475. "that the city intellectuals . . . bourgeois decadence": Kerouac, *Vanity*, p. 272. Death of Leo: J. K. to Joe Chaput, November 15, 1968, in possession of Joe Chaput, Lowell; Interview with A. G.; Kerouac, *Vanity*, pp. 270–280. "Life is too long . . .": Jack Kerouac, *Desolation Angels* (New York: Coward-McCann, Inc., 1965), p. 290.

VI   "A WESTERN KINSMAN OF THE SUN"

"A Western . . .": Kerouac, *Road*, p. 7. Kerouac in the summer of 1946: Goldman, *Decade*, p. 59; J. K. to J. C. H., June 1963, Interview with L. C.; Kerouac, *Lonesome*, p. v. "fragments of a great confession": Johann Wolfgang Goethe, *Dichtung und Wahrheit* (New York: Horizon Press, 1969), p. 305. William and Joan Vollmer Burroughs: W. S. B. to A. G., September 1, 1946. Ginsberg's publication: Allen Ginsberg, "Paterson: No.

1," Passaic Valley *Examiner,* September 14, 1946, p. 7. "that cockroach": A. G. Journal, no date. New Year's Eve 1946: A. G. Journal, December 31, 1946; Kerouac, *Cody,* p. 198; Interview with L. C.

Kerouac meets Cassady: Kerouac, *Cody,* pp. 338–343, 296–299; Kerouac, *Road,* pp. 10–20. "sideburned hero of the . . .": Ibid., p. 11. "young jailkid hung up . . . a wild yea saying . . . In other words we've . . . was the one and only holy . . . natural tailor of . . . Yes, of course, I know . . . inwardly realized . . .": Ibid., pp. 7, 11, 6, 6, 9, 7. Cassady as cowboy: Gary Snyder to Alfred G. Aronowitz (tape-recorded interview), May 1959. "a million disorderly images . . .": Kerouac, *Cody,* p. 51.

"unnatural son of a . . .": Neal Cassady, *The First Third* (San Francisco: City Lights Press, 1971), p. 1. Cassady background: Kerouac, *Cody,* pp. 48–56, 80; Cassady, *Third,* pp. 1–72; Interview with C. C. "My dear fellow . . .": J. K. to Alfred G. Aronowitz (interview), May 1959. Background of Brierly: Ivan Goldman, "Jack Kerouac's Denver Friends Formed Theme for Novel," The Denver *Post,* December 29, December 30, December 31, 1974, and January 1, 1975. "the poet is much more . . .": Kerouac, *Cody,* p. 215. Cassady meets Ginsberg: Cassady, *Third,* pp. 118–121; Kerouac, *Road,* p. 8; Interview with A. G. "the holy conman . . . dark mind": Kerouac, *Road,* p. 8. "energetic efficiency . . . staring into each other's . . . total accident . . . curious, envious, humorous . . .": Interview with A. G. Kerouac compares Cassady-Ginsberg to himself and Sammy Sampas: Kerouac, *Cody,* p. 345.

Neal's book list: N. C. to A. G., March 1947. "soberly (and severely) . . .": A. G. Journal, March 4, 1947. Cassady's departure: Ibid., Kerouac, *Road,* p. 9; Kerouac, *Cody,* p. 343. "The Great Sex Letter": N.C. to J. K., March 7, 1947. Further correspondence: N. C. to J. K., March 13, March 27, April 15, May 20, 1947: N. C. to A. G., March 6, 10, 14, 20, April 10, 1947. "almost paranoid fear . . .": N. C. to A. G., March 20, 1947, "dirty, double crossing . . .": as quoted in N. C. to A. G., April 10, 1947. Biography of Carolyn Cassady: Carolyn Cassady, "The Third Word," unpublished manuscript in the possession of C. C. "Closer to relating . . . unselfish": Interview with C. C.

America in 1947: Perrott, *Days of Sadness,* pp. 341–355; Keith Olson, "The GI Bill and Higher Education," *American Quarterly* 25 (December 1973): pp. 596–610. "Money has changed hands": as quoted in Jeanne Perkins, "Emily Post," *Life,* May 6, 1946, p. 59. "Red Image": Leslie Adler, "Red Fascism in America: American Attitudes Towards Communism and the Cold War" (Ph.D. dissertation, University of California at Berkeley, 1970), pp. 1–170. "Poetry is not a turning loose of emotion . . .": as quoted in David Daiches, "The New Criticism," in Robert Spiller, *A Time of Harvest* (New York: Hill & Wang, 1962), p. 96.

On the road to Denver: Kerouac, *Road,* pp. 11–34. "they can't put . . . cute suburban cottages . . . Maw, rustle me up . . . for the hugeness outside . . . Damn damn damn . . . Wow!": Ibid., pp. 14, 18, 19, 30, 31–32. In Denver: Goldman, "Denver Friends," December 30, 1974, p. 27; Kerouac, *Road,* pp. 35–50; Allen Ginsberg, *Visions of the Great Rememberer* (Amherst, Mass.: Mulch Press, 1974), pp. 2–3; A. G. Journal, undated; Carolyn Cassady, "Word," pp. 40–46; Interviews with A. G. and C. C. "Why, Ja-ack, we . . .": Kerouac, *Road,* p. 38. "a hood": Bob Burford in Goldman, "Denver Friends," December 30, 1974. "the man with the dungeon . . .": Kerouac, *Road,* p. 44. "you redeemed yourself . . .": A. G. to J. K., August 1947.

Kerouac in Marin City: Kerouac, *Road,* pp. 50–66. "cop souls . . . sneak out into the . . .": Ibid., pp. 54, 59: New Waverly, Texas: "Herbert Huncke Interview," *unspeaka-*

ble visions of the individual 3 (1974): p. 6; William S. Burroughs Jr., "Life With Father," *Esquire* (September 1971), pp. 113–117; N. C. to J. K., September 3, 1947; Kerouac, *Cody*, pp. 120–150; A. G. to Louis Ginsberg, September 3, 1947. "sad prophetic Jew": A. G. to J. K., August 1947. "If you want to know . . . juvenile delinquents": Ibid. Bea Franco: Kerouac, *Road*, pp. 66–80. Return to New York: Ibid., pp. 80–89.

Fall of 1947: N. C. to J. K., October 5, 1947, (Columbia). N. C. to J. K., November 21, December 25, 1947, January 7, 1948. Anti-Communism in the U.S.: Richard Freeland, *The Truman Doctrine and the Origins of McCarthyism* (New York: Alfred A. Knopf, 1972), pp. 27, 208–247; Athan Theoharis, *Seeds of Repression* (Chicago: Quadrangle Books, 1971), passim. Writing *The Town and the City:* J. C. H. to J. K., November 30, 1948. "rooted in earth . . .": Kerouac, *Town.*, p. 5. "wild self-believing . . .": Kerouac, "Origins of Beat," p. 32. "The depth of a woman's . . . all merciless and . . . A child, a child, hiding . . . family falling apart . . . the whole legend of . . .": Kerouac, *Town*, pp. 69, 155, 190, 235, 287. Screwing the ground: Holmes, *Declare*, p. 73.

"Astounded at its depth . . .": Interview with A. G. "felt that all . . . permanent form": A.G. Autobiographical Fragment for Psychiatrist, undated (1948). "the only eccentric . . .": A. G. to J. K., undated (1948). "Beat me up . . .": Interview with A. G.; A. G. to J. K., April 15, 1948. "the wire is still . . .": Naomi Ginsberg to A. G., undated. "Hallucinations . . . apocalyptic statements": A. G. to N. C., undated (Spring 1948).

"great intellectual poet . . .": A. G. to J. K., undated (Spring 1948). "monumental, magnificent, profound": A. G. to Lionel Trilling, June 1, 1948. Charles Scribner's Sons and Alfred Kazin: J. K. to A. G., May 18, June 5, 1948. Cassady's state of mind: Cassady, "Third Word," pp. 124–140; N. C. to A. G., July 1948; N. C. to J. K., June 16, 1948. "The idea of you . . .": A. G. to N. C., Summer 1948. "Bullshit . . . I can't . . .": N. C. to A. G., July 1948. Ranch idea: N. C. to J. K., June 16, July 5, 1948; Interview with C. C. "I just don't . . .": Cassady, "Third Word," p. 154.

"By 1948 it had . . .": Kerouac, "Origins of Beat," p. 32. Kerouac meets John Holmes: Holmes, *Declare*, pp. 47–77; Interviews with A. G. and J. C. H. "too lyrical . . . structure . . . the potential and costs . . . purity . . . going to *some* serious fate": Holmes, *Declare*, pp. 47, 47, 74, 48, 48. "solemnly radical undergraduate": Ibid., p. 47. "New York migraine liberals . . . naked on a plain": as quoted in John Clellon Holmes, *Go* (Charles Scribner's Sons, 1952), p. 22. "tramp transcendentalist . . . Right?": Holmes, *Declare*, p. 68. "inquisitive dormouse . . . Does your wife approve . . .": Ibid., p. 50. "sweet and generous": Interview with A. G. "widen the area of . . .": as quoted in Holmes, *Declare*, p. 61.

Allen Ginsberg and Blake: A. G. in Kazin, *Writers*, pp. 200–204; A. G. to N. C., Fall 1948. "Ah, Sunflower": Alfred Kazin, ed., *The Portable Blake* (New York: Viking, 1946), p. 110. "This is what I . . . been existing in": A. G. in Kazin, *Writers*, p. 202. "The Sick Rose": Kazin, *Blake*, p. 107. "dream like and white . . . the nightingale at last": A. G. to N. C., Fall 1948. "We are inexistent until . . .": A. G. to J. K., Fall 1948.

1948 Election, current events: Robert Griffith, "Truman and the Historians," paper presented to the Organization of American Historians, April 1974. "an illusion of . . . conspiracy": Robert Griffith, *The Politics of Fear* (Lexington, Kentucky: University of Kentucky Press, 1970), p. 143. Films: Leslie Adler, "Red Fascism," pp. 427–429; Interview with J. C. H.; Norman Friedman, "American Movies and American Culture, 1946–1970," *Journal of Popular Culture* 3 (Spring 1970): pp. 815–824. Best sellers: Alice Payne Hackett, *Seventy Years of Best Sellers*, 1895–1965 (New York: R. R. Bowker Co., 1967), p. 179. Kerouac and politics: Holmes, *Declare*, p. 198; J. K. to J. C. H., November 18–19,

1948; Interview with J. C. H. *"Issues . . . issues . . .* kind of American existentialism": Ibid. "It's sort of furtiveness . . .": Holmes, *Declare,* p. 106. "You know . . . a beat generation": Jack Kerouac to Alfred G. Aronowitz, January 1959.

Fall 1948: Interview with J. C. H.; N. C. to J. K., October 4, 1948. Kerouac's experimental writing: Jack Kerouac Journal entry of November 29, 1948, in Andreas Brown, ed., *A Creative Century* (University of Texas Library Catalogue) (Austin, Texas, University of Texas, 1972), p. 17. "Well, I've decided . . .": as quoted in Holmes, *Go,* p. 9. Kerouac on Ginsberg: J. K. to A. G., December 15, 1948. *"fallen* angel . . . future fancy": A. G. to J. K., December 1948. Kerouac thinking of Cassady: Kerouac, *Cody,* p. 342.

Neal Cassady at Christmas 1949: Cassady, "Third Word," pp. 160–180; Holmes, *Declare,* p. 199; Kerouac, *Road* pp. 91–96; Kerouac, *Cody,* pp. 338–350. "Everything is fine, God . . . *Now!* . . . Now is the time . . .": Kerouac, *Road,* pp. 99, 100, 100. "That's right! That's right!": Holmes, *Declare,* p. 199. "Whither goest thou . . .": Kerouac, *Road,* p. 99. William Burroughs correspondence: W. S. B. to J. K. and A. G., June 5, 1948; W. S. B. to A. G., January 10, January 16, January 17, 1949, and Telegram, January 10, 1949. "Pull My Daisy": Jack Kerouac, *Scattered Poems* (San Francisco: City Lights Press, 1971), p. 6; Interview with A. G. "I didn't want to interfere . . . follow": Kerouac, *Road,* p. 110.

Trip to San Francisco: Ibid., pp. 110–142. "Don't worry 'bout . . .": Ibid., p. 116. "Factualism": W. S. B. to A. G., November 9, 1948. "Crime is simply . . .": Ibid. "If he does not feel . . .": W. S. B. to J. K., March 15, 1949. Mayan Calendar: Daniel Odier, *The Job: Interviews with William S. Burroughs* (New York: Grove Press, 1970), pp. 28–39. "He seems much more sensible . . .": W. S. B. to A. G., January 30, 1949. "And for just a moment . . .": Kerouac, *Road,* p. 142. Sale of "The Town and the City": J. K. to Ed White, March 29, 1949, as reproduced in *Mano-Mano* 2 (Summer 1971): no pagination. Talk with John C. Holmes: Interview with J. C. H. "I'd like to lay . . .": Holmes, *Go,* p. 208.

VII LITRICHUH AND THE ROLLING TRUCKS

Party: Interviews with L. C., A. G., H. H., and J. C. H. "just provincial French enough . . .": Interview with H. H. "vision haunted mind . . . sordidness of self": Allen Ginsberg, *Empty Mirror* (New York: Totem Press/Corinth Books, 1961), pp. 7, 9. "North polar fixed . . .": A. G., "Autobiographical Fragment for Psychiatrist," (1948). Allen Ginsberg and Herbert Huncke: Ibid.; Interviews with A. G., H. H., and J. C. H.; Kramer, *Ginsberg,* p. 225; Holmes, *Go,* pp. 220–240. "like a saint of old": Ginsberg, "Autobiographical Fragment." Burroughs on Huncke: W.S.B. to A.G.,: January 30, 1949. William Burroughs' arrest: Confidential source; Burroughs, *Junkie,* pp. 85–115; W. S. B. to A. G., March 26, April 13, 16, 1949. "Besides, if you really . . .": Ginsberg, "Autobiographical Fragment."

Allen Ginsberg arrest: Ginsberg, "Autobiographical Fragment"; Kramer, *Ginsberg,* pp. 225–226; A. G. to J. K., undated (May 1949); "Wrong Way Auto Tips Off Police," New York *World Journal,* April 22, 1949, p. 1; "Wrong Way Turn Clears Up Robbery," *New York Times,* April 22, 1949, p. 1. "But really, why get . . . the window": Holmes, *Go,* p. 235; Interview with A. G. Cassady on Kerouac and Huncke: N. C. to J. K., June 1949, Kerouac's move to Colorado: J. K. to A. G., May 23, July 5, 1949; J. K. to J. C.

H., June 24, July 26, 1949; A. G. to J. K., June 13, June 15, 1949; A. G. Journal, May 23, 1949. "Yeats' Plotinus-inspired . . .": J. C. H. to A. G., July 6, 1949.

Allen Ginsberg in "bughouse": Kramer, *Ginsberg,* pp. 128–130; Ginsberg, "Sunshine Interview," p. 20; A. G. to J. K., June 17, July 13, 1949; J. K. to A. G., June 10, July 5, 1949; A. G. to N. C., May 20, 1949. "confused and impotent . . .": A. G. to N. C., June 10, 1949. "I'm Prince Myshkin . . . Kirillov": Ginsberg, "Sunshine Interview," p. 20. "herded around . . .": W. S. B. to J. K., June 24, 1949. Kerouac's reaction to Ginsberg's situation: J. K. to A. G., June 10, July 5, and July 26, 1949. Giroux visit to Colorado: J. K. to J. C. H., June 24, 1949; J. K. to P. W., November 18, 1963; Kerouac, *Cody,* p. 292. Cassady's pleas for help: N.C. to J.K., July 16, 1949. "Go thou, die hence . . .": Kerouac, *Cody,* p. 295.

Kerouac's San Francisco visit: Cassady, "Third Word," pp. 244–261; Kerouac, *Road,* pp. 148–170; Interview with C. C. "Jack! I didn't . . . fell apart in me": Kerouac, *Road,* p. 150. "Holy Goof": Ibid., p. 160. "Entirely irresponsible to the . . .": Kerouac, *Cody,* pp. 356–357. "But now he's alive . . . fault of God": Kerouac, *Road,* p. 161. San Francisco to New York: Ibid., pp. 170–201; Kerouac, *Cody,* pp. 355–374. "the ideal state of . . .": W. S. B. to J. K., September 26, 1949.

"On the Road" as a Denver businessman: J. K. to A. G., February 26, 1950. Burroughs on Reich: W. S. B. to A. G., December 24, 1949, May 1, 1950. Burroughs on politics: Ibid. "every conceivable diversion": W.S.B. to A.G., September 26, 1949. "the only columnist in my . . .": W. S. B. to A. G., December 24, 1949. "sniveling, mealymouthed tyranny": W. S. B. to J. K., January 1, 1950. Kinsey: Francis Sill Wickware, "Report on Kinsey," *Life,* August 24, 1948, pp. 86–92. "Proofs Book One . . .": Robert Giroux to J. K. via telegram, November 1, 1949, at Harcourt, Brace, Jovanovich. Kerouac's "love letter" to Ginsberg: J. K. to A. G., January 13, 1950. "Decade of Parties": Holmes, *Declare,* p. 217. "us by a commodious . . . longing for": J. K. to Charley Sampas, December 27, 1949, as published in the Lowell *Sun,* October 23, 1969, p. 45.

Alger Hiss trial: Allen Weinstein, "The Symbolism of Subversion," *Journal of American Studies* 6 (no dates): pp. 165–179; Griffith, *Politics of Fear,* pp. 43–50. "general annihilation beckons": Albert Einstein, as quoted in Goldman, *Decade,* p. 137. New Critics: Murray Krieger, *The New Apologists for Poetry* (Minneapolis, Minnesota: University of Minnesota Press, 1956), passim; Bruce Franklin, "The Teaching of Literature in the Empire," *College English,* March 1970, pp. 548–557; Malcolm Cowley, "T.S. Eliot's Ardent Critics—and Mr. Eliot," New York *Herald Tribune* Book Review, March 13, 1949, p. 1; Daniel Aaron, "Review of Spiller, et al's, *Literary History of the U.S.,*" *American Quarterly* 1 (Spring 1959): pp. 169–173.

"almost a major . . . unreadable": "War and Peace," *Newsweek,* March 13, 1950, p. 80. "a rough diamond . . . exaggerated": John Brooks, "Of Growth and Decay," *New York Times Book Review,* March 5, 1950, p. 6. "radically deficient . . . treated": Howard Mumford Jones, "Back to Merrimack," *Saturday Review,* March 11, 1950, p. 18. "ponderous, shambling . . . tiresome": "Briefly Noted," *New Yorker,* March 25, 1950, p. 115. "after midnight in voices . . .": Norman Mailer, "Up the Family Tree," *Partisan Review* 35 (Spring 1968): p. 236. Kerouac's visit to Lowell: Interviews with Jim Sampas, Roland Salvas, and Tony Sampas; Charles Sampas, "Sampascoopies," Lowell *Sun,* March 19, 1950, p. 35.

Kerouac as fraud like Vautrin: J. K. to J. C. H., June 23, 1963. "Christ is at our . . .": J. K. to A. G., February 26, 1950. *Neurotica* and Jay Landesman: Holmes, *Declare,*

p. 17; Jay Landesman to Alfred G. Aronowitz, July 9, 1959; A. G. to J. K., March–April 1950. "drawing rooms full of . . .": Holmes, *Go,* p. 122. Kerouac's feelings on *Town and City:* "blurb," *Publisher's Weekly,* March 2, 1950, p. 146; J. K. to A. G., April 1950; J. K. to J. C. H., May 1–3, 1950; J. K. to Jim Sampas, August 1, 1950, in possession of Jim Sampas.

Denver-Mexico trip: J. K. to N. C., December 14, 1950; Kerouac, *Cody,* pp. 375–390; Kerouac, *Road,* pp. 204–250. "like a burning shuddering . . . Hot damn! . . . lazy and tender . . . There's no *suspicion* . . . *Sí, sí, dormiendo* . . .": Ibid., pp. 211, 220, 224–225, 241, 226. "Fellaheen eternal . . . straightforwardness": Kerouac, *Cody,* p. 88. "completely and godlikely aware . . .": Ibid., p. 298. Cassady's marriage to Diana Hansen: Cassady, "Third Word," p. 300; N. C. to J. K., July 22, 1950; Kerouac, *Cody,* p. 390; Interview with C. C.

Mexico City visit: Ibid., p. 96; J. K. to A. G., June 27, 1950; J. K. to Jim Sampas, August 1, 1950, in possession of Jim Sampas; J. K. to J. C. H., July 11–12, 1950. "Great Walking Saint": Ibid. "We are doomed . . .": Ibid. Writing in the Fall of 1950: Interview with J. C. H.; Kerouac, *Cody,* p. 24. Godly state: J. K. to A. G., October 1950. "I'm a man, I'm . . .": A. G. to J. K., June 8, 1950. "to destroy all in your . . .": A. G. to J. K., October 1950. "the sheer ecstasy of utterly . . .": N. C. to A. G., November 25, 1950.

Bill Cannastra: Holmes, *Go,* p. 21; Kerouac, "The Art of Fiction," pp. 75–76; John C. Holmes "Interview," Knight, *Beat Diary,* p. 51; "Climb from Subway for Drink Kills Rider": New York *Daily News,* October 12, 1950, p. 2. "tantalizing aura of doom": Holmes, *Go,* p. 21. "Do you want me . . .": Kerouac, "The Art of Fiction," pp. 75–76. "a couple of collaborations . . .": Jack Kerouac to Alfred G. Aronowitz, January 1959. Joan Haverty and marriage: Interviews with J. C. H., L. C., A.G., and H. H.; J. K. to N. C., December 14, 1950; N. C. to J. K., December 5, 1950; Joan Haverty Kerouac, "My Ex-Husband, Jack Kerouac, Is an Ingrate," *Confidential,* August 1961, pp. 18, 53–57. "full of youth and . . .": J. C. H. to A. G., December 12, 1950. "without real sadness . . . of the night": A. G. to N. C., December 18, 1950. "true peasant . . . to see this": N. C. to A. G., November 25, 1950.

Neal Cassady's visit to New York: Cassady, "Third Word," p. 281; J. K. to A. G., January 11, 1951; Kerouac, *Road,* p. 251; Interview with J. C. H. "frosty fagtown New York": N. C. to J. K., January 8, 1951. Cassady's letters: N. C. to J. K., September 25, 1950, February 6, 1951; N. C. to A. G., November 15, 25, 1950. "SO HORRIBLY . . .": As quoted in Cassady, "Third Word," p. 332. "At any particular time . . .": N. C. to A. G., November 25, 1950. "reads with spew and rush . . .": A. G. to N. C., December 18, 1950.

Writing of *On the Road:* Joan Kerouac, "My Husband," p. 55; J. K. to J. C. H., May 16, 1963; Interviews with J.C. H., A. G., and L. C., John C. Holmes Interview in Knight, *Beat Book,* p. 40. "I shambled after . . .": Kerouac, *Road,* p. 9, "rueful work of a wounded . . . Boddhisattva prophet": Interview with A. G., "He didn't know . . . yet": Interview with J. C. H. "the writing is dewlike . . .": A. G. to N. C., May 7, 1951.

Retyping *On the Road:* Interviews with A. G., J. C. H., and L. C.; N.C. to A.G., May 15, 1951; J. K. to J. C. H., July 14, 1951. "He is afraid to foretell . . .": A. G. to N. C., May 7, 1951. "crooked road of prophecy": J. K. to J. C. H., July 14, 1951. "the sales manager would not . . . like Dostoyevsky": J. K. to P. W., November 18, 1963.

Separation from Joan Kerouac: Joan Kerouac, "My Husband," p. 56; Interviews with J. C. H. and L. C.; Joan Kerouac to J. K., August 8, 1951, in possession of Eugene Brooks.

Summer 1951: N. C. to J. K., June 20, August 25, 1951. Summer Reading, 1951: J. K. to J. C. H., July 14, 1951; J. K. to A. G., July 16, 1951. "I want deep form . . .": Holmes, *Declare*, p. 78.

VIII THE BREAKTHROUGH

Bobby Thomson: John Drebinger, "Giants Capture Pennant, Beating Dodgers 5–4 in 9th on Thomson's 3-Run Homer," *New York Times,* October 4, 1951, p. 1. "trembled with joy and . . .": Kerouac, "Origins," p. 179. Kerouac's love for October: J. K. to J. C. H., June 1963. Source of writing changes, stay in VA Hospital and Lee Konitz: Ibid.; Kerouac, "The Art of Fiction," p. 66. "Blow as Deep . . .": Interview with J. C. H.; Jack Kerouac, "Belief and Technique for Modern Prose," in Robert Creeley and Donald Allen, eds., *The New American Story* (New York: Grove Press, 1965), p. 269. Ed White and concept of sketching: J. K. to A. G., May 16, 1952; A. G. Journal, June 1953.

Influence of Neal's letters: J. K. to Alfred G. Aronowitz, January 22, 1960. Wilhelm Reich: Interview with A. G. Yeats: J. K. to A. G., May 16, 1952. Movies in abstract: J. K. to J. C. H., June 1963. Origins in *Town and City:* Interview with A. G. "Time is of the essence": A. G. Journal, June 1953. Honesty in writing: J. K. to A. G., May 16, 1952. "the direct approach . . .": John Crowe Ransom, "Glossary of the New Criticism," *Poetry,* February 1951, p. 155. "When you depend entirely . . .": R. P. Blackmur, Ibid., p. 161. "pathetic, laconic, no great . . .": Harrison Smith, "The Young Generation," *Saturday Review,* December 1, 1951, p. 13.

Diner, movie theater sketches: Kerouac, *Cody,* pp. 3, 5, 10, 11, 16, 19, 31. "the flash of their mouths . . . I dig jazz . . . a great rememberer . . .": Ibid., pp. 7, 40, 103. Leaving Richmond Hill, *President Adams,* Cru, San Diego: Ibid., pp. 92–114; Jack Kerouac, "Piers of the Homeless Night," in *Lonesome,* pp. 1–16. Return to San Francisco to teach Neal: J. K. to J. C. H., July 14, 1951.

"You see, she was a . . . I caught her with . . .": Cassady, "Third Word," p. 409. Life at 29 Russell St.: Interview with C. C.; Cassady, "Third Word," pp. 402–477; J. K. to A. G., May 10, 1952. February 8, 1952: Interview with C. C.; Cassady, "Third Word," pp. 417–421; Kerouac, *Cody,* p. 331. Kerouac's affair with Carolyn Cassady: Interview with C. C.; Cassady, "Third Word," pp. 421–432. "My best gal . . . I thought it would be nice": Ibid., p. 427. "Remember when we . . . should have": Ibid., p. 432. "tender and considerate lover": Interview with C. C.

"mind would add extra . . .": Cassady, "Third Word," p. 91. "engulfed in ideas": N. C. to A. G., May 15, 1951. Taped conversations, February-March 1952: Kerouac, *Cody,* pp. 127–244. "You're not going to get . . . sadness of it all": Ibid., p. 156. Analysis of *Visions of Cody:* Interview with A. G.; Ginsberg, *Visions of the Great Rememberer,* passim. "the art lies in . . .": Ibid., p. 14. Neal's prediction of historians: N. C. to J. K., June 20, 1951.

Pat Henry and life in the Russell St. attic: J. K. to J. C. H., June 17, 1952. "crazy dumbsaint . . . of the individual": Kerouac, "Belief and Technique," p. 269. "Begin not from . . .": Jack Kerouac, "Essentials of Spontaneous Prose," in Robert Creeley and Donald Allen, *The New American Story* (New York: Grove Press, 1965), p. 271. Shape in writing rather than form: Interview with Michael McClure.

"like bop, we're getting . . .": Kerouac, *Cody,* p. 296. Shed Hammett-Burroughs: J. K. to N. C., April 1955. "not so much concerned with . . .": Holmes, *Declare,* p. 69. "What I'm beginning to discover . . .": Ibid., p. 81. "Jackie Kerouac, 6–B . . . let me tell the story": Kerouac, *Cody,* pp. 249, 251. "dream golden, not . . . about the wonders of . . . instinctive communication . . . the red brick wall . . .": Ibid., pp. 249, 258, 258, 279. "Mind is shapely . . .": Allen Ginsberg, "Notes on Having Finally Recorded *Howl,*" in Thomas Parkinson, *A Casebook on the Beat* (New York: Thomas Y. Crowell Co., 1961), p. 28.

"you muster up . . . the death of Hollywood . . .": Kerouac, *Cody,* pp. 281–282. On the movie *Sudden Fear:* Lawrence J. Quirk, *The Films of Joan Crawford* (New York: The Citadel Press, 1969), p. 182. "Homeric warrior . . . baby food, come . . . the leader . . . empty-minded, vacant . . . great spindly tin-like . . . King": Kerouac, Cody, pp. 303, 304, 304, 318–19, 353, 377.

"an athlete of . . .": Unpublished poem by Michael McClure. [It should be noted that Kenneth Rexroth linked Beat with Parker and Pollock in "Disengagement: The Art of the Beat Generation." The idea had occurred to me well before I saw this essay, and my development of it is radically different.] Charlie Parker: Frank Kofsky, *Black Nationalism,* pp. 15–43; Ross Russell, *Bird Lives,* passim; Interview with Max Roach. "naked passions . . . romanticism": Kofsky, *Black Nationalism,* p. 30. "the style was not . . .": Russell, *Bird Lives,* p. 182.

Jackson Pollock: B. H. Friedman, *Energy Made Visible* (New York: McGraw-Hill Book Co., 1972), passim; Bernice Rose, *Jackson Pollock: Works on Paper* (Greenwich, Conn.: New York Graphic Society Ltd., 1969), passim. "Technic is the result . . .": Rose, *Pollock,* p. 16. "artist of genius": Jack Kerouac, "Are Writers Made or Born," *Writer's Digest,* January 1961, p. 14. "Experience of our age": Rose, *Pollock,* p. 16. "He sensed rhythm . . .": Lee Krassner in Friedman, *Energy,* p. 181. Art as process: Interview with Robert Creeley. "the only creative thing . . .": Friedman, *Energy,* p. 88. Pollock and concept of accident: Rose, *Pollock,* p. 66. "in the painting": Friedman, *Energy,* p. 77.

Kerouac at maturity: J. K. to J. C. H., March 12, 1952. "the perfect executive . . .": Allen Ginsberg in "The Craft Interview," *New York Quarterly* 6 (Spring 1971): p. 15. "You'll come to death . . . memory and dream . . . I was born . . . now it's atom bombs . . . part of a general . . . the enigma of . . . something secretively wild . . .": Kerouac, *Sax,* pp. 202–3, 5, 17, 76, 22, 28, 102.

Sources of *Dr. Sax:* J. K. to J. C. H., June 1963. "nothing works in the . . . the universe disposes . . . something that can't . . .": Kerouac, *Sax,* pp. 240, 245, 180. "losses and exasperations": J. C. H. to J. K., May 1963.

"I think Jack is . . .": A. G. Journal, April 13, 1953. "so passionately did I . . .": Holmes, *Declare,* p. 82. Kerouac's attitude on editing: J. K. to J. C. H., March 12, 1952. Thoughts of a breakdown: J. K. to A. G., March 12, 1952. "Whore Whore Whore": A. G. to N. C. and J. K., February 15, 1952. Kerouac on John C. Holmes: J. K. to A. G., April 8, 1952. Joan Haverty: Ibid. Phil White: Interview with H. H.

"should be more connected to . . .": A. G. to N. C. and J. K., February 15, 1952. "You *must* have a . . .": William Carlos Williams to A. G., February 27, 1952; Kramer, *Ginsberg,* pp. 134–135. "eavesdroppings on my . . .": A. G., "Introduction to 'Empty Mirror,'" undated typescript (Texas).

Kerouac's reaction to "Empty Mirror": J. K. to A. G., March 15, 1952. Kerouac lectures on spontaneous prose: Ibid. "you are the wisest of . . .": C. C. to A. G., April

8, 1952. "make love to wife . . .": N. C. to A. G., May 20, 1952. Peyote and materialism: J. K. to A. G., May 10, 1952; Cassady, "Third Word," pp. 452–453. "The Mysteries of America": J. K. to J. C. H., March 12, 1952. "so big, so sad . . .": Kerouac, *Lonesome*, p. 17.

IX   AMONG THE FELLAHEEN OF MEXICO AND MANHATTAN

Mexico: Jack Kerouac, "Mexico Fellaheen," in *Lonesome*, pp. 24–37. "My name is Enrique . . . get high? . . . We'll take the snake . . . the Earth is an . . .": Ibid., pp. 26, 26, 28, 22. "world citizens, world pacifists . . .": N. C. to J. C. H., November 20, 1950. "timeless gaiety . . ." and pure land: Kerouac, *Lonesome*, pp. 22, 24.

Panchos: Kerouac, *Road*, p. 230. "we would be as poor . . .": Ibid., p. 246. "the essential strain of the . . .": Ibid., p. 229. "with the Indians . . .": N. C. to A. G., July 10, 1952. "African world fellaheen . . .": Kerouac, *Lonesome*, p. 22.

AEC, deodorants: *Life*, May 17, 1952, passim. "it makes not one . . .": N. C. to A. G., July 10, 1952. Politics: I. F. Stone, *The Haunted Fifties* (New York: Vintage Books, 1969), pp. 14–77; Robert Griffith, "Truman and the Historians," p. 10. Korea: "Truce Beam Casts Ironic Light," *Life*, July 24, 1952, p. 39. Atlantic Records: Charles Gillett, *Making Tracks* (New York: E. P. Dutton Co., 1974), p. 51.

Laws against: Kerouac, *Lonesome*, p. 21. Kerouac worried about Burroughs, his own divorce: J. K. to A. G., May 10, 1952. Joan Vollmer Burroughs' death: Interviews with A. G. and L. C.; A. G. to N. C., September 7, 1951; William Burroughs, Jr., "Life with Father," p. 113. "Heir's Pistol Kills His Wife": New York *Daily News*, September 8, 1951, p. 3. "wealthy cotton grower": Ibid. "I have been laying . . . correct": W. S. B. to A. G., undated (1951). "the problems and difficulties . . .": W. S. B. to A. G., December 20, 1951. "sexuality back somewhere . . .": as quoted in W. S. B. to J. K., March 26, 1952. Lewis Marker, "Queer": W. S. B. to A. G., June 4, 1952.

"nothing else to do": William Burroughs in Kazin, *Writers*, p. 145. "the excerpts from your . . .": W. S. B. to J. K., April 3, 1952. Kerouac as "Factualist": J. K. to A. G., undated (1951). Kerouac's reaction to Burroughs, life at 212 Orizaba St.: J. K. to A. G., May 10, 1952; J. K. to N. C. and C. C., May 27, 1952. "He has developed . . .": W. S. B. to A. G., May 15, 1952.

Burroughs and junk: Burroughs, *Junkie*, p. 122. "I got the horrors . . . grown inside it": Ibid., 133. "Ah, I feel awful, I . . .": W. S. B. as quoted in J. K. to J. C. H., June 3, 1952. "Wig": J. K. to C. C., June 3, 1952. *Dr. Sax* as a vision from shroud: J. K. to A. G., May 18, 1952; *A Bibliography of Works by Jack Kerouac*, Ann Charters, compiler (New York: Phoenix Book Shop, 1967), p. 13. Brothels: J. K. to N. C., June 3, 1952.

Kerouac's book plans: J. K. to A. G., May 18, 1952. "Hold Your Horn High": J. K. to J. C. H., June 3, 1952. "Blow baby blow!": Cassady, "Third Word," pp. 497. June 1952 plans: J. K. June 3, 1952. Kerouac's feeling of blankness with Neal, and advice to him: A. G. to C. C., July 1952; J. K. to C. C., June 3, 1952. "terrified of going into . . . clean up messes": A. G. to J. K., May 15, 1952. "I don't see . . . put down, man?": A. G. to J. K. and W. S. B., June 12, 1952. "A holy mess . . . how far you can go": A. G. to N. C., July 3, 1952.

Carl Solomon: Interview with A. G.; Interview with Carl Solomon in Knights, *Beat Book*, pp. 88–101. "I have not been mad . . . many realities": Carl Solomon, *Mishaps*,

Perhaps (San Francisco: City Lights Press, 1966), pp. 20, 13. "loss of respect for . . . undertipped head waiter": Carl Solomon to J. K., December 13 [1951] (Columbia). "a jackass . . . royal house": Carl Solomon to J. K., February 6 [1952].

Kerouac response to Ginsberg on *On the Road:* J. K. to A. G., June 20, 1952. "usually surly . . . insufferable": W. S. B. to A. G., August 20, 1952. "paranoid": W. S. B. to A. G., July 13, 1952. "uncut kick that . . . final fix": Burroughs, *Junkie*, p. 149. Kerouac's visit to chapel: Kerouac, *Lonesome*, pp. 34–36. "We are good . . . forgive him": W. S. B. to A. G., September 5, 1952.

"We are but poor . . . we weren't ever": A. G. Journal, July 18, 1952. Kerouac in Rocky Mt. and his return to San Francisco: J. K. to J. C. H., October 12, 1952; N. C. to J. K., August 27, September 2, 1952; Cassady, "Third Word," p. 517. Kerouac quarrels with Cassadys: N. C. to A. G., October 4, 1952, and J. K. to A. G., November 8, 1952. "quite a few people . . .": A. G. Journal, October 1952. Kerouac spite letter to Ginsberg: J. K. to A. G., October 8, 1952. October 1952 in San Francisco: Jack Kerouac, "October in the Railroad Earth," in *Lonesome*, pp. 35–78. "Energy for sex . . . working to pluck . . . commuters of American . . . end of land sadness": Ibid., pp. 46, 77, 37, 37.

Kerouac on Holmes loan, *Go:* J. K. to J. C. H., October 12, 1952; Interview with J. C. H. "lost children of the night": Holmes, *Go*, p. 17. "nakedness of mind . . . resources on a single number": John C. Holmes, "This is the Beat Generation," as published in *Declare*, p. 110. Letters to editor about "This is the . . .": Interview with J. C. H. Kerouac on article: J. K. to J. C. H., December 9, 1952. Invites Carolyn to Mexico, Neal's reaction: Interview with C. C.; Cassady, "Third Word," pp. 344–350. Kerouac's thanks to Ginsberg: J. K. to A. G., November 8, 1952. Visit to Mexico: J. K. to J. C. H., December 9, 1952; J. K. to N. C. and C. C., December 1952. "All hung up . . . but (no?) wiser": A. G. to N. C., January 1953. Kerouac's reaction to friends in New York: J. K. to N. C. and C. C., January 10, 1953.

Maggie Cassidy as Proustian love story: J. K. to C. C., February 1953; Charters, *Bibliography*, p. 15. "before the war . . . would turn mad . . . with just a touch . . . death is sweet": Kerouac, *Maggie*, pp. 7, 23, 31, 34. Spring 1953: J. K. to C. C., March 20, 1953. Blurb for *Junkie:* J. K. to A. G., February 21, 1953; J. K. to J. C. H., March 9, 1953; Interviews with A. G. and J. C. H. "yours most respectfully and in . . .": A. G. to J. K., February 24, 1953. "a learned vicious, Goering . . .": A. G. Journal, April 15, 1953. San Luis Obispo, thoughts of Thoreauvian life: J. K. to A. G., May 7, 1953. "loneliness angel": Jack Kerouac, *The Subterraneans* (New York: Grove Press, 1958), p. 4. Voyage of the *Carruth:* Jack Kerouac, "Slobs of the Kitchen Sea," in *Lonesome*, pp. 80–111. "sparkle glow . . . gut joy": Ibid., p. 88. Fear of alcoholism and "inability to be gracious . . .": Kerouac, *Subterraneans*, p. 4.

TV: Peter C. Rollins, "Victory at Sea: Cold War Epic," *Journal of Popular Culture* 3 (Spring 1973): pp. 463–482. "I Believe": Hughson F. Mooney, "Songs, Singers, and Society," *American Quarterly* 3 (Fall 1954): pp. 221–232. "Rosenbergs are pathetic . . .": A. G. to N. C., June 23, 1953. "Power of Attorney for Allen Ginsberg from Jack Kerouac," June 30, 1953. "You are right . . .": M. C. to A. G., July 14, 1953. Publishing difficulties: Interviews with M. C. and A. G.; A. G. to J. K., October 8, 1953.

"Mardou Fox" is a fictitious name. Kerouac affair with Mardou Fox: Kerouac, *Subterraneans*, passim; Interviews with Mardou Fox, L. C., and A. G. "What are you reading . . . hip without being . . . big paranoic bum . . . strange intellectual . . . Yeah

well they never . . . and of junkies man . . . buy this brooch . . . a great electrical . . .
happening all the time . . . so hip, so cool . . . eyes for that hysterical . . . city decadent
intellectual . . . I thought I saw . . . sweetly but nonetheless . . .": Kerouac, *Subterraneans,*
pp. 9, 2, 9, 9, 40, 40, 32, 42, 42, 69, 56, 79, 63, 65. Kerouac as lover: Interviews with C.
C., Mardou Fox, A. G., L. C., and Dody Müller.

Gregory Corso biography: Corso in Knights, *Beat Book,* p. 26; G. C. to A. G.,
undated (1958). "a refinement of beauty . . .": Allen Ginsberg, Introduction to *Gasoline,*
by Gregory Corso (San Francisco: City Lights Press, 1957), p. 7. "parental hydra, as it
were": Gregory Corso, "When I was Five I Saw a Dying Indian," *Evergreen Review,*
August 1967, p. 29. Corso jail terms: Gregory Corso "Biography," in Donald Allen, ed.,
The New American Poetry (New York: Grove Press, 1960), p. 429; Gregory Corso in
remarks at "Kerouac Symposium," Salem State College. Meeting of Corso and Ginsberg:
Interviews with A. G. and G. C. "Why, I know her . . .": Interview with A. G.; Kramer,
Ginsberg, p. 138. "her little girl-like . . .": Kerouac, *Subterraneans,* p. 94. End of affair:
Ibid., pp. 117–141.

"A Baudelaire's poem . . .": Ibid., p. 13. "Three full moon . . .": Charters, *Bibliogra-*
phy, p. 8. "redeemed": Kerouac, *Subterraneans,* p. 25. Kerouac feared her vagina: Ibid.,
pp. 104–105. "And I go home . . .": Ibid., p. 152.

Lost weight writing: Kerouac, "The Art of Fiction," p. 90. William Burroughs visit:
Interviews with A. G., L.C., and W. S. B. "astounded, horrified, and pruriently . . .":
Interview with A. G. Burroughs' journey: William Burroughs and Allen Ginsberg, *The*
Yage Letters (San Francisco: City Lights Press, 1968), pp. 1–45. "whores and pimps and
hustlers . . . as a bad boy": Ibid., pp. 8, 8, 14, 17, 42. "Essentials of Spontaneous·Prose":
Charters, *Bibliography,* p. 53. "were ultimately going to schlup . . .": Kramer, *Ginsberg,*
p. 138.

Post dinner address: J. K. to A. G., and W. S. B., November 21, 1953. Earlier negative
comments on Gore Vidal: J. K. to A. G., May 16, 1952. Encounter with Vidal: Kerouac,
Subterraneans, pp. 73–74; A. G. to N. C., September 4, 1953; Gore Vidal, *Two Sisters*
(Boston: Little, Brown, 1970), p. 213. "Boastfully queerlike . . .": A. G. to N. C.,
September 4, 1953.

X THE DHARMA ROAD

Throwing the I Ching: Holmes, *Declare,* p. 57; A. G. Journal, July 27, 1953. "as
Byron saw ruins . . . solitude of jungles": A. G. to N. C., December 1953. Kerouac,
Cassady, Ginsberg plans: J. K. to N. C., and J. K. to N. C. and C. C., December 10, 25,
1953, and J. K. to N. C. and C.C., January 25, 1954, and J. K. to C. C., December 3,
1953, and N. C. to J. K., December 4, 1953, and A. G. to N. C., November 14, 1953.
Kerouac's dreams: Jack Kerouac, *Book of Dreams* (San Francisco: City Lights Press, 1960),
pp. 11–12. "sheepish guilty idiot turning out . . .": Ibid., p. 20. Kerouac attitude to
publishers: J. K. to C. C., December 3, 1953.

"Repose Beyond Fate": Jack Kerouac, "The Last Word," *Escapade,* October 1959,
p. 112. "and saw golden swarms . . .": Ibid. "Existence is suffering . . . eight fold path":
William McGovern, *An Introduction to Mahayana Buddhism* (New York: E. P. Dutton
Co., 1922), pp. 160–174. The wheel, mythology: Ibid. "all composite things are . . .":
"Gatha of Impermanence," in D. T. Suzuki, *Manual of Zen Buddhism* (New York: Grove

Press, 1960), p. 15. "Pursue not the outer . . .": "On Belief in Mind," Ibid., p. 4. Kerouac's Buddhist practice: Kerouac, "The Art of Fiction," pp. 84–85. "hearts and flowers . . . imaginative part . . . Edgar Guest sensibilities": Interview with P. W. Media articles on Buddhism: *Reader's Guide to Periodical Literature* (New York: H. W. Wilson Co., 1944–1954), passim; "Temple Gardens," *House and Garden,* April 1952, p. 94; "Brooklyn Buddhist," *Life,* March 18, 1950, p. 14. Allen Ginsberg and Chinese art: A. G. to N. C., May 14, 1953.

Neal Cassady and Edgar Cayce: Interview with C. C.; Cassady, "Third Word," pp. 584–587. Kerouac at San Jose Library: Interviews with A. G. and C. C. "All composite things are . . .": *Diamond Sutra,* Dwight Goddard, *A Buddhist Bible* (New York: E. P. Dutton Co., 1938), p. 50. Religious arguments between Kerouac and Cassady: Cassady, "Third Word," pp. 580–600. "But a *soul,* man . . . nothin' . . . period": Ibid., pp. 590, 626. "the sound of silence . . .": Kerouac, *Angels,* p. 77. A matter of cosmic style: J. K. to A. G., March 1954. Kerouac on Cayce as dualistic fraud: Ibid.

Departure from Cassady home and "San Francisco Blues," Cameo: Jack Kerouac, *Scattered Poems,* ed. by Ann Charters (San Francisco: City Lights Press, 1971), p. 65; N. C. to A. G., April 23, 1954; J. K. to A. G., May 1954. Kerouac decision on where to go: J. K. to A. G., March 1954. "stone cocks a thousand . . .": A. G. to N. C. and C. C., January 1954. "long sinister pagan candles": A. G. to N.C., C. C., and J. K., March 4, 1954. Ginsberg's physical and spiritual growth in Mexico: Picture at Columbia; Maurice Lin, "Children of Adam: Ginsberg, Ferlinghetti and Snyder in the Emerson-Whitman Tradition" (Ph. D. dissertation, University of Minnesota, 1973), p. 105. Kerouac's lessons on Buddhism to Ginsberg: J. K. to A. G., May 1954. "—lights out . . . dead stop trance": Kerouac, *Scattered,* p. 27. Kerouac and literary business in May 1954: J. K. to A. G., May 1954. "monotonous and probably without . . .": Mark Van Doren, as quoted in Ibid.

Kerouac and Joseph McCarthy: Interview with L. C. McCarthyism: see Robert Griffith, *The Politics of Fear: Joseph R. McCarthy and the Senate* (Lexington, Kentucky: University of Kentucky Press, 1970); Michael Paul Rogin, *The Intellectuals and McCarthy* (Cambridge, Massachusetts: M.I.T. Press, 1967); Athan Theoharis, *Seeds of Repression* (Chicago: Quadrangle Books, 1971). Suburbia: Goldman, *Decade,* pp. 263–281; "The Lush New Suburban Market," *Fortune,* September 1953, pp. 105–112. Popular books: Hackett, *Seventy,* p. 195. "I snapped the side . . .": Mickey Spillane, *The Big Kill* (New York: Signet Press, 1951), p. 41. Kerouac on Spillane: J. K. to A. G., April 8, 1952. Committee for Cultural Freedom: Christopher Lasch, "The Cultural Cold War: A Short History of the Committee for Cultural Freedom," in Bernstein, *Towards a New Past* (New York: Vintage Books, 1969), passim.

"McCarthy's got the real . . .": Interview with L. C. Kerouac on Al Hinkle's radicalism: J. K. to A. G., August 23, 1954. "I feel sickened by the . . .": Kerouac, *Dreams,* p. 85. On writing of "cityCityCITY:" J. K. to A. G., July 14, 1955; Jack Kerouac, "cityCityCITY," in LeRoi Jones, ed., *The Moderns* (New York: Corinth Books, 1963), pp. 250–265. "carefully cultivated for years . . .": Ibid., p. 264. "you dirty whore": Interview with L. C., Sterling Lord: Interview with A. G. "Trust in the Lord": Ibid. Cowley assistance: J. K. to A. G., August 23, 1954; Interview with M. C. "unpublished narrative 'On . . .'": Malcolm Cowley, "Invitation to Innovators," *Saturday Review,* August 21, 1954, p. 38.

Kerouac as Taoist: J. K. to A. G., July 30, 1954. "to see the world from . . .": Kerouac, *Angels,* p. 230. Kerouac shows manuscript to Corso and Fox: J. K. to A. G., July 30, 1954. "was very straight, it wasn't . . .": Gregory Corso in Knights, *Beat Diary,* p. 14. "A Dream

Already Ended" and "Little Sutra": J. K., dated 1954 (Columbia). Kerouac and Cassadys: J. K. to N. C. and C. C., April 23, 1954; J. K. to C. C., July 2, 1954. Kerouac on Rorschach Test: J. K. to C. C., August 26, 1954. Ginsberg evicted by Carolyn Cassady: A. G. to J. K., September 7, 1954. Kerouac's reply: J. K. to C. C., August 26, 1954. Carolyn Cassady apologizes: C. C. to A. G., September 20, 1954. Allen living a "straight" life: A. G. to J. K., September 7, 1954. Burroughs and Ginsberg and Kerouac: Kerouac, *Angels*, p. 322; W. S. B. to J. K., April 22, May 4, September 3, 1954; J. K. to A. G., August 23, 1954; A. G. to N. C. and C. C., May 12, 1954; J. K. to A. G., October 26, 1954; A. G. to J. K., undated (September 1954), November 8, 1954; W. S. B. to J. K., December 7, 1954. "I say we are . . .": W. S. B. to J. K., May 24, 1954.

Visit to Lowell: Kerouac, *Angels*, pp. 49, 65; Interview with Jim Curtis. Ginsberg's visit, Buddhist lectures: J. K. to A. G., October 26, November 24, December 7, 1954; A. G. to J. K., November 26, 1954; Interviews with A. G. and Eugene Brooks. Taste buds and Buddha: J. K. to C. C., August 26, 1954. "golgotha-robot-eternal . . .": A. G. to J. K., November 8, 1954. Kerouac's dream of Walden: Kerouac, *Dreams*, p. 159. "AT THE LOWEST BEATEST . . . release his own mind": Jack Kerouac journal entry of December 19, 1954, published as "Jack Kerouac Tells the Truth," *Robert Lowry's Book U.S.A. 1* (Fall 1958): no pagination. Joan Haverty and paternity suit, and meditations after: J. K. to A. G., January 18, 1955; Interview with Eugene Brooks. Reaction of Kerouac after trial, and "Dhayana of Complete Understanding": J. K. to A. G., January 18, February 10, 1955.

Kerouac conciliates with Cassadys: J. K. to N. C., undated (late March 1955). Bird Parker's death: Interview with J. C. H; Russell, *Bird Lives!*, p. 300. Jack on Neal as writer: J. K. to A. G., January 18, 1955. "Buddha Tells Us": J. K. to A. G., April 20, 1955. Kerouac as great Buddhist writer: J. K. to A. G., April 20, 1955. Kerouac feels like Cézanne: J. K. to C. C., April 15, 1955. Publication: Charters, *Bibliography*, pp. 35, 52. "I guess you're going . . .": A. G. to J. K., May 10, 1955. On Ginsberg as Jewish writer: J. K. to A. G., May 11, 1955. Kerouac "past enlightenment": J. K. to A. G., May 20, 1955. Depressing spring, publishing news: J. K. to W. S. B., May 1955; J. K. to A. G., May 27, July 14, 1955. "You think you're God": Ibid. Visit to New York: J. K. to A. G., June 27, June 29, 1955. "thatched hut in Lowell": as quoted in J. K. to A. G., July 14, 1955. Ginsberg's plea to Kerouac: A. G. to J. K., June 1, 1955; J. K. to A. G., July 14, 1955.

Mexico City with Garver: J. K. to A. G., August 7, 1955. Writing "Mexico City Blues": Charters, *Bibliography*, p. 17. "jazz poet blowing a . . .": Jack Kerouac, *Mexico City Blues* (New York: Grove Press, 1959), no pagination. Analysis of *Mexico City Blues*: Interview with A. G. "in Jesus, Buddha . . . no direction to go . . . Dharma Law / . . . remove my name / . . . I get tired . . . the wheel of the quivering . . .": Ibid., 10th, 36th, 66th, 125th, 130th, 211th choruses. "a permissible dream": Ibid., 51st chorus.

"Born to Die": Jack Kerouac, *Tristessa* (New York: Avon Book Division, 1960), p. 40. "I am sad because . . . My Lord, he pay . . . Excuse . . .": Ibid., pp. 22, 31, 38. "resenting and resisting": Interview with A. G. "Hebraic-Melvillian bardic . . . a lament for the Lamb . . .": Allen Ginsberg, "Notes on *Howl*," pp. 27, 28. "I saw the best minds . . .": Allen Ginsberg, "Howl," from *Howl and Other Poems* (San Francisco: City Lights Press, 1956), pp. 3–27. "LET'S SHOUT . . . EARTHQUAKES": as quoted in Bruce Cook, *The Beat Generation* (New York: Charles Scribner's Sons, 1971), p. 27.

XI   A REVOLUTION OF PROPHECY AND LIVING THINGS

Jack on train: Jack Kerouac, *The Dharma Bums* (New York: Viking Press, 1958), pp. 3–6. "were about transcending . . . of experience": Interview with Paul Krassner. American culture, GNP: "Ten Amazing Years, 1947–1957," *U.S. News and World Report,* December 27, 1957, p. 78. "A Truman Democrat . . .": Stone, *Fifties,* p. 184. "perfect model of the . . .": Martha Saxton, *Jayne Mansfield* (Boston: Houghton-Mifflin Co., 1975), p. 130.

"written by an unemployed . . .": "Wanted: An American Novel," *Life,* September 12, 1955, p. 48. Hemingway and *Life:* James Steel Smith, *"Life* Looks at Literature," *Journal of Popular Culture* 6 (Fall 1972), p. 17. Literary scene and security: John Aldridge, *In Search of Heresy* (New York: McGraw-Hill Book Co., 1956), p. 6; Malcolm Cowley, *The Literary Situation* (New York: Viking Press, 1956), p. 14. "Thus, the arriving poet . . .": John Ciardi, "Poverty on Parnassus," *Saturday Review,* July 28, 1956, p. 8.

James Dean: Venable Herndon, *James Dean, A Short Life* (Garden City, New York: Doubleday and Co., 1974), passim. San Francisco: Kenneth Rexroth, in Charles Farkas, "A Whole World West of Yale" (Senior Honors Thesis, Princeton University, 1973), Chapter I, passim. Kerouac's ride to San Francisco: Jack Kerouac, "Good Blond," *Playboy,* January 1965, pp. 139–140. Peter Orlovsky: Ginsberg, "Sunshine Interview," passim; Kramer, *Ginsberg,* pp. 43–45; A. G. to J. K., December 29, 1954; Interview with A. G. Karamazov family: P. O. to A. G., January 22, 1958. "a big strange dumbbell . . .": Interview with A. G. "so goofy he lets . . .": J. K., as quoted in A. G. to Howard Schulman, October 16, 1961, as published in Knights, *The Beat Book,* p. 77. "a naked boy with his . . .": Ginsberg, "Sunshine Interview," p. 11. "I do, I do . . . eternal place": Ginsberg, "Sunshine Interview," p. 13. Kerouac blesses affair: J. K. to A. G., January 18, 1955. "Why don't you do . . . who will like you": Ginsberg, "Sunshine Interview," p. 12; Kramer, *Ginsberg,* p. 43.

Milvia St. cottage: Kerouac, *Bums,* p. 17. Six Gallery reading: Kerouac, *Bums,* pp. 14–16; Gary Snyder Interview in Knights, *The Beat Diary,* p. 143; Interviews with P. W., M. M., L. F., and A. G. "a cat with a flannel . . . this is all right": G. S. to Alfred G. Aronowitz, March 1959. "Six poets at Six . . .": Postcard on file in City Lights Press Collection, University of California at Berkeley, Berkeley, California. "a new and truly wild . . .": M. M. to Alfred G. Aronowitz, March 1959. "like bringing two ends . . .": Philip Lamantia in Farkas, "A Whole World West," p. 16. Cora Dubois, "The Dominant Value Profile of American Culture," *American Anthropologist* 57 (December 1955): pp. 1232–1239. Obedience and Civil Rights: H. H. Wilson, Civil Liberties in the U.S. Today," *The Political Quarterly* [London] 30 (April–June 1959): pp. 171–184. "Power is everywhere . . .": "Statement of Purpose," *Liberation,* March 1956, p. 3. Language: Howard Junker, "As They Used to Say in the Fifties," *Esquire,* August 1969, pp. 70–71. "voice was deep and . . .": Kerouac, *Bums,* p. 15.

Rexroth biography: David Meltzer, *The San Francisco Poets* (New York: Ballantine Books, 1971), pp. 9–34. Ferlinghetti biography: Paul Carroll, "Interview with Lawrence Ferlinghetti," undated typescript in City Lights Press Collection. "the only place I knew . . .": Ibid. "180 lbs. of poet meat": Kerouac, *Bums,* p. 17. Whalen biography: Interview with Philip Whalen. "Me imperturbe . . .": Whitman, *Leaves,* p. 9. Kerouac and Gary Snyder: Kerouac, *Bums,* passim. "Peace and purposefulness": Ibid., p. 21. Cassadys and

Los Gatos: Cassady, "Third Word," pp. 572–600. Kerouac's binge: J. K. to J. C. H., October 12, 1955. "wiry, suntanned, vigorous": Kerouac, *Bums*, p. 10.

"poet, mountain man, Buddhist . . . to himself": Ibid., p. 22. "rip rap (steps) on the . . .": Gary Snyder, *Myths and Texts* (New York: Totem Press/Corinth Books, 1960), p. 43. "enable the traveler . . .": Richard Howard, *Alone with America* (New York: Atheneum, 1969), p. 486. "the city's not so . . .": Gary Snyder, *The Back Country* (New York: New Directions Press, 1968), p. 54. "greatly enjoyed tricks . . .": G. S. to Alfred G. Aronowitz, March 1959. Snyder biography: Interviews with G. S. and P. W.: David Kherdian, *Six Poets of the San Francisco Renaissance* (Fresno, California: The Giligia Press, 1967), pp. 47–49; Barbara Harte and Carolyn Riley, *Two Hundred Contemporary Authors* (Detroit: Gale Research Company, 1969), pp. 260–261. Charge of Communism on Snyder: Kerouac, *Angels*, p. 75. "the greatest piece of religious . . .": G. S. to Alfred G. Aronowitz, March 1959.

"dreamy": Kerouac, *Bums*, p. 13. "Zen ideas are only . . .": J. K. to Alfred G. Aronowitz, January 1959. "the invention of . . . essential teaching of Buddha": Kerouac, *Angels*, p. 276. "a split that didn't exist": G. S. to author, December 15, 1975. Zen: D. T. Suzuki, *Manual of Zen Buddhism* (New York: Grove Press, 1960), passim; Garma C. C. Chang, *The Practice of Zen* (New York: Harper & Row, 1959), p. 182; Eugen Herrigel, *Zen in the Art of Archery* (New York: Vintage Books, 1971), passim. "spit forth truth . . .": Herrigel, *Archery*, p. 71. "His body of love . . .": as quoted in Suzuki, *Zen*, p. 37.

Mountain trip: Kerouac, *Bums*, pp. 36–88. "Comparisons are odious . . . Here now, the earth . . .": Ibid., pp. 55, 66. "harmony with nature . . . external harmony": Thomas Parkinson, "The Poetry of Gary Snyder," *The Southern Review* 4 (Summer 1968): p. 619. "as in most . . .": G. S. to author, December 15, 1975. "A skin bound bundle . . .": Snyder, *Myths*, p. 44. "As poet, I hold . . .": Gary Snyder, as quoted in Parkinson, "The Poetry of Gary Snyder," p. 632. "so and so equally empty . . .": Kerouac, *Bums*, p. 69. "When you get to . . . *it's impossible to fall* . . . you just have to . . .": Ibid., pp. 82, 85, 86.

"who refuse . . . dropouts": Ibid., p. 97. "hopefully decentralized . . .": G. S. to author, December 15, 1975. Kerouac's visit to Los Gatos: Interview with C. C., Cassady, "Third Word," pp. 673–679. Natalie Jackson: Interviews with A. G. and C. C.; C. C. to Alfred G. Aronowitz, March 1959. "now they know . . . you *fool*": Kerouac, *Bums*, pp. 110–111. Cross-country travel and alone at Christmas: Ibid., pp. 117–137; J. K. to C. C., December 30, 1955.

"I'm gonna die": Kerouac, *Bums*, p. 137. "Death is the only . . .": Kerouac, *Gerard*, p. 123. On writing *Gerard:* Charters, *Bibliography*, p. 29; Kerouac, *Angels*, p. 29; Interview with Tony Sampas; "Jack Kerouac's New Book," Chicago *Daily News*, August 24, 1963, p. 6. "rackety typewriter": Ibid. "Who will be the . . . laceries—I say": Kerouac, *Gerard*, p. 40. Visit to New York City: J. K. to P. W., February 7, 1956; L. C. to A. G., February 13, 1956. Lookout job: J. K. to C. C., February 11, 1956. "Pure Essence Buddhism": J. K. to P. W., February 7, 1956. Reincarnation and psychic experiences of Kerouac: J. K. to C. C., March 2, 16, 1956. "Book of Prayers": J. K. to P. W., March 6, 1956. "dealing in outblowness . . .": Kerouac, *Bums*, p. 46. Dreams of Dinah Shore: Kerouac, *Dreams*, pp. 31–32.

Swift departure for California: J. K. to P. W., March 19, 1956. Mill Valley scene: Interviews with A. G. and John Montgomery; Kerouac, *Bums*, pp. 161–189; Gary Snyder to author, December 15, 1975; J. K. to J. C. H., April 17, 1956. "The Book" and "The Duluoz Legend:" Notebook I, dated April 6, 1956, in Berg Collection, New York Public

Library. "Old Angel Midnight": J. K. to L. F., April 5, 1959. "All right, Kerouac . . . Sutra": Charters, *Bibliography*, p. 20. "During that timeless . . . perfectly": Jack Kerouac, *The Scripture of the Golden Eternity* (New York: Totem Press/Corinth Books, 1960), p. 64. "Did I create the sky . . .": Ibid., p. 1.

Last days at Mill Valley: J. K. to J. C. H., May 21, 1956; Kerouac, *Bums*, pp. 189–215. Allen Ginsberg: Mark Van Doren to A. G., May 21, 1956; William Carlos Williams to A. G., March 17, 1956. "MAY YOU USE . . .": Kerouac, *Bums*, p. 215. Robert Creeley: Interview with Robert Creeley; *Black Mountain Review* 7 (Autumn 1957): passim. "for the personal voice . . .": Martin Duberman, *Black Mountain* (New York: Doubleday and Co., 1973), p. 355. Lookout on Desolation Mountain: Kerouac, *Angels*, pp. 1–30; Kerouac, *Bums*, pp. 216–235; Kerouac Journal, July–August, 1956, Berg Collection, New York Public Library; Kerouac, "Alone on a Mountain Top," *Lonesome*, pp. 118–129. "little shadowy peaked . . .": Ibid., p. 122. "I'm alone I will . . .": Kerouac, *Angels*, p. 26. "what is the meaning . . .": Kerouac, *Lonesome*, p. 126. "mad raging sunsets . . .": Ibid., p. 129. August 7th nightmare: Kerouac, *Angels*, pp. 30–31. Killing a mouse: Ibid., p. 87. "Just be . . . just flow" . . . "wait, breathe, eat . . .": Ibid., pp. 27, 27.

XII THE ANGEL TRAVELS

Seattle: Kerouac, *Angels*, pp. 90–126. Voting for Eisenhower: Interview with M. M. "so elegant so snide . . .": Kerouac, *Angels*, p. 128. San Francisco: Ibid., pp. 132–212; Kerouac, "Origins of Beat," p. 31; Interviews with A. G. and M. M.; M. M. to Alfred G. Aronowitz, March 1959; A. G. to J. K., August 12, 1956; J. K. to P. W., October 1956. "vision of the freedom . . . warring societies": Kerouac, *Angels*, p. 85. "Jackson me boyy . . . Penny" [pseudonym used by Kerouac in *Angels*] . . . Words! . . . million dollar outfield . . . Hand in *hand* . . .": Ibid., pp. 145, 164–166, 166, 206, 168. "comrades . . . join or die": M. M. to A. G. A., March 1959. "You hate me . . . exception of Jack": Kerouac, *Angels*, p. 212; J. K. to P. W., October 1956.

"Celebrated Good Time . . .": Publicity postcard, on file in City Lights Press Collection. "a young will . . . to this region": Richard Eberhart, "West Coast Rhythms," *New York Times Book Review*, September 2, 1956, pp. 8, 7. "New Buddha . . .": Ginsberg, *Howl*, dedication page. "Hold back the edges . . .": William Carlos Williams, Introduction to *Howl*, by Allen Ginsberg (San Francisco: City Lights Press, 1956), p. 3. "NAOMI GINSBERG DIED . . .": Eugene Brooks to A. G., June 9, 1956 (Telegram). Naomi Ginsberg's funeral: Eugene Brooks to A. G., June 11, 1956. "I ride freight trains . . . freight train!": Kerouac, *Angels*, p. 192. "Every once in a while . . .": Interview with P. W. "walking talking poetry in the . . .": Kerouac, *Angels*, p. 205.

Los Gatos: Cassady, "Third Word," p. 717; G. C. to C. C., Undated (1958); A. G. to J. K., October 1956. "growing narrower in its . . .": Kerouac, *Angels*, p. 238. "I'm studying hobo": Kerouac, *Lonesome*, p. 181. "to dream all day . . . in book form": Kerouac, *Angels*, p. 229. "nail her . . . weak and sick": Kerouac, "The Art of Fiction," pp. 90–91. Mexico: Kerouac, *Angels*, pp. 230–261; Kerouac Journal, October 15, 1956, Berg Collection; Charters, *Bibliography*, p. 31; Kerouac, *Tristessa*, pp. 82–150; J. K. to P. W., November 1956. "long sad tales . . .": Kerouac, *Tristessa*, p. 126. "ingrown toenail packed . . .": J. K. to Alfred G. Aronowitz, January 1959.

"I don't know, I don't . . . an aching mystery . . . like a tiger sometimes . . . and I will die, and you . . . dramatize the way . . . the street of nausea . . . nobody *cares*":

Kerouac, *Angels*, pp. 89, 26, 48, 127, 244, 258, 258. "poor, sick and nowhere": G. C. to L. F., November 13, 1956. "nakedness . . . what's that?": Kerouac, *Angels*, p. 240. "It's time for you . . . no prophetic poets?": Ibid., pp. 259–261.

New York City: J. K. to J. C. H., December 13, 19, 1956, January 10, 1957; Kerouac, *Angels*, pp. 278–298; J. K. and A. G. to N. C., January 1957; Diane DiPrima, *Memoirs of a Beatnik* (New York: Olympia Press, 1969), p. 168. Visit to Corso: J. K. to P. W., December 31, 1956; G. C. to L. F., March 25, 1957; Kerouac, *Angels*, pp. 286–290. "How can you confess . . .": Ibid., p. 287. Mémère: Ibid., pp. 292–294.

Joyce Glassman: Interviews with Joyce Glassman Johnson and L. C.; Kerouac, *Angels*, p. 299. Visit to Dr. Williams: Interviews with A. G. and P. O.; Kerouac, *Angels*, p. 296. "Lotsa bastards out . . .": Allen Ginsberg, *Indian Journals* (San Francisco: Dave Haselwood Books/City Lights Press, 1970), p. 61. Typing poems for *Combustion:* Interviews with A. G. and Louis Ginsberg; G. C. to L. F., January 21, 1957. "All you do is . . .": Kerouac, *Angels*, p. 298. Visit to Old Saybrook: Interview with J. C. H.; Holmes, *Declare*, p. 57. New York scene and approaching fame: J. K. to N. C. and C. C., January 25, 1957; Michael Grieg, "The Lively Arts in San Francisco," *Mademoiselle*, February 1957, pp. 142–43, 190; Dan Balaban, "Three 'Witless Madcaps' Come Home to Roost," *Village Voice*, February 13, 1957, p. 3. "Don't shoot . . . forgive men": Ibid.

Voyage to Tangiers: J. K. to J. C. H., June 23, 1957; Kerouac, "Big Trip to Europe," in *Lonesome*, pp. 135, 138; Kerouac, *Angels*, pp. 310–311. "light and gay": Kerouac, *Lonesome*, p. 135. "nothing but Mind": Ibid., p. 138. "tanned, muscular, and vigorous": Kerouac, "The Last Word," *Escapade*, August 1960, p. 114. Tangiers: J. K. to J. C. H., June 2, 1957; William Burroughs, Jr., "Life with Father," pp. 113–114; Kerouac, *Lonesome*, pp. 141–148; Kerouac, *Angels*, pp. 314–327; P. O. to Ron Lewinsohn, May 3, 1957, (Texas). "I'm just a hidden agent . . . carrying lambs": Kerouac, "The Last Word," p. 114. Further Tangiers: W. S. B. to A. G., October 8, 1957; A. G. to N. C., April 24, 1957. "trying to arrive at a . . .": W. S. B. to J. K., February 12, 1955. "horrible sickness": W. S. B. to A. G., October 8, 1957. "I am shitting out . . .": Kerouac, *Angels*, p. 319.

"stiff officious squares . . . postured actually secretly . . . my doing": Ibid., pp. 327, 328, 328. France: Kerouac, *Lonesome*, pp. 151–166. "too fucking professionally morose": G. C. to L. F., April 16, 1957. London: J. K. to J. C. H., November 8, 1957. *"Aimer, Souffrir . . ."* as précis of *Town and City:* J. K. to P. W., April 28, 1957.

Return to United States: Kerouac, *Angels*, pp. 339–343. *Peyton Place:* Hackett, *Seventy*, p. 203; Grace Metalious, *Peyton Place* (New York: Julien Messner, 1957). "Is it up . . . hard?": Ibid., p. 124. Kerouac on rock and roll: Interview with J. C. H.

"silk bloomers, rosaries . . .": Kerouac, *Angels*, p. 339. Trip to Berkeley: Ibid., pp. 346–350. Life in Berkeley: Ibid., pp. 340–350; J. K. to N. C. and C. C., March 1957; J. K. to P. W., April 30, 1957; J. K. to N. C., May 15, 1957; J. K. to Alfred G. Aronowitz, January 1959; P. W. to A. G., May 18, 1957; J. K. to J. C. H., June 23, 1957; Interviews with C. C. and P. W. "Keep low and poor . . .": J.K. to P.W., April 30, 1957. Neal Cassady and *On the Road:* Interviews with C. C. and A. G.; Kerouac, *Angels*, pp. 362–369. "shifty-like": Ibid., p. 369.

Orlando cottage: Gabrielle Kerouac to P. W., July 29, 1957; Kerouac, *Angels*, p. 370. Mexico City: Ibid., p. 371; J. K. to P. W., July 12, 1957; Jack Kerouac, *Big Sur* (New York: Farrar, Straus, and Cudahy, 1962), p. 19. Orlando: J. K. to P. W., August 19, 1957. "bunch of hard up . . .": A. G. to Eugene Brooks, August 10, 1957.

Evergreen Review: (undated), Issues One and Two. "only a good deal more so . . .": Kenneth Rexroth, "San Francisco's Mature Bohemians," *Nation*, February 23, 1957, p. 159. Reaction to *Evergreen:* Louise Bogan, "Verse," *New Yorker*, April 13, 1957, pp. 172–174; George Baker, "Avant Garde at the Golden Gate," *Saturday Review*, August 3, 1957, p. 10; "New York's Spreading Upper Bohemia," *Esquire*, July 1957, pp. 42–46.

Howl trial: Interview with L. F.; Jake Ehrlich to Alfred G. Aronowitz, March 1959; "Press Clippings File," City Lights Press Collection; David Perlman, "How Captain Hanrahan Made *Howl* a Bestseller," *Reporter*, December 12, 1957, pp. 37–39. "Making a Clown . . .": San Francisco *Chronicle*, June 6, 1957, p. 22. "Cops Don't Allow . . .": San Francisco *News*, August 4, 1957, p. 17. Kerouac's reaction to trial: J. K. to P. W., April 30, 1957. Writing of first review of *On the Road:* Interview with Gilbert Millstein. Joe Gould: "Joe Gould Dead at Pilgrim State," *Village Voice*, August 21, 1957, p. 1.

XIII   SUCCESS, MORE OR LESS

"historic occasion . . . a major novel": Gilbert Millstein, "Books of the Times," *New York Times*, September 5, 1957, p. 27. "enormously readable . . . our lives": David Dempsey, "In Pursuit of Kicks," *New York Times Book Review*, September 8, 1957, p. 4. "verbal goofballs": Carlos Baker, "Itching Feet," *Saturday Review*, September 7, 1957, p. 19. "infantile, perversely negative": Gene Baro, "Restless Rebels," New York *Herald Tribune Book Review*, September 15, 1957, p. 4. "lack[ed] seriousness": Thomas Curley, "Everything Moves, But Nothing Is Alive," *Commonweal*, September 13, 1957, p. 595. "like a slob . . .": Benjamin DeMott, untitled, *Hudson Review* 10 (Winter 1957–1958): p. 111. "series of Neanderthal . . .": R. W. Grandsden,. "Adolescence and Maturity," *Encounter*, August 1958, p. 84. "wild and incomprehensible . . .": "Briefly Noted," *New Yorker*, October 5, 1957, p. 198. "more convincing as . . .": Phoebe Adams, "Ladder to Nirvana," *Atlantic*, October 1957, p. 180. Ganser syndrome: *Time*, "The Ganser Syndrome," September 16, 1957, p. 120. "Kerouac has appointed himself . . . me the fountain pen": Herbert Gold, "Hip, Cool, Beat and Frantic," *Nation*, November 16, 1957, p. 349. "not just a writer . . .": Arthur Ossterreicher, *"On the Road,"* *Village Voice*, September 18, 1957, p. 5.

"a kind of tireless . . .": John Ciardi, "Writers As Readers of Poetry, *Saturday Review*, November 23, 1957, p. 33. "celebration of the . . .": Frederick Eckman, "Neither Tame nor Fleecy," *Poetry*, September 1957, p. 387. "exhibitionist welter of unrelated . . .": James Dickey, "From Babel to Byzantium," *Sewanee Review* 65 (July-September 1957): p. 510. "dreadful little volume . . .": John Hollander, "Poetry Chronicle," *Partisan Review* 24 (Spring 1957): p. 298. "Poetry has been attacked . . .": Ginsberg, "Notes on *Howl*," in Parkinson, *Casebook*, p. 30.

"Big Day for Bards at Bay," *Life*, September 9, 1957, p. 105. "a product of Rexroth's . . .": Norman Podhoretz, "A Howl of Protest in San Francisco," *Commentary*, September 16, 1957, p. 20. Best-seller list: *New York Times Book Review*, October 13, p. 2. "novel of resignation . . .": Dwight Macdonald, "By Cozzens Possessed," *Commentary*, January 1958, pp. 36–37.

Dream: J. K. Journal, September 6, 1957, Book 5, Berg Collection. Sales, New York scene: J. K. to N. C., October 29, 1957; J. C. H. to A. G., November 29, 1957. "my liquid

suit of armor . . .": Interview with Jim Curtis. "I can't stand to meet . . . fuck him now!":
Interview with J. C. H. "in an age of total . . .": Gore Vidal, *Two Sisters*, p. 6. "clammed
up almost totally . . . before the cops": Jerry Tallmer, "Back to the Village—But Still On
the Road," *Village Voice*, September 18, 1957, pp. 1, 4. "You know what I'm thinking
. . . to feel?": J. K., in Holmes, *Declare*, p. 83. "A tough young kid . . .": J. K. to L. F.,
October 15, 1957.

Sales and writing *Dharma Bums:* J. K. to P. W., undated (Fall 1957); J. K. to L. F.,
undated (November 1957); J. K. to J. C. H., November 8, 1957; Charters, *Bibliography*,
p. 11. "god knows the revolution . . .": A. G., as quoted in J. K. to L. F., November 12,
1957. "as complicated as Flaubert . . . more sensational": Interview with P. W. "He went
. . . bones of things": G. S. to author, November 28, 1975. "You old son of a . . . lay
Jesuit?": Charters, *Bibliography*, p. 11. "Colleges being nothing . . .": Kerouac, *Bums*, p.
39. "that there are other things . . .": Interview with P. W.

Village Vanguard: Dan Wakefield, "Night Clubs," *Nation*, January 4, 1958, p. 19;
Interviews with A. G., John Montgomery, Gilbert Millstein, and Alfred G. Aronowitz;
Alfred G. Aronowitz, "The Beat Generation—Beaten?," New York *Post*, December 26,
1957, pp. 5, 10; Howard Smith, "Jack Kerouac: Off the Road, Into the Vanguard, and Out,"
Village Voice, December 25, 1957, pp. 1, 2. "I'm no Jackie Gleason . . . poet": Aronowitz,
"Beaten," p. 10. Mémêre: J. K. to P. W., January 7, 1958. Kerouac, "The Rumbling
Rambling Blues," *Playboy*, January 1958, pp. 57–63. Hentoff: Nat Hentoff, "What Time
Does the Next Balloon Go Up, Mr. Kerouac?," *Village Voice*, January 8, 1958, p. 1. "Now
there are two . . .": Kenneth Rexroth, "The Voice of the Beat Generation," San Francisco
Chronicle, February 16, 1958, p. 8. Anaïs Nin: Edwin Fancher, "Avant-Gardist with a
Loyal Background," *Village Voice*, May 27, 1959, pp. 4, 5. "Kerouac leaves you with
no . . .": Ralph Gleason, "Kerouac's 'Beat Generation,' " *Saturday Review*, January 11,
1958, p. 75. "a phenomenal ear . . . great musician . . . a way of being": David Amram, "In
Memory of Jack Kerouac," *Evergreen*, January 1970, pp. 41–48. "I'm a story teller . . . it's a
beautiful answer": James Breslin, "The Day Kerouac Almost, But Not Quite, Took
Flatbush," *Village Voice*, March 5, 1958, p. 3. "When you take . . .": David Amram,
Vibrations (New York: The Macmillan Company, 1968), p. 295.

"like a self destructive . . . in one mind": "Mike Wallace Asks Jack Kerouac What
Is the Beat Generation," New York *Post*, December 1, 1958, p. 3. "We love everything
. . .": Charters, *Bibliography*, p. 60. "Beat Mystics," *Time*, February 3, 1958, p. 56. "The
Beat Generation believes . . . natural Immanence": "On the Road Back," San Francisco
Examiner, October 5, 1958, p. 22; Jack Kerouac, "Lamb, No Lion," *Pageant*, February
1958, pp. 160–161. "psychic havoc of the . . . psychopath . . . for his cowardice: Norman
Mailer, "The White Negro," in *Advertisements for Myself* (New York: Berkeley Medal-
lion Books, 1959), pp. 312, 320, 320. "God . . . show me his face": Jack Kerouac, as quoted
in Holmes, "The Philosophy of The Beat Generation," *Esquire*, January 1958, p. 57.
"specifically moral . . . inviolability of comradeship . . .": Holmes, "Philosophy," as
published in *Declare*, p. 122. "my little brother . . .": Ibid., p. 125. "ragged, beatific
. . . high, ecstatic, saved": Jack Kerouac, "Aftermath: The Philosophy of the Beat Generation," *Esquire*, March 1958, pp. 24–26.

"Latrine laureate . . .": "The Blazing and the Beat," *Time*, February 24, 1958, p.
104. "celebrates the self . . .": David Dempsey, "Diary of a Bohemian," *New York Times
Book Review*, February 23, 1958, p. 4. "American actual speech . . .": A. G. to Louis
Ginsberg, June 1958. "Believe me, there's nothing . . .": Henry Miller, "Introduction to
The Subterraneans," as published in Parkinson, *Casebook*, p. 231.

"come 1500 miles to turn . . .": Jack Kerouac, "On the Road to Florida," *Evergreen,* January 1970, p. 64. "Cauterize my wounds . . .": Joyce Glassman, as quoted in Ann Charters, *Kerouac* (San Francisco: Straight Arrow Press, 1973), p. 299. Life on Gilbert Street, spring–summer 1958: J. K. to J. C. H., March 14, April 13, July 21, 1958; Stanley Twardowicz, at "Jack Kerouac Symposium"; J. K. to P. W., May, June, July 1958; P. W. to A. G., March 19, 1958.

Late summer, 1958: J. K. to P. W., July 18, 1958; P. W. to A. G., June 29, 1958. Rexroth attacks: Interviews with William Everson and M. M.; Kenneth Rexroth, "Revolt: True or False," *Nation,* April 26, 1958, pp. 378–379. "Herbert Gold is right . . .": Kenneth Rexroth, "The Voice of the Beat Generation Has Some Square Delusions," San Francisco *Chronicle,* "This World" section, February 16, 1958, p. 3. "I've *lived* in the kind . . .": "Daddy-O," *New Yorker,* May 3, 1958, pp. 29–30. Kerouac on Rexroth: J. K. to J. C. H., April 13, 1958; J. K. to P. W., February 1958.

Ginsberg's return: J. K. to A. G., March 20, 1958, and P. O. to A. G., March 20, 1958. "face all them aroused . . . sound horrible": A. G. to J. K., undated (Summer 1958). "actually it only seems to be . . .": A. G. to Louis Ginsberg, November 30, 1957. "The general image . . .": A. G. to J. K., October 6, 1959. "the poets and writers will . . . in this country": Ward Cannel, "Success Spoils Ginsberg," in "Columbiana Clip File," (no reference as to source), Columbia. "now you don't have to worry . . .": A. G. to J. K., September 28, 1957. Beat Hotel: Robert Palmer, "The *Rolling Stone* Interview: William Burroughs," *Rolling Stone,* May 11, 1972, pp. 48–56. "due to loss of . . .": A. G. to J. K., January 4, 1958. "Those who have doubts . . .": A. G. to J. K., January 11, 1958. "revolution of consciousness . . . on both sides": A. G. to Louis Ginsberg, February 2, 1958.

Cassady's arrest: C. C. to Alfred G. Aronowitz, March 1959; Interview with C. C.; C. C. to A. G., July 20, 1958; J. K. to P. W., August 4, 1958; A. G. to J. K., June 26, 1958. "uncool . . . heroic, but . . .": Interview with A. G. "I'm sorry about his wife . . .": Interview with C. C. Mémère and Cassady's arrest: W. S. B. to A. G., July 24, 1958; J. K. to G. C., October 13, 1958. Jack as Candide: J. K. to P. W., August 4, 1958. Beats and American left wing: David McReynolds, "Youth 'Disaffiliated' from a Phony World," *Village Voice,* March 11, 1959, pp. 1, 4, 5. "protest without program": James Breslin, "The Beat Generation: A View from the Left," *Village Voice,* April 16, 1958, p. 3.

"Blessed, blessed oblivion": George B. Leonard, "The Bored, the Bearded and the Beat," *Look,* August 19, 1958, pp. 64–68. "equally far out": Herb Caen to Alfred G. Aronowitz, March 1959. *Playboy:* Sam Boal, "Cool Swinging in New York," *Playboy,* February 1958, pp. 21–25; Noel Clad, "A Frigid Frolic in Frisco," Ibid., pp. 22, 29–34. "sick refrigerator[s] . . .": Herbert Gold, "The Beat Mystique," *Playboy,* February 1958, pp. 35–40. Best sellers: Hackett, *Seventy,* p. 206. Eugene Burdick, "The Innocent Nihilists Adrift in Squaresville," *The Reporter,* April 3, 1958, p. 30. "Obituaries": Robert Dunavon, "The Revolution in Bohemia," *Saturday Review,* September 6, 1958, p. 13; Guy Daniels, "Post Mortem on San Francisco," *Nation,* August 2, 1958, p. 53.

"Don't let Madison Avenue . . .": A. G. to J. K., October 29, 1958. "I'm too literary . . .": as quoted in Marc Schleifer, "Here to Save Us, But Not Sure From What," *Village Voice,* October 15, 1958, p. 9. "cancer": A. G. to Ron Lewinsohn, October 28, 1958. "Yeah, I'm almost . . . makes sense": A. G. to J. K., September 17, 1958. Kerouac at time of visit to Suzuki: J. K. to G. C., October 13, 1958. Visit to Suzuki: Interview with A.

G.; J. K. to Alfred G. Aronowitz, January 1959; A. G. to J. K., October 29, 1958; J. K. to P. W., November 4, 1958; Winthrop Sargeant, "Profile of D. T. Suzuki," *New Yorker*, August 31, 1957, p. 44. "When . . . right now . . . When the Buddha was . . . green tea": J. K. to Alfred G. Aronowitz, January 1959.

"This time it should . . .": A. G. to J. K., September 17, 1958. "poet of the pads . . .": Holmes, *Declare*, p. 68. "naive": Marcus Klein, untitled, *Hudson Review* 11 (Winter 1958–1959): p. 620. "juvenile": Charles Poore, "Books of the Times," *New York Times*, October 2, 1958, p. 35. "adolescent": Anthony West, untitled, *New Yorker*, November 1, 1958, p. 175. "How the Campfire Boys . . .": "The Yabyum Kid," *Time*, October 6, 1958, p. 94. "vicious, animal-like": "Moonstruck Bop-Beater," *Newsweek*, October 6, 1958, p. 92. Nancy Wilson Ross, "Beat—and Buddhist," *New York Times Book Review*, October 5, 1958, pp. 5, 14. Robert P. Jackson, untitled, *The American Buddhist*, October 1958, p. 1. "extraordinary mystic testament . . .": Allen Ginsberg, "The Dharma Bums," *Village Voice*, November 12, 1958, pp. 3, 4. Gary Snyder, "Notes on the Religious Tendencies," *Liberation*, June 1959, p. 11.

Dreams: J. K. Journal, December 1958 through May 1959, Notebook I, Berg Collection. "pearly mystical . . . and felt sad": John Updike, "On the Sidewalk," *New Yorker*, February 21, 1959, p. 32. "inarticulate hero": Robert Brustein, "America's New Culture Hero," *Commentary*, February 1958, p. 425; Robert Brustein, "The Cult of Unthink," *Horizon*, Spring 1959, p. 41. "surly and discontented expression": Brustein, "New Hero," p. 425. "self indulgent . . . inwardly conformist": Brustein, "Unthink," p. 41. "Kerouac, McClure, and the . . . every page": Ibid., p. 92. "spiteless": Kerouac, "Jack Kerouac's Answer to the 'Cult of Unthink,' " unpublished manuscript in the possession of Alfred G. Aronowitz.

"hostile to civilization . . . mystical doctrines . . . solidarity with . . . an anti-intellectualism . . . kill . . .": Norman Podhoretz, "The Know-Nothing Bohemians," *Partisan Review* 25 (Spring 1958): pp. 307, 307, 308, 317, 317. Kerouac on Goethe: J. K. to Alfred G. Aronowitz, May 25, 1959. "comprehend the nature of awe . . .": Holmes, *Declare*, p. 137.

Brandeis Forum: J. K. to Alfred G. Aronowitz, January 1959; J. K. to P. W., January 10, 1959; Marc D. Schliefer, "The Beat Debated," *Village Voice*, November 19, 1958, pp. 1, 2; Kingsley Amis, "The Delights of Literary Lecturing, *Harper's*, October 1959, pp. 181–182. "It is because I am Beat . . . Love your lives out": [all quotations from Forum] Transcript of Forum, November 1, 1958. "Look, we've done all . . . by moonlight": Interview with A. G.

XIV *ON THE ROAD* IN A CORVETTE STINGRAY

Kerouac's affair with Dody Müller: Interviews with Dody Müller, L.C., A. G.; J. K. to Alfred G. Aronowitz, January 1959. Northport in early 1959; J. K. to P. W., January 10, 1959; J. K. to J. C. H., February 21, 1959. "He is very calm and . . .": P. O. to C. C., January 10, 1959. "sweet and kind": Interview with Dody Müller. Mémêre: Interview with Dody Müller. "despicable . . . obscene": Ibid. "lover's quarrel": Ibid. "Immaculately-sick-clean": Ibid. Dody seen as witch: Interview with L. C.

Pull My Daisy: Interview with Alfred Leslie; David Amram, *Vibrations*, pp. 313–353; Various materials concerning the published film script of *Pull My Daisy* in Grove Press Collection; Walter Gutman, *The Gutman Letter* (New York: Something Else Press, 1969), pp. 30–33, 52, 101; Interview with A. G. Development of film: Interview with

Alfred Leslie. "This is supposed to be real . . . alive and spontaneous!": Amram, *Vibrations*, p. 314. "Early morning . . . poor tortured socks": Transcript of *Pull My Daisy*. "brilliant": Peter Bogdanovich, as quoted in "Movie Journal," *Village Voice*, January 5, 1961, p. 6. "sign post . . . of purity . . .": Jonas Mekas, "Movie Journal," *Village Voice*, November 18, 1959, p. 47. "refreshing . . . of kidding": Dwight Macdonald, *On Movies* (Englewood Cliffs, New Jersey: Prentice-Hall, 1969), pp. 310–311. "played into the hands of . . .": J. K. to Alfred G. Aronowitz, January 1959.

Chicago Repression: *Chicago Review* 12 (Spring 1958), *Chicago Review* 12 (Summer 1958), *Chicago Review* 12 (Autumn 1958); Paul Carroll to A. G., January 9, 1959; Paul Carroll Interview in David Ossman, *The Sullen Art* (New York: Corinth Books, 1963), pp. 17–20; John Ciardi, "The Book Burners and Sweet 16," *Saturday Review*, June 27, 1959, pp. 22, 30.

"that remedy all singers . . .": Allen Ginsberg, "Kaddish," in *Kaddish and Other Poems, 1958–1960* (San Francisco: City Lights Press, 1961), p. 7. "There, rest. No more suffering . . .": Ibid., p. 9. Chicago Reading: Bruce Cook, *The Beat Generation*, (New York: Charles Scribner's Sons, 1971), p. 77; Interview with A. G., Nelson Algren, "Chicago is a Wose," *Nation*, February 28, 1959, p. 191. "You don't know . . . this is a drag": "Fried Shoes," *Time*, February 9, 1959, p. 16. "spat on the appearance . . . created things": A. G., P. O., and G. C., "Letter to the Editor," *Time*, March 9, 1959, p. 5.

Alfred G. Aronowitz: Interview with Alfred G. Aronowitz. Alfred G. Aronowitz, January 12, 1960; J. K. to C. C., April 17, 1959. "only paid *fourteen* . . . we're bourgeois": Jack Kerouac as quoted in Alfred G. Aronowitz, "The Beat Generation," New York *Post*, March 10, 1959. Neal Cassady: A. G. to C. C., January 10, 1959; N. C. to C. C., July 18, 1958; N. C. to Alfred G. Aronowitz, March 1959; N. C. to J. K., June 12, 1959; C. C. to A. G., January 28, 1959; A. G. to J. K., May 12, 1959. "Giving those three . . .": N. C. to J. K., June 12, 1959.

"That's not writing . . .": as quoted in Janet Winn, "Capote, Mailer and Miss Parker," *New Republic*, February 9, 1959, p. 27. Flimsy local article: Val Duncan, "What Is the Beat Generation?," *Newsday*, August 3, 1959, p. 11C. "Bad taste . . . incoherent": David Dempsey, "Beatnik Bogeyman on the Prowl," *New York Times Book Review*, May 3, 1959, pp. 28–29. "psychopathic fantasy . . . stupefying in its . . . Barefoot Boy . . .": Barnaby Conrad, "Barefoot Boy with Dreams of Zen," *Saturday Review*, February 2, 1959, pp. 23–24. Lawrence Lipton, *The Holy Barbarians* (New York: Julian Messner, Inc., 1959).

Early 1959, columns and Avon anthology: J. K. to C. C., April 17, 1959; J. K. to P. W., March 15, 1959, April 19, 1959. Evaluation of Lord and publications: Interview with A. G., Ann Charters, *Bibliography*, p. 15. *Holiday* magazine: Kerouac, "The Vanishing American Hobo," *Holiday*, March 1960, p. 60; Kerouac, "The Roaming Beatniks," *Holiday*, October 1959, p. 82; J. K. to J. C. H., April 28, 1959. Unpleasant spring, exposure: Ibid. "It's wild . . . was and still is Lowell": Pertinax, "Kerouac on Kerouac," Lowell *Sun*, April 17, 1959, p. 5. "Old Angel Midnight": J. K. to L. F., Ferlinghetti, May 22, 1959. *Pull My Daisy* première: J. K. to J. C. H., May 25, 1959.

"The Beginning of Bop": Jack Kerouac, "The Last Word," *Escapade*, May 1959, pp. 103–104. "position in the current . . .": *Escapade*, June 1959, p. 105. "unnatural": August 1959, pp. 103–104. "bloody and sad and mad": November 1959, pp. 103–104. "The mad road, lovely . . .": April 1960, pp. 103–104. "the greatest composer who ever . . .": December 1960, pp. 103–104.

"joyless ambitions": A. G. to J. K., July 1, 1959. Kerouac's mood at the time: J. K. to Dick Huett, June 1959, Grove Press Collection. "naked and unashamed . . .": Alfred Kazin, "The Alone Generation," *Harper's*, October 1959, p. 129. Beats as anti-intellectuals: Irving Howe, "Mass Society and Modern Fiction," *Partisan Review* 26 (Summer 1959): pp. 420–436. "unwashed eccentricity": John Ciardi, "Epitaph for the Dead Beats," *Saturday Review*, February 6, 1960, p. 13. "the aristocrat that all . . .": Diana Trilling, *Claremont Essays* (New York: Harcourt, Brace and World, 1964), p. 22. "without the promise . . . miserable children . . . passionate love poem": Diana Trilling, "The Other Night at Columbia: A Report from the Academy," *Partisan Review* 26 (Spring 1959): pp. 27, 27, 29.

"muggles": Caroline Freud, "Portrait of the Beatnik," *Encounter*, June 1959, p. 44. "a combination of nausea and . . .": Ralph de Toledano, "The Poetry of the Beats," *National Review*, November 18, 1961, p. 347. *Playboy:* "The Playboy Philosophy," *Playboy*, January 1963, p. 50. "adolescent": Richard Hofstadter, *Anti-intellectualism in American Life* (New York: Random House, 1962), p. 420; Leo Marx, *The Machine in the Garden* (New York: Oxford University Press, 1964), p. 218. "a sad, mentally sick . . .": as quoted in "Sickniks," *Newsweek*, May 22, 1961, p. 56; "Life of Beatniks Linked to Stress," *New York Times*, April 2, 1959, p. 37. Frances J. Rigney and L. Douglas Smith, *The Real Bohemia* (New York: Basic Books, Inc., 1961). "Priest Belittles Beat Generation," *New York Times*, September 8, 1958, p. 21. Catholic Intellectuals on Beat: William G. Herron, "The New Barbarians," *Cithera* I (November 1961): pp. 39–45; Samuel Hazo, "The Poets of Retreat," *Catholic World*, October 1963, p. 33; Clayton C. Barbeau, "The Plight of the Beat," *America*, November 12, 1960, p. 210.

"Recent history is the . . . secret police systems": Allen Ginsberg, "Poetry, Violence, and the Trembling Lambs," *Village Voice*, August 26, 1959, pp. 1, 8. "the Beat Generation is youth . . .": Gregory Corso, "Variations on a Generation," in Parkinson, *Casebook*, p. 90. Army Corporal: "New Chill in the Cold War," *Life*, February 10, 1959, pp. 23–25. TV: "New Programs," *Life*, February 2, 1959, pp. 48. Maynard G. Krebs: CBS files, CBS headquarters, New York. "We're not criticizing . . .": Bill Becker, "Beatniks Battle for Own Hangout," *New York Times*, August 30, 1959, p. 67. TV Beatnik criminals: "On the Road Back: An Interview of Jack Kerouac," San Francisco *Examiner*, October 5, 1958, p. 18.

New York Police Raids: "Disguised Police Make New Raids," *New York Times*, November 23, 1959, p. 33. "and we don't actually show . . .": Albert Zugsmith to Alfred G. Aronowitz, March 1959. "Beat Playmate": *Playboy*, July 1959, p. 47. *A Real Cool Cat* and sweat shirts: Tim Ross, "The Rise and Fall of the Beats," *Nation*, May 27, 1961, pp. 456–458. "Beatnik Fly," "Sugar Shack": Leo Walker, *The Wonderful Era*, pp. 160, 179. Cartoon: *Esquire*, June 1963, p. 53.

"James Jones. Jack Kerouac . . .": Harriet Frank, "Beauty and the Beatnik," *Saturday Evening Post*, July 11, 1959, p. 129. "the hairiest, scrawniest . . . to deserve this?": Paul O'Neill, "The Only Rebellion Around," *Life*, November 30, 1959, pp. 47, 113, 114, 119, 131; Paul O'Neill, "The Only Rebellion Around," *Reader's Digest*, April 1960, p. 64. "cool us in . . . things like that": "Squaresville U.S.A. vs. Beatsville," *Life*, September 21, 1959, p. 31.

Fall 1959: Charters, *Bibliography*, pp. 56–57; A. G. to J. K., October 6, 1959; J. K. to P. W., November 1959; J. K. to J. C. H., October 14, November 8, 1959; Interviews with J. C. H. and A. G. "I've always wondered what ever . . .": Kenneth Rexroth,

"Discordant and Cool [Review of *Mexico City Blues*], *New York Times Book Review*, November 29, 1959, p. 14. Later reviews of *Mexico City Blues:* Robert Creeley, "Ways of Looking," *Poetry*, June 1961, pp. 197–198; Anthony Hecht, "The Anguish of the Spirit and the Letter," *Hudson Review* 12 (Winter 1959–1960): pp. 593–603.

Trip West: Interview with Alfred Leslie; N. C. to J. K., October 27, 1959. *Steve Allen Show:* Interview with J. C. H.; Pertinax, "Sometimes It's Sour Grapes," Lowell *Sun*, November 24, 1959, p. 33. San Francisco: Herbert Feinstein, "Passion on the San Francisco Screen," *American Quarterly* 12 (Summer 1960): pp. 205–210; J. K. to L. F., December 6, 1959; P.W. to A. G., December 3, 1959. Return East: Jack Kerouac, Albert Saijo, and Lew Welch, *Trip Trap* (Bolinas, California: Grey Fox Press, 1973), passim; Interview with M. M. "politics and politicians, intricate crimes . . .": Kerouac, Saijo, and Welch, *Trap*, p. 5. Northport, Benzedrine, "Beat Traveler" and a hermitage: Lew Welch, *How I Work*, p. viii; J. K. to J. C. H., January 21, 1960; J. K. to P. W., January 18, 1961; J. K. to P. O., March 23, 1960.

Ferlinghetti: J. K. to L. F., February 1, 1961; "Poems Read in Class Stirs Inquiry Here," *New York Times*, April 14, 1960, p. 23. New York City Beatniks: " 'Village' Beatniks Heckle Firemen," *New York Times*, June 11, 1960, p. 23; "80 Beatniks Protest," *New York Times*, June 13, 1960, p. 32.

North Beach: Michael Grieg, "The Old Beat Gang is Breaking Up," San Francisco *Examiner*, September 28, 1958, p. 18. "too much publicity . . .": Ralph Gleason, "Begone, Dull Beats," *The New Statesman*, June 2, 1961, p. 868. Gilbert Millstein, "Rent A Beatnik and Swing," *New York Times Sunday Magazine*, April 17, 1960, pp. 3, 28, 30. Neal Cassady's release: J. K. to C. C., April 20, 1960. You cook, I'll write . . . "You're a whirlpool . . .": An Arthur Freed Production, *The Subterraneans*, 1960. Spring 1960: J. K. to P. W., April 12, 1960.

XV COLLAPSE

Kerouac's nervous breakdown: Jack Kerouac, *Big Sur* (New York: Farrar, Straus and Cudahy, 1962), passim. "so ugly, so lost . . . One fast move . . .": Ibid., pp. 3, 7. "Kennedy has a jewel . . .": Norman Mailer, "Superman Comes to the Supermarket," in Harold Hayes, ed., *Smiling Through the Apocalypse* (New York: The McCall Publishing Company, 1969), p. 6. "shy drunken Catholic Boddhisattva": Interview with A. G. Kerouac's vote: A. G. to J. K., undated (Fall 1960). Spring 1960: Interviews with Dody Müller, A. G., L. C., and J. C. H.; Ann Charters, *Bibliography*, p. 19; J. K. to L. F., June 23, 1960; J. K. to P. O., May 12, 1960; P. O. to A. G., May 13, June 8, 29, 1960.

Kerouac disillusioned: Interview with A. G. "I don't want to . . .": Ibid. "I wish you were . . .": A. G. to J. K., June 6, 1960. "What I thought was . . . had it nearly . . .": Ginsberg, *Yage Letters*, pp. 49–51. Ginsberg in Peru: A. G. to Howard Schulman, October 16, 1961, in Knights, *Beat Book*, pp. 77–78. "completely lost strayed . . .": Ginsberg, *Yage*, p. 54. "Drive me crazy, God . . .": Allen Ginsberg, "The Magic Psalm," in *Kaddish and Other Poems* (San Francisco: City Lights Press, 1961), p. 93. "God answers with my . . .": Allen Ginsberg, "The Reply," in Ibid., p. 94.

Ferlinghetti's offer and Kerouac's sickness: J. K. to L. F., July 2, 8, 21, 1960. Train ride: Kerouac, *Sur*, p. 5. Philip Whalen: J. K. to P. W., March 15, 1959; P. W. to A. G., July 26, 1960. "aerial roaring mystery . . .": Kerouac, *Sur*, p. 10. Bixby Canyon: Ibid., pp. 10–13; Author's observation. "Mien Mo Mountain": Jack Kerouac Journal, February

8, 1960, Notebook 5, Berg Collection; Kerouac, *Sur,* p. 16. First three weeks at Bixby: Ibid., pp. 14–44. "keep concentrated on the fact . . . that after all . . . Oh my God we're . . . GO TO YOUR . . .": Ibid., pp. 24, 24, 36, 41.

"sneering dark glasses": Ibid., p. 45. Hitching to San Francisco: Ibid., pp. 44–47. "I really don't know how to tell you . . . a little dotty": Ibid., pp. 50, 51. "That's all anybody loves . . .": Interview with C. C. Visit to Cassadys: Ibid. Visit to Saijo; Kerouac, *Sur,* pp. 78–82; "Sam Johnson": Ibid., pp. 86–88.

Party at Bixby: Interviews with L. F., C. C., and M. M.; Kerouac, *Sur,* pp. 89–110. "It was at moments . . . this is intellectual . . . put-down questions": Interview with M. M. "*O mon Dieux, pourquoi . . .* Man is a busy little . . .": Kerouac, *Sur,* pp. 114, 120.

"A band of angels . . . I don't like *On the Road . . .* ones in the bunch": Carolyn Cassady, "Third Word," pp. 896, 899–900. Jacky: Kerouac, *Sur,* pp. 144–149, 166, 193; Interview with Lenore Kandel. Philip Whalen: Interview with P. W.; Kerouac, *Sur,* pp. 160–165. "You said that . . . with the world": Ibid., p. 162. Stop at Los Gatos: Interview with C. C. "for being a member . . . devoid of human beingness": Kerouac, *Sur,* p. 166, 193.

"automatic directionless circle . . . STOP THAT . . .": Ibid., pp. 199, 201. Return to San Francisco, Long Island: J. K. to N. C., undated (September 1960); P. W. to A. G., September 7, 1960; J. K. to L. F., September 14, 1960; J. K. to P. W., September 1960; Interviews with P. W., C. C., and L. F., "I took a lot more . . .": A. G. to J. K., September 19, 1960.

XVI   WAITING

Fall 1960: J. K. to L. F., February 29, March 4, April 25, May 4, May 16, 20, 28, June 3, September 24, undated (October), October 18, 1960. "the selfhood of death . . . *Jésus, pourquoi tu . . .* ties all mankind together . . . in their sleep": Kerouac, *Dreams,* pp. 139, 174, 3, 3. Drugs: Timothy Leary, *High Priest* (New York: World Publishing Co., 1968), pp. 49–123; Interview with A. G., "I think I'll take . . . in a day": Interview with A. G.

"Oh those Jews . . . dirty old cunt": Ibid; A. G. to J. K., undated (October, 1960); J. K. to P. W., February 2, 23, 1961. Politics: J. K. to L. F., February 1, undated (March 1961), May 25, August 9, 1961, April 28, 1962. Gagarin: J. K. to J. C. H., August 9, 1961. "Jewish Ukraine": J. K. to Ellen Lucey, January 19, 1961 (Columbia). Cholly Knickerbocker: J. K. to L. F., April 28, 1962. Jackals: J. K. to Nanda Pivano, January 5, 1961, in Knights, *Beat Book,* p. 56. "harassed Norman Mailer . . . to be of the Beatnik clan": Louis Sobol, "Kerouac Protests Legend," New York *Journal-American,* December 8, 1960, p. 25. "Colette to Kerouac": J. K. to P. W., April 10, 1961. Northport furor: J. K. to P. W., March 30, 1961; J. K. to N. C., April 3, 1961.

Joan Haverty and Courts: J. K. to N. C., undated (1961); Charles McHarry, "On the Town," New York *Daily News,* January 11, 1961, p. 56. Alcoholic: J. K. to P. W., March 30, 1961. "Buried alive in the blues . . . ": Nick Gravenites, as quoted in Myra Friedman, *Buried Alive* (New York: Bantam Books, 1974), p. 211. Orlando: J. K. to L. F., May 25, August 28, 1961. Mexico: Charters, *Bibliography,* p. 31; J. K. to Nanda Pivano, October 24, 1961, in Knights, *Beat Book,* p. 56. "I got to look like . . . I shall bullwhip the . . . modern America of crew . . . a wondrous of contradictions . . . suspicious paranoid . . . for little favors": Kerouac, *Angels,* pp. 230–1, 347, 239, 239, 291, 348.

"Mao . . . Eternity and the . . . in graves death": Ibid., pp. 348, 348, 276. Quit literature: J. K. to L. F., undated (August, 1961). "Worth the telling . . . everything . . . *O Why Is God* . . .": Kerouac, *Sur*, pp. 19, 19, 23. Writing of *Big Sur*, Fall, 1961: J. K. to P. W., October 17, 1961; J. K. to L. F., October 23, 1961; J. K. to C. C., October 17, 1961; Interviews with A. G. and J. C. H.; Charters, *Bibliography*, p. 27.

Anthologies: Thomas Parkinson, ed., *A Casebook on the Beat* (New York: Thomas Y. Crowell, 1961); Donald Allen, ed., *The New American Poetry* (New York: Grove Press, 1961); Gene Feldman and Max Gartenberg, *The Beat Generation and The Angry Young Men* (Freeport, New York: Books for Libraries Press, 1958); Seymour Krim, *The Beats* (New York: Fawcett Publishers, Inc., 1960). Ginsberg on *New American Poetry*: A. G. to Louis Ginsberg, March 8, 1960. "one loves only form . . .": Charles Olson, "I, Maximus of Gloucester, to You," in *New American Poetry*, p. 8. Poetic community: Robert Duncan in Ginsberg, *Verbatim*, p. 131. "Rivals": Donald Hall, Robert Pack, Louis Simpson, *New Poets of England and America* (New York: Oxford University Press, 1960); Donald Hall, "The Battle of the Bards," *Horizon*, September, 1961, pp. 116–121; Cook, *Generation*, p. 135. Earth literature: Michael McClure, Lawrence Ferlinghetti, and David Meltzer, *Journal for the Protection of All Beings*, "Love Shot Issue" (San Francisco: City Lights Press, 1961).

"invented . . . the author of a dull . . .": Leslie Fiedler, *Waiting for the End* (New York: Stein and Day, 1964), pp. 164, 164, 248. Critical view of Allen Ginsberg: M. L. Lowenthal, "Seven Voices," *The Reporter*, January 3, 1961, p. 46; George Oppen, "Three Poets," *Poetry*, September 1962, pp. 329–337. *Tropic of Cancer:* Hackett, *Seventy*, p. 215. "The young people who have . . .": William Byers, "I Call on Jack Kerouac," *The Last Word* (Northport, Long Island, High School's literary magazine) Spring 1960, pp. 4–5, 32–33.

"this impossibly/hard life": Jack Kerouac, "Poem on Dr. Sax," *Bastard Angel* 1 (undated), p. 7. New York City and Court: Interview with Eugene Brooks; J. K. to J. C. H., December 29, 1961; Eugene Brooks to A. G., December 3, 1961, April 27, 1962. "I demand that . . .": Kerouac, *Scattered*, p. 37. Ginsberg opinion: A. G. to Louis Ginsberg, May 22, 1962. "Beat Bard Denies He's . . .": Alfred Albelli, New York *Daily News*, March 14, 1961, p. 3. "just cares about his self . . .": G. C. to A. G., March 9, 1962. "I don't know anything . . .": Alan Ansen to A. G., October 24, 1965.

Henry Miller petition: J. K. to J. C. H., April 17, 1962. Sale to Farrar, Straus: J. K. to J. C. H., June 8, 1962. "Inhumanly independent of . . . void preaching guru": A. G. to J. K., May 11, 1962. Summer 1962: Ibid.; J. K. to L. C., June 7, August 11, 1962. J. K. to L. F., June 15, 1962. J. K. to P. W., June 19, 1962. "Lady Cunt": J. K. to N. C. and C. C., August 11, 1962.

Maine and Cape Cod: J. K. to C. C., October 21, 1962; J. K. to L. F., October 6, 1962. "dreary": Interview with J. C. H. Visit to Old Saybrook: J. K. to J. C. H., August 8, September 3, 1962; Interviews with J. C. H. and Shirley Holmes. Lowell: Interviews with George "GJ" Apostalakis, Tony Sampas, William Koumantzelis, Greg Zahos, Manuel "Chiefy" Nobriga, Jay Pendergast, James Curtis, and Charles Jarvis; Pertinax, "Kerouac, Joyce, Proust," Lowell *Sun*, October 24, 1962, p. 7; J. K. to J. C. H., October 9, 1962. "Some day they'll take down . . .": Interview with James Curtis.

Jack Kerouac, James Curtis, and Charles Jarvis, "Dialogues in Great Books," September 19, 1962 (tape recording of radio program, in possession of Tony Sampas, Lowell). "I am Lewis Milestone . . . and I have followed him . . . went back to a vision . . . only fast . . . it's a sin!": Ibid. "treated people good": Interview with Tony Sampas. "more of the grape": Interview with Manuel Nobriga. "table thumping . . . is QUEBEC": Pertinax, "Conversation with Kerouac," Lowell *Sun,* September 20, 1962, p. 7. "a vast collection of . . .": "Dialogues" tape in possession of Tony Sampas. Kerouac and churches: as quoted in Pertinax, "Kerouac Remembers Them All," Lowell *Sun,* October 25, 1962, p. 7. "the price is too high . . .": Interview with Greg Zahos.

"on the right road at . . .": Herbert Gold, "Squaring off the Corners," *Saturday Review,* September 22, 1962, p. 29. "a sense of structure and . . . novel to date": William Wiegand, "A Turn in the Road for the King of the Beats," *New York Times Book Review,* September 16, 1962, pp. 4, 42. *Playboy:* (untitled) *Playboy,* September 1962, p. 48. "Vogue perfume ad": Jean Shepard, "Amid Dark Spectres," New York *Herald Tribune Book Review,* September 16, 1962, p. 7. "confirmed one-vein literary miner . . . a child's first touch . . .": "Lions and Cubs," *Time,* September 14, 1962, p. 106. "committed the worst crime . . .": Ralph Gleason, "The Beatific Vision vs. the Beat Scene," San Francisco *Sunday Chronicle,* "This World Magazine," May 21, 1961, p. 28. Kerouac not a Jew, and extreme bravado: J. K. to C. C., October 21, 1962.

Iroquois: Interviews with Paul Bourgeois and Tony Sampas; J. K. to L. F., October 6, 1962; J. K. to J. C. H., October 9, 1962; A. G. to J. K., October 11, 1962. "Moon-Cloud Chief . . . being obliterated by . . . Chief wants to . . . I intend to find out . . .": Jack Kerouac, "Among the Iroquois," *City Lights Journal* 1 (1963): pp. 43–45. Tony Sampas' home, Orlando, move to Northport: Pertinax, "On the Road with Marty and Jack," Lowell *Sun,* October 26, 1962, p. 5; Interviews with Manuel Nobriga, Lucien Carr, Tony Sampas, and Greg Zahos; J. K. to Tony Sampas, October 9, 1962, (Lowell); J. K. to Francesca Carr, October 22, 1962; J. K. to N. C. and C. C., November 28, 1962.

Burroughs: William Burroughs, *The Soft Machine* (New York: Grove Press, 1966); William Burroughs, *The Nova Express* (New York: Grove Press, 1964); William Burroughs, "My Mother and I Would Like to Know," *Evergreen Review,* June 1969, p. 35. "pure and unpremeditated legal lunacy": L. F. to A. G., June 13, 1958. "prose written in bone . . .": Norman Mailer, "Some Children of the Goddess," in Harry T. Moore, ed., *Contemporary American Novelists* (Carbondale, Illinois: Southern Illinois University Press, 1969), p. 54. "a frozen moment . . . every fork": William Burroughs, *Naked Lunch* (New York: Grove Press, 1962), p. v. "modern inferno": W. S. B. to A. G., November 26, 1957. Dr. Benway: W. S. B. to A. G., October 19, 1957. "the ideal product . . . to his product . . . control . . . like junk": Burroughs, *Lunch,* pp. vii, vii, 164, 164.

"The only American novelist . . .": as quoted in Cook, *Generation,* p. 168. Mary McCarthy: Mary McCarthy, "Burroughs," in *The Writing on the Wall,* (New York: Harcourt, Brace and World, Inc., 1970), pp. 42–53. "trash": John Wain, "The Great Burroughs Affair," *New Republic,* December 1, 1962, p. 22. "second growth Dada": "King of the YADS," *Time,* November 30, 1962, p. 96. *Partisan Review:* Lionel Abel, "Beyond the Fringe," *Partisan Review* 30 (Spring 1963): pp. 108–112. Books: Hackett, *Seventy,* p. 218. James Bond: Richard Carpenter, "007 and the Myth of the Hero," *Journal of Popular Culture* 1 (Fall 1967): pp. 80–89.

Lenny Bruce: Albert Goldman, *Ladies and Gentlemen, Lenny Bruce* (New York: Ballantine Books, 1974); Interviews with Paul Krassner and J. C. H. "kike dirty mouth . . .": Ibid. "alienated conservative": Goldman, *Lenny,* p. 646. "John Baby": "Religions Incorporated," on Fantasy Records, 1970, "The Best of Lenny Bruce." "Remember this,

I'm . . .": John Cohen, ed., *The Essential Lenny Bruce* (New York: Ballantine Books, 1967), p. 69.

Pop songs: Herbert Goldberg, "Contemporary Popular Music," *Journal of Popular Culture* 4 (Winter 1971): pp. 579–589. Bob Dylan: Anthony Scaduto, *Bob Dylan* (New York: Signet Books, 1972); Bob Dylan, *Writings and Drawings* (New York: Alfred A. Knopf, 1973). "other people out there like me!": Interview with A. G. "Brecht of the Juke Box": Jack Newfield, "Brecht of the Juke Box," *Village Voice*, January 26, 1967, p. 1. "first poet of the mass . . .": Ralph Gleason, as quoted in David DeTurk and A. Poulin Jr., *The American Folk Scene* (New York: Dell Publishing Co., 1967), p. 4. "another fucking folk . . . well, okay, he's good": Interview with J. C. H.

Northport: J. K. to P. W., December 13, 1962, January 14, February 23, 1963; J. K. to J. C. H., April 4, June 23, 1963. Cassady divorce and Neal Cassady's visit to Northport: J. K. to C. C., February 21, August 16, 1963. Popular Culture: William Manchester, "Then," *New York Times Sunday Magazine*, November 4, 1973, pp. 37, 63–65. "self-indulgence": Robert Phelps, "Tender Kerouac," New York *Herald Tribune Book Review*, September 8, 1963, p. 3. "garrulous hipster yawping": Saul Maloff, "A Yawping at the Grave," *New York Times Book Review*, September 8, 1963, pp. 4–5. Kerouac on *Visions of Gerard* reviews: J. K. to J. C. H., October 5, 1963. "tin-eared Canuck . . . a fraud": "Children Should Be . . ." *Newsweek*, September 9, 1963, p. 93.

Ginsberg's travels: Allen Ginsberg, *Indian Journals* (San Francisco: Dave Hasel-wood/City Lights, 1970), passim; Ginsberg, "The Change," in *Planet News* (San Francisco: City Lights, 1963), p. 61; A. G. to J. K., May 8, 1963. "The SNAKE's all took care of . . . when eyes say yes": A. G. to J. K., October 6, 1963. "Kali, Durga, Ram . . .": Ginsberg, *Indian Journals*, p. 37. Kerouac's reaction to Ginsberg: J. K. to J. C. H., December 11, 1963.

XVII   THE VILLAGE IDIOT

"village idiot": Interview with Gerard Wagner. "Once you gave it back . . . than anti-Semitic": Interview with A. G. "he was full of shit": Interview with J.C.H. Kerouac and identity: Interviews with Tony Sampas, Billy Koumantzelis, Walter Full, A. G., L. C., and J. C. H. "I'm old, ugly, red . . .": Ginsberg, "Sunshine Interview," p. 4; Interview with A. G.; A. G. to J. K., undated [February 1964?]. "romantic, handsome . . . doomed": Ginsberg, "Sunshine Interview," p. 9.

"the expansion and regeneration . . .": Eric Mottram, *Allen Ginsberg in the 60s* (Seattle, Washington: Unicorn Bookshop, 1972), p. 4. "an ethical revolt against . . .": Jack Newfield, *A Prophetic Minority* (New York: Signet, 1966), p. 15. Politics: Ronald Berman, *America in the Sixties* (New York: Grosset and Dunlap, 1968). "Documents on Police Bureaucracies": Unpublished manuscript by Allen Ginsberg, April 1964, (Columbia). "technology has . . .": Ginsberg, *Verbatim*, p. 77.

Kesey, LSD: Tom Wolfe, *The Electric Kool-Aid Acid Test* (New York: Farrar, Straus, 1968); Interviews with Jerry Garcia, Paul Krassner, and A. G. "doors of perception": William Blake, *The Collected William Blake* (New York: Viking Press, 1949), p. 72. "suddenly people were stripped . . . of this country": Ken Kesey Interview, *The Realist* May–June, 1971, p. 4. "holy primitive, the holy . . . get thoughtful": Interview with Tom Wolfe. "subjects that . . .": Interview with Jerry Garcia. "the yoga of a man . . .": Kesey,

Realist, p. 148. "you understand": Wolfe, *Acid Test,* p. 14. Kerouac on Kesey: J. K. to P. W., October 17, 1961. "we should have gone . . .": Interview with A. G.

Beats and Rock: Robert Palmer, "William Burroughs, The Rolling Stone Interview," *Rolling Stone,* May 11, 1972, pp. 48–56; Grover Lewis, "Boz Scaggs' Life," *Rolling Stone,* November 23, 1972, p. 50; Craig Copetas, "David Bowie," *Rolling Stone,* February 28, 1974, p. 26; Myra Friedman, *Buried Alive* (New York: Bantam Books, 1974); Michael McClure, "The Poet's Poet," *Rolling Stone,* March 14, 1974, p. 34; Gwyneth Cravens, "Hitching Nowhere; The Aging Young on the Endless Road," *Harper's,* September 1972, pp. 66–67, 69. "Jack Kerouac was . . ." Chet Flippo, "A Style Is Born," *Rolling Stone,* December 15, 1977, p. 21.

St. Petersburg, Nin's death: Jack Kerouac, "My Ideas About the Major League Race," *St. Petersburg Independent,* July 16, 1965, p. 6; Charters, *Bibliography,* p. 63; J. K. to P. W., January 10, 1965; J. K. to J. C. H., October 16, December 8, 1964, March 2, 1965. Best sellers: Hackett, *Seventy,* p. 224. "Bumbling Bunyan . . . Buddhists behave": *Time,* May 7, 1965, pp. 110–111. "a great deal to say . . .": Samuel Bellman, "A Fevered Snowflake," *Saturday Review,* July 12, 1965, p. 47. "obsolete": Charles Poore, "An Elegy for the Beat Syndicate of Writers," *New York Times,* May 4, 1965, p. 41. "disaster . . . inconsequential epic": Saul Maloff, "A Line Must Be Drawn," *New York Times Book Review,* May 2, 1965, p. 4. "exhibitionistic cults of . . .": Poore, "Elegy," p. 41. "Probably no other . . . when we see one": Dan Wakefield, "Jack Kerouac Comes Home," *Atlantic,* July 1965, p. 69.

Paris: Jack Kerouac, *Satori In Paris* (New York: Grove Press, 1966), pp. 1–102; J. K. to C. C., July 1965; J. K. to J. C. H., July 21, 1965. "have pity on us all . . . a tale that's told for . . .": Kerouac, *Satori,* pp. 11, 10. International Beatdom: "The Beatniks' Friend," *Newsweek,* August 23, 1965, p. 36; J. Anthony Lukas, "Beatniks Flock to Nepal," *New York Times,* December 26, 1966, p. 1, 2, 11; Herbert Lottman, "A Baedeker of Beatnik Territory," *New York Times Sunday Magazine,* August 7, 1966, pp. 40, 46, 53, 113; Richard Kostelanetz, "Ginsberg Makes the World Scene," *New York Times Sunday Magazine,* July 11, 1965, pp. 22–23, 27, 28, 30, 32.

The Wild Boar: J. K. to J. C. H., February 18, 1966; Interview with Gerard Wagner. "a man who invested . . . the most democratic . . . 'your cunt stinks' . . . Chevalier Gerard Alvin . . . would lead you to . . . 'I'm not a spokesman' . . .": Ibid. "I finally found a . . . best of all . . . fuck it all": A. G., N. C., and C. C. to J. K., October 1, 1965. "Who answered that phone . . . in yo han', y'heah?": Carolyn Cassady, "Third Word," p. 1012.

Fall 1965 through move to Cape Cod: J. K. to Tony Sampas, November 29, 1965. Gabrielle Kerouac to P. W., December 17, 1965, (Columbia); J. C. H. to A. G., December 21, 1965; J. K. to J. C. H., September 18, 1965. "I doan like dem dere . . . God be justified: Interview with Jacob Roseman, "and we'll bat out an . . .": Interview with J. C. H. Charters: Ann Charters, *Kerouac* (San Francisco: Straight Arrow Press, 1973), pp. 349–355. Mémêre: J. K. to J. C. H., September 22, 1966. "her asshole and her mouth": Interview with Dody Müller. Hyannis and marriage: Joe David Bellamy, "Jack Kerouac's Last Years: An Interview with Robert Boles," *The Falcon* 1 (Summer 1970): pp. 5–12; Stella Kerouac: as quoted in Barry Gifford, *Kerouac's Town* (Berkeley, California: Creative Arts Publishing Company, 1977), p. 52. Marriage: Frank Falacci, "Lowell Girl Wed to Jack Kerouac," Boston *Sunday Herald,* November 20, 1966, p. 9.

XVIII IT'S TRUE: YOU CAN'T GO HOME AGAIN

"deserted twilight streets . . .": "Jack Kerouac's New Book," Chicago *Daily News*, August 24, 1963, p. 6. Kerouac at Nicky's: Interviews with Tony Sampas. Hippies and the Be-In: Interviews with M. M. and A. G.; Leonard Woolf, *Voices from the Love Generation* (Boston: Little Brown & Co., 1968).

Gary Snyder: Gary Snyder, *The Back Country* (New York: New Directions Press, 1968); Gary Snyder, *Earth House Hold* (New York: New Directions Press, 1969); Gary Snyder, *Myths and Texts* (New York: Totem Press/Corinth Books, 1960); Gary Snyder, *Regarding Wave* (New York: New Directions Press, 1970); Gary Snyder, *Turtle Island* (New York: New Directions Press, 1974); Kherdian, *Six Poets*, pp. 50–55; Don McNeill, "Gary Snyder, Poet, Doubter of Cities," *Village Voice*, November 17, 1966, p. 20. "the revolution has happened . . .": Interview with P. W. "individual insight into the . . .": Snyder, *Earth*, p. 92. "If civilization / is the . . .": Gary Snyder, "Revolution in the Revolution in the Revolution, *Wave*, p. 39. "new race of longhaired . . .": as quoted from Lawrence Ferlinghetti, *Tyrannus Nix*, in Maurice Lin, "Children of Adam", p. 197. "I owe everything to . . .": Interview with Stewart Brand. "Kerouac came back to . . .": Ray Mungo, *Total Loss Farm* (Boston: Beacon Press, 1970), pp. 33–34.

Kerouac in the bars of Lowell: Interviews with Greg Zahos, Walter Full, Nick Sampas, Tony Sampas, Bill Koumantzelis, John Mahoney. "What's your story?": Interview with Greg Zahos. "He stood for something": Interview with John Mahoney. "crazy asshole dreamer drunk": Interview with Walter Full. "He was real drunk and he was . . .": Interview with James Upton. Kerouac and his relatives: Interviews with Doris Kerouac and Armand Kerouac. "no literature in his books . . . *not* a drunk": Ibid. "a different person": Interview with George "GJ" Apostalakis. "these New York fellas did to him": Scotty Beaulieu, in remarks at Kerouac Symposium. "He could have been a professional . . .": Interview with Fred Bertrand.

"Always glad to buy . . . I went out . . . Now I KNOW . . . Tell me about . . . I couldn't take it . . . big money . . . I'm home Stella . . . a mill rat . . . You're my brother . . . I haven't been right . . . stole my ideas . . . Man, that guy . . .": Interview with Joe Chaput. " 'cause they created Gods with . . .": Interview with Greg Zahos.

"You know, there are only . . .": as quoted in Ruth Kligman, *Love Affair* (New York: William Morrow and Co., 1974), p. 127. Kerouac's privacy at home: Interview with Greg Zahos. TV movies: Interviews with Bill Koumantzelis and Walter Full. Reading Bible: Interview with Walter Full. Telephone: J. K. to Joe Chaput, July 18, 1968 (Lowell); in possession of Joe Chaput; Interview with Walter Full. Kerouac visiting churches: Interviews with Charles Sampas, Tony Sampas, and William Koumantzelis. Writing *Vanity of Duluoz*: Berrigan, "The Art of Fiction," p. 70; J. K. to J. C. H., May 22, 1967. Analysis of *Vanity of Duluoz* based on: Interview with A. G. "Insofar as nobody . . . Vanity . . . wise guy . . . I could have gained a lot . . . was telling everybody to go . . .": Kerouac, *Vanity*, pp. 7, 276, 171, 171, 95. "controlled folly": Carlos Castaneda, *Journey to Ixtlan* (New York: Simon and Schuster, 1973), p. 69.

"potboiler of broken convictions . . .": Kerouac, *Vanity*, p. 106. "lecher fondling . . .": Ibid., p. 74. "God, man, I rode around . . .": Berrigan, "The Art of Fiction," p. 78. "And I wasn't trying to create . . . get laid": Cook, *Generation*, p. 89. "Let me tell you, a true writer . . .": Ibid., p. 88. "FEELING is what I like . . .": Berrigan, "The Art of Fiction," p. 65. "you insane phony . . . Frankly I do feel that . . . Notoriety and public confession . . .": Ibid., pp. 85, 89, 98.

"the consciousness of the writer . . .": Interview with J. C. H. Use of Interview Form: Jerome Ellison and Franklin T. Gosser, "Non-Fiction Magazine Articles: A Content Analysis Study," *Journalism Quarterly*, Winter 1959, pp. 27–34. Jill Johnston as "beatnik": Jill Johnston, *Lesbian Nation* (New York: Simon and Schuster, 1973), p. 73. Charles Bukowski: Interview with L. F. Beat and encounter groups, mysticism: Interview with Tom Wolfe. "the Jews have corrupted . . . Boy, I'm gonna teach . . .": Interview with Joe Chaput.

Sales of *Vanity of Duluoz*, Charters, *Bibliography*, pp. 37, 75. Writer in Residence: J. K. to Charles Jarvis (no date given), as cited in Charles Jarvis, "Angel Goof," on deposit in Lowell Public Library; Interviews with Charles Jarvis and James Curtis. "You professor weirdo": Jarvis, *Visions of Kerouac*, p. 14. "What was the influence . . . Go fuck yourself!": Interview with Jay Pendergast. "I saved your school . . . remember that?": Interview with Greg Zahos.

"I get in a group . . . else to do . . . My God, I've killed . . .": Carolyn Cassady, "Third Word," pp. 1082, 1082, 1085. Neal's death: Charles Bukowski, "Open City," *Los Angeles Free Press*, July 26, 1968, p. 7; N. C. to A. G., May 1967; Interview with C. C. "Shut up . . . be dead": Ibid.

"Don't *tell* them . . .": Interview with Georgette Zahos. "I don't want to fuck . . .": Interview with J. C. H. "Jesus is in my house, no sex . . .": Interview with Gerard Wagner. "Don't use that word . . . and he wasn't that good": Interview with J. C. H. "Don't discipline them . . . about kids": Interview with Georgette Zahos. Trip to Europe: Interviews with Greg Zahos, Tony Sampas, Nick Sampas, Walter Full, and Joe Chaput; J. K. to J. C. H., April 1, 1968; Gregory McDonald, "Off the Road," Boston *Sunday Globe Magazine*, August 11, 1968, p. 8.

"After Me, the Deluge": U.P.I. teletypescript, courtesy of Alfred G. Aronowitz (undated, unpaginated, and unedited). "the great white father and . . . intellectual forebear of . . .": Ibid. "new reasons for spitefulness": Interview with A. G. "shiny hypocrisy . . . money glut . . . quite understandably alienated . . . no better plan to offer . . . believe in the written word . . . parasites": Kerouac, "After Me, the Deluge."

Visit to New York: Interviews with Doris Kerouac, A. G., L. C., W. S. B., Tony Sampas, Bill Koumantzelis, and Joe Chaput. William Burroughs: Daniel Odier, *The Job* (New York: Grove Press, 1970); Eric Mottram, *The Algebra of Need* (Buffalo, New York: Intrepid Press, 1970); William Burroughs, "Academy 23: A Deconditioning," *Village Voice*, August 6, 1967, pp. 5, 21. "to make people aware of the true . . .": William Burroughs in Kazin, *Writers*, p. 174. "high as the Zen master is high . . . this is the space age . . .": William Burroughs, "The Day the Records Went Up," *Evergreen Review*, November 1968, p. 76.

"A kind of record of the . . .": Kramer, *Ginsberg*, p. 144. "Mind is shapely . . .": Ginsberg, "Notes on Howl," Parkinson, *Casebook*, p. 28. Allen Ginsberg: Interview with A. G.; Eric Mottram, *Allen Ginsberg in the 60s* (Seattle: Unicorn Bookshop, 1972); Paul Carroll, "The *Playboy* Interview: Allen Ginsberg," *Playboy*, April 1969, pp. 81–92, 236–244. "include a larger consciousness . . . all sentient beings": Alison Colbert Interview with Allen Ginsberg, transcript on file, (Columbia). "Get the fuck off . . .": Interview with Joe Chaput. "I don't care what . . . all right": Interview with Bill Koumantzelis.

"The Firing Line" program: undated transcript, courtesy of William F. Buckley. "apparently some kind of Dionysian . . . good kids . . . beat mutiny . . . being a Catholic": "Buckley transcript," p. 7. "No, no. I thought . . . there are people who make a rule . . . I'm not connected . . . next to his": Ibid., pp. 31–2, 19, 34, 34.

"Goodbye, drunken ghost": Interview with A. G., "I'll be able to walk": Interviews with Tony Sampas and Joe Chaput. Janet Kerouac visit: Interview with Doris Kerouac. Hurried departure of the Kerouacs: Interviews with Manuel Nobriga, Bill Koumantzelis, and Tony Sampas.

XIX ENDGAME

Move to Florida; Interview with Joe Chaput; J. K. to Tony Sampas, December 5, 1958; J. K. to Joe Chaput, November 15, 1968. Kerouac unable to obtain a decent advance: J. K. to Andreas Brown, March 23, 1969, (Columbia).

"credit card sensibility": Andrew Sarris, "More Babbit than Beatnik," *New York Times Book Review*, February 26, 1967, p. 5. "Road to Nowhere": Thomas Lask, "Road to Nowhere," *New York Times*, February 17, 1968, p. 27. "infantile . . . Good Old Days": Peter Sourian, "One Dimensional Account," *New York Times Book Review*, February 18, 1968, pp. 4, 51. "best book": "Sanity of Kerouac, *Time*, February 23, 1968, p. 96. "There's an air of Finality": John C. Holmes, "There's An Air of Finality in Kerouac's Latest," *National Observer*, February 5, 1968.

"John, you've just got . . .": as quoted in Kramer, *Ginsberg*, p. 165. Allen Ginsberg: Barry Farrell, "The Guru Comes to Kansas," *Life*, May 27, 1966, p. 78; Morris Dickstein, "Allen Ginsberg and the 60's," *Commentary*, January 1970, pp. 64–70; M. L. Rosenthal, "Poet and Public Figure," *New York Times Book Review*, August 14, 1966, pp. 4, 28. "The literary world has swung . . .": Thomas Lask, "Guru and Faculty Adviser," *New York Times*, May 17, 1969, p. 27. "we talk about our assholes . . .": Allen Ginsberg in Kazin, *Writers*, pp. 287–288. "What Ginsberg forced us . . .": Paul Zweig, "A Music of Angels," *Nation*, March 10, 1969, pp. 311–13.

City Lights: 1974 "City Lights Press Catalogue"; Peter Collier, "Lawrence Ferlinghetti: Doing His Own Thing," *New York Times Book Review*, July 21, 1968, pp. 4–5, 24. "It is not they . . .": Cook, *Generation*, p. 119. "liars . . . female spinster": Louis Simpson, "On Being a Poet in America," *The Noble Savage* V (1962): pp. 24–33; Louis Simpson, "Poetry in the Sixties. Long Live Blake! Down With Donne," *New York Times Book Review*, December 28, 1969, pp. 1, 2, 18. "Well, he was the first . . .": Allen Ginsberg, as quoted in John C. Holmes, "Gone in October," *Playboy*, December, 1972, p. 98. "Pic": Jack Kerouac, *Pic* (New York: Grove Press, 1972); Interviews with Robert Creeley, J. C. H., and A. G.; Stella Kerouac, as quoted in Barry Gifford, *Kerouac's Town* (Berkeley, California: Creative Arts Publishing Company, 1977), p. 52. "Shit, it's a story of life . . .": Jack McClintock, "This Is How the Ride Ends," *Esquire*, March 1970, p. 98. "tedious": Kerouac, *Pic*, p. 4. Kerouac beaten up: Interview with Joe Chaput.

"We are forces of chaos and anarchy . . .": Martin Balin, "Volunteers," Ice Bag Music, 1969. Telephone calls: Interviews with Jim Sampas, John C. Holmes, Carolyn Cassady, Gregory Zahos, and Tony Sampas. Call to Bob Burford in Ivan Goldman, "Bob Burford's Summer of 1947," The Denver *Post*, December 30, 1974. "Carolyn . . . take a leak": Carolyn Cassady, "Third Word," p. 1111. "call me back if . . . ": Interview with J. C. H. "The Beat Spotlight": Stella Kerouac in Gifford, *Town*, p. 52.

Death: Alfred G. Aronowitz, "Kerouac Gone," *New York Post,* October 21, 1969, p. 6; Lowell *Sun,* Obituary, October 21, 1969, p. 1. "Stella, help me": Interview with Jay Pendergast. "I'm hemorrhaging . . .": Stella Kerouac, in Gifford, *Town,* p. 53. "Gone in October": John C. Holmes, "Gone in October," *Playboy.* "in the name of American poetry": as quoted in Ibid., p. 98.

Obituary: Joseph Lelyveld, "Jack Kerouac, Novelist, Dead; Father of the Beat Generation," *New York Times,* October 22, 1969, p. 11. Editorial: "He Hit the Road, Jack," Boston *Globe,* October 25, 1969, p. 6. "We should say a prayer . . .": as quoted in Holmes, "October," p. 162. Other obituaries: "End of the Road," *Time,* October 31, 1969, p. 10; "Jack Kerouac, R.I.P.," *National Review,* November 4, 1969, p. 1104; Lester Bangs, "Elegy for a Desolation Angel," *Rolling Stone,* November 29, 1969, p. 36. "I feel bad about Kerouac . . .": Ken Kesey interview, *The Realist,* May–June 1971, p. 51. "And as long as America . . .": Gregory Corso, *Elegaic Feelings American* (New York: New Directions, 1970), pp. 5–6.

Wake and Funeral: Interviews with Allen Ginsberg, Tony Sampas, Bill Koumantzelis, and Gerard Wagner; Douglas Crocket, "Kerouac, King of the Beats," Boston *Evening Globe,* October 24, 1969, p. 41; Vivian Gornick, "Jack Kerouac; The Night and What It Does to You," *Village Voice,* October 31–November 6, 1969, pp. 1, 27; Stu Werbin, "The Death, the Wake, and the Funeral of Jack Kerouac," Cambridge *Phoenix,* October 30–November 5, 1969, pp. 8, 9. "All of you! Why didn't you . . .": as quoted in Holmes, "October," p. 158. Later visitors to grave: Gifford, *Town,* p. 14; Interview with A. G. "He honored death, too": Ibid.

Manuscript Locations

Correspondence between J.K. and N.C. and C.C., and from A.G. to J.K., except when otherwise noted, is on deposit at the Humanities Research Center, University of Texas, Austin.

All other letters to and from A.G., and correspondence from J.K. to W.S.B., except when otherwise noted, is on deposit at Butler Library, Columbia University, New York.

Letters from J.K. to L.F., and other correspondence to L.F., are on deposit at the City Lights Collection, University of California, Berkeley.

Letters from J.K. to M.C. are on deposit at the Newberry Library, Chicago.

Letters from J.K. to P.W. are on deposit in the Philip Whalen Collection, Reed College, Portland, Oregon.

Certain notebooks of J.K. are in the Berg Collection, New York Public Library.

Materials on the film *Pull My Daisy* are located in the Grove Press Collection, Syracuse University.

Index

"After Me, the Deluge" (Kerouac), 335
Aldrin, Buzz, 343
Algren, Nelson, 238
Allen, Donald, 233, 297, 298, 341
Allen, Steve, 249, 275
"America" (Ginsberg), 218
"America's New Culture Hero" (Brustein), 257
Amis, Kingsley, 258, 259
Amram, David, 245–46, 262, 263
Anderson, Cliff, 319
Anderson, Joan, 133
Anslinger, Harry, 313
Apostolakis, George "GJ," 15, 17, 22, 23, 24, 27, 29, 45, 51, 105, 118, 126, 150, 189, 296, 301, 327
Armstrong, Neal, 343
"Army" (Corso), 264
Aronowitz, Alfred G., 265–67
Artaud, Antonin, 120, 298
Ashe, Penelope, 343
Ashton, Dore, 238
Ashvagosha, 179, 183, 215
"Atop an Underwood" (Kerouac), 48
Auden, W. H., 93, 104, 203
Avakian, George, 37
Avalokitesvara, 195, 209, 215, 219

Balaban, Dan, 231
Barnes, Djuna, 93
Bateson, Gregory, 337
Baudelaire, Charles, 66, 93, 175
Beard, The (McClure), 265

"Beat Book, The" (Aronowitz), 267
"Beat Generation, The" (Cowley), 194
Beat Generation, The (Kerouac), 262
Beat Generation and the Angry Young Men, The (Feldman and Gartenberg), 297
Beats, The (Krim), 297
Beat Scene, The (McDarrah), 276
"Beat Traveler" (Kerouac), 276
Beckett, Samuel, 167, 238
Beckwith, Jacques, 299
"Beginning of Bop, The" (Kerouac), 268
Bellow, Saul, 303
Bentley, Elizabeth, 108
Berg, Peter, 325
"Berry Feast, The" (Snyder), 205, 238
Bertrand, Fred, 15, 18, 22, 24, 25, 27, 327
Bigarini, William, 277
Big Sur (Kerouac), 296, 297, 299, 302, 303, 308, 317, 321
Blackmur, R. P., 140
Blake, William, 74, 107, 111, 116, 117, 119, 135, 136, 162, 194, 281, 300, 310, 312, 314, 341, 346
"Blow As Deep As You Want to Blow" (Kerouac), 139
Bly, Robert, 298
Bodenheim, Maxwell, 239
Bogan, Louise, 224, 238
Boldieu, Scotcho "Scotty," 15, 22, 24, 31
"Book, The" (Kerouac), 216
Book of Dreams (Kerouac), 190, 276, 292–93

Book of Prayers (Kerouac), 214
"Book of Sketches" (Kerouac), 267
Bourgeois, Albert, 14
Bourgeois, Paul, 303–4, 336
Bowles, Paul, 176
Brand, Stewart, 298, 326
Brando, Marlon, 212, 229, 242, 249, 250, 257, 279
Breslin, Jimmy, 342, 346
Breton, André, 153
Bridges, Harry, 36, 205
Brierly, Justin W., 92, 98, 127
Brooke, Rupert, 25
Brooks, Eugene, 72, 117, 190, 194, 224, 295, 299
Brooks, Van Wyck, 36, 234
Brossard, Chandler, 297
"Brothers, The" (Kerouac), 35
Broughton, James, 238
Broyard, Anatole, 297
Bruce, Lenny, 305, 306–7, 313
Brustein, Robert, 256, 257, 294
Buckley, William F., 336, 337, 338, 340
Buddha Tells Us (Kerouac), 193, 194
"Buddhist Anarchism" (Snyder), 298
Budenz, Louis, 108
Bukowski, Charles, 331
Burford, Beverly, 98, 126
Burford, Bob, 98, 344
Burlingame, E. W., 183
Burroughs, Mrs. Joan Vollmer, 59, 75, 76, 79, 89, 99, 117, 123, 128, 157, 158, 340
Burroughs, Julie, 99
Burroughs, William, Jr., 99, 128
Burroughs, William S., 64–65, 67–89, 98, 99, 101, 111–23, 126, 128, 129, 133, 143, 145, 150–53, 157–59, 160, 163, 169, 175–76, 186, 188–89, 194, 195, 197, 218, 224, 230, 232–36, 243, 245, 251, 253, 264–68, 281, 293, 296, 300, 305–7, 313, 315, 328, 336–37

Caen, Herb, 253, 307
Cage, John, 218, 255
Camus, Albert, 93
Cannastra, Bill, 130–31, 167
Capote, Truman, 267, 337–38
Carney, Mary, 28–31, 36, 39–40, 54–55, 102, 169, 189, 301, 320, 327–28
Carr, Lucien, 62–74, 80, 81, 89, 101, 122, 124, 130, 131, 135, 157, 175, 184, 186–88, 194, 214, 228, 230, 248, 260, 266, 283, 287, 294, 304, 308, 322, 336
Carson, Rachel, 210
Carus, Paul, 183
Casebook on the Beat, A (Parkinson), 297
Cassady, Mrs. Carolyn Robinson, 94, 97, 98, 100, 101, 104, 105, 110–12, 114, 118, 121, 127, 128, 136, 141–43, 153–54, 160–61, 163–65, 168–70, 178–82, 184, 188, 192, 207, 212, 213, 225, 236, 252–53, 262, 263, 277, 285, 287, 289, 296, 297, 299, 300, 303, 309, 310, 320–22, 329, 333, 334, 343–44
Cassady, Cathy, 110, 142, 225, 309
Cassady, Curtis, 132
Cassady, Jamie, 142, 225, 309
Cassady, Jimmy, 91
Cassady, John, 142, 225, 309, 321, 333
Cassady, Mrs. LuAnne, 90, 92, 93, 97, 98, 104–5, 112, 113, 114, 121, 237
Cassady, Neal, 89–94, 95, 97–101, 103, 104, 108, 110, 111–15, 118, 120–22, 126–36, 139, 141–47, 151–54, 156, 160–61, 162, 164, 165, 167, 168, 173, 175, 178–82, 186, 188, 189, 192–93, 203, 206–7, 212, 213, 217, 222, 225, 229, 234, 235, 237, 242, 244, 248–54, 256, 261–63, 266–67, 269, 275, 277, 285–92, 300, 303, 309, 313–15, 320–22, 324, 333–34
Cassady, Mrs. Neal, *see* Hansen, Diane "Di"
Cassady, Mr. and Mrs. Neal, Sr., 91
Castaneda, Carlos, 330
Cayce, Edgar, 180–81, 182, 189, 192, 207, 212, 213, 217, 222, 267
Céline, Louis-Ferdinand, 74, 85, 93, 193, 238, 246
Cerminara, Gina, 180
Chambers, Whittaker, 108, 119, 124
Chandler, Billy, 19, 31, 45, 51
Chaput, Joe, 327–28, 332, 336, 337, 340
Charters, Ann, 322
Chase, Hal, 89, 92, 98
Ciardi, John, 200–1, 241, 269
"CityCityCITY" (Kerouac), 186–87, 194
Cocteau, Jean, 302
Coffey, Peggy, 28, 29, 49
Cohn, Roy, 171, 186
Cohon, Peter, 325
Colette, 294

Commoner, Barry, 337
"Coney Island of the Mind, A" (Ferling-hetti), 238, 276–78
Cook, Bruce, 330–31
Coplon, Judith, 124
Corso, Gregory, 174, 175, 188, 194, 195, 218, 222–29, 231, 234, 238, 243, 244, 250, 251, 254, 259, 262–65, 268–71, 278, 296–99, 301, 331, 341, 345, 346
"Côte d'Or" (Sampas), 60
Cowley, Malcolm, 171, 187, 194, 212, 215
Cozzens, James Gould, 242
Crane, Hart, 93, 113
Creeley, Robert, 218, 223, 274, 297, 341, 346
Cru, Henry, 35, 58, 98–99, 141, 184
"Cult of Unthink, The" (Brustein), 257
Cunningham, Merce, 218
Curtis, James, 301–2

"Dakar Doldrums" (Ginsberg), 104, 112–13
Dali, Salvador, 229, 279
"Dark Brown" (McClure), 286
Dastou, Ed, 21
Dean, James, 201, 248, 257
Debray, Regis, 332
De Kooning, Willem, 202, 218, 268
Dempsey, David, 169
"Denver Doldrums and Dolours" (Ginsberg), 104
Desolation Angels (Kerouac), 225, 226, 295–96, 316–17, 321
Dharma Bums, The (Kerouac), 210, 244, 246, 250, 254, 255–56, 276, 298, 308, 325
Dickey, James, 241
Dies, Martin, 36
Dionne, Scoopie, 21
DiPrima, Diane, 229
"Disaffiliation and the Art of Poetry" (Lipton), 264
Dr. Sax (Kerouac), 19, 150–51, 159–60, 164, 171, 184, 254, 267, 268, 303, 304, 308, 332, 345
"Dr. Sax, Faust Part III" (Kerouac), 17–18
Dodge, Mabel, 239
Donachie, Father, 270
Dorn, Ed, 218
Dostoyevsky, Fyodor, 49, 50–51, 63, 101, 106, 119, 134, 135, 170, 175, 201, 296

"Dream Already Ended" (Kerouac), 188
Dreyfus, Jack, 262
Duluoz Legend, The (Kerouac), 216, 316
Duncan, Robert, 188, 223, 264, 297
Durgin, Russell, 105
Durrell, Lawrence, 238
Dylan, Bob, 267, 305, 307–8, 346

Earth House Hold (Snyder), 298, 325
Eberhart, Richard, 223–24
Eddy, Mona Kent, 266
Ehrlich, Jake "The Master," 239
Einstein, Albert, 124, 183, 185
Eisenhower, Dwight D., 156, 171, 184, 199, 220, 221, 269, 280, 293
Electric KoolAid Acid Test, The (Wolfe), 314
Eliot, T. S., 59, 83, 96, 120, 217
Ellis, Anita, 263
Elvins, Kells, 159
Empty Mirror (Ginsberg), 153
"Epitaph for the Dead Beats" (Ciardi), 269
"Essentials of Spontaneous Prose, The" (Kerouac), 176
Ettor, Joe, 12
Everett, Rae, 135
Everson, William (Brother Antoninus), 238, 242

Fadiman, Clifton, 273
Farrell, James T., 185
Faulkner, William, 217
Feldman, Gene, 297
Ferlinghetti, Lawrence, 205–6, 227, 231, 238, 242–44, 264, 268, 276–77, 279, 281, 284, 286, 289, 291, 292, 294, 296–98, 303–5, 307, 326, 338, 341
Fiedler, Leslie, 298
"Filthy Writing on the Midway" (Mabley), 264
Finneral, Huck, 301, 302
First Third, The (Cassady), 91, 152
Fleming, Ian, 294
Flynn, Elizabeth Gurley, 36
"For the Death of 100 Whales" (McClure), 204
Fourchette, Jean ZouZou, 11, 18
Fox, Mardou, 171–74, 175, 179, 183, 188, 214, 248, 320
Franco, Bea, 100, 114
Frank, Robert, 249, 262, 263

Freed, Alan, 157
Frost, Robert, 22
Fugate, Carol, 247
Full, Walter, 326
Fuller, Buckminster, 218
Furey, Ralph, 43, 76

Gagarin, Yuri, 295
Gaillard, Slim, 160
Garcia, Jerry, 314, 325
Gartenberg, Max, 297
Garver, Bill, 84, 194, 195, 196, 225, 226,
    227, 237
Gasoline (Corso), 243
Gauthier, Armand, 13
Genet, Jean, 120, 193, 233
Gide, André, 67, 74, 93
Gilbert, Eddie, 34, 35, 39
Gillespie, John Birks "Dizzy," 82, 106,
    179, 255
Ginsberg, Allen, 63–67, 72–81, 85, 86, 89,
    92–99, 101, 103–5, 107–8, 110–13, 115–
    20, 122, 123, 126, 130–36, 144, 146,
    149–53, 156–59, 161–63, 165, 167–78,
    180, 182–84, 188–90, 192–94, 196–98,
    201–4, 206–8, 212, 213, 217, 218, 222–
    31, 233–35, 237, 238, 241, 243–45, 249–
    59, 261–64, 267–71, 274–76, 280, 281,
    291, 293, 296–300, 307, 308, 310–13,
    315, 319–22, 324–26, 328–31, 335–38,
    340–42, 345–47
Ginsberg, Louis, 75, 118, 120, 230
Ginsberg, Naomi, 103, 118, 120, 224, 264,
    312
Giroux, Robert, 115, 120, 123, 125, 135,
    152, 194, 299
Glassman, Joyce, 230, 231, 236, 243, 249,
    260
Gleason, Ralph, 238, 245, 277, 303, 307,
    308
Go (Holmes), 152, 159, 165, 167, 169
Goddard, Dwight, 181, 183
Goethe, Johann Wolfgang von, 23, 49, 65,
    88, 139, 164, 258
Gold, Herbert, 241, 250, 253, 254, 297,
    303
Golden, Harry, 253
"Good Blond" (Kerouac), 316
Goodman, Paul, 218, 241, 337
Gordon, Max, 245
Gould, Joe, 239

Graham, Billy, 181, 247
"Green Automobile, The" (Ginsberg), 175
Grieg, Michael, 231
Gubichev, Valentin, 124
Guest, Edgar, 180
Guevara, Che, 332
Guttman, Walter, 262

Hall, Donald, 297–98
Hamill, Pete, 342
Hammett, Dashiell, 16, 77
Hanrahan, Captain William, 238
Hansen, Diane "Di," 122, 127, 128, 132,
    141
Harriman, Averell, 156
Harrington, Alan, 106, 114
Harrington, Michael, 253, 312
Hauptmann, Bruno, 18
Haverty, Joan (Mrs. Jack Kerouac), 131,
    132, 134, 135, 141–42, 152, 157, 162,
    191, 193, 230, 236, 295, 299, 322
Hecht, Anthony, 274
Heller, Joseph, 193
Hellman, Lillian, 242, 244, 262
Hemingway, Ernest, 23, 48, 129, 200, 283
Henry, Pat, 144
Hentoff, Nat, 245
Hersey, John, 109
Hinkle, Al, 112, 113, 186, 237
Hinkle, Helen, 112, 113, 121
Hiss, Alger, 108, 124
Hitler, Adolf, 18, 31, 46
Hoffman, Abbie, 335
Hoffman, Dr. Albert, 313
Hoffman, John, 203
Hoffman, Judge Julius, 265
Hofstadter, Richard, 270
Hold Your Horn High (Kerouac), 160
Holiday, Billie, 37, 38, 143, 160
Hollander, John, 241, 298, 341
Holmes, John Clellon, 83, 92, 105–10,
    115–19, 122, 123, 126, 129–31, 134–36,
    145, 151, 152, 159, 160, 165, 167–70,
    174, 178, 183–84, 217, 230, 232, 239,
    242, 243, 247, 255, 258, 275, 300, 301,
    303, 306, 308, 309, 311, 321, 322, 329,
    331, 341, 344–47
Holmes, Mrs. Marian, 152
Holmes, Mrs. Shirley, 300, 301, 346
Hook, Sidney, 185
Hoover, J. Edgar, 36

Horn (Kerouac), 136
Horn, Clayton, 239
Howe, Irving, 201, 269
Howl (Ginsberg), 196–97, 202, 204, 206, 217, 223, 224, 235, 237, 238–39, 241, 254, 258, 271, 308, 310, 312, 325, 337, 341
"How to Meditate" (Kerouac), 183
Hughes, Howard, 96
Humphrey, Hubert, 184
Huncke, Herbert, 83, 84–85, 99, 100, 105, 109, 116, 117–18, 119, 152, 276
Huxley, Aldous, 71, 74, 186, 255, 337

"Imitation of the Tape" (Kerouac), 145–46
"In the Ring" (Kerouac), 332
"Invitation to Innovators" (Cowley), 187

Jack Kerouac Explores the Merrimack (Kerouac), 15
Jackson, Natalie, 212–13, 252
Jackson, Phyllis, 169
Jarrell, Randall, 224, 227, 229
Jarrell, Mrs. Randall, 227
Jarvis, Charles, 301–2, 332, 333
"Jazz of the Beat Generation" (Kerouac), 187, 193, 208
Jennison, Keith, 194
Joan Anderson Letter (Cassady), 192
"Joan Rawshanks in the Fog" (Kerouac), 146
Johnston, Jill, 331
Jones, Howard Mumford, 125
Joseph, Chief, 298, 325
Josselman, Michael, 185
Joyce, James, 59, 74, 93, 303, 316, 333, 341
Junkie (Burroughs), 151, 158, 169, 170, 305

Kaddish (Ginsberg), 264, 298, 310
Kammerer, David, 65, 68, 69, 70, 71, 73, 74, 77, 102, 332
Kandel, Lenore, 265, 289, 290, 296, 325
Kauffman, Bob, 277
Kazin, Alfred, 104, 110, 269
Kennedy, John F., 280, 293, 294, 304–5, 306, 309, 312, 313, 316
Kennedy, Mrs. John F., 280, 294, 304
Kennedy, Robert, 335
Kerouac, Caroline ("Nin"), 4–8, 28–30, 57, 104, 111, 112, 136, 141, 142, 160, 164, 192–94, 213–15, 229, 236, 260, 261, 295, 300, 316, 321, 347
Kerouac, Doris, 327, 339
Kerouac, Mrs. Edie, *see* Parker, Edie
Kerouac, Mrs. Gabrielle Mémêre Levesque, 4–9, 13, 15, 17, 22, 29, 30, 33, 36, 46–49, 51, 57, 60, 72, 78–79, 85–86, 88, 95, 98, 99, 101, 102, 104, 105, 111, 112, 115, 116, 118–20, 122, 123, 126, 127, 129, 132, 134, 136, 139, 141, 142, 150, 152, 160, 163, 164, 168–70, 173, 175, 177–79, 184, 187, 191, 193, 194, 213–15, 219, 229, 230, 235–37, 245, 249, 250, 253, 260–61, 266, 274, 278, 280, 283, 284, 290, 291, 293–96, 299, 300, 303, 304, 306, 308, 309, 311, 316–18, 321, 322, 324, 326–28, 332, 334, 335, 336–40, 342–44, 346
Kerouac, Gerard, 4–9, 11, 15, 17, 20, 22, 24, 62, 68, 78, 79, 90, 135, 163, 193, 195, 206, 213, 214, 248, 261, 278, 284, 291, 302, 328, 329, 347
Kerouac, Hervé, 15, 327, 339
Kerouac, Janet Michele, 136, 152, 191, 299, 339
Kerouac, Mrs. Joan, *see* Haverty, Joan
Kerouac, Leo Alcide, 4–7, 9, 10, 12–16, 21–23, 26, 27, 29, 30, 33, 34, 46–49, 51, 54, 55, 57, 60, 67, 71, 72, 79, 85–87, 89, 102, 108, 129, 135, 145, 150, 156, 163, 178, 186, 195, 214, 226, 248, 284, 287, 293, 294, 304, 312, 334, 344, 347
Kerouac, Mrs. Stella, *see* Sampas, Stella
"Kerouac's Sound" (Tallman), 297
Kesey, Ken, 314–15, 333, 345
Khrushchev, Nikita, 269, 271, 293
King, Martin Luther, Jr., 335
Kinsey, Alfred, 84, 123
Kline, Franz, 202
"Know-Nothing Bohemians, The" (Podhoretz), 257–58
Korzybski, Alfred Habdank, 74, 93
Koumantzelis, Billy, 302, 320, 336, 346
Krassner, Lee, 149
Krassner, Paul, 199
Krim, Seymour, 268, 297
Kristol, Irving, 185
Kyger, Joanne (Mrs. Gary Snyder), 300, 310

Lamantia, Philip, 153, 203, 205, 264

Lancaster, Bill, 76
Landesman, Jay, 126
Lasky, Melvin, 185
"Last Word, The" (Kerouac), 268–69
"Laughing Gas" (Ginsberg), 264
Laughlin, James, 254
La Vigne, Robert, 202, 279
Lawrence, D. H., 106, 136, 217
Lawrence, Seymour, 184
Leahy, Frank, 30
Leary, Timothy, 293, 314, 328
Lebris, Ulysse, 318
Lekas, Paul, 346
Lenoir, Henri, 277
Lerner, Max, 109
Leslie, Alfred, 262, 263, 275
Leslie, Hube "the Cube," 253, 277
Levine, Steve, 325
Levitt, William, 95
Lindsay, Vachel, 205
"Lion for Real, A" (Ginsberg), 269–70
Lipton, Lawrence, 264, 267, 274
Little, Lou, 30, 33, 34, 45, 47, 54
"Little Sutra, The" (Kerouac), 188
"Lively Arts in San Francisco, The" (Grieg), 231
Lonesome Traveler (Kerouac), 280
Lord, Sterling, 187, 192, 193, 233, 242, 249, 267, 268, 299, 332, 336, 338, 346
Love Book, The (Kandel), 265
Lowell, Robert, 298
Lowry, Malcolm, 341
"Lucien Midnight," see "Old Angel Midnight" (Kerouac)
"Lysergic Acid" (Ginsberg), 264

Mabley, Jack, 264
MacArthur, Douglas, 140
McCarthy, Joseph R., 124, 157, 184–86, 187, 195
McCarthy, Mary, 306
McClure, Michael, 147, 203–4, 218, 223, 231, 238, 242, 257, 264, 265, 273–74, 286–88, 297, 298, 313, 324–26
McCorckle, Locke, 216
McCullers, Carson, 176
McDarrah, Fred, 276
MacDonald, Dwight, 95–96, 242, 263
McHugh, Vincent, 239
McIntosh, Ralph, 238
McReynolds, David, 253

"Magic Psalm" (Ginsberg), 281
Mahoney, John, 327
Mailer, Mrs. Adele, 190
Mailer, Norman, 125, 190, 231, 247–48, 280, 293, 294, 305, 306, 317, 331
Malamud, Bernard, 303
Mansfield, Helen, 14, 15, 18, 22
Mao Tse-tung, 293, 312
Marker, Lewis, 157, 158
Marx, Leo, 270
"Mass Society and Modern Fiction" (Howe), 269
Matus, Don Juan, 330
Maxwell, Morty, 35, 39
Mayé, Mohammed, 234
Mazur, Hank, 48, 54
Mekas, Jonas, 263
Melody, Little Jack, 116–17
Meltzer, David, 298
Melville, Herman, 55, 136, 145, 151, 268, 303, 329
Mémêre, see Kerouac, Mrs. Gabrielle Mémêre Levesque
Memory Babe (Kerouac), 250
Merton, Thomas, 298
"Mescaline" (Ginsberg), 264
Metalious, Grace, 235
"Mexican Girl, The" (Kerouac), 193
Mexico City Blues (Kerouac), 195–96, 208, 213, 237, 243, 254, 259, 267, 274, 307, 346
Michaux, Henri, 238
Miles, Josephine, 238
Miller, Henry, 238, 249, 298, 300
Millstein, Gilbert, 167, 239, 240, 294
Minh, Ho Chi, 343
Monk, Thelonius Sphere, 82, 174, 179, 254, 269
Montagu, Ashley, 258, 259
Montgomery, John, 209–10, 211, 217
Morales, Adele, see Mailer, Mrs. Adele
Moran, Frank, 49
Morland, Dusty, 153
Morrisette, Mrs. Caroline ("Nin"), see Kerouac, Caroline ("Nin")
Morrisette, Charles, 28, 57
Morrisette, Father Armand "Spike," 13, 346
Müller, Dody, 260–62, 280, 281
Müller, Jan, 260
Mungo, Ray, 326

Murao, Shig, 238
Murphy, Danny, 301
Murrow, Edward R., 43
"Myth of the Rainy Night, The" (Kerouac), 119, 120, 150

Nabokov, Vladimir, 300
Naked Lunch, The (Burroughs), 218, 232–33, 243, 264, 265, 305–6
Nelson, Donald, 52
New American Poetry, The (Allen), 297, 298, 341
Newfield, Jack, 312
Newman, Jerry, 168, 184, 263
Nichols, Luther, 239
Nietzsche, Friedrich, 65, 66, 73, 77, 89, 164
"Night Words" (McClure), 238
Nin, *see* Kerouac, Caroline ("Nin")
Nin, Anaïs, 245
Nixon, Richard M., 221, 280, 343
Nobriga, Manuel "Chiefy," 302, 328, 329
"Notes on the Religious Tendencies" (Snyder), 256, 297
Nothing More to Declare (Holmes), 309

O'Brien, James, 71
O'Connor, Flannery, 201
"October in the Railroad Earth" (Kerouac), 166, 218, 233, 238, 245, 280, 297
"Old Angel Midnight" (Kerouac), 216–17, 236, 243, 264, 268, 276, 283
Olson, Charles, 218, 297
O'Neill, Paul, 273–74
On the Road (Kerouac), 118, 120, 122–23, 129, 133–36, 145, 146, 148, 151, 152, 162, 165, 171, 184, 187, 192–94, 212, 214, 223, 228–31, 236–37, 239–45, 247, 250–55, 257, 258, 262, 265, 266, 271, 272, 275, 285, 287, 303, 304, 312, 315–16, 319, 325, 342, 344
"On the Sidewalk" (Updike), 256–57
Oppen, George, 298
"Origins of the Beat Generation, The" (Kerouac), 258–59
"Origins of Joy in Poetry, The" (Kerouac), 264
Orlovsky, Amiel, 202
Orlovsky, Julius, 202, 320–21
Orlovsky, Lafcadio, 202, 222, 225, 226–27, 228

Orlovsky, Nicky, 202
Orlovsky, Peter, 202, 217, 222, 225–28, 230, 231, 233, 234, 251, 254–55, 260, 262–64, 268, 269, 276, 281, 296, 300, 320–21, 345–47
"Other Night at Columbia, The" (Trilling), 269

Pack, Robert, 297–98
Parker, Charles "Bird," 82, 83, 106, 143, 147–48, 149–50, 179, 192, 234, 248, 320, 328
Parker, Edie, 58–62, 68–73, 75, 119, 122, 231, 236, 346
Parkinson, Thomas, 297
Patchen, Kenneth, 206
Peale, Norman Vincent, 109, 185
Peebles, Mooney, 262
Pegler, Westbrook, 123
Pendergast, Jay, 301, 333
Perse, St. John, 93
"Philosophy of the Beat Generation, The" (Holmes), 248
Pic (Kerouac), 342–43
Picasso, Pablo, 149, 329, 341
Pictures of the Gone World (Ferlinghetti), 206
Planet News (Ginsberg), 341
"Plus Ça Change" (Whalen), 204
Podhoretz, Norman, 242, 256, 257–58, 294, 297
"Poetry, Violence, and the Trembling Lambs" (Ginsberg), 270
"Police" (Corso), 264
Pollock, Jackson, 147, 148–50, 242, 257, 329
"Pome on Dr. Sax" (Kerouac), 298–99
Porter, Arabelle, 187
Post, Emily, 95
Pound, Ezra, 172, 203, 208, 217
"Power" (Corso), 264
Prescott, Orville, 239
Proust, Marcel, 93, 132, 135, 143, 145, 164, 192, 206, 228, 261, 302
"Pull My Daisy" (Kerouac, Ginsberg and Cassady), 113, 126, 263
Pull My Daisy (motion picture), 212, 244, 262–63, 264, 268, 275

Queer (Burroughs), 158

Rachou, Madame, 251
Ransom, John Crowe, 96, 140, 201, 258
Real Bohemia, The (Rigney and Smith), 270
Reed, John, 25, 239
Regarding Wave (Snyder), 325
Reich, Wilhelm, 113, 123, 139
"Reply, The" (Ginsberg), 281
"Revolt: True or False?" (Rexroth), 250
Rexroth, Kenneth, 188, 193, 201, 203, 205, 206, 207, 217, 218, 223, 238, 239, 242, 245, 250, 267, 274, 326, 341
Rexroth, Martha, 218–19
"Rhapsody in Red" (Sampas), 60
Rigney, Francis, 270
Rimbaud, Arthur, 62, 66, 68, 71, 73, 74, 92, 93, 111, 308
"Rimbaud" (Kerouac), 292
Rivers, Larry, 262
"Road Runner, The" (Whalen), 238
"Roaming Beatniks, The" (Kerouac, Corso, Ginsberg and Orlovsky), 268
Robbins, Harold, 298, 343
Robinson, Carolyn, see Cassady, Mrs. Carolyn Robinson
Robinson, E. A., 22
Rockefeller, Courtney, 42
Romney, Hugh, 343
Roosevelt, Franklin D., 14, 21, 47
Roseman, Mr. and Mrs. Jacob, 321–22
Rosenberg, Ethel and Julius, 124, 171
Rosenthal, Irving, 264
Rosenthal, M. L., 298
"Rose of the Rainy Night" (Kerouac), 118–19
Ross, Nancy Wilson, 256
Rosset, Barney, 299–300
Roth, Philip, 343
Rubin, Jerry, 335
"Rumbling Rambling Blues, The" (Kerouac), 245
Rusk, Dean, 304
Russell, Vicki, 84, 89, 92, 102, 116–17, 130, 172
Rynne, Elmer, 30

Sahl, Mort, 250
Saijo, Albert, 275–76, 285
Salinger, J. D., 303
Salvas, Roland, 15, 22, 24, 25, 28, 29, 126
Sampas, Charley, 30, 46, 124, 125

Sampas, Jim, 126, 344
Sampas, Nick, 324, 326, 334
Sampas, Sebastian "Sammy," 24–25, 30, 40–42, 45, 46, 48, 49, 52–53, 55, 60–63, 93, 126, 135, 302, 322, 323, 344
Sampas, Stella, 302, 322–23, 324, 326, 328, 329, 333, 334, 337, 340, 342, 344, 346
Sampas, Tony, 302, 304, 321, 324, 327, 328, 334, 344
Sandburg, Carl, 205
Sanders, Ed, 336, 337, 338
"San Francisco Blues" (Kerouac), 182
"San Francisco's Mature Bohemians" (Rexroth), 238
Saroyan, Aram, 330, 331
Saroyan, William, 23, 48, 100, 145, 330
Sartre, Jean Paul, 167, 238
Satori in Paris (Kerouac), 319, 322, 340
Schine, G. David, 171
Schlesinger, Arthur, Jr., 185
Schorer, Mark, 239
Schwartz, Delmore, 201
Scripture of the Golden Eternity, The (Kerouac), 216, 217, 267, 280
"Sea" (Kerouac), 283, 286, 317
Sea Is My Brother, The (Kerouac), 53, 54, 59, 76
Secret Mullings About Bill (Kerouac), 237
Seton, Ernest Thompson, 208
Seyrig, Delphine, 262–63
Shakespeare, William, 42, 59, 143, 215, 219, 261, 302, 303, 320, 329
Shapiro, Meyer, 119
Sheperd, Frank, 127
Sheresky, Dick, 34, 35
Shields, Karen, 182
Shulman, Max, 272
"Siesta in Xbalba" (Ginsberg), 183
Silliphant, Stirling, 272
Simpson, Louis, 297–98, 341
Smith, L. Douglas, 270
Smith, Luxy, 11, 23–24
Smith, Paul, 285, 286, 287
Snyder, Gary, 203–12, 214–18, 220, 223, 229, 235, 238, 244, 250, 254, 256, 264, 275, 297, 298, 300, 308, 310, 313, 320–21, 324–26, 337
Sobol, Louis, 294
Soft Machine, The (Burroughs), 336
Solomon, Carl, 119, 120, 151, 152, 162, 164, 165, 193, 197

Some of the Dharma (Kerouac), 183, 190
"Sonnet I" (Ginsberg), 104
Spectorsky, A. C., 268
Spender, Stephen, 185
Spengler, Oswald, 18, 55, 74, 77, 78, 93, 155, 237
Spicer, Jack, 238
Spillane, Mickey, 185, 295
Spiller, Robert, 124
Starkweather, Charles, 247
Stein, Gertrude, 317
Stevenson, Adlai, 184, 221, 280
Stone, Jesse, 157
Sublette, Al, 160, 164, 170, 182, 190, 194, 275
Subterraneans, The (Kerouac), 172, 175, 176, 188, 228, 230, 233, 248–50, 255, 266, 275, 278, 287, 308
Subterraneans, The (motion picture), 277–78, 279, 281
"Summertime in a Mill City" (Sampas), 25
Susann, Jacqueline, 343
Susskind, David, 267
Suzuki, D. T., 254–55, 264
Symphony Sid, 122

Taft, Robert A., 156, 184
Tallman, Warren, 297
Tate, Allen, 96
Taylor, Cecil, 190, 229
Teresa of Lisieux, St., 9–10, 17, 167, 180, 199, 252
Thelin, Ron, 325
"This Is the Beat Generation" (Holmes), 167, 168
Thomas, Dylan, 272
Thoreau, Henry David, 3, 40, 55, 119, 179, 190, 194
"Three 'Witless Madcaps' Come Home to Roost" (Balaban), 231
Town and the City, The (Kerouac), 88, 92, 94, 95, 101–5, 110, 115, 116, 120, 123–26, 134, 139, 142, 145, 150, 162, 234
Toynbee, Arnold, 255
Trilling, Diane, 75, 185, 269, 270
Trilling, Lionel, 75, 104, 269, 298
Tristessa (Kerouac), 196, 225, 226, 267, 281
Trotsky, Leon, 85
Truman, Harry, 81, 108, 113, 124, 128

Turtle Island (Snyder), 325
Tynan, Kenneth, 276

Updike, John, 256–57

Van Doren, Mark, 42, 44, 76, 104, 115, 119, 120, 184, 217
"Vanishing American Hobo, The" (Kerouac, Corso, Ginsberg and Orlovsky), 268
Vanity of Duluoz (Kerouac), 49, 304, 308, 316, 329–30, 332, 340–41
"Variations on a Generation" (Corso), 270–71
"Veille de Noël, Une" (Kerouac), 35
Vidal, Gore, 125, 176–77, 243
Villanueva, Esperanza, 196, 225–26
Visions of Cody (Kerouac), 142, 143, 144–47, 150, 152, 158–62, 171, 267, 269, 274, 275, 307, 346
Visions of Gary (Kerouac), 237
Visions of Gerard (Kerouac), 213–14, 299, 309–10
Vollmer, Joan, *see* Burroughs, Mrs. Joan Vollmer
Voznesensky, Andrei, 341

Wagner, Gerard, 319, 320, 346
Wakefield, Dan, 245, 317
Wake Up (Kerouac), 193
"Wales Visitation" (Ginsberg), 326
Wallace, Mike, 246, 247
Warren, Henry Clarke, 183
Warren, Robert Penn, 201
Watts, Alan, 264
Weaver, Raymond, 76
Weber, Hugh, 299
Wechsler, James E., 258, 259, 264–65
Weil, Jerry, 272
Welch, Joseph, 186
Welch, Lew, 275–76, 284–86, 289, 290
"West Coast Rhythms" (Eberhart), 223–24
Whalen, Philip, 180, 203, 204, 206, 214, 218, 222–24, 235, 236, 238, 244, 250, 252, 254, 259, 264, 268, 274, 275, 279, 282, 284, 286, 288, 291–94, 297, 308, 313, 324, 325
"Wheel of the Quivering Meat Conception" (Kerouac), 346
White, Ed, 92, 98, 126, 139

White, Phil "Sailor," 83, 84, 152–53
"White Negro, The" (Mailer) 247–48
Whitman, Walt, 40–41, 44, 45, 46, 206, 295
Whole Earth Catalogue, The (Brand), 298, 326
Wild Boys, The (Burroughs), 336
Williams, William Carlos, 89, 104, 153, 203, 217, 224, 230, 341
Williams, Mrs. William Carlos, 230
Wilson, Edmund, 300
Winchell, Walter, 32
Wingate, John, 243, 249
Witt-Diamont, Ruth, 224, 227
Wolfe, Ben, 68
Wolfe, Nero, 76–77
Wolfe, Thomas, 44–45, 46, 48, 68, 80, 88, 103, 104, 106, 301
Wolfe, Tom, 314

Wong, Victor, 286
Woods, Edwin, 157
Wouk, Herman, 303
Wynn, A. A., 151, 162
Wyse, Seymour, 36, 38, 83, 160, 234, 294

Yablonsky, Lewis, 336, 338
Yage Letters, The (Burroughs and Ginsberg), 175
Yeats, William Butler, 66, 71, 74, 77, 93, 119, 120, 139, 314
Young, Celine, 65–66, 68–69, 72, 73, 89
Young, Lester "Prez," 37, 38, 45, 127, 147, 154, 160, 259

Zahos, Greg, 301, 302, 303, 329, 333, 334, 344
Zugsmith, Albert, 272, 294

About the Author

DENNIS MCNALLY was born in Fort Meade, Maryland, in 1949. He holds a doctoral degree from the University of Massachusetts and has written about Kerouac and the Beats for scholarly journals. He lives and writes in San Francisco.